Helping
Troubled Children
and Youth

Robert P. Cantrell

and

Mary Lynn Cantrell,

Editors

AREA

AMERICAN RE-EDUCATION ASSOCIATION

Memphis, TN   2007

HELPING TROUBLED CHILDREN AND YOUTH

Continuing Evidence for the Re-ED Approach

Book 2 in the Troubled and Troubling Child Series

Edited by Robert P. Cantrell and Mary Lynn Cantrell

Copyright © 2007 by: American Re-EDucation Association

259 N State Street, Suite 200

Westerville, OH 43086-1331

Printed in Memphis, TN

Library of Congress Control Number: 2007938364

ISBN 9780978535605

To purchase copies, consult the publisher's website: www.re-ed.org

Please Note: Any errors or omissions found in this volume are inadvertent.

Dedication

To Teacher-Counselors everywhere, in and out of Re-ED programs.
In all their roles and job titles, their work brings hope to
children and families like the ones whose stories follow.

The AREA logo is a drawing of the sculpture "Come Play" by Katharine
Blackman Haven. The original was on Nicholas Hobbs' desk. An enlarged
bronzed casting stands in front of the Nicholas Hobbs Laboratory of Human
Development at Vanderbilt University.

The Life Tim Wanted

I met Tim when he was 17, after a suicide attempt in the local river. Diagnosed with schizophrenia at a very young age, he had lived through years of struggles at home and in "treatment." Now 17, Tim was sure he would never experience a "normal life" — that he would always be a "freak."

Our program at the time was a typical cookie cutter residential program with point sheets, level system, and consequences leading to some level of success for almost any chient. But Tim struggled in this environment. His desire for perfection escalated him into crisis if he missed points needed for the level he wanted. At times his paranoid thinking convinced him that staff were preventing him from attaining the level he felt he should be on, creating crises. Then there were the voices that mocked him for missing points, for not achieving, constantly reminding him that he was a "freak." Although we shared very few common points of reference, our efforts to work with Tim continued, with staff assuming that his lens of understanding was similar to ours.

Our team felt pretty defeated as we discussed some ideas with Tim's parents. Then we decided to try something that was radically different for us. Little did we know that we were about to bring several Re-ED principles (then barely known to us) into our work with Tim.

The first step was to get Tim involved in his own treatment decision-making. His doctor wanted to try an old school, potentially dangerous medication. Instead of just informing Tim, then making the changes, we met with Tim and educated him about the med: that in order to start the new med he'd have to be completely free of his current ones. Tim was terrified of coming off his meds, for although they were not as beneficial as everybody would have liked, any change in meds usually sent Tim spiraling downward. Those were painful to watch and indescribable to experience. We left the decision to Tim. With the support of his family and the team, Tim opted to take a chance. He equated this to being the "most terrifying thing he'd ever done."

Once med changes were in place, we rewrote Tim's living conditions, asking the entire program to drop all old ways of dealing with Tim's less desirable behaviors. No more point sheets, no more level system, and no more standard consequences for specified behaviors. If we were taking kids out and Tim was in a good frame of mind to go, he got invited. Tim had a clean slate and was, as of this time, "perfect."

Working with Tim now became present tense. We lived in the here and now with him, and helped him allow himself to do the same. We didn't allow Tim to use the story of his past to write the script for his future. We accepted what Tim had to offer in the moment, praised him for what he had to offer, no matter how much or little it seemed to be, and worked to build connections on any level with what Tim found important, interesting, and entertaining. We valued Tim as the Expert on Tim. When he told us the voices were very strong at night when he showered and it was difficult to get up mornings to shower, we didn't remain rigid, forcing him to adjust to our options. Instead, we found a time in the early afternoon when he could shower.

The climb up from that very dark hole that Tim lived in was not perfect, but with each hiccup, Tim realized that we would not be daunted, nor would we allow him to be daunted. Tim continued to be our expert on Tim. We discussed our ideas with him, and any idea he brought to us led to extensive conversation and consideration.

What happened was impressive. Tim became more confident, more functional, and happier. Going home for Thanksgiving with the story that "holidays are always bad," he returned to proclaim his time with family as "the best family holiday I can remember!" With this new story he looked forward to Christmas, and although he would become stressed thinking about all the past Christmases that had gone poorly, we reminded him that the story of family holidays had been rewritten by Tim just a few weeks ago. This was another opportunity to do the same. Tim had a terrific Christmas.

Tim still had his difficulties; he still climbed the counter on occasion, or swore profusely, or sat conversing with his miniature Christmas tree. But helping Tim through this situation was easier and more productive because we weren't people "trying to force him to do what they wanted." The world was no longer doom and gloom because Tim had racked up a long list of consequences, leaving him feeling powerless and overwhelmed. Now it was about helping Tim live, develop trust, and explore his feelings instead of making excuses for them. Real people who shared some of themselves with Tim, and valued what Tim had to share with them of himself, met Tim in real time.

Tim turned 18 while he was with us. He and his parents faced legal issues such as custody and power of attorney, even as they processed and accepted the reality that Tim would not be returning home. His family, whom we now knew well, continued to show phenomenal strength and determination to help Tim be successful. When discharge was delayed, Tim continued to trust that everybody was working with him and in his best interest. Meanwhile, he worked with a skills trainer to learn the city bus system. A cell phone was provided in case he became lost, stuck, or anxious. We would stop and say to one another, "Did you ever think Tim would be out riding a bus alone to a destination? WOW!"

Tim eventually moved to a foster home, where he functioned with some independence. He went to school, worked a few hours at the school coffee cart, and visited his family frequently. Education and empowerment had led him to feel more control of his life.

Tim still calls us on occasion to tell us what's going on in his life. He has a new foster home, a new case manager, and a new psychiatrist. The earlier Tim would have considered these changes to be guaranteed crises. His interests have not changed much, but his self-confidence and his ability to handle his "rough spots" have.

I really can't tell you all that we learned from Tim in our work with him, but his successes fuel our desire to be mindful in our work with all the other kids we come in contact with. We think, "How can we apply what we've learned to working with this other child?" We didn't sit down with a list of the Re-ED principles and talk about how we were going to implement them, but in hindsight that's pretty much what took place. Our program had just rewritten itself with the help of some very trusting and brave people -- Tim and his family.

Recently, I was talking to Tim on the phone. As he was telling me all he was experiencing and doing, I said to him, "Tim it sounds like you are living that 'life' that a year ago you were sure you'd never be able to live." He paused, then with a little chuckle, said "Heh, YEAH!"

- - - Tom Moore

From Dropout to Entrepreneur

Tom greeted me just inside the front door of his business, with a friendly handshake and forthright eye contact. A tall man with a warm smile, he invited me to have a seat in his small tidy office, the hub of his thriving business. Tom spoke openly about his frustrating lack of success in school which persisted until his mid-teens. That was when, through his mother's perseverance, they found the Re-ED program.

Tom vividly recalls the day he graduated from SECEP (South Eastern Cooperative Educational Program), especially the book bag his teachers gave him in anticipation of his certain success in his new "regular" high school. Mrs. Robertson gave him a dictionary which he uses to this day. Increasing his spelling skills has been an ongoing objective since he chose it as a weekly goal while a student in Miss Midgette's Re-ED class. He missed so much of school during the years when his peers were learning spelling patterns, word families, phonetics, and irregular spellings. Today, the dictionary is supplemented with a spell check system and the help of his loyal office manager.

During the late '60s and early '70s, Tom was a youngster who didn't fit the box. School meant confinement, having to fight against staying awake late at night and sleeping late in the morning. Nothing at school motivated him to disrupt his natural circadian rhythms and go to school where, he states, the classroom was like "uncontrolled lock-down." Unfortunately, his teachers had little training in classroom management or positive behavioral interventions. He learned to defend himself by being absent, avoiding the chaos, disruption, and threats.

Recognizing that Tom "learned differently" and did not readily respond to traditional instructional methods, but lacking the skills or training to provide alternative programming, his 3rd grade teacher allowed him to spend most of his days in the classroom coat room playing. In sixth grade, for the same reasons, he and a peer were frequently sent to a nearby dump to dig up dirt for the teacher's plant collection. It was not a positive learning environment for this bright young athletic boy, whose learning style did not conform to the norm.

Discouraged, unmotivated, and feeling he was falling further and further behind in academic skills, Tom dropped out of school in the seventh grade. For an entire year, he refused to go to school. His mother, by then a divorced working parent of two young sons, did her best to advocate for him. She appealed again and again to her local school board to provide some services for Tom. Finally, she heard about a relatively new program in the area, called SECEP.

Now in his teens, Tom was given two options: attend school at SECEP or go to a detention facility. Tom chose SECEP. Immediately upon enrollment, and for the first time in his life, school became supportive and positive. Miss Midgette's classroom was structured, expectations were clear, and Tom did not feel as if school had to be a battleground to retain control of his lunch money. Most importantly, individualized learning styles were acknowledged, and Tom began to complete his assignments. He remembers that Miss Midgette "got on my case" about the importance of regular attendance. Motivated by success and support, he attended consistently and progressed. His second year in the program, he was assigned to the teaching team of Mr. Hill and Mrs. Robertson. Tom smiles and recalls that Mr. Hill was like Fred Rogers of "Mister Roger's Neighborhood" — easy-going and caring. Mr. Hill even wore a cardigan sweater and tennis shoes, like Mister Rogers. He and his teaching partner, the beloved Mrs. Robertson, "made it difficult to go wrong," according to Tom. "They made me feel adult -- and good about myself."

After steadily working his way through Re-ED, Tom reintegrated to his home zoned high school. Already eighteen, however, he realized after consulting a guidance counselor that graduation was still a long way away. So he opted for a vocational technology program, obtained his GED, and was accepted at the VoTech center for a four year apprentice sheet metal program. Thirteen years in the sheet metal trade solidified his work ethic, and he knew it was time for a career move. He began selling security systems, door-to-door. Here Tom's honest, forthright, and personable manner paved the way for success. He quickly worked his way up from Sales Rep to Manager, until he supervised 16 sales reps, 12 installers, and 1 coordinator. Seven years ago, he started his own business. Initially working out of his home, he built his company at a fast pace until it outgrew his home office. Today, he leases a suite in a local executive park. Pictures of his wife and children hang proudly on the walls of his office, and his name on the door announces his hard-earned status as owner.

Tom says he is grateful for the opportunity he received some twenty-five years ago to turn his life around.

Jimmy's Story

When I visited his classroom, I was careful to interact with all five of the students. But it didn't take Jimmy long to figure out that I was really there for him, and he clearly enjoyed having a visitor. When told by his teacher, Rob, to do an errand, he patted my arm and said, "C'mon." Out in the hallway, he went directly to his destination, smiling at students and teachers who spoke to him. Jimmy is an exceptionally friendly student, outgoing and eager to please.

I found myself having great fun spending the morning with this group of five challenging students and their three staff members. The classroom is structured and cheerful, arranged for optimum success with each individual student — a happy place. This day, the class was making peanut butter pinecones to feed the birds — a delightful, ecologically aware, springtime activity. I watched Jimmy and his classmates each choose a pine cone, spread peanut butter on it, and roll it in birdseed. Then, along with their teacher, school community trainer, and teacher assistant, we all trooped out to a tree just outside their window where the students hung their pinecones. One of Jimmy's services. During Rosa's last hospitalization, the hospital staff felt Rosa required something different, and Connections was contacted. They hoped Connections would help her find new ways to be successful enough to stay at home.

Rosa lived in Puerto Rico before coming to Cleveland; she is bilingual. Her parents speak limited English. Luis, a Connections Community Support Case Manager who is fluent in both English and Spanish, was called in to help. Luis was the best thing that could have happened for Rosa, even though she didn't initially see it that way. He was persistent. No matter how hard Rosa tried to push him away, he was there. Every morning he called her house to tell her he expected her to take her medications, find her way out of bed, and get herself to school. As things changed, Luis decided that it would be good for Rosa to work with another staff person and learn how to trust another adult. Jill and Rosa quickly developed a healthful relationship.

Rosa has a strong and supportive family. Her 84 pound mother is a force to be reckoned with, and Rosa's mother was not going to let her fail. Together, Rosa, her family, and the Connections staff identified three primary goals for Rosa – preventing her threatened removal from home, staying in school, and gaining emotional stability.

Rosa has met each of these challenges. She is now emotionally stable, and no longer requires medication. She has not been hospitalized since the event that led her to Connections. She determined that her high school environment was not good for her, so she is enrolled in a GED program. She talks about going to college and looks forward to a career in the medical field. Removal from home is not a risk anymore. In fact the opposite is true – her mother desperately wants her to stay at home and go to college in Cleveland because she is such a strong and positive force in their family.

Rosa profoundly understands Hobbs' statement that, "Life is to be lived now, not in the past, and only in the future as a present challenge." She can now see a bright future for herself. She will tell you, smiling, that she is truly happy. Rosa has discovered inner strength. She now sees the hope for herself that Luis, Jill, and Rosa's family all saw before.

Starting from Scratch:
Learning How to Be a Teacher-Counselor

In 1962 we started Project Re-ED without techniques, but we did start with a philosophy. A clear philosophy guides you in how to respond to students, and leads the way toward interventions. Fortunately, we were able to talk to wise professionals about how to develop our role.

Carl Rogers told us something that became a core therapeutic point for Re-ED. Therapy isn't a process. It's the outcome that tells you whether something is therapeutic. It's as simple as this: *successful living is healing*. Those four words underlie everything we do in Re-ED. Just experiencing success toward worthy goals makes someone stronger. As early T-Cs, we talked a great deal about what would help us achieve this end.

We realized it's likely a long time before a troubled kid has a full day of successes. But there are many opportunities for tiny bits of success to occur during the day. Children might have a successful experience and not even be aware of it, because they are so geared to look at their failures. We learned that one of our jobs is to watch for successes that happen, whether it is as simple as the child saying "Thank you" to someone or completing a math problem or catching the ball -- tiny bits of success. All learners need feedback, so we are constantly alert for bits of success to happen. Watch for them; if your feedback is honest, it will be important to the learner and encourage more effort.

Planning for students' successes is the underlying objective of everything we do. From the way we structure seating in the classroom, the kind of assignments we give, and the goals we help them set, we are aiming at successful experiences for the child or the adults in his world. We create structures to encourage success. When rules describe productive ways to behave, stated positively, they give us many opportunities to point out success. (We avoid negatively stated rules that focus on misdeeds and shape us to respond to negative behaviors.) Our goals also have no negative words in them. Instead, they describe successful ways to behave in words that are understandable for everyone.

Rituals add structure to complex situations that can help create order, restore order, or encourage order. They add meaning to events we hope students will value, like graduations. Even our structures for talking with students can help them increase their chances for successes by helping them figure out the relationships between behaviors and their results.

Re-ED is open ended and changes over time, but successful living is the goal we all share.

— Robert Slagle was in the first group of
Cumberland House teacher-counselors.

Foreword

Reading this volume, it is abundantly clear that Nick Hobbs was both a philosopher and an interventionist. He envisioned a world in which principles could guide action and, in turn, could make children, families, and communities maximize their potential. Amidst the current emphasis on evidence-based treatments and outcomes research, it is refreshing to read this volume and to be reminded of the intentions, integrity, and optimism that spawned Re-ED. It also brings into focus both the enormous potential of Re-ED for meeting the needs of troubled children and youth and the challenges in utilizing such a framework in the contemporary world.

Bob and Mary Lynn Cantrell have done a wonderful job of bringing Re-ED into focus with a volume that is aimed at a broad and shifting audience. As they state in the introduction, this book will be helpful to long-time Re-EDers who want to preserve and enhance the culture of the intervention. It provides invaluable information to novices who want to learn about the approach, understand its history, and contemplate its use in their programs. And it reaches out to the broader professional, consumer, and advocacy community to understand the potential role of Re-ED in child-serving systems. In line with the inclusive participatory nature of Re-ED, the volume includes a refreshing variety of voices: professionals who have worked in programs, agency directors, parents, youth, and academics. These perspectives come together to provide a richness and texture that is rarely found in discussions of contemporary mental health interventions.

The book begins where it must, with Hobbs' original 12 principles of Re-ED. Re-reading these, their validity seems so obvious: trust is essential; feelings should be nurtured; groups are major sources of instruction; benefits of community must be experienced; intelligence can be taught; competence makes a difference; self-control can be taught; physical experiences help define ourselves; now is when life is to be lived; time is an ally; ceremony and ritual give order; and joy should be built into each day. These tenets provide a powerful grounding for the Re-ED approach, and the remainder of the volume provides background, descriptions, guidance for implementation, and research that explore these essential features. But the truly wonderful thing about this volume is that it is not a regurgitation of Hobbs' earlier volumes or of decades-old vision about effective programming. Rather, following Hobbs declaration that Re-ED must "guard against hardening its beliefs into cement of dogma and orthodoxy... the strength of Re-ED programs lies in their always 'becoming' by virtue of staff who are always 're-inventing' them..." (p. 45), the volume is organized around a smaller set of principles, six that have recently been distilled to capture the essential and defining elements of Re-ED. These, based closely on Hobbs' original principles, are: (1) a strength-based view; (2) an ecological approach; (3) an emphasis on teaching, learning, and competence; (4) an emphasis on interpersonal relationships; (5) a focus on developing adults to fill teaching and counseling roles in children's lives; and (6) the essential role of questioning and searching in the intervention process.

Part I provides the background to the rest of the volume. It begins with Hobbs' principles and shows how these have guided current efforts to operationalize and distinguish Re-ED. Chapter 3 provides a transcript of a student's petition to graduate from a Re-ED program. At first glance, it seems out of place — a verbatim transcript of an exit interview just as the reader is getting caught up in the academic discussion of what Re-ED is, how it's been studied, what its essential elements are. But as you read it, you realize that it crystallizes what the whole volume is about. It's not just about research, a model, or evidence: it's about kid's lives. Throughout the volume, just when it's tempting to get drawn into the academic and programmatic details of Re-ED, chapters like this one leap out to grab you and say: "Remember, this is about kids and families. It's about using sound principles to work with kids to help them do their best and achieve their potential. This isn't about feeling good about ourselves because we have a great model. It's about feeling good about the world because we have a framework and tools that can make a difference in kids' lives."

All of the volume's sections highlight the tremendous potential of Re-ED to positively influence the lives of children and families. Part II gives the reader an inside look at what it means to focus on strengths rather than pathology. While such a shift in language is common in contemporary mental health services, a true shift in thinking is not. Chapters 4-7 immerse the reader in this different way of thinking, how it looks, how it feels, and what it takes to make it an underpinning of intervention.

Part III focuses on families and ecologies. It reminds us of Re-ED's essential view that "children's problems do not reside inside the child, nor do they reside solely in others." Rather, each child functions in his/her own world (ecology), and problems arise from discord within these ecologies. "The child and the elements of that world share both in the problems and their solutions" (p. 71). This section reminds us of what a pioneer Hobbs was in his view. This ecological view is now routinely cited as Bronfenbrenner or when referring to interventions such as Multisystemic Therapy, but Hobbs was key in setting the stage for this type of thinking and, more importantly, for its implications in working with families and youth.

Parts IV and V provide a reminder of just how much work is involved in making all of this happen. Developing competence and finding/creating professionals who can do this work is a difficult business. No matter how much the philosophy focuses on success, joy, and trust, the day-to-day reality of working with youth who come to mental health programs is tough. These chapters provide a delightful blend of philosophy (to make it clear why you'd want to do what needs to be done) and details on how it can actually be done. This section illustrates that philosophy alone is never enough, and that Re-ED has decades of experience in figuring out how to translate that philosophy into action.

Part VI provides a key set of ideas that must be incorporated if Re-ED is going to continue to exist and grow. It focuses on building relationships. The development and nurturing of trusting relationships is one of Re-ED's core principles. Chapter 31 helps to align Re-ED with the contemporary focus on non-specific elements of treatment in its discussion of therapeutic alliance. But the Cantrells made a very wise decision in this section: relationships aren't only critical for what happens within Re-ED, they're also essential to Re-ED's future. Chapter 28, "Starting a Grassroots Movement," shows how efforts at external linkages and relationships can grow out of needs and successes within a program. The types of connections, technical assistance, and community described in this chapter point toward the potential of Re-ED to extend its reach, while recognizing the costs and limits that such reaching out can bring.

Part VII most directly addresses the "Continuing Evidence" portion of the volume's title. For all of its strengths and appeal, Re-ED has been criticized for its relative absence of empirical studies. This section highlights the studies that have been done. Early work (in the 1970s) by Weinstein (Chapter 29) compared youth in the initial Re-ED programs with untreated similar youth from their home communities. On a wide range of outcomes (self-concept, behavioral adjustment, academics, maternal ratings of improvement), youth in Project Re-ED settings did better than comparison group youth. Studies in the 1970s examined effects of utilizing Re-ED approaches in public schools. More recently, outcomes from several Re-ED programs were reported (Chapters 30, 32, 33).. All of these results are positive. So why isn't Re-ED viewed as an evidence-based program? The answer is fairly clear: Re-ED has focused its energies on serving youth, not on conducting and publishing studies. Collectively, the available research suggests Re-ED as a "promising" approach. Individually, though, there are too few studies and those that have been done lack random assignment, sufficient sample size, and enough publications in peer-reviewed journals to meet contemporary criteria for "evidence." Meadowcroft, Cantrell, and Cantrell's work on a fidelity measure (Chapter 31) can hopefully be used in coming years to conduct quasi-experimental studies to add to this literature. Hopefully, this section (and the entire book) will re-kindle interest in Re-ED and spark a wave of research that will provide the types of evidence it needs to be included in discussions of empirically validated approaches.

As readers go through this volume, they will be struck repeatedly by how much sense it all makes. How much could we accomplish if we changed our view; understood ecology; viewed time as an ally; focused on strengths and built competences; thought about transactions and fit rather than pathology; partnered with families; focused on building trusting relationship; etc.? Hobbs and Re-ED were in the vanguard of a shifting paradigm on mental health in the early 1960s. In many ways the principles that Hobbs envisioned fed into the reconceptualization that formalized itself as the CASSP principles of the mid-1980s. So, in many ways, pieces of what Hobbs and the early Re-EDers developed have become central to contemporary thinking about appropriate treatment for children and youth. But the volume also makes it clear that this forerunner and visionary is currently at risk of being trampled and lost in the aftermath of the changes that have swept the field. What is it that keeps Re-ED alive? And what are the "interventions" that can be applied at this point to overcome its challenges and lead it to its most promising future?

This volume reminds the reader repeatedly that Re-ED continues, not because it has spent its time on self-promotion, marketing, and dissemination, but in spite of a relative absence of these activities. Hobbs published articles and a book on Re-ED. There have been a handful of studies completed, and there is a national organization (the American Re-Education Association) devoted to the model. The power of Re-ED is not in the scant infrastructure or publicity that it has developed. Rather the power of Re-ED is in the commitment of practitioners in agencies across the country who base their approaches on the Re-ED framework and who continue to work diligently with and on behalf of troubled youth and their families. Re-ED has provided a framework and training ground for a vast network of professionals across the country. Even if they are no longer working in a Re-ED program, the philosophy, solid training, skills, and wholistic approach to treatment remains with them and infuses their efforts. In many ways, the 25 programs that are currently sponsoring or associate members of AREA are only the core of Re-ED's influence and reach. Given its strong theoretical underpinnings and coherent model, its influence extends well beyond the parameters of these agencies. It has influenced over a generation of mental health professionals and public policy.

But this focus on "doing good" isn't enough in the current era of evidence-based treatment, outcomes-based performance reviews, pay for performance, and menus of reimbursable evidence-based practices. All of this emphasis requires empirical studies (preferably randomized controlled trials), enormous resources and infrastructure, publication of results in peer-reviewed journals, and dissemination/replication studies to assess fidelity, transportability, and magnitude of impact. In many ways, this volume emphasizes the potential down side of the evidence-based movement. There is no question that everyone wants to see better outcomes for youth and families. However, as the chapters in this volume so clearly convey, not everything that happens in treatment can be easily measured. And reducing a model to its measurable components threatens to strip away the underlying philosophy, commitment, and vision that create coherence in a program and lead to the types of outcomes we're all trying to achieve.

This is not to say that rigorous studies should not be done or that anecdotal evidence is sufficient. However, this volume forces us, as a field, to think about what we're trying to achieve and to determine the best ways to learn what we need to know to provide the best possible services to youth without losing the essential nature of the intervention in the process.

This volume does a wonderful job of reminding us of the connectedness of things: of youth to their ecologies, of treatment providers and families to each other, of communities, but also to the ebb and flow of historical time and the world. Hobbs and Re-ED are usually seen as ahead of the curve in children's mental health in the U.S., but as Chapter 38 reminds us, the idea for the approach was inspired by the educateur model in post-WWII Europe. The principles of Re-ED are timeless statements of essential ideals, not only for treatment but for successful living. At the same time, even these principles have been evaluated, revised, and repackaged to ground Re-ED as it has evolved during the past 45 years. The collective chapters here remind us that Re-ED has been around for much longer than many of the evidence-based models that currently command so much attention from researchers, policy makers, and funders. It is based on principles of development, treatment, and relationships that supersede simplistic short-term or outcomes-based lenses. This volume serves as a much-needed booster to guide Re-ED into the future. It provides an introduction for a new crop of professionals just entering the field, a reminder to those of us who have been around for a while, and a broad window for a wide variety of potential stakeholders to think carefully about what we want to achieve, how we want to get there, and what we'll need to know and do to make it happen.

Betsy Farmer
Tom Farmer
State College, PA

Preface

This book is the second volume in a series begun by Nicholas Hobbs' 1982 book, *The Troubled and Troubling Child* (reprinted in 1994 by the American Re-Education Association to meet requests for it by member agencies and other professionals). The first volume reflects the ecological view of services to those children and their families who have found growing up "troubled and troubling." Like Nick Hobbs, we prefer this term to the more common ones used in mental health and special education (children with "emotional disturbance," "behavioral disorders," or "challenging behaviors.") They are, most of all, children and youths with the same precious individualities, needs, hopes, and potentials for growth of other children who may have found growing up less difficult and less painful by whatever accidents of birth and fortune. Our troubled children, too, can be helped to find strengths within themselves and others, and to experience the joys in life that can come from belonging, learning, helping, and just plain fun.

Hobbs' first book shared the heritage of Project Re-ED and its aftermath over the twenty years from the first students in 1962 to 1982. This volume attempts to perform a similar function for the subsequent twenty-five years, as the philosophy and practices sought both more definition and more widespread adaptation to the range of services our troubled and troubling children and their families need. What we have learned from these children and from their families is extraordinary and constantly unfolding. Their courage and their perseverance have inspired both staff and other parents and students who must work to find the strength to continue. We hope these pages can begin to share some of that learning with readers.

In this volume you will hear from youths, families, staff members, and even visitors. We hope you will find it of some assistance.

Robert P. Cantrell and Mary Lynn Cantrell
November, 2007

Acknowledgements

Our sincere thanks go to:

Positive Education Program which bore the costs for writing, editing, and initial preparation, and whose leadership and staff could not have been more helpful and supportive — especially Frank Fecser whose patience and personal support through all the barriers life can throw at us, made the book possible.

The "Wizards" group at West Bridge in Cleveland and their teacher-counselors (Rob Cooper and Juliann Fausel), who made the "Come Play" statue on Nick Hobbs' desk come to life so that Ryan Smith could photograph them for the book's cover.

Ryan Smith, who designed the book cover, Jay Baker (from Youth Villages) who completed the covers, and Margaret Houston whose many hours of careful transcription served as the beginnings of some chapters.

Allison Urschel, who created the basic Pagemaker format for the book, did many of the initial software transfers and all of the final cleanup and packaging for the printer, while answering scores of technical questions with skill and patience — wonder woman!

Connie Mills who filled the valued liaison role — coordinating layout needs with the Youth Villages Public Relations staff, proofings, interfacing with the printer, and keeping us all laughing throughout.

xxx

Deanna Blackledge, Youth Villages PR director, who freed Connie and Allison up to do this work, and to Patrick Lawler who offered their help – without which AREA could not have published the book and made it inexpensive for practitioners and students.

Scott Condon, whose librarian skills, computer literacy, and willingness to help secured our ISBN approval, numbers, and barcodes for this and future AREA publications.

AREA's Board members who initially requested the book, supported requests, and extended patience through years of projected timelines interrupted by life events, and especially Mark Freado and Carolyn Hartzell who provided detailed assistance whenever needed.

AREA members and others who confirmed facts and descriptions or read portions and offered editorial suggestions, especially Terry Cooper, Bob Slagle, Tom Valore, Lee Maxwell, and Diane Bricker — and Sarah Hurley for special attention to the research section.

All the authors, each of whom thoughtfully consolidated the skills and experiences they gained in "doing Re-ED," and put them into written form to share with readers — and whose patience with our many requests, from beginning to end, is much appreciated.

Larry Brendtro and Nick Long, editors of the *Reclaiming Youth* journal, who invited AREA to produce the summer 2002 Re-ED issue and then gave us permission to reprint any part of it for the book.

Jim Kauffman, who gave us permission to reprint Nick Hobbs' "The Art of Getting into Trouble" speech, from his 1974 book with C.D. Lewis, *Teaching Children with Behavior Disorders.*

Betsy and Tom Farmer, who graciously agreed to write the foreword – citing their positive experiences with Re-ED over the years as they said yes to our request (including Tom's early undergraduate introduction to Wright School fieldwork and later employment there, and Betsy's interaction with Re-ED staff on evaluation research studies while at Duke); we know this was no insignificant interruption of their busy schedules as professionals nationally known for their commitment to children's mental health and special learning needs.

Tom Hobbs and family, for their continuing support of Re-ED staff and AREA agency members' requests.

Family and friends who patiently asked over 5 long years how the book was coming, and were understanding of our preoccupation, who offered assistance, even if we couldn't take them up on it – most of all our daughter Kymber Rock (a Re-ED fan since she was a 5 year old playing in the late afternoons with Cumberland House's youngest group, the Whippoorwills, while her mom worked in the Pathfinder classroom) who volunteered her computer skills and attention to detail, and came through willingly when we accepted.

The many Re-ED ers from the past whose legacies continue to inform and inspire us – they have given us all much to live up to.

Contents

Helping
Troubled Children
and Youth

Continuing Evidence
for the Re-ED Approach

Part I

Introducing Re-ED

Re-ED programs have used an ecological approach to serve troubled and troubling children and youths, along with their families, in sites spread across the United States since 1962. The term is an acronym that comes from the first program's title: Project Re-ED (Re-education for children with Emotional Disturbance). The approach was conceived by Nicholas Hobbs and his colleagues, and then tested and developed in the first two Re-ED sites, both five day short-term residential treatment centers: Cumberland House in Nashville, Tennessee and Wright School in Durham, North Carolina.

The Re-ED approach largely works from an ecological competence model which sees each troubled and/or troubling child as a member of a unique ecosystem that has become sufficiently discordant to lead to their referral for special services. This ecological problem solving approach builds competence through positive experiences, while demonstrating inherent respect for children and their families. Everyday activities become opportunities for growth if employed therapeutically. As Carl Rogers told the first Re-ED staff group, "Successful living is healing."

Essential Elements

Re-ED has always been difficult to define, largely because its practices are principles based. (Hobbs' 12 principles are provided in chapter 1.) In an effort at further definition, some recent empirical work asked if characteristics seen by experienced Re-ED staff as essential in Re-ED programs differed significantly from those seen as essential by a sample of staff members working in a more traditional mental health program. (This study is described in more detail in chapter 31.) The six essential elements identified include:

(1) A *focus on the child's strengths* (and the resources available in the ecosystem to help it achieve its capacity for wellness) actively replaces the usual emphasis on pathology.

(2) The *ecosystem* in which the child functions is where needs are to be met, strengths recognized, and interventions enacted.

(3) Increased *competence* in many arenas is the goal of intervention for all the ecosystem's members, including Re-ED workers.

(4) *Relationships* are fostered, built, and maintained as critical elements of successful living; skills for forming constructive relationships are actively sought.

(5) Individuals who are ongoing members of the child's life (e.g., parents, teachers, and others in the ecosystem) are valued as agents of change, capable of improving skills for their natural roles as *the child's teachers and counselors*.

(6) *Questioning* helps us respect the constant need for review and evaluation, recognizing that any ecosystem (family or program) must remain dynamic and open to better ways to meet our own and others' needs.

We know we share these beliefs and characteristics with other professionals and service groups who do not identify with "Re-ED" and may never have even heard the term. Many of these beliefs and ideas have become part of our national zeitgeist in mental health, and we have found many like-minded colleagues.

A National Organization

The Re-ED philosophy has been adapted to a wide variety of service options, starting in 1962 with short-term residential treatment, a day school in 1967, school preventive intervention programs in 1970, and a neighborhood child advocacy project in 1971. Since then many adaptations have appeared, both residential and community-based: day treatment, preschool intervention, treatment foster care, in-home services, and a wide variety of others. These sites serve a wide range of children who have been identified as eligible for services in one or more systems, or are at risk for identification.

In 1980 several of these programs joined to form the American Re-EDucation Association (AREA), recognizing their mutual interests and their desire to maintain contact, sharing their products and experiences. Today AREA is a national organization of member programs and individual members representing approximately 6,000 staff serving about 40,000 children and families each year. Member agencies operate service programs in 18 states and in some European countries. (The last section of this book contains more detailed descriptions of the fourteen current sponsoring member agencies. Also included are a brief history of Re-ED's development and biographical information about Nicholas Hobbs.)

Purpose, Scope and Sequence of the Book

The purpose of this book is threefold:

(1) to assist Re-ED programs in preserving and enhancing the culture;

(2) to assist interested programs in understanding and accessing Re-ED philosophy and practices;

(3) to acquaint the larger professional and consumer community with both what Re-ED is today and what evidence it has to offer in support of the effectiveness of the approach.

The scope of the book, like Re-ED itself, is broad-based, if not comprehensive. Our programs serve those children most in need, in their infinite variety. The potential for adaptation of this philosophy and its principles-based practices seems limitless. Someone once asked Nick Hobbs, then in his sixth decade of life, about the types of Re-ED adaptations he could envision we needed. He said, smiling, "I can see the need for a great many Re-ED centers. Lately, I've been thinking about one for senior citizens."

This book cannot be "sufficient" to meet the needs of any one reader, but it tries to describe in some detail what Re-ED has become after almost five decades serving children and families. Hopefully, it serves as a resource guide, summarizing evidence accumulated for the approach (ample early on, but less so recently, with service money unaccompanied by evaluation or research funds).

Following this introduction are the three chapters in Part I. The first provides the 12 Re-ED principles guiding the development of program practices. The second discusses the continuing evidence for the approach, and gives an overview of the empirical development of six Re-ED essentials. Chapter three follows with Alex's story, a transcription of his formal meeting with staff to petition for graduation from a Re-ED program.

Other chapters in this book are organized into sections for each of the six essential elements described above:

Part II	Focusing on Health and Strength
Part III	Strengthening Families and Ecologies
Part IV	Developing Competence
Part V	Valuing the Teaching and Counseling Roles
Part VI	Building and Maintaining Relationships
Part VII	Questioning and Growing

An eighth part describes our current member programs and some of their major activities in a look at Re-ED's past, present, and future.

We believe the rich heritage of this approach is apparent in services that still join with families, schools, and community agencies to alleviate discord and enhance success in the lives of troubled and troubling children and youths, from birth to young adulthood.

Most importantly, future research must establish whether Re-EDness (in the sense of programs whose operations are measurably consistent with Re-ED philosophy and practices) continues to make a difference for children, families and communities. Early results have been encouraging, but the work remains ongoing – as the services are ongoing.

In the services themselves, we see the results as we see our work – one child (and family) at a time. The chapter that follows, *Alex's Petition to Graduate*, is an example of what keeps us going – the kind of continuing evidence we can see in our programs.

References

Cantrell, R.P. & Cantrell, M.L. (1976). Preventive mainstreaming: Impact of a supportive services program on pupils. *Exceptional Children, 42,* 381-386.

Weinstein, L. (1974). *Evaluation of a program for Re-Educating disturbed children: A follow-up comparison with untreated children.* Washington, D.C.: Department of Health, Education and Welfare. (Available through ERIC Document Reproductions Service, ED-141-966.)

3

Alex's Petition to Graduate

The following is a transcript of a videotaped *Petition to Graduate* meeting held at a Re-ED program, which provides an example of the philosophy, its principles, and biases in action. Alex's account of his Re-ED journey tells about engaged parents, trusting relationships, sound ecological assessment and service delivery, a focus on competence, caring staff, and the pursuit of joy. Alex was referred to our program at 15 years of age. Alex, his family, and the staff spent three years working and learning together to reach the goals that Alex speaks to in his culminating story. All staff questions and comments are italicized; more than one staff member is speaking. The non-italicized words are his.

Good afternoon Alex. You have written a fine petition and collected the necessary preliminary signatures that indicate your readiness for this final meeting. We are here to discuss, and for you to defend, your readiness to graduate from our program. We would like to follow the outline of your paper which includes the behaviors that led to your referral to us, how you addressed those behaviors, and your future challenges and plans. Why don't we go back in time and talk about why you were referred, your experience at your previous school.

Okay, starting at my old school, I had a lot of anger problems with a lot of the staff and students. I showed a lot of anger and aggression toward them. I felt that I had some problems and instead of teachers helping, they made things worse. Certain teachers were always setting us problem kids up—that's what they called us—calling us on, saying "You think you're tough; come on and hit me, I dare ya." So anger and aggression. And I also eventually got into doing a variety of drugs, and that's about it. That's all I can think of now.

Was there one significant incident that you had in your former school that led to you being referred to us?

Oh yeah! Well, this teacher, Mr. A., he was one out of that group of teachers that made things worse for any kid who had any kind of problem; he was like the leader of them. One day I was sent to the office, again, and on the way down to the office, Mr. A. appeared, like out of nowhere, and started telling me all sorts of things about how I was never going to be anything, about how I'm nothing, that I was the worst kid that ever came into that school and how I belong in jail, and everything else. When we got in the office with the principal, everything was a little different. He [Mr. A.] changed and said stuff like, "So I'm really worried about you, Alex. I want to see you grow, I want to see you succeed" and everything else. Then, when the principal left, Mr. A. put his hand on my shoulder and began talking his negative stuff, he wouldn't quit and that's the last thing I remember. But from things I heard, I got up and I hit him and made him feel it. We got into it pretty bad.

I remember you talking about that. You described him as a person who typically behaved this way.

With me and with other problem students, or whatever you want to call us.

Okay, so what were you trying to show him at that point?

That he was smaller than me. He always made everyone feel small.

So you had problems with anger and disrespect and with using drugs and alcohol. What would you say is different now? What has changed?

Well I came here and I found a lot of different ways to deal with my anger and my aggression—a lot more control. And, I don't use drugs anymore.

What are some of the ways that you control and cope with your anger?

It depends on my surroundings. If I'm at home, I'll work out usually, or I'll leave, if that's the only option. I'll just go to my friend's house or whatever there is to do. If I'm at work, sometimes I can talk it out with my buddy, which helps me calm down. When I'm in school, if I have the option when I'm aggravated, I just put my head down and I can think about it in my head.

We've talked a little bit about how Mr. A. made you feel. You said you wanted to take matters into your own hands and show him who's boss and knock him down to size. Is that about it?

Uh huh.

We've never seen that here. Why not?

I never had a reason to, here.

What does that mean? What was different?

All of you just handed me respect and trust from the start. You gave it to me as a person. You didn't treat me like I needed to be walked around with my hand held. You treated me like—however old I was—with just as many rights as anybody else. I never had that in a school. I didn't want to lose it.

It's a powerful thing to feel, isn't it?

Yes. The bad stuff wasn't just with Mr. A. He did it a lot—sometimes more than other teachers, but he was just at the right place, at the right time, or I guess the wrong place and time. But it was more of my attack at the school. I was wrong in what I did, but I needed help and they never helped; they just wanted to get rid of me.

When you first got here to our program, you said you were handed trust. When you walked into the classroom, how was it conveyed to you? How did you feel it? How did you know?

I just knew it, I don't know, it was just at that level, I knew. I guess it came through, you could just feel that these people were real. Oh yeah, they kept their word on everything too. And, if I said something, staff would believe me. I could tell it wasn't fake. And they were fair, with everyone.

So part of it is that they kept their word, and it sounds like you weren't singled out.

Yeah, that was one thing I saw, that all the people had the same thing. Everybody was just like me, pretty much. Other people had other problems, but I was no different from everybody else — so there wasn't any room for singling out, but even if there was, they didn't — my teachers Mr. D., Ms. J. or no other staff here.

What happened when you would have a problem here? If you were upset about something or when you were in the classroom and you were irritated with other kids, how was that different?

Hum, okay. Usually, we just talked it over. Ms. J. took me out in the hall a few times and talked to me. She'd ask me, "What happened?" instead of yelling, "Look at what you did!" Before she went to another staff to talk to them about my problem, she'd go to me to find out my story.

Is that respect? Is that trust?

Definitely. It's more like Ms. J. would think there's his story first, he's the one involved in the situation, then I'll go to the staff and get their side.

I know we talked a little bit about the behaviors that got you here and we talked about the things that have changed. My question is, "Why did they change?" What was the turning point?

The major turning point was first getting off of drugs. That made me a little smarter, a little wiser, or whatever you want to call it. Clearer, I could see things differently, a little clearer. I saw everything differently. I could relate to things differently. My anger didn't boil up as quickly, or as long. I think that was one of the major turning points. And more trust. I had more people behind me trying to get me to do the right things and helping me.

Why do you think you got off of drugs here, and not at the other school?

At the other school it was easier to get and I didn't want to get off. I had no reason to.

Why do you think you were using those drugs?

There were a lot of reasons. They were fun and I guess, I used them like an escape. Trying to forget and trying to escape.

Trying to forget something in particular?

A lot of things, most probably what went on at the school. I used a lot before, during, and after school and on the weekend. I remember not using as much on weekends—not needing as much.

I know you didn't give up drugs immediately after you came here. In fact, an incident occurred early on, during a camping trip. How did that incident affect things?

I know I screwed up a lot of people's plans and fun because of it. I know I kept people up late hours. I made a few people drive places I know they didn't want to drive; to come out from home in the middle of the night to help me and the staff. I don't remember too much of that night. I can remember my age dramatically increasing, maturing, but that's about it.

What about after the incident, when you came back to school and your classroom talked about it?

Nobody really seemed to be angry — more disappointed I think. This was the first camping trip of the year, and then, I didn't know what camping trips were really like. I was just guessing by how everybody talked about them, that they were fun. I guess what I thought was fun was a little different than what the group thought. I knew I had ruined people's fun.

Can you remember just after the incident, before you were to encounter the group? What were your feelings about what to expect? Were you concerned?

At first, yes, but Ms. J. helped me. She told me to meet her before school started. I had to talk to her first before everybody else was there. I don't remember the conversation because it was awhile ago, but I remember that it wasn't like, "You screwed up!" She talked to me like I was a person. Looking back, I think she prepped me for the meeting so I would control myself.

Trust and respect again?

Yeah.

Was it different than consequences that you faced at the other school?

Well, at the other school, when I got consequences I was happy because it meant I could stay home and do anything I wanted, which was good for me. But here I wasn't happy with myself. I felt I had let people down and I didn't like feeling that way. At first, I thought it was going to be like everything else when I messed up, punishment, isolation, never letting it go. But when I found out it wasn't, I think that was another thing that really made me realize this school was a lot different from my old school. The consequence wasn't go home for 5 days or 10 days. Then you have to have a remedial drug class, and then a fine and be labeled as a junkie for the rest of the time that you're there. Here, it's more like you made a mistake. You deal with it like a man, and here's your consequence and that is it. When it's over, it's over. They don't keep bringing it up like at my old school. Nobody brings it up unless I do.

One of the things I remember real clearly is your interaction with dad. Not only did you have problems with authority figures in school but, you had a lot of problems interacting with dad as well. A lot of anger there. Would you agree?

Uh huh.

How would you characterize your relationship with dad now?

I would say we're best friends.

Why do you think the relationship changed?

I saw it changing when I began to quit drugs, and as time progressed we could finally sit down and talk. And since I was showing that I would talk, and he was beginning to show that he would talk, you know it just kinda landed. I think mom and dad attending parent group with you guys really helped open some doors. I don't know what you did on those nights, but it worked. They understood my problems better, and I reacted to them in a different way. I got a job the summer before I came back to school. I was still using drugs, and when I got off of them, things just started to get a little bit better. You know, one day at a time. In the morning I could walk by him and just say, "Hi." The next day I could say, "Hi, Dad, how are you doing?" Soon, I was drinking coffee with him in the morning.

What else occurred in your relationship with your dad?

Another time came when I wanted to join the Army National Guard. I needed his signature, because I was 17. Even though things were a lot better, I still wasn't sure how he'd react. I told him I had papers to enlist in the Guard and before I could throw in, "Dad, this is what I want. I *really* want this. Can you please sign?" He said, "Where do I sign?" He looked proud. I think I showed him a lot of responsibility on my part and dedication, showing I do have a goal.

You didn't expect that reaction?

I wasn't sure what to expect. It showed me that he had enough trust that I could do it. Enough trust that I wasn't going to mess it up. Enough respect for me. I think Dad felt that this is what my son wants and I think he's mature enough to get it and do it. It's like what I think his reaction was to me coming home from Boot Camp. That reaction showed me his feelings which I think brought our relationship a lot closer, and now our relationship is even closer than it was then. Me going away, and going through the toughest time in my life so far, getting letters from him and sending letters to him and everything.

Respect and trust from home also?

Yeah, and when he came to Boot Camp graduation and I saw him with the video camera just running towards me, and my mom mauling me and hugging me and kissing me. Getting all the tears on me, and my dad doing the same thing. I knew things were different. We could never go back to those old ways.

You shared something with us before about the significance of joining the Guard and being at Boot Camp. Why is that such a significant event between you and your father?

He did the same thing. He's been through Basic Training. He was at the same place I was, his barracks were across the street. He had almost the same job. Technology has changed a little so there's a little difference, but all in all we have the exact same job. Basically he's done the same thing that I've just completed.

Did that feel good, or did you not want to do the same thing?

That made me feel good and also when my Dad was in the Army, he excelled quite a bit, and when I excelled, it was like we could talk about things more. When I got home, he finally started talking about Vietnam and things to me because he knew now I was old enough to handle it. I'm in the Army myself now.

Just after Christmas, we had a most memorable parent group here. Mom and dad came to parent group. And like so many other groups, your dad was talking about how proud he was of you. At one point he reached into his pocket and pulled out this little gift that you had given him and he had tears coming down his face as he talked to us about that gift. Can you talk about that gift and its significance?

Well, the last time my dad went to Vietnam he showed me his trooper stuff and two Army commendation medals. On one it had V for Valor. No matter how many problems we had, I always held him in high respect because of those medals, 'cause I know what he had to go through; he showed me the scars, what he had to go through to get those. I've read all the articles on what he had to do. So when I went looking for Christmas presents, I decided instead of getting another Fireman's statue, I decided to get him a Brass Zippo lighter and had the words *American Hero* engraved on it, and the date on it 12/25/1999 — because to me that's what he is.

He is to us as well. I have to mention that he was not the only one with tears on his face during that meeting.

I heard.

What are your plans for the immediate future and the long term?

Immediate future, I plan on working full time at a local fitness center for now and I'll see how that goes. I'm getting moved up to Program Director, which is sales. I'm also going to be attending Emergency Medical Training School at a Career Center, a 4 hour class twice a week to get my national certification. Those will be my short term goals; and for long term, basically finishing up my training with the National Guard and this coming summer Artillery School, and taking the test for the fire department.

Sounds good. Thanks for bringing this in today (photograph of Alex in uniform). What do you think? Is this you now?

I think so.

Well, you've done a great job. You've come a long way in a relatively short amount of time. It's pretty phenomenal —from a kid who was very angry, disrespectful, and using— to this (holding up Alex's photograph) young man in the Guard. (pause) Short and long term goals and a great relationship with his dad and family. (pause) Most of all you should feel proud of yourself. Any final thoughts?

It's hot in here.

It is hot in here!

Alex, could you please let this group know about the offer you made to me?

I told Ms. J. that if you ever need anyone to talk to anybody about my experience, just let me know and I could talk to them.

That would be nice. It's always better to hear it from the guys than from us.

If you need a drill sergeant I could help you with that.

We may need that too. ...Well, what do you think? Shall we grant this graduation?

Definitely.

[Staff present at this meeting were Margaret James (Teacher-Counselor), Miriam Robinson (Liaison T-C), Dennis Koenig (School Psychologist), and Tom Valore (Center Coordinator). All were staff of the West Shore Day Treatment Center operated by the Positive Education Program.]

This transcript was provided by Thomas G. Valore, PhD, currently Director of Staff Development for the Positive Education Program in Cleveland, OH.   Valore@pepcleve.org

Part II

Replacing Pathology: Focusing on Health and Strength

Choosing to Think Differently

Hobbs made active choices that promoted positive change, proposing the

> *"...model provided by education – with its emphasis on health rather than illness, on teaching rather than on treatment, on learning rather than on fundamental personality reorganization, on the present and the future rather than on the past, on the operation of the total social system of which the child is a part rather than on intrapsychic processes exclusively"* (Hobbs, 1982, p. 16).

This decision consciously made wellness paramount, using the idiom of education to frame everyone's view of the troubled and troubling child as first and foremost a child with his or her own capabilities, hopes, and dreams, as well as fears, illusions, and needs. This "child first" view frames our thoughts in a different way, shapes our awareness of their strengths and accomplishments, and reminds us they are not the same as their weaknesses and failures.

Hobbs was early in pointing out this difference in the 1960 planning for Project Re-ED. He recognized the importance of language, that words shape thoughts, that thoughts frame perceptions and create selective awareness. He believed that the cognitive sets created by these perceptions shape both behaviors and others' responses to those behaviors which confirm or disconfirm our original assumptions. By focusing on pathology and abnormality, we may create even more of the same.

Hobbs was particularly concerned about the effects of labeling children. At the request of the Secretary of Health, Education, and Welfare, he initiated a 1972 national study (called the Project on Classification of Exceptional Children) that involved a wide range of national leaders interested in classification issues. Two books resulted: one, written by Hobbs, summarized the project's findings, exploring categories, labels, and their consequences (1975a); a second edited book (1975b) consisted of chapters by project colleagues across the country and served as a sourcebook for the national group's recommendations. Using new words to describe a child can be strange to many who are accustomed to the former language and the ideas associated with them. This cognitive dissonance we experience when a new idea doesn't "fit" can feel punishing, but it can also begin to disconfirm our original thinking and reshape viewpoints.

Choosing a Model and Investigating Theories

The *foundation* of an approach or a program is its *philosophy and values*, the associated beliefs and principles that ultimately shape its processes. From that foundation, the entire *first floor* (using a building metaphor) would be the selection or creation of a *model*, and the investigation or development of *related theory*. Hobbs saw the outgrowth of this new emphasis on strength and learning for troubled and troubling children, and their families, as both an ecological and a competence model. An ecological competence model would be related to a somewhat different set of theories and research than a pathology based model. This approach would be concerned with learning theory, emphasizing social learning theory, and would seek out research on emotional de-conditioning and skill instruction – as well as a broad range of areas not traditionally included in the mental health intervention repertoire.

Effects on Intervention Choices

Models selected and their supporting theories give rise to the concrete tools programs employ when enacting an approach to serve children and families. The *second floor* of the program "building" must have workable and efficient *structures and strategies*. The wellness based view looks for interventions that build on ecosystem strengths and commit to positive goals and strategies. The assumption is that children and their families are both learners and teachers, just like all of us. Conscious acceptance of those roles accelerates openness and growth.

Hobbs described some simple but highly affirmative beliefs that guided the early (and later) Re-ED programs:

"[T]hat young people have a tremendous desire to learn and to do well; that their feelings are intrinsically valid and quite as important as their thinking; that destructive and self-defeating behavior must be faced; that young people can help each other sort things out and arrive at good choices; that the world is rich in things to learn; that life is to be savored at each moment; and that decent, caring adults are absolutely essential in the lives of children if those children are to grow up strong in body, quick of mind, generous in spirit (Hobbs, 1982, p. 20).

Inclusion of Medical Services

When need is indicated, medical consultation is sought and valued, as are all other disciplinary consultations. We are especially grateful for the new medical model described as "bio-psycho-social" by the physicians trained in forward thinking medical schools and facilities. We would add "-educational" (or a synonym for learning) and find it much like an ecological model.

Medication is not a usual feature of Re-ED intervention. In those cases where there are clear medical indications of both its need and effectiveness, however, our staff and families are more likely to include it in the intervention plan. In the years since Re-ED started, psychoactive medications have exponentially increased in number, in specificity of known effects, and in information on side effects. We maintain our stance that medication is almost never the sole intervention, its effects are closely and continually observed, and the child is never encouraged to attribute his behavior (appropriate or inappropriate) to having taken or missed his medication. Attributing positive (or negative) changes to the effects of medication, without acknowledgement of the child's own efforts, can be destructive.

Brain research, both in general and in the specific, is also becoming a major contributor to our field's bank of interdisciplinary intervention resources. Especially useful is the rapidly growing body of clinical research studies targeting the massive effects of trauma often associated with the experiences of troubled and troubling children (e.g., Perry, 2001b). We do well to learn continually from and with each other as professionals.

Replacing Pathology with a Model for Strength and Wellness

This substitution of wellness for a pathology-based view is not so unusual now as it was at the time when Hobbs and his colleagues proposed it in the late 1950's and early 1960's. Medicine and psychotherapeutic approaches had less to offer at the time, and the promise of a new and broader ecological-competence paradigm has proved both productive and long-lived. (Parts III and IV, immediately following this section, will explore the key concepts of "Ecology" and "Competence," respectively.)

This section (Part II) examines the first one of six Re-ED essentials, exploring some of the implications and results of this basic decision to adopt a wellness and strength-based view, made by Hobbs and his colleagues almost five decades ago. Part II includes:

Terry Cooper's report (chapter 4), written for his supervisor to summarize his reactions after visiting a Cleveland Re-ED program, was shared by his supervisor with a friend and former colleague. The friend himself directs a large Re-ED agency, knew the book was being written, and requested permission to send it to us. We asked Terry and his supervisor if we could include it, and they agreed. Like many of our member agencies, they recognized themselves in many of our beliefs and practices; about two years later Cal Farley's joined the American Re-Education Association as a sponsoring agency.

Also in this section, Adam (chapter 5), nearing completion of his Re-ED stay in an alternative school, describes what he found there and what about it was important to him. Our students are our teachers, on a continuing basis.

One of the most critical aspects of Re-ED programming is the extraordinary effort that goes into planning for success. Proactive forethought and carefully planned provisions act preventively to reduce the need for adults to react to crises and solve problems. In chapter 6, Jim Doncaster, Teacher-Counselor in the early years of Re-ED and later supervisor-trainer-administrator in other Re-ED programs outside Tennessee, shares valuable components of this proactive programming.

Nick Hobbs acknowledged a debt *"...for the importance of purpose and of joy in the life of children to Anton Makarenko of the Soviet Union"* (Hobbs, 1982, p. xvii). When asked which of Re-ED's 12 principles is their personal favorite, many Re-ED staff respond quickly with: "A child should know some joy in each day." Janice Moore (chapter 7) gives her view of the importance and functions of joy in working with troubled and troubling children and youth.

References

Hobbs, N. (1975a). *The futures of children: Categories, labels, and their consequences.* San Francisco: Jossey-Bass.

Hobbs, N. (1975b). *Issues in the classification of children: A source-book on categories, labels, and their consequences.* San Francisco: Jossey-Bass.

Hobbs, N. (1982). *The troubled and troubling child.* San Francisco: Jossey-Bass.

Perry, B. D. (2001b). The neurodevelopmental impact of violence in childhood. In D. Schetky, & E. Benedek (Eds.). *Textbook of child and adolescent forensic psychiatry* (pp. 221-238). Washington, D.C.: American Psychiatric Press, Inc. www.ChildTrauma.org

4

A Visitor's View: Report to Mark Strother of Cal Farley's

Terry Cooper

The Positive Education Program (PEP), located in Cleveland, Ohio, has a number of programs serving children and families. This site report focuses on PEP's Midtown Center for Youth in Transition (Midtown). Tom Valore, PEP's Program Director in charge of training, was the primary contact for this visit. The goal of this visit was to observe a mature program serving youth which operates according to the principles of Re-Education of Troubled Youth (Re-ED) as derived from the book by Dr. Nicholas Hobbs, *The Troubled and Troubling Child.*

PEP's literature states that Midtown's program goal is to address the needs of troubled young adults who are facing a difficult transition to independent adult living. Essentially, Midtown is a day treatment center for youth who have exhausted the resources of public schools in their effort to graduate and become independent. Midtown is located in a large multi-story building just down the street from PEP's main office. Even though it is situated in downtown Cleveland, Midtown's students come from all over the surrounding county.

The majority of the visit was spent in one classroom, with most of the time spent observing an ongoing interaction between a group of Midtown teacher-counselors (T-Cs) and Edison, age 17, who had been attending classes at Midtown for less than six months. This one day observing Edison was far more instructive about PEP's implementation of Re-ED principles than any formal presentation or tour might have been.

In the time that Edison had been at Midtown, it is likely that his behavior would have already resulted in a discharge from most other institutions. Behaviors such as those presented by Edison often provoke counter-aggressive responses from staff, counter-aggression which leads to spiraling conflict cycles and fruitless power struggles ending in restraint or seclusion. In fact, Edison's placement at PEP was the most recent stop in a life marked by multiple failed placements, school failure, and ineffectual treatment strategies.

Edison was born outside the United States. He was adopted by American parents soon after birth. Apparently, the adoptive family had or developed significant problems, because staff reported that he had a family history of parental conflict and physical and substance abuse. Observing Edison, it was evident that he had significant developmental difficulties. He had some speech and language difficulties which often made it difficult to understand him.

Tom and I arrived at the classroom during a general tour of the building. We had not planned to stay, but did stay when the lead teacher reported that they had a restraint that morning. The teacher noted that it was their first restraint in months, so Tom decided to investigate. What began as a casual walk-through tour became a fascinating study of a mature Re-ED program at work.

The classroom was relatively small with a variety of small desks and tables arranged around the room in no apparent pattern. Two teacher's desks were placed head to head against each other and positioned against a wall. Two doors led into the classroom. One was the main entrance into the hall. The other led into a small office housing a clutter of desks, phones and filing cabinets. Later, this seemingly random design was revealed to be critically important to the functioning of the classroom.

The classroom environment appeared casual and unhurried. Several students were working on a variety of tasks ranging from writing on paper to working with small boxes full of gears and small parts.

Neither teachers nor students seemed to be disturbed by the presence of a visitor. Many of the typical trappings of a classroom, such as cheery bulletin boards and wall decorations, were missing. Everyone, except for Edison, appeared busy and calmly focused on their particular task.

In Edison's case, his task was "being restrained." The lead teacher, Sharon Novak, explained before we entered the classroom that Edison was engaged in a "self-restraint." Puzzled, Tom and I entered to find Edison lying on the floor by himself, with his arms wrapped tightly around his own torso and his legs crossed over each other. At first, it seemed like a prank, but Edison's serious demeanor made it clear it was serious business. Sharon told us that upon Edison's arrival that morning, he had begun attempting to engage staff and students in a conflict. After unsuccessfully attempting to redirect Edison, she suggested to him that if he really wanted to have a serious conflict, he should save his energy and go straight to the final stage. Edison's history in previous placements had been to engage in conflicts leading to restraints. Knowing this, Sharon suggested that he simply get down on the floor, assume a restraint position, and get comfortable. She told him that after a while, staff would join him on the floor. In this way, no one got hurt or tired. Tom and I entered shortly after Edison had complied with the suggestion, thus his position on the floor.

Since no one seemed to be paying much attention to Edison, I still thought it was something of a joke. But Tom explained that Edison had a long history of physical aggression, and on Friday of the previous week, Edison had spit in Sharon's face in an attempt to provoke counter-aggression. However, in the six months Edison had been attending classes at Midtown, staff had yet to be involved in a restraint with him.

With the situation ongoing, Tom, Sharon, and I sat down at an empty desk and began discussing the classroom program. All during this time, students came in and out of the classroom without seeming to notice Edison. Other than the occasional glance to check on him, neither Tom nor Sharon paid any particular attention to Edison.

Sharon seemed particularly unperturbed by Edison's actions. Her reaction could not be characterized as apathetic. Instead, it seemed to be a very calm, very determined effort not to engage in counter-aggressive responses to Edison. Even so, her calm was not a pose adopted over an anxious concern. She seemed generally at ease, as did the other students and staff.

After a short time, Edison got up from the floor and went to his desk which faced the far wall from where we were sitting. He sat down, and pulling his black leather jacket over his head, placed his head on the desk. No one reacted to him or gave him new instructions, other than to praise him for making better decisions. I asked Sharon about this limited response. She said that Edison's routine was such that he knew exactly what work he was to do, and when he was ready, he would begin working.

A few more minutes passed. Edison raised his head, and peeking out from under his jacket, began attempting to get the other teacher, whose desk was close to Edison's but faced in the opposite direction, involved in a verbal confrontation. Edison's efforts consisted of making statements that he was not going to do his work, and no one could make him. These statements were laced with profanity, most of which was directed at the teacher. The teacher's consistent and low key response was to remind Edison that he would respond to him when Edison was ready to work and could address him in an appropriate manner.

This went on for more than 30 minutes. Finally, Edison appeared to scribble on a paper, and took it to the teacher. He threw the paper on the teacher's desk, with the statement "Here, bitch, is your fucking math paper." The teacher continued to calmly remind Edison what he needed to do. Edison's response was to continue to attempt to provoke a confrontation. He alternated this with what appeared to be efforts to work on his papers, followed by a retreat under the jacket, followed by another attempt to provoke the teacher. After some time, my comfort level increased to the point where I was observing Edison less intensely. Thus it was to my surprise when I looked up later in the morning, to see Edison calmly walking to the teacher's desk to hand in his completed work.

The postscript to the morning's event involved Tom Valore. As soon as it appeared that Edison was stable and engaged, Tom casually approached Edison to introduce himself. Standing by Edison's desk, Tom stuck out his hand and said, "Hi, I'm Tom." Edison's reaction was swift and startling. He leapt from his desk, putting it between the two of them, and cried out in a tone both defensive and aggressive, "Get the fuck away from me!" Tom quickly moved back, hands held out to his sides, reassuring Edison and saying, "No problem. I hadn't met you yet and I just wanted to." Within ten minutes, Tom was sitting by Edison's desk, chatting happily about the leather jacket Edison was wearing. The conversation culminated with Edison and Tom leaving the classroom to go downstairs to the cloakroom to view Tom's leather jacket. As they left the room, they were having a serious discussion about the care and maintenance of leather jackets.

This might seem a typical and trivial incident in the life of a youth-serving organization. However, while the incident may have been trivial, it is not typical of how youth such as Edison are typically served. Indeed, in far too many situations, Edison's behavior would have at best resulted in expulsion from the classroom, and at worst in a restraint.

This raised several questions. Why was Midtown's response to Edison so different? What issues does this vignette raise for other programs seeking to engage in strength-based program principles? What principles were the foundations of Sharon and Tom's response to Edison?

Sharon and Tom's response to Edison was extraordinary in that it was not so much a measure of their self-control as it was an indication of their belief in Edison's strengths and capacities. In many programs, the prognosis for Edison would be dim and limited. As it was, the current picture gave little reason for optimism. Given Edison's limited coping skills and apparently meager assets, a casual observer might be excused for thinking that Edison's chances for graduation from the Midtown program would seem poor at best. To put it bluntly, Edison seemed more likely to be a candidate for marginalization within and without the special program.

Yet almost inexplicably, the PEP staff appeared to genuinely admire and respect Edison. They did not accord him any lesser status nor treat him with any less regard than any other person in the room. Their response was not passive or patronizing. Simply, they appeared to look past and through Edison's behaviors and limited coping strategies. Instead of seeing the deficits, they seemed to see a unique and interesting human being, with as much capacity to enjoy life and contribute to the community as anyone else in the room, including the adults present. Watching the staff at work, it seemed evident that Re-ED seemed much more than a theory of practice – it was a way of life.

Thus it was obvious that Edison was an end unto himself. What mattered to the staff was Edison – not the program, not an outcome, not a theory, not their own comfort or job security – it was Edison that mattered. Thus the Re-ED principles seemed to be a natural and logical expression of the staff's core belief and value systems. It is critically important to understand that unlike other programs visited, the PEP program infrastructure and program design facilitated and enhanced the expression of these core beliefs by staff and youth.

For example, the Re-ED principle that "Time is an ally" was clearly supported. Edison's classroom was designed around students working with individual instructional plans. Each student clearly knew what they were to do. The classroom environment was driven not by the needs of the external environment (i.e., schedules, bells, curriculum, program agendas), but by the needs of the students in the classroom. Teachers were under no pressure to bring a process or task to conclusion in such a way that would create more behavior management issues later in the day. Indeed, Edison spent much of the morning in a resistant posture. It appeared that the morning was being wasted. But in the end, Edison completed his work, and the problems of the morning did not extend into the rest of the day. When Edison's problem was over, it was over. The critical element in achieving this was that the staff did not have to bring Edison into compliance in order to move him to another program or class.

Midtown teacher-counselors also demonstrate the Re-ED principle that "Self-control can be taught." The staff did not respond to Edison by controlling his behavior, but by constantly reinforcing his efforts at self-control while giving no reinforcement to his attempts to get someone else to own his problem. Similarly, they worked on the principle that "Intelligence can be taught." This was evident in their work with the other students in the room. Most of these students had come to Midtown with histories similar to Edison's. They were engaged in a variety of tasks, some of which did not appear to be traditional vocational or academic activities. The explanation for this was that each student was working on something which promoted development of their particular intelligence and allowed them to experience competence (as per the principle "Competence makes a difference".)

Not only did staff attitude and performance provide a demonstration of Re-ED principles at work, but the design and staffing of the classroom were also critically important. The classroom was a small community in itself. Unlike most classrooms, the door to the hallway was open allowing students and staff to move freely in and out of the room. Visitors were not a disruption, but a normative part of the environment. It was clear that the classroom process was based on trust between students and staff. There was an ease and comfort evident in the way staff and students interacted. No one was distracted or deterred by Edison's antics. Instead, everyone seemed to accept them as something normal, and students continued to work and interact in a relaxed and productive fashion.

This calm atmosphere was supported by the proximity of other staff. The attached office was where the vocational and liaison teacher-counselors worked. This meant that an adult was always readily available to a student. It also meant that students could see the adults as a team rather than as isolated individuals. Sharon told me that students knew that if there was a problem at home, it was likely that the liaison teacher-counselor would hear about it the same day (the liaison teacher-counselor's counterpart in other institutions would be a caseworker.) The liaison teacher-counselor's conversation would be overheard by the academic and vocational teacher-counselors, who could discuss it and make adjustments in the student's classroom or work environments as needed. Or, an employer might call the vocational teacher-counselor to discuss a concern about a student's workplace performance. The issue would then be discussed with other teacher-counselors, and adjustments made as needed.

Thus to the students, the staff team was seamlessly present at the various parts of a student's day. In fact, Tom reported that it was not unusual for teacher-counselors to get calls from home during non-school hours requesting assistance. Staff had been known to arrive at a student's home to help deal with challenges that would have negative consequences in school or work. This willingness to go the extra mile, according to Sharon, was because each staff member knew that the others would "get their back" while they were away. Sharon reported that the physical proximity allowed staff to easily communicate and plan coordinated responses to student issues. But most importantly, she reported that the proximity made it possible for her to feel like part of a team. This core team is critical to the development of community in the classroom and throughout the program.

It was obvious that the pervasive posters listing the twelve Re-ED principles were more than window dressing. These principles have apparently been essential to the creation of a shared set of values among the staff team. These values were made evident to the students through the actions of the staff as well as through the ubiquitous posting of the principles in corridors, classrooms, and offices. Unlike many other programs, these principles and values are not ideals to strive for, but are reflective of the reality being lived out on a daily basis. This leads to another critical question: How did this come about at PEP, when other facilities struggle to develop consistently applied strength-based programs?

The first and most obvious answer is that PEP was founded on Re-ED principles. As a result, the staff team was hired with these principles in mind. The programs were developed to achieve outcomes based on them. According to Tom, much has changed since PEP's founding, but the focus on these principles has remained a constant point of reference.

One of the Re-ED principles is that "a child should know some joy in each day." PEP's leadership has obviously figured out that it is difficult for children to know joy at a school if the employees don't experience some joy as well. This doesn't mean that PEP is an "adult welfare" agency. Instead, it is very clear that the well-being of children and youth is the sole purpose of PEP's programming. But the PEP environment is one which promotes positive relationships for adults and children. The aforementioned design of the classroom is a case in point. Rather than having the service delivery split across several locations, where team members only meet for routine meetings and during a crisis, the camaraderie of the team is supported by the proximity of their work space. Sharon reported that one of the most outstanding reasons for her twelve years of service was the knowledge that she worked with people who were connected with each other in ways that crossed typical workplace boundaries. Tom modeled this in that he appeared to know a great deal about the life situations of the staff we met, and in his casual chat with them, displayed an interest in them as friends and colleagues. Because of this relational and professional dynamic, Midtown "reflects and transmits a shared understanding of what it means to be a good person," as is called for in a recent press release concerning a national report on the needs of children (Commission on Children at Risk, 2003).

This proximity enables the Midtown classroom to more fully function according to Hobbs' ecological model of treatment and care. Through the simple reality that the Midtown teacher-counselors get to see issues from a shared perspective, the classroom staff can more easily plan and respond according to ecological principles as outlined by Hobbs.

According to Hobbs, a Re-ED school becomes part of a child's ecosystem for the explicit purpose of increasing the adequacy of the system with respect to the development of the child. The school is ecologically oriented in order to recognize that the functioning effectiveness of a child may be substantially affected by environmental influences, logistical arrangements, and individual-environment transactions. This orientation results in an assessment that leads to an enablement plan rather than a service plan.

Of course, such a plan requires that the Midtown program address more variables than the typical program. An enablement plan requires the staff to be present and informed across the scope of the youth's ecosystem. Such an approach can be costly, making the need for maintaining ongoing funding a perpetual crisis. As such, Midtown and PEP face the same funding, contract, and service jurisdiction challenges any other urban youth serving organization faces. The city of Cleveland is facing a fiscal crisis that may force substantial funding cuts across the board for all human service contracts. It is unlikely that PEP could or will escape the impact of such cuts. PEP also faces the challenges of working with a complex human service bureaucracy that makes consistent care of youth difficult as they move through the various levels and authorities of the bureaucracy.

Admirable as the Midtown model is, it may have limited applicability to other programs, since it did not have to transform itself into a strength-based program but was developed this way from the beginning. Programs serving youth from traditional clinical and deficit models may find it difficult to make the changes to strength-based culture and theory of practice. Indeed, it is important to note that PEP is as much a culture as it is a program. The PEP "brand" is something in which the staff invest a great deal of ownership and pride. Their work and personal spaces seem permeable in a way that traditional providers may find challenging or even inappropriate.

Also, PEP's labor pool is located in the middle of a diverse urban population. This makes it easier for PEP to be highly selective about their hires. PEP seems to have little of the "warm body" staff profile that afflicts many programs, particularly residential ones. This allows PEP to hire and retain people who buy into the unique culture and community of facilities like Midtown. It is my belief that PEP is able to hire and retain quality staff as much on the basis of the culture as of the specific mission or skill set.

This has allowed PEP to hire teacher-counselors, rather than just teachers or caseworkers. This is a critical point in understanding the Midtown experience. It was evident that PEP's teacher-counselors embodied Hobbs' description of the characteristics of a successful teacher-counselor.

According to Hobbs, a teacher-counselor should have the ability to experience, accept, and handle feelings with minimum distortion, to tolerate anxiety without dulling, to exercise authority, and to refresh themselves independently of their work. They should demonstrate a commitment to children, and engage in effective interpersonal relationships with adults. They should have skills in general and special teaching, and be informed about the general culture.

But most important, and this was evident in the staff's response to Edison, a teacher-counselor is one who is good at working with young people and believes in them. A teacher-counselor is someone whose self-realization is linked to the full development of youth. Thus the teacher-counselor should be concerned with the specific learnings required by a particular child to regain access to normal opportunities for learning in home, school, and community from which the child has been excluded because of their unacceptable behavior. Certainly the prior statement describes Edison's needs and history, and this approach was evident with every student in the classroom. Midtown's classrooms were working examples of Hobbs' concept of treatment consistency.

In the final analysis, even if PEP's program practices are not always directly applicable to other institutions, PEP's Re-ED model should not be dismissed. Instead, PEP should be an inspiration and starting point for any program seeking to develop a strength-based program and culture.

References

Commission on Children at Risk (2003). *Hardwired to connect: The new scientific case for authoritative communities.* New York: Inst. for American Values, 1841 Broadway, Suite 211, NY 10023 http://www.americanvalues.org/html/hardwired.html#Press

Author's Note

This report was submitted to Mark Strother of Cal Farley's, Amarillo, Texas. All names of students and staff, excepting Tom Valore and Sharon Novak, were changed to protect privacies.

Terry Cooper, MSW, is Director of Cal Farley's Institute in Amarillo, Texas. terrycooper@calfarley.org

5

A Teen Talks: Adam's Story

Adam

The reason why I wasn't going to school was because [pause] I'm working and I'm not going to get credit for it so I just have to say forget it. So I never came to school after [they told me] that. I would just cut school. And then it got to be a habit, a bad habit ….

One day I met with them [at the old school] like a Friday or a Thursday, and then the next Monday, I was getting ready to go to school and my Dad said, "Well, you're not going there anymore; we're taking you here." Then they kind of just dropped me off here at MT [Re-ED program] and I've been going here ever since….

I just didn't feel like I needed to be here. Actually attending MT made me realize there was stuff I needed to work on. My attendance for example. There were a lot of things at home going on that were bothering me, but I had teachers and I had people that really cared and worried about my well being, worried about me coming to school everyday and me getting my work done and really wanted to see me graduate. It was easier coming to school because if I had a bad day I had Ms. N or Mr. R or Ms. B, I had someone to talk to when I was really upset or when I had stuff that was bothering me. When I had stuff that was really going on at home….

They asked me what did I want to do, instead of this is what you're going to do.

…. I felt like I had a lot of choices. If I didn't like one situation,

39

I could always put myself in another situation, and it just made me feel better. I felt relieved. They actually made me want to come to school, because I hate school. I hate school. I hate school; I don't like school! I had people who made me want to come to school, so thank you for that. It made me feel like somebody was in my corner, too.

I always knew what was going on…. [T]here was never really a time that I didn't know what my plan was. I always had a plan [a skill emphasized and taught at MT]. I always knew where I was going. I always knew the steps that I had to do to carry out that plan.

Because of me attending MT, I feel like I can go to college and probably accomplish something, get a real job instead of one of these fast food joints, make some real money. They make you feel like anything is possible if you put your mind to it, and I like that. They kind of motivated me to do things that I normally wouldn't do, like come to school and go to work and get an education. They really teach you the importance of an education and they work with you to achieve that goal.

 If I were to say something to students, I'd tell them to let the staff help them, because can't nobody help them unless you let them help them….

What made me start letting y'all help me was [pause], no matter how I treated y'all, regardless if I was having a bad day, it was like you still wanted to help me. No matter how I was acting, you still wanted to help me whether I had a funky attitude or whether I had a nice attitude; that let me know it was more than just a job. Most teachers act like they want to help you — as soon as you blow them off, they're like, "Oh, all right," and then they don't want to do anything for you. So once I saw that, I was like, "OK, they really want to help. So I might as well, to be sitting here all day, I might as well get up and do something." So that's why I let y'all help me. And plus it needed to be done. And I was going through so much at the time, I couldn't do it by myself. So I let y'all help me.

I was successful because the teachers at MT respected me; they listened to my problems. They always gave me choices; they gave me hope. They really made school fun. *I enjoyed it!*

6

Antecedent Management &Maximization: Setting the Stage for Success in Re-ED Programs

James R. Doncaster

"What that young person needs is discipline" is a statement all of us have heard at one time or another. Perhaps it is true, but not in the sense which implies needed punishment. Discipline is better viewed as the process whereby external event relationships become internalized associations, whereby controls from without, in the parlance of Fritz Redl (Redl & Wineman, 1952), become "controls from within." While consequations are typically considered controlling events, the key to behavior change may well be proper antecedent events coupled with reinforcement (ideally positive).

For Re-EDers, the accent has always been on properly aligning antecedent conditions for a young person in order to elicit a fairly accurate response that can be positively reinforced. We have found that how we set the stage is critical to what is enacted upon it; it is the former (the antecedent or setting event) that informs and influences the latter (the young person's behavior). Our challenge is to set the stage for success, to capitalize on antecedent processes and arrange setting events so that success becomes more probable than failure for individuals or groups.

Although there are many ways this antecedent maximization principle plays out in Re-ED programs, this chapter focuses on four processes. First is the power of expectancies to influence outcomes.

41

By combining expectancies with the second process, the power of a therapeutic relationship, success begins to be more probable.

The third antecedent process, precision programming, derives from the principles of the competence model (White, 1959; Bricker, 1967; Cantrell, 1974; Cantrell & Cantrell, 1995). A good competence assessment by perceptive and sensitive teacher-counselors sets the academic and social bars at just the right height for young persons to be challenged, yet still succeed.

The fourth antecedent is the Re-ED practice of clearly communicating expectations to a young person or group, using behavioral rehearsal with one or all, when necessary. Establishing "points of order" in group life during which expectations are communicated, revisited, or evaluated actualize this practice. All four processes are explored in detail below.

The Power of Expectancies

"Treat people as if they were what they ought to be and you help them become what they are capable of being."
— Goethe

Nicholas Hobbs, the father of Re-ED, characterized a teacher-counselor as *"a decent adult... a person of hope, quiet confidence, and joy; one who has committed himself to children and to the proposition that children who are disturbed can be helped by the process of reeducation"* (Hobbs, 1982, p. 82). Belief in a young person's capacity for change, belief in one's own ability to forge a therapeutic relationship and be a catalyst for change, and belief in the re-education approach as the means by which change is brought about: these have become the hallmarks of Re-ED programs and the teacher-counselors who staff them. But it was not always so.

In the early days of the first Re-ED programs, teacher-counselors struggled to find the successful paths to teaching and treating troubled young people. For the staff, theory had yet to be translated into effective practice, and faith had yet to be bolstered by experience. As children and adolescents exhibited the maladaptive behaviors that brought them into treatment, teacher-counselors often became discouraged. Many knew failure. Staff turnover ran high (Hobbs, 1982).

Over time, however, the staff came to know success. While many teacher-counselors left, many stayed. Those who stayed tended to be those who were able to forge relationships with the young people and who were successful in their efforts to help them grow and overcome the difficulties that had brought them into residential care. The successes of these pioneering teacher-counselors were chronicled, their practices defined, shared, built upon, added to, and embellished. Many of them became program leaders who taught other teacher-counselors what worked and supported the new staff in times of crisis. As success bred success, faith in the re-education process became an experience-based conviction.

Dr. Frank Hewitt, the special education professor who originated the "engineered classroom," conducted a tour of Re-ED programs prior to launching a teacher-counselor training program at UCLA in the early 80s. After commenting in his report about the *"enthusiasm and commitment of the staff"* he made the following observations about them (as cited by Hobbs, 1982).

"Most importantly, they were believers; they took everything they did very seriously. I was really impressed by their attention to detail and their constant efforts to convey to their charges that everything going on was important and for a purpose. This sense of purpose and meaningfulness is in marked contrast to the confusion, vagueness, and coldness I have often felt in other residential climates. This seriousness and sense of purpose was contagious and readily discernible among the children and adolescents themselves.

"One thing that concerned me was whether they were simply extra-special young people who could make any program work or whether or not there was something in the reeducation process itself that activated the many fine qualities which I saw. I believe the reeducation process had a great deal to do with their enthusiasm and dedication. There was an expectancy that their efforts would be effective in helping the children and as this visibly occurred it was self-perpetuating" (Hobbs, 1982, pp. 32-33).

Expectancy effects are nothing new. According to Weinberger and Eig (1999, p. 359), *"There are overwhelming data attesting to the power of expectancies in medical treatment.... [P]lacebos and therefore expectancies can affect just about anything. A. K. Shapiro and Morris (1978) argued that most medical procedures before the 20th century owed their effectiveness to placebo or expectancy. Expectancy is an extremely powerful variable in human health functioning."*

Hobbs certainly was aware of the body of research on placebos and expectancies. He references Rosenthal and Jacobson's seminal work exploring the power of expectancies in educational settings in his book *The Futures of Children* (1975). The finding that students can, and often do, perform up to teacher expectations was named "The Pygmalion Effect" by Rosenthal and Jacobson (1968). Their study affirmed Hobbs' beliefs and became a rallying cry for more than one generation of teacher-counselors. "Set the bar high," goes the refrain "for the kids will live up to, or down to, your expectations."

Hobbs (1978) spoke directly to the importance of expectancies in the treatment of children:

"In the past few years I have come to appreciate more and more the power of expectancies in influencing the behavior of us all, including the children with whom we work" (p. 65).

Then speaking of his earlier work in the Classification project, he added:

"We did find evidence of the overwhelming influence that institutions have on the development of children. Each institution, whether family, church, or school, community center, hospital, correctional institution, or Re-ED school has its own metaphorical imperatives. These get expressed in myriad ways in the ambient expectations of the ... program. [They] are seldom defined, indeed the people involved (staff, children, parents) become so imbued with institutional expectations that they seem altogether natural and fitting and thus become unavailable for questioning. Paradoxically, specialized treatment institutions tend to confirm and extend the difficulties they are intended to remedy. Thus hospital wards for disturbed children tend to evoke sick behavior; institutions for the mentally retarded have impoverished learning programs; and juvenile correctional institutions tend to be schools for crime.... Re-ED schools have created an altogether different

set of expectancies for emotionally disturbed children and their families: the expectancy of competence, of trust and mutual acceptance, of shared efforts to help a child, of confidence in the child himself, of adventure, zest, joy" (p. 65).

Hobbs, who forever argued that Re-ED must guard against hardening its beliefs into a cement of dogma and orthodoxy, who argued conversely that the strength of Re-ED programs lies in their always "becoming" by virtue of staff who are always "re-inventing" them, concluded: *"A good exercise for a Re-ED staff is to re-examine this question: What expectancies are in fact operating in our school?"* (1978, p. 65). Given the apparent connection between beliefs and outcomes, staff raise belief systems to the level of consciousness, question their most basic assumptions, and attend to the alignment of expectancies with program values and goals lest there be program drift, stagnation, or worse.

The instilling of a belief system (in this case belief in the principles and processes of re-education and the catalytic impact they can have on a young person) cannot be left to chance. Rather it must become part of the formal training regimen of an organization. Organizational success could well hinge on such a process, according to IBM's Tom Watson, Jr.:

> *"[A]ny great organization–one that has lasted over the years–... owes its resiliency ...to the power of what we call beliefs and the appeal beliefs have for people. ...[A]ny organization, in order to survive and achieve success, must have a sound set of beliefs on which it premises all its policies and actions. Next, ...the most important single factor in corporate success is faithful adherence to those beliefs. And, finally,...an organization...must be prepared to change everything about itself except those beliefs as it moves through corporate life."* (Peters & Waterman, Jr., 1982, p. 280).

One belief, the belief in the child and his or her capacity for growth and change, takes us naturally to the second antecedent condition: the therapeutic relationship.

The Therapeutic Relationship

For the teacher-counselor, genuine belief in one's self, the re-education process, and the young person can set the stage for success, but does not ensure it. Positive expectancies, while they may influence the ensuing reality, do not determine it. A relationship between a teacher-counselor and a troubled youth is the second antecedent, the second critical variable in the Re-ED success equation. According to Hobbs, *"Trust between child and adult is essential, the foundation on which all other principles rest, the glue that holds teaching and learning together, the beginning point for re-education"* (1982, p. 22).

Troubled children, almost by definition, have impaired relationships with adults. Often the products of aberrant learning histories, most have concluded that adults cannot be relied upon and should not be trusted. While a conventional child looks naturally to an adult for support and direction, the troubled child may well see the same adult as a potential source of derision, rejection, or even harm. To forge a trusting relationship in the face of this mistrust is the challenge every teacher-counselor faces with nearly every troubled child served.

The literature on resilience resonates with the importance of relationship between adult and child. According to some resilience scales, the more relationships with adults that are formed, up to a point, the more likely a child is to grow to be a "survivor," that is, a healthy adult capable of giving and receiving love. Still, a child's survival begins with the forging of a single trusting relationship. How critical is relationship for a troubled child? Waln Brown (1995), president of the William Gladden Foundation and author of the autobiographical *The Other Side of Delinquency*, found it odd that he is so often asked to address child-care workers when these professionals had *"written me off"* when he was a *"very disturbed and disoriented youth"* (p. 18). Many labels such as "neurotic, schizoid, schizophrenic, high psychotic potential" (p. 18) and other such diagnoses had been attached to his files and had followed him throughout his childhood. Fortunately, there were other professionals who saw his potential and invested in providing him with opportunities to prevail. *"They are the true heroes in my life; without their altruism and dedication I would have proved the doubters correct"* (Brown, 1995, p.18).

Brown singled out one man, a probation officer who took a special interest in him, as the one who made all of the difference:

"…[W]hat I have come to realize is that he, more than any person other than myself, had the most influence in determining how my life has turned out. He was the one steadfast influence in an otherwise tumultuous childhood. He was the difference between what I am and what I might have become. He was a believer, and he believed in me" (p. 19).

Brown concludes with this admonition:

"To you, the professionals who work with emotionally and behaviorally disordered children like I once was, I have tried to impart what I deem to be my most critical insight, the product of a lifetime of introspection: Don't give up! Don't ever give up!" (p. 19).

Belief in a child's ability to achieve potentiality if given opportunity to do so seems a likely starting point for relationship building. Holding to that belief in the face of indifference or hostility–not giving up! – appears to be equally important for the teacher-counselor if the child is to succeed.

Certainly Hobbs thought so. To nurture trust, the teacher-counselor *"must be a whole person, not a detached therapist"* (1982, p. 247), able to hold to belief in a child when the child has lost faith in himself and able to weather the storms that arise. While insisting that there are no exact formulas, Hobbs did suggest some cognitive and behavioral strategies for relationship building:

"What does it take, this building of trust between teacher and child? First of all, …to gain the trust of a child, …believe that the problem of trust is real and that progress toward its solution will mean progress toward the child's learning. Then …have time or take time simply to be with the child. One must also …recognize the child's distrust and …accept without dismay–or retaliation–his swift and sure thrusts to hurt and keep others away; …recognize that a child's feelings have a validity quite independent of other people's reality; …modulate expectations of a child's achievement until success, however modest, becomes his frequent joy; …be patient, infinitely patient; …be utterly dependable, …keep one's word; …seek help from objective observers of one's own behavior with the child, for one cannot always distance himself properly from a self-defining commitment; …use private resources for personal understanding and support, especially when the going

is tough; and ...be genuinely content, no, joyous, when a child begins to catch fire with learning, however limited or grand his flame may be. It can be done; we vouchsafe that" (1982, pp. 250-251).

Recent research has made it *"clear that the therapeutic relationship is causally relevant to treatment outcome"* (Weinberger & Eig, 1999, p. 371). Identifying factors that influence successful relationship formation has become an object of study. Pressley Ridge has undertaken a five year study to examine therapeutic alliance. The research, a collaborative effort of the Pressley Ridge Institute and Vanderbilt University, has isolated several personality and behavioral factors related to building and sustaining positive relationships between teacher-counselors and the youth in their care. While a fuller discussion of the findings can be found in the chapter by Rauktis, Andrade, and Doucette in this book, one of the key personality traits associated with high levels of alliance is "genuineness" or the ability to be "real."

Other behaviors and traits identified as instrumental in teacher-counselors' forming positive relationships and managing resistance include: (1) high levels of warmth, or empathy; (2) low anxiety and stability of mood; (3) flexibility; and (4) knowing and effectively implementing the program's treatment strategies. The project continues to provide data that are proving helpful in teacher-counselor selection, training, and supervision.

Competence Makes a Difference

Give a man a fish and he will eat for a day;
Teach a man to fish and he will eat for a lifetime.
                                                    —African Proverb

"Competence makes a difference; children and adolescents should be helped to be good at something, and especially at schoolwork," states the pivotal, third Re-ED principle (Hobbs, 1982, p. 22). That "something" may be anything–building a teepee fire, riding a bicycle, turning a pot on a potter's wheel, or playing a tin whistle. Often that "something" relates to school work. The most common characteristic of a severely emotionally disturbed child or adolescent is academic underachievement. Rarely does a young

person come to a Re-ED program on grade level; indeed, most enter our programs two to three years academically deficient.

The relationship between low academic performance and emotional difficulties, while unclear, appears to be one of interaction rather than causation (Hobbs, 1982). Learning difficulties may give rise to emotional or behavioral problems, or emotional problems may deleteriously impact learning, depending on individual and situational variables. Both conditions in the short term produce stress and both over the long term can create lower self-esteem.

Underachievement in school is the most common characteristic of an SED child. According to Nicholas Hobbs (1982, p. 252):

"The common assumption that emotional disturbance causes reading difficulties leads to the conclusion that the emotional difficulty must be cleared up before progress can be made in ...reading. This is a too-simple conception of the relationship between symptom and cause. All evidence calls at least for an interaction hypothesis to account for the frequent improvement in adjustment following improvement in basic academic skills."

In view of the interactional nature of learning and emotional and behavioral difficulties, neither should await the other for redress. Rather, both should be addressed simultaneously.

Teacher-counselors commonly use two models to increase the probability of success with troubled youth. One, the competence model, is used primarily for assessing skill levels and components, preparatory to formulating intervention strategies. In Re-ED programs, this model is typically associated with the academic arena, though the competence model lends itself equally well to framing skill assessment and programming in any venue or diagnosing the cause of an emotional outbreak.

The Competence Model

As noted, most troubled and troubling young people have known failure in the classroom. For some, emotional difficulties have interfered with learning, causing academic performance to plummet. For others, learning problems have given rise to apathy and withdrawal or hostility and aggression. In either case, without proper intervention, troubled youths fall further and further behind peers and more and more into cycles of failure and frustration. What is asked of them seems reasonable enough; it is what is asked of all of their classmates. Unfortunately, what is asked of them is no longer within their means to produce. (See Figure 1 below.)

The Competency Model

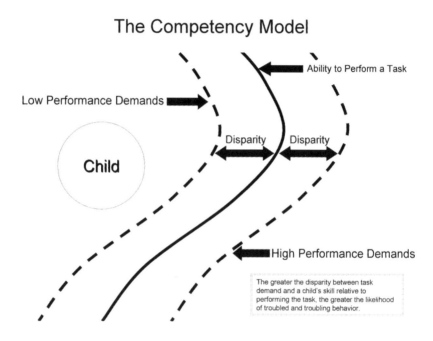

The greater the disparity between task demand and a child's skill relative to performing the task, the greater the likelihood of troubled and troubling behavior.

The process of re-education begins with assessment, and assessment begins with the Competence Model as a referent. The Competence Model, articulated for problem behaviors by W. A. Bricker in 1967 (Cantrell, Cantrell, Valore, Jones, & Fecser, 1999), addresses the relationship between an organism and the environmental demands placed upon it. When applied to a child, the model holds that the more task demands meet, or just exceed, the child's ability to perform the task, the more likely the child is, if properly motivated, to perform the task. Conversely, the greater the disparity between task demand and the child's ability to perform the specific task, the greater the likelihood that the task will produce stress and, over time, eventuate in off-task behavior. The greater the disparity between a task's demands and a child's skill relative to performing the task, the greater the likelihood that troubled and troubling behavior will ensue. Complex division problems given to a student who is unable to perform multiplication tasks, for example, will perplex and frustrate the student. If the disparity between the task demand and the student's ability is not reduced, over time the student's behavior is likely to become increasingly more discordant. Likewise the student who goes unchallenged, who is given the same steady diet of long division when she is capable of performing advanced math, will become bored and equally frustrated. The end result is the same: off task or emotional "garbage" behavior.

For a Re-ED student, once the student's performance level and component skills are determined, targeted teaching can begin. Initially, because the classroom teacher-counselor is aware that the student has known much failure in school, he/she may set the task bar slightly under the student's ability level to avoid overwhelming the student and to begin the process of confidence building. In the days ahead, the bar will be inched upward, however, so that the student may grow in both competence and confidence.

The principles inherent in the Competence Model apply equally to programming in settings outside the classroom. A teacher-counselor would not presume to ask a new student to lead a group meeting, for example. The student would have neither the frame of reference nor the skill to do so successfully. Rather, through a process involving repeated demonstration, encouragement, assistance, and support, the student grows to handle program and life demands.

With time, the skillful teacher-counselor learns to intuitively approach all planned activities, whether for an individual or a treatment group, in a manner consistent with the Competence Model. In this way activities are task analyzed and skill sequenced prior to being taught. Thus, swimming and water safety are taught before canoeing, mastery of canoeing on flat water precedes the challenge of white water, and riffles are tackled long before Class III rapids are even considered. Such an approach all but guarantees successful living experiences for a young person, and as Re-EDers have always maintained, "successful living is healing."

The PIE Model

The second model, for lack of a better term, is referred to by Re-EDers as the PIE model, PIE being an acronym for Planning-Implementation-Evaluation. The conceptual model of Planning-Implementation-Evaluation no doubt was borrowed by Re-ED, though its applications to our work with troubled young people may be somewhat unique. The practices emanating out of this model bring stability to our classrooms and residences and help guide troubled young people through the challenges inherent in all settings. The model, as applied in Re-ED settings, is aimed at antecedent control. With its emphasis on the clear articulation of expectations, it is one more means by which we set the stage for success with those in our care.

This model emphasizes clear expression of expectations with children preparing to undertake a task (planning), the carrying out of the task (implementation), and the review of task performance (evaluation). It is commonly used to address behavioral and emotional difficulties in Re-ED programs. Just as the competence model lends itself to use in both the academic and behavioral realms, so, too, can the PIE techniques be applied in all settings.

Stephen Covey, author of The Seven Habits of Highly Effective People, advises, *"Seek first to understand, then to be understood"* (1989, p. 235). The competence model is the paradigm by which teacher-counselors seek to understand the student's difficulties within contexts. Performance data, gathered from assessments formal and informal, can be understood against the backdrop of the competence model, and potentially effective intervention strategies plotted. The first component of the PIE model is the basis by which teacher-counselors seek to clearly communicate expectations with troubled young people. This serves to decrease the misunderstandings that can confound interactions and lead to behavioral problems. The competence model, with its emphasis on understanding, and the PIE model, with its emphasis on being understood, are both stage-setting models.

In group work, applying the PIE model begins with a *point of order* that sets the stage for planning. For a treatment group, a point of order is established when individual members of the group cease their respective activities and come together, usually at the request of a teacher-counselor. The coming together may involve movement, as in the case of a dispersed group "huddling up," but always involves focusing the attentions of the individual group members. Typically in Re-ED programs, points of order are established to: (1) set or clarify expectations for an activity, (2) problem solve, or (3) evaluate an undertaking; though they may be used for a raft of other purposes as well. Group life would be chaotic without them. Indeed, one of the first tasks teacher-counselors have with a newly formed group is the inculcation of respect for points of order so that any call for one is heeded.

An example may help to clarify. At Pressley Ridge's Ohiopyle wilderness program, boys are assigned to one of six treatment groups, all of which have Indian names. We will focus on one brief activity for one group, the Iroquois group, for the purpose of illustration. As background, Iroquois is a transition group traditionally comprised of soon-to-be-graduated members from the other treatment groups. As such, the Iroquois group, while not devoid of problems, is more mature and self-directing (if not more cohesive) than the other treatment groups, as they progress through PIE cycles.

This example shows how the role of a teacher-counselor (T-C) in a group varies from day to day, task to task. He or she gives to the group what it cannot give to itself. When a group is performing responsibly, the teacher-counselor may assume a posture more facilitative than directive, as shown here in the example, following.

T-C, as the last boy arrives in the ready area: "*Alright, we're all here. Everyone is moving pretty quickly this morning. I appreciate that. I especially appreciate Tom here. Although he admittedly has had problems getting going in the past, he was the first one here this morning. My hat goes off to you,*

Tommy. OK, Iroquois, what's next?"

Tom (beaming): *"We're headed down to dining hall."*

T-C: *"Right! And what do we need to keep in mind as we move down the trail?"*

Billy: *"Keep our hands and feet to ourselves."*

T-C: *"Absolutely. If we can do that, we've got it made. What else?"*

Tyrone: *"Stay together as a group."*

T-C: *"Good one, Tyrone. We haven't had a problem with that one for a while, but it sure is important. Other expectations?"*

Robert: *"Respect."*

T-C: *"What's that mean to you, Robert?"*

Robert: *"Watch our language. Don't 'dis' anyone."*

T-C: *"Excellent. Any others?… All right, gentlemen, do we think we can do that?"*

Group: *"Yea!"*

T-C: *"Then let's go. Single file. Tom, will you take the lead, please?"*

And off they go, with their prognosis for success significantly improved by this single antecedent event, this planning point of order. One of two things is now likely to happen. They will arrive at the dining hall without incident, or they will experience a problem in route. Either event will result in a second point of order. Let's deal with the problem scenario first: As the group is moving down the trail, Tom reports to his teacher-counselor that Billy has just stepped on the back of his leg and has muddied his pants.

T-C (matter-of-factly): *"Ok, Let's huddle up."*

Group: *"What? What happened? What's going on?"*

T-C: *"Tom, please share with the group what just happened."*

Tom: *"Billy's messing with me. He's always messing with some body and holding us up."*

T-C: *"What happened, Tom?"*

Tom: *"He (pointing to Billy) got the back of my pants all muddy. And these were clean, too!"*

Billy: *"It was an accident."*

T-C: *"Tom, do you think it could have been an accident?"*
Tom: *"No!"*
T-C: (Scanning the group) *"Group? Does anyone have any thing to add?"*
Tyrone: *"I think it was an accident. Billy was turned around talking to me when he ran into Tommy..."*
T-C: *"Billy, is that what happened?"*
Billy: *"Yep. It was an accident. That's what I said."*
T-C: *"Do you have anything to say to Tom?"*
Billy: (Pause) *"Sorry, Tom."*
T-C: *"Are you alright with that, Tommy, or do we need to talk about it some more?"* (Tommy nods his head). *"OK, what else can be done?"*
Robert: *"Billy could help clean off the mud at the dining hall."*
T-C: *"Billy?"*
Billy: *"Fine with me."*
T-C: *"Tommy, does that work for you?"*
Tom: *"I guess so."*
T-C: *"OK, sounds like we've got a plan. Will someone run through it for me to make sure we're all on the same page?"*

Following the reiteration of the plan, trail expectations are reviewed once more and the group resumes its task. So goes a problem-solving point of order.

The second scenario assumes that the group made it to their dining hall ready area without a problem. A new point of order is now established to evaluate their performance and to address what comes next.

T-C: *"Alright, Iroquois, we made it! How'd we do?"*
Group (chorus of voices): *"Great. Good. Fine. We're bad!"*
T-C: *"What is it we said we were going to do? Girard, you've been quiet this morning. Can you help us out?"*
Girard: *"Stay together. Keep hands and feet to ourselves. Respect one another. I think that's it."*

T-C: *"Thanks, Girard. Good memory! And did we do that, Iroquois?"*

Group: *"Yep. Betcha. Uh huh."*

T-C: *"Absolutely, we did it. Just last week we were having problems on the trail. Now look at us! Everyone turn to the guy on his right, and give him a pat on the back for a job well done. Okey dokey, we're going into the dining hall now. What do we need to remember?"*

And so it goes; the PIE process is applied to all things great and small, wherever new behavior or relatively new behavior is being learned or rehearsed. Weekly planning sessions are followed by carrying out the weekly schedules, which in turn are followed by weekly evaluations which give rise to a new cycle of planning, implementation, and evaluation. Re-ED days conclude with an evaluation of the day and each group member's contributions to it, followed by looking ahead to the morrow. Transition points, formerly times of difficulty for troubled youth, become points of order through which behavioral expectations are articulated and performances evaluated. Through this simple means, teacher-counselors modulate the experience of the youth in our charge, clarify what each task and situation is asking of them, help them at the point at which they encounter difficulty, and finally, teach them to reflect upon their behavior and to appreciate their individual contributions and accomplishments.

Conclusion

Re-ED programs of today begin with the end in mind. Of critical importance is staff selection. We seek out and hire people who possess a natural affinity for working with youngsters, people of warmth, stability, energy, and commitment. Knowing that outcomes are influenced by expectancies, we strive to influence the belief systems of teacher-counselors through training and supervision activities that impart hope, optimism, idealism, and other positive life values. Firm in the belief that meaningful and lasting behavioral change must be built on the bedrock of relationship, we stress the molding of therapeutic alliances between our staff and the young people we serve.

Finally, we seek to equip our teacher-counselors with the assessment skills essential to knowing where to begin the re-education process, and with the communication and intervention skills necessary to help bring order from chaos for troubled youngsters. With that, our stage is set for success, and we can proceed confident in the knowledge that our work up front will yield growth and joy in the youth we serve.

References

Bricker, W. A. (1967). Competence as a key factor in the study of children's deviant behavior. *Mind over Matter*. Nashville, TN: Tennessee Department of Mental Health.

Brown, W. K. (1995). Don't ever give up: The power of belief in promoting a turnaround. *Reclaiming Children and Youth: Journal of Emotional and Behavioral Problems, 4*(2), 17-19.

Cantrell, M. L. (1974). *Maladaptive behavior as a function of skill/demand discrepancies: An empirical investigation of the competence model.* (Doctoral dissertation, George Peabody College for Teachers, 1974). *Dissertation Abstracts International, 35,* 7718-7719.

Cantrell, M. L. & Cantrell, R. P. (1995). Competence: Building it and building on it. *Reclaiming Children and Youth, 4,* 20-24.

Cantrell, M. L., Cantrell, R. P., Valore, T. G., Jones, J. M., & Fecser, F. A. (1999). A revisitation of the ecological perspectives on emotional/behavioral disorders. In L. M. Bullock & R. A. Gable (Eds.), *The third mini-library series: What works for children and youth with E/BD: Linking yesterday and today with tomorrow.* Reston, VA: Council for Children with Behavioral Disorders.

Covey, S. R. (1989). *The seven habits of highly effective people: Restoring the character ethic.* New York: Fireside.

Hobbs, N. (1978). Perspectives on Re-Education. *Behavioral Disorders, 3*(2), 65-66.

Hobbs, N. (1975). *The futures of children: Categories, labels, and their consequences.* San Francisco: Jossey-Bass.

Hobbs, N. (1982). *The troubled and troubling child.* San Francisco: Jossey-Bass.

Peters, T. J., & Waterman, Jr., R. H. (1982). *In search of excellence: Lessons from America's best-run companies.* New York: Warner Books.

Redl, F., & Wineman, D. (1952). *Controls from within: Techniques for the treatment of the aggressive child.* New York: Free Press.

Rosenthal, R., & Jacobson, L. (1968). *Pygmalion in the classroom: Teacher expectation and pupils' intellectual development.* New York: Holt, Rinehart, and Winston.

Shapiro, A. K., & Morris, L. A. (1978). The placebo effect in medical and psychological psychotherapies. In S. L. Garfield & A. E. Bergin (Eds.), *Handbook of psychotherapy and behavior change.* (pp. 369-410). New York: Wiley.

Weinberger, J., & Eig, A. (1999). Expectancies: The ignored common factor in psychotherapy. In I. Kirsch (Ed.), *How expectancies shape experience.* Washington: American Psychological Association.

White, R. W. (1959). Motivation reconsidered: The concept of competence. *Psychological Reviews, 66,* 297-334.

James R. Doncaster, MA, is Director of Training for Pressley Ridge in their central offices in Pittsburg, PA.
jdoncaster@pressleyridge.org

7

Joy in Each Day

Janice D. Moore

The last (but not least) of Dr. Nicholas Hobbs' twelve principles of re-education is "In growing up, a child should know some joy in each day and look forward to some joyous event for the morrow" (Hobbs, 1982, p. 285). Dr. Hobbs knew the importance of joy in our lives for health and good functioning. A leading college dictionary defines joy as "a feeling or state of great delight or happiness; keen pleasure; elation" (Nichols et al., 2001, p.716). Joy is as individual as each of our faces and at the same time is as universal as its simplest expression, the smile. Most of us take for granted the joy in our lives and seldom stop to contemplate it or even acknowledge to ourselves just how much joy our lives contain. For some of those we serve, however, there is either little joy at all or it is so overpowered by intense negative feelings that they can scarcely perceive it. Others we serve are deeply impacted by depression or have been socialized in environments in which only negative feelings were acknowledged. These individuals often know neither how to appreciate the joys that are in their lives nor how to plan for joyful experiences.

As service providers for these individuals, it is easy to get so caught up in helping them better manage their daily lives and cope with their problems that the notion of joy in their lives becomes the furthermost thing from our minds. We can become so involved in helping those we serve cope with all the tragedy and difficulty in their lives that we allow our stress to interfere with appreciation of the joy in our own lives. Helping our consumers, our coworkers, and ourselves to experience some joy in each day is one of the easiest things we can do; it can yield great benefits.

It is easy to forget how a simple act can make a big difference in a day. One such day occurred when I was working at a long term, child/adolescent residential psychiatric hospital. Our children and youth at that time were a rather intense group, and it had been a particularly rough few days with several new youths entering, a number of fights occurring between them, and other outbursts regularly "disturbing the peace." While preparing to leave the house to go to work that morning, I was thinking about how serious and unhappy the faces of the youths had been over the past few days. On a momentary impulse, I grabbed my daughter's Tickle-Me-Elmo on my way out the door. Throughout the day I started it laughing and handed it to various residents. Without fail, every one of them began to laugh or at the very least, developed a huge ear-to-ear grin. Other youths standing near the one holding the Elmo wanted to hold it. Before the day was over, every single one of the more than thirty enrolled had held Elmo at least once, and all of us were rewarded with their joyous smiles and laughter.

It is important for us to spend time thinking about ways to bring joy, laughter, and happiness wherever we go, sharing it with those around us. Simple acts like copying and handing out an appropriately funny joke or cartoon, recounting something funny that happened to us, or sharing a favorite poem or song can make a big difference in someone's day. We can build fun into activities with our youths, our trainings, and meetings with our colleagues, encouraging others to share with us the joys in their lives.

For those whom we serve, it is also important to help them identify and learn to appreciate the joys that they experience in their own lives. Many of them will tell you that they do not have any joy to appreciate. One way to help is to give them examples of the simplest of pleasures -- things like seeing a child smile, feeling a gentle breeze on your face, or touching the warm fur of a kitten. Then challenge them to look for, and write down, five such simple joys that they experience before they see you next. Simple activities can help all of us learn to "stop to smell the roses." Asking someone to think of and share one simple thing that recently made them smile can be the beginning of learning to appreciate the simple pleasures of life. Just the act of thinking about, and sharing with others, experiences such as the laughter of a young child at play, the beauty of a sunset or a field of flowers, or a funny thing that happened to you can bring back a smile not only to the teller, but also to others who hear of it.

There are countless other ways to incorporate the concept of "joy in each day" into our work. By so doing, we not only create some of those moments of joy, but also teach the art of creating and appreciating such moments to those around us. My husband, Mike, is a case manager who has worked for years with adults with chronic mental illness. A female client he has worked with for many of these years has a continually serious, solemn demeanor; she seldom ever smiles or laughs. Mike has made it his personal challenge to make her laugh every time he sees her. Throughout this time, the jokes, actions, and just plain silliness that he and his co-workers have used to successfully accomplish their goal, have been a great source of laughter and joy not only to this woman, but also for others who were around to witness them.

We all have heard and read about the effective healing power of laughter. Most of us don't even need the growing body of supportive research to believe it. Yet in our ever accelerating, fast paced and high-pressure society, it is at the least, very difficult for the most "*well adjusting*" of us to take time to relish the joy in our lives. (I point up the phrase "well adjusting" because one of my psychology professors wisely said many years ago that he doesn't believe there is any such thing as a "well adjusted" person. He believes that since there are constantly new things in our environment to adjust to, the best we can hope for is to be "well adjusting.")

All our lives are filled with many difficulties, stressors, challenges, sad events, and even tragedies. This is all the more true of the individuals with whom we work. Life should be enjoyed for the great gift it is. What better gift can we give than that of ensuring that others experience and learn to appreciate joy, every day of their lives?

References

Hobbs, N. (1982). *The Troubled and Troubling Child.* San Francisco: Jossey-Bass Inc.

Nichols, W. R., et al. (Eds.). (2001). *Random House Webster's College Dictionary.* (2001 Second Revised and Updated Random House ed.). New York: Random House Inc.

Janice D. Moore, MA, is a therapist with Centerstone's Therapeutic Preschool Program in Davidson County, Tennessee. janice.moore@centerstone.org

Part III

Strengthening Families and Ecologies

Working in the child's ecology has been a central tenet of Re-ED since its beginning. Nicholas Hobbs (1982) acknowledged indebtedness *"...for concepts of ecological systems to Kurt Lewin, Ludwig von Bertalanffy, Roger Barker, Phil Schoggen, James G. Miller, and most recently, Urie Bronfenbrenner...."* (p. xvii). More and more, current approaches recognize the importance of broadening their intervention scope to the child's ecosystem. Troubled and troubling children, and their families, benefit from this expanded view of "severe emotional or behavioral disorders." The same positive expectancies that often help our students behave in positive ways serve to encourage other ecosystem members to act constructively as well.

Families in Re-ED: Pioneering in Partnerships with Families

The 1950s were indeed grim times for children with mental health needs—no rights, few services, long term treatment — if any. The times were also extremely difficult for their families, who faced widespread assumptions of parental blame, nonexistent community support, and frequent isolation. When Nicholas Hobbs and his colleagues envisioned a new "ecological approach," they saw families as involved participants. They asked NIMH to fund a new kind of therapeutic school, describing it as a place where the language of health is consciously employed and "teacher-counselors" create lively experiences to coax children into health. They also expected "students" to stay as short a time as necessary, going home on weekends while in treatment – with home goals to help everyone prepare for their return home in 4 to 6 months. Staff roles called "Liaison teacher-counselors" worked intensively with families and community agents; all became partners striving to accomplish mutual goals for each student's quick and successful return home. Each Re-ED school began with two liaison staff, but parents' desire to problem solve with teacher-counselors when the children returned to school on Sunday night soon necessitated a liaison for each team serving a group of children.

Cumberland House School opened in 1962 in Nashville, TN and Wright School in Durham, NC in 1963. By the late 1960s, Re-ED schools functioned across Tennessee, all with staff who met with parents to develop and carry out "Ecological Enablement Plans."

In 1970, the national Joint Commission on Mental Health of Children gave Project Re-ED its unqualified endorsement, saying: *"Because of its proven effectiveness, in terms of both cost per child and success in restoring the child to home, school, and community, the commission recommends that the Re-ED model be adopted and extended as one of the many needed kinds of services for emotionally disturbed children"* (Joint Commission on Mental Health of Children, p. 44).

Soon after Peabody faculty William and Diane Bricker began work with Re-ED students and staff in 1965, they asked the mother of a child with autism to work with them as they taught her son new skills and behaviors. Vanderbilt student John Ora observed their work before going to the University of Kansas for additional graduate training. He returned to Nashville with an innovative idea, and in 1969 initiated the Regional Intervention Program (RIP) at Peabody College. Ora trained mothers by helping them teach their own preschoolers' new behaviors, using procedures developed by Robert Wahler at the University of Tennessee. In this program, trained mothers then help other mothers learn the same skills; few professional staff are needed, compared to traditional programs. Long term follow-up of these children showed that their significant gains maintained over years, with impressive cost savings (Strain & Timm, 2001). RIP's parent implemented programs operate in Tennessee today, thanks to strong parental support across the state, despite constant state budget cuts in mental health and children's services. A mid 1970s dissemination grant allowed RIP to train staff for service replications in other states as well.

Evolution of Family Participation in Early Re-ED Programs

The expanding role of families in Re-ED programs can be traced through program histories, the first an example in Ohio. Rico Pallotta's visits to Nashville in the early 1970s led to the creation of the Positive Education Program (PEP) in Cleveland, where PEP staff work with children and their individual family members. In 1975 PEP started its first of 10 Re-ED day schools for school age youngsters, involving parents through liaisons and parent support/training groups. In 1976, PEP opened the first of 2 Early Intervention Centers (now Early Childhood Centers) for preschoolers and their parents, RIP replications with parents as well as professionals on staff. In 1978 they obtained a brief grant to hire a Parent Education Coordinator, then inducted the first of several parents with children in the program onto the PEP Board of Trustees where they have been represented since.

Parent satisfaction surveys became a part of PEP's annual evaluations about 1982. To date, well over 90% of parents' responses consistently express satisfaction with the services they and their children receive. A 2001 MetNet Consumer Satisfaction Survey of mental health programs for children was conducted for the Cuyahoga County Mental Health Board by the University of Dayton's Center for Business and Economic Research. Results corroborated PEP's own parent satisfaction surveys; more than 90% expressed satisfaction with PEP services.

About 1987 PEP started a central Parent Advisory Council which soon requested and received a family specialist role at central office (since there was no longer funding for the Parent Education Coordinator). In that same year, PEP day treatment's first Family Services Aide was hired. By 1990, parents of PEP students were hired as Family Service Aides in all the Day Treatment Centers, and Parent Advisory Boards were formed in each center. PEP also began hiring parents to contact other parents for the one year follow-up studies. Early in the 1990's, contacts with professional and family advocates led to parent affiliations with the Federation of Families for Children's Mental Health, providing the families with an active national network.

Throughout this time, other Re-ED programs were making significant family commitments. Pressley Ridge developed PRYDE (Pressley Ridge Youth Development Extension), an early therapeutic foster care program in 1978, and moved on to support the development of Wraparound services to meet the needs of many children and families in the seven states they serve. Youth Villages became a major provider of MST intensive in-home services (Multisystemic Treatment, Henggeler, 1993) to families inside and outside Tennessee. Youth Villages has made an agency wide commitment to supporting or finding permanent families for every child and youth they serve. They strive to meet that goal in all they do, and celebrate each child when that goal is attained.

National Family-Centered Leadership

In 1975 Hobbs established the Center for Study of Families and Children as part of Vanderbilt University's Institute of Public Policy Studies. Since then, this center has functioned as a hub for research, publications, and advocacy for families. Hobbs' Re-ED book, *The Troubled and Troubling Child*, published the year before his death in 1983, expressed strongly how Re-ED practitioners viewed their work with family members. He reminded us that parents are not sources of contagion; they are responsible collaborators in making the system work for their children. In 1984 Hobbs and colleagues' book, *Strengthening Families*, made a strong case for families' place in public policy and the potential benefits to society as a whole of providing services to meet families' needs.

Valuing and teaming with family members is not new in Re-ED. Partnering with kids and their families is an integral part of both our foundational values system and our operational structures.

Strengthening Ecologies

Part III opens with chapter 8, the editors' overview of the ecological approach — its development, basic premises, and implications for service. The next two chapters present the case for families of troubled and troubling children and youth, written by a group of parents at a Re-ED program who frequently work together to help other families in the program. They offer the unique perspectives only family members can give on two critical areas: their learning and their teaching. In chapter 9, parents of PEP students share their experiences over the years learning from their children and the professionals who serve them; they describe both some painful learning we all wish they had not encountered and some helpful learning which made a positive difference for them and their children. In chapter 10, Valerie Rudar and the Family Support Liaisons, show what they have done to inform and train staff in their program about the potential assistance they have to offer and the needs of parents who bring their children there for help.

Chapter 11 describes the parents teaching parents program still operating in Tennessee. The Regional Intervention Program is presented first from the perspective of a staff member, E. Ann Ingram. Miki Martin then gives the view of a parent served by the program, years after her family's participation.

Chapter 12, the last in Part III, demonstrates how Re-ED's principles-based ecological approach was adapted for use in a service that is seldom delivered using this perspective: a Diagnostic Assessment Service. Robert Spagnola and his colleagues' explanation of how they operationalized the basic tenets of the approach demonstrates the breadth of its applicability.

References

Hobbs, N. (1982). *The troubled and troubling child.* San Francisco: Jossey-Bass.

Hobbs, N., Dokecki, P. R., Hoover-Dempsey, K. V., Moroney, R. M., Shayne, M. W., & Weeks, K. H. (1984). *Strengthening families.* San Francisco: Jossey-Bass.

Henggeler, S. (1993). Multisystemic treatment of serious juvenile offenders: Implications for the treatment of substance abusing youths. In L. S. Onken, J. D. Blaine, & J. J. Boren (Eds.), *Behavioral treatments for drug abuse and dependence: National Institute on Drug Abuse Research Monograph 137.* Rockville, MD: NIH Publication No. 93-3684.

Joint Commission on Mental Health of Children. (1970). *Crisis in child mental Health: Challenge for the 1970s.* New York: Harper & Row, 1970.

Strain, P. S., & Timm, M. A. (2001). Remediation and prevention of aggression: An evaluation of the Regional Intervention Program over a quarter century. *Behavioral Disorders, 26*(4), 297-313.

8

The Ecological Approach

Mary Lynn Cantrell & Robert P. Cantrell

Nicholas Hobbs smiled as he said that the word "ecology" has been "polluted by the environmentalists." Hobbs' humor had special meaning in his role as a major conceptualizer of the ecological view on troubled and troubling children and youth, on their needs and how to meet them. Ecological concepts have shown themselves to be important in the education and treatment of children and youth with emotional and behavioral problems, playing significant roles in intervention planning for individual children as well as in policy and system planning for these individuals as groups.

From this perspective "Severe Emotional Disturbance" is not seen as something existing in the child but as the expression of discordant transactions between the child and others in his world. The child is an inextricable member of a unique ecosystem comprised of the child and the people who interact with him in the settings where they spend time. The child acts on this ecosystem, as well as being acted upon by it. The "SED" label appears when ecosystem members can tolerate no longer the discord in the system, and they seek help or change that leads to formal identification. The task of intervention is *"...helping the significant members of the ecosystem, including the child or adolescent, take the steps necessary to enable the system to work reasonably well — that is, within tolerable levels of discord"* (Hobbs,

1982, p. 183). Identification of, and emphasis on, ecosystem strengths are critical components for accomplishing changes.

Hobbs (1982) defines ecology as *"the study of the complex interaction of energies in natural systems"* (p. 189). Biological sciences originated the use of the term, but professionals applying the concepts of natural ecology to serving troubled and troubling children and youth have found them highly useful. The interdependent nature of organisms, both on their natural surroundings and on each other, form a central tenet of ecological concepts. Health of the members of an ecosystem denotes a relative harmony occurring over a period of time. The nature of that delicate balance is dynamic rather than static. At the ecosystem's best, balance regenerates continually as its members function. At its worst, introduction of a new or potentially toxic element, or even the declining function of a member, can send the ecosystem off balance, threatening all its members. There are obvious parallels with human social ecologies.

William Rhodes (1967, 1971, 1972) described the development of the ecological approach in the late 1950's and early 1960's, saying,

"We felt that 'disturbance' was a relative term, that different settings saw different kinds of behavior as 'disturbed' depending on the cultural values and expectations of that setting, as well as the particular predilections of the child's own parents and teachers....We felt that, to avoid the negative influence of institutions, treatment had to be in a setting as nearly like the child's natural habitat as possible...." (Hobbs, 1982, p. 183).

The term *ecology* offered significant additions to the concept of *environment*, with their view of mutual exchanges between ecosystem members.

Hobbs recognized the natural affiliation between the ecological view and competence building. He chose to adopt

"...the model provided by education — with its emphasis on health rather than illness, on teaching rather than on treatment, on learning rather than on fundamental personality reorganization, on the present and the future rather than on the past, on the operation of the total social system of which the child is a part

rather than on intrapsychic processes exclusively" (Hobbs, 1982, p. 16).

Healthy ecologies are dependent on the competence of their members.

Basic Premises

The premises of an approach determine how situations are analyzed and how interventions are designed and implemented. Cantrell, Cantrell, Valore, Jones, and Fecser (1999) summarized the following beliefs underlying the ecological perspective.

- *"Children's problems do not reside inside the child, nor do they reside solely in others.*
- *Each child functions in a unique 'world' (ecosystem or 'ecology' specific to him or her). He or she is an inseparable member of that small social system made up of the child, family, school, neighborhood, and other community units where he spends time. (The ecosystem may even include some people and places where he spends a great deal of mental energy, if not time).*
- *When discord exists in the ecology, it occurs in the interactions of the child and members of his 'world.'*
- *The child and the elements of that 'world' share both in the problems and their solutions.*
- *The child and family are partners with professionals in planning and in accomplishing solutions. Each maintains responsibility for participation in their mutual growth.*
- *Education and treatment efforts occur in settings as close to the child's home and home school settings as possible.*
- *Careful assessment and analysis before planning an intervention is important to effecting change.*
- *What occurs (and how it occurs) during assessment and analysis sets the tone for collaboration in intervention. Intervenors foster collaboration when they are clearly facilitators, committed to problem solving and not to assigning blame.*

- *The strengths of the child and of the people in his ecology are an important focus for analysis and intervention. Areas of need or problems offer targets for change. Strengths become critical elements of support for those changes.*
- *Discovery and choice of interventions involve identifying key logs in the logjam of difficulties. Pragmatic goals and practical interventions foster small, early successes that help everyone maintain their efforts.*
- *Small changes in multiple locations can have large effects on overall functioning.*
- *Building competence in everyone involved produces lasting change.*
- *Successful living, experienced one day at a time, is therapeutic. Ideally, therapeutic skill building events and interactions are an integrated part of the day's ongoing activities"* (Cantrell, et al., pp. 7-8).

When strategies and techniques fail, and they inevitably do at times, guiding concepts provide a strong basis for decision making. With a shared philosophy that undergirds both how helpers view problems and come to solutions, different strategies are more easily generated. The ecological perspective provides a value base from which therapeutic and educational experiences, which build competence in the child and other ecosystem members, can be developed and refined.

Implications for Treatment and Education

The philosophy directing development of ecological strategies led to a series of biases with implications for intervention.

Language is important; it can affirm, and it can damage. Words carry excess meaning, and our word choices have both intended and incidental consequences. A term often carries assumptions on which people base decisions and subsequent action. When a term applies to an individual, professionals must consider whether the implied assumptions and their consequences are in the best interests of that person. Official designations of mental illness or delinquency lead to interventions by social agencies "serving the ill" or "correcting the delinquent," independent of their ability to meet that individual's critical needs. Hobbs (1982) deliberately chose to describe children with serious behavioral and emotional disorders as "troubled and troubling." He also avoided the term "case manager" because *"....no one wants to be a 'case,' and no one wants to be 'managed'"* (p. 214).

Where professionals adopt the ecological perspective, they prefer using the least stigmatizing terms available, the language commonly used for children in general. When forced to use more pathology based terms (often to meet funding requirements), Re-ED professionals are uncomfortable with the necessity. They make an effort to use the mandated terms in formal reports, but work to avoid them when talking about a child (or group) and are even more vigilant when making decisions on their behalf.

Children (and adults) learn in the context of well planned, meaningful days — one day successfully accomplished after another. The goal is to make each day in a child's life full and purposeful. This poses a constant challenge for teacher-counselors and other Re-ED staff –

"...to design a daily program so engaging, so varied and new yet orderly and stable, ...so filled with success in matters large and small, so unconcerned with failure, so appreciative of individuality and of common purpose, so evocative of a sense of community, so finely modulated to the needs of a particular child and a particular moment, ...so filled with good talk, so fatiguing, so rewarding to children and teacher-counselors alike...that the disturbed child finds himself immediately committed to a new way of living at once more satisfying to himself and more satisfactory to the people in his life" (Hobbs, 1982, pp. 88-89).

These days require commitment, resources, and careful planning from administrators, teacher-counselors, and teams. Students learn from the planning when they are meaningfully included. When such days occur, a child is more likely to behave in adaptive ways, less likely to his being described as "disturbed." On a good day, a visitor to a Re-ED program may wonder why these children are in special settings. On a bad day, staff support one another as best they can. Later, they debrief what went wrong, discussing how it might have gone better, if the problems call for sticking with prior plans or reconsideration of a plan. If they have come to the end of their understanding or creativity, they ask who else may be able to help. They know that not all days can be good ones, but work nevertheless to make them all good.

Important therapeutic agents are already in the child's life; not all are professionals. The most central natural agents in a child's ecosystem usually include parents, teachers, relatives, extended family, and sometimes professionals in community agencies. Given support and information, they can be co-planners and partners in implementing the interventions needed for success. Where natural agents can carry out planned changes, they lay the foundation for more productive transactions with the child.

Liaison staff model how ecological stressors can be addressed, and strengths or resources used to solve family problems. But ultimately, it is the ecosystem members who are most invested in its long term health. *"...[A]n important strategy in liaison work is to teach the liaison function to one or more adults who are important in the life of a child, and to the adolescent when old enough and competent, so that the ecosystem can function effectively and meet new crises without external assistance"* (Hobbs, 1982, p. 214).

In Re-ED programs, parents and caretakers are not just "involved." They participate in all phases of planning and helping their child. *"They are also encouraged to participate as:*
- *Members of parent support groups, gaining from and giving help to other parents.*
- *Representatives on parent advisory groups, contributing to design and review of the school's mission, goals, process decisions, and outcome reports.*
- *Family in staff roles, which increases new parents' opportunities for contact with those who have seen some success, as well as known the pain.*

- *Trustees or board members, who maintain the ultimate responsibility for the program's continuing operation and continual improvement"* (Cantrell, et al., p. 18).

The goal is a satisfactory world for the child, where successful days are more common than unsuccessful ones, and where the ecosystem can function largely independently — without massive professional help. Rejecting the designation of the child as "ill," Re-ED also abandons cure as a goal. We seek, instead, to help the members of the child's world learn to function with reasonable satisfaction. We become part of that ecosystem temporarily, until it appears likely to continue to work without us. This may require significant improvement in a single component of need, or smaller improvements for a number of others. Improvements come from "successful days," when each child (or significant other) comes close to mastery of the day and holds hope for success tomorrow.

"Mother, near the end of her time at the Early Intervention Center with her preschooler: 'Things aren't perfect — and maybe they never will be, but I feel we're in control now — 90% of the time, and the other 10% we're working on'" (Cantrell, et al., 1999, p. 19).

Systematic ecological analysis and intervention planning help achieve these ends. Hobbs (1982) called what teacher-counselors do "precision programming" and outlined its sequence:

"(1) shared identification and definition of a problem; (2) agreement on means to effect desired changes; (3) specification of outcomes sought, preferably in behaviors that can be counted, measured, or consensually validated; (4) assignment and acceptance of responsibilities for carrying out the plan by specified target dates; and (5) periodic evaluation of progress and redefinition of the problem — in a continuing cycle" (p. 87).

He stressed the need for communication among all involved — sharing goals, means, and desired outcomes if they are to be achieved. Intervention occurs within the purposeful day, planned with and eventually carried out largely by natural agents – with the purpose of maintaining, long past Re-ED's involvement. Empowering families requires that problem solving skills be imparted to one or more members of the childs world (and/or the adolescent) so that the ecosystem can function both more effectively and more independently by means of their increased competence.

Interventions best build on ecosystem strengths, commit to affirmative goals, and use positive strategies. The belief that positive change can occur inspires us to program for it. Identifying potential sources of strength in both the child and others, sometimes through negative episodes, takes us to interventions we would otherwise miss. The child leading a group in an antisocial effort displays there his leadership skills and aspirations; these could likely be channeled into a more pro-social activity. The parent who precipitates arguments with an adolescent about curfew violations shows concern about the youth's whereabouts, and may well be willing to engage in needed surveillance. The teacher frustrated with the failure of efforts to help the child, and expressing the lack of other options, may well be open to new ones if given support, models, and encouragement. Decoding, reframing, and pulling out dormant possibilities can uncover important helper strengths.

In brief, we see our children as learners – as are their families and the rest of us. Careful planning for purposeful days with personal meaning for students, encourages all of us to explore new skill areas. Developing plans with family members to build new skills can achieve more purposeful days for them all. Using a systematic approach can encourage them to use it themselves. Modeling the search for potential strengths can show to others that strengths can be uncovered in unlikely places.

Service Templates

Hobbs recognized many whose conceptual work served as precursors to the ecological perspective. Cognitive or visual templates help bridge the gaps between theory and practice, guiding or assisting ecological analysis and planning for ecosystems in difficulty. Some commonly used templates are described below.

Ecosystem Maps and Diagrams

Visual depictions can summarize a great deal of information about ecosystems in an efficient package. Ecological maps, a frequently used template, employ a series of Venn diagrams. The child's circle drawn in the center of these overlapping circles shows the child to be the defining member of this ecosystem. Overlaps between other settings and the child's circle represent the learning he has experienced in that setting — ways of feeling, thinking, and behaving. Stars on the map represent strengths; needs are designated by gray dots. Both stars and dots are placed on the map to best show where the strength or problem exists: primarily for the child, for another member, or in their interaction. Figure 1 presents an example.

Figure 1. An Ecological Map For Alan

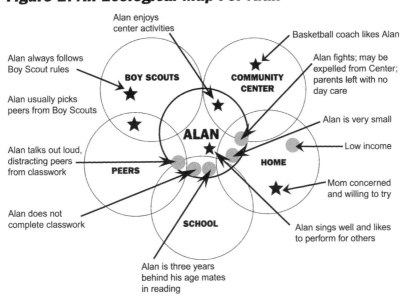

Typically, as children become older, their maps and diagrams show increasing complexity in their ecology. After analysis is completed, and interventions for logjam difficulties are planned, listing those interventions in boxes placed beneath the needs they target or the strengths employed can be helpful.

Ecological Analysis and Enablement Plans

Ecological assessment and intervention planning culminate in a written individual plan that is devised for (and with) the child and family, teacher, and other central members of the ecosystem. Hobbs presented a model for such a plan (1982, p. 203). The one page plan had eight columns, the first column listing each *service required*. The remaining columns ask seven questions for each service listed in column one. (1) *Who's responsible* (for initiating and monitoring the service)? (2) *By whom* (will the service be provided)? (3) *By what date?* (4) *At what cost?* (5) *Source of funds?* (6) *Criterion* (for success of service)? (7) *Follow-up* (needed)? The plan provides a brief, clear, and simple reminder of their goals and responsibilities for all ecosystem members.

The "Heuristic"

Ecological assessment and planning is simple only with the most simple ecosystem discords, but simple problems typically do not reach the point of referral requesting special assistance for a child with "severe emotional disorders." It is difficult to learn quickly the complex process for helping most complex ecosystems. The process involves stagewise intervention, requiring that many pieces of information be sought, found, and organized into patterns that make sense and can be addressed. The "heuristic" used in the Prevention-Intervention Project (PIP) guided staff in ecological assessment and problem solving (Cantrell & Cantrell, 1980). It was developed to decrease the training time involved for individuals to become both effective and efficient ecological problem solvers. The "heuristic" guide provided questions to (1) identify current functioning in different settings or functioning areas, (2) set goals for change, and (3) plan for stagewise approximations toward stated objectives. When PIP's ecologically oriented school support teachers used the heuristic guide completely and in sequence in their ecological assessment and planning, they met objectives in less time than when they did not. This statistically significant finding was true regardless of ecosystem problem difficulty level or of which support teacher was the problem solver.

As responsible professionals, we are constantly reminded that we are temporarily joining the lives of real children, family members, and school staff. Applying our learning from professional training to these real lives seldom is easy. Following is an outline of a process for ecological assessment and intervention planning. An example of how it was used with one child is provided in Cantrell, et al. (1999).

A Brief Outline for Ecological Assessment and Planning

A. Introducing the Child
    Who is s/he? How old is s/he?
    Where and with whom does s/he live?
    Where does s/he go to school?
    What does s/he enjoy doing?
    What does s/he do well?
    Who is important to this child?
    Who else fills / could fill a special need for this child and family?

B. Assessing the Discord
    What are the central areas of discord?
    What specifically does the child do or not do that is problematic?
    Where, when, and how frequently does s/he do it?
    How do others react?
    What appears to be maintaining this problematic behavior?

C. Planning the Intervention
    How can we change the situation (antecedents) to encourage
      more productive behavior?
    What adaptive behavior(s), competing with the problem,
      would we like to encourage?
    What can be used to strengthen the adaptive behavior?
    How can we remove the consequences maintaining the problem?
    How can we feasibly and naturally structure the situation with
      cues to encourage productive behavior?
    How can we feasibly and naturally structure consequences to

strengthen it?

How will we know when we have met our goal?

How can we build in a continuous evaluation system?

D. Implementing and Monitoring the Plan

How will we introduce the plan's changes and set them into motion?

When or at what points will we make evaluation decisions?

How will we decide if the plan should be continued, revised, faded, or discontinued?

What will we do when we have reached our specified goal?

How will we exit from the intervention plan?

What follow-up procedures will be instituted?

E. Providing Follow-up Support

Are changes being maintained? Is further follow-up necessary? What really happened?

Not always will we hear what we want to hear. As with us all, there are times when students and their families make less than optimal choices, and the consequences are less than optimal as well. A naive young professional asked Hobbs what kind of success rates we should expect? "Should we strive for 100%?" His answer was that if we were always completely successful, that would be sad, because it would only mean we weren't trying to help the ones who needed us most.

An Expanded Ecological Perspective

As the research and literature in our field grow, we discover *new tools for ecological change*, and the perspective itself enlarges. As the impact of biogenic disorders or factors on humans and their transactions is made clearer, medical professionals appear more frequently on the ecological team. The impact of cognitive beliefs and strategies can be seen in the behavior of ecosystem members, and options are posed for introducing more satisfying thoughts and actions through cognitive approaches. As the field gains new information on the relationships between past learning and current behavior, we discover new ways to teach and re-teach. As we strive to understand the contributions of culture to harmony and discord in ecosystems, we can work to become more culturally knowledgeable and more responsive. As we explore the developmental nature of how we learn to care about others, we can help children and youth perform caring acts and experience for themselves the deep personal satisfactions of helping.

References

Cantrell, M. L., Cantrell, R. P., Valore, T. G., Jones, J. M., & Fecser, F. A. (1999). A revisitation of the ecological perspectives on emotional/behavioral disorders. From L. M. Bullock & R. A. Gable (Series Eds.), Third CCBD Mini-Library Series: *What works for children and youth with E/BD: Linking yesterday and today with tomorrow*. Reston, VA: The Council for Exceptional Children.

Cantrell, R. P., & Cantrell, M. L. (1980). Ecological problem solving: A decision making heuristic for prevention-intervention education strategies. In J. Hogg & P. Mittler (Eds.), *Advances in mental handicap research*: Vol. 1. (pp. 267-301). Chicester, England & New York, NY: John Wiley Publishers.

Hobbs, N. (1982). *The troubled and troubling child*. San Francisco, CA: Jossey-Bass.

Rhodes, W. C. (1967). The disturbing child: A problem of ecological management. *Exceptional Children, 33*(7), 449-455.

Rhodes, W. C. (1971). Ecological models of emotional disturbance. In J. Paul & W. C. Rhodes (Eds.), *Models of emotional disturbance*. New York, NY: Wiley.

Rhodes, W. C. (1972). *Behavioral threat and community response*. New York, NY: Behavioral Publications.

Mary Lynn and Robert Cantrell are currently Research Consultants for the Positive Education Program in Cleveland, Ohio.
   mlc8648@sbcglobal.net   rcantrell8648@sbcglobal.net

9

Parenting a Troubled and Troubling Child

Parents of PEP Students

One Parent's Story

Our son started to experience panic attacks when he was about seven years old. He didn't have any problems before that time period. He was a happy go-lucky little kid, did well in social situations, had lots of friends — did well in nursery school, kindergarten and first grade, and then all of a sudden he experienced these panic attacks. In fact, he was in the house when he experienced his first one. Of course, he didn't tell us about it...for probably two weeks, but he would run, grab his foot, and say his foot hurt. And then about two weeks later he called me aside and said, "Mom, it's not my foot, I have these strong scary feelings inside me. I don't know where they are coming from. It's nothing outside that's scaring me. It's something inside me and I thought they would go away by themselves and I didn't want to worry you and dad."

I told the neurologist that he went to. I explained it, and he said, "Well, he didn't say that to you. Those are adult words." I said, "No, that's how he explained it to me. He's a verbal little kid and that's how he explained it to me." But anyway, the panic attacks subsided, and then his behavior changed and we went to all kinds of professionals. Medical professionals like I said, the professionals at the public schools, and nobody could seem to help us. When I asked for their help, they said basically, they just didn't want that behavior in the public school.

And when I asked medical professionals for help like, "Is there a support group?" They said. "Oh, it's just like ADHD; go to an ADHD group." But it wasn't ADHD. And so that was very difficult.

Through the different hospitalizations with our son, they just said he needed to be in residential treatment; you can't keep him at home, you can't keep him safe at home. But I knew if there was something out there that could help us during the day, we could work with him in the evening. That's when we kept having these meetings at school and we would have representatives from the Special Education Center come, and one of them suggested PEP [Positive Education Program]. I think our school system just wanted to get rid of us and close the door and that was it, but the rep talked to the school people about PEP. My husband and I said, "It sounds like that might work."

Even though we thought it might work, it was very difficult for us when we went to see the day treatment center. It was disheartening. I really felt sad that it had come to this. But after being there for half an hour with the professionals and staff members at PEP, I knew we were at the right place — because the attitude was different. We were going to be part of the team and it wasn't just talk; we were actually going to be part of the team. They were going to listen to us, and they proved themselves to listen to us at every turn in any problems that we have. Also, the other thing is that they asked us what were our child's strengths. No other professional asked us about any strengths. They were always looking for the pathology, the illness, what was wrong. PEP looked for the strengths and they built on the strengths.

The major turning point in dealing with our son's emotional and behavioral problems came when my husband and I sat in a small cramped office at the Day Treatment Center. Up until that point we spent our time trying to understand everything that was happening to our son that was making his behavior and his whole persona change so radically. Psychiatrists gave us numerous diagnoses: separation anxiety disorder, post traumatic stress disorder, oppositional defiant disorder, bipolar disorder, etc. and numerous medications to treat these disorders. We lived in the world of the abnormal, focusing on pathology and illness. We didn't know how to live as a family anymore. Up to this point we had seen so many professionals both in the academic and in the medical arenas. We were told by an academic professional that in twenty five years he never witnessed behavior as severe as our son's. Medical professionals said that we needed to place our son in residential treatment. None of these professionals gave us what the PEP staff gave us that day.

What they gave us was *HOPE*. It wasn't hope that our problems would go away. They didn't give us empty promises or talk of a cure. The staff gave us the tools to start living a successful life again. They gave us something to hang on to. What they gave us was a definite shift in *ATTITUDE*. Yes, our son had a diagnosis. In fact he had a litany of diagnoses. But what the PEP staff saw when they met our son was not a disorder but an eight year old boy who had potential but had some problems to work through so that he could reach that potential. It was the first time in a long time that anyone actually asked us about our son's *STRENGTHS* as opposed to his deficits. When we met the staff who would be working with our son, we knew that he was in the right place.

As time went by, we knew that as a family we were also in the right place. My husband and I and even our older son were considered an integral part of the team. We were respected and listened to. We were either invited to, or asked for, input regarding treatment team meetings. The passport was invaluable in keeping both school and home informed. Any comments made through the passport were able to be immediately addressed. This helped to strengthen our family as a whole.

And the other thing with PEP is, sure he might have a diagnosis of an illness, but he has to live in the real world and that's what they instilled upon him and upon us too. We didn't just say, "Oh poor kid. He's got this diagnosis so he can't do this, he can't do that." We worked with the staff members and that really made a difference.

Another turning point was when we were touring the DTC for the first time, and the coordinator pointed out the 12 Re-ED Principles hanging in a frame on the wall. He explained to me how these 12 principles were incorporated into the daily lives of the students at PEP. I read them and saw how simply stated but how powerful they were. I decided at that moment to assimilate these principles into my everyday interactions with my younger son and ultimately with every member of the family. I had a simple but strikingly different approach to going forward in my life with my family. By incorporating these principles into our lives, our family flourished. Following are some examples of how I saw to use these principles within our family.

"Time is an ally…" was most evident when I would journal every night before going to bed. I could actually see the progress we were making even though at times it seemed like baby steps. Things were improving. In working with *"Competence makes a difference…"* I would give my son a task I knew that he could handle and that would give him a feeling of competence. The more competent he felt, the more he would take on. It empowered him to strive for more at home and at school. *"Communities are important"* really had an impact for me. At times I felt very isolated and felt that people didn't understand. How could they? I didn't have a handle on it myself. Once I let my guard down and let old friends in, I understood that a lot of them just didn't know what to say or how to help. After talking to one of my friends, she understood our need for respite. She took it upon herself to call 10 other family friends and for 10 weeks we had 2 to 3 hours of respite every Monday night. My husband and I spent uninterrupted time with our older son. We went grocery shopping in peace. We went for a walk. Simple things that you take for granted. *"There should be some joy in each day…"* is probably my most favorite. There are so many small joys that you can help others experience. I made it a point for my younger son, no matter how difficult his day was, to have some simple joy every day. Some examples are popping popcorn, drawing together, looking at the night sky on a cold, clear evening bundled in a blanket, reading together, making his favorite dinner, etc. It is also healthy to experience some joy each day for yourself. It rejuvenates you and replenishes your well being. It makes you better able to parent effectively. These are just a few examples that helped us return to living successfully as an intact family.

I hope that gives you some insight from a parent's perspective. In May of this year we attended our son's graduation from college. As you can see, he [former PEP student] and our family have come a long way, thanks to the caring and dedicated staff at PEP.

Other Parents Sharing Their Perspectives

The following is the transcript of a taped discussion among parents, talking about their own and their children's experiences.

Learning to Understand

P1 — "Our kids have taught us a lot – they've taught us to laugh at ourselves when we make mistakes. It also helped me understand.... I know I had some judgmental attitudes about people with all different kinds of issues before I experienced this. I mean, even things like substance abuse; I used to just think, why don't they just stop? Look what they're doing to their life; why don't they just knock it off? And then I have this kid and people are just saying, 'Well, just tell him to knock it off. Why doesn't he just stop?' And then I realized, through living with a person with these kinds of struggles, they can't just shut it off. They're missing the chemicals or whatever, part of their brain that helps them control that. And all of a sudden the light bulb went off and I thought about people with different kinds of mental illness, people with substance abuse issues, and it was like I never would have had that level of understanding had I had that perfect, well-behaved kid that I thought I was going to have, dreamed about having. I wouldn't have developed as a person, the way that I have."

Finding Out Their Child Has a Real Problem

P2 — "The kids are good teachers. ...A lot of parents beat themselves up, because... they don't know what's going on with these kids. Like one of you said, she went to all of these different professionals, and they couldn't give her any answers. After I found out that my child had ADHD, I felt really, really bad that I was a whupping mama. I felt so bad, ... I can't believe I abused my child. ... I just didn't know he had this issue, but he was a terror, he was different from any kid that I had ever seen. And of course I thought he was just being a boy and then realized, no, he's got more going on.... He was ADHD, but he was very aggressive.... very fast. He could get out that window. It would take my brother and sister to catch him every time he ran, because I could not catch him. He was really fast. I'm talking like three people running down the street.... It was tough.

"When he went to pre-school, he choked a boy until the boy changed colors. That was my first indication something is really wrong with this child. He couldn't go to pre-school unless I was there. So I sat up at pre-school with him everyday. Then he went to kindergarten. I would walk him to school, and it was no short walk. I would come back home and as soon as I walked in the door and took my shoes off, the phone would ring. I had to walk back up there and go get him. Then it got to the point where in order for him to be in kindergarten, I had to sit there with him. The last straw was when he took a one inch wood block. He broke it in half and I said, 'This child is going to kill somebody.' And the principal referred us to PEP."

P3 — "I know things now that back then I was troubled with. When my son was a baby, you couldn't hold him; he didn't want to be held. He just did not want to be held. You just lay him down and put him to sleep — he was fine. When he was nine months old, he was hurting himself. And you knew, he would hit his head, and hit his head, and hit his head — and to try to tell the pediatrician there's something not right here; to not want to be held, never cry, just to not want to have anything to do with anybody. And as he got older, he became more self-destructive and you didn't see that in any other kid.... What did I do wrong? Parents will blame themselves.

"As he got older it got worse: Banging his head on the wall, very destructive to himself.... cut himself... You should see his arms now. He's got scars all down his arms. He cut himself when he was fourteen, fifteen. That was fifteen years ago. They didn't talk about that fifteen years ago."

P2 – "I wanted my son, but I didn't know what to do with this kid, because he was really different from any kid I had ever seen. When we got to EIC [Early Intervention Center, now ECC, Early Childhood Center] he was diagnosed, I think when he was three or four, with ADHD.... I kind of felt like I was alone, because no one in my family was dealing with this. When one staff person came to me and said that her kid would actually be bashing onto her hand with his teeth, I realized that he hasn't got it that bad; he's not hurting me. He's tearing up the house and he's fighting folks at school, but he's not hurting me. I thought, 'Well, I'm not alone.' So I didn't feel that bad; I felt a little more relaxed, and not blame myself so much.... "

P4 — "...That's what's going on with one of my twins. She has the room set up — jumps from couch to couch.... Now the other twin, just the other day she took her bare fist and punched the bathroom window."

Learning How to Advocate

P2— "One of you asked me earlier about being a young mom and how it affected my interactions with professionals in the school system.... I try not to be aggressive, because that's not the route I want to go, but I try to stand up for my rights and the rights of my son. And a lot of times because I'm young and I was there by myself a lot they would try to talk over me and I wouldn't let them. And they probably said, 'Oh my goodness, here she comes,' because once I got PEP behind me, that was it. I felt secure in standing up for my rights and for my son's rights.... The wonderful thing about PEP is, if you've got questions, even if you're out of the program, you can call and ask them.... There are a lot of parents that don't have that support. They're a wonderful support system."

Having No Support

P2 (cont'd) — "I didn't have any support in the family, because they didn't know.... I couldn't call them for any advice. I couldn't call them just for a listening ear.... When I first went to PEP, I was excited about it. You know. My son is going to get help. I'm going to learn all these new techniques. 'You're letting people tell you how to raise your child.' What? What's your advice on how to raise them? They didn't have any advice for me. It got to the point I didn't care what they thought. At family gatherings I was talked about. You know, 'Oh she doesn't know what she's doing. That boy is running her crazy. She's got those people telling her what to do.' I ignored them. This is my baby, I've got to raise him until he's eighteen plus; I don't care what they think. It was hurtful that I didn't have anybody to talk to about it.... and it was even harder when I didn't have anybody to watch him when I went to work.... Then I get in our parent group the support I couldn't get at home from my family. I was able to get it with other families, because they knew what I was going through.

"I got a lot of negative feedback from my family when I first went to PEP, but after embracing some of the techniques that I was learning — then they wanted me to help *them* with *their* kids: 'Well, let me ask you this question.' Or, 'Come over here and watch her for a minute. She's doing this.' Oh, you want my help now.... "

No Drugs for My Child!

P2 (cont'd) — ".... It's super hard. Like for me, I didn't want my son on drugs. So that meant no drugs. I didn't care if it was to keep him calm, I don't want him on nothing. And I waited some years; people kept telling me, you know he would do a lot better. Okay, I don't care what you say; he's not taking *no* medicine. When he got to be five, he needed some medicine. I had had it, and I said I'm going to try a little bit. I had my little notebook and I wrote down how he was acting and everything, because I wanted to monitor him very closely.... 'Why did I wait so long?' But my thing was, I've seen people on drugs. I didn't want my son to have anything to do with that stuff."

P5 – "You saw people abusing."

P2 – "Exactly. So I didn't want any prescription drugs or street drugs in his system. That was ignorance, because I didn't know."

P6 — "That's what the professionals have to realize, because it's so new.... We don't know what they know. They're trying to shove something down our throat, and we're trying to get as much knowledge as we can before we say, 'Okay, let's go that route.'"

P5 – "You don't know which professional to believe, because you've had professionals give you so many different stories; it's like, 'I don't know that they are telling me the right thing, so I'm going to wait until I find out a little bit more before I make a move on something.'"

P2 – "They may have been talking about Ritalin for years, okay? For a parent this may be their first time hearing of Ritalin.... They don't give you any background information. 'This will help your child calm down.' Okay, what else will it do? Parents have a lot of questions and a lot of the time you have that hour meeting, that's not enough time to get all your questions answered before you're ready to put him on something...."

Working Together as a Whole Family

P6 — "A lot of times my son would run away from home and I would call... About two or three staff members would come over; I specifically remember Tom Valore at one point talking to my oldest son to see what his perspective was, and talking to my husband, and talking to me. He talked to the whole family and that seemed to help the most too, because this also addressed the whole issue: that we're still a family and we're not going to be an intact family if a problem's always going to be pointed at one person. He would always be seen as the one on the outs. But our younger son always felt close to all the rest of us, so it was real important that there was conversation and dialogue between all of us.

"And the PEP program is the only program of all the services that I have sought and received for my son that ever asked how I was doing, or the other three kids in the family were doing, or how dad was doing. You know the psychiatrist was focused on his patient, the school was very focused on the student for whom the IEP meeting was being held or whatever, and nothing about how are you guys doing.

"I remember this one psychiatrist...was having a talk with our son, and here he is eight years old. Afterwards I asked, 'Well, how did it go?' He said, 'Well, I can't divulge anything to you because he's my client; you're not.' I said, 'Well, he's my eight year old son.' And he said, 'Well, I will tell you one thing, he didn't have anything bad to say about you.' That's not what I meant. I asked how the session went. Was it productive? And I never got that with any PEP staff members. We were all working together.

"We've had wonderful successes with other psychiatrists and I can say even when our son had trouble with the police, you could have one policeman that would say, 'What's the matter with this kid?' and another one speak very empathetically and say, 'I see that you're having a very difficult time with your son and I hope you can get the help that he needs.' He just had more compassion and more understanding of what was going on. And here they're both in the same profession."

Rational Depression

P4 — "When I first came to ECC I was torn down. I mean I was at my wits' end. But I knew why I was there. To get my twins some help and to get some help for myself. You know, because my parenting skills are not great, but there's a lot of things they gave me that I wasn't expecting. That's what broke me down. So when I got to ECC I didn't want to be there. I just did not want to be there. I knew I had a purpose for being there but I didn't want to be there. I was depressed. I was very depressed."

P2 — "You feel like you're all alone. You're struggling with this kid and thinking what was wrong with him. And I realized once I got to EIC that he had his issues, but I needed to change so I could help him. I try to instill that in parents now: it's not that you were the cause of those problems, but he was giving you different problems that typical parenting didn't handle. I wasn't using the skills within myself to help him to cope with what he was going through. That's what I try to tell parents now. You can't just say, 'Okay, I'm coming to this program and he's going to be fine,' because in just a while he's got to come home with you. We know Grandma's rule and all that kind of stuff because our grandmothers did it to us. But when you're stressed out you don't think about all that kind of stuff, unless somebody's going to keep drilling it into your head and it's going to become a part of you."

P4 — "Even though I didn't want to be at ECC I knew I was there for a purpose and I came every single day; and I was involved in the classroom. I was involved; I did all the sessions — even though sometimes I was broke down, I still went. And they still opened the door for me. What I did was, I told them that I didn't want to be there, I mean, because I was depressed; so I told them that I didn't want to be there. When I told them, that's when they started communicating with me more, and we even got together a personal caring group. We got to talk about everything that happened to us in our life. And in that group, I learned a lot about myself."

Being Accepted

P2 — "It's interesting that we talked about how kids are so beaten down from other places that when they get to a certain place they can do things at PEP and they're still accepted. PEP understands their issues."

P6 — "They see the kids for who they are. They don't see all disability. You know, they see that, but they look past it. I think that's where we come into play a lot of times at the centers, being parents of these kids.... it's like just see the person first. Try and get beyond that and reach him in a different way."

P2 – "The wonderful thing about PEP is, the kids are accepted. I told you about the one kid that came to EIC — adorable little thing. He had gotten kicked out of pre-schools all across the city; couldn't stay in a pre-school. And his mom, she was afraid he was going to get kicked out too. His attitude to staff was, 'I'm going to fight, and I'm going to kick you and I'm going to get kicked out of here.' The staff member got to his level and said, 'Honey, you can do whatever you want, we're not kicking you out.' That was unbelievable to him. When I looked at the mom's face, she couldn't believe it either.

"We've got some parents that when they come to the center they are so scared the kids are going to hurt the staff. One said, 'I don't want her to hurt anybody.' I said, 'Oh, she'll be all right. They're not going to let her hurt them.' And the mom said, 'Well, if she hurts somebody, you guys call me and I'll come and get her.' I said, 'It's going to be all right. They can handle it.' A lot of parents don't believe that, but the kids do their thing and the staff still accepts them and loves them."

P1 — "And they accept the parents wherever they are too. Just like the kids can come in with all kinds of severe stuff, parents come in with a variety of skill levels, a variety of acceptance, a variety of some-times mental health problems of their own — and they are accepted universally and they know that they are accepted.

"Another FSL [Family Support Liaison] and I went to a presen-tation earlier this year. The professional was presenting on working with resistant parents or something like that and some of the techniques were very good. They're not that different from the techniques we learned at PEP, but a few people in the audience were asking questions and making comments about ... 'Well, what about the parents that just won't do it or just won't follow through?' I about fell off the chair when I heard his response was, 'Well, I just fire them. I just do a Donald Trump on them. You're fired!' And I thought, 'Thank God my kids receive services in a place that doesn't fire parents!'

"And it was more appalling to me that I'm sitting there in an audience of probably a hundred or seventy-five or so professionals who work with kids and families and no one flinched at that, besides me. I about fell off the chair when I heard it and I thought, 'No one else is bothered by that,' because I kind of expected there to be a little grumbling around me or a few under the breath comments about, 'Well, we don't fire families at *our* agency.' I don't know what agency these folks were from but they weren't from PEP, and we don't fire families at PEP. *Or kids.*"

P2 – "Some parents come in and they're so drained, so worn out, they just need someone to empathize with them, they need somebody to be a listening ear and to help them. When I went to EIC, I felt relieved. When I started talking to the other parents... I'm thinking okay; my problems are not as bad as theirs; let me see if I can help them. And then when you help somebody else, it helps you in return. That speaker's not the kind of professionals we want in our program!"

P5 – "So, what you would say about a PEP professional is that no matter how much you tell them you don't want to be there (and you really try hard so maybe they won't force you to do some of the things that you know you need to do), they don't give up on you. Even though you may have turned them off, they didn't turn you off. The point I'm trying to make is that there are a lot of professionals who, if a parent gives them the slightest inkling that they are not interested, they'll give up on them and they'll move on to another parent, because they're not going to waste their time with you."

What the Principles Mean to Parents

P5 – "Instead of embracing the Re-ED principles and understanding that *Competence Makes a Difference*, maybe this parent just needs to feel competent and maybe just have the slightest success and then they'll be more receptive to getting help or having me help them or whatever."

P7 — "Or maybe they need to build up the *trust* that *is essential* before they can even start utilizing any of those helps; first, you have to establish credibility and that can take a long time."

P2 — "Especially when your trust has been torn down so many times. Before you get to PEP, you go through a lot of stuff. (long pause) It's amazing what a caring person can do."

Schools Can Target Children Unfairly

P7 – "I didn't think my son belonged here at PEP."

P2 — "But the school district was saying he should?"

P7 — "Yeah, there was a lot that was going on at the time. First of all, they weren't too thrilled about having a little black kid in a *certain area* — bottom line. They talked about diversity, but actually it was not there. If you ask me, it's still not there. There was a teacher that whatever he said, or looked, or whatever; she didn't like him — period. I don't care what he did or could have done, this woman just didn't like my kid. So he was kind of like targeted. They would call me about little things that he supposedly had done. Actually, they called me one day when my son was home sick. They called me to tell me what all he was doing that day and I said, 'This is an amazing kid, because he's in the bed. He's doing all these amazing things!'

"My son was eight when they sent him to PEP. Then I actually had a chance to relax a little, first time in a while. They didn't call constantly. I wasn't getting those calls. I didn't have to go up to the school. Life was good."

P5 – "It didn't feel like anybody was stacking the deck against your child?"

P7 – "Right, right. At the time my son started, I don't care what anybody says, he had the best two teachers ever, which were Kevin

Jackson, which I think everybody knows, and Karen M — she's no longer with PEP, but they were the best two teachers in the world. KJ, as we called him, loved basketball and he would come and get my son and take him over to the college and play basketball with him. He actually talked to me like he really cared. And I think that was the turning point. PEP really helped me out a lot, and I'm to the point now that I'm ready to help somebody else. I've been with PEP a long time."

P2 – "So even though you didn't want him at PEP because you didn't think he warranted being here, you appreciated it. Because once he got here, he got the attention that he needed."

P7 – "By the same token, I was reluctant. I really didn't want him to go back to public school.... Because it seemed like such a long time that I was going through all this trauma with the public system and now he was there at PEP and life was good. "

P5 – "How long was he there?"

P7 – "My son was there, I think he was shy a couple of weeks of a year."

P5 — "He needed that positive environment to build himself back up, because God knows what would have happened if he had stayed in that horrible environment."

P7 – "Yeah, because it was taking its toll on him also. You know, 'If I'm going to be accused of this, why not do it?'"

P5 – "What would you say would be the turning point for you... or the turning point for your kids?"

P4 — "...Learning the techniques. Even though I did struggle at home, because I'm dealing with teenagers and I'm dealing with five year olds. At first..., I was just hollering and screaming, whopping, but now, I don't do that. My son taught me not to do that. He came to me and said, 'Mom, screaming and hollering is not going to make me listen to you.' He told me that."

Don't Give Up!

P5 – "You're going to get tired; you're going to get burned out trying them, and you're going to give up, but you've got to pick yourself back up and keep trying — and that's the same with professionals. They may have a parent who may not follow through many, many times, but you can't give up. You've got to keep embracing those Re-Ed principles and instill them in parents."

P2 – "You can't give up. They don't know what that parent has gone through that makes them resist it. It could be the professional's approach. Nick Hobbs said the parent is the expert on their child. You cannot sit down with a parent and tell them that you need to do this, this, this, and this. Hold it, back up, listen to what the parent has to say first. They are the experts. They may not be using all the techniques right away, but they know their child. If Nick Hobbs could be around to tell them all that, it would be wonderful."

P4 – "When we first moved up from Cleveland to Cleveland Heights, they didn't want to give my children the services that they needed just because we were new, but I went in there and I explained to them what had gone on in the previous schools and what my children were going to do, and everything I told them happened."

P2 – "Because you are the expert."

P4 -- "I am the expert."

P2 – "You know those kids and a lot of the professionals just don't know that. But I do have to say things happen for a reason, and our kids have taught us a lot, and we, in turn, have to help others."

P4 — "And I find myself doing it everyday."

P2 – "You can't help it. It's like having good news; you cannot keep it within yourself. ....You don't have to raise your voice at a child, just talk to them. And make them look at you; make eye-contact and that's something so many parents don't do. PEP has done a great justice for me and my family."

Empowering Parents through Leadership Roles

P5 – "I guess the turning point for me was the model of parents helping other parents. When they asked me to take on the responsibility and be in a leadership position of teaching another parent what I had learned, for me that was so empowering... I felt, 'Wow, I must be doing something right.... they're asking me to show somebody else how to do it'.... That was the turning point for my whole family. The more confidence I had, the better parent I became."

P2 – "I think mine came right before I got hired: where I could see that I was making a change in other people's lives.... It made me feel good that I was teaching my husband. He was using the techniques, they were working — so we were together as a family. And then the other people in the program at PEP and EIC, I was able to help them, so then I was feeling confident in myself, so I said, 'Okay this stuff works and I'm good at using it!' I was the praise queen — soon as somebody walked in the door, I'd praise them,... just praise, praise, praise, and that's something I didn't do at home before. Praise him for what? Doing what he's supposed to do?"

P4 — "I really felt good about myself at ECC, being asked to be a part of the parent advocacy program. Me? Why me? I didn't want to be there, but when I got up there and I got myself comfortable, it's like, I was just at home...."

Lasting Effects

P2 – "Not only can we use what we learned to help our children, we can also use them to help our family's children and our grandchildren.... and I use all of those techniques, all of them.

"Well, we say, changing the world one child at a time. And it does work. In Parent Group, I tell parents, 'I don't teach you anything I don't believe in. I know about the Re-ED principles.' I say, 'These techniques work. They may not work right away, but you've got to have some endurance, because they will eventually work.'"

P5 – "That's what is so incredible about Re-ED. It is with you forever. If you have professionals that embrace it, who in turn teach us as parents how to embrace it, it will carry on for generations to come. That's what's so incredible about it."

The parent who wrote the initial portion of this chapter, and the parents who participated in the taped discussion for the second portion, all have now, or have had in the past, a child or youth in Positive Education Program. Those whose children are no longer at PEP are currently on staff as Family Support Liaisons, helping other parents.

10

Parents Providing Training:

Parent-Professional Partnerships
Parents and Professionals Growing Together
Why Re-ED?

Valarie Rudar & the Family Support Liaisons

I. Parent-Professional Partnerships

Parent/professional partnerships in the field of children's mental health have always been, and always will be, a huge challenge — and an ever-evolving journey. When it comes to developing respectful, thoughtful, and effective partnerships with families, we were fortunate to be the heirs of Nicholas Hobbs' thinking, which was so counter to most of the thought of his time, and unfortunately, often remains today. Re-ED and PEP, however, have been in the forefront of working along with, and advocating for, parents since Re-ED was born in 1962.

In 1989, in an effort to implement the spirit of Hobbs' philosophy of truly partnering with parents and gaining full family participation, Positive Education Program (PEP) wrote a grant to hire the first Family Support Liaison (FSL) in the day treatment service area. This first FSL was the parent of a child previously enrolled in the PEP program. The role of this parent was to provide direct peer support for parents of new and current children attending PEP, enhance parent participation in center activities such as parent group, and act as a liaison to bridge any communication gaps between parents and staff. By 1990, parents of PEP students were hired as FSLs in all Day Treatment Centers (DTCs). Over the years the FSL role has been professionalized. Today the FSL is an integral member of the support staff team in the DTCs, participating in the intake process, treatment staffings, support staff meetings, home visits, and facilitating parent groups.

The first FSL was Carlyn Lewis; she set the bar high for all to follow. Current FSLs are: Stacy Bush, Millie DeMent, Beverly Jeffries, Norah Joseph, Karen Mullins, Edie Richardson, Kathy Surmitis, Mary Rita Urban, Lasondra Whitney, and Cossondra Williams.

Paying a Debt to Nick Hobbs

We recognize how much we owe to Hobbs' "out of the box" thinking in the 1950's and '60's. His ideas created the way our professionals interact with families. We believe that without him our partnerships would be just like everyone else's out there, and we wouldn't have the success stories we have to tell. That kind of partnership greatly empowers us as parents.

As a parent, I was a fortunate product of PEP's Early Childhood Centers (ECCs, formerly the EICs, based on the Regional Intervention Program or RIP model from Nashville, Tennessee). I was given the gift of having professionals, in the words of Nick Hobbs, "act as consultants" and view me as "the expert on my child," offering their support for what I believed to be the best interests of my child and family. The working relationship we had, based on that respect, was nothing like what I had experienced with other professionals. The result was a sense of empowerment that ensured my growth as a person and a professional, as well as the successes of both my child and my family.

Therefore, as I moved into my coordinating position as Family/Community Liaison for PEP, I was looking for a way to continue enhancing parent-professional partnerships across the organization. PEP appreciates a long and valued association with Trina and David Osher, and through them with the Federation of Families for Children's Mental Health. My search led me to their website, where I found a list of training opportunities they offered for parents and professionals. Their training progam, *Creating Better Partnerships: One at a Time* (Federation of Families for Children's Mental Health, 2002) met the challenge of partnerships head on by training parents and professionals together.

This one-day workshop brings parents and professionals together to explore the value and challenge of authentic working partnerships. Participants work together to develop critical insights and skills necessary to foster enhanced communications among family members and professionals, to strengthen their working relationships, and ultimately to create better outcomes for families. We needed a uniform training which introduced partnering with parents to staff in PEP's service areas outside ECC, where service provision is not so inextricably tied to parents as it is in the ECCs.

PEP's administration adopted and embraced this curriculum. In September 2005 we trained about 15 teams of parents and professionals to act as facilitators. We formed a parent-professional partnership committee. Its charge was to develop ways to integrate this program into the training continuum. Our first training of parents and staff occurred in April 2006. The Federation's curriculum met our needs with minimal adaptation. We want to acknowledge in the section below all the individuals and groups they acknowledge in the written curriculum. The four paragraphs below are quoted from page 7 of the special adaptation for PEP of the curriculum entitled *Creating Better Partnerships: One at a Time, Family-Professional Partnership Training*.

"This work is a compilation of many people's ideas, work, and experiences. It has been captured and organized in this new format to bring the best and the most current into one easy-to-use resource for trainers.

"The Regional Research and Training Center at Portland State University developed one of the earliest training models focused on improving family-professional partnerships in the children's mental health arena in the late 1980's. That model, produced in partnership with families and professionals, has been used extensively around the country. Modifications have emerged as deeper understandings of the challenges and strategies to good partnerships have developed. In addition,

new writings have come out such as the National Peer Technical Assistance Network's 'Learning from Colleagues: Family/ Professional Partnerships Moving Forward Together' in 1998. That same year, two volumes of 'Systems of Care: Promising Practices in Children's Mental Health' focused on collaborations with families in improving systems of care. They were 'Volume I: New Roles for Families in Systems of Care' and 'Volume II: Promising Practices in Family-Provider Collaboration.'

"The training model offered in these pages builds upon the early works and writings in the children's mental health arena, but is also influenced by the works of The Peter F. Drucker Foundation for Nonprofit Management; leaders in the ''Dialogue' field; and Don Miquel Ruiz's book, 'The Four Agreements.' The Federation of Families recognizes the thousands of good people who endeavor daily to build respectful, thoughtful, and effective relationships to improve the lives of children with mental health issues and their families" (Federation of Families for Children's Mental Health, 2002, p. 7).

The following quoted materials outline the training module purposes, contents, and sequence.

"Modules in Sequence Included in Creating Better Partnerships

"Module One: Introductions and Overview

"Purpose of this Module is to set the context, orient the participants, and create an environment for open and honest exploration of the value and the challenges of parent-professional partnerships.

"Module Two: Surface Feelings

"Purpose of this module is to demonstrate what makes each 'side' angry with the other and what each "side" appreciates about the other. This generally results in recognition of similarities between families' and professionals' feelings about working with one another and an increased empathy toward one another.

"Module Three: A Deeper Look

"Purpose of this module is to give participants an opportunity for self-reflection and to try to recognize and be aware of what is behind the reactions and feelings they shared during the exercise in Module Two. While this is an important knowledge base for anyone intending to effectively participate in partnerships, it is critical if the training outcome selected (Module Five) is "Individual Goal Setting."

"Module Four: Relationship Skills

"Purpose of this module is to introduce skills for building honest, open and authentic dialogue between people and, then, to offer an opportunity to practice the skills with each other.

"Module Five: Creating Better Partnerships

"Purpose of this module is to create Individual Goals for Creating Better Partnerships based on the 12 Re-ED principles.

"Module Six: Closing

"Purpose of this module is to close the day with good intentions. The questions discussed are: What's the hardest thing about partnering together?   What are the most important things you learned today? What did you see? What did you feel? What did you hear?" (Federation of Families for Children's Mental Health: Special Adaptation for PEP, 2002, pp. 10-15).

Training participants provided the following information as part of the module exercises.

Participant Responses to Module One Exercises

Concepts Exercise: **"What does safety here mean to you?"** produced: No foul language, All comments are respected, Ask the question, No shame or blame, Feel comfortable to express an opposing view, No question is stupid, Be open minded, Speak for yourself, Don't be opinionated or judgmental, Don't take comments personally.

Partnerships: **"What one word comes to mind when you think about partnerships?"** produced: Trust, Challenging, Sharing, Scary, Knowledge, Fondness, Communication, Changing , Respect, Openness, Team, Continual, Collaboration, Conflict, Hard work!,

Compromise, Risky, Confident, Dependability, Growing, Security, Necessity, Emotional, Giving, Support, Receiving, Frustration, Balance, Safe, Common sense, Listening, Aggravating, Boundaries, Flexible, Resolution, Process.

The following four were added at the end of the day: Enriching, Do-able this year, Experience, Joy, Fun.

Assumptions Exercise: **"What do we assume when we see or hear one of these phrases?"** Participants were asked to finish these phrases as sentences, based on the limited information given. Their answers follow.

I'm afraid to drive…. produced: Had a bad experience; Panic attacks; No insurance; Can't afford a car, I'm a minor; People drive too fast; I have a physical disability; Public phobia; Afraid of police; Too many tickets, license taken away; Car could break down; Wants other person to go with them; Safety concerns due to child's behavior; Afraid to drive in bad weather; Been in an accident; Can't see well; Never learned to drive; Afraid of failing temp test; Mental health issues; Claustrophobia; Developmental delay.

I want my check cashed in quarters…. produced: Relies on public transportation; Works; Saving "state" quarters; May not have a washing machine, May want to feel the weight of money; Teenager wants video game money; No home phone; Can only count by 25; Money for parking meters; They can identify what they want; Need quarters to wash or for bus fare; Mental health issues (OCD or DD); I want to play the slot machine; Emergency pay phone money; Makes me feel like I have more money; Toll booth money; Blind.

I want my father to go to the appointment with me…. produced: Insecure; Dad is not in the home; Dad may be the support person; Need transportation from dad; Young child; Wants more time with dad; Dad needs to discipline or control; Dad needs to be more involved; Child wants dad to understand; May need to work at something with dad; Fathers know better; Dad will protect me; Strange (enmeshed) relationship with dad; Likes to be with dad; Person knows what he wants; Afraid of doctors; May not be comfortable advocating for self; Reason to see dad/quality time; Could be mad at his mom;

No insurance.

I can't write my name...... produced: Their hand could be
broken; They could be illiterate; They could be deaf; Maybe they
never learned; May not be able to write in English; May be blind;
May be oppositional; Child-attention seeking; Cerebral palsy,
or physically impaired (no arms); Developmental delay; Not
confident; Paranoid (identity theft); Have been enabled (learned helplessness); Doesn't like his/her name; Afraid to sign away rights.

Participant Responses to Module Two Exercises

**Professional's responses to "Parents make me angry
when...."** produced: Can't make contact; Don't show up for meetings;
Don't return calls; Sabotage treatment plans; Show up unannounced
at school and expect a meeting; Neglect children medically; Higher
expectations for their children than for themselves; Don't return
paperwork; Accept no personal responsibility and blame; Not willing
to work for change; Take advantage of children financially (SSI); Use
corporal punishment/abuse; Ask for help and don't follow through;
Give half information—secretive.

Professional's responses to "I appreciate parents who...."
produced: Keep appointments; Follow through; Keep trying;
Honest; Make needs known; Welcome communication; Keep
professionals informed of changes; Willing to work with us; Parents
who tell you they are mad at you; Focus on positive in their kids;
Understand we don't have all the answers; Support interventions;
Open minded to new ways of thinking; Trust; Parents who encourage
their children/supportive; Spend time with their children; Take the
initiative; Advocate for their child; Who say "no."

**Parent's responses to "Professionals make me angry
when...."** produced: They go by book knowledge and not by life
knowledge; Judgmental about my motives as a parent; They don't
communicate everything unless I ask; They tell me how to run my life;
I'm not recognized for the life knowledge I bring to the table; They try
to tell me how to raise my child and they don't even have children;
They blame the parents; Make decisions about treatment before

talking with me; They focus on the weaknesses in my child or our family; Don't try to understand the families' cultural needs; They assume that parents don't care about or love their child.

Parent's responses to "I appreciate professionals who…." produced: Recognize my strengths and that of my family; Take time to really listen; Respects my knowledge regarding my child's needs; Explain ABC language; 'Family driven' is truly practiced; Ask my advice; Support my decisions even though they don't agree; Involve me in the treatment plan; Share their knowledge with me as an equal; Share my vision for my child; Are helpful and go beyond the call of duty; Don't view me as the problem; Be truthful and honest in a respectful way; Call you back with information; Admit they don't know and seek out the answer; Truly listen to what I have to say; Feel that they can learn something from me; Work with me; Treat me like I actually have intelligence; Work with my schedule; Not judgmental; Make me feel comfortable; Realize that I'm doing the best I can; Respect my life experience as much as their book knowledge; Communicate back to me that they understand my point of view; Realize that we as parents have other responsibilities other than our child; Inform me of the consequences and how it will be perceived.

Summary of Evaluation Results

#1. *"Identify yourself as family member or professional"* produced: 11 family members; 11 professionals; 7 as both

#2. *"Did training improve ability to engage in family/ professional partnerships?"* produced: 24 yes; 1 no; 5 great refreshers. Some comments made by participants that said yes: Made me more aware I'm not the "expert" with parents but a collaborator; Now I can open up more in a positive way, instead of being so negative; Provided me with a lot of info to start engaging f/p partnerships; Taught me to never assume anything; ask questions, and really listen; Very helpful to hear what professionals view as barriers in working with parents.

The comment made by the person who said no: I feel I already practice the skills we discussed.

#3. *"Did you feel respected and safe during the training?"* produced: All participants indicated yes. However, one person indicated that the car exercise was uncomfortable for them.

#4. *"Ways training curriculum could be improved"* produced: Need to further adapt for our agency; More instruction on how to be good trainers; I need to use the curriculum first before I can comment; Discuss ways to implement program for our agency; Follow-up practice for dialogues would be helpful; A little shorter (2x); More demonstrations on how to present training; Put modules pages and comments together; Type up flip chart pages generated at this training and distribute; Have further training available.

#5. *"What ways could trainers improve delivery of curriculum?"* produced: Delivery was - excellent, good, great, fine (4 separate responses); Great team work; Delivery was excellent, professional, and most importantly "real;" Maybe use power point, drawings or diagrams of some sort; Trainers were easy to listen to; We weren't bored; More in depth, Viewing and discussing videos of role-plays of "best" and "not so great" practice.

#6. *"Is there anything else you would like to tell us about your experience?"* produced: Better than I expected; I'm energized; Very helpful-have info to share with colleagues; Very uplifting; Trainers were well prepared; Kept my attention; Good participation from group-liked the way trainers gave group "chill" time; I was very comfortable and wanted to share my thoughts; Shouldn't assume "ice breakers" positive experience for all— Some laughter is nervous; Helped me focus on priorities I want to work on for the year; I really enjoyed training with all the professionals and hope to do more; Driver's seat ice-breaker took too long and didn't really seem to have a point.

II. Parents and Professionals Growing Together

Training Created by PEP Parents

At the end of the school year in June 2004, the Family Support Liaisons (FSLs) provided an in-service entitled "Let's Grow Together" designed to enhance home-school relationships and develop empathy for both staff and parents. This in-service demonstrated that staff and parents have more similarities than differences. We wanted staff to better understand that even "difficult" parents want their kids to do well, but are often unaware of how to make that happen.

PEP's Parent Advisory Council has an ongoing goal of finding ways to enhance communication and relationships between parents and staff. This, as well as the success of the parent panel over the years in the summer institute (since 1981), contributed to the development of this in-service.

Goals. We listed the following goals for this training:

— To enhance empathy of staff towards parents/families of emotionally disturbed youth at PEP

— To provide staff and parents an opportunity to discuss issues related to parent-school mental health partnerships

— To encourage staff to identify and write one objective for the next school year whereby they would further develop their interactions and partnerships with parents and families.

Schedule and Structure. A half day (approximately 3 hours) was scheduled. Four different sites were set up across PEP involving staff from two day treatment centers at each site. Each trainer panel had four parents, representing a good mix of child's age, race, and disability. To develop a safe, comfortable environment permitting an open and honest dialogue, parents on the panels were not at the site where their child attended school.

Content. During the first 10 minutes of in-service, staff listened to a CD of actual comments, positive and negative, commonly made regarding parents/families, a brief explanation about why they were listening to this CD, and how it tied into the agenda for the day. (The team of FSL's at each site wrote their own explanations.)

The bulk of the morning consisted of parent panel presentations, lasting approximately 1 ½ hours. Then we had a question and answer period that led to a dialogue between parents and staff. For the closing task, one FSL made nice cards with envelopes so that each staff member could write a goal for enhancing their partnerships with parents, seal it, and then re-open it once they returned in the fall. FSLs reported that many staff had the cards posted or set up on their desks throughout the school year to remind them of their goal.

Follow-up. As a follow-up to that in-service, FSLs focused on the importance of the12 Re-ED Principles and how they apply to staff working with parents. This consisted of highlighting two Re-ED principles per month and relating each to Re-ED's philosophy on parent involvement and partnership in the treatment process. Most centers would give the FSL some time at the center staff meeting to discuss ways to implement the principles. Each center had different ways of implementing the principles. The following were provided as handouts distributed for these follow-ups.

Hobbs' Principles as Stimulus Materials for Our Parents

"Life is to be lived now, not in the past, and lived in the future only as a present challenge" (Hobbs, 1982, p. 22). Often with our students parents feel a strong sense of failure and may feel responsible when their child experiences difficulties. They also need to experience periods of success that renew their bodies and spirits. We need to do everything possible to help structure successes by helping them move forward, not dwelling on past mistakes, while being mindful of their own needs and capabilities.

"Communities are important..., but the uses and benefits of community must be experienced to be learned" (Hobbs, 1982, p. 22). Parents feel isolated when they have a child with difficulties. Communities provide support and a sense of belonging, a sense of self esteem and empowerment, and a connectedness for the entire family. We need to help parents become aware of, and learn how to access, these services and resources in their community. Examples of community are church, clubs, recreation centers, and support groups.

"A child should know some joy in each day and look forward to some joyous event for the morrow" (Hobbs, 1982, p. 23). We believe that a joyous experience is important and immediately

therapeutic for both our students and our parents as well. Parents experience some of their most joyous events when they can identify and communicate their strengths at parenting, or when they learn about the successes of their child.

Joy should also be reciprocal: teacher to child, child to teacher, parent to child, child to parent, teacher to parent, parent to teacher. The more we experience joy, the more joy we can give to others.

"The group is very important to young people; it can be a major source of instruction in growing up" (Hobbs, 1982, p. 22). Parents are our allies, a part of our team, and we must not allow them to be excluded. We must involve them in every aspect of our program and gather their input regarding IEPs, ISPs, intake, and especially parent group. Parent group and the sharing of experiences about their children provide parents with a sense of motivation, instruction, and a human relatedness which most have not experienced.

"Ceremony and ritual give order, stability, and confidence to troubled children and adolescents, whose lives are often in considerable disarray" (Hobbs, 1982, p. 22). Parent group, assemblies, field trips, graduations, and parties are times of ceremony and enrichment. If parents are involved in these activities, there will be more positive interaction, more follow through. Barriers will be removed, and they are more likely to approach the center when requested.

"Competence makes a difference; children and adolescents should be helped to be good at something, and especially at schoolwork" (Hobbs, 1982, p. 22). Many times parents come into our program with a broken spirit, lacking confidence as a parent. They have been through so much with their child before coming to PEP. This broken spirit may come across as disinterest, hostility, belligerence, even anger. Acceptance without judgment is the beginning point in the process of re-education. Our job is to help parents realize their strengths and to feel empowered, which will help mend their broken spirit, and boost their confidence. A parent must believe in himself/herself; only then will we start seeing positive results.

"The cognitive competence of children and adolescents can

be considerably enhanced; they can be taught generic skills in the management of their lives as well as strategies for coping with the complex array of demands placed on them by family, school, community, or job; in other words intelligence can be taught" (Hobbs, 1982, p. 22). Much like their child, many parents who come to our program have deficits in both concepts and problem solving skills. Remember, you can't know what you have never been taught. We can help parents learn the process for problem solving, and new ways to approach parenting. They can learn to use behavior management skills and to utilize resources. Parent group is a wonderful, non-threatening, supportive way that parents can come together and learn new problem solving skills. Please encourage your parents to attend and feel free to come, too.

"Time is an ally, working on the side of growth in a period of development when life has tremendous forward thrust" (Hobbs, 1982, p. 22). Implementing the "time is an ally" principle in our interactions with parents is not an easy task. Sometimes progress with a child, or our ability to build a relationship with a parent, seems to move at a snail's pace. Many times we see no progress at all. This is when we need to remember time is on our side. More time allows for the opportunity to keep communication open, improving the chances of developing a working relationship. We won't see results overnight, but as professionals, utilizing time as an ally, we can help parents learn and grow along with their children and us.

"Self-control can be taught and children and adolescents helped to manage their behavior without the development of psychodynamic insight" (Hobbs, 1982, p. 22). Just as many parents come to our program without certain concepts and problem solving skills, they also may need guidance in learning self-control; this also may be something they have never been taught. Helping parents learn to identify feelings and triggers to maladaptive behaviors is one of the best skills we can give them.

"The body is the armature of the self, the physical self around which the psychological self is constructed" (Hobbs, 1982, p. 22). What we like about this Re-ED principle is the emphasis on involving

all aspects of your body in a given activity, producing a greater awareness of what you are capable of doing. It's an exercise in self-discovery. Just as our students need to engage in physical activities to experience a connection, so do their parents.

"Feelings should be nurtured, shared spontaneously, controlled when necessary, expressed when too long repressed, and explored with trusted others" (Hobbs, 1982, p. 22). Many parents who come to our program, like their child, are variously incapacitated in the management of their feelings. Many experience anger, fear, resentment, anxiety, and depression. Parents need as safe and secure a forum for expressing themselves as our students do. Every contact we have with a parent is an opportunity to really listen to what they are saying and feeling. There are parents whose feelings run deep. Helping them unravel these feelings by meeting them where they are right now today, not where we would like them to be, is the first step to developing a meaningful relationship with us. We know this can be difficult at times. However, parent group presents a wonderful opportunity for parents to express their feelings in a safe, supportive environment.

"Trust between child and adult is essential, the foundation on which all other principles rest, the glue that holds teaching and learning together, the beginning point for re-education" (Hobbs, 1982, p. 22). Development of trust is the first step in the process of re-education. Nothing can undermine a relationship more completely than lack of trust. If parents don't trust us, why should their children? By the time many children come to PEP, their parents' trust in "systems" has been destroyed; they have likely not experienced a trusting relationship with a professional. This impacts their relationship with us. Therefore, our "system" needs to be trustworthy. We need to nurture trust with parents. This can be a daunting task. We need to keep the relationship with parents consistent, predictable, and genuine. One way of establishing that trusting relationship is to listen, really listen without being judgmental.

III. Why Re-ED?

The Family Support Liaisons' Workshop

Parents hired by the Positive Education Program as staff to help other parents with children now in the program designed a workshop to share with new (and perhaps old) PEP professional staff the perspectives of parents like the ones they now serve. The workshop's objectives were to promote: (a) an increased knowledge of the Re-ED philosophy, (b) a heightened awareness of current utilization of the Re-ED philosophy with parents, (c) a greater sensitivity to parents' perspectives, and (d) the importance of the role that Re-ED can play in treatment within families' ecologies.

What Is Re-ED? Nicholas Hobbs initiated the Re-Education of Emotionally Disturbed children as a dynamic child and family centered approach to treatment which remained an open paradigm, incorporating new treatments as their validity and utility become known. Its primary, individualized objective is to restore the ecology of each troubled child to a "tolerable level of discord."

What's Different About Re-ED?

The FSLs led staff in discussing each of the following important characteristics of a Re-ED program.

Provides an ecologically-based approach. These concepts were very radical in the 1960's. Re-ED was, and still is, a new concept of working with children, their families, and the supports in their community, helping all members of the child's world to function in a reasonably satisfactory manner - a concept that looked to develop plans with family members to empower them to build new competencies and achieve purposeful days.

Seeks re-education of everyone in the child's ecology. The ecological concept involves not only the re-education of children but also the re-education of parents, regular teachers, relatives, professional people, and our own staff.

Sees parents as primary change agents. The parents of a troubled child are, and must be, central agents in efforts to help the child and younger adolescent. Empowerment of parents is a critical

concept in Re-ED strategies. It abandons the notion of blaming parents for the difficulties of their children and rejecting them for their inadequacies. It seeks to identify and use their strengths to enhance their competences, their skills.

Recognizes parents as true experts, not as sources of contagion. Parents must be recognized as special educators, true experts on their children; professional people must learn to consult with parents. *"The tendency to blame parents must be guarded against, especially by young staff who have not themselves experienced the humbling complexities of a parent's role....However, to accept parents as the true experts on their children is a difficult concept for professional people to learn"* (Hobbs, 1982, p. 219).

Abandons cure as a goal. *"The goal is not a perfect world for the child, [or parents], but a satisfactory one where successful days are more common than not...."*(Cantrell, Cantrell, Valore, Jones, & Fecser, 1999, p. 19) — where the*"motivation to persevere results from setting clear goals and recognizing when small successes towards these goals occur"* (Cantrell, et al., 1999, p. 12). The end result is successful moments turned into successful days for both child and family.

Doesn't look at what's wrong with people. Re-ED is *"interested in what it is that keeps ecosystems from working;...not interested in what's wrong with people — not the child, or the parents, teachers, or any others"* (Hobbs, 1982, p. 217). Instead, it seeks to help all the members of the child's world learn to function in a reasonably satisfactory manner.

Identifies strengths as a critical element. Strengths of the child and the people in his/her ecology are important areas for analysis and intervention. Strengths are critical to bring about changes. *"Examining the potential sources of strength in the child and others in the child's world (even within negative episodes) leads us to develop interventions that otherwise might be overlooked"* (Cantrell, et al., 1999, p. 20). Helpers can often identify strengths not normally recognized, where others might see only weaknesses.

Builds competence to produce lasting change. The ultimate

goal for troubled and troubling children, and for their families, is successful living. To help them reach that goal, we must give them hope, and assist them in learning to choose and succeed with more satisfying steps toward creating better lives for themselves. *"The achievement of competence, step by step, in matters small then large, is an attractive challenge not only to children and adolescents, but to teacher-counselors as well"* (Hobbs, 1982, p. 87). This holds true especially for parents.

A great example of how building competence produces lasting change is a student's mom who is challenged with some developmental delays of her own. DTC staff worked to help her build confidence across areas, such as exposing her to staying away from home overnight. PEP offers all parents who consistently attend and actively participate in Parent Group throughout the year an opportunity to attend an overnight Amish retreat. After this trip she had a sense of achievement and confidence not witnessed before.

Emphasizes importance of language. We must use the least destructive and most positive language we can. *"Words carry excess meaning; our word choices have consequences. Often, a term carries with it assumptions on which people will base decisions and then act. When the term applies to a human being, we are obligated to consider whether the assumptions implied by the term and the consequent actions are in the best interest of the person involved"* (Cantrell, et al., 1999, p. 15).

The Labels Exercise

The FSLs had posted words as pejorative labels on walls around the room before participants entered. Referring to those posted, they introduced an activity, with the following: It's hard to admit, but most of us, consciously or not, label some parents and caregivers in our programs. We may not speak these labels aloud, but they definitely impact the way we interact with families.

The "Abusive" or "Irresponsible" Parent. Often these labels are based on objective facts: We may consider a dad an "abusive parent" because of well-documented incidents of abuse. We might

consider a mom "irresponsible" because of the past times she's left her young children home alone, or partied away the grocery money. We might consider another mom as "difficult" because when we've talked with her, her screams and curses were repeatedly aimed at us. Another mom becomes known as "a drama queen" or "histrionic" because of her multiple calls each week about the latest "crisis."

We need to remember Hobbs stressed that *"life is to be lived now"* (Hobbs, 1982, p. 22). What happened in the past may *not* be what is happening in the present. When we remember this, we give a parent the chance to start over, try again.

Next, FSLs serving as presenters give examples of how these labels may have been applied to us as parents and how each of us may have internally labeled a parent in this way such as those below.
Examples:
— I've worked with parents whose documented history of physically abusing their children left me a little more suspicious of bruises or injuries on their child than with parents who, as far as I knew, have always been kind, patient, and gentle with their children. Does this mean we shouldn't be vigilant about assuring that children whose history includes abuse are safe? No, just that we need to be aware of how our internal "label" of that parent may affect our reactions. This can work both ways in that we might be tempted to dismiss marks on the "saintly" parent's child, thinking, "I'm sure he must have bumped into something, because that parent wouldn't hurt her child."

— We all realize that parents are not always consistent about their children getting to school each day on time. We may label them "lazy," "irresponsible," or as "enabling" parents who let their child stay home any time he doesn't feel like attending school. Sometimes I've found myself rushing to assumptions when a child missed another day, or arrived late. Perhaps I think the parent overslept again or was making excuses for their child who just preferred not going to school. Then I learn the child was hospitalized with an illness or they had an accident on the way to school. How might my interactions with that parent differ *before* versus *after* obtaining that last bit of information?

The "Non-Compliant" Parent. Non-Compliant Parent may be the most frequently used label, in several forms: No-Follow-

Through-Parent, No-Consequences-Parent, Wants-Us-To-Do-All-the-Work-Parent, Not-Willing-To-Put-Forth-Effort-Parent, and others. But perhaps a parent's reluctance or refusal to implement recommendations results from many years of not being able to achieve changes; perhaps professionals made unhelplful suggestions. Parents are experts on not only their child. They also know their family's dynamics and how able they are to implement suggestions. A strategy's success depends upon a parent's willingness and ability to carry it out.
Examples:

— Staff might recommend that the child not be allowed to engage in desired activities until a task is completed or as a consequence for negative behavior, but the mother feels unable to physically deal with the aggressive outburst that this withholding will create. Chances are, she will not consistently follow through on the recommendation because she fears the child will act out aggressively. The mother may need additional training in safe methods of physical restraint, or alternatively, the mother could practice withholding during times when there is another family member (or trained respite provider) available to help with physical management of the child.

— Staff may develop a Premacked schedule to help a child perform less-preferred daily activities. However, due to her own difficulties with routines, schedules, and organization, the child's mother seldom, if ever, implements the schedule. It might be necessary to help the mother work on her organizational skills before asking her to implement a structured schedule for the child. Another option could be having the mother start off implementing a predictable schedule for one small part of the day.

Parents as "Sources of Contagion." Another reason why we sometimes label parents is that they may present themselves as disinterested, irresponsible, apathetic, or irritable. Our natural tendency is to conclude that the affect we see displayed is linked to the child's problems. Hobbs referred to this as seeing the "... parents... as sources of contagion" (Hobbs, 1982, p. 28). This natural tendency gets reinforced, because surely there are times when parents' behaviors do lead to children's problems and can negatively impact progress.

However, we need to remain open to the possibility that, in some cases, the parent's behavior or affect is the *result* of living with a very challenging child, not the cause. It may also result from accumulated negative experiences the parent has had with other service providers or even with friends, relatives, and neighbors. The following are examples of unusual parent-child interactions that may not truly reflect what their surface patterns appear to suggest.

Examples:

— A parent seems to display no physical affection towards their preschool-age child. Be careful not to assume this means the parent doesn't like or love the child, is cold and distant, or harbors deep resentment toward him. It *could* be that the child is troubled by tactile defensiveness and that in the past any attempts at physical affection by the parent were met with extreme negative reactions from the child. You'd stop hugging a child too if he kicked or bit you every time you did!

— You notice a parent often seems highly irritable towards their child. While this certainly can have a negative effect on the child's behavior and needs to be explored, it's possible this parent starts every day with a positive spirit and easy-going demeanor, only to be met with negativity, non-compliance, aggression, etc. from the child at every turn. Even Mother Teresa herself might be a little testy after a day like this parent has had! Encourage a positive approach, but understand when parents aren't able to keep this going at all times.

— Every time you see this parent, he seems sleepy and disinterested. You've wondered if he might be on drugs. There may be more going on than you realize. He may be working three jobs but hasn't mentioned this to you. He may be caring for an ailing parent or disabled sibling after putting in a full workday and taking care of his own household and family obligations. There might be a child in the home who doesn't sleep through the night, and this parent is chronically sleep-deprived. There could be medical problems that haven't been disclosed. Keep an open mind to all possibilities.

— Remember that we don't always know the life events that may have led to differing affects.

Professionals, Don't Give Up On Us!!

As a parent of two children with disabilities, one of my major continuing goals is to enhance parent-professional partnerships. My experience as both parent and professional demonstrated what we all know to be critical to ensuring a positive outcome for the child and family: the effectiveness of the teamwork relationship we have with each other. For over 25 years of participating in and facilitating numerous parent panels, or making individual presentations regarding these partnerships, the main objective is always to encourage open, honest dialogue that will help parents and professionals see and understand each other's perspectives. One comment invariably arises: "You're different, not like most parents I work with. You're involved, and you seem to really care."

In a recent training, one staff member gave a specific example. A mom of one of her students is not at all involved with her child to the point of neglect, to the point that the team had to report that neglect to County Children's Services. The staff member's frustration with the mom runs deep, because for the period of time that county was involved in the case, the mom "snapped to," got much more involved, and was no longer neglectful. But, as soon as the county was out of the picture, she went back to being uninvolved and neglectful again.

The parents there all felt, and understood the staff member's frustration. In our effort to help alleviate some of that frustration, our responses came from our hearts — based on our own journey from that place of despair and hopelessness that we felt, as well as our experiences as parent-professionals who have worked with these same kinds of challenges.

The initial response to the staff member's story from most of the parents in the training was, *"The parents you see present here today are not the same parents we were when our children first came to PEP. We have come a long way --after a long, arduous journey. We still struggle today. Even though some of our children are adults now, we still have crises from time to time. We too were uninvolved, and were probably considered the 'non-compliant parent.' But because of the strong dedication and resolve of PEP staff, meeting us where we were, really believing that they were facing a set of very complex circumstances surrounding parents who needed a tremendous amount of support and intervention, as opposed to parents who didn't care, PEP staff didn't give up — no matter how disengaging we may have been."*

Many parents who end up on PEP's doorstep have had numerous contacts with other professionals; they may not have experienced any success from those attempts. After failure, it is very hard for parents to open up and accept that what professionals are bringing to the table can make a difference. Some of us will be eager and ready for any help we can get, and others will be very distrustful, angry, and distant to the point of being considered uncaring — or as the parent in this case, being neglectful. That doesn't mean however, that she does not care or love her child. This parent is obviously at the bottom of her barrel, and needs a lot of caring support — and time to embrace what professionals have to offer.

Many of us have been there. For us the difference was a professional we could trust who wasn't going to judge us for making some of the poor choices we'd made. We had professionals that saw something in us that we couldn't see in ourselves. We couldn't see it because we were either so overwhelmed, suffered from mental health issues of our own, and/or had lost all hope that we could improve or that things could get better for our child and family. They recognized some element of strength amongst circumstances that other professionals couldn't see and then build upon. If professionals believe we can't, or don't want, to grow, learn, and change, then professionals will miss that element of strength in us that may be the turning point.

Breaking out of the mold of the "typical professional" is not an easy task. We fiercely tested the skill, patience, and resolve of the PEP staff that worked with us. A message to professionals: You will have many frustrating moments and failures, but remember change is enormously difficult and takes a long time --but *please don't give up on us.* You never know when something will click, and the parent that you least expect to rise to the occasion, will do so -- giving a level of satisfaction and accomplishment even greater than with the parent who didn't present such a challenge. We desperately need you to help us recognize and build on our strengths; give us hope that we can rise to the challenge and that our child and family will get better.

My response, in an effort to help relieve some of the staff member's frustration, was to point out that even though this parent is sending signals that maybe she does not care about her child, there is at least one strength there—she did what she needed to do to keep her child. If she had not cared for this child, she would not have risen to the occasion for even that short period of time. Build on that strength, somehow. She may be depressed; she may be so overwhelmed that she has just shut down. I was at that point many times. Parents, like teachers, are only human; it is impossible to maintain constant, optimal performance, day in and day out. We all experience that roller coaster of resolve. Some of us have the resources, strength, and support to regain the top of the hill, but many of us need tremendous support for longer periods of time.

A Different Way of Thinking

A 1980 video of Nick Hobbs when he came to speak to PEP staff made a difference for me, dramatically changing how I viewed certain parents and students that I have worked with, and will work with in the future. He pointed out the difference between viewing a student as a "problem student that will never change" as opposed to a "system or ecology that is not working." He said that a crisis or critical situation is a time for creating options, for thinking outside the box. He told about an 11-year-old boy named "Bobby Washington." Bobby came to them after being in various placements that had not worked due to his violent outbursts. When he came to Re-ED, he could not read or differentiate between letters and numbers. He had a measured I.Q. of 50, but showed signs of being brighter than that; he could play the piano a little bit by ear.

During his first Re-ED day Bobby had four or five fights, and wounded a couple of other students. They knew that day what a "critical situation they had" (notice Nick did not refer to Bobby as a problem student or bad kid). After a month or so they were not making much progress with Bobby. The Teacher-Counselor came to him and said she could not tolerate Bobby any more. He had attacked her that day and she felt she had failed miserably. The team had numerous meetings over the next week, trying to decide what to do with Bobby. The one suggestion that kept arising was for them to send him back to Central State Hospital (where he would be put in a locked ward, sedated, and become a custodial patient — eventually a likely inmate in the state penitentiary). However, the team decided to keep him at Cumberland House. They put together a comprehensive plan that addressed multiple needs. The most critical of those needs was to get him to feel competent at something, so they started to teach him to read and provided him with piano lessons. About a month or so after they had implemented the plan, Nick was on campus, and Bobby came running across the grounds yelling, "Mr. Hobbs, I can read! I can read! I can read!" Bobby went on to success, and at the time of the video in 1980, Bobby was 24 years old, had a job, and was married with a child of his own.

The compelling factor for me in this story was how Nick had helped the team reframe their views of Bobby. He helped them see it was the system surrounding Bobby that was inadequate — not that Bobby was an out of control, problem child who couldn't or didn't want to change. With this story, Nick demonstrated that a careful selection of the terms we use to describe the students and parents we work with directly impacts how we interact with them and what interventions we choose to generate and implement. No matter how uninvolved, uncaring, or disengaged a parent may seem, there is some strength to build upon if we choose to view the parent's actions as symptoms of a complex set of circumstances that signal a need for a lot of support - not as the actions of a "problem parent" who can't or doesn't want to change. Am I saying that all parents will respond positively to others' efforts and rise to the occasion? No, but echoing the words of Nick Hobbs, *"There are some parents that have so few resources and supports of their own that they can't respond to the level we believe they should. But they're few and far between. We bring them along as far as we can — we don't give up"* (Hobbs, 1980).

Another comment/question that arises is, "Sometimes the parent is the problem because they have been found to have either physically or sexually abused the child. How can you still consider those parents as the experts on their children?"

My response is, "Yes, that kind of abuse causes *major* problems for a child, and is certainly very serious." Any parent that has been guilty of this kind of abuse has most likely been a victim of abuse himself or herself. They obviously have never been taught parenting skills or proper ways of coping and managing their stress and/or anger. This does not excuse their choice of behavior, but these are parents who need our help the most, ones we should really be working hard with to find a way to help them break that cycle. We should not be writing them off, or discounting their assistance with their child because they have been abusive. The absence of all these kinds of skills does not mean that a parent doesn't know their child better than anyone else. They still have expertise to offer.

Experts don't always make the right choices for a lot of reasons, often due to other areas where they don't have skills. Still, even with their own problems and skill deficits, as Hobbs said, parents do know their child – and make powerful allies when you stick with them.

References

Cantrell, M.L., Cantrell, R.P., Valore, T.G., Jones, J.M., & Fecser, F.A. (1999). A revisitation of the ecological perspectives on emotional / behavioral disabilities. In Bullock, L.M. & Gable, R.A. *What works for children and youth with E/BD: Linking yesterday and today with tomorrow.* Reston, VA: Council for Children with Behavioral Disorders, a division of the Council for ExceptionalChildren.

Federation of Families for Children's Mental Health (2002). *Creating better partnerships: One at a time. Family-professional partnership training: Special adaptation for PEP, Cleveland, Ohio* (2005). Alexandria, VA: Author.

Hobbs, N. (1980). Cleveland Symposium: Transcript of videotaped presentation. Cleveland, OH: Positive Education Program.

Hobbs, N. (1982). *The troubled and troubling child.* San Francisco: Jossey-Bass.

Valarie Rudar is Family & Community Liaison for Positive Education Program in Cleveland, Ohio.
Vrudar@pepcleve.org

The Family Support Liaisons (Stacy Bush, Millie DeMent, Beverly Jeffries, Norah Joseph, Karen Mullins, Edie Richardson, KathySurmitis, Mary Rita Urban, Lasondra Whitney, and Cossondra Williams) each serve in the parent support role at a Positive Education Program Day Treatment Center, each center serving students 6 to 18; centers are spread across northeast Ohio.

11

Teacher-Parents: The Heart of Regional Intervention Program

E. Ann Ingram

Since its inception in 1969, the Regional Intervention Program (better known as RIP) has relied on parents as the primary therapists and behavior change agents for their preschool age children with challenging behaviors. From the very first weeks of their participation in RIP, parents are taught and given the opportunity to: (1) record and analyze data, (2) write behavior programs using principles of applied behavior analysis, (3) conduct social skills training sessions, and (4) implement behavioral interventions in a variety of settings.

Who teaches these very complex skills? Parents!

After completing the active treatment phase, parents begin to "pay back" the program for services received. Among the duties included within the payback phase is the training and support of new families who have entered the program. Under the guidance of the program's professional staff, the "payback parents" gain confidence in their own newly gained skills as they share them with others. New parents find hope as they hear testimony from the payback parent about how these techniques have changed the behaviors of their own child. Since the parent is told prior to beginning training that they will be expected to share their knowledge with others during their payback period, the importance of understanding and retaining the information increases.

Not only do payback parents assist with training, they may also serve as lead teachers in RIP classrooms and conduct program tours. The goal of a RIP site is for parents to assume active roles in program operation and to be indistinguishable from staff in the eyes of a program visitor.

Parents are actively recruited to serve on program advisory boards and to serve as paid staff members. Successful graduates of RIP are hired to serve in case management, classroom coordination, and technical assistance roles for children enrolled in child care and school settings.

As parents become confident in their abilities to change the behaviors of their own child and to share these skills with other parents, this empowerment often transcends the RIP experience into other areas of their life. Frequently, RIP graduates move on to become agents of system change within their community and beyond. They lead support groups, are child advocates who attend M-team (multi-disciplinary) meetings with other parents, and are members of local early intervention councils. Recently, several graduates have joined the new national service movement: AmeriCorps RIP Partnership. Through this continued service to RIP, they earned educational awards which many have used toward a career goal in children's mental health.

Does this empowerment stand the test of time? One of the original parents who enrolled in the program in 1969 recently moved to a community that did not have a RIP. She began a community education campaign, tirelessly retelling the story of how the program taught her skills to manage her child's difficult behavior and the ensuing success. She even shared tales of how these skills have been handed down across generations, now that she's a grandmother. Due primarily to her efforts, funds were located and the program is now in operation. She continues to serve on the program's advisory board, and to make referrals during her day to day activities when she sees young mothers struggling with their toddlers somewhere in the community.

Over the years, parents have demonstrated the power of gaining confidence and competence by teaching others in Re-ED programs such as RIP. This power can do far more than affect the parents' own lives and those of their families. Their empowerment is evidenced by their leadership of family support groups, grassroots movements to improve or increase services, and participation on child advocacy boards and councils. *Competence truly makes a difference for parents* – not only in the lives of their own children but also in the lives of many others.

Parent Power: My RIP Journey
Miki Martin

When my family first entered the Regional Intervention Program (RIP), I knew that we were there because my daughter had behavior problems. I had no idea that I was there to learn skills that would change our lives!

In the beginning, I learned that I would be expected to "pay back" the program for the services I received for my own child by helping other families. At first, this made me somewhat anxious. I was the one asking the program for help and they were expecting me to help others. What were they thinking?

Then I learned that the person who would be my Case Manager was a parent who had graduated from the program. She was very knowledgeable and was able to teach me the skills I needed to observe, analyze, and implement programs to change my daughter's behavior. The support that she was able to give me as a parent who shared similar experiences, both the triumphs and frustrations, was extremely useful. And if we ran into any stumbling blocks along the way, there were always professional staff members available to assist when needed.

During each session, I learned to do more and more until I was not only comfortable with using the techniques with my own child but also with other children in her group. Before I knew it, I was doing my payback as the Lead Teacher in the RIP Classroom. Being able to talk with new parents about their issues, and relating to them as parents facing similar circumstances as my own, gave me strength to deal with my daughter's needs. The RIP Payback phase of treatment is an empowering experience that can change your life direction.

My experience at RIP has given me the competence and the confidence to work not only individually with parents, but also with parent groups and even groups of professionals. After my completion of RIP, I became a Parent Staff member and have worked part-time in the program for 10 years. My interest in teaching parenting skills also led me to my work with the Responsible Parenting Project in which I provide education and support for teen parents in their homes and schools.

Over the years I have noticed a need for parents of children beyond the preschool age to have access to a parent-to-parent support system similar to what is available in RIP. A group of interested community members were successful in establishing the Tennessee Voices for Children Support Group and I currently serve as the Parent Facilitator.

My work with the families in RIP also opened my eyes to my responsibility to be an advocate for all children in my community. Therefore, I try to give as much of my time as possible to serve on local committees where I believe my experience as both a parent and a provider of services to families of children with challenging behaviors will be valuable. My current affiliations include The Family Resource Center, the Early Childhood Network, and the Child Care Committee Task Force.

My next goal is to move beyond local service delivery and make an impact on the state level and beyond. I've made my first step with my participation on the Tennessee Department of Mental Health's Region V Planning Committee.

As I look back, I'm amazed by the direction my life path has taken since that first day I walked through the RIP door. And the best part is that I can watch this cycle each day as I work in RIP and see the domino effect of parents empowering other parents -- parent power at its best.

At the time of writing, Miki Martin, AA, was a RIP Case Manager.

E. Ann Ingram, MEd, is Program Manager for Centerstone's Early Childhood Programs; her office is located in Columbia, TN.

   eann.ingram@centerstone.org

12

Principles-Based
Diagnostic Assessment

*Robert Spagnola, Leslie Wilton,
Keith Brown, & April Shepherd*

Positive Education Program's Diagnostic Assessment Service (PEP DAS) responded to requests from the county's mental health board to provide functional ecological diagnostic assessments for children and adolescents with behavioral and emotional disorders who were referred to the Department of Children and Family Services.

As DAS staff, we embrace Nicholas Hobbs' vision of providing all services through the ecological approach. When we intervene, there are already discordances existing between the youth and others in his or her unique world. Unfortunately, the youth has already begun to add to his /her ecosystem by acting out and, of course, he/she is being impacted by that same ecosystem.

The intervention we provide is both ecological assessment and help for the youth and her/his caregiver(s) as they step through the therapeutic recommendations. These recommendations enable the caregiver and the youth to regain a modicum of equilibrium in their shared ecology so that it can function reasonably well. Recommendations need to be delivered in a setting as similar to and as close to the child's home setting as possible, so a diagnostic consultant goes out into the child's environment. In-the-office assessment batteries don't help us do our job, although we do use some standard measures.

Through our assessments and recommendations, we attempt to alter the environment in therapeutic ways.

We subscribe to the concept that caring adults are absolutely essential if youth are to grow and become productive citizens of the world; we are caring adults while we work on behalf of a child, identifying and supporting the caring adults in his/her life. Recommendations and interventions on their own aren't helpful unless the youth or caregiver experiences them as being practical, so we strive for "do-able" actions and help ecosystem members in the "doing." We understand that small early successes are in-roads to maintaining lasting success.

We complete a careful functional diagnostic assessment and analysis before planning any recommendations that will positively impact his or her environment. Each consultant is committed to problem solving. We recognize problems as opportunities for change, opportunities to facilitate or increase the youth's psychological growth. We incorporate clients' strengths as a component of effective change, synergistically increasing the youth's coping ability along the way.

How does a diagnostic assessment service embrace the tenets of Nick Hobbs, the basic premises of the Re-ED philosophy? PEP's DAS operates in harmony with the twelve core Re-ED principles (Hobbs, 1982, pp. 22-23), using them as a guide to ensuring that all our clients' needs are met.

"Life is to be lived now..."

Now is when life is to be lived. It is vital to teach youths and their families not to look back at failures, but forward, towards the future. Our functional diagnostic assessment has as its core value a belief that the youth and family already have various strengths on which to begin the rebuilding process towards higher functioning. These strengths, whether they be strong spiritual beliefs, a desire to implement changes to help recreate structure in the life of a child, a commitment to the child's educational pursuit, or others of equal importance, all are factored into this strengths-based diagnostic assessment process. Focus on and use of these strengths can go a long way towards improving the child's joy for life and a promising vision of the future.

"Trust... is essential"

While engaging our youths, we seek to earn their trust. Our staff thoroughly believe that in order to engage the youth we are assessing, we must gain their trust and the trust of their caregivers. Oft-times the youth has lost trust in those he/she had counted on in the past. Thus, re-establishing trust is crucial if the eventual success of intervention is to be realized. Not only must the intervention be demonstrably sound (a quality therapeutic proposal on the face of it), the youth and the caregiver must also feel that it's worthwhile to engage in because it holds future promise of beneficial change.

The youth must trust that going to therapy, associating with a big brother or big sister, tutoring, or attending a survivors of domestic violence group will be important and can contribute to a more personally satisfying future for her or for him. Trust is essential as a means for providing children and youths with viable opportunities for a better future.

"Time [must be treated as] an ally"

Meeting the youth and caregiver in a timely fashion is crucial. The thirty day turnaround time must be carefully used if a functional diagnostic assessment is to be ultimately effective as an intervention. Positive action taken on a child's behalf as early as possible in his/her life is helped by the forward thrust toward growth we see in young people. Taking no action, or taking negative action, can make of time an enemy.

Once a consultant completes the initial intake, it is important to make contact with the caregiver as soon as possible to let them know there is a service that will make therapeutic interventions easily and immediately available to the youth and his/her existing environment. This therapeutic intervention will make a difference in re-establishing equilibrium in the caregiver's existence and in the client's daily, routine functioning.

Once the recommendations are made to the referring agent, the caregiver, and the youth, the consultant then follows up with the referring agent to determine whether recommendations have been implemented and how successful the outcomes were. Occasionally other recommendations are needed, especially if some impediments to implementing the original recommendations have arisen unexpectedly. The time it takes to keep everyone informed, and to follow up, is critical time.

"Competence makes a difference"

We believe individuals can become effective and efficient problem solvers. We first assess what the child can do well, and point out his areas of competence. We know emotional behavior is a signal that the individual is not competent in that situation, that he or she lacks the skills to meet the demands placed on him or her there. We communicate the value of continual learning, for everyone, and involve them in problem solving. Through our recommendations we seek to effect personal and ecological change across time together, thus providing a foundation for the youth to build upon. Remembering small, early successes helps maintain the client's sustained efforts for increased competence and personal success into the future.

"Self control can be taught"

Family, peers, and community often devalue and reject a child or adolescent whose behaviors are seen as unacceptable. Inappropriate emotional behavior is often the result of the child being unable to meet the demands made by the environment in that situation. For children and adolescents, learning how to manage these unacceptable behaviors will allow them to build relationships with others, and hopefully to build new skills as well. Showing belief in a child's ability to change in the ecological assessment process sets the stage for the child to develop more skills. As these skills emerge, they increase the numbers of favorable interactions between the child and members of his/her ecology.

"Intelligence can be taught"

Inherent in the Re-Ed philosophy is the belief that children have a tremendous desire to learn and do well (even when they do not show it). Many children we work with have difficulties with problem solving. Treatment recommendations can include opportunities for experiences that can enhance learning and problem solving, helping them develop overall coping skills and more easily navigate interpersonal relationships. During the ecological assessment, more formal learning needs which have not yet been addressed within schools or by other systems may also be identified. In interviewing not only the child and his or her family, but also others involved (such as the school), these needs can be identified. Treatment recommendations can serve as the catalyst for intra-system involvement and collaboration for change. Treatment recommendations can also serve to educate the client and family regarding existing supports already available to help change occur.

"Feelings should be nurtured"

In the ecological assessment process, the diagnostic consultant strives to approach each child, family, and system from within a strength-based attitude and frame of mind. Each person has an opportunity to identify concerns and needs. Each also has an opportunity to discuss what they would like to see changed, and which strengths they possess would help to support those changes. Recommendations are also reviewed with the child, family, and other systems' representatives to ensure that they correspond to the desired goals stated. Only by identifying and nurturing the strengths of each contributor to the intervention process, can true and long lasting change occur. Giving opportunities for expression and accepting the feelings of youth and of each ecosystem member, help build trust in the process of seeking mutually optimal outcomes.

"Groups [are] a major source of instruction"

Families are of primary importance because they are a child's first teachers. Family groups provide the contexts for early learning and serve as a bridge between the child and their larger environment. Supporting families is critical to supporting change for their child.

Other children and adults can also help a child to increase problem solving and begin to make better choices. That is why recommendations almost always encourage participation in groups where appropriate modeling and support are available. These inter-actions with others are important to helping the child recognize the interdependency among people and systems, and especially their personal impact on others. It is more difficult to begin to make changes while alone and independent from others, than to make changes with the guidance and support of a group system that is already functioning well. Small changes across multiple arenas can produce longer lasting and larger impacts in the overall functioning of a child.

"Ceremony and ritual give order, stability and confidence..."

Hobbs goes on to say that the lives of troubled children and adolescents are often in disarray. When we assess a child's ecology for evidence of this principle, and the need for it, we look for signs of their rites of passage. We also look for indications of multi-cultural diversity as we try to understand the client's realm, ecosystem, and cultural beliefs. These arenas give us the opportunity to get into their world to understand the differences that exist between different cultural beliefs, and see what types of "rites of passage" may, or may not, be beneficial to their development. Part of the recommendations would include identifying discordant areas where structured routines could be developed (as family rituals) to help solve problem times (such as calming down chaotic mealtimes), or finding areas of more positive affect in their lives and then using those areas to help them grow.

"The body is [defined as] the armature of the self"

The physical self is the center around which the psychological self is organized. It's important when we do our diagnostic assessment that we understand if there are any health concerns. Specifically, we want to rule out any medical needs before concerning ourselves with any diagnostic labels. This is very important because there may be situations or clusters of characteristics that are solely due to medical concerns rather than psychological or mental health issues. The important thing here is to check on nutrition, exercise, and/or sleeping habits. These are important because, as we know, these habits do affect how we act and function psychologically from day to day, impairment or not. There may be special medical needs of the client, or special medical needs of the parents or caregivers involved with the client, that also may participate in the problems the child is enduring.

"Communities are important for children and youth..."

Hobbs adds that the uses and benefits of the community must be experienced to be learned. Again, part of our diagnostic assessment is to identify which parts of the community have been beneficial to the child and which parts have not. We identify areas of strength in the community that may be beneficial for the child, in order to increase caretaker awareness and thus help with the child's developmental growth. Community resources (such as Big Brothers, Big Sisters, YMCA, or a program that we have here called The Young Marines) can serve as differing types of positive influences on these children. Persons within these community resources can also become very positive role models that many of these kids don't have in their lives. Identifying potential role models is an important plus for an intervention plan.

"A child should know some joy each day, and look forward to some joy on the next "

Many times we encounter children and adolescents who have not been able to benefit from much joy in their lives because of dysfunctional elements or patterns within their ecosystem. Many children haven't had the opportunity to be a child and know childhood's joy and fun. So identifying strengths and weaknesses in the "joy each day" area will also help with recommendations for the future, especially those aimed at letting the child be a child.

We feel it is important to attempt to step into the psychological shoes of the child. We attempt to immerse ourselves in understanding each one's entirely unique ecology. We identify areas of strength and weakness in all its realms. By identifying the holes or gaps within the child's situation that contribute to discord, we feel we can help lead to healing. And if you can initiate healing in one area, you can begin healing in other areas as well.

As Carl Rogers told the early Re-ED staff, *Successful living is healing.*

Reference

Hobbs, N. (1982). *The troubled and troubling child.* San Francisco, CA: Jossey-Bass Inc..

Robert Spagnola, MSSA, is a Diagnostic Consultant at Positive Education Program in Cleveland, Ohio.
Spagnola@pepcleve.org

Leslie Wilton, MSW, is a Diagnostic Assessment Consultant for Tapestry, a service operated by Positive Education Program in Cleveland, Ohio.
Lwilton@pepcleve.org

Keith Brown, MA, is currently Assistant Director, Mental Health Services, Eldercare Services Institute for the Benjamin Rose Institute in Cleveland, Ohio.
kbrown@benrose.org

April Shepherd, MS, is Clinical Associate at the Phoenix Point Day Treatment Center operated by Positive Education Program in Cleveland, Ohio.
Ashepherd@pepcleve.org

The Art of Getting into Trouble

Nicholas Hobbs

"Life is always highly problematic and what you become will rest in no small measure on the kinds of problem situations you get yourself into and have to work yourself out of. It is exceedingly difficult for a person to take thought and alter the quality and character and direction of his life. However, he can choose the direction he would like his life to take and then put himself deliberately in situations that will require the evolution of himself toward the kind of person he would like to become.

"It is deep in the nature of man to make problems for himself. Man has often been called the problem-solver, but he is even more the problem-maker. Every noble achievement of man – in government, art, architecture, literature, and above all, in science – represents a new synthesis of the human experience, deepening our understanding and enriching our spirit. But each such noble achievement creates new problems, often of unexpected dimension, and man moves eagerly on to face these new perplexities and to impose his order upon them. And so it will be, world without end.

"To know a person, it is useful to know what he has done, another way of defining what problems he has solved. It is even more informative, however, to know what problems he is working on now. For these will define the growing edge of his being.

"We sometimes think of the well-adjusted person as having very few problems, while, in fact, just the opposite is true. When a person is ill or injured or crushed with grief or deeply frightened, the range of his concerns becomes sharply constricted; his problems diminish in scope and quality and complexity.

"By contrast, the healthy person, the person healthy in body and mind and spirit, is a person faced with many difficulties. He has a lot of problems, many of which he has deliberately chosen with the sure knowledge that in working toward their solution, he will become more the person he would like to be.

"Part of the art of choosing difficulties is to select those that are indeed just manageable. If the difficulties chosen are too easy, life is boring; if they are too hard, life is defeating. The trick is to choose trouble for oneself in the direction of what he would like to become at a level of difficulty close to the edge of his competence. When one achieves this fine tuning of his life, he will know zest and joy and deep fulfillment" (Hobbs, 1971/1974, pp.164-165; see reference on page 140).

Part IV

Developing Competence

Competence building among all the child's ecosystem members, including Re-ED workers and other community agents, is essential to Re-ED philosophy and practice. Competence is neither a fixed state nor a set of skills, but a continually growing repertoire of skills and awareness that allows one to respond to changing situational demands and keep on learning from them. Identification of key competence roadblocks in troubled ecosystems is prerequisite to effective intervention and helping. This view of us all as continual learners (children, families, ourselves, and others) is what makes Re-ED not just a competence model, but a *shared competence model*, toward the goal of successful living.

Learning and Teaching -- Everywhere

Learning and teaching of all kinds is important, and we are all both learners and teachers though it is difficult to be sure we are teaching (and learning) what is most beneficial in the long run. What behavior change strategies are consistent with our values and biases about helping and intervention programming? What skill instruction advances can help us enlarge academic and other repertoires of our students (and others)? Surely it is the size, breadth, and depth of those repertoires that determine how free we are to manage the demands of many settings – how free to choose which environments and demand sets define the way we want to live, the life problems we want to pursue. The challenge to choose what we want to become by placing ourselves in *positions of just manageable difficulty of our own choosing* is the subject of a 1971 commencement address made by Nicholas Hobbs (1974) which is valued by many who have read it. Thanks to Jim Doncaster, we have its full text to provide on the page prior to the beginning of this introduction.

Hobbs recognized the contributions to Re-ED thinking made *"...for concepts and techniques of behavior management to Joseph Wolpe, especially, and also to B. F. Skinner and Sidney Bijou; for the importance of meaning and structure in learning to Sidney Pressey and Jerome Bruner;... for the uses of metaphor and games in learning to Eli Bower;... and for concepts of the malleability of intelligence to Reuven Feuerstein"* (1982, p. xvii).

Hobbs' friend and colleague, Campbell Loughmiller (1979) provided major guidance to the early Re-ED staff on the value and use of the outdoors as a setting for building competence.

"Camp can simplify things, remove kids from school and other settings where defeat and despair have become their constant companions. Camp can give these children new opportunities to learn about themselves and others, about skills they will need to manage in this world. The woods simply provide a congenial setting for adults and young people to work together...." (American Re-Education Association, 1986, p. 37).

In these settings, T-Cs (teacher-counselors) encourage students *"to discover for themselves what learning entails and why learning is so important for them to value as an end in itself. ...[T]he child who refuses to take a poncho along on a hiking expedition is allowed to learn in a sudden downpour that no amount of complaining will stop the rain. Over a camp cookstove, the child who will not participate in the cooks' chores learns how such a non-cooperative attitude can affect his or her peers...the ones shouting for 'Food, now!' or the ones trying to excuse the tardiness of the meal"* (American Re-Education Association, 1986, p.38).

Competence Building

In opening Part IV with chapter 13, Bridget A.Walker and Frank A. Fecser provide an overview of the essential elements of any Re-ED classroom or other program component that make it both therapeutic and competence building for those it serves. It is broadly applicable to the wide range of service settings, and can be used as a base for both program self assessment and initial planning. Of particular importance is the piano analogy the authors provide in the Integrated Programming section, making a strong case against artificial disciplinary divisions.

In the second (chapter 14), Claudia Lann Valore explains the crucial role of instruction and skill building in Re-ED settings, in particular with academic skills for troubled and troubling students. The relationship of emotional, behavioral, and academic difficulties is re-examined, and the therapeutic value of skill building explained.

In chapter 15, Felicia Demchuk and Carole Geraci Sever visit the remaining original Re-ED center (Wright School), look specifically at their academic program, and describe what they find out. The school's staff provide updated information on what has developed and changed since the visit. (Re-ED programs do indeed re-invent themselves as situations indicate need, or new information and resources become available.) The school's behavioral and social-emotional programming is equally impressive, but the visitors were asked to focus on their exceptional academic system.

One of the most easily misinterpreted of the 12 Re-ED Principles deals with the nature of intelligence. It is still difficult for many to believe that Hobbs meant what he said when he wrote: "Intelligence can be taught." In chapter 16, the author explains what she finds in the literature that supports what some see as an extraordinary statement — that children can be taught to be more intelligent!

Chapter 17 presents an empirical study of the competence model that interprets emotional behavior as reflecting a less than optimal relationship between environmental demands and the individual's skills relative to those demands. The model can assist us in identifying ecological goals and in interpreting students' emotional behavior.

The perspective on competence of the parent of a troubled and troubling child can be as basic as one's view of survival. Chapter 18 provides that important perspective from a parent who can look back over years of difficult learning.

References

Hobbs, N. (1971, May). *The art of getting into trouble.* Commencement address to the graduating class of Peabody Demonstration School. Reprinted in Hobbs, N. (1974). A natural history of an idea: Project Re-ED. In J. M. Kaufman, & C. D. Lewis (Eds.), *Teaching children with behavior disorders* (pp. 164-165). Columbus, OH: Charles E. Merrill.

Hobbs, N. (1982). *The troubled and troubling child.* San Franciso: Jossey-Bass.

Loughmiller, C. (1979). *Kids in Trouble: An Adventure in Education.* Tyler, TX: Wildwood Books.

Smith, B. G. (Ed.). (1986). *Ideal Elements of Re-ED.* American Re-Education Association.

13

Elements of an Effective Re-EDucation Program for the 21st Century

Bridget A. Walker & Frank A. Fecser

In the 1993 article, *A Model Re-Ed Classroom for Troubled Students*, Fecser outlined what he described as the "key ingredients" of an effective Re-ED classroom. The article focused on elements central to classroom staff in the 1990's. Because issues such as referrals, regulations, and program development were often handled at the supervisory level, front line staff were able to focus primarily on daily activities and student needs. Today, however, regulatory mandates and new information guiding best practice place additional demands on front line staff. Increasingly, direct service staff are necessarily involved in program planning and development as well as implementation.

The 1996 National Agenda for Children with Behavior Disorders addressed the need for evolution in the field of special education and mental health. It challenged professionals who serve troubled children and their families to assure that they are informed of developments in the field and are implementing best practices (Osher & Hanley, 1996). Nicholas Hobbs (1982), the founder of Project Re-ED, recognized that practice is dynamic; he wrote that Re-ED programs are always in a state of "becoming," constantly re-inventing themselves in response to the needs of the children and families, as well as to progress in the field. As Re-EDucation moves into the 21st century, it is appropriate to examine current research and implications for practice.

Effective Re-ED classrooms integrate diverse strategies and approaches into a comprehensive and dynamic therapeutic learning environment. This chapter identifies four critical areas of best practice in successful classrooms: (1) program foundation and philosophy, (2) structure and predictability, (3) program content and climate, and (4) individual programming. Figure 1 diagrams these elements and their components. It is our hope that by organizing essential elements in this way, we can provide a template to assist in program self-assessment. When considering the extent to which these elements and best practices are present in a setting, it may be helpful to imagine what a program visitor might find if he or she were to walk in tomorrow unannounced.

While the focus of this chapter is on school-based services for students with Emotional or Behavioral Disabilities, these elements are applicable in other settings, such as residential and other therapeutic group care situations. The same components are applicable as well in programs that serve students with disabilities related to the autism spectrum. We recognize that the elements discussed in this chapter would be operationalized quite differently in each of these settings; conceptually, however, they remain a comprehensive outline of how best practices can be integrated to support effective interventions for children and youth with challenging behaviors. We urge providers in these settings to examine how these elements and best practices can be adjusted and implemented to address the unique needs and challenges of their programs.

Element 1: Program Foundation and Philosophy

"Ecology means the study of the complex interaction of energies in natural systems. It seems an apt term to express our concerns for children in settings and for mobilizing the natural resources of a system in the service of a child or an adolescent" (Hobbs, 1982, p. 189).

Values, Beliefs, and Goals

The foundation of any program lies in its orienting philosophy. Re-EDucation believes in the importance of work within the ecology,

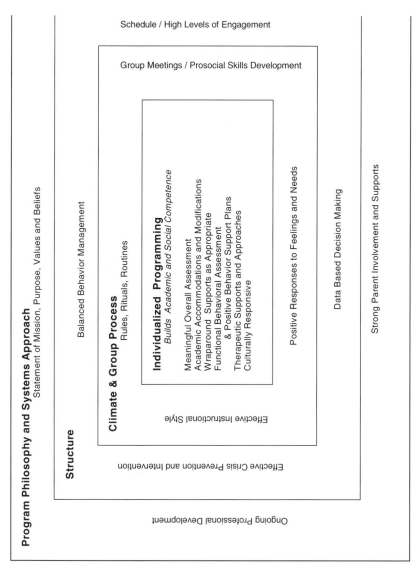

Figure 1. Elements of an Effective Re-EDucation Program for the 21st Century

Program Philosophy and Systems Approach
Statement of Mission, Purpose, Values and Beliefs

Structure   Balanced Behavior Management

Climate & Group Process
Rules, Rituals, Routines

Individualized Programming
Builds Academic and Social Competence

Meaningful Overall Assessment
Academic Accommodations and Modifications
Wraparound Supports as Appropriate
Functional Behavioral Assessment
& Positive Behavior Support Plans
Therapeutic Supports and Approaches
Culturally Responsive

Effective Instructional Style

Effective Crisis Prevention and Intervention

Ongoing Professional Development

Schedule / High Levels of Engagement

Group Meetings / Prosocial Skills Development

Positive Responses to Feelings and Needs

Data Based Decision Making

Strong Parent Involvement and Supports

addressing the dynamic interactions of settings and individuals central to the life of a child. Re-ED focuses on the strengths inherent in each child, employing a variety of perspectives and approaches to problem solving. The starting point for a healthy operating philosophy rests in its statement of mission, values, and purpose. As Fecser summarized in 1993,

"A clearly stated values system is the foundation of any community, be it an entire school or a single classroom. Our values system establishes the ethics of good practice and provides a standard against which our actions and decisions can be measured" (p. 15).

Staff, students, and families involved in a program must have a common understanding of a program's purpose and goals in order to work as a team. Yet this aspect of program development and implementation is often overlooked. Through their work with Project Destiny, Cheney and Barringer (1999) found that when a program's mission statement, vision, and objectives are evident throughout all aspects of the program, actively present in decision-making and program planning, they serve as a solid base on which to build all other aspects of service. When faced with difficult program decisions, the mission statement and operational philosophy serve to guide the problem solving process, helping staff make decisions that are aligned with the program philosophy and long range plans.

Purposes Served

Another critical aspect of a program's operational foundation is a clear delineation of when and how children and families enter a particular program or level of service, as well as when and how they are supported in reintegrating into other settings or services. Clear referral and reintegration processes address such questions as: (a) What are the challenges and needs this program is designed to address? (b) How do we know if we are effectively meeting a child's needs? (c) How do we know when a child is ready for a less intensive or a different type of service or setting? (d) How do we go about helping a child reintegrate into another school and/or community setting? The answers to these questions must be clarified both philosophically and pragmatically, clearly communicated in program descriptions, referral packets, and other literature, as well as apparent in practical daily activities. With these issues understood, staff and families have a clear sense of role, direction, and purpose lending a significant positive momentum to day-to-day experiences.

Child and Family Focus

Meaningful involvement of parents and caregivers in program planning and implementation is fundamental to making a positive impact on the natural ecology of each child. *"In Re-ED,"* Hobbs (1982) said, *" parents are no longer viewed as sources of contagion, but as responsible collaborators in making the system work"* (p.28). Additionally, both the National Agenda and IDEA 97 (USDE, 1997) have placed a heightened emphasis on increasing meaningful parent involvement in program development and implementation. Programs encourage greater involvement by recognizing parents and caregivers as essential partners in supporting and serving each child, rather than as another problem that needs intervention. For example, in many programs parents and caregivers are moving from the role of passive consumer into active roles as advocates or trainers, establishing networks of support for other families facing the challenges of parenting troubled children. This network of support transcends the "formal" setting of the program, reaching families in their homes and communities and resulting in positive changes for the family as well as the individual child (Cheney & Barringer, 1999; Cheney & Osher, 1997). Naomi Karp (1993) of the Federation of Families urges professionals and parents to examine their assumptions and attitudes about one another, and build a set of common values that can lay the groundwork for mutual respect and collaboration as they work together. The Federation of Families for Children's Mental Health (www.ffcmh.org), the Research and Training Center on Family Support and Children's Mental Health at Portland State University (www.rtc.pdx.edu), and the PACER Center (www.pacer.org) provide resources and supports for family members and professionals interested in increasing family involvement in their programs.

Investing in Staff

A successful program reflects the skills of its staff and requires ongoing professional development. Serving troubled children and their families is highly challenging and demanding. As a result, administration must assure that staff are informed of emerging research and effective practice through systematic training. Also required are well thought out and defined job descriptions, access to professional journals and publications, and opportunities to collaborate with other professionals. Additionally, the increasing shortage of well-prepared professionals means that programs need to invest considerable resources in staff development. Abundant, systematic professional development opportunities increase staff retention, job satisfaction, and subsequent program stability (Gersten, Keating, Yovanoff, & Harness, 2001). Unfortunately, the realities of tight budgets and full program schedules often result in sacrificing staff training during difficult times. Lack of training then contributes to a cycle of burnout, decreasing morale, lower effectiveness, and high turnover which leads to increased error and risk. Skilled and motivated staff are a program's most valuable resource, deserving of continued investment.

Element 2: Program Structure

"Learning occurs in the context of well planned, purposeful, and meaningful days" (Cantrell, Cantrell, Valore, Jones, & Fecser, 1999, p.16).

Children with emotional or behavioral problems require a structured and predictable environment. They respond best when expectations are clear and consistent, and changes in routine are kept to a minimum. Interpreting the optimal degree of structure, however, is tricky business. Well-meaning staff may create a rigid structure, overly concerned with external control and reduction of problem behaviors at all costs, thereby losing the natural reinforcement inherent in a dynamic and interactive learning community. In their landmark study, *At the Schoolhouse Door: An Examination of Programs and Policies for Children with Behavioral and Emotional Problems* (1990), Knitzer and Steinberg extensively studied the everyday life of EBD classrooms, visiting 26 programs in 13 states that had been identified as "exemplary," as well as conducting numerous interviews with practitioners and parents. The authors found that few specialized programs were implementing a balanced approach to behavior management embedded within meaningful educational activities. Instead, the authors "repeatedly found pervasive boredom and apathy" (Steinberg and Knitzer, 1992, p.146) in classrooms, leaving children with high levels of wait time and little individualized instruction or group interaction. Behavior management in these programs was characterized by an "over reliance on control" in which the emphasis on order and externalized behaviors took the place of true educational interaction. The authors referred to this phenomenon as the "curriculum of control," and they found that overly controlled settings tended to produce both poor academic and behavioral outcomes.

Ongoing research in the last decade has found that despite the best intentions and efforts of professionals, this same phenomenon is true today and a large discrepancy continues to exist between recommended practices and daily reality in programs designed to meet the needs of students with challenging behaviors (Maag, 2001; Wehby, Symons, & Canale, 1998). Sadly, this situation assures that students with EBD have little chance of addressing the learning and behavioral deficits that triggered their specialized programs in the first place. Responsiveness to emerging student needs and interests is as essential as consistency. Skilled teacher-counselors understand that structure and predictability take different forms as the needs of the child change. Consistent classroom structure can evolve to encourage the emerging social and cognitive development of the child.

Building Positive Structure

Effective behavior management is fundamental to successfully striking this balance. Ideally, adults can consistently enforce rules, develop a clear system of both positive consequences and mild response costs for behavior, use effective limit setting, and, perhaps most importantly, provide much higher rates of positive reinforcement than negative consequences in their interactions with students. Well designed and meaningful point systems, level systems, and token econo-mies can be helpful behavior management tools. Nevertheless, teacher-counselors who readily use social reinforcement such as praise, prox-imity, and attention, rather than relying primarily on external types of reinforcement systems or punishment, tend to have fewer behavior problems and see greater academic and social gains in their students (Maag, 2001; Sutherland, Wehby, & Copeland, 2000). The most effective praise statements are genuine and specific, helping the student understand what aspects of their behavior are on target. This is true even when a student is attempting appropriate behavior; a specific praise statement can help to shape and guide the emergence and generalization of pro-social and academic skills (Rhode, Jenson, & Reavis, 1997; Walker, Colvin, & Ramsey, 1995).

Limit Setting

Strong behavior management also includes the ability to use effective limit setting when necessary, intervening early in emerging problems rather than waiting to react until the problem behavior has intensified and becomes a "crisis" (Nelson & Roberts, 2000; Wehby, Symons, & Canale, 1998). In *The Tough Kid Book*, Rhode, Jenson, and Reavis (1997) describe attributes of effective limit setting: (1) Use statements rather than question format; (2) Be close to the child; (3) Use a quiet, firm voice; (4) Be non-emotional; (5) Look directly at the child; (6) Give him/her time to comply; (7) Do not nag; (8) Describe the request; (9) Make more start "do" requests than stop "don't" requests; and (10) Follow through as necessary with either positive reinforcement for compliance or limits for noncompliance.

Effective limits are logical, in that they have direct relevance to the problem behavior and the situation, are predictable to the student, and are designed to address the intensity of the student's behavior and emotion. For example, a student who is not complying with a direction to complete an assignment might be required to work on that assignment at a different time, completing it before s/he has the opportunity to participate in a desirable activity such as recess or free choice time. Limits outlined for a student in the midst of an emotional outburst are immediate and focus on maintaining safety and helping the child regain self-control. Limits in a classroom are best designed to allow staff access to a range of responses to behaviors, given individual student differences. For example, interventions designed to reduce the frequency and intensity of "shouting out" would look quite different for a student with oppositional-defiant disorder than for one with Tourette's disorder.

Structure must offer staff a range of responses to use with emerging problem behaviors which give students an understanding of expectations and consequences for behaviors. In order to be effective, negative consequences must be appropriate and relevant for the problem behavior, understandable and predictable for the student, and provide an opportunity for the student to learn more appropriate response skills to use next time (Rhode, Jenson, & Reavis, 1997; Walker, Colvin, & Ramsey, 1995).

It is also important that most behavior problems are handled by frontline staff. External administration or agencies (such as police) should become involved only in connection with serious offenses, and then as part of a planned strategy rather than as a reactive response to a significant disruption. This assures that students understand that they remain accountable and connected to their frontline staff, even under the most difficult circumstances.

Planning the Day

Scheduling and pacing activities to promote active student involvement and success throughout the day also helps reduce the opportunity for bored students to get into trouble. Planning for high levels of positive interactions between staff and students, and assuring that even "unstructured" time is well planned and supervised, can do much to keep everyone on track. A daily schedule, followed as consistently as possible, lends a sense of order and stability. The Premack Principle (Premack, 1965), often referred to as "Grandma's rule," can be particularly helpful when planning a daily schedule. The Premack Principle establishes that more difficult or less interesting tasks are positively reinforced when followed by activities of higher interest.

The likelihood of completing a challenging academic task is increased if it is followed by an attractive interactive activity. If the group game is contingent upon the group's completion of the reading assignment, motivation is increased for most students.

Students benefit when actively engaged in learning activities for the greatest possible amount of time; this behavior is commonly measured and referred to as "academic engaged time (AET)." When activities are well planned, engaging, and paced appropriately, students are more likely to meet both behavioral and academic goals and objectives. Tracking the time within an activity that a student is actually working on an assigned task, one clearly geared to his or her skill and ability level, can help teacher-counselors assure that daily activities, lessons, and schedules are designed to maximize student success. In general, 80% of the designated time is considered an acceptable rate of AET (Walker, Colvin, & Ramsey, 1995).

Using Data for Decision Making

To help staff determine if the current structure of the program is indeed generating the desired outcomes for students, effective and systematic data collection techniques are used to monitor daily functioning, drive program planning, and evaluate student progress (Sugai & Lewis, 1999). This means that selected information reflecting each student's daily performance is recorded and reviewed frequently. Student and classroom data often reveal trends and patterns that suggest adjustments in the structure and behavioral supports needed for each student and/or the group as a whole. All too often, data are collected via complicated systems which are seldom used effectively. This perpetuates the tendency for staff and family members to be reactive to a student's behavior rather than proactively responsive. To avoid bogging staff down with paperwork and to assure that data remain meaningful, any data collection system needs to be efficient, easy to maintain, and meaningful to staff, students, and families. In order for the data system to have relevance and meaning for students, they must understand the system and be involved in implementing it, to the extent that such involvement is developmentally appropriate. Finally, parents and caregivers can become more effective members of the child's team if kept informed about their child's academic and behavioral progress through daily notes, home/school passports, report cards, or other means.

In programs designed to serve students with challenging behaviors, level systems are commonly used to track and monitor student performance, as well as to provide structured access to reinforcement and certain activities. In recent years there has been increasing concern about many aspects of level systems, as well as legal challenges regarding their use (Scheuermann & Webber, 1996; Smith & Farrell, 1993). One concern is that level systems frequently emphasize punishment of undesirable behaviors, rather than focus on structures which track and monitor student growth and progress. This occurs when the language and implementation of the system concentrate on reducing problem behaviors (such as aggression or defiance) rather than attending to the presence of desired behaviors (such as time on task or complying with requests). Often level systems "standardize" access to social activities, and even to learning activities. However, a number of legal challenges have determined that this standardization of services and support violates the earlier foundations requiring an individually designed program (Scheuermann & Webber, 1996).

To address these concerns, Scheuermann and Webber recommend that reinforcement systems be administered outside the context of the level system and that the level of reinforcement be adjusted, based on the individual needs of each student. An example of this type of system is a well conceived token or point system which promotes individualized decision making for each student. Such a system is carefully designed and monitored to be sure that it is implemented in a manner that can be continually individualized for each student, and focuses on documenting growth and mastery of new skills. They also suggest that staff interested in using level systems regularly evaluate their system to assure that it is aligned with current research and legal guidelines (1996).

Preventing and Managing Crises

Even in an environment providing high levels of motivation

to manage behavior, students with emotional or behavior problems are still likely to become flooded and lose control of their behavior. Recognizing this, teacher-counselors use effective crisis prevention and early intervention strategies. Program structure includes a clear process for addressing and redirecting the early emergence of problem behavior, as well as for responding to the various levels of escalating behaviors with appropriate, corresponding intervention strategies (Walker, Colvin, & Ramsey, 1995). Staff who are routinely trained in and regularly practice crisis intervention strategies, verbal de-escalation techniques, and therapeutic physical interventions are best prepared to turn a student's "crisis" into an opportunity for teaching and learning. Understanding of the Conflict Cycle (Long, Wood, & Fecser, 2001; Long, 1996, 1986), which illustrates how well-meaning adults can be unintentionally drawn into power struggles with students, is a critical precursor to producing change. Knowledge of the Conflict Cycle can help the teacher-counselor respond more effectively to an escalating student without mirroring the student's behavior.

Skilled staff work continually to maintain a sense of physical and emotional safety for both staff and students. Yet, when working with seriously emotionally disturbed children and youth, the possibility of physical crises is a reality not to be denied. Responsible programs ensure that staff are well trained in a reputable physical crisis intervention approach, such as Crisis Prevention Intervention or Therapeutic Crisis Intervention.

Debriefing Crises

Because crisis situations often provide powerful teaching opportunities for troubled children and youth, teacher-counselors must be prepared to take advantage of these "teachable moments." To do so, staff must know how to use supportive post crisis intervention techniques such as debriefing, problem solving, and reintegration discussions in a manner that maintains student dignity and rebuilds relationships. Strategies such as *Life Space Crisis Intervention* (LSCI) (Long, Wood, & Fecser, 2001) can be particularly effective at such a time. LSCI helps staff understand the hidden or disguised issues driving a child's problem behavior and use that understanding to help the student gain some insight into self-defeating patterns of behavior. To assure that crisis interventions are utilized effectively, safely, and consistently, it is important that staff routinely debrief crisis situations and make any necessary programmatic adjustments based on what they may have learned from the experience. Debriefing with trusted colleagues also helps to relieve the stress that lingers for staff who must regularly respond to crisis situations.

Element 3: Program Climate & Group Process

"The constant challenge in a Re-ED program is to help groups build cultures that sustain children and adolescents in their efforts to manage their lives in ways satisfying to themselves and satisfactory to others (Hobbs, 1982, p. 332)."

Choices made about the inclusion of techniques, strategies, and activities define the day-to-day content of a program. The way in which the critical elements and best practices of a program come together creates a palpable "feeling tone" or climate in the program. This climate reflects how the students and staff interact as a group, as both a learning and therapeutic community. A healthy program climate provides its members a sense of identity, cohesion, and belonging which encourages more appropriate behavior and facilitates success. A program where the overall climate is not well developed often experiences a higher level of disruption, sees less cooperation, and requires more external controls (Valore, 1991).

Group Development

A positive group climate and healthy group process do not emerge spontaneously. They require an understanding of the stages of group development, the nature of group functioning, and a great deal of planning (Valore, 1991, 2002). To accomplish this successfully, staff must employ the dynamics of effective group management as the group progresses through its formative stages. Establishing a group identity (through such activities as selecting a name and mascot), contributing productively to the group, determining group goals, and participating in group strategies for accomplishing those goals, all help bring the group together and establish a sense of belonging, interdependence, and mutual interest. Supported by the skilled facilitation of a teacher-counselor, a group may decide, for example, that they want a new, larger computer monitor for their classroom. They would then plan how they might earn the funds for such a purpose, with each group member playing an important role in moving toward and finally achieving that goal.

Rules, Rituals, and Routines

Positive group process is maintained through the use of meaningful rules, rituals, and routines that are integrated into the schedule and environment in a way that promotes student success, minimizes opportunities for disruptive behavior, and builds group identity and cohesion. Classroom or group rules that are developed with input from every group member have greater meaning and power to influence student behavior. Rules are most effective when they are visibly posted, positively stated, easy to understand, clearly identifying behaviors for success, and consistently enforced (Walker, Colvin, & Ramsey, 1995). A clear indicator of whether the rules have real meaning in a community is to ask a student to explain the rules, expectations, and classroom routines to others. If the student is able to do so in a way that indicates s/he has a basic understanding of the rules, their meaning, and their function for the group, it is a good indicator that s/he is well integrated into the daily experiences of the community.

Meaningful routines are "essentially good habits" (Fecser, 1993) that are established and practiced to facilitate transitions, classroom activities, handling disruptive behaviors, and managing emergencies such as fire and earthquake drills. Consistent signals and cues (such as transition signals like "give me five [seconds]" or "take a quiet minute") are used by staff and students for communication, and promote in students a sense of predictability and order, as well as personal involvement and responsibility.

Another powerful aspect of a positive group process is the use of rituals involving both staff and students. These mark, and make even more significant, many desirable life or learning events (such as acknowledging student progress, birthdays, or a staff member's or student's joining or leaving the group). Rituals help students establish a sense of group membership and acknowledge the many expectations and responsibilities that come with being a part of the community.

Group Meetings

Along with the social learning that emerges naturally from participating in a community, pro-social skill development is enhanced when staff and students participate together in well managed group meetings (such as meetings structured for problem solving, goal setting, group business, or positive feedback). For such meetings to be effective, students are taught the steps and elements of effective group meetings, and participate in facilitating meetings as they are individually ready. When a new student or staff member joins the group, experienced members gain from sharing the steps and expectations for a meeting. These meetings allow students to experience the impact they can have when they contribute as a member of a community. They provide predictable, structured opportunities for students and staff to learn from one another, as well as to use the pro-social skills they are learning in a concrete, meaningful way.

Pro-social Practice

Providing targeted, direct instruction on pro-social skills (such as self management, effective communication, or making and keeping friends) is also necessary. Such learning experiences build on the natural power of peer influence, and are particularly effective when the structure of the program includes opportunities for students to practice new skills in realistic, but supported social situations (Gresham, 1998). Students who are instructed in effective feedback skills and provided with structured opportunities to give and receive feedback, can improve their group and individual social skills. For example, in a daily goal meeting students have the chance to identify and discuss their progress towards a specific goal for their day, while also receiving feedback on their individual successes from other students in the group. Excellent social skills programs are readily available, such as the *Skillstreaming* series (McGinnis & Goldstein, 1984) and *PRE-*

PARE Curriculum (Goldstein,1988), the *Thinking, Feeling, Behaving* series (Vernon, 1989), the *Tough Kid Social Skills Book* (Sheridan, 1995), the *Clear Thinking* curriculum (Nichols, 1999), the *ACCESS curriculum* (Walker, Todis, Holmes & Horton, 1988), as well as others. Each is most effective as an integrated part of a continual teaching milieu where their "lessons" can be recalled in day to day situations.

Along with more structured approaches to teaching social skills, adventure and experience based activities also provide a dynamic and interactive approach to promoting group development and cohesion; they create ample opportunities for students to practice pro-social skills (Forgan & Jones, 2002). This approach to using games and outdoor activities in order to create powerful learning experiences for students has become increasingly popular in the past decade. Several resources have been published which outline games and activities that can be used in a wide variety of situations. These include *Adventures in Peacemaking* (Kreidler & Furlong, 1986), *Silver Bullets: A Guide to Initiative Problems, Adventure Games, and Trust Activities* (Rohnke, 1984), and *Cowtails and Cobras II: A Guide to Initiatives, Ropes Courses, and Adventure Curriculum* (Rohnke, 1989). Re-ED has valued and used outdoor activities since the early 1960's, and staff have welcomed such resources with enthusiasm.

Staff Responsiveness

In addition to more structured forms of positive feedback, a healthy program climate includes positive responses to feelings and needs. While difficult to operationalize, this concept may be one of the most important features in an effective Re-ED program. Because "trust between child and adult is essential, the foundation on which all other principles rest, the glue that holds teaching and learning together" (Hobbs, 1982, p. 245), teacher-counselors must be sensitive to student needs and aware of the importance of their interactions. They must respond to feelings and issues that may underlie an eruption when a child is having difficulty, not just react to the surface behavior itself.

For example, if a student is usually on task during early morning work but arrives one day visibly distracted and noncompliant, a sensitive staff member would talk quietly with the student in an attempt to understand what might be driving the behavior rather than relying on the classroom behavior management system to control the problematic surface behavior. By giving the student the opportunity to find words to express what s/he is feeling, the adult might learn that the student is struggling with issues outside the classroom. The staff member then has a "teachable moment," an opportunity to decode the situation with the student by linking the student's feelings with the problem behaviors. Together they can then generate more appropriate ways to express and own the feelings, manage the behavior, and work toward stabilization of the underlying issue. Such support sends the message that staff are interested in helping students understand their reactions to experiences and find successful ways to express their feelings. These interactions provide a series of real life, in-the-moment lessons in interpersonal skills.

Communication Enhancement

A student's responsiveness within a community increases when taught effective ways to communicate needs, feelings, and issues through learning strategies such as active listening and conflict mediation. As a student learns to use self-control and communication strategies (such as "I Statements"), staff provide cues and reinforcement until they become a more natural part of the student's behavior. To create an overall tone of mutual respect within the group, staff teach students to listen to the perspectives and opinions of others and to acknowledge the contributions of others within the group. These are skills that will serve students well throughout many aspects of their lives; by using them in daily experiences they are more likely to generalize them successfully. To help social skills generalize, teacher-counselors continuously model effective feedback and supportive communication styles with one another and when interacting with students and family members. Children learn what they live.

Effective Instruction

Successful learning is a powerful change agent for troubled children, who often have a history of academic failure. In Re-EDucation programs, a high level of emphasis is placed on success in academic and vocational learning, as well as behavioral and social progress. Elements of effective instruction are used throughout all aspects of the program, rather than simply consolidated into the "official" academic parts of the schedule under the purview of the "certified teacher." In the spirit of the true teacher-counselor, each staff member needs to understand the basic components of effective instruction and use them effectively in a variety of activities from outdoor education experiences or social skill groups to daily math lessons.

Implementing a variety of instructional strategies throughout the day (varying cooperative or experiential learning, direct instruction, group and individualized instruction), creates a rich and rewarding learning climate which is naturally reinforcing for students. To help students experience themselves as competent, successful individuals, teacher-counselors plan carefully. Lessons and activities selected are developmentally and cognitively appropriate, keyed to individual interests to provide intrinsic motivation, and designed so that students experience frequent success (Lann Valore, 2002). This learning often occurs when staff are able to develop creative, alternative activities that involve acquiring and mastering academic skills without focusing solely on traditional paper and pencil tasks. For example, science, math, and interpersonal skills are all needed when a class plans and builds a small greenhouse, then sells the plants they grow in order to buy new equipment for the gym. This approach to instruction allows staff to lead a student who is unfamiliar with academic success, "step by step to a successful encounter with learning" (Hobbs, 1982, p. 255). Success, in turn, contributes positively to program climate because students who are actively involved in learning tend to exhibit far fewer behavior problems.

Integrated Programming

Blending successful academic experiences with meaningful responses to a child's feelings and needs within a single, powerful learning and therapeutic environment makes Re-EDucation programs dynamic and effective. This blending of academic and therapeutic modalities is analogous to a pianist playing a lovely piece of music. The movement of each hand across the keyboard is critical to the expression of the piece. At times the notes and chords of one hand may sound with more emphasis. Moments later those played by the other hand may do so, but it is this ongoing interplay of notes, sounds, and cadence played by each that comes together to express the melody beautifully. To the listener, the different movements of each hand are unimportant, because they blend together to create a powerful musical experience. So also a seamless blend of meaningful learning and therapeutic experiences in a Re-ED classroom creates a powerful climate supporting change and growth for children and families.

As important as this integration of approaches is, this blending also creates some of the most significant systematic challenges for Re-ED programs. Because of funding and regulatory issues for educational and mental health services, many barriers to truly blending these services exist. Returning to the analogy of the pianist, many state and federal funding systems are structured so that the pianist is required to play with each hand on a separate piano, and never to play with both hands at the same time, even though both systems want to hear the same piece of music performed. As a result, those involved in effective Re-ED programs must constantly work to educate and inform regional, state, and federal agencies on the critical importance and the effectiveness of integrating learning and therapeutic approaches to meet the needs of troubled children and their families.

Element 4: Individualized Programming

"Important helper strength in the education and treatment process lies in decoding, reframing, and pulling out the dormant potential, searching for strengths where some might see only weaknesses" (Cantrell, Cantrell, Valore, Jones, & Fecser, 1999, p.20).

Educational and Behavioral Assessment

While the first three components of best practice address the ecological context within which the child is served, the core of every program lies in meeting the individualized needs of each child. Some troubled children are struggling with significant learning deficits and/or disabilities while others are highly capable academically but deeply challenged emotionally and/or behaviorally. The first step in individualizing a program involves a thorough assessment of strengths and needs. This includes identifying a student's unique learning styles, along with social/emotional and developmental needs, so that a successful program can be created. A thorough assessment enables the teacher-counselor to craft an effective academic and behavioral program that includes accommodations or modifications which might support both the academic and social success of the child. Individualized curricular modifications which address learning needs, styles, and preferences reduce incidents of problem behaviors and increase the student's engagement in learning (Kern, Bambara, & Fogt, 2002; Kern, Delaney, Clarke, Dunlap, & Shields, 2001).

Ecological Assessment and Programming

An ecological assessment, including the roles and involvement of family members, other care providers, and relevant community connections should be included. In many areas today ecological planning is referred to as a "wraparound model." Most commonly the wraparound process is used to support the child whose needs are so significant that they are impeding multiple life domains and/or requiring the involvement of multiple agencies (Eber & Nelson, 1997; Eber, Nelson, & Miles, 1997). In order for teacher-counselors to contribute to ecological planning, they must be familiar with ecological goals and intervention options. They may have or develop contacts at other agencies who can provide needed types of support for the student and/or family, such as public health, child care, or employment services.

Staff successful in implementing ecological or wraparound strategies understand how to advocate for a child's or family's needs within the larger social service network, and they have a schedule that allows them to make contact or attend necessary meetings. This can be particularly difficult for staff who are also primarily responsible for the daily operations within the classroom, making phone calls or meetings during the school day a challenge. Many Re-ED programs address ecological needs through the role of the Liaison Teacher-Counselor or other community-based professional whose primary responsibility is providing support to the home and involved community members. Other programs allow flexible scheduling and extra duty pay to compensate staff for attending extra evening meetings. However this need is met, effecting positive change throughout the ecology of the child must extend beyond the traditional program boundaries and the hours of the school day.

Functional Behavioral Assessment and Positive Behavior Support Planning

Another important assessment component that has been thrust into the spotlight in recent years, since being included in the 1997 re-authorization of the Individuals with Disabilities Education Act (IDEA), is Functional Behavioral Assessment (FBA). A meaningful FBA assists staff in understanding the context of a child's behaviors through analysis of the sequence the problem behavior typically takes, which is known as the behavior pathway. The behavior pathway identifies events that: (1) make the behavior more likely to occur (setting events), (2) typically trigger the problem behavior (antecedents), (3) clearly define the behavior of concern (problem behavior), and (4) occur directly after the behavior, making it likely to continue (reinforcement). Additionally, the behavior pathway asks professionals to define an acceptable alternative behavior that the student could learn which will provide the student with the same reinforcement as the problem behavior. This aspect of the pathway is critical to motivating the student throughout the process of learning new behaviors. Finally, the pathway asks the team to define the desired behaviors which may then be supported throughout the ecology by other types or levels of reinforcement in the long run.

The information gained in completing behavior pathways helps the IEP team build an individualized Positive Behavior Support Plan (PBS). This PBS plan emphasizes strategies to support the child in achieving academic and social success by directly addressing skill deficits and other needs that interfere with appropriate behavior (Sugai & Lewis, 1999; O'Neil, Horner, Albin, Sprague, Storey, & Newton, 1997). The PBS plan includes strategies that address each component of the behavior pathway, thus providing staff with a range of responses to the entire context of the child's behavior.

Once the initial FBA and PBS are completed, both are monitored and updated regularly throughout the child's involvement in the program. In most cases it becomes part of the child's Individual Education Plan or IEP. In the past few years, professionals and families have become increasingly aware of the need to utilize the FBA/PBS process when building a student's individualized program, although there are many questions about how it should be implemented and supported. A number of agencies can provide resources and strategies to assist professionals and family members in better understanding and implementing the FBA and PBS process. These include the Center for Positive Behavior Interventions and Supports at the University of Oregon (www.pbis.org), the Center for Effective Collaboration and Practice (www.cecp.org), the BEACONS Project at the University of Washington (http://depts.washington.edu/beacons), and the Kentucky Behavior Homepage (www.state.ky.us/agencies/behave/bi/fba.html).

Social / Emotional Development

To address emotional and/or mental health issues the child is experiencing, the therapeutic aspect of a child's program is individualized as well. In Re-EDucation programs these interventions are not limited to ongoing psychotherapy, but instead focus on techniques and modalities that strengthen the child's social and cognitive development, including teaching problem solving, increasing self and social awareness, and enhancing self-control. The goal of these strategies is to help children come to understand how their thoughts, feelings, and perceptions may be contributing to problem behaviors (Jones, 1987).

Just as effective instructional techniques are used in all classroom activities, therapeutic intervention is infused in all daily activities, including academics. Play, art, drama, and music activities provide opportunities for therapeutic expression and growth (Hileman, 1996). Cognitive behavior modification strategies can become integrated into a child's daily program in both group and individual experiences (Maag, 2003). For example, exploring and expressing feelings can be incorporated into a language arts unit on poetry in which students are introduced to a variety of feeling words and expressive poetry, then supported in writing and publishing their own poetry that explores their favorite feeling words. Or a student struggling with maintaining attention in groups may benefit from a series of music therapy sessions in which the student learns how to listen for and maintain a steady drum beat and rhythm. In this manner, academic, therapeutic, and behavioral goals can be met within a single engaging learning experience. The goal of this type of therapeutic support is not for the child to gain deep personal insight into the origin of their difficulties, but rather to enhance the child's ability to successfully participate in their own childhood experiences. *"The students learn that they can think about their behavior, about their relationships with other people, about their future. They learn that they do not need to be the victims of impulse or the persuasion of others — in sum that they can take thought and control their behavior here and now"* (Hobbs, 1982, p. 266).

Cultural Responsiveness

Finally, in order to truly individualize a child's program, it is important that all aspects of the child's program be culturally responsive. Staff members, volunteers, and family members need to have ongoing learning experiences in multicultural issues and awareness, access to information and materials related to a variety of cultural perspectives, and access to curriculum resources reflecting diverse cultures and perspectives. This responsiveness should not be limited to ethnic diversity, but should include awareness of the effect of socioeconomic status on experiences and perspectives as well (Payne, 2001). A climate of mutual respect must be developed within the program that supports a meaningful, ongoing dialogue between program staff, students, family, and community members regarding diversity issues and needs. In this way, existing or emerging problems can be identified and addressed before they interfere with the success of a child's program, and issues such as the disproportionate representation of children of color in special education can be addressed (Garcia & Malkin, 1993; Townsend, 2000).

In Conclusion

"The many competencies acquired in the Re-ED experience may permit a child or adolescent to accurately say, 'I am a competent person'" (Hobbs, 1982, p.257).

Clearly, the challenge of meeting the needs of our troubled and troubling children is not an easy one. Thankfully, our profession continues to benefit from the research, advocacy, and the practical experience of committed professionals, community, and family members throughout the world. Because of their efforts, we continue to come to a better understanding of what strategies and approaches can make a difference in the lives of children in need. The ongoing challenge lies in assuring that the necessary training and resources are available to those who have dedicated their lives to supporting troubled children and the families that love them.

Through the balanced implementation of the elements outlined here, a dynamic and effective program can be developed that meets the needs of troubled children and their families, while creating a reasonable working environment for staff members and volunteers. By regularly reviewing a program's progress in all four critical areas, administrators and staff can assure that they are creating a strong and viable program that has the potential to make a significant impact in the lives of the troubled children and youth that they serve for years to come.

References

Cantrell, M. L., Cantrell, R. P., Valore, T. G., Jones, J. M., Fecser, F. A. (1999). A revisitation of the ecological perspectives on emotional/behavioral disorders. In L. M. Bullock & R. A. Gable (Eds.). *The third mini-library series: What works for children and youth with E/BD: Linking yesterday and today with tomorrow.* Reston, VA: The Council for Children with Behavior Disorders.

Cheney, D., & Barringer, C. (1999). A transdisciplinary model for students' social and emotional development: Creating a context for inclusion. In J. Scotti & L. Meyer (Eds.) *Behavior intervention: Principles, models, & practice.* (pp. 3-26). Towson, MD: Paul Brookes.

Cheney, D., & Osher, T. (1997). Collaborating with families. *Journal of Emotional and Behavioral Disorders, 5*, 36–44.

Eber, L., & Nelson, C. M. (1997). School-based wraparound planning: Integrating services for students with emotional and behavioral needs. *American Journal of Ortho-Psychiatry, 67*, 385-395.

Eber, L., Nelson, C. M., & Miles, P. (1997). School-based wraparound for students with emotional and behavioral challenges. *Exceptional Children, 63*, 539–555.

Fecser, F. A. (1993). A model Re-ED classroom for troubled students. *Journal of Emotional and Behavior Problems, 1*, 15–20.

Forgan, J. W., & Jones, C. D. (2002). How experiential adventure activities can improve students' social skills. *Teaching Exceptional Children, 34*, 52 - 58.

Garcia, S. B., & Malkin, D. H. (1993). Toward defining programs and services for culturally and linguistically diverse learners in special education. *Teaching Exceptional Children, 26*, 52-58.

Goldstein, A. P. (1988). *The Prepare Curriculum: Teaching pro-social competencies.* Champaign, IL: Research Press.

Gresham, F. M. (1998). Social skills training: Should we raze, remodel, or rebuild. *Behavioral Disorders, 24*, 19-25.

Gersten, R., Keating, T., Yovanoff, P., & Harness, M. K. (2001). Working in special education: Factors that enhance special educators' intent to stay. *Exceptional Children, 67*, 549–567.

Hileman, L. R. (1996). Exploring drama with emotionally disturbed adolescents. In N. J. Long & W. C. Morse (Eds.) *Conflict in the classroom* (pp. 526-532). Austin, TX: Pro-Ed.

Hobbs, N. (1994). *The troubled and troubling child.* Cleveland, OH: American Re-Education Association.

Jones, V. F. (1987). Major components in a comprehensive program for seriously emotionally disturbed children and youth. In R. Rutherford, Jr., C. Nelson, & S. Forness (Eds.). *Severe behavior disorders of children and youth* (Vol. 9, pp. 94-121). Austin, TX: Pro-Ed.

Karp, N. (1993). Collaboration with families: From myth to reality. *Journal of Emotional and Behavioral Disorders, 1*, 21-23.

Kern, L., Bambara, L., & Fogt, J. (2002). Class-wide curricular modifications to improve the behavior of students with emotional or behavioral disorders. *Behavioral Disorders, 27*, 317-326.

Kern, L., Delaney, B., Clarke, S., Dunlap, G., & Shields, K. (2001). Improving classroom behavior of students with emotional and behavioral disorders using individualized curricular modifications. *Journal of Emotional and Behavioral Disorders, 9*, 239–247.

Knitzer, J., & Steinberg, Z. (1990). *At the schoolhouse door*. New York: Bank Street College of Education.

Kreidler, W. J., & Furlong, L. (1986). *Adventures in peacemaking: A conflict resolution activity guide for school age programs*. Hamilton, MA: Project Adventure, Inc.

Lann Valore, C. (2002). Spitting from windmills: The therapeutic value of effective instruction. *Reclaiming Children and Youth, 11*, 85-89.

Long, N. J. (1986). Stages of helping emotionally disturbed students through the reeducation process. *The Pointer, 30*, 5-20.

Long, N. J. (1996). The conflict cycle paradigm: How troubled students get teachers out of control. In N. J. Long & W. C. Morse (Eds.) *Conflict in the classroom* (pp. 526-532). Austin, TX: Pro-Ed.

Long, N. J., Wood, M., & Fecser, F. A. (2001). *Life space crisis intervention: Talking to children and youth in crisis*. Austin, TX: Pro-Ed.

Maag, J. W. (2003). *Behavior management: From theoretical implications to practical applications*. San Diego, CA: Singular Publishing.

Maag, J. W. (2001). Rewarded by punishment: Reflections on the disuse of positive reinforcement in schools. *Exceptional Children, 67*, 173-186.

McGinnis, E., & Goldstein, A. P. (1984). *Skillstreaming the elementary school child: A guide for teaching social skills*. Champaign, IL: Research Press.

Nelson, R., & Roberts, M. (2000). Ongoing reciprocal teacher-student interactions involving disruptive behaviors in general education classrooms. *Journal of Emotional and Behavioral Disorders, 8*, 27–37.

Nichols, P. (1999). *Clear thinking: A psychoeducational program for preteens, teens, and young adults.* Iowa City, IA: Riverlights.

O'Neill, R. E., Horner, R. H., Albin, R. W., Sprague, J. R., Storey, K., & Newton, J. S. (1997). *Functional assessment and program development for problem behavior: A practical handbook.* Pacific Grove, CA: Brooks Cole Publishing.

Osher, D., & Hanley, T. V. (1996). Implications of the national agenda to improve results for children and youth with or at risk of serious emotional disturbance. In R. J. Illback & C. Michael Nelson (Eds.). *Emerging school-based approaches for children with emotional or behavioral problems* (pp. 7-36). Binghamton, NY: Haworth Press.

Payne, R. (2001). *A framework for understanding poverty.* Highlands TX: Aha! Process.

Premack, D. (1965). Reinforcement theory. In D. Levine (Ed.), *Nebraska symposium on motivation* (pp. 123-188). Lincoln: University of Nebraska Press.

Rhode, G., Jenson, W., & Reavis, K. (1997). *The tough kid book: Practical classroom management strategies.* Longmont, CO: Sopris West.

Rohnke, K. (1984). *Silver bullets: A guide to initiative problems, adventure games, and trust activities.* Dubuque, IA: Kendal/Hunt Publishing Company.

Rohnke, K. (1989). *Cowtails and cobras II: A guide to initiatives, ropes courses, and adventure curriculum.* Dubuque, IA: Kendal/Hunt Publishing Company.

Scheuermann, B., & Webber, J. (1996). Best practices in developing level systems. In L. M. Bullock & R. A. Gable (Eds.) *Best practices for managing adolescents with emotional/ behavioral disorders within the school environment.* (pp.

21-30). Council for Children with Behavioral Disorders Mini-Library Series on Emotional/Behavioral Disorders. Reston VA: Council for Exceptional Children.

Sheridan, S. M. (1995). *The tough kid social skills book.* Longmont, CO: Sopris West.

Smith, S. W., & Farrell, D. T. (1993). Level system use in special education: Classroom intervention with prima facie appeal. *Behavioral Disorders, 18,* 251-264.

Steinberg, Z., & Knitzer, J. (1992). Classrooms for emotionally and behaviorally disturbed students: Facing the challenge. *Behavioral Disorders, 17,* 145-156.

Sugai, G., & Lewis, T. J. (1999). What works for children and youth with E/BD: Linking yesterday to tomorrow. In L. M. Bullock & R. A. Gable (Eds.), *The third mini-library series: What works for children and youth with E/BD: Linking yesterday and today with tomorrow.* Reston, VA: The Council for Children with Behavior Disorders.

Sutherland, K., Wehby, J., & Copeland, S. (2000). Effects of varying rates of behavior specific praise on the on task behavior of students with EBD. *Journal of Emotional and Behavior Disorders, 8.* 2-8.

Townsend, B. L. (2000). The disproportionate discipline of African American learners: Reducing school suspensions and expulsions. *Exceptional Children, 66,* 381-391.

U.S. Department of Education, Office of Special Education Programs. (1997). *Eighteenth annual report to Congress on the implementation of the Individuals with Disabilities Education Act.* Washington, DC: Author.

Valore, T. G. (1991). *The Group Meeting Cohesion Profile: A reliability and validity study.* Unpublished doctoral dissertation, Kent State University, Kent, Ohio.

Valore, T. G. (2002). Sharing adventure: The group is important. *Reclaiming Children and Youth, 11,* 90-94.

Vernon, A. (1989). *Thinking, feeling, and behaving: An emotional education curriculum for children.* Champaign, IL: Research Press.

Walker, H. M., Colvin, G., & Ramsey, E. (1995). *Antisocial behavior in school: Strategies and best practices.* Pacific Grove, CA: Brooks Cole Publishing.

Walker, H. M., Todis, B. J., Holmes, D., & Horton, G. (1988). *The Walker social skills curriculum: The ACCESS adolescent curriculum for communication and effective social skills.* Austin, TX: Pro-Ed.

Wehby, J. H., Symons, F. J., & Canale, J. A. (1998). Teaching practices in classrooms for students with emotional and behavioral disorders: Discrepancies between recommendations and observations. *Behavioral Disorders, 24,* 51–56.

Bridget Walker, PhD, is on the faculty of the College of Education, Seattle University   walkerb@u.seattleu.edu

Frank Fecser, PhD, is Chief Executive Officer of the Positive Education Program in Cleveland, OH. fecser@pepcleve.org

14

Spitting from Windmills: The Therapeutic Value of Effective Instruction

Claudia Lann Valore

"To do well in spelling or arithmetic, especially for students who expect and dread failure, is to know a sharp delight. It is like spitting from the top of a windmill"
(Nicholas Hobbs, 1982, p.287).

The schedule indicates an academic period — it's right there on the wall, prominently displayed with cute color-coded clocks showing the start and stop times for MATH. The noise level in the room is only a few decibels below that of the previous FREE TIME period. A few students are industriously working on a black-line worksheet. The teacher's aide hovers. Waiting for their time with the teacher, two students are giggling, kicking each other under the table they share in a dance that, if not interrupted, will soon erupt into a pushing match or full-blown fight. One student sits off by himself in a corner, surrounded by a sea of crumpled papers, strewn books, food wrappers, and a coat that he uses as a pillow with the hood pulled over his head. Three others sit at their desks, workbooks out, pencils in hand, eyes everywhere but on their work. Occasional insults, looks, giggles, or small items are tossed back and forth among them. One student is wandering the room muttering about a lost book and stupid math. The teacher is crouched at William's desk, showing him yet again how to compute a problem. Not completely tuned out to the class, she looks up, scanning the room. She says, "John, sit down."

To the two at the table, she says, "Hands and feet to self, please!" Regarding the sleeper, she fleetingly decides to leave him alone. She goes back to William and his worksheet.

The Dilemma

Is the previous picture an exaggeration? An anomaly? Sadly not. According to Walker, Forness, Kauffman, Epstein, Gresham, Nelson, and Strain (1998), *"Substantial numbers of educators seem to ignore the concept of best practices and rely upon a hodgepodge of activities, unplanned curricula, and conceptually incompatible interventions to accomplish teaching, learning, and management goals"* (p. 8). Though there are pockets of excellence and many effective classrooms with highly skilled and dedicated teachers and supportive staff, far too many classrooms for students with behavior disorders or emotional disturbance (B/ED) look like the opening scenario. Some are in regular school buildings. Others can be found in a variety of alternative settings from special schools and treatment centers to locked facilities. It is no wonder teachers burn out and leave the field, transfer to regular education, or worse, become numb to chaos and return every morning to just make it through another day. It is no wonder that far too many students fail to learn, fall further behind, and often eventually drop out. Only one-third of them complete school (Gunter & Denny, 1998). It is no wonder that principals and others responsible for student success feel ineffective, frustrated, annoyed, and even embarrassed. Parents are blissfully ignorant, or detached and unconcerned, or worried but helpless or hopeless, or battling the staff and system for something better on behalf of their child. Scenarios like these are lose-lose situations. No one is happy, feeling competent or satisfied with the outcomes. Everyone wants change, but the question of "Where to start?" seems impossible to answer.

A Solution

Many, if not most, troubled and troubling children are underachieving, experiencing learning difficulties or disabilities, or at best making painfully slow progress in a curriculum several grade levels below their peers. In 1966, Nicholas Hobbs wrote, *"Underachievement in school is the single most common characteristic of emotionally disturbed children"* (p. 1110). In more recent years, the connection between low achievement and serious behavior problems has been well documented (Epstein, Kinder, & Bursuck, 1989; Kauffman, 1997; Walker, Colvin, & Ramsey, 1995).

When charged with educating these students who also present challenging and sometimes overwhelming behavior and/or emotional problems, a teacher and other school professionals often do not know which to tackle — behavior or academics. Popular practice seems to support the idea that classroom behavior must be "brought under control" before academic instruction can occur. Re-ED programs have long held the belief that both behavior and academic learning require direct, effective, and rigorous attention simultaneously. Add to this list group process strategies and techniques and you have the three major elements of an effective and therapeutic Re-ED classroom.

In 1982, Hobbs wrote in *The Troubled and Troubling Child*:

> *"Research evidence today underscores the importance of academic competence in a child's achievement of personal integration and social effectiveness, and it contradicts the long-held assumption that the seriously disturbed child must be treated for his illness before he can become an effective learner. All our experience suggests that the causal direction of the relationship between emotional disturbance and learning competence may be, for many children, the reverse of that traditionally posited. The most probable relationship is interactional, so that early and continuing address to both adjustment and learning problems is indicated"* (p. 23).

More recently, the nature of the relationship between achievement and behavior problems has been declared as clearly reciprocal (Kauffman, 1997; Scott, Nelson, & Liaupsin, 2001; Walker et al., 1995). Other recent work in the area of functional behavioral assessments supports this reciprocal or interactional relationship by showing clear patterns of inappropriate behavior that maintain academic and social failure (Dunlap, Kern-Dunlap, Clarke, & Robbins, 1991; Lewis, Sugai, & Colvin, 1998; Skiba & Peterson, 2000). It would seem that the research and current body of literature concurs with what Re-ED has long held to be true.

Competence as a Therapeutic Goal

Re-ED's third principle states, *"Competence makes a difference; ... children and adolescents should be helped to be good at something, [and] especially at schoolwork"* (Hobbs, 1982, p. 251). In 1966, Hobbs shared an early version of the Principles of Re-ED in a presentation to the 74th Annual Convention of the American Psychological Association. Of this principle, he said,

> *"It means first and foremost the gaining of competence in school skills, in reading and arithmetic....If a child feels that he is inadequate in school, inadequacy can become a pervasive theme in his life....We regard it as sound strategy to attack directly the problem of adequacy in school"* (p. 1110).

Dr. Hobbs is often also quoted by those in Re-ED as having said, *"Schoolwork is the business of children."* Thus, teacher-counselors have always held the status of being the most critical professional in Re-ED programs, as they are the ones working day-in and day-out with the children, who must carry out the program minute by minute, using every opportunity to engage the children in successful, purposeful endeavor. This is no easy task; Hobbs went on in his address to say,

> *"It requires utmost skill and finesse on the part of the teacher-counselor to help a disturbed child move into an area where he has so often known defeat, where failure is a well rooted expectancy, where a printed page can evoke flight or protest or crippling anxiety. The teacher-counselor need make no apologies to the psychotherapist with reference to the level of skill required to help a disturbed child learn"* (p. 1110-1111).

From Failure to Success

By the time children or adolescents reach Re-ED programs they have often experienced a lifetime of failures across a variety of settings. But school is often the place where their behavioral and/or emotional problems first become manifest and their downward spiral of failure takes on momentum (Hobbs, 1982). At school, children and adolescents are faced with expectations they are unable to meet. Discrepancies between their skills and the demands made on them result in inappropriate behavior (Cantrell, 1974; Cantrell & Cantrell, 1995). They cannot sit still, or their poor reading becomes painfully public, or they cannot keep pace with their peers on even simple tasks because they are so disorganized. These failures bring on disapproval and criticism from within and without. Highly stressed, the children feel incompetent, stupid, angry, or depressed. Teachers, parents, and peers censure and punish. Such negative interactions often lead to more frequent or intense maladaptive responses. Discipline problems may escalate or students may withdraw into themselves, both reactions often driven by the function of avoidance. Disruptive, challenging, or depressed behavior often invites rejection. All of this creates or affirms in the student a self-concept of incompetence and inadequacy, and a pattern of living in which failure breeds failure.

Re-ED programs strive to reverse this downward, destructive spiral by teaching children new ways of living, by operationalizing in our work the belief that successful living is healing. A promising place to start this healing process is with academics. There is an arsenal of knowledge regarding effective instructional practices that can be used to almost guarantee task success and thus, academic learning. Though too little attention is paid to academics in the B/ED literature (Gunter & Denny, 1998; Ruhl & Berlinghoff, 1992), there still exists more than enough information and knowledge regarding effective instruction. We know how to plan, manage, implement, and evaluate instructional programs effectively (Ysseldyke & Christenson, 1993), if only we use this skill. We know how to analyze and sequence tasks and how to provide skill instruction so that children are able to meet expectations (Cantrell, 1971). Further, a body of literature is emerging regarding specific, promising instructional strategies and practices to use with children who have emotional and/or behavioral disorders (Cegelka, Fitch, &

Shaughnessy, 2001; Shaughnessy, 2001). We can combine diagnostic-prescriptive or precision teaching with sound design and effective instruction to plan well, teach well, arrange the environment, and set expectations that put children in situations that are *"just manageably difficult"* (Hobbs, 1965).

By using this Just Manageable Difficulty (JMD) principle familiar to Re-ED, and asking children to engage in learning at a pin-pointed level of appropriate challenge, the learner not only "gets it right," but also experiences a true sense of success, accomplishment, and growth. Every successful incident can be used to create new feelings of capability and to provide multiple opportunities to receive praise, recognition, and approval. Motivation is positively channeled, and when enough of these experiences have occurred, they eventually serve to reduce fear, anxiety, and hostility. No longer do children and adolescents seek to avoid school or find schoolwork inherently aversive. Willingness to risk emerges as trust is established between student and teacher-counselor, allowing the student to fully participate, engage, and learn. As skills, knowledge, and successful learning experiences accumulate, the child's concept of self changes from "failure" to "competent individual." Success breeds success!

Effective, Therapeutic Instruction

It is beyond the scope of this chapter (and the expertise of this author) to explore in detail and definitively answer the complex question: What is effective instruction for students with B/ED, and how is it done? As stated earlier, our field's literature is woefully inadequate with regard to academics. But all is not lost! Experience is a great teacher; Re-EDers have been teaching troubled and troubling children and adolescents successfully for many years. That, combined with looking to the broader literature from special and regular education on teaching and learning, creates a powerful knowledge base from which to work. When looking at the question from that angle, the problem becomes a paradox. On the one hand, we don't have the answer. On the other, we have so much information available to us from which to draw that we are overwhelmed by choice!

One thing we know for sure. Teaching, or providing effective, therapeutic instruction, is both a science and an art. It draws upon and affects the heart as much as the head of both teacher and learner. While true for all, this is magnified when working with troubled and troubling kids. The science of teaching and learning is critically important, but the art of the teacher-counselor is typically what sets them apart. Hobbs spoke of *"the skillful hand and responsive heart"* of teacher-counselors (1982, p. 253). They are skilled indeed. These skills are enhanced with dogged determination to never give up, to be patient and kind, empathic and supportive, but to artfully set high expectations and to convey their contagious belief that every student will learn and be successful through the development of their competence.

Heart and art won't do it alone. Warmth, joy, care, trust, and nurturing a climate of high expectations for learning must be accompanied with instructional skill. Good teaching requires a firm grasp of theoretical knowledge regarding principles of learning and instruction. It also requires an arsenal of pedagogic methods, strategies, and tactics and their sophisticated, deliberately planned use.

Underlying all these skills and applications is the need to also understand the nature and needs of children and adolescents with severe behavior and emotional problems. Some are pretty safe bets – providing order, predictability, and consistency in the classroom through the use of rules, rituals, routines, and schedules have become second nature to most teachers. All children benefit from these types of positive behavioral supports, but children and adolescents with E/BD typically need them to thrive in the classroom. Other needs include highly individualized presenting problems that require modifications, accommodations, and interventions designed for specific children. Teacher-counselors adapt and adjust all they do for individual students and presenting situations. If *"teaching children to read is rocket science"* (National Reading Panel video, 2000), then teaching troubled and troubling children and adolescents is quantum physics! Needless to say, it is hard, hard work that takes heart, extraordinary knowledge and skill, a good dose of creativity and invention, relentless effort, resilience, and an ability to find joy and encouragement in every success, no matter how small. It is no wonder that in Re-ED, teacher-counselors are so valued.

When overwhelmed by information, an excellent strategy is to find or create an organizational construct which is as simple as possible. The Mastery Teaching model is one that has done just that. Madeline Hunter equated teaching with decision-making, based on the combined knowledge of research-based principles of learning and a keen sensitivity to the individuality of students (1982). These decisions, in their simplest form, address three questions: What to teach? How to teach? What will students do?

Combine Hunter's ideas with those of Ysseldyke and Christenson (1993), and what emerges is an ever-repeating cycle of instruction. It can be viewed as a four-step planning and implementation process: what to teach (assessment and content), how to teach (methods & strategies), teaching (implementation), and monitoring progress (evaluation). Within each step is a multitude of considerations, choices to be made, and professional knowledge to employ. In Figure 1, this "simple" four-step cycle is used to organize and categorize a long, yet no doubt incomplete, list of strategies, sources of information, and various ideas for consideration in making decisions about the teaching and learning process.

In Figure 2, an even broader view of the process is presented. This model of effective instruction is one that combines models from both regular and special education to present a conceptual approach that attempts to synthesize the two. Either one alone seems inadequate. The regular education models fail to recognize the challenges teachers face when working with young people who are far behind, reluctant to engage, or challenged by severe learning disabilities. Special education practices of focusing solely on the child's profile and engaging in individualized, diagnostic-prescriptive instruction has resulted in curricula that are unable to keep pace with what schools expect children to learn. Legislation such as the "No Child Left Behind Act" (2002) has exacerbated the problem and raised the stakes for all. Recently

Figure 1
Whoever Said Teaching Was <u>Easy</u>?!
(when there's so much to consider)   **123**

GO!

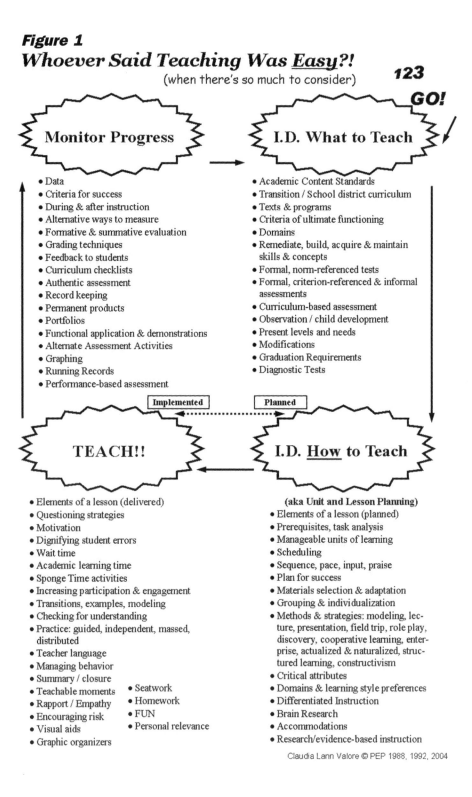

Monitor Progress

- Data
- Criteria for success
- During & after instruction
- Alternative ways to measure
- Formative & summative evaluation
- Grading techniques
- Feedback to students
- Curriculum checklists
- Authentic assessment
- Record keeping
- Permanent products
- Portfolios
- Functional application & demonstrations
- Alternate Assessment Activities
- Graphing
- Running Records
- Performance-based assessment

I.D. What to Teach

- Academic Content Standards
- Transition / School district curriculum
- Texts & programs
- Criteria of ultimate functioning
- Domains
- Remediate, build, acquire & maintain skills & concepts
- Formal, norm-referenced tests
- Formal, criterion-referenced & informal assessments
- Curriculum-based assessment
- Observation / child development
- Present levels and needs
- Modifications
- Graduation Requirements
- Diagnostic Tests

Implemented ← → **Planned**

TEACH!!

- Elements of a lesson (delivered)
- Questioning strategies
- Motivation
- Dignifying student errors
- Wait time
- Academic learning time
- Sponge Time activities
- Increasing participation & engagement
- Transitions, examples, modeling
- Checking for understanding
- Practice: guided, independent, massed, distributed
- Teacher language
- Managing behavior
- Summary / closure
- Teachable moments
- Rapport / Empathy
- Encouraging risk
- Visual aids
- Graphic organizers

- Seatwork
- Homework
- FUN
- Personal relevance

I.D. How to Teach

(aka Unit and Lesson Planning)
- Elements of a lesson (planned)
- Prerequisites, task analysis
- Manageable units of learning
- Scheduling
- Sequence, pace, input, praise
- Plan for success
- Materials selection & adaptation
- Grouping & individualization
- Methods & strategies: modeling, lecture, presentation, field trip, role play, discovery, cooperative learning, enterprise, actualized & naturalized, structured learning, constructivism
- Critical attributes
- Domains & learning style preferences
- Differentiated Instruction
- Brain Research
- Accommodations
- Research/evidence-based instruction

adapted to incorporate the latest movement toward standards-based education, we offer this as another "simple" organizational construct to make sense of what we know about instruction, to prompt considerations, and to guide decisions regarding this incredibly complex process.

Providing effective instruction can be, and usually is, a rather daunting challenge to even the most seasoned and experienced teacher-counselor. It cannot be done well without careful planning, continuous learning, reflection, and a commitment to professional excellence. In our field, it also requires a deep belief *"that children who are disturbed can be helped by the process of re-education"* (Hobbs, 1982, p. 82). Teacher-counselors know that helping includes rigorous attention to the building of academic competence and learning efficacy in every one of their students.

A Transformation

So what might that math class look like in a Re-ED classroom? Experienced, skilled teacher-counselors know that time is a valuable asset not to be wasted, and the lesson must be carefully planned and executed in order to create a therapeutic learning environment:

"If each moment of a child's day can be programmed with exciting and relevant behavior changing, skill building, competence enhancing activities, there is less opportunity and need to engage in the old maladaptive, inappropriate, unproductive habits; sound, constructive learning and growth can occur" (Hobbs, 1969, p. 6).

The cute color-coded clocks indicate that it is time for math. The teacher-counselor has already informed the students that Choice Time is nearing its end, and the previously taught and well-practiced routine for transitioning into math is underway. As she gathers materials for two different lessons that will be directly taught this day, she comments on positive behaviors observed during the choice time period and reinforces appropriate behavior by thanking students who are getting ready. She has reminded them that the Puzzle Corner will be available during the last ten minutes of the period to those who finish

Figure2

Effective Instruction

Effective Instruction is a term inclusive of planning, managing, delivering, and evaluating instruction (Ysseldyke & Christenson, 1993). To be effective, it must also be assumed that the many elements of programming are also included, such as assessment (diagnostic and curriculum-based), individualized academic planning (goals and objectives), and instructional event planning (Hunter, 1982). Following a lesson, it assumes that evaluation will take place. Evaluation includes monitoring student performance and achievement as well as evaluating the lesson and the instructional technique.

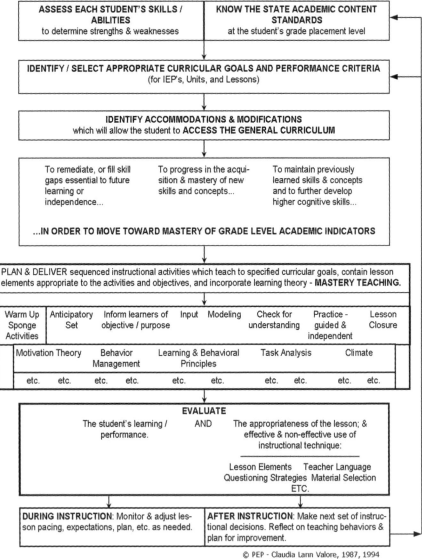

their tasks (carefully individualized) to criteria. She approaches the sleeping student and quietly informs him that he'll be working on the computer today (a last minute change of plans to encourage engagement), and asks him to go "fire it up." She directs the students' attention to today's math groupings and assignments on the blackboard, which were written there before school started.

One student goes to the "Think Tank" (a corner area blocked off with a bookcase) to take a test under the watchful eye of the associate teacher-counselor who can monitor the area from where he sits during this period. Students at their desks are working at independent practice, having already demonstrated a clear understanding and mastery of the process of long division. Three other students are assigned to engage in continued guided practice with the associate teacher-counselor (or ATC), who has asked them to bring their math boxes (manipulatives) to the table. They are given a quick task to work on together so he can briefly excuse himself because a student working at his seat raises his hand for help. William hands over one of his question cards and asks, "Is this right?" After asking whether or not he really wants to spend the card by asking this question now (building independence is a goal for William), the ATC checks the problem, smiles, and says, "We knew you could do that." He goes back to the table and provides feedback to the students on their successful completion of the task and tells them he appreciates their patience.

On the teacher-counselor's way over to the three who have moved their desks together for a lesson with her, she casually makes tally marks next to several names on a well-used laminated chart that reads "Academic Bonus Points." John, a wandering student, sees this and changes his course, going directly to the shelf that houses the math books. He gets his book, and heads toward his desk. The teacher puts a tally mark next to his name. She says, "John, you'll be timing yourself on the facts today, so please get the stopwatch and the answer sheet envelope, so you can check your work when you're done." After finishing the lesson she is about to deliver to the small group, she'll send them off to the Puzzle Corner because they won't be quite ready for independent practice of the skill taught today. She goes to the student working on the computer, rests her hand on his shoulder, and watches quietly for ten seconds. She proceeds to monitor John while he graphs his results on his ongoing line graph; later she will introduce how to represent the same information in a bar graph. She'll then have him pull specific flash cards for the facts he missed for immediate review and homework practice. While he's doing that, she checks on the work of the independent workers and provides immediate feedback with instructions to correct any errors before going to the Puzzle Corner, time-permitting. There is grumbling, but not much because it is what they expected. Correcting work is as much routine as is the schedule or rules, and the teacher-counselor strategically ignores their complaints.

About two minutes before the end of the period, one of the teacher-counselors will warn the group that math is almost over. Materials will be put away, papers collected, and a quick evaluation of the period will occur. Students will be asked to comment on how they performed, and the next period will begin with the day's student group leader calling for a "quiet 30 seconds" and a review of the classroom rules and procedures for group meeting (their next period).

Spitting from Windmills

Achieving academic competence is healing. For any student, especially those who do not necessarily expect it, success is exhilarating, motivating, and joyful. *"It is like spitting from the top of a windmill"* (Hobbs, 1982, p. 287). Effective instruction for the pursuit of student learning and achievement is more than a task of this honorable profession we call "teaching." It is a primary therapeutic intervention and one taken most seriously by teacher-counselors who believe and truly understand the philosophy and practices of Re-ED. Teacher-counselors know, from Re-ED training and experience:

> *"School is the very stuff of a child's or adolescent's problems, and, consequently, a primary source of instruction in living, in the achievement of competence. Special therapy rooms are not needed; the classroom is a natural setting for a constructive relationship between a disturbed youngster and a competent, concerned adult"* (Hobbs,1982, p. 252).

Dr. Hobbs said it simply, and best, from the earliest years, *"So in Re-ED, school keeps. It is not regarded, as it is in many mental health programs, as something that can wait until the child gets better"* (1966, p. 1111).

References

Cantrell, M. L. (1971). *Academic Programming in the Re-Education School.* The Information-Dissemination Office, Tennessee Re-Education Program, Tennessee Department of Mental Health (Available from the Positive Education Program, Cleveland, OH web-site: http://www.pepcleve.org.

Cantrell, M. L. (1974). *Maladaptive behavior as a function of skill/demand discrepancies: An empirical investigation of the competence model.* (Doctoral dissertation, George Peabody College for Teachers, 1974). *Dissertation Abstracts International, 35*, 7718-7719.

Cantrell, M. L., & Cantrell, R. P. (1995). Competence: Building it and building on it. *Reclaiming Children and Youth, 4*, 20-24.

Cegelka, P. T., Fitch, S., & Shaughnessy, M. (2001, November). *Developing Effective Instructional Practices with BD Teachers: A Data-based Teacher Supervision Model.* Presented at the TECBD Conference, Tempe, AZ.

Dunlap, G., Kern-Dunlap, L., Clarke, S., & Robbins, F. (1991). Functional assessment, curricular revision, and severe behavior problems. *Journal of Applied Behavior Analysis, 24*, 387-397.

Epstein, M. H., Kinder, D., & Bursuck, B. (1989). The academic status of adolescents with behavioral disorders. *Behavioral Disorders, 14*, 157-165.

Gunter, P. L. & Denny, R. K. (1998). Trends and issues in research regarding academic instruction of students with emotional and behavioral disorders. *Behavioral Disorders, 24*, 44-50.

Hobbs, N. (1965). *The Professor and Student or The Art of Getting Students Into Trouble.* Paper presented at the 48th Annual meeting of the American Council on Education, Washington, D. C.

Hobbs, N. (1966). Helping disturbed children: Psychological and ecological strategies. *American Psychologist, 21*(12), 1105-1114.

Hobbs, N. (1969) The philosophy of re-education. *Mind over Matter, 14*(1), 5-8.

Hobbs, N. (1982). *The troubled and troubling child: Re-Education in mental health, education, and human services programs for children and youth.* San Francisco: Jossey-Bass.

Hunter M. (1982). *Mastery teaching.* El Segundo, CA: TIP publications.

Kauffman, J. M. (1997). *Characteristics of emotional and behavioral disorders of children and youth* (6th ed.). Columbus, OH: Merrill.

Lewis, T. J., Sugai, G., & Colvin, G. (1998). Reducing problem behavior through a school-wide system of effective behavioral support: Investigation of a school-wide social skills training program and contextual interventions. *School Psychology Review, 27*, 446-459.

National Reading Panel (2000). *Teaching children to read.* [videotape]. (Available from NICHD Clearinghouse, http://www.nichd.gov/publications/nrppubskey.cfm).

No Child Left Behind Act (2002). (Available from NICHD Clearing house, http://www.nichd.gov/publications/nrppubskey.cfm).

Ruhl, K. L., & Berlinghoff, D. H. (1992). Research on improving behaviorally disordered students' academic performance: A review of the literature. *Behavioral Disorders, 17*, 178-190.

Scott, T. M., Nelson, C. M., & Liaupsin, C. J. (2001). Effective instruction: The forgotten component in preventing school violence. *Education and Treatment of Children, 24*(3), 309-322.

Shaughnessy, M. R., (2001, November). *Effective Academic Instructional Practices for Students with Behavioral Disorders: A Review of the Research Literature.* Presented at the TECBD Conference, Tempe, AZ.

Skiba, R., & Peterson, R. (2000). School discipline at a crossroads: From zero tolerance to early response. *Exceptional Children, 66*, 335-346.

Walker, H. M., Colvin, G., & Ramsey, E. (1995). *Antisocial behavior in school: Strategies and best practices.* Pacific Grove, CA: Brooks/Cole.

Walker, H. M., Forness, S. R., Kauffman, J. M., Epstein, M. H., Gresham, F. M., Nelson, C. M., & Strain, P. S. (1998). Macro-social validation: Referencing outcomes in behavioral disorders to societal issues and problems. *Behavioral Disorders, 24,* 7-18.

Ysseldyke, J., Christenson, S. (1993). *TIES-II: The instructional environment system-II.* Longmont, CO: Sopris West.

Claudia Lann Valore, MEd, is Chief Program Officer for Positive Education Program in Cleveland, Ohio.   CValore@pepcleve.org

15

Academics in a Re-ED Program: A Visit to Wright School

Felicia Demchuk & Carole Geraci Sever

Upon driving onto the Wright School campus, a first-time visitor immediately notices that there are some *great* climbing trees on their front lawn. Here is a school where children can be children: they can climb trees, laugh, run, and feel safe. Clinical Coordinator Julia Huff-Jerome did confirm that the trees are great for climbing, and whenever the kids are outside, there are bound to be a number of kids (and sometimes a few staff) in the trees. In true Re-ED fashion, there is even a ritual for determining which trees the kids can climb. They must progress from the "learner" tree; then by working with peers and staff and showing competence, they can advance to the more challenging trees.

At Wright School, learning to climb trees is an apt metaphor for what children do every day. With the help of peers and staff, under the guidance of Re-ED, the children learn to master the challenges of both trees and life, one limb at a time.

We are here to see everything — how they "do Re-ED." Since we've heard they have a particularly excellent academic program, this paper will focus primarily on how they build these skills in their students.

History and Structures

Housed in a building from the 1920's (originally built for an orphanage), Wright School opened in 1963 as one of the two original

Project Re-ED programs. Today, it may be the only Re-ED program still in existence that follows most of the initial Re-ED organizational framework. As in the past, the program still serves a total of 24 children at a time, with three groups of eight students who live and attend school together, building group cohesion. Like Project Re-ED, the current group of students at Wright are ages 8 through 13 years old, although they sometimes range from 6 to 14. Each group has a name, and thereby an identity around which they develop rituals and customs. Currently, the three groups are named the Olympians, the Royals, and the Eagles. (In the Eagles group, behavioral levels range from "nestwarmer," the lowest level, to "High Flier." Those who are getting ready to graduate are called "Senior Eagles.")

Like the treatment program developed for Project Re-ED, this is a short - stay residential program; most children attend Wright School for about six months. Wright School operates as a year-round, 12-month program. During the summer months children follow the same schedule of full-day school and evening residential Re-ED activities. The staff has developed learning and group cohesion-building routines and rituals that mirror the changing seasons: garden planting and tending from spring through fall, sled riding in the winter, hikes on the Eno River, and, of course, tree climbing whenever possible.

Staffing patterns continue to follow the initial plan of Project Re-ED with Day, Night, and Liaison Teacher-Counselors. As time has passed and as we have learned more about the kinds of services that children need to overcome life challenges, more roles have been added to support children attending Wright School. The teacher-counselors (T-C) continue to be the most central staff member in the lives of students. At Wright School, each group of 8 children has a Lead Day T-C, a Day T-C Assistant, Lead Night T-C, Night T-C Assistant, Liaison T-C, and Overnight T-C Assistant. The clinical leadership team consists of five coordinators who facilitate various components of the treatment and educational process. Three Clinical Case Coordinators provide leadership to the teacher-counselors in the three treatment groups. Each clinical coordinator additionally facilitates an independent work group that focuses on the continuous quality improvments of school wide initiatives for academic programming, therapeutic programming, and ecological programming. A Resource Coordinator supervises the clinical social worker and a flexible resource team whose members include the third shift staff and four and a half teacher-counselor assistants who serve as first responders for crisis management, individualized interventions, and cover leave for the treatment team staff. Supporting all the teams, the Assessment and Evaluation Coordinator provides leadership to the educational diagnostician/reading specialist and speech language pathologist in assessment and individual/small group interventions, manages contracted clinical services from psychiatry, psychology, occupational and physical therapy, and does some program evaluation activities. Support staff provide the necessary and valued technology, fiscal, clerical, food management, housekeeping, and maintenance services.

Day and Night and Liaison T-Cs are licensed special education teachers. Often staff members have "risen through the ranks," starting in supportive roles, gaining the skills, training, and licensure they need to move into these leadership roles. As a result, a number of staff members have worked for Wright School for a long time, and a few staff spend most of their careers with this program.

Therapeutic Living Arrangements

The Wright School building is designed so that each of the three treatment groups has a separate wing which contains their living room, classroom, and sleeping rooms. A day at Wright School is very predictable for children, with close supervision and structure as well as a consistent routine. T-Cs individualize the level of adult regulated structure whenever possible to help children generalize lessons in self-management as they prepare to leave the treatment program. All three groups share a common dining room where meals are served family style, with each group eating together with their T-Cs. A few days each week kids eat in an "open" format – that is, they choose their own seat, and teachers sit apart from the kids to simulate a public school cafeteria setting.

As with the original Project Re-ED program, children go home on the weekends to live with their family and practice their new skills. The Liaison T-C works with both families and communities so that significant adults in the child's ecology are practicing new skills, too. In some cases, however, the community case managers and the Wright School LT-C may arrange for respite care on the weekends, because either the child or the parent /foster family is not yet able to provide a safe environment on the weekend.

Curriculum: The Academic Focus

The majority of academic instructional time at Wright School focuses on the core subjects of reading, written language, and math. These are all taught in blocks of time. Children are ability grouped for language arts and math instruction, based upon initial formal and informal diagnostic assessments. Julia Huff-Jerome noted that treatment teams initially expressed conflicting opinions about ability grouping, where students leave their primary group for at least some instructional lessons. T-Cs now agree, however, given students' vast differences in academic achievement, it works well to have them ability grouped. Debbie Simmers, Director, said that kids are best ability grouped for remediation; "In the short amount of time we have these kids, we are trying to provide as much remediation as we can." The important functions of the group to create cohesion, as well as commitment to help with each others' growth, remain robust because all time other than core academics is spent with the treatment group.

Academic Remediation Programs

Wright School T-Cs work to identify language arts and mathematics instructional programs for students based upon evidence of the instructional programs' proven effectiveness for skill acquisition by special learners with remedial academic needs. For reading remediation, Wright School uses the Wilson Reading Program and Hill Center methods. T-Cs have found the programs to be useful and successful. Both programs are incorporated into classroom instruction, and additionally, are offered on a one-on-one basis as supplements to regular instruction.

[Editor's note: See www.wilsonlanguage.com and wilsonlanguage.com/further_reading.html for research study references and other documentation about the program. See www.hillcenter.org/general/overview.html and www.hillcenter.org/newsevents/outreach_article.html for information about their programs for specific learning disabilities and/or attention deficit disorders.]

Children who are on grade level participate in daily classroom instruction, but do not receive pull‑out intervention. All children reading one standard deviation or more below what would be expected for their chronological age receive Wilson intervention. Evenings, students participate in the Accelerated Reader (AR) Program. Wright School has purchased the software and books, and continues to build their AR library through purchases and donations. *[Editor's note: See http://www.sbc.mps.k12.mi.us/AR_program.htm. This program provides a list (~ 100 pages long!) of Accelerated Reader (AR) books for students to read, answer questions about their readings, and earn points towards ultimately receiving recognition on the AR bulletin board.]*

As part of written language instruction, Wright School uses the University of Kansas Sentence Writing Strategy (which provides much information for teaching children with learning disabilities), along with portfolios, graphic organizers, the "Four Blocks" framework (Cunningham & Allington, 2003), and other strategies. Recently, Wright School teachers adopted a writing program from a local independent school, which is a base program for language mechanics. *[Editor's note: See http://kucrl.org/archives/ls/sentence.shtml which describes the programs, outlines a new addition to the now two‑level program, which is less complex in order that younger students can learn how to write simple sentences. Persons wishing to purchase the programs are required to undergo professional development instruction in use of the programs.]*

Day T‑Cs focus on language arts and math instruction. Resource T‑Cs develop weekly theme based instructional units on science and social studies. Night T‑Cs are also responsible for academic programming. They teach the "Healthful Living" curriculum which is part of the North Carolina Course of Study; it includes instructional content for health and life skills, as well as physical education and human growth and development. *[Editor's note: See http:// www.ncpublicschools.org/curriculum/health/ and http:// www.ncpublicschools.org/curriculum/health/scos/toc for additional information.]* The Wright School evening curriculum includes group instruction in social skills, dealing with anger, and coping/problem-solving. Evening teacher-counselors also organize and support structured homework sessions for students.

Wright School's academic program must comply with North Carolina state mandates. The prescribed state Course of Study, like Ohio's, requires that a "sixth grade student is instructed to meet sixth grade objectives, using sixth grade materials." Each North Carolina public school student must also participate in a state mandated testing program, based on content from the Standard Course of Study, and must pass "Gateway" tests at grades three, five, and eight. The Gateway tests are "high stakes" tests; that is, a child must pass these levels before they are promoted to the next grade. The state uses the test information to track the progress of school districts, individual school buildings, and individual student growth, in compliance with the No Child Left Behind Act. (Because Wright School is a short-term program and students are in residence for less than a full school year, Wright School does not have to meet the strict NCLB requirements to show adequate yearly progress [AYP] through high stakes testing. Regardless, academic instruction at Wright School is designed to bring students as close as possible to grade-level achievement. The focus on the "three R's" helps students make significant gains in language arts and math. Academic outcomes, as measured by admission and discharge standardized assessments, indicate that their students make substantial progress during their length of stay.) *[Editor's note: See http://paws.wcu.edu/bp19383/gateway.html which gives a detailed explanation of each of the Gateway "stages" for North Carolina schools.]*

Wright School is fully funded by the Department of Health and

Human Services through the NC Division of Mental Health/Developmental Disabilities and Substance Abuse Services. They receive some federal funds for exceptional children, including IDEA (VI-B) funding, but no direct funding through the NC Department of Public Instruction.

The Diagnostic/Assessment Program

Wright School has an Assessment Team consisting of an Assessment and Evaluation Coordinator, an Educational Diagnostician, a Speech Language Pathologist, and a Clinical Social Worker to evaluate each child's academic skills, language, and social/emotional self-reports upon admission to the program. (In addition to serving as the assessment team, these highly skilled professionals also provide individualized and small group direct education and therapy services as needed.) Wright School requests multi-disciplinary and psycho-educational evaluations for all children referred to the treatment program. School districts send any assessment information they have on the children, but because they do not function as the referring agency, it is sometimes a challenge to obtain a complete pre-admission psycho-educational battery.

The evaluation is completed during the first two weeks the child is in residence. Wright has a "no reject" policy if children fall within the appropriate age range. Children have been admitted with verbal IQs ranging from between the first and second percentile (on a standardized measure of intelligence) to the "gifted" range, although many children are admitted with significant academic deficits. Wright School also serves children who fall in the range of high functioning autism spectrum disorder.

Formal Academic Assessments

A formal academic diagnostic assessment is performed by the Wright School Diagnostician. Children are assessed with a standardized academic achievement test, such as the Woodcock Johnson III (WJIII) as both a pre - and post-test. *[Editor's note: See http:// www.riverpub.com/products/wjIIIComplete/index.html for a description of the depth and coverage of the batteries. Also, see: http://www.wiley.com/WileyCDA/WileyTitle/product-cd-*

*0471419990,descCd-description.html?print=true for a descrip-
tion of a companion book by one of the authors, Nancy Mather,
on the WJIII, its reports, recommendations, and strategies.]*

If indicated, the Diagnostician will do the more in-depth assessments that are part of the WJIII. In addition, she may complete a
battery of other assessments that might be appropriate for that child,
including additional math assessment, the Qualitative Reading Inventory and, at times, the OWLS written language assessment. *[Editor's
note: See http://occawlonline.pearsoned.com/bookbind/pubbooks/
leslie_awl/chapter0/deluxe.html for an introduction to how this book
helps in the assessment of reading ability in students from the emergent stage through high school levels. Also see http://
ags.pearsopnassessments.com/Group_p.asp?nGroupInfoID=a3370
for additional descriptions of the OWLS scales.]*

The Speech Language Pathologist performs a complete language
assessment on every child, even if they have never been referred for
SLP services. The language portion of the curriculum is presented in
greater detail in its own section below.

While the student is in the classroom and the T-Cs are awaiting
the testing/assessment results, the T-Cs collect informal assessment
data designed to supplement the formal information. After the initial
assessment process is completed, the student is placed in a reading
and math group appropriate for his achievement level, and the treatment team meets to discuss all essential information and develop treatment goals. The Day T-C writes the student's Individualized Education Program (IEP), the Night T-C writes the treatment plan, and the
LT-C creates the service plan which includes ecological goals identified by the family and the community, all of which are shared jointly in
the student's assessment team meeting.

Tracking Progress

Monthly written reports provide on-going documentation of student progress in the areas of academics, behavior, and the ecology.
Throughout his or her stay, each child's programming is reviewed during monthly Utilization Review sessions. This session is attended by all
staff working with the child; it is designed to review academic and

behavioral programming, including student progress in school, at home, and in the community.

T-Cs continue to assess students daily, using standard curriculum-based assessments, as well as teacher-designed tools. At the end of their stay, most children are re-assessed using an alternate form of the Woodcock Johnson III to gauge academic progress. The Clinical Coordinator leads the preparation of a comprehensive discharge report in conjunction with all T-C staff from that team. This includes test information, behavioral information, and performance information. The discharge report also identifies specific instructional strategies which have been shown to work (or not to work!) with each of the students and their families. Upon discharge, the majority of the children return to their home school district. Some students will be placed in separate or self-contained classrooms, but many school districts in North Carolina meet all student needs through inclusion services after elementary school. During the child's stay at Wright School, the LT-Cs work with home districts, and in some cases with receiving teachers, to prepare them for the child's return. If the child lives locally, they may be allowed to live at Wright for a brief time while they transition back to their home school, or they may be allowed to attend the school program at Wright while they transition back home. This is not often an option, as a result of the distances children travel from their homes all over North Carolina.

The Importance of Language

All students at Wright School are given a complete language assessment upon entry, whether or not they qualified previously for language services; all students receive academic instruction designed to remediate language deficits and enhance language skills. Staff members at Wright School are reminded regularly by their Director and the Speech Language Pathologist (SLP) that there is a significant co-occurrence of behavioral difficulties and language disorders (Benner, Nelson, & Epstein, 2002). In spite of the fact that many children appear to have "good" language skills on the surface, they are sometimes unable to use language for problem-solving or social skills.

Staff know that these deficits often surface as behavioral problems.

Standard school testing often fails to assess receptive, expressive, and pragmatic language, so children's language deficits may have never before been identified or addressed. To further complicate matters, when children are "full of feelings" and overwhelmed by emotions, their ability to use language may be further compromised; they may be unable to use language to solve their problems, as many typical children might.

As a result, there is an on-going effort for teacher-counselors to modify their classrooms, including their verbal and written instructions, and what they teach the children to do. Over the past decade the SLP has done a lot to train T-Cs and others in the children's ecologies to provide modifications and accommodations designed to help children learn to use language more effectively.

Nina Lorch, Wright School's Speech Language Pathologist, talked to us about their language program and its important place in Wright School's competence building. The goal is to provide children whose language ability levels vary with opportunities for as much access to information as possible. Modifications and accommodations made for a child who cannot read and who has difficulty processing language will not detract from the learning experience of any other child involved in the lesson; in fact, many of the other children may also have varying degrees of language and learning problems. By accommodating for different languare levels, instruction becomes reinforcing for them all, including those with a host of other problems.

Writing down the steps for a particular skill enables children who cannot remember what was said to return to the written rubric time and time again. Using pictures or icons enables children who cannot read to see from the picture what is being discussed and helps them learn the content when the process is gone over aloud. The pattern of pre-sentation must be consistent across topics and content, so children can start to build up internal expectations and linkages to past lessons that have incorporated the same information in the same framework. They can begin to say to themselves, "Oh yeah, this is what we do every day. We go over the schedule and I'm starting to remember that is what we said." The teacher uses the same processes to set expectations until, finally, the children internalize the patterns and expectations.

Staff actually talk to students about language that can help children be successful in the classroom, such as how to ask for help or how to get a teacher's attention in an appropriate manner, or techniques for getting more time to think of an answer, particularly "cool" ways. Teachers can post lists of all the "cool" ways to gain processing time like, "Could you run that by me again?" or, "I'm sorry, I didn't catch that." These are techniques for avoiding the slightest hint of stigmatizing the child for not being facile with language. These "cool" strategies are made part of the ongoing practice within the classroom culture and kids are praised for using the "cool" approaches, so that they become part of their daily repertoire.

One often sees groups of kids going around school practicing language-based social skills. The little boy in the Olympians who graduated today had a real problem making conversation with people until staff broke conversation down into its component parts and taught him how to do each one of them. Think about the parts of a conversation. If you are going to carry on a conversation with someone you have to: (a) look at who you are talking to, (b) pay attention to them, (c) wait your turn to say something, and (d) while you are waiting, you have to remember what you were going to say. Then, you have to (e) respond to what the other person is saying, and, (f) while staying on the topic of your conversation, you have to say something back to the other person.

To most of us, conversational turn-taking and all the other elements of a conversation are like breathing, but to this little boy it was six different things he had to remember how to do at once. Wright School staff started out with him practicing with his therapist, a graduate intern who worked with him. Next, they had him practice with a variety of people, until finally the whole school was the playing field for his conversational practice, the SLP told us.

"We often use the same step-by-step process for moving skills from the therapy room to the larger group. Or, if the classroom group is doing skill building within their classroom, they eventually begin to practice in front of other people in the school. Along the

way we work on a lot of other pragmatic skills such as: ignoring, teasing, accusing (and its counterpart, dealing with being accused), and all those other social skills — like interrupting or apologizing — that are needed in everyday interactions with other people. All of these behaviors are about language, how it's used effectively instead of ineffectively. Many Wright School kids, even those with otherwise intact language skills, fall down markedly in the effective use of language in social situations.

"It is so much fun to give these kids the keys for breaking the language/social codes. For example, it's really fun to walk into a classroom and say, 'I really like to call on people who are raising a quiet hand and smiling at me.' I only have to do that once and the next time I walk into the classroom, I'm facing a sea of smiling faces and raised hands; they know what they want — my attention. I've told them what I want and it's not a mystery to them anymore; whereas, for five years the social language process hasn't worked for them. But now they've been told the code, the secret." Ms. Lorch enjoys describing their discoveries and the behavior changes she sees as a function of simply cuing them in, sharing the secrets.

In summary, tell children what the rules are for reaching their social goals. This is a major part of the problem for children who are transitioning from using language in the home setting to the school setting. At home children may not have to talk in complete sentences. Everyone just sort of knows what's being talked about (the context is clear), so the child doesn't have to be very specific and, what's more, they can talk whenever they want. Then comes school and school has rules like, "You can't talk until you raise your hand and someone calls on you." Furthermore, someone can tell you your turn is over, even though you haven't finished speaking and you have much more to tell everybody. Or, children don't know there's a difference between how you talk to your brother and how you talk to an adult — they don't know the rules that we have absorbed over a long period of time, like we've learned how to breathe.

Thus, this process has to become a whole school curriculum;

everybody has to be "in" on the teaching process, not just a speech pathologist who might see a child once or twice a week or who may go into a classroom once a week. *"Since we started making it a 'whole school process' it has become a big part of our culture for all of us. Our teachers here know they could teach a college course in language modification geared for children with language difficulties because each of them have had to do it and they know how it works."*

Simple Language Classroom Techniques

The following concrete examples provide simple techniques that can be used in every classroom or home setting.

1.   Written schedules don't work for non-readers, or for children who have language processing deficits. On every classroom schedule, icons are used in addition to the printed word.

2.   Day T-Cs are very careful about how they place children in classroom seating assignments, based upon listening strengths and needs.

3.   T-Cs have been trained to ask questions designed to maximize student learning and success. It is critical to help hesitant children practice answering questions, and answering them correctly so they can build their confidence and self esteem. Teacher-Counselors are taught the hierarchy of question difficulty, and how to phrase questions so children can answer successfully. T-Cs have also been taught how to make their classrooms a safe place for children to ask questions. Children with language processing problems may not know how to ask questions, and may have spent much of their lives being punished for seeking information when they're confused or need help. Wright classrooms teach the children how to ask for help, and let them practice asking for that help, both in and out of the classroom.

4.   T-Cs are also taught how to give information to children with language processing problems, and how to check for understanding.

The staff members at Wright School know it is important for children at different ability levels to have as much access to language information as possible. The modifications discussed here do not take away from the learning experienced by any of the children, regardless of their language needs. The following is the report of an actual reading lesson, taught by Mandy Sitz, the Day T-C of the Olympians.

A Wright School Reading Lesson

This lesson involved eight students, who were divided into two smaller groups. Mandy worked with the lower functioning group first, while the T-C Assistant worked with the other group. It was clear that there was a great deal of trust between teacher and students, as well as student to student, in spite of the fact that at least one of the students had only been in the program a few days. Classroom expectations and routines were well established, and students and teachers treated everyone else with a great deal of respect. Though this observer did not conduct a formal praise to criticism ratio assessment, it was obvious that there was constant praise, and little (if any!) criticism. The process of instruction, direction, re-direction, and questioning was flawless. Here is a summary of her instruction.

Mandy began the session with a review of the Wilson Reading Program practice. She used the letter flash cards with the students, and did a quick review of sounds, then tapping sounds in words, and reading words in word families. She reviewed the Wilson sentences with the students.

She presented the teacher-made lesson, which was tied into a poetry reading presentation that was being given by the older classroom. It was also tied into a story to which the children had previously been exposed about Anansi the Spider. The students were excited after this anticipatory discussion took place, and eager quiet hands were in the air to answer Mandy's questions.

Mandy wrote the title of the poem, *Spiders Are Everywhere*, on the whiteboard, and discussed the fact that it was written by a seven year old. She talked to the children about why it was exciting that someone their age could have written a poem that was published on the Internet.

T-C — "We are reading a poem, *Spiders Are Everywhere*, by Josh."

T-C — "Can you read the title out loud?"

Students — Read the title in unison.

There was discussion about how each child felt about spiders; each was encouraged to talk, and there were no "wrong" answers.

T-C — "I want you to read through the poem, and underline any words you know. For example, we know this word" (points to the word "spiders" on the whiteboard).

T-C — Asks a student to read the word she is pointing to.

Student — Reads the word.

T-C — Underlines the word.

T-C — "When you see the word "spiders" in your poem, what will you do?"

The student — "I will underline it."

T-C — Asks another student, "When you see this word (points to "spiders" on the whiteboard) what will you do with it?"

Student — "Underline it."

T-C — "Does anyone see another word they know?" pointing to the title on the whiteboard.

The student — "Everywhere."

T-C to all students — "Can you point to the word 'everywhere' on your papers?"

Students all point to the correct word.

T-C asks another student — "What do you do to that word?"

Student — "I will underline it."

T-C asks another student — "Why do we underline it?"

Student — "Because it is a word I can read."

The students then successfully completed the assignment, because they completely understood it, based upon Mandy's excellent presentation. More great instruction followed, but this description is intended to show how language issues were taken into account in talking to the students, and how they all (even some very low functioning children) were able to understand the assignment, and complete the task successfully. This assignment provided the opportunity for every child to feel like they could correctly accomplish the task, and it was clear they felt proud that they completed it correctly.

A Summary Impression

It is always inspiring to watch master teachers at work, and especially at a school that serves troubled and troubling students whose needs are so great they have been sent to a residential center. Wright School's Re-ED Teacher-Counselors take their roles as both Teachers and Counselors very seriously. They recognize their students' strengths and use them to grow beyond their weaknesses, seeing as Nick Hobbs did, *"...that young people have a tremendous desire to learn and to do well;...that the world is rich in things to learn...."* (Hobbs, 1982, p. 20).

They know that learning and growing in and of themselves can be fun, pure pleasure for the children and for the adults who help them. As staff in Re-ED programs, our collective and individual efforts to become more competent, in the wide range of areas where competence is called for, pay off for our students and for ourselves.

"Competence makes a difference," indeed – for our children and youth, and for the adults in their lives.

References

Benner, G., Nelson, J. R., & Epstein, M. (2002). Language skills of children with EBD: A literature review. *Journal of Emotional and Behavioral Disorders, 10*(1), *43-59.*

Cunningham, P., & Allington, R. (2003). *Classrooms that work: They can all read and write* (3rd ed.). Boston: Allyn & Bacon.

Hobbs, N. (1982). *The troubled and troubling child.* San Francisco: Jossey-Bass.

Felicia Demchuk, MEd, is Educational Services Director for Positive Education Program in Cleveland, OH. Fdemchuk@pepcleve.org

Carole Geraci Sever, MEd, is Staff Development Associate on the training staff at Positive Education Program in Cleveland, OH. Csever@pepcleve.org

16

Intelligence Can Be Taught ...Really

Elaine Harper

"The cognitive competence of children and adolescents can be considerably enhanced; they can be taught generic skills in the management of their lives as well as strategies for coping with the complex array of demands placed upon them by family, school, community or job; in other words, intelligence can be taught"(Hobbs, 1982, p.265).

Intelligence...

Intelligence has always been intricately woven into understanding human development and learning. Theorists have debated many issues regarding intelligence. For Re-ED, the way intelligence is defined and the belief that it can be taught and improved are essential characteristics from which our practices are based. While intelligence has traditionally been viewed as an unchangeable entity, Re-ED views intelligence as multidimensional and malleable.

Several theorists propose theoretical backdrops consistent with that view. Piaget (1952) saw intelligence as developmentally constructed in the mind of the learner as it changes from concrete to abstract stages of understanding. Vygotsky (1978) viewed intelligence as a function of activity mediated through material tools, psychological tools, and other human beings. Feuerstein's (1979) theory of structural cognitive modifiability sees intelligence as a function of experience that can be changed through guided mediation. Gardner (1983), theorist of multiple intelligences, says intelligence is made of eleven realms of knowing for use in solving problems and creating products in a culture. Goleman (1995) recognizes emotional intelligence as a higher predictor of success in life than traditional IQ, including self-awareness. Sternberg's (1988) view is that intelligence is triarchic with analytic, creative, and practical components that need to be balanced for optimal functioning. Others have additional perspectives, both recognizing the multidimensionality of intelligence and demonstrating its malleability. Re-ED embraces the *multidimensionality of intelligence* and seeks to capitalize on each student's strengths and then utilize those strengths to remediate deficits.

Furthermore, Re-ED is responsive to the possibilities that intelligence may be recognized and expressed differently in various cultures.

Can Be...

Perhaps the most powerful characteristic about Re-ED's notions regarding intelligence is that it is changeable. Through the teacher-counselor's relationship with the student and the teacher-counselor's *belief that positive change is possible*, the student is encouraged to see their potential for change even before they observe it for themselves. In the literature we find that the belief itself that positive change can occur has led to fewer instances of depression and mental health issues than where students lack that belief (Dweck, 2000).

Taught...

Re-ED acknowledges that the teaching of intelligence, cognitive competence, and generic skills happens in a multifaceted approach to learning that encompasses, by deliberate design, an endless variety of situations. Certainly, a day treatment center classroom containing all the elements "stocked" with sound academic programming and effective behavior management cultivates intelligence. Ideally, competence-"stretching" academic programming serves as effective behavior management.

The therapeutic camping trip experience is another venue for generalizing cognitive skills learned in one context carefully into another. Re-ED programs providing other services cultivate the teaching and learning interactions, too. Experiences provided in the home and the community can also be included in the "teaching" of intelligence. A host of literature has demonstrated the *remarkable impacts on children's IQ scores made by enriched early experiences* (Hunt, 1961; Skeels, 1966; Espy, Molfese, & DiLalla, 2001).

Really.

Teachers, parents, and schools can be *merchants of hope to students struggling both to learn and to demonstrate what they have learned.* "Durelle," for example, came to our classroom branded as not very intelligent, unable and unwilling to learn. He was often disruptive, disrespectful, and unable to manage his anger. He spent long periods of time refusing to engage in our program. He was the oldest of three school age children whose mother had recently died. As we got to know him, I was stunned and horrified as he told us about his past experiences in school, including a teacher telling him he was "the devil himself."

I ran into "Durelle's" dad several years later on a Saturday while I was grocery shopping. "Thank you," he said, "I want you to know that PEP (Re-ED) saved my son's life." He went on to tell me that after completing PEP, "Durelle" got a part-time job and worked while he finished high school. "Durelle" wanted to go to the Marines, yet he worried that he wouldn't pass the testing. Proudly, he did. At the time I had run into his dad, "Durelle" had been married for a year and they were planning for a baby.

"Durelle" had validated for himself and for me the words of Hobbs. He had learned *"skills in the management of* [his] *life"* as well as *"strategies for coping with the complex array of demands placed upon* [him] *by family, school, community* [and] *job."* He had learned intelligence (Hobbs, 1982, p. 265).

Accepting the evidence that intelligence can be taught allows,

even motivates, us to help kids grow. Growth implies change.
Accept the evidence and believe *"intelligence can be taught."*

References

Dweck, C. (2000). *Self theories: Their role in motivation, personality, and development.* Philadelphia, PA: Psychology Press.

Espy, D. A., Molfese, V. J., & DiLalla, L. F. (2001). Effects of environmental measures on intelligence in young children: Growth curve modeling of longitudinal data. *Merrill-Palmer Quarterly, 47*(1), 42-73.

Feuerstein, R., Rand, Y., Hoffman, M., et al., (1979). Cognitive modifiability in retarded adolescents. Effects of Instrumental Enrichment. *American Journal of Mental Deficiency, 83*, 539-550.

Gardner, H. (1983). *Frames of mind: The theory of multiple intelligences.* Basic Books.

Goleman, D. (1995). *Emotional intelligence: Why it can matter more than IQ.* New York: Bantam.

Hobbs, N. (1982). *The troubled and troubling child.* San Francisco, CA: Jossey-Bass Publishers.

Hunt, J. McV. (1961). *Intelligence and experience.* New York: Ronald Press.

Piaget, J. (1952). *The origins of intelligence in children.* New York: W. W. Norton.

Skeels, H. M. (1966). *Adult status of children with contrasting early life experiences, A follow-up study.* Society for Research in Child Development.

Sternberg, R. J. (1988). *The triarchic mind: A new theory of human intelligence.* Viking Adult.

Vygotsky, L. (1978). *Mind in society: The development of higher psychological processes.* Cambridge, MA: Harvard University Press.

Elaine Harper, MEd, is Education Coordinator for Positive Education Program in Cleveland, Ohio.
Eharper@pepcleve.org>

17

Where Skills Meet Demands: An Empirical Study of Competence

Mary L. Cantrell & Robert P. Cantrell

The continuing pursuit of competence has been a mainstay construct in the Re-ED repertoire. Most of us were introduced to its implications by Nick Hobbs who invited the graduating seniors of the Peabody Demonstration School to a different, more challenging way to live a life. "Put yourself in just manageable difficulty, of your own choosing," he said, and many Re-EDers ever since have adopted that mantra as their own (Hobbs, 1971). Why is this view important to us as helpers? And why is competence so important in helping troubled and troubling youth and their families?

The goal of this chapter is to: (1) explore the relationship of emotional behavior to situation specific competence and its acquisition, (2) present an empirical study investigating the parameters of those relationships in one behavioral setting, and (3) explore the situational and psychological mechanisms by which the pursuit of competence relates to a growth-oriented way of living.

The Concept of Competence

Among the many thoughtful scholars who studied the concept of competence and its implications was Harvard's Robert White (1959). White challenged the conventional view of competence and its place in motivation with his scholarly article, *Motivation Reconsidered:*

The Concept of Competence. In this treatise he explored the biological and ecological demands imposed on organisms that forced them to adapt to changing environmental conditions or die without progeny.

William Bricker (1967) expanded the concept by adapting its premises to the study of children's emotional (or deviant) behaviors. He saw the presence of non-productive behavior as signaling a mismatch between an individual's skills and the setting's demands made on those skills. A series of informal studies counting inappropriate behaviors under three conditions (demands significantly above, slightly above, and below the child's skills) showed the lowest incidences of these behaviors consistently occurred in the "demands slightly above skills" condition (Cantrell & Cantrell, 1995). Would a formal study also corroborate Bricker's thesis?

An Empirical Study of Competence and Maladaptive Behavior

To test the empirical validity of White's and Bricker's competence premise, M. L. Cantrell (1974) performed an experimental study of the competence concept under three comparative conditions. Participants were public school second graders from six elementary school classrooms, and their teachers.

In each of the six classrooms, the three students scoring closest to each of the 10th (low), 50th (mid), and 90th (high) percentiles on the Metropolitan Achievement Test (MAT) Math section were chosen for behavioral observation. Across the six classrooms, these students represented three student groups: (a) low math achievers, (b) mid math achievers, and (c) high math achievers. Each selected student was observed for three weeks, while three different math lessons were taught to the entire class for one week each. Each week of lessons aimed at one of the three functioning levels: low, middle, and high.

Materials for the three weeks' math instruction were developed using Stern, Stern, & Gould's 1965 Structural Arithmetic series. Lessons were prepared for the specific skill needs determined by skill assessments of each 3 person target group in each day's lesson, teachers were provided with worksheets, teacher directions, and demonstration materials.

Classroom behaviors were observed as all three levels of math lessons were experimentally taught to each of the three levels of students: i.e., (a) Low math functioning students during low, mid, and high level math lessons; (b) Mid math functioning students during low, mid, and high level math lessons, and (c) High math functioning students during low, mid, and high level math lessons. To remove the effect of lesson order, presentation order was varied to cover all six possibilities (LMH, LHM, MLH, MHL, HLM, HML), each classroom receiving the three weeks of lessons in one of the six orders.

Classroom observers were trained to 70% or higher agreement with a criterion observer using videotaped classroom sessions for three children and the teacher before the actual experiment began. Observers did not know the math instructional level for any of the nine students they were observing in each classroom. Each target student in a classroom was assigned a number from one through nine and observed in that order. Students were observed in turn for five seconds each, recording one of four behavioral categories: TA = task attentive; NA = task non-attentive/non-disruptive; D = task non-attentive/disruptive; and U = unratable. After a group of three students was observed for five seconds each, the next (or fourth) five-second interval was used to rate the teacher's statement during that interval as positive, neutral, negative, none, or unratable. When all nine students had been observed once and the teacher had been observed three times, the process would begin again. This rotation continued until the 30 minute observation had ended. An audio signal through an earplug attached to a cassette player provided observers with the numbered five second intervals from one to nine.

Hypotheses. The experimental hypotheses tested whether emotional or dysfunctional student behaviors would vary as a function of experimentally manipulated math instructional demands on students whose math skills were currently below, at, or above the expected level of math functioning for second grade. It was hypothesized that the greatest incidences of inappropriate behavior would occur where the disparity between skill level and lesson level were highest (such as low group during high lesson, or high group during low lesson).

Results. To compare non-attentive (NA) and disruptive (D) behaviors for each group under each lesson, three factor analyses of variance were performed. Results for the disruptive behaviors (D) are most relevant to the competence model hypotheses. Different groups did behave differently during the different lessons, as indicated by the significant groups by lessons interaction for disruptive, non-attentive behaviors ($F = 8.305, p < .001$).

The *low math group* demonstrated the least disruptive behaviors during the low lessons, more disruptive behaviors during the mid lessons, and most disruptive during the high math lessons, although these mean differences were not large enough to be statistically significant.

The *mid math group* were most disruptive ($p < .01$) at the low math instructional level, and dropped significantly ($p < .01$) when the mid math lesson was taught, but did not demonstrate significant levels of disruptive behavior during the high math lesson level.

The *high math group* were most disruptive at the low math instructional level, somewhat less disruptive when the mid math lesson was taught, and least disruptive when the lesson level went to high math; these mean comparisons were significant ($p < .01$).

Only the low math group demonstrated gradually increasing levels of D as the lessons' difficulty levels went from low, to mid, to high. The other two groups' lowest levels of D and NA behavior occurred when the instructional level being taught was the next step up in difficulty. Cantrell concluded that:

> "...[T]he finding that, in almost all cases, groups were not significantly more disruptive during that lesson which was immediately above their own appears to indicate that dealing with slightly difficult demands is indeed reinforcing.... [W]here two-step discrepancies existed in this study, however, as with the low group in the high lesson and the high group in the low lesson, relatively higher proportions of disruptive behavior occurred. This effect corroborates evidence that task failure and/or frustration is aversive" (pp. 36-37).

Optimal vs Problematic
Skill-Demand Discrepancies

This study's empirical results support the conclusion that maladaptive behaviors can be functionally related to skill/demand discrepancies (differences between a situation's expectations for behavior and the individual's skills in that arena of behavior). As skill/demand discrepancies grow larger, the reinforcing/punishing aspects of those gaps appear to reflect shifts in students' maladaptive social behaviors.

A significant aspect in the study of competence in children and youths is the limitation placed upon their options for handling situations where they are not competent because of their age. Adults in a stressful "demand greater than skill" situation have options generally not available to younger ones: (1) They can attempt to negotiate demands, making them more realistic. (2) They can seek out

Figure 1. Skill Below Demand

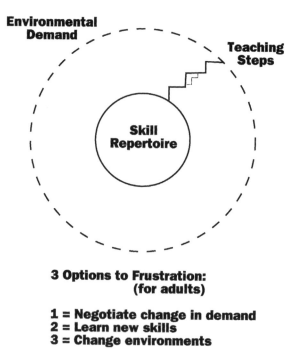

opportunities to increase their skills, or break down skill steps they find too large. (3) They can change settings, and therefore situations, if all else fails. None of these are normally available to children, who are dependent upon adults to construct these options for them. Figure 1 provides a symbolic representation of the dilemma and these options.

The relationships between student competencies and situational demands, with their potential for being either reinforcing or punishing depending upon the magnitude of the gap between skills and demands, have utilitarian, diagnostic value for professionals. These observations are useful during the professionals' initial assessments of troubled children's ecologies and in the day-to-day decisions that teacher-counselors face.

"...[I]ndividual or group increases in disruptive behavior should give rise to questions like the following: For whom is this task material too difficult or too easy? How could it be broken down into smaller steps or speeded up? How could prompts be added or removed? How could it be revised to allow for a higher degree of match with the diverse individual skill repertoires represented in this classroom? Further, how could scheduling of reinforcing consequences be arranged to optimize working rates for students where available materials are not ideally suited to their needs?" (Cantrell, 1974, pp. 39-40)

Skill Problem, Demand Problem, or Different Problem Altogether?

Skill/demand discrepant situations can appear in a wide range of guises. Interpersonal conflicts, such as control/counter-control cycles, or effects of trauma, serve as some examples, each involving complex learning from unique reinforcement and punishment histories. But competence is a lifelong pursuit, a continuous process - not a state of being, static or otherwise. "Is this person competent?" The answer is, "It depends" — on current skills facing the demands of the moment. Competence is more a process of becoming than of being, a state of doing and learning from a long succession of successes and failures.

Re-ED is concerned with the processes of competence attainment by children, teaching them effectance skills. Once a person has begun the life-learning process, there is often an increased willingness to engage the world, testing oneself against an ever-changing mosaic of situations that offer opportunities for using one's skills (at their current level of proficiency) in response to the demands (or enticements) of the situation, in hopes of enlarging one's effectance repertoire. In time, this pattern of engagement evolves into a personal style of approach to learning in many arenas, no longer an infrequent event. Competence as a reinforcing process for living an ever-expanding life, one day at a time, comes from grappling with "just manageable difficulties of your own choosing" (Hobbs, 1971).

At no point in this process is success from that point forward guaranteed (a state of "competence" attained), but each grappling with a challenge teaches both what works and what doesn't. It is said that Thomas Edison tried about 6000 substances while searching for a durable filament for his light bulb. Most substances failed. When asked why he continued in the face of such repeated disappointments, he replied something like, "These were not failures; I now know a lot of materials that don't work." Did Edison start his career with this persistent faith in his inventive genius, a generalized competence for invention? Likely not, but he had learned something invaluable from his first success: *how to persist* in pursuit of his next success, and the next and the next, each time pitting his slowly growing set of skills against sometimes unique, sometimes similar demands of each new unknown. With each new challenge, he could look back and say to himself, "I've solved problems like this before; I can solve this one as well" until his ability to persist in pursuit of answers became legendary.

That is the essential process of competence. Cumulative successes slowly overcome one's tendency to abandon the quest for task mastery prematurely. Successes become a larger part of life: "I can do it — like the other kids." "I believe I can solve this problem, and help this kid."

More difficult to detect, however, are the signs of a failed compe-tence history turned into *avoidance at all costs*, sometimes accom-panied by a performance that includes minor to major mayhem. "Who cares? What kind of a dumb question is that?" can start a reaction that escalates to a full blown crisis. To those with the knowledge and experience to see beyond surface behaviors, at least two options exist for coping with a child with a large pack of failures on his/her back, as suggested above by Cantrell (1974): reduce the difficulty level of the demand, teach the skills to meet the demand, or both. Once a child (or an adult) has developed a taste for being competent, it becomes "like eating peanuts - no one can eat just one."

If Re-ED's emphasis is on discord in the child's ecosystem rather than within the child, the beginning point of helping may be informal interviews with system members, assessing key competence discrepancies in the child's world - the child's, others', and our own as helpers. Once identified, changes become possible.

"Competence and anxiety stand in a reciprocal relation, and this gives the sense of competence special importance in development. At the root of anxiety is a feeling of helplessness" (White, 1959, p. 53). We are in the business of helping children and adults gain competence in a wide range of important arenas, helping them to feel and be less helpless in the face of life's difficulties.

References

Bricker, W. A. (March, 1967). Competence as a key factor in the study of children's deviant behavior. *Mind Over Matter.* Nashville, TN: Tennessee Department of Mental Health.

Cantrell, M. L. (1974). Maladaptive behavior as a function of skill/ demand discrepancies: An empirical investigation of the competence model. (Doctoral dissertation, George Peabody College for Teachers, 1974). *Dissertation Abstracts International, 35,* 7718-7719.

Cantrell, M. L., & Cantrell, R. P. (1995). Competence: Building it and building on it. *Reclaiming Children and Youth, Summer,* 20-24.

White, R. W. (1959). Motivation reconsidered: The concept of competence. *Psychological Reviews, 66,* 297-334.

Mary Lynn Cantrell, PhD, is currently Research Consultant to the Positive Education Program in Cleveland, OH. mlc8648@sbcglobal.net

Robert P. Cantrell, PhD, is currently Research Consultant to the Positive Education Program in Cleveland,OH. rcantrell8648@sbcglobal.net

18

A Parent Talks about Competence

I remember how overwhelmed and confused I felt. I had three little boys ranging from an infant to seven years old, a husband who worked seven days a week late into the night and unable to offer any emotional support. I felt pulled in so many different directions, unable to concentrate on any one thing long enough to complete it correctly. Every day I felt like I was frantically treading water, barely able to keep my head above it. The only way I knew to handle stress was by just skimming over things, and addressing what I thought to be the top priority for that day.

Before coming to PEP, I had been through two other programs with my son: one at a well-known university and the other at a major local hospital. Each program was very different, and tried to convince me that the way I was handling things before I came to them was ineffective (if not just plain wrong), and their way was going to work. Each professional believed that his or her way was the right way. I do believe in some absolutes in life, so it was very hard for me to know for sure that if I really followed through, any of it would work. Was what this person suggesting really the right choice? Was it worth the radical change and disruption it would cause in our lives? How could I choose which was right? After all, the different professionals couldn't even agree. I remember, I really wanted to be "the cooperative parent" so I always nodded my head in agreement to intervention suggestions, all the while thinking, dear Lord, how on earth am I ever going to be able to do that?

I felt like our family was this buoy bobbing around in the water, never being able to drop anchor to gain any kind of stability. One thing I did know for sure was everyday I tried my best to keep things running as smoothly as possible, with what little energy and resources I had. However, I'm sure this was not the perspective of anyone on the outside looking in, because I wasn't able to follow through on the things I had agreed upon.

When we first came to PEP, I thought this was just another program with all the "hot tips." These professionals seemed so efficient and organized. There was no way they could possibly understand what my chaotic world was like. It took time for me, but I finally was able to put my guard down, and realize I was very wrong. People actually truly cared, and listened. I felt like I was part of a bigger picture, one that was really going to work for my son and our family as a unit.

The turning point for me was when I saw small improvements in my son's behavior, and got help in my home with critical parenting skills to help me manage my two younger boys. Finally, some of those absolutes in life I mentioned earlier became more visible. I began to have more confidence in the professionals making the suggestions, as well as my ability to follow through with them. The progress came in very small baby steps, but even those small accomplishments encouraged me to stay the course. This is where I found time to truly be an ally. Re-ED and the caring dedicated staff at PEP became the anchor our family so desperately needed to finally stabilize the buoy.

Whoever said helping was easy?

The way we respond to another's behavior can be helpful or harmful. Some thoughts from an experienced, early liaison teacher-counselor can help us think about the consequences we employ with children – or with other adults.

"Nobody can change anyone else's behavior, but we can change our own behavior."
(p. iii)

"If we perceive ourselves as punishers, then that is what we will be and punishing is what we will do. It is critical not to administer consequences out of a punitive mind set. It teaches [others] to be angry. Rather, we are trying to help the child learn about strong character and good choices. If we know that our motive is to help..., if we respect and love the individual..., then we will know that we are using the consequence for them and can [respond] without hesitation. We can feel sad that they have chosen an inappropriate behavior and wish they had not done so." (p. 35)

"Another essential teaching for children is to see parents and teachers make mistakes, admit them, and make new choices. They will learn that they too can make mistakes, admit them, and choose differently in the future. Children will be more apt to choose appropriate behavior when allowed to learn from their mistakes and to see adults do the same." (p. 44)

— Jeanie Sloan Williams, MA,
Inseparable Partners: Behavior and Consequence

Part V

Valuing the Teaching and Counseling Roles

The heart of any helping program is in the people who interact directly with children and their families. Positive changes come from what happens in their interchanges. Learning results from the experiences where teacher-counselors create meaningful events, and troubled youth (and their families) encounter those events, successfully or otherwise. What happens before these events (planning and preparing for success) and what happens afterward (reviewing, and celebrating or rethinking) are extremely important to the quality of that learning. Helpers also learn from these experiences, of course.

Teacher-Counselor (or T-C) is the name traditionally given that role, but in today's Re-ED programs, T-Cs come with many different job titles. Funding often influences both role definitions and titles. But the functions of teacher-counselors are critical, and Re-ED programs work to maintain them. Most Re-ED sites are full of T-Cs, people in all kinds of roles, who connect with youth and care enough to invest in their growth. They may be secretaries, maintenance staff, or food service workers as well as supervisors and administrators. Young people respond to those who laugh and listen, and they are often good at distinguishing caring from manipulation. The formal T-C role, however, is a professional commitment with the preparation to make work with these youth a life choice. They value learning for themselves and others, and work to acquire teaching and helping skills -- regardless of their job title. They value choice for their charges, seeing constructive self direction as the end goal for each one.

Where discord has led a family or community to seek help for a child, it seems clear that the child's natural early teachers and counselors (adults in the ecosystem) need help. Re-ED concentrates the benefits of the teaching and counseling roles in an intense experience with professional Teacher-Counselors (T-Cs) who serve as *catalysts for positive change.*

The Teacher-Counselor Role

Creating environments for change is a tall order. Re-ED staff hope to create experiments in successful living for both the child and members of his world. T-Cs responsible for children are challenged to work together —

"...to design a daily program so engaging, so varied and new yet orderly and stable, so exuberant, so filled with mystery, exploration, and discovery, so physical, so meshed with the growth of the child's mind, so rich in human interchange, so responsive to mood, so tranquil and safe as occasion demands, so unconcerned with failure, so appreciative of individuality and of common purpose, so evocative of a sense of community, so finely modulated to the needs of a particular child and a particular moment, so joyous, so aware, so full of good talk, so fatiguing, so rewarding to children and teacher-counselors alike – in sum, so resonantly normal – that the disturbed child finds himself immediately committed to a new way of living at once more satisfying to himself and more satisfactory to the people in his life.... Such a day is by no means easy to make happen" (Hobbs, 1982, p. 89).

After twenty years of Re-ED program operation, Hobbs discussed what to look for in selecting staff who can plan and create such days. *"We would continue to stress commitment to children, beyond doubt; but we would be disposed to add such words as sensitive, resolute, creative or inventive, exuberant or zestful or quietly purposeful, serious and joyous altogether, inquisitive, enthusiastic, warm and affectionate, stern even, professional in the demanding sense of that word, playful perhaps, resourceful surely, responsible, and aware – aware of themselves, of their world, of children in all their marvelous simplicity and complexity"* (p. 98-99).

He added other considerations: physical stamina, patience, tolerance for sustained intimacy with other adults as well as children and adolescents, *"...a bit of the antic spirit, a gentle sense of the absurd in life, a real appreciation of fun"* (p. 99).

Hobbs acknowledged Re-ED's conceptual and scholarly debts "...for the theory and practice of reeducation to Robert Lafon, Henri Joubrel, and Robert Preaut of France, Catherine McCallum of Scotland, and Jeannine Guindon of Canada..." (1982, p. xxvii). The *educateur* filled a unique niche in the lives of Europe's post World War II troubled youth. They were both teachers and counselors, purveyors of hope and skill that inspired Project Re-ED's conceptualizers.

But the ecological model that U.S. teacher-counselors employ led them to recognize the teaching and counseling potential of ecosystem members. They recognized that teaching and counseling can be as simple as caring, listening, and investing oneself in children's growth – and at the same time, as complex as life and learning. They learned to ask other adults to invest more in the child, too. They saw that most of us respond positively when others deliberately assume that we want to increase our competencies and maximize our skills to accomplish goals that are important to us. This is especially true if those asking are sensitive to our current uncertainties, feeling overwhelmed or depleted or confused. Given small steps with likely success at each step, we find ourselves doing things we were not sure we could. When helpers *"act as if" the motivations of others are constructive*, the others' ability to act constructively grows. Holding these expectations for partnering with parents and home school teachers has paid off, confirming this belief over years of Re-ED service.

Programs: Constructions of Knowledge and Skills

Filling this critical function, regardless of which programmatic role a "teacher-counselor" fills, requires a complete set of necessary skills.

Using the building analogy employed in an earlier section to describe essential pieces of a functioning program, the T-C in any role needs:

A firm foundation of Re-ED *philosophy and values*, with grounding principles;

A ground floor consisting of the *ecological competence model*, and how to use it;

A second floor of workable *structures and strategies* which implement the model;

A third floor of *individual provisions* and adaptations, to fit each child and ecosystem;

And a protective roof with two heavy duty slopes that keep the building strong:

Teamwork and collaboration to assure mutual problem solving and action, and

Data-based decision making at both the child and the programmatic level.

Program planners address all of these components, both in their program operations and in their staff training.

"Natural Child Workers"?

Nick Hobbs referred to the "natural child worker" with great respect. He described individuals who by virtue of personal characteristics and experiences liked being with children, connected and interacted easily with them, and were willing to work on behalf of their optimal development. Over the years, professionals in Re-ED programs have discussed the relative contributions of natural characteristics vs training to effective T-Cs. Early on, selection of "naturals" was likely essential, since knowledge for training staff how to work with troubled and troubling youth was relatively sparse. The role of training became more important as strategies accumulated from Re-ED experience and the literature offered more useful information on how to help children with serious needs.

One study (reported in chapter 23) lent some interesting information related to this discussion. Empirical clustering of teacher groups based on their different patterns of *behavioral knowledge* and *attitudes toward teaching* produced interesting results. Two groups of High attitude teachers were found, one with High behavioral knowledge and the other with Low behavioral knowledge. Only one group of Low attitude teachers emerged, and they were also Low in behavioral knowledge. *There was no group of teachers High in knowledge who were also Low in positive attitude in the study sample.*

Personal characteristics that help staff make contact with and relate to children therapeutically, however, are still central considerations. Model T-Cs would seem to come from Re-ED programs which *select their candidates carefully*, *train them thoroughly* in the structures of programming and intervention, *provide supervision* from experienced staff who can serve as wise mentors, and *encourage their continual growth* and learning.

One area of constant learning for us all appears to be cultural responsiveness to the diverse histories and ethnic / social cultures of our students. Our charges continue to teach us, as one young woman from the inner city so succinctly taught the drama teacher who was expecting his young actors to demonstrate wide ranges of emotion: "This is the ghetto. We don't have emotions here." The unstated message was not lost on that teacher; emotions betray vulnerability that youths could not afford in their world (2006 PBS airings of *My Shakespeare: Romeo and Juliet with Baz Luhrman*).

Living the Teaching-Counseling Roles

Chapters in this section all deal with how agents helping a troubled ecosystem fulfill their teaching and counseling roles. Although all but one of these authors function in professional roles, they recognize that not all therapeutic agents are professionals. The content applies, perhaps with some adaptation, to those carrying out any of the teaching and counseling functions.

In chapter 19, Paul Filipek shares reflections on the cognitive views and motivations that sustained this highly valued Teacher-Counselor across 21 years of working and playing daily with troubled and troubling children and youth.

In the following chapter 20, Nicholas Long moves from being *in the role* to learning how to *grow in that role*. He points up the critical functions of mentoring for all of us as we work with troubled and troubling youth. You may recognize some of the missteps, and the learning that followed, as having counterparts in your own journey — whatever your role.

In chapter 21, Mark Freado and Gino DeSalvatore outline basic elements in operating a therapeutic program. They discuss use of these elements in planning or upgrading a program to provide Re-ED services, whether in community or residential settings. Re-ED services have always recognized the critical nature of connecting with youth and the difficulty of using social reinforcement in children's lives.

James Jones and Jeffrey Kepner, in chapter 22, provide a close look at how teacher attention affects the behaviors of students, constructively or otherwise. Years of observation and use of attention in classrooms have led them to some basic principles and practices which they share in their explicit training for teachers in the schools they serve. Their information has implications for staff and parents in other situations where adult attention affects behavior, with the added proviso that for seriously troubled children a higher praise to criticism ratio is often needed initially for change to occur. We don't want our own behavior to accidentally shape or maintain behavior in our children which is ultimately destructive for them (and for us as well).

Chapter 23 looks at Hobbs' hypothesized existence of "Natural Child Workers" in the ranks of professional educators. Robert Cantrell describes the design and results of an empirical study of this hypothesis in public schools. Teachers skilled in managing behavior also had positive attitudes toward students and teaching. By year's end their students with learning problems had significantly higher achievement scores, without hindering the achievement of high performing students in their same classrooms.

What motivates individuals to persevere in these difficult teaching and counseling roles? Angie's story in chapter 24 answers that question.

19

On Being a
Teacher-Counselor

Paul Filipek

There is a story told that when Michelangelo was asked how he was able to create his magnificent statue of David from the badly marred piece of marble that so many other sculptors had rejected, he replied, "I simply chipped away everything that was not David." In his humble view, Michelangelo recognized that a potential masterpiece was locked inside the marble; he just needed to use his skill to uncover it. I think this is similar to what a Teacher-Counselor (T-C) does. T-Cs help to uncover everything in a troubled and troubling child's behavior that is not part of the masterpiece that is the whole child, freeing the child to then begin successful movement towards his/her goals. If there were a thirteenth Re-ED principle I believe it might read, *Sometimes we must look beyond the facts to see the truth.* Just as there is something in the sculptor (part talent / part training) that enables him to look beyond the marble to see a masterpiece, there are qualities or perhaps values, shared by many, if not all, T-Cs that enable them to see the whole child amid the rough exterior of troubling behaviors. While the tools or skills of T-Cs are many, two of the most important are their powers of observation and description.

I believe that the most effective Teacher-Counselors are good observers who can communicate their findings in simple, clearly understood language. This is particularly crucial to the treatment process because our students are highly diverse individuals who come with a variety of troubles, but all appear to share in common some form of receptive and/or expressive language deficit or difficulty. The T-C serves initially as the narrator of her/his students' lives, providing an external voice which reports unmistakable observations of how a student behaves and what consequences result from that behavior. T-Cs describe actions and outcomes, both positive and negative, until students can do this for themselves. This approach generally begins supportively, with the T-C drawing the student's attention to something that he or she is doing well, regardless of how seemingly insignificant the action might appear. We strive to "catch" the child being appropriate or making a good choice. These observations are frequently delivered in the form of praise, and nearly always emphasize action and outcome.

T-Cs also observe and describe how a student appears to feel following a particular action. This feedback is a necessary precursor to the goal of helping the student learn that one's thoughts control the way one feels. This process is repeated over and over until a student has internalized the feeling-behavior connection well enough to begin using his or her own positive self-talk to change the way they are feeling. Over time, as students slowly learn through experience to trust the T-C, they begin to see themselves as more than just their referral behaviors. A student begins to look beyond his/her troubles to see themselves as a person deserving and capable of success and happiness.

Through verbalizing or reflecting observations, the Teacher-Counselors teach their students to become skilled observers of their own lives. Many of our clients are already somewhat skilled at observing others. Some are especially skilled at recognizing vulnerabilities in others that can be pushed, like buttons, to yield a desired and frequently negative reaction. Yet these same children are often poor observers of themselves in their social interactions. To them, life seems unpredictable, full of random and often unfair events over which they have little control. To counter these perceptions, treatment days are filled with rich experiences and skill building activities designed to increase the probabilities for their individual and group successes. The T-C stands ready and alert for opportunities to facilitate successes when needed and, perhaps more importantly, to act as a verbal historian lest a student's success be inaccurately self-attributed to luck or to the activity's just "being easy." T-Cs are always on the lookout for those priceless teachable moments which are like the tiny fissures in marble that, when struck precisely, will yield a desired form or outcome. When students can observe and describe for themselves what they do and what results, even in the most rudimentary terms, life is no longer something that just happens to them. They can begin to take some responsibility for their experiences and begin to choose what their lives will be. They are well launched on their journey toward becoming Re-EDucated. The masterpiece begins to more fully emerge.

Teacher-Counselors are a highly diverse and resilient lot. We wear a variety of hats because this "calling" is not so much tied specifically to a degree or particular educational background, as it is dependent on a commonly held philosophy founded on the principles of Re-ED. All who serve troubled and troubling children in a Re-ED program are considered to be Teacher-Counselors, custodian and coordinator alike. We communicate diversity and resilience by living and modeling them, and in so doing we help our students recognize and value their own diversity, and discover that they too are resilient. We meet problems with a positive attitude, whether the student's or our own, viewing difficulties as opportunities for new growth and success. We are teaching so much more than mere optimism or that every glass is "half full." We are teaching that sometimes the glass is "empty" and we may be thirsty for a time, but we will learn skills to survive.

A unique opportunity was presented to me a few years ago when my 21-year-old son worked as a T-C in a summer one-on-one aide position in the youngest classroom at my center. After one particularly trying day, he came home frustrated and exhausted, asking me, "Why would you ever want to do this for a living?" Remarkably, a few weeks later, he came home still exhausted but also excited as he announced that his little charge "...didn't spit on me or pee on himself! More importantly, he tied his shoes when I asked him to because he finally understood that he would then be able to go outside and play!" Then he added, "How could you not love a job like this?" Why would a T-C choose to do this hard and, at times, unrewarding work? Perhaps, like the sculptor who painstakingly labors over a badly marred piece of marble to carve a masterpiece, T-Cs are gifted with the ability to hold the vision of a masterpiece hidden within the marble (or troubles), and to communicate that image to students until each can hold the vision for themselves.

Paul Filipek, MEd, is Staff Development Associate on the training staff at Positive Education Program in Cleveland, Ohio.
Pfilipek@pepcleve.org

20

On Becoming a Teacher-Counselor

Keynote Address at the Seattle, Washington Conference of the American Re-Education Association

August 9, 2003

Nicholas J. Long

I am honored to be invited to speak at this National Re-Education Conference because I believe in the Re-ED philosophy. I love the Re-ED programs and I admire the dedication and the competency of the Re-ED staff. Now as many of you know, I'm at the end of my professional career, and many of you are at the beginning part of your professional career. My challenge is, what can I talk about that might have some meaning and relevance to beginning Re-ED staff. After much thought, I've decided to talk about the role that frustration and failure play in the development of your professional skills. This is an unusual topic, so I'm going to begin with a personal story.

About six months ago I received a telephone call from a graduate student in New England. She was taking a survey course in Emotional Disturbance. Each member of the class was assigned to select a leader, call that person, and then have a summary of what contributions that leader made to the field. I listened and I said, "This is very interesting. Tell me, how did you happen to select my name." She hesitated and then said, "Well actually, I was absent the day that they selected names, and the only two remaining names that were left were yours and Raymond Dembinski." I said, "Well, I've got to tell you something, I'm really pleased you selected my name because as you know, *"Everybody Loves Raymond."* She didn't laugh. So I sent her my vitae, and four weeks later she called and she said, "Dr. Long, you sure have had a lot of different experiences with disturbed kids." Then she asked, "Can you identify any one reason or characteristic that motivated you professionally?" I thought this was a good question. In fact I had never really thought about it, and as I did, I said, "Well first, I wanted to be professionally competent, but the skills of helping troubled children and youth were very difficult to learn. In addition, my impulsivity, my immaturity, and my naive understanding of the complexity of human behavior kept getting in my way. In fact, they continued to put me in harm's way, so the result was that I ended up in many student conflicts. I messed up; I made the situation worse, and by any standards at that time I would be labeled as a professional failure. The only reasons I survived in this field were due to my supervisors and mentors who continued to believe in me and to support me when I no longer believed in myself." She said she didn't understand this explanation. So I said, "Let me tell you about Fritz Redl."

Fritz Redl?

Fritz Redl once wrote (and he was correct when he said it), there is no such thing as the great psychiatrist, psychologist, social worker, teacher, or crisis person. Only ordinary human beings, ordinary men and women who decided to take on the struggle and are dedicated to reclaiming troubled children and youth — troubled children and youth who have been rejected, abused by their families, failed by their schools, alienated by society. What Redl implied is no one is born with the complex skills of being competent with emotionally disturbed students. These professional skills can only be learned slowly over time and in reality situations. These reality situations guarantee that young staff will have many opportunities to strike out professionally, to fail, and to feel inadequate during their early years.

The stresses that beginning staff face when they try to reclaim troubled children and youth are significantly different from those men and women face who choose occupations that are emotionally safe, predictable, and are not demanding. These occupations may not be rewarding or intellectually challenging, since the adults are able to master all the necessary job skills within three to six months. In addition, they don't have to face the fears of failure, nor do they generally have to deal with the underlying concerns of being criticized and rejected by their customers. This is certainly not true in our profession. In our profession, we cannot achieve professional competence by avoiding the psychological pains of failure. Instead we learn to recognize these feelings and to understand that these painful conditions are a way of facilitating new learning and insight.

Let me say it this way. It is impossible for you to learn the complex skills of helping troubled children and youth without feeling absolutely miserable at times. These feelings of misery exist in a psychological gap. They exist in the gap between our feeling of initial failure and our hope for subsequent success. This is the gap between what we wish to be and what we are at this moment in time. Initially, this gap includes all of our psychological feelings of humiliation, regrets, inadequacies and guilt. However, there is good news. If we give up blaming others for our misery, and we rid ourselves of self-deception, this gap actually becomes the essential link to acquiring new skills. For example, all of us, I'm sure, have experienced the pain of being rejected by someone we love. The feeling of rejection during this time is real and powerful — and often consuming. But what's fascinating is that simultaneously, as we deal with these feelings of rejection, there also opens up the possibility of new insights into our underlying personal issues around emotional dependency. This is particularly true if you hear yourself saying over and over again, "You know I can't live unless Mary continues to love me. My life has no meaning without Mary. I will never love anyone else as I love Mary." Now these irrational statements, if you have support, can also become the basis of really examining our personal emotional luggage we carry around with us all the time. Proust described this process when he wrote, "We don't learn anything of significance until we are in pain." We are in pain because something did not happen that we hoped would happen.

Why Suffer?

Descartes wrote, "I think; therefore I am." Proust wrote, "We suffer; therefore we think." Let me say it again: we suffer; therefore we think. I believe in this statement. I believe this is an important statement. We know happiness is good for the body, but suffering expands the mind. Let me give you an example. When my car is running smoothly, I am not motivated to understand the dynamics of the internal combustion engine. When my cholesterol number is low, I'm really not motivated to start counting fat calories. However, if I am told my number exceeds that for low risk, and I'm at risk of having a heart failure, then I'm highly motivated to learn new eating habits. It seems paradoxical that when our life is blissful and running smoothly, we're not motivated to search into the deeper meaning of life or relationships. In plain language, if it's fixed and running well, don't mess with it. But this leads us to two new concepts: *painless learning* and *painful learning*. Painless learning really occurs when we take graduate courses, read journals and books, and attend national conferences like this. This is simply called the acquisition of intellectual knowledge. Painful learning occurs when we are engaged in a conflict with a troubled student, face to face, and the emotions are heating up and we don't have the slightest idea about what to do next.

"Whose Knife?"

I had my first consultation with Dr. Fritz Redl, when I was 21 years old. I was a counselor in a camp for delinquent boys run by the University of Michigan. I found a knife in one of my campers' foot-lockers. So I approached Jerome and I said, "I found this knife in your footlocker. Tell me about it." He looked at me and said, "I have no idea how that knife got in my footlocker! In fact, that's not even my knife." He added, "I bet somebody put it in there to set me up so I would get into trouble." He said, "Who do you think it was?" Suddenly I had no idea what to say. I told Dr. Redl about this incident and I asked him how much of what Jerome told me should I believe. He smiled and he said, "Nicholas, believe only half of what he said," and I said, "Which half do I have to believe?" And he kind of looked at me like a real Guru and he said, "You'll know after you have had more experience with delinquent boys, and by that time you will have developed what we call clinical insight." So I left feeling really good. I had some new insights. I'm going to develop some clinical insights, and then I said to myself, "What is *clinical insight?* How do you get it? Who teaches it to you? And how long does it take?" Later I really understood that clinical insight couldn't be taught; we each have to discover it ourself.

Learning from troubled children is a personal journey no one else can take for you. It's something we have to do for ourselves.

The reason why these journeys are so difficult is because troubled students take beginning staff to new, dark, and strange emotional places they have never experienced or thought about. Troubled students expose them to intense feelings that staff have never felt before. And troubled students behave in ways in which they flood young staff with irrational behaviors that exceed the staff's level of tolerance and acceptance. When all of these forces impact on the management skill of the young staff, what are the chances that a beginning staff will manage a student conflict successfully?

I'm going to suggest several analogies. After I describe an analogy, I want you to shout out whether the winner will be a troubled student or staff. All right? Now here's analogy number one. If a troubled student and staff are playing chicken, and a staff is driving a Pinto, and the troubled student is driving a tank, which one will get run over? Number two. If a troubled student is a shark, and the staff is a life guard, tell me, which one will get bloodied? Number three. If a troubled student and staff are in a conflict situation and the troubled student has a stun gun, which one will get shocked? You're right, it will be the staff. Let's face it; the playing field between a beginning staff and a troubled student is not level. The troubled student has all the advantages and the beginning staff will have all the feelings of inadequacies.

Fortunately, these painful experiences are also the times that promote clinical insights. For a long time I didn't understand how clinical insights develop, but now I have figured it out. Clinical insight begins during that psychological gap between our initial failure and our subsequent success. It emerges slowly, first as a thought. Then the thought becomes a fragmented message. The message grows in intensity until it echoes in our head and we say to our self, "I messed up. I will never do that again! There's got to be a better way of understanding this student and managing this situation." This message of self awareness is critical, because once we say that, then we can move from the feeling of self blame into the possibility of learning from this conflict. When this happens, all of the feelings of inadequacy and guilt begin to lose their power to injure us psychologically. Now we feel more hopeful because this crisis became a source of new insight and competence.

Why So Slow?

Unfortunately, it is my painful duty to tell you there are no short cuts to this learning process. This process does not take weeks or months; it takes years. I believe it takes about ten years of failing and learning with troubled students before we really feel competent and comfortable helping them. You'll probably want to ask, "Why does it take that long?" Because after ten years of being with troubled students, interacting with them, living with them and feeling with them, we have visited most of their dark and strange places. They are no longer strange to us anymore. By this time we are comfortable and not overwhelmed by the intensities of their feelings. We know their feelings are intense, but they do not last long. By this time we also can manage a greater degree of students' deviancy and behaviors without becoming counter aggressive. And finally, by this time we have suffered successfully and developed the clinical insights to know which half of Jerome's story we should believe. Now, I want to share with you the many times in my early career that I messed up, and I said to myself, "Never do that again, Nicholas. There's got to be a better way of understanding and living with and managing these kids."

Too often, we believe the leaders or experts in our field are smarter than we are. They write textbooks, give invitational lectures, and appear to have an answer to most of the problems we have with our students.

The truth is most of our experts are not smarter, but just older. They have had more frontline experiences with troubled students. They have failed, suffered, and learned from their experiences. Let me validate this assumption by sharing with you some of my failed attempts of helping students in a crisis during my early years.

"How Do I Get Them to Bed?"

My first experience with children occurred when I was a senior at college. I was a math major. I accepted a camp counselor's job during the summer for regular pre-adolescent boys. I had eight 8-year old boys in my cabin for the four weeks. The only problem I had with this group was that I couldn't get them to settle down after washing up in the group bathroom prior to bedtime. They always returned in a hyperactive state led by two of the more aggressive boys. I decided that if I could get these two boys to come to the cabin first after the bathroom, I could manage them. Then, I was convinced the rest of them would fall in line. So, I had this great idea. It was really a bright idea. I was young and strong so I told the campers the first two kids who returned from the bathroom could punch me in the stomach. What? You heard it. The first two kids could punch me in the stomach. I felt this would appeal to the two aggressive kids who would be motivated to return quickly. The system was really quite simple: I would stand by the cabin door, the two boys would return from the bathroom. They would walk up to me and say, "Ready?" And I tighten my stomach muscles and say, "Ready," and they would punch me in the stomach. Then they would go into their cabin and I'd say, "Now you've got to settle down." Much to my surprise and satisfaction they did. Now the story becomes complicated. That very weekend, I had Saturday night off. My replacement counselor was sick and the camp director, Dr. Mace Matthews, decided to put my boys to bed. I always looked up to Dr. Matthews. He was a terrific therapist. He was standing by the cabin door and Jason runs up to him and says, "Are you ready?" And he says, "Ready for what?" Jason says, "Ready for this." Boom! And he punched Dr. Matthews in the stomach. When I got back the next morning there was a great buzz going on. My friends came up to me and said, "Ahhh! Nicholas, you are in deep trouble." But come to think of it, they didn't use the word trouble.

The next morning, Dr. Matthews called me into his office. I was feeling anxious and fearful of being confronted about my behavior. He asked me to sit down and quietly said, "I'm sure you heard about last night." I said, "Yes sir." "Now tell me Nicholas, what was going through your head, that you would allow your campers to hit you in the stomach?" Well, I explained that I had this bedtime problem and I was trying to solve it. He looked at me in a kind of puzzled way and said, "In other words this wasn't a macho act that illustrated you're immune to pain?" I said, "No, sir." He thought and said, "In other words, your behavior was trying to solve a bedtime problem?" I said, "Yes, sir." He said, "In other words, this technique you used was a failed attempt of a creative process." I said, "I never thought of it that way, sir." "Well," he said, "Listen. You had the right idea. You were trying to find a solution to manage these two aggressive boys. Unfortunately, you just had all the wrong behaviors." I was surprised and said, "What do you mean?" He said, "Did you learn anything from this experience?" I said, "Well, the first thing I learned is, I would tell my campers never to hit the director in the stomach." Dr. Matthews smiled and said, "Well, yeah, that's okay. But try to go a little deeper." I thought and said, "Well, it's the idea that you shouldn't hit any adult." He said, "That's right. But for a behavior management technique to be successful, it has to meet two criteria. The first criterion is it must be teachable and effective for all staff, and second, the management technique must protect kids from their own aggressive and sexual impulses." I left this meeting feeling relieved. My feelings of anxiety were gone. Afterwards my friends rushed up to me and said, "What happened? Did he fire you? Did he give you holy hell?" And I looked at them and said, "No, I learned that my failed attempt of problem solving was a byproduct of creativity." They laughed, but I remembered. Not only did I remember this conversation then, but I remembered it when Frank Fecser and I were taking Redl's LSI concepts and trying to translate them into specific skills. We decided to include this particular concept into what was called the New Tool Salesmanship Intervention. This is a reclaiming skill in which the adult identifies the student's positive intention or right idea, although he had the wrong behavior. It is a strategy which supports, rather than humiliates a student.

How Do You Get That Magic?

My second experience was in 1952. I had just finished my master's degree in child development at Michigan. It was summertime and I didn't have a job. As I was walking around campus, I looked at a bulletin board, and I saw this announcement:

Wanted: Camp Counselors! Eight Weeks, Six Free Graduate Credit Hours, Free Room and Board, while earning Six Hundred Dollars. I thought, "Wow, this is a miracle." This was the solution to my summer problem. I thought it was a perfect match. So I became a counselor at the Fresh Air Camp for delinquent boys. When I tried to relate to these kids, I was totally shocked. I was shocked by everything I saw, and everything they said. All of my previous graduate training had little or no impact on my ability to work with these campers. These boys would fight, yell, spit, taunt, and set each other up at the slightest provocation or disappointment. It was a totally new experience for me. It was at this camp that I was exposed to Redl's concept called *Life Space Interviewing.* I was in awe, absolutely in awe, of Bill Morse and Dave Wineman, who would talk with a camper who was in a rage. Often they would have to carry him up to the camp office, what we called the LSI room, and listen to this angry camper. At the end of the session this camper crisis would turn into a meaningful life experience for the camper and he would leave feeling OK. As a 22-year old graduate student, it looked like magic, and I thought Bill Morse and Dave Wineman were the magicians. You remember the slogan, "I want to be like Mike?" Well, I wanted to be like Bill Morse and Dave Wineman, but this seemed to be an impossible goal. How could I ever learn those skills? They didn't have any notes; they just related and they did it.

At the end of the camp, Bill Morse came up to me and said, "I just received a federal grant and I'm going to need a full time graduate assistant. Are you interested in a Ph.D. program and being my assistant?" I did not hesitate. I jumped at the offer without a blink. This decision changed my life.

During the first summer at camp, I learned some important concepts. I discovered most troubled students are motivated not to seek improvement, but to find ways of justifying their behavior. The next concept I learned is that a crisis wasn't a handicap. It wasn't something that you avoid, but a unique opportunity. This was a new and interesting idea. Also, I learned it is possible that during a crisis a camper will verbally abuse you, but by using certain skills this can become the most unique opportunity to enhance your relationship with him. What an idea!

The next year, I returned to Fresh Air Camp. I was knowledgeable about the program and I anticipated no surprises. In fact, I said to myself, I was going to be one of the best counselors at this camp. This time I had a group of eight 10 to 12 year old delinquent boys for four weeks. I decided to keep my group so programmed they would not have a minute to act out or get involved in negative activities. To prevent this, I came prepared with a variety of magic tricks, coin tricks, verbal games, and jokes. Every time I felt my group was being taunted or being set up by some other groups, I would restructure the situation and get them involved in these activities.

My weekly supervisor at the camp was Dr. Lee Salk, Jonas Salk's brother. Lee Salk was a famous clinical psychologist in New York City who had a weekly column on how to manage children. During my second session with Dr. Salk, he said to me, "Nicholas you look a little tight, how are you?" "Oh," I said, "I'm fine, no problem. I've got it under control."

You've got to realize all the campers were just running wild. It was a crazy, chaotic experience. By the third week, MY group was the only group out of ten cabins that did not have a major group crisis or blowup. Boy, I was pleased! I was doing well. During my supervision time, Dr. Salk said to me, "Nicholas, I need to tell you, you look extremely stressed and I'm concerned about you. Can you share with me what you're feeling?" I said, "No, I've got it under control – no problem," and I said to myself, "Only five more days! I'm going to make it!" Then everything fell apart.

It happened at dinnertime. Tyrone was bitching about having to clean up the table, even though it was his assigned time. He complained Jason made a deliberate mess in his area that he had to clean up, and he wasn't going to clean up Jason's g- d— table.

And I said to him, "Tyrone, this is your responsibility and you can stay here all evening until you clean it up. I'm taking the rest of the group back to the cabin because we're going to play softball, in ten minutes." So we left. I told the kids to walk back to the cabin. Then I ran around and peeked into the dining room window. I saw Tyrone cleaning up the table. I ran back to my cabin and said to the boys, "Let's wait a few minutes because Tyrone will be coming and we want to include him in the group." Tyrone came walking along the lane. When he was about 10 or 15 steps from the cabin, I jumped up and I walked over to him. I stuck out my hand and said, "Tyrone, I am really pleased that you are here and that you did the dishes." He gave me a sarcastic look and said, "I didn't do those f— — — dishes." I had a melt down! I grabbed him by the arm and turned him around, took two steps and realized his feet were not touching the ground. He smiled at me and said, "I did it. The dishes are done." The boys heard this. They realized I had lost control. They realized I had an impulse breakthrough. I can't describe the chaotic scene that followed. One boy turned around and punched another boy in the mouth; two boys ran down to the waterfront, swearing and screaming. Another boy climbed on top of the roof of the cabin with a loudspeaker, and he shouted, "Nick the volcano blew his top. Nick the volcano blew his top! Come see, come see." Within that moment, within that brief time span, I went from the best counselor to the worst counselor at camp. I felt humiliated; I felt I let everybody down, and I decided to quit and leave this camp. I couldn't take this anymore. It was too overwhelming, too painful. And then Bill Morse and David Wineman, rounded up the kids and they did their magic. Later, they rounded me up, and they put Humpty Dumpty back together again.

What did I learn? I learned something that has been with me all of my life. I learned that management begins with us and not our students. It begins with our ability to be in touch with our feelings and to know what's going on inside us. We must understand when we're stressed; understand when we're tense; understand when we have counter aggressive feelings that are real and powerful. We have to own them and to acknowledge them in order to be in control. We need to say *Yes* to acknowledge the existence of these feelings, and *No* to the expression of those feelings in behavior. This concept has been a theme during my professional career. Management begins with us, and techniques without self-understanding are meaningless.

"What Happened to the Keys?"

Two years later I finished my PhD, and I was considering a job at Ohio State University in Child Development. Dr. Morse called and said that the University of Michigan Medical Center had just built the first independent children's psychiatric hospital and wanted to create a therapeutic day program. He wanted to know if I would consider being the principal. I was surprised by the offer and said, "I haven't been trained to be a principal." He said, "No one has been trained to be a principal, but if you take it, we can use it as a field placement for my graduate students, and I would be willing to supervise you." I said, "In that case, I'll do it." I suddenly became principal of this school. We hired most of the staff from the Fresh Air Camp, so we had some camaraderie. We had some similar beliefs and values, and we started to train graduate students. It was an exciting and challenging time.

About six months later, one of the graduate students was substituting for one of our teachers. At the end of the day, she came to my office and said, "Nicholas, I've got a problem. I was about to dismiss the boys and I noticed my keys, that I'd put on the top of my desk, are missing. I asked the group and they said they knew nothing about it." I said to myself. "Principals have attributed authority. Students are more likely to do something if the source of power comes down to the classroom and asks them." I knew how to handle this situation. I went to the classroom and said, "Boys, I know you have a new teacher here and I'm sure it has been fun. You boys have been teasing her, but the keys are gone and she really needs them, so I would appreciate it if you could return them. This is what we're going to do. We're going to walk out the doors and get a drink of water. We're going to come back in five minutes and we're going to find the keys on the teacher's desk." We went out and came back — no keys. Then I moved to plan two. I said, "I have a better idea. This is what we are going to do; I'm going to give each boy in this class a 3 X 5 card. I have a slotted box here. I am sure it's very difficult for whoever took the keys to show them in front of his peers. So this time, all you've got to do is simply write where they are — like in the desk drawer, basket, bookcase. This way no one will know that you took the keys, and you won't have to face any peer rejection or concern. I'm going to give you ten minutes to do this." Then we walked out. We waited, we came back in. The box was sitting on the table. And the boys were smiling. I opened the box. The first slip I read said, "F— you, Long." I opened the second one; it said, "F— you, Long." I opened all of them. All of them said, "F— you, Long." This is when I learned for the first time the *Power of Group Negative Leadership.* I learned some behavior is not a function of individuals, but a function of the group dynamics.

The group members act like one personality and decide how to behave. This was a new idea at the time. It was one that bothered me because I said, "Teachers need to know what roles these kids are playing, independent of their personality." So over time a group of us studied this question and developed what we called the L-J Sociometric Technique for Classroom Students. It was a simple technique. You have the names of the students in your classroom on the blackboard, and you say, "I want you to write down the names of two students in this class you like the most, two kids in this class you like the least, and two kids in this class who can make other students fearful of them." These data are put into a matrix table, and four group roles can be identified in your classroom.

First is the *Significantly Preferred Student.* When you look at the data, this is the student who has significantly more positive choices than anyone else. If you have to appeal to the group for strength, you appeal to this student first because he is the key student who can influence the other members of the group.

The second one is the *Significantly Rejected Student.* This is a student nobody likes; most everyone says, "I can't stand that guy." This student tends to be the group's scapegoat, since he's not ignored, nor is he feared.

The third one is the *Significantly Ignored Student*. When you look at the data, no one likes him, no one rejects him, and no one fears him. Psychologically, he has no impact on what's going on in that group. He is the silent, withdrawn student.

The fourth one is the *Significantly Feared Student*. There are two variations of this role. One is the classic type in which this feared student is not rated as being liked or rejected. He's just feared. On the other hand, you have a different dynamic in the classroom where the most feared student is also the most preferred student. If this happens, he's the student who's going to say, "F— you, teacher," and the group is going to nod their heads and go along with it.

One of the limitations we have in this field is that we've not paid enough attention to the group dynamics. In a study many years ago in Washington, D.C., we had one classroom group that had an incredibly positive attitude. It was the kind of group where if the teacher was sick someone would say, "Let's write her a letter," and they would do it. It was just the perfect combination of peer interaction that was supportive to prosocial learning and acceptance. However, there are other classroom groups in which you have significant peer rejection. When you have two students in class who are significantly rejected, these students frequently reject each other. With this group dynamic, the teacher is going to have a difficult time managing the class.

Why Do We Do That?

The next year Dr. Redl called me. At this time, Dr. Redl was carrying out the first longitudinal study of hyperactive, aggressive, delinquent boys. He had selected eight of the most aggressive adolescent boys on the eastern seacoast. Each one of these boys had a different diagnosis, but they all had similar behavior. They were children who hated. The only time they would join forces and support each other was when they wanted to attack a staff. One evening Redl called me and said, "Nicholas, our director was attacked and now has a hernia. He has quit and I'm wondering if you would like to come to NIMH and be the Chief of our Children's Treatment Residence?" When Redl called, what is one going to do? I crossed myself and said, "Thank you Lord." I thought this was an opportunity not to miss. I also was smart enough and had enough experience to say, "Well, I'll do it under one condition — if I can bring my two colleagues: Vic Steoffler and Chic Young." He said, "Agreed." So, we went to NIMH. The three of us moved to Bethesda, MD. At this time, there were six of the adolescent boys in the program, and the place was out of control. We had to make immediate changes, and felt we had to model the values and skills we were trying to implement. Since the three of us were trained at Fresh Air Camp, we had common skills and beliefs. The boys were confused because they could not split the three of us. We were all doing the same things and they never knew if they were talking with Nick, Vic, or Chic. And after about two months, the boys began to settle down. But then something troubled me.

Practically every day a staff was involved in student "take down." There was some conflict that came up between the counselors and the boys that resulted in a physical restraint. I began to think, "This doesn't make sense. These are kind hearted, competent staff who chose to work with these troubled youth. These are not hostile, rejecting adults. I could understand this problem if untrained adults were working with these youth. They would end up fighting with them all the time. But why would staff who have the skills, who have the background, and who have the training end up continually restraining these youth." I said, "There had to be an intervening variable that's triggered this counter-aggressive reaction by staff." We talked about it, looked at other behavioral models, but nothing helped. After a lot of discussion, I came up with a concept called the *Vicious Cycle* which was the precursor to the Conflict Cycle. It was a precursor because every time anyone tries to solve a new psychological problem, the solution is so complicated it can only be understood by the originator. Over time, we began to make this concept more user friendly, and we ended up with the *Conflict Cycle Paradigm* which is easier to understand and teach. Later we added the cognitive process to the *Conflict Cycle*. The sequence was: A stressful incident occurs, and creates an irrational belief. The message of the irrational belief is: "This should not happen — this is terrible!" The irrational belief triggers feelings. The feelings drive the behavior, the behavior incites others, and then others escalate it which creates more stress. This cycle goes around and around until the student behavior gets crazy. As we studied this process we had this insight: If staff follow their feelings and do what is natural or normal with troubled students, the conflict is going to get worse. We discovered a student in stress will create in the adult his feelings, and if the adult is not trained, that adult is going to mirror the student's behavior. So student aggression gets what? It gets adult counter aggression. Student depression gets adult counter depression; student ambivalence gets adult counter ambivalence, and that's the way it goes.

What is fascinating is that for years we have talked about how teacher behavior or adult behavior affects children. In the Conflict Cycle Paradigm, we're talking about how student behavior influences and determines teacher behavior. If a teacher does what seems logical during a crisis, the teacher is going to escalate the conflict cycle. But on the other hand, if a teacher is aware that the student's goal is to get her to act out (and fulfill his prophecy), then the teacher will have new choices. The teacher understands that the troubled student is behaving like a Director of a play, who is using his skill to cast the adult into a role with specific behaviors which are different from his personality. For example, you're a tolerant person, but if I'm an aggressive student, I'm going to cast you into the role of a mean son-of-a-b----. I'm going to work on you until I make you lose control and scream at me. When this happens, I have fulfilled my prophecy that all adults are mean and aggressive. The Conflict Cycle model became essential in helping us to understand this dynamic relationship.

"Where Are the Fire Extinguishers?"

Another stressful incident occurred at the NIMH treatment center. When I arrived for the four o'clock shift I was told the fire extinguishers were missing. I called the boys together and I said, "This is a serious issue, because we're in violation of the law, and we've got to find the fire extinguishers. I'm asking you all to look around the house and outdoors." Well, for 20 minutes the boys looked around and did not find them. Then I said, "Okay, now we have to do it one more time, but we've got to get more creative because they have to be here." Norman, one of the troubled students, said, "Long, can I go with you?" I said, "Sure." So we went upstairs. We looked under the beds. We looked in the closets. We looked in the bathrooms. We looked behind the shower curtains, and we couldn't find them. By this time I was getting frustrated. I made what is called the inductive leap to a conclusion. I said, "Norm, just stop and let me say something to you. I think the reason why you decided to come with me is that it's really hard for you to tell me where the fire extinguishers are. This is your way of telling me." He said, "What do you mean? Are you accusing me? Do you think I took the fire extinguishers? Do you think that I am lying to you?" He got more and more excited until he blew up and tried to hit me. We had to restrain him which took about a half hour. Then we went to the bathroom and washed up. Simultaneously, the dinner bell rang. As we were walking down the stairs, I noticed John, looking like that Cheshire cat. He was leaning against the wall, enjoying the scene. When I came down, he said, "Whew, Long, sounds like you had a lot of trouble with Norm up there." I said, "Well, we had an incident, but we resolved it and things are cool." And he said, "O-oh." Just then Norman came walking down the stairs and John smiled and asked him, "Hey, Norm, do you like Long?" Norman said, "I HATE that son-of-a-b----." Suddenly the whole incident was reactivated and we had to restrain Norm one more time. And after this stressful incident, I thought, "What happened? How could John start a fight without ever throwing a punch? John was successful because he knew the right words, at the right time to fuel Norm's aggressive impulses, causing him to blow up." As we developed our concept of Manipulations of Body Boundaries in LSCI, we defined this pattern as one of our six diagnostic patterns. This pattern is about false friendship, about how peers exploit others for their own pleasure. This concept has been one of our most teachable and effective reclaiming interventions.

How Do We Teach – and Learn?

Now the last incident that I would like to share with you happened in 1968. I was returning from Chicago to Washington, D.C. My wife and I were on a flight, sitting about two seats behind a mother and a four-year old boy. The four-year old boy was acting up. He was standing up, turning around, making faces, making demands, and the mother was absolutely doing everything wrong. She had no idea of the difference between reinforcing good behavior and bribing kids. She was constantly bribing him around his inappropriate behavior, and the kid was not responding. I remember saying to my wife, "Jody, if I could have one hour with that woman I could teach her two or three techniques which would make her life better with her son." We deplaned and were walking down the corridor when I left to go to the restroom. Jody was hanging back, and as this woman walked by she stopped, turned to her son, and said, "See that man going into the bathroom? He was my college professor, and he taught me everything I know about children."

After that comment, I decided to distinguish the difference between intellectual knowledge and behavioral skills. Those of you who have completed our LSCI certification course, you know we have built our training around 26 competencies you have to learn. There are three parts to each competence. The first is: Do you understand it intellectually? I'm sure this woman could talk about behavior management. The second question is, can you demonstrate it? Can you use the competency effectively? Clearly she could not use her intellectual knowledge. Finally, can you internalize the skill, make it a part of your life, and teach it?

How Do We Get There?

Let me summarize. Redl was right when he said there are no great teachers, psychologists, social workers, staff — only ordinary men and women who dedicate themselves to reclaiming troubled children and youth. For beginning staff, the road to developing professional skills is difficult. It is filled with multiple kinds of psychological mine fields. As a result, when you get knocked down, beat up, and run over — you have to remember that failure is not about your personality. Failure is about learning. It's about being able to have the right skill, at the right time, with the right student. And it is something you can learn either painlessly or painfully. However, when you turn your failure into a learning opportunity, it does lead to advanced insights — what we call *clinical insight*.

Let me talk with the supervisors and the mentors in this group. You realize beginning staff are going to foul up. They're going to mess up. You need to be as supportive and as compassionate towards them as you are with troubled students. I have found you have great tolerance towards kids. You can tolerate inappropriate behavior while looking for student strengths. But when it comes to beginning staff, the feedback sounds like this: "You're an adult, you should know better. Why in the h— did you behave that way?"

We have to be able to support and to care for beginning staff when they no longer want to support themselves. I'm going to leave you with this one thought. Sometimes you're going to see a beginning staff who has failed and then you're going to say to him, "You know, your technique was a failed attempt of a creative solution." You had the right idea but the wrong skill. Let me show you another way of responding in the crisis!

Nicholas J. Long, PhD, is an esteemed pioneer and continuing contributor to the field of education and treatment for troubled and troubling children and youth. His contributions have spanned the decades in which this service area became a recognizable field, in roles that include direct service to children and youth, supervision and administration, university teaching, and authorship. His writings include the multiple editions of the text series "Conflict in the Classroom" (originally written with William C. Morse and Ruth Newman), "Life Space Crisis Intervention" (with Mary M. Wood and later Frank A. Fecser), the LSCI training materials (with Frank A. Fecser), "The Angry Smile: Managing Passive Aggressive Behavior" (with Jody E. Long), and numerous others. He is the founding director of the Life Space Crisis Intervention Institute which certifies LSCI trainers who teach the program to practitioners from around the world. He co-founded and co-edited the Journal of Emotional and Behavioral Problems (now Reclaiming Youth: the Journal of Strength-Based Interventions) with Larry Brendtro. Dr. Long was given the American Re-Education Association's Lifetime Award in 1989. He remains a valued friend and consultant to practitioners in schools and service programs around the world.
njllsci@aol.com

21

Creating or Fine Tuning a Re-ED Focused Program

Mark D. Freado & Gino DeSalvatore

Contemporary child and adolescent mental health approaches contain a number of service delivery models, ranging from community-based family services to in-patient psychiatric hospitalization. Each service delivery type contains characteristic precepts about how the service is rendered. Individual programs, however, vary in their missions, goals, and philosophies that guide delivery of what they believe youth need to help them succeed in their immediate settings and beyond. Many programs specify their philosophical foundations and then develop, implement, and evaluate the treatment structures they believe will help youth and their families become self-sufficient. Re-ED programs employ an ecological model and operate in support of the child's ecology; they are values-based and principles-driven.

This chapter provides a philosophical and operational framework that can be used to create or refine a Re-Education based program. Re-ED principles can be implemented for any type of service delivery model, including residential care, day treatment, alternative school programs, or school-based services. The framework provided here for *becoming* a Re-Education based program can be used to *modify* an existing program that is exploring new ways to grow, or to *design* and plan a new program.

Programming for Troubled and Troubling Youth

The overall goal of any organization that works with troubled and troubling youth is to help these young people become more independent, solve problems in a safer and more socially acceptable manner, and integrate successfully within the daily life of their community. How providers across the theoretical spectrum accomplish this end varies from program to program, although on analysis, there are themes, components, and areas common to each of them. Successful Re-Education programs have built on the contributions of pioneers in our field, borrowing and incorporating concepts and strategies from a number of theories to aid their programming. Brief mention of some of these contributors can help an interested reader put Re-ED in a historical context and perhaps assist in constructing a program.

Early Contributors to the Field

As an early pioneer, August Aichorn (1925) contributed much to work with youth problems. His thoughts on "companions with whom a child lives" (p. 113), on the child's environment, and more specifically on striving to make the worlds of disturbed youth as natural as possible while decreasing conflict in their environments were innovative in their day and added to our understanding of work with troubled children.

Organizations can profit from an understanding of therapeutic milieu and those who contributed to the development of milieu intervention. A therapeutic milieu contains the structures necessary to create order, help establish boundaries, and provide a format for treatment. Translated, the word "milieu" means nothing more than "environment." Simply put, a therapeutic milieu is an environment which contains elements that are therapeutic in nature and are used to help youth change maladaptive patterns of behavior. While this may sound simple, putting the theory into practice is difficult. Professionals who contributed to the development and refinement of the use of therapeutic milieu include Aichorn (1925), Redl and Wineman (1957), Trieschman, Whittaker, and Brendtro (1969), and Cotton (1993). After the mental health devastations of World War II, other professionals in Europe followed similar lines of environmental endeavors (Hobbs, 1982, pp. 83-85).

Therapeutic Management

The therapeutic milieu is not something quickly put together or developed. Therapeutic management, and its place in the process of socialization, must be carefully planned if our work is to be therapeutic rather than custodial in nature. According to Cotton (1993),

"...therapeutic management is to the care of emotionally disturbed children what normal socialization is to childrearing....Therapeutic management consists of adult-child interactions and interventions that take place in the children's living situation that are designed to protect, engage, and teach children. The goal of therapeutic management is to heal suffering, contain and modify maladaptive behavior, promote development of greater competence and build a stronger and more valued sense of self for emotionally troubled children [and youth]" (Cotton, 1993, p. 6).

Therapeutic management is not a specific therapy itself; rather, it incorporates and weaves many therapies and interventions into the fabric of daily living (Cotton, 1993). Cognitive-behavior therapy, family systems work, psychopharmacology, and insights from child and adolescent development can all be part of the milieu, providing what children need. Corrective opportunities and events added within the milieu can help emotionally disturbed youth get "back on the track of positive development."

Therapeutic management relies on the abilities of staff to relate and interact directly with the youth; however, the interaction is a two-way street. The youth, the family, and/or other members of the ecology must also be active participants in this process. Many youth referred to Re-ED programs have discords in their interpersonal lives leading to high levels of distrust for the adult world. The qualities of their interactions often determine how easily trusting and teaching processes will be learned. Many youth have been labeled as "relationship resistant" (Trieschman, Whittaker, & Brendtro, 1969, p. 52). Viewed from within this conceptual framework, such youth avoid forming relationships with an adult initially. Establishing relationships with them requires patience, careful communication, and creativity in dealing with both their reluctances to respond to social reinforcements and their out-and-out rejections of the adult world (Trieschman, Whittaker, and Brendtro, 1969).

Hobbs and Re-Education

Nicholas Hobbs (1966; 1982) focused on the individual ecosystems defining each child's world. He added new emphasis on families and communities, demonstrating their importance in identifying (and remediating) the discords in the child's world which caused them to be viewed as "troubled or troubling." While testing the development of ecological intervention in residential schools, he made a commitment to short term treatment (4 to 6 months), returning children to their homes on weekends where they could work with their families on goals aiming toward their early return. He urged using the language of childhood rather than pathology in our work with youth, calling them "students," rather than clients or patients or residents. He advocated the use of Re-ED principles in the operation of many services working with youth, both intensively and preventively, in settings like schools and community centers. He envisioned the Teacher-Counselor role, teachers who were also counselors, listening, helping problem solve, modeling a different way -- in short, staff who connected with their kids and planned days of positive learning.

Any program that proclaims itself a "Re-Education program" should be familiar with the teachings and writings of Nicholas Hobbs (1982). Hobbs articulated the 12 principles developed in Re-ED, explained the "ecological model," and expressed thoughts on such issues as health, interdependence, competence, and reducing discord within the ecology. He imbued Re-ED with a focus on wellness and strength, teaching rather than punishment, and learning rather than compliance.

Basic Components in Successful Programs

Six basic components are essential to a Re-Education program's functioning, including: (a) safety, (b) staff skill support, (c) structure and organization, (d) youth involvement, (e) validation of individual worth, and (f) program evaluation. The order by which the essentials are addressed and developed is important, as each builds on the previous component.

Component 1: Safety

Of all the elements crucial for any successful program, safety is paramount. This component refers to the ability of the program to address behaviors that originally led to the youth's being identified as troubled or troubling. A program cannot be successful if a child or youth believes that their aberrant behavior can "destroy" its purpose. At the same time, a program cannot be successful if the setting's culture is laden with practices that are physically or psychologically damaging. Regardless of the "acting out" reasons for which they were sent to us, these youth were victims as well. As a result, many have learned to be survivors, developing strategies they believe can protect them from being hurt, but which may actually be hindering their ability to learn and develop. Youth cannot channel their emotional and psychological energies into doing what it takes to improve, engaging in their own positive growth, if they are anxious about their well-being and safety.

In either the initial development or the re-tooling of a program, the following elements should be contemplated, addressed, implemented, and continually evaluated in order to maintain safety. The goal is to increase each youth's use of safe and healthy behavioral choices to satisfy their needs, without relying on acting out to get what they want. Safety standards require we do the following:

Assure physical safety in the setting and provide for management of dangerous behavior. Employ standard protocols for prevention and management of unsafe behaviors; these would address situations such as suicide precautions, destruction of property, aggressive acting out, and running away behavior. Many behavioral crises can be avoided by involving youth in decision making about their physical environments. Involvement helps invest them in both the culture of the program and its physical surroundings. It is not enough to effectively supervise students; we must also give them strong reasons to stay, and every positive experience contributes to these reasons.

Ensure psychological safety by: (a) Conducting appropriate background checks on employees; (b) Training and supervising staff, preparing them to intervene with youth in a respectful and professional manner; (c) Responding to any staff member's less than optimal conduct with a youth in a timely and decisive manner; (d) Creating and maintaining standards for student - student interaction by modeling and teaching values and respect in all our interactions; (e) Providing opportunities to practice what is taught and learned; (f) Using teaching interventions and taking advantage of teaching moments when they arise; and (g) Adapting our supervision of our youth as their needs and behaviors indicate the need for changes in surveillance.

Our responsibility to provide for the safety of the youth we serve, can sometimes mean that youth are physically controlled by staff, using state approved and, often, internationally recognized methods. Staff members are trained by certified instructors in carefully selected, competency-based methods, instead of using medical or mechanical restraints. Re-ED programs are not pro-restraint; they are pro-safety. They take very seriously the training and supervision of staff to use flexible and creative arrays of verbal and non-verbal interventions when youth are experiencing crisis situations. Physical restraint is truly a last resort, used in a manner to ensure safety of both youth and staff.

Constant maintenance of order and control is highly over-rated. In programs serving troubled and troubling youth, there has to be room for the expectation that kids will act out, and that the program will allow them ways to express what is troubling them while ensuring their safety. Otherwise, too much containment can suppress the creativity, staff initiative, and "thinking outside the box" often necessary for success. Over-containment can create and reinforce a sense of isolation in both adults and youth that hinders connections and growth. Only vigilance and ongoing discussions within treatment teams can help staff avoid this pitfall.

Component 2: Staff Skill Supports

Hobbs (1966) said about the teacher-counselor:

"But most of all, a teacher-counselor is a decent adult; educated, well-trained; able to give and receive affection, to live relaxed, and to be firm; a person with private resources for the nourishment and refreshment of his own life; not an itinerant worker, but a professional through and through; a person with a sense of

significance of time, of the usefulness of today and the promise of tomorrow; a person of hope, quiet confidence, and joy; one who has committed himself to children and to the proposition that children who are disturbed can be helped by the process of Re-Education" (pp. 1106-1107).

Hobbs (1982) emphasized the importance of selecting the right staff for positions in our programs. Hiring child workers who seem to be "naturals" with children makes programs more effective than can training processes alone. Selecting teacher-counselors with certain innate abilities for creating and sustaining meaningful relationships with students sets the stage for their sharing their knowledge and creativity with others, reinforcing in one another the resilience to restore their focus and energy regularly. As they become more effective, the teacher-counselors regularly contribute to the on-going development of the training program.

Preparing Staff. Bob Slagle, an original Re-ED teacher-counselor and a mentor to many subsequent teacher-counselors, often speaks of "starting from a point of order." Applied to the preparation of new teacher-counselor staff, "starting from a point of order" means having pre-service training in place that helps them know what to do before they are "alone with kids." Aside from organizational orientation and personnel issues, pre-service training provides a foundation for understanding the philosophy and principles of Re-ED, introduces staff to the mission, purpose, and values of the program in which they will be working.

Initial interactions between teacher-counselors and their students must start from a point of basic staff competencies. Some programs maintain a pre-service training program for new teacher-counselors prior to their assuming direct care responsibilities; others prefer to provide this as part of an on-the-job training process. Whether the pre-service training occurs as a separate component or in the context of on-the-job training, specific elements should include the following.

Values and Principles
    1.   Organization's mission and values
    2.   Re-ED philosophy overview and Re-ED principles

Orientation to Youth and Families
1. Nature of youth and referral sources
2. Understanding the needs and interests of the youth and families served
3. Expectations for developing relationships with youth and families (professional demeanor and responsible behaviors)

The Therapeutic Process
1. Assessment, planning, implementation, and evaluation
2. Student and family involvement in the process

Foundational Skills Training
1. Connecting skills
2. Competence building skills
3. Understanding the Conflict Cycle of Life Space Crisis Intervention (Long, Fecser, & Wood, 2001)
4. De-escalation skills
5. Effective listening and communication skills
6. Opportunities to practice skills (video models, role play, feedback, supervision)

Counter Aggression
1. Understanding aggression (origins, functions, and forms)
2. Our own buttons (staff triggers and reactions, how to objectify our responses)
3. Skills to minimize and avoid power struggles

Building Team Strength. New staff also need the opportunity and means to become part of a strong, supportive professional community to become part of a team. Supervisors, and to some extent administrators, must perceive new staff as part of the team, rather than as individuals apart from the team. The goal is to establish a culture where crisis is seen as opportunity and is used to help both staff members and youth grow. Accomplishing this may involve the entire professional community, both those directly responsible for the program as well as those whose function is to support the program. When staff members are perplexed by the problems of a youth, or challenged by the youth's behaviors, they should be expected to both seek and support help and guidance from their extended team.

Relating to Youth. Identifying student needs, and providing them with support before a crisis occurs, reduces the need for extreme crisis intervention. There is a delicate balance here, however. Prevention is not always desirable; if we "control" an environment too effectively, students do not have a chance to learn and practice the skills necessary for success in other environments. It is not enough to teach them to "be good" where we have them; we are also responsible for teaching them to do well wherever they are. An understanding of normal child and adolescent development helps staff members see troubling behavior in perspective, relative to their agemates.

Relationship building requires reinforcing when things go well, teaching what is needed, and supporting youth throughout their experiences in the program. Staff are expected to have purposeful, meaningful, personal, and professional connections with youth. Sam, a 16 year old female, explained it this way at the girls group home in Clarksville, Tennessee:

"The first day I got here I made my mind up these people can't help me, they can't do anything for me and they certainly can't change me. Boy, was I wrong. I spent a little time with them and after awhile, they grew on me. Then I realized they were proving me wrong. I wasn't around people who were here only for the money; these people really do care! For some of us, they were all we had. The people here gave me more than anyone could imagine. These people adjust their time and lives to help us and don't get anything but more stress. They have given me a chance to accept me for me. To them I owe my debt of gratitude. When I first got here, I'm surprised the staff didn't quit; that's how bad I really was. They taught me how to follow rules even though I might not like them. They helped me see that I am not perfect; at least I can say I am trying my best."

Loughmiller (1965) spoke of the relationship between a staff member and child:

"This simple development of faith in a boy is one of the greatest achievements a counselor attains in his work. It makes all the difference in the world whether he sees a boy as a hell-raiser who is trying to disrupt everything the group undertakes, or whether he sees him as a frustrated, insecure boy who is trying with all his might to find a satisfactory way of living with others. As this faith develops and becomes an entrenched habit with a

counselor, his job becomes easier and his work becomes more effective" (p. 11).

The following elements help prepare staff to build positive relationships with youth:

Developing one's personal qualities. This means allowing the best of me (e.g., interests, talents, skills in music, photography, writing, camping, etc.) to be part of who I become as a teacher-counselor.

Teaching staff to establish and maintain a balance between teaching, counseling and limit setting, based on the needs of the children and youth we serve.

Providing skill-based interventions to use in tough situations, such as Life Space Crisis Intervention (Long, Fecser, & Wood, 1991), Response Ability Pathways (Brendtro & duToit, 2005), Aggression Replacement Training (Goldstein & Glick, 1987), curricula for social skills and anger management, and other counseling skills.

Taking initiative to connect with and get to know youth as individuals, begin to build rapport and plant the seeds of trust, and create opportunities for belonging.

"Hanging in" with youth through their problem behaviors, without giving up on them, building trust in the fact that your caring is not just short term.

Establishing and maintaining program limits for consequences of extreme behavior, without ejecting a youth from the program, whether residential, day/educational, or family-based.

Providing a process for transition that maximizes a youth's chances for successful transition within her or his ecology.

Making program values explicit and shared so that what we do reflects what we believe.

Component 3: Organization and Structure

Structure and organization in Re-ED programs are used to adapt services to meet the ecological needs of our youth. These services can be delivered through a variety of program approaches, with each one's operational forms defining the ways in which staff and youth (and their families) participate, interact, and address the issues facing them. Types of program structure can range from secure and restrictive to guidance and teaching. They can be intensive, 24 hour a day residential programs, school support or stand alone special alternative school settings, therapeutic foster care and family based services, or others developed by creative Re-ED organizations. Structures define the "laboratory" in which youth live and/or work, where they perform the "experiments" necessary for growth. Without the structures which define and clarify, staff members must spend a great deal of time and energy reacting to or controlling problems, overusing safety components. In essence, if more time is required to maintain safety, less time is available to seek growth.

In a principles-driven system, structure and organization should be flexible, allowing programs the freedom to develop unique treatment components or provisions that enhance opportunities for youth to change. Structure and organization are dynamic processes that must be constantly evaluated, and changed if needed to accommodate the strengths, degree of problems, and changing needs of individual youth and their families. Highly rigid and dogmatic approaches can stifle creativity and hinder adaptations based on needs, or on differences in the level of experience and skill of staff.

One way to evaluate organization and structural needs is through a "program development meeting." This meeting brings professionals and youth together to discuss issues that deal with structural elements; it helps match programmatic needs of youth with skill and expertise levels of the human resources available. Changes in organization and structure occur through consensus within the meeting.

In a Re-ED program, structure and organization are designed to: (a) focus on strengths; (b) emphasize learning; (c) promote changes in children and youth, rather than control them; (d) address symptoms and needs; (e) replace maladaptive patterns of behavior by teaching more successful living skills; (f) assist youth to consider consequences of actions, and help them learn control of impulses through analysis of choices; (g) allow for creativity and adaptation of the program to meet all needs;

(h) identify, support, and develop each child's strengths, skills, and competencies; (i) provide an atmosphere of openness to new or different interventions that are philosophically consistent; (j) develop rituals and ceremonies to handle problems, celebrate successes, and provide predictable structures for both staff members and youth.

For example, Ritual and Ceremony can be used as a structure to promote youth investment. Each Friday afternoon at Wallace Academy in Nashville, Tennessee, the school schedules a "Circle Ceremony" in the cafeteria. The ceremony celebrates the students' successes throughout the week in each class, gives praise and recognition to group accomplishments, and honors staff members who have gone above and beyond the call of duty that week. Over time, youth (and staff members) come to value these regular Friday events.

Component 4: Youth Participation and Involvement

We involve youth in our programs in a variety of ways that are consistent with the following two beliefs. First, experiential learning is accomplished by what we *do with* youth in our care, rather than what we *do to* them. Second, the basis for services in Re-ED programs derives from the individual needs and interests of each youth and his/her family. Programs vary in opportunities for involvement with peer groups or family members. Some programs emphasize group process in one continuing group; some operate in individualized ways with youth participating in specific groups; others involve trained staff working in the home of the family; and some incorporate some or all of these elements and more, as part of an intensive ecological program.

All Re-ED programs stress the importance of building relationships as the cornerstones for change. Daily activities are critical vehicles used to promote growth, and energy is placed into proactive planning for each day.

Behavior management systems for teaching and feedback. Almost all programs have some form of behavior management system in place to energize and evaluate each youth's progress toward agreed upon goals. A behavior management system may be largely social or based on daily or weekly accumulations of points of some kind, for some tangible reward, activities, or privileges. These systems may also include levels through which youth move up or down, depending on their behaviors. Some programs avoid points and levels systems and evaluate progress through observation, documentation, and ongoing discussion between the youth and those providing treatment and support. Whatever the approach, we believe it is important to note that the behavior management system as typically implemented, should not be viewed or promoted as the total program, but only as one tool.

Behavior management systems provide primary feedback, important for investing youth in their own positive changes. Information from behavior management systems generally tells us two things: (a) how each youth is doing within the behavior management system; and (b) how the program or system needs changing, based on how all youth are working overall.

In May, 1971 Nicholas Hobbs delivered a commencement address entitled, *The Art of Getting into Trouble* to the graduates of the Peabody Demonstration School. In this essay he shared his thoughts about personal growth through accepting "just manageable" challenges and difficulties "of our own choosing." If we ask more of kids than they can reasonably achieve based on their abilities, we set them up to fail. If challenges are too easy, nothing is learned, no growth is achieved, and there is no joy in accomplishment. Growth occurs between these two extremes, where demands are challenging, but possible.

Principles-driven organizations (like Re-ED programs) pay attention to what data tell us about our own effectiveness, and respond by adapting the program's approach to better meet the needs of the youth. Program adaptations include lowering initial expectations to allow the youth to experience some success, then gradually raising them as the youth's competence increases. Another adaptation ensures that where the system demands certain performances (such as speaking to each other respectfully), those behaviors are being modeled and explicitly taught by teacher-counselors as they work with youth. Once taught, opportunities are devised that place youth in positions that cue positive practice of those skills in a variety of situations, thus encouraging healthy development to proceed and generalize. Behavioral systems must include skill building experiences to teach the expected behaviors and produce successful outcomes.

Behavioral systems that plan for behavioral fluctuations. Where behavioral systems are used, it is worth considering a level system whereby youth earn levels that cannot be lost. Instead of moving up and down levels on a daily or weekly basis, youth learn a series of skills to meet clear criteria for a given competence level. Once that level has been attained through teaching, practice, and review, the youth and staff know those competencies are present and the level of achievement can be awarded.

Students may not consistently demonstrate these skills, however. There may be times that privileges associated with a given level are not provided because of their actions. When sanctions are imposed, they should be temporary and the level maintained; staff then engage in problem solving with the students to analyze difficulties, helping them regain the privileges of their level. This facilitates competence building and relationship development with teacher-counselors.

Successes in facing the challenges of each day are the bases for most of the meaningful, positive changes that youth experience in a Re-ED program.

Component 5: Validation of Individual Worth

Developing a sense of one's own worth is essential. Many youth in our programs lack the ability to self-evaluate, have lowered self-esteem and a flawed concept of themselves, often as a result of neglect, abuse, abandonment, or poor adult or peer role models. A youth's sense of self must be nurtured, re-built, and supported to build hope. Youth can find this nurturing foreign and uncomfortable. They are not accustomed to differences from what they have been led to believe about themselves or others. As a result, they may sabotage our best efforts at praise and rewards. Finding the right time and opportunity for reinforcing the notion that they are valuable and that there is good in them is sometimes difficult, even for the most experienced and knowledgeable staff.

Personal validation builds on trust and develops over time with our youth. At the beginning, many youth respond best to external motivation (where positive reinforcements are typically concrete, tangible, and delivered by others). With conscious program changes where reinforcements are paired with external sources of personal validation for the youth, over time s/he progresses to an independence where youth can reward themselves and find intrinsic satisfactions. The journey towards validation occurs on an hour-to-hour, person-to-person, group-by-group, and family-by-family basis, carried out through hundreds of therapeutic interactions - within group process, scheduled activities, formal feedback times, and in spontaneous and unconditional positive events. Ideally, these life affirming activities occur from the time youth awake to the time they go to bed, consistently implemented by all adults with whom they interact, at home or in the program. In fully functioning Re-ED programs all personnel (including parents and/or guardians) come to see their role as therapeutic, helping the child to live successfully.

A number of key elements must be part of the validation process, if we are to build and maintain a positive and rewarding program culture. An aura of respect, good feelings, and success permeating all aspects of the program fosters its image as a place where change and positive growth occurs. Validation involves self-esteem, feedback, and positive relationships.

Self-Esteem. The validation process ultimately targets development, enhancement, or restoration of self-esteem as its goal. Self-esteem helps youth cope with stress, provides feedback about who they are as individuals, and reinforces their skills for "making it" in life. According to Cotton (1985), there are three main sources of self esteem: (a) esteem held for others, (b) esteem for one's own competencies, and (c) esteem as one's individual view of "self" develops as filtered by both others' and their own competencies. Programs concentrate on: (a) learning how to *select worthy others and esteem them*, (b) developing ever broadening *skills as a personal growth learner*, and (c) addressing our views of *self through reflection and feedback*.

Service learning projects can also help youth to learn both the value of others and their own by what they can do to help someone else.

Feedback. Typically, programs share information with youth about how well they participate in the program, their accomplishments, and what needs to be addressed further. This feedback is best provided in an objective, non-confrontational, and neutral manner.

Youth need both formal and incidental feedback on their skills and what they can contribute to the program and society. Informal feedback comes from both adults and peers, with some of the most important feedback coming from interactions occurring every day: understanding looks, humor, and repeated, consistent recognition of their gifts in many small ways.

Relationships. Teacher-counselors are prepared for their meaningful, combination role through training, then continually supported through effective supervision to fulfill their important responsibilities. Our youth often arrive lacking a lasting, meaningful connection with a caring, trusted adult; their developmental Circle of Courage is broken at "Belonging" (Brendtro, Brokenleg, and Van Bockern, 1990). Gaining trust can enable them to progress through the four quadrants represented by the circle, from Belonging through Mastery to Independence, and on to Generosity. Since teacher-counselors and youth spend much time together engaged in a wide array of situations - teaching, learning, having fun, problem solving, and resolving crises, there are many chances for relationships to be created and sustained.

As a sense of mutual respect develops between each professional staff member and each youth, the youth learns to trust that adult to both help and teach her/him to help themselves. No matter what problems arrive with the youth, staff must respect and embrace each youth's potential, helping him/her to live life unburdened by overwhelming baggage or past problems.

Component 6: Program Evaluation and Outcomes

A final, crucial component in any effective Re-ED program design is measurement of both outcomes and other areas known to effect differences in a program's impact. Commitment to program integrity leads us to ask these questions:

Who are we? And are we who we say we are? Programs should decide on, and express their place in the community's continuum of services. Not only must they decide what types of problems they will address, but also the intensity of the services they will provide. For example, Wallace Academy, an alternative school program of Centerstone, Inc., serves the Nashville, Tennessee School System. It was established to serve public school students removed from school for aggressive behaviors. Wallace Academy accepts and works with these students; it does not kick them out of the program for displaying aggressive behavior.

Are we serving the youth that the system/community needs us to serve? When a program establishes a connection with a community referral source to serve a particular type of youth, intake systems should be set up to say yes to those referrals. An intake process that rises to meet challenges does not admit youth who can be served elsewhere, nearer to the community. It does not look for "easy" children, who have fewer acting out behaviors, or who appear to have a better prognosis and outcome. It welcomes those who need its services most.

Are we doing what we have pledged to do, and are we doing it well? In order to be effective, a program must have an established service delivery system that addresses the problems of the youth we serve. For example, when our Re-ED program serves students who have run away from other programs, we act proactively. First, we provide support to them and others in their ecologies, helping them find reasons to stay. The second level of response is preventive; increasing the youth's competence and understanding can help decrease acting out behavior. Working creatively to avoid ejecting or discharging youth from the program for behaviors evident at intake promotes further confidence that we are addressing the needs of those we serve.

Do we have outcome measures to determine consumer well being and satisfaction (for youth, family, and purchasers of service)? For example, Pressley Ridge has conducted outcome studies for over 20 years, measuring how youth perform in the program, how they left the program, and finally how they performed within school, family, and community one year post discharge. This information helped Pressley Ridge change and adapt its programs to serve their youth and families better and provide services designed to have lasting impact.

Conclusions

Successful programs require planning, skill, and a sound values-based and principles-driven foundation from which to work. We believe successful and effective programs weave the components outlined in this paper into the fabric of life in each service setting. Guided by principles and values, programs can and should promote and teach healthy, successful, and positive growth.

References

Aichorn, A. (1925). *Wayward youth*. Vienna: Internationaler Psychoanalytischer Verlag.

Brendtro, L. K., Brokenleg, M. & Van Bockern, S. (1990). *Reclaiming youth at risk: Our hope for the future.* Bloomington, IN: National Educational Service.

Brendtro, L. K., & duToit, L. (2005). *Response ability pathways: Circle of courage.* Cape Town: Pretext Publishers.

Cotton, N. S. (1985). *A developmental model of self-esteem regulation: Part I.* New York: Hatherleigh Co.

Cotton, N. S. (1993). *Lessons from the lion's den.* San Francisco: Jossey-Bass.

Goldstein, A. P., & Glick, B. (1987). *Aggression replacement training.* Champaign, IL: Research Press.

Hobbs, N. (1966). Helping disturbed children: Psychological and ecological strategies. *American Psychologist, 21*(12), 1105-1115.

Hobbs, N. (1971, May). *The art of getting into trouble.* In J. M. Kaufman, & C. D. Lewis (Eds.), *Teaching children with behavior disorders* (pp. 164-165). Columbus, OH: Charles E. Merrill.

Hobbs, N. (1982). *The troubled and troubling child.* San Francisco: Jossey-Bass.

Long, N. J., Fecser, F., & Wood, M. (1991). *Life space crisis intervention: Talking with students in crisis.* Austin: PRO-ED.

Loughmiller, C. (1965). *Wilderness road.* Austin, TX: The Hogg Foundation for Mental Health.

Redl, F., & Wineman, D. (1957). *The aggressive child.* New York: Macmillan.

Trieschman, A. E., Whittaker, J. K., & Brendtro, L. K. (1969). *The other 23 hours.* New York: Walter de Gruyter, Inc.

Mark D. Freado, MA, is the Executive Director of the American Re-Education Association, in Westerville, OH, Director of Re-Education Training and Consultation at Pressley Ridge in Pittsburgh, PA, and Vice President/CFO of Reclaiming Youth International in Lennox, SD mdfreado@re-ed.org or mfreado@pressleyridge.org

Gino DeSalvatore, MS, is the Director of Residential Treatment and Academy Services for Centerstone, based in Nashville, TN. gino.desalvatore@centerstone.org

22

Learning to Use Selective Attention: How and Why

James M. Jones & Jeffrey A. Kepner

One challenge every teacher faces is keeping students' attention during instructional activities. Unless students attend to the learning task, they will not transfer information into short term memory and then into long term memory. Two methods can increase a teacher's effectiveness in keeping students focused on the lesson: (1) Selective attention, and (2) Starting from and returning to a point of order. This chapter shares our method for teaching others to employ these useful teaching skills.

Selective Attention

There are two basic elements to using one's attention productively in the classroom: (1) Classifying the type of attention you are giving, and (2) Shifting the proportions of types you are using.

Classifying Two Kinds of Attention. Selective attention is a process whereby the teacher makes decisions about which students will receive attention and what type of attention they are going to receive at any point in time. We label any teacher attention to appropriate behavior (i.e., on-task) as *praise*, and any attention to inappropriate student behavior (off-task, disrupting, spacing out, etc.) as *criticism*. For example, if a teacher attempts to redirect a student from current inappropriate behavior by telling him or her to get back on-task, we label that redirect a *criticism*. If the teacher smiles at a student who is on-task, we label that teacher behavior a *praise*.

The Four to One Ratio. Our goal is a praise to criticism ratio that approaches four praises for every one criticism. This highly positive ratio is important because many students find all types of attention reinforcing – even negative attention. Our criticism or nega-tive attention used to redirect the student does so by attending to the negative behavior. These "redirects" may work for the moment, but the inappropriate behavior often returns later. Despite its return, however, the teacher is "tricked" into thinking the *criticism redirect* has worked because it was initially effective. As a result of this perceived success, he or she continues to use criticism as redirects – even if over time, inappropriate behavior is increasing. Overall, it is a losing strategy.

Types of Positive Attention to Positive Behavior (Praise)

The goal is to increase the amount of attention that students receive for being on-task. There are many ways to accomplish this goal, since there are many ways to attend to student behavior. *Verbal praise* is one example of attending to appropriate student behavior. We can make verbal comments about a student's behavior. Another is to move into the physical space of a student, a form of attention we call *proximity*. We can also touch a student (e.g., touch or pat on the back) when he or she is on-task, labeled as a *physical*. Teachers can use gestures as signals.   They can also do some or all of these in combination. For example, the teacher can move into the physical space of a student and praise that student at the same time. We label that teacher response as a *praise proximity*. If the teacher touches the student while praising, it is a *praise physical*. Teachers can also use empathetic statements when students are on-task; "I know it's tough for you to keep at it, but you're really staying with that assignment."

Evidence for Use of Selective Attention

These concepts are not new. Madsen, Becker, & Thomas (1968) were three of the first authors to speak about "catching the child being good;" Re-ED staff started using this research finding in about that same year. Later, Brophy and Good (1986) cited multiple sources in the literature that speak to these concepts. Marzano (2003 a) points out that the research shows that students need feedback to distinguish between behaviors that are appropriate and those that are not. The author also points out that the classroom needs to be physically arranged in such a way as to facilitate a teacher's flexible use of proximity for each student.

Research has demonstrated teachers can increase a student's motivation to attend to task by reinforcement (Kamins & Dweck, 1999). Learning how to use these concepts, however, is not easy. How does one go about teaching these strategies? After having observed and taught hundreds of teachers to use these techniques, we arrived at what seems to be a common starting point. We begin by observing a teacher's classroom behaviors in a structured manner across key areas. When we count teacher behaviors, we find that most of their responses are rated as "other" responses because they are not paying attention to any specific child behavior. For example, if a teacher is standing at the board and says, "Take out your books," he or she is not attending to any particular student behavior. This says to us that the teacher is not always noticing or coding students' behaviors independently as appropriate or inappropriate, nor acting accordingly.

Starting with Proximity

To make teachers aware of student behaviors, we first teach them to use proximity as an attention device. Proximity is a valuable tool for a variety of situations. A teacher can use proximity while he or she teaches, when giving directions, or during seatwork activities. Verbal praise, though important, plays a limited role in the selective attention process. In many situations, verbal praise interferes with the flow of instruction. Proximity is far more efficient. A teacher can "cruise" the classroom, pause in areas where students are on-task, and teach at the same time. Another reason why we start with teaching how to use proximity is that most teacher movement is random or undirected, without apparent instructional purpose. When a teacher uses proximity for appropriate student behavior, it produces two positive effects.

First, that student receives attention for doing the right thing, and second, the teacher slightly raises the student's anxiety level. This second reason often puzzles teachers; they ask why they should raise the anxiety level in their students. Brain scientists tell us that mild anxiety helps attention and learning in general (Wolfe, 2001). There is an old saying. "If you have no anxiety you will not get out of bed in the morning. If you have too much anxiety, you will not get out of bed in the morning." Producing an optimal level of anxiety helps teachers seize the learner's attention. Moving into the physical space of a student raises anxiety slightly, moving their attention and learning into the optimal range.

Using proximity becomes a little more complicated when there are several students on-task. A rule of thumb is to move into the proximity of a student who is more likely to become off-task. This idea is easy to understand, but often difficult to implement. Students who are troublesome often elicit counter-aggressive feelings in adults (Long, Morse, and Newman, 1976). For example, Tommy is constantly (or so it seems) talking to his neighbor. This behavior is irritating to the teacher. Over time, the teacher develops negative feelings toward Tommy. We don't normally gravitate towards students who elicit these types of feelings. We often lower our expectations for them and pay a lot of attention to them when they are doing the wrong thing. We are more likely to move towards students who do what we want or what we expect. Countering these natural inclinations is difficult, but important if we want to increase on-task behavior.

Accessibility

We need to make a conscious, deliberate effort to move into Tommy's area when he is on-task, and our attention ratio needs to be at least four praises to one criticism for him, as for the others. Sometimes, we place these less cooperative students away from the rest of the group (e.g., in a corner) because they seemingly cannot handle the stimulation of being around others. When we relocate these students, they are now out of the teacher's cruising pattern, and using proximity for their on-task behavior is more difficult. We need to make a conscious effort to move into their area so that we can move near them whenever we see positive behavior. Placing our target students in areas that are easily accessible helps us use the proximity technique.

A Trap: Legal Off-Task Behavior

During seatwork time, another proximity rule comes into play. Often, two or more students will raise their hands as a signal for help. The teacher moves from one student to the next to give the necessary help. During our observations, we find that while one student is getting his or her question answered, others raise their hands. When this occurs, we are accidentally teaching students that they can "legally be off-task" as long as their hand is raised and they are quiet. A large number of learning minutes are lost to this legal off-task time.

Timing Proximity. We have two solutions to legal off-task behavior. First, be sure to stop in areas where students are working independently. There appears to be an optimal time period to spend in the proximity of a student – three seconds. If the teacher spends less than three seconds, there seems to be decreased impact. If the teacher spends more than three seconds, he or she may be teaching the child to be dependent. We call this the three-second rule. Our informal data collection has led us to discover a second interesting point. Most teachers take about a step a second when moving around the classroom. By applying the three-second rule, they actually take fewer steps while producing students who pay more attention to task.

Using "Stump." A third grade teacher invented this second technique, which she called "Stump." After contemplating this legal off-task phenomenon which we had pointed out in her classroom, she drew a picture of a tree stump and wrote four rules on it. These rules were listed: "Re-read the question. Go on to the next problem. Ask your neighbor. Ask the teacher." Her clever heading on the tree stump poster is "Stumped?" She reviews the "Stump" technique before each seatwork activity, indicating students are to go through all four rules in order. Afterward, before answering any question, she asks the student, "Did you do Stump?" By using this technique consistently, observations showed she reduced the number of "legal" off-task minutes by over 50 per cent. Prorated over a 180-

day school year, a teacher's use of "Stump" can impressively increase the number of students' actual learning minutes.

Prior Learning Interferes

A primary difficulty that teachers face when learning to attend selectively is that it goes against what they were taught. Most educators have seen or been instructed to use proximity as a control mechanism when students are off-task. In fact, in a recent publication, Marsano (2003 a) states that subtle attention to the target student should be the first technique tried when a student is violating the rules. However, if a teacher is using proximity to redirect off-task students, the question becomes, "Who is directing whom?" It seems that by doing the wrong thing the off-task students are controlling the teacher's behavior. Instead, we instruct teachers to move near to students who are doing the right thing, thereby assuring that students will spend more time learning in the long run.

Unlearning and Relearning

Teachers often tell us that proximity redirections to students who are being inappropriate are effective; they therefore find it difficult to give them up. As discussed earlier, criticism usually does work for the moment. The problem remains that such criticism may accidentally teach students to be off-task since a student's inappropriate behavior still results in the teacher's attention. The critical issue is which result one focuses upon: immediate? or long term? Which behaviors are actually changing over time? Are off-task instances becoming more frequent, or are on-task instances lasting longer? Instructing teachers in this concept may sound simple, but one of Murphy's Laws applies here: "Nothing is as simple as it appears." When we work with teachers on this concept, we warn them that using proximity for appropriate behavior is counterintuitive. Using proximity when students are on-task goes against our intuitive thinking which tells us to move into the off-task student's area. Generally, we want teachers to move into the proximity of students who are on-task, not off-task, since on-task behavior is what we hope to strengthen.

Becoming a Natural

While teachers are learning this concept, they have to think about their own behavior as they are teaching - a difficult task. The good news is that after they practice the technique for approximately nine weeks, it generally becomes much more automatic. If the teacher uses these strategies consistently, he or she will get more students to pay more attention. However, like any other management tool it will have no impact if not used consistently.

After he or she can attend selectively and do it consistently, the teacher is ready for the next step. Often several students are already on-task. We want the teacher to move into the proximity of students who are more likely to soon be off-task than on-task. In other words, go first to students who habitually struggle to stay on-task and go *while they are on-task*. Once again, this is counterintuitive. We tend to gravitate to students who share values similar to our own and who look and act in familiar ways. We do not tend to move toward those who are causing us a problem. When students give us an opportunity to attend to them for doing the right thing, we need to seize it.

Direct Address

As is the case with all management plans, there are exceptions to the rule. If a student engages in an unsafe situation, we immediately attend to that behavior. If the student's behavior will result in a contagion effect (i.e., other students are either joining in or are about to join in), we will give direct attention to that behavior. If the behavior is inherently reinforcing, we will interrupt it. Inherently reinforcing behaviors are those the student actually enjoys. For example, if a student is talking to his or her neighbor, the conversation itself is reinforcing. The student may or may not respond to a reminder given by praising another student's appropriate behavior (called a "praise cue" and explained below). If he or she does not respond, we need to address this behavior directly in order to get it to stop. We call this attention "direct address." Selective attention does not imply that all criticism is bad. Remember, we are talking about a ratio or proportion in which students receive far more attention for doing the right thing than the wrong thing.

Praise Cues

This is not to imply that teachers should ignore all inappropriate behaviors other than those that are unsafe, contagious, or inherently reinforcing. There are other techniques that can be used. Sometimes teachers can "cue" the target child by praising a different child who is behaving appropriately. For example, if a child calls out, the teacher can praise another child who is raising his hand. The goal is to cue the target child using minimum teacher attention. We call this a *praise cue*. A related technique is called a *third party cue*. For example, let us say the teacher is working one on one with a child named Tommy, and the teacher's rule states that students are not to interrupt. A student leaves his seat and interrupts. The teacher can carry on a conversation with the one on one student and make the target child the "third party," as in this example, "Tommy, are we supposed to get out of our seat when we have a seatwork assignment?" Tommy will probably say, "No." The target student will hear the conversation and usually return to his or her desk. In this way, we minimize the amount of attention given to the target child and the inappropriate behavior, while still getting our point across.

Closing the Loop

Many teachers tell us they have tried praise cues, but that praise cues did not work. Often a praise cue does not work because the teacher makes a critical error. After students follow the cue, they are ignored; there is no reinforcement to strengthen their direction-following behavior. By the teacher not recognizing publically that the target child has followed the cue, the student receives no recognition for the appropriate behavior. When a teacher does use attention to recognize a student for "cue following," the technique is called "closing the loop."

The Rule of Two

A guideline for timing applies here; we call it the *rule of two*. If a teacher tries two praise cues and the target child fails to respond, the teacher should directly attend to the target child. If the child then follows the direction, recognize it openly. In addition, we have found that if three or more students are engaged in disruptive behaviors, praise cues seem to be less effective, perhaps because the noise level is too high. In this case, the recommended method is "returning to a point of order," which is discussed later.

Physical Attention

After the teacher learns to use proximity and praise cues, we instruct the teacher in the use of physical attention. As the teacher moves around the room while teaching an assignment, he or she has the opportunity to touch students gently on the shoulder or pat them on the back while moving. We have found that the teacher can actually deliver a high rate of praise in a short interval with this action. We also believe that physicals are higher level reinforcers, more effective in keeping most students on-task.

Phrasing Verbal Praise

So far, we have been discussing ways to praise students non-verbally. Now we turn to verbal praise as a method of recognizing on-task behavior. Two major guidelines exist for use of verbal praise. First, use both the student's name and the behavior, rather than "thank you" or "I like the way..." In other words, recognize the student by name and specify the behavior that he or she is demonstrating. It might be, "Tommy has his book out" instead of "I like the way that Tommy has his book out." Voice tone is also important. Our voice tone needs to show joy and celebration for success. Praising in a rote manner loses effectiveness.

Once again, we may be contradicting what most educators were taught. Many were taught to use "I like the way" as a praise statement. We know, however, that the brain pays attention to things that are novel and tends to ignore the familiar. How many times do you think students have heard the statement, "I like the way?" As a result, it is no longer novel and they tend to tune out, thus decreasing the effectiveness of the praise statement. Students tend not to tune out teacher statements that begin with the student's name. In addition, we ultimately want students to know that they are behaving appropriately for themselves, not just to please adults.

Timing Verbal Praise

Next, time praise for when it is most effective. Generally speaking, verbal praise is most effective just after the teacher has given a direction, but is not yet engaged in direct instruction. An example would be to follow a teacher direction such as "Take your books out" with verbally praising students who are complying. Another example is recognizing when a student is following a rule. If a student raises his or her hand to answer a question, the teacher can say, "Tommy has his hand up." We call this praise "*going public*." There are two advantages to *going public*: (1) we are recognizing appropriate behavior, and (2) we are using the appropriately behaving student as a model for other students.

More about Variety: Combinations and Gestures

Remember the other ways that teachers can attend to on-task students, many of which are combinations that reduce the chances for student "tune-outs." For example, we use praise and proximity together. When we move into a student's area and praise that student at the same time, we call it a "*praise proximity*." Likewise, when we praise a student while touching that student, we call that a "*praise physical*." When we are in the proximity of an on-task student and converse with that student, we call it a "*proximity verbal*." We can also communicate with on-task students nonverbally by gesture: smiling, winking, nodding, or giving a hand signal. When we coach teachers, our goal is to have a wide variety of praise behaviors. If we use the same praise behavior over and over, the praise becomes less effective because of satiation. Again, we are trying to have a 4 to 1 praise-criticism ratio. Over time we can teach students that we pay a lot more attention to them when they pay attention to the teacher.

Empathy and Mediation

Two other powerful ways to attend to students who are on-task involve use of empathy and mediation. When we use an empathetic praise statement, we comment on the behavior and the effort that went into it. For example, if Jeff has a hard time completing his homework, we can say, "Jeff, you have your homework done. Good for you! I know that getting it done was difficult for you." The last part of this statement is the empathetic portion. Empathy is a natural human bonding technique, one reason why it is so powerful.

Mediation is an attending statement that teaches cause and effect. We begin by praising the behavior and then asking the child to identify the consequence of the appropriate behavior. For example, we would say, "Jeff, you turned in your homework. What do you think is going to happen because you were able to get it done?" The student is helped to increase awareness of the good things that follow appropriate behavior.

Criticism

Let us return to the proper role of criticism (i.e., attention to inappropriate behavior by direct address). Once again, not all criticism is inappropriate. There are behaviors that should not be ignored. First, we do not ignore behaviors that are health and safety issues. We also do not ignore those behaviors that are inherently reinforcing to the student. Lastly, when we have tried two praise cues and the student fails to respond, we redirect the target child by direct address. We believe that *redirection works best when we start it with the phrase, "The rule is —."* Once again, the key is in the ratio. Recent research stresses balance between praise and criticism (Marzano, 2003 b); our balance is weighted to the side of praise so that we achieve a ratio of four praises for every one criticism. An example is, "Tom, the rule is no talking to our neighbor during study time." We think that stating the rule helps depersonalize the criticism.

The 90 Second Scan

So far we have talked about a variety of selective attention techniques that apply during large group instructional activities. The techniques can also be implemented when the teacher is working in a small group (like reading) with the larger group working on a seatwork activity. We find that effective teachers scan the large group every 90 seconds. What usually happens is that teachers only comment if there is a problem. We encourage teachers to comment on appropriate behavior when they see it during their scanning as long as it does not interrupt the flow of instruction.

Figure 1 reviews the major elements teachers need to remember in order to implement selective attention processes effectively.

Figure 1. Using Selective Attention

Prevention	Remediation
As you move around the room, use proximity and/or physical attention techniques for students who are on task.	Praise cue if two (or fewer) students are off task. If the cue works, close the loop by praising the target student.
Three-second rule for proximity states that as you move around the classroom, pause in an on-task student's area for three seconds before you move. Try not to be tethered to the front of the room (board).	Use no more than two praise cues. If the target student fails to respond, say, "The rule is..." When the target student responds to the rule prompt, praise the target child.
When there are several students on task, choose the student who is least likely to be on task. Students who struggle with attention need more attention when they are on task than those students who do not struggle.	If more than two students are engaged in an inappropriate behavior, return to a point of order. This is similar to starting from a point of order, but we are only going to use ten seconds instead of twenty and we are only going to review the rule that is being violated.
When calling on students who are following the expectations (e.g., hand raised), "go public" with why they were called on. For example, say "Tommy has a quiet hand."	
90 second scan rule: When your group is divided (e.g., you are with a reading group and the large group is doing seatwork), scan and comment on an average of every 90 seconds.	

Starting from a Point of Order, and Returning to a Point of Order

Over the years school research has clearly stated that effective teachers protect instructional time by establishing effective routines to keep housekeeping (or transition) time to a minimum (Cotton, 1995). In addition, when students are in transition from one activity to another, we can "get their brains ready to learn" by using the strategy discussed next.

Twenty Quiet Seconds

We begin the use of a Point of Order by first telling the class that they must take twenty quiet seconds. During the twenty quiet seconds, the class is instructed to think about the rules that apply to the upcoming activity. The teacher begins the time with a verbal cue to "Start;" then she or he immediately praises the first two students who begin the "quiet time." This verbal praise is delivered in a "quiet voice" so the teacher can model the expectation. We praise the first two because we want to create a "sense of urgency." We want to get the quiet time completed as quickly as possible. Some teachers report that students complain because they were not recognized, and teachers often view this "what about me" response as a negative. We feel just the opposite, because when a student says that, he or she is asking, "What do I need to do to get recognized?" Now we have a highly motivated student. The teacher's reply to this statement should be, "Let's see how fast you get started the next time." The probability of that student starting quickly has now increased. It is incumbent upon the teacher to remember this fact and praise that child if they begin quickly. What we really want is for all students to want to "be first" to start the quiet minute. This helps protect instructional time.

Rule Review

Once the quiet time is completed, the teacher calls on various students and asks them to name a rule. This "rule review" sets the stage for appropriate behavior. We feel that very few students set out to deliberately violate rules. Often, they just forget. Rule review acts as a reminder, after which use of selective attention begins. Of course, no technique works all the time. If more than two students begin engaging in a disrupting behavior, the teacher can "return to a point of order" by requiring the students to "take ten (or twenty) seconds," using the same ritual of starting from a point of order. We are using this technique instead of praise cues because a greater number of students are involved in the inappropriate behavior, and the whole group is involved in coming to a "point of order."

Summary: The Overview

We have covered a lot of ground. Let us summarize. First, start from a point of order. Ask for twenty quiet seconds and praise the first two students who comply. Second, review the rules of the instructional activity. Begin instruction and pay attention to on-task students. When students go off-task, make a decision. If two or fewer students are disrupting, use a praise cue. If the cue works, close the loop by recognizing the behavior. If the cue does not work, try one more. If two cues still do not work, use direct address by stating, "The rule is…" If three or more students are disrupting, use a return to a point of order routine. Be careful that your use of proximity does not reinforce dependency. Pay attention to independent work and teach students to do "Stump." Use mediation and empathy whenever you have the chance; they are powerful reinforcers. Finally, remember that no technique works if not used consistently. With practice, these will become automatic, and you will have more students on-task and fewer discipline problems.

A Management Summary
Using Selective Attention and Point of Order

Start from a point of order.
      Ask for 20 quiet seconds
      Praise the first two complying students.
Review the rules.
Begin instruction, attending to on-task students.
If students disrupt (or go off-task):
      One or two students - Use a praise cue
      Students return to task - Recognize the behavior.
      Cue doesn't work -- Use second praise cue.
      Two cues don't work -- State "The rule is ...."
      Three or more students -- Return to a point of order
         routine.
Remember:
      Don't let proximity reinforce dependency.
      Pay attention to independent work.
      Teach students to do "Stump."
      Use mediation and empathy whenever you can.
      No technique works unless used consistently.

References

Brophy, J., & Good, T. (1986). Research linking teacher behavior to student behavior: Potential implications for instruction. In M. C. Wittrock (Ed.), *Handbook of research on teaching*, (3rd ed.). New York: Macmillan.

Cotton, K. (1995). *Effective schooling practices: A research synthesis 1995 Update*. Portland, OR: Northwest Regional Educational Laboratory.

Kamins, M. L., & Dweck, C. S. (1999). Person versus process praise and criticism: Implications for contingent self-worth and coping. *Developmental Psychology, 35*, 835-847.

Long, N., Morse, W., & Newman, R. (1976). *Conflict in the classroom: The education of children with problems.* (3rd ed.). Belmont, CA: Wadsworth.

Madsen, C. H., Jr., Becker, W. C., & Thomas, D. R. (1968). Rules, praise, and ignoring: Elements of elementary classroom control. *Journal of Applied Behavior Analysis, 1*, 139-150.

Marzano, R. (2003a). *Classroom management that works: Research-based strategies for every teacher*. Alexandria, VA: Association for Supervision and Curriculum Development.

Marzano, R. (2003b). *What works in schools: translating research into action*. Alexandria, VA: Association for Supervision and Curriculum Development.

Wolfe, P. (2001). *Brain matters: Translating research into classroom practice*. Alexandria, VA: Association for Supervision and Curriculum Development.

James M. Jones, MEd, is currently School Psychologist for the Clark County School District in Las Vegas, Nevada. jmj1246@aol.com

Jeffrey A. Kepner, MS, is currently School Psychologist for the Clark County School District in Las Vegas, Nevada. Jkepner2@cox.net

23

An Empirical Search for "Natural Child Workers" in the Public Schools

Robert P. Cantrell

Nicholas Hobbs outlined his beliefs about the qualities of effective teacher-counselors in Re-ED programs in *The Troubled and Troubling Child* (1982), saying that the ideal teacher-counselor's competency is evidenced by their *"skillful management of individual children and adolescents, groups, and ecosystems, as facilitators of change"* (Hobbs, 1982, p. 87). He added that *"teacher-counselors agree that some of the most satisfying moments are generated by successful achievement in school. To do well in spelling or arithmetic, especially for students who expect and dread failure, is to know a sharp delight. It is like spitting from the top of a windmill"* (Hobbs, 1982, p. 287).

But where do these teacher-counselors come from? According to Hobbs, from within life's very same pool of candidates that produce regular teachers, but with some essential qualities and propensities:

"She has to have technical skills of a wide-ranging character. She must be able to work effectively with her teammates. She has to be able to do things with competence and assurance, so that she can have heart and mind to respond personally to children.... [making] professional use of experiences acquired over a lifetime, and, for this very reason, such people are available for professional work of high caliber without extensive professional training" (Hobbs, 1982, p. 89).

The Prevention-Intervention Project (PIP) enabled us to investigate these assertions as PIP attempted to validate use of the Re-ED philosophy within public schools. With Hobbs' prescriptive descriptions in mind, we hypothesized that there were teachers within the proposed experimental and control schools who already possessed many of these qualities and whose personal philosophies about teaching would mesh well with Re-ED beliefs.

Further, we predicted that some of these teachers had already absorbed more accurate lessons about behavioral principles than others, even before exposure to formal training in such procedures. We also predicted that they would be generally more favorably disposed towards the children they taught. Additionally, we predicted that these knowledge and attitude characteristics would produce more positive and encouraging interactions with their pupils than criticisms. And finally, we predicted that these personal qualities and their attendant teaching processes would significantly accelerate their pupils' academic accomplishments.

In this study Cantrell, Stenner, and Katzenmeyer (1977) used data gathered during PIP's first year with first grade teachers and their pupils, focusing on three criteria Mitzel (1960) had suggested as the most important in determining teacher effectiveness: (a) entering teacher characteristics, (b) teacher and pupil interactions across the year in classrooms, and (c) measures of pupil change such as academic achievement.

Question and Purpose

This study tested whether approximations to Hobbs' "ideal teacher-counselor" existed within the public schools themselves. Specifically, the question was whether there were regular first grade teachers among the PIP schools whose discernible patterns of knowledge, attitudes towards children and teaching, and classroom teaching practices would produce greater academic gains from their pupils than teachers not possessing these attributes. In other words, would these teacher groups with differing factor profiles of behavioral knowledge and attitudes produce significantly different student academic outcomes?

Participants, Instruments, and Initial Analyses

Factor structures of two measures of teacher attributes were first determined using two separate teacher groups. The first teacher group was 872 teachers working in three different sections of the country. They provided data for a factor structure analysis of our measure of teachers' *behavioral knowledge* applied to classroom setting predicaments (Alternative Classroom Strategies Inventory, ACSI, Cantrell & Cantrell, 1969). The second teacher group supplied results for a second factor structure study of their *attitudes toward teaching and students* (Minnesota Teacher Attitude Inventory, MTAI, Cook, Leeds, & Callis, 1951). This group was composed of 153 first, second, and third grade teachers and their principals in PIP's experimental and control schools distributed across PIP's five school systems.

Two instruments were also administered to these teachers' students; *intelligence* was measured by the Otis-Lennon Mental Ability Test (Otis & Lennon, 1967) and *achievement* by the Metropolitan Achievement Test (Durost, Bixler, Wrightstone, Prescott, & Balow, 1971).

Interactions between teachers and their students were measured by a Classroom Observation Schedule (COS) adapted from Flanders' (1960) Interaction Analysis Categories. Twice monthly, trained observers used the COS to observe classroom teachers for 30 minutes per session. Each 30 minute observation was broken down into successive ten second intervals. Each ten second interval started with codes for classroom antecedent events, followed by codes for target child behaviors and associated consequences.

Several interlocking studies were performed to determine: (a) if patterns existed between teachers' knowledge of behavioral principles and the measure of teacher attitudes, and (b) to investigate any effects these patterns might have on classroom interactions and students' academic achievements.

Teacher Knowledge of Behavioral Principles: ACSI Factors

The ACSI was a 60 item, unpublished experimental test of knowledge of behavioral principles at work in common classroom situations. The respondent's task was to choose among four alternative solutions or procedures for dealing with the classroom situation that served as each item's "stem." Only one of the four procedures was behavior theory defensible as the best approach to the problem posed. Each item addressed a different basic principle found in the behavioral literature. This instrument was administered to first grade teachers at the beginning (pre-test) and end of the initial school year of PIP. Pre-test measures were used to determine the group memberships of teachers in the analyses described below.

Two major factor analytic studies on the ACSI (Maxplane rotation), using the 872 teachers produced two error strategy factors and three behavioral knowledge factors, as described below.

ACSI 1 was termed *Traditionally Authoritarian Control Strategies* and consisted of control tactics espoused by teachers in a behaviorally erroneous manner to persuade pupils to cease and desist unwanted behaviors.

ACSI 2 was labeled *Well-Intentioned Strategies That Are Sure to Backfire*. Here the goals were appropriate, but the behavioral strategies chosen were highly likely to produce effects opposite from those intended. These "backfire" events were largely gleaned from the research literature on behavior modification (e.g., Ullmann & Krasner, 1965; Bricker, 1967) and from consultative experiences with teachers and parents (Cantrell, Cantrell, Huddleston, & Wooldridge, 1969).

ACSI 3 was termed *Selective Attention*. High scores on this factor implied knowledge about how to deliver and use consequences to motivate or shape appropriate behaviors in the classroom.

ACSI 4 was *Structuring Contingencies* and emphasized the use of naturally occurring consequences for changing pupils' behaviors.

ACSI 5 was labeled *General Classroom Programming*. High scores implied that the teacher understood and could use the total behavioral gestalt of a classroom situation to resolve problem issues.

Reliability studies on the ACSI using both raw scores and factor replicability approaches (Katzenmeyer and Stenner, 1975) were performed. A one year test-retest reliability coefficient on the measure using raw scores was 0.82. With another group and another testing, the split-half reliability (Kuder-Richardson 20, N = 153) was

0.85. A factor replicability coefficient of r = 0.89 was obtained for ACSI 3; ACSI 4 produced r = 0.74; and ACSI 5 produced r = 0.39. No replicability studies were performed on the two error strategies (i.e., ACSI 1 and ACSI 2).

Teacher Attitude About Students and Teaching: MTAI Factors

The second factor analytic study dealt with teacher attitudes about students and teaching as measured by the MTAI. Teachers and principals in the experimental and control schools responded to the MTAI measure on the same testing schedule as the ACSI. Again, a Maxplane rotation factor analysis was performed on these data for the 153 principals and teachers in the project. A seven factor solution was obtained for the factors. Their interpretive labels follow.

MTAI 1 was labeled *Student Irresponsibility vs. Student Self Direction.* Agreement with the items of this factor implied a rejecting view of children, combined with the view that a child should subject him/herself to the will of the teacher. Disagreement implied a view of children as responsible and capable of self-direction.

MTAI 2 was labeled *Authoritarian vs. Supportive Approach to Pupils.* Agreement with these items implied rigidity and a "tight ship" view regarding children and education, especially if the scores were high. Disagreement or low scores on this factor implied a supportive and helpful orientation toward children and teaching.

MTAI 3 was labeled *Positive Acceptance vs. Rejection of Children.* Agreement with these items implied that children have certain positive attributes that can be acknowledged without putting the teacher's role as an adult at risk.

MTAI 4 was labeled *Expectation and Enforcement of Pupil's Submission to Authority.* Agreement with these items implied a teacher's belief that pupils are to submit to authority without question. Disagreement implied a non-absolutist approach to children and hesitancy about easily using punishment.

MTAI 5 was labeled *General Dissatisfaction with Children and Teaching vs. Satisfaction with Teaching and Children.* This was a difficult factor to generalize verbally, except for the prediction that high scoring teachers on this factor would probably also be high in overall criticism aimed at the whole class, would likely teach from a stationary point in the class, and would be more variable in their use of punishment than would teachers disagreeing with these items.

MTAI 6 was labeled *Maintenance of Teacher-Pupil Distance*. Disagreement with these items suggested less teacher need for absolute control over teacher-pupil interactions and less need for deference from the student. Agreement suggested that a teacher believed that students should make teaching easier, and that distance between teachers and pupils should be maintained.

MTAI 7 was labeled *Disbelief vs. Belief in Student Freedom*. Agreement inferred that pupils benefit more from being task-oriented, with the approach to learning being set by teachers or schools. Disagreement implied a more easygoing approach, emphasizing pupils' independent learning.

Student Intelligence and Achievement: O-LMAT & MAT

Two major pupil measures, the *Otis-Lennon Mental Ability Test* (Primary II, Form J; Otis & Lennon, 1967) and the *Metropolitan Achievement Test* (Durost, et al., 1971), were given to all first graders in the Prevention-Intervention Project during the fall of the initiation of the project and again at the end of first grade. All experimental and control schools' first graders were tested.

Mental ability scores and fall achievement scores were used in a multiple regression equation to predict year-end achievement scores. Residual scores from this multiple regression were used to measure whether students at three IQ levels (low IQ, range 50-89; mid IQ, range 90-104; or high IQ, range 105-135) achieved academically by year's end at, above, or below what would have been expected from their mental ability and pre-achievement scores alone.

Teacher and Student Classroom Behaviors: (COS)

Thirty minute classroom observations were obtained twice-monthly in both experimental and control group teachers' classrooms. The 30 minute sessions were broken down into 10 second sampling intervals. The first three seconds of each interval were used to code teacher verbalizations. We used Flanders' (1960, p. 20) teacher verbalization categories (*Accepts feelings, Praises or encourages, Accepts or uses ideas of student, Asks questions, Lecturing, Giving directions, Criticizing or justifying authority,* and *Silence or confusion*) for this portion of the observation.

The next three to four seconds captured the responses of a "target child" (TC) in the classroom. In the experimental schools this child was the pupil nominated by the teacher as the child the multi-person team (teacher plus two support teachers plus parents) had agreed to work together to help, with the goal of preventing this child from falling further behind academically and/or behaviorally. The target child observation categories (Cantrell, et al., 1977, p. 175) were *Handraising, Child response, Child initiative, Attentive posture, Non-attentive, Disruptive, Silence/confusion.* These categories attempted to capture the on-going TC behaviors embodied in these 10 second samples that might be used to document helpful vs. non-helpful classroom interactions, showing how the classroom behavioral ecologies changed as support teachers and project consultants dealt with key problem "knots" experienced by teachers, children, and their families.

The third three to four seconds captured the consequences intended or obtained by the TC during that 10 second interval. The consequence categories were: *Teacher positive, Teacher negative, Peer attention, Teacher and peer attention, and No consequence* (Cantrell, et al., 1977, p. 175).

In addition, observers captured one or more of 10 classroom formats being used by the teacher (e.g., lecturing, individual tutoring, etc.), one or more of 10 classroom formats for the target child (e.g., seatwork, small group, etc.), and the content subject being taught during the observation (e.g., reading, math, etc.). If changes occurred, new formats were captured at the point of change.

Reliability and quality control were monitored through videotaping procedures that occurred simultaneously with the live observations. Each ten second interval was numbered and the audio count was loaded onto the videotape through a mike mixer and into the data collector's earphone. Criterion raters randomly sampled and re-rated two tapes per month for each rater in the school districts. Data collectors maintained an average of 80% agreement with criterion raters' ratings collapsed across all the teacher verbalization, TC response, and consequence segments (Cantrell, Wood, and Nichols, 1974).

Teacher Profile Analysis Study

There were 138 first grade teachers and their principals in PIP experimental and control schools who participated in the initial teacher and principal testings and subsequent cluster analysis procedures. Of this group, there were 40 first grade teachers for whom teacher tests, classroom observations, and student achievement data were complete and available for first year project analyses.

The knowledge (ACSI) and attitude (MTAI) measures were combined into profiles for each teacher and subjected to cluster analysis (presage variables); then, the pupils of those cluster groups were examined for achievement gains across the year (outcome variables), as well as concomitant teacher-pupil interactions (process variables) in the classroom.

The cluster procedure produced three distinct cluster groups, labeled (a) the Positive Contingency Manager teachers, (b) the Traditional Non-Authoritarian teachers, and (c) the Traditional Authoritarian teachers, on the basis of cluster-weighted combinations of items on the ACSI and MTAI test results.

The Positive Contingency Manager teachers (PCM, $N = 26$) demonstrated high factor scores on variables characterized as *structuring classroom contingencies*, *knowledge of selective attention strategies*, and *general classroom programming strategies*, (Cantrell, et al., 1977, p. 176). Of this group of 26, 41% were control school teachers from the original data set of 138, minus the principals. The PCM teachers were the lowest of the three teacher clusters on choosing behaviorally erroneous strategies when problem solving on the ACSI. On the MTAI, this group espoused high positive attitudes and acceptance for children, and high levels of belief in children's responsibility. They did not support the idea that children should automatically submit to authority. In addition, (a) PCM teachers were not dissatisfied with children and teaching, (b) they did not believe that the traditional teacher-pupil distance should be fostered, and (c) they showed a high belief in student freedom. Overall, these teachers distinguished themselves as the *high knowledge, positive attitude* group.

The next group, Traditional Non-Authoritarian teachers (TNA, N = 6, of which 64% were from control schools), generally showed low knowledge of behaviorally correct classroom strategies, but were very similar in their attitudes to the PCM teachers concerning children and teaching. Overall, these teachers were referred to as the *low knowledge, positive attitude* group.

The Traditional Authoritarian teachers (TA, N = 8, of which 41% were from control schools) produced high factor scores on behaviorally erroneous problem solving strategies, low knowledge about selective attention strategies, and relatively low positive acceptance of students. They strongly believed that students were irresponsible. They showed general dissatisfaction with teaching and children. This *low knowledge, negative attitude* group also strongly believed that distance should be maintained between teachers and students.

Interestingly, there was *no group demonstrating high behavioral knowledge and negative attitudes* towards students or teaching.

Teacher Profile Groups and Classroom Observation Results

Membership in one of the three teacher groups (PCM, TNA, or TA) was used as the criterion variable in a multiple discriminant analysis. For this analysis the independent variables for predicting differential group membership were rates of different categories of classroom verbalizations across the year's classroom observations for each teacher.

Two discriminant functions resulted from this analysis. One discriminant dimension was labeled *Positive Responsiveness to Pupils*, based on the pattern of the discriminant function weights. The other discriminant dimension was labeled *Teacher Initiated Directiveness* (Cantrell, et al., 1977, p. 177).

Profile results showed that the PCM teachers were the most verbally positive (praises/encourages), while the TA teachers were the most verbally negative (criticism, giving directions). The TNA group fell in between the PCM and the TA groups on positive verbalizations. However, of the three teacher groups, the TNA group used the most teacher-oriented, direct approach with their pupils (lecturing, accepts/uses ideas). The PCM teachers were mid-way between the TNA and the TA groups on this dimension.

Student Achievement and Teacher Profile Groups

First grade pupils ($N = 1,000$) of the PCM, TNA, and TA teacher groups were divided into IQ thirds using their pre-test results on the *Otis-Lennon Mental Ability Test*. The low IQ group ($N = 329$, IQs 50-89), the medium IQ group ($N = 334$, IQs 90-104), and the high IQ group ($N = 337$, IQs 105-135) were also cross-classified by which of the three teacher cluster groups the teacher to which they had been assigned at the first of the year belonged.

The hypothesis was that effective teaching would produce year-end student achievement above and beyond what could be statistically expected solely from each student's IQ and entering levels of academic achievement at the beginning of first grade. Residual scores between pupils' actual post-year achievement scores and their predicted achievement scores were used as each pupil's dependent variable in a three teacher groups (PCM, TNA, TA) by three IQ levels (low IQ, medium IQ, and high IQ) analysis of variance.

Because of significantly lower variability in residual achievement scores for the high IQ pupils when compared with the residual scores of the two other IQ groups, the assumption of homogeneity of variance for a three by three-way analysis of variance could not be met. A separate one-way analysis of variance for the high IQ pupils' residual achievement scores across the three teacher cluster groups did not result in significant differences across the three cluster groups of teachers ($F = 0.13$, n.s.).

The remaining two student groups (middle IQ and low IQ) for each of the three teacher groups (PCM, TNA, TA) were subjected to a two by three-way analysis of variance. There were significant differences in achievement residuals across the three teacher cluster groups for both IQ levels, in favor of achievement gains by the PCM teachers' pupils ($F = 3.81$, $p < .025$). The PCM teachers helped their students achieve significantly more by year's end than was predicted statistically from their IQs and academic achievement scores at the beginning of their first grade year. The other two teacher groups (TNA and TA) did not produce academic accomplishments for their students beyond what was predicted from their pupils' mental ability and academic achievement levels at the beginning of the year.

These findings are made more meaningful by the realization that *PCM teachers were able to teach low and middle IQ pupils more effectively than the other teacher groups, without simultaneously penalizing the academic achievements of their high IQ pupils.*

Summary of Results and Discussion

The results of this study for the Positive Contingency Management teachers support Hobbs' (1982) characterizations of the ideal teacher-counselor. PCM teachers demonstrated the "technical skills of a wide-ranging character" (p. 89), particularly as those skills relate to knowledge of how to deal with classroom problem situations. The PCM teachers also demonstrated a greater degree of "heart and mind to respond personally to children" (p. 89) by their significantly higher rates of verbally positive responses to pupils in the day-to-day classroom instructional processes. These verbally positive interactions with their pupils were maintained across the school year, along with a moderate rate of teacher-initiated instructional procedures. PCM teachers' professional knowledge elements and continuing positive interactions with pupils produced significant achievement results in their low IQ and middle IQ pupils without significantly impeding the academic achievements of their high IQ pupils.

These year-long results support the following statement. Apparently there *are* teachers who already think along the same lines as Hobbs has described - the "natural teacher-counselors" of the world. This group seemed to have a head start for continual learning about how to help and teach children, and probably their families. Two significant questions remain. How do we employ what we know about the "Positive Contingency Managers" in selecting and placing them in roles where these entering attributes are most important and effective? And even more importantly, how do we create and deliver the experiences needed for individuals in the other two groups to learn and change?

One strategy for helping teachers learn and change may be to help them solve their students' problems before those student difficulties escalate. Most teachers are highly motivated to solve student problems when concerns about a student first arise; helping a teacher solve problems at that point may short-circuit what frequently becomes an escalation of the student's problems. The traditional referral process to psychological or other services often shifts the dynamics of teacher-pupil interactions. A desperate-for-help teacher may be tempted to resort to building (perhaps even unknowingly aiding) a worst case scenario in order to move the child to the top of the list for services, where others may assume responsibility.

The argument can be made that both Traditional Non-Authoritarian and Traditional Authoritarian teachers can profit from increased knowledge of behavioral principles for positive use in their own classrooms with their "problematic" students. *The fact that the cluster analyses in this study did not find a high knowledge-negative attitude teacher group may indicate that teachers who know more about how to manage and teach children by positive means tend to like both children and teaching.* School administrators might find it helpful to identify teachers who approximate PCM teachers within their own schools, and team them with less experienced teachers to resolve student difficulties.

References

Bricker, D. D. (Ed.) (1967). *Cumberland House Studies in Behavior Modification.* Nashville, TN: Department of Mental Health, State of Tennessee.

Cantrell, R. P., & Cantrell, M. L. (1969). *Alternative Classroom Strategies Inventory.* Unpublished experimental test.

Cantrell, R. P., Cantrell, M. L., Huddleston, C. M., & Wooldridge, R.L. (1969). Contingency contracting with school problems. *Journal of Applied Behavior Analysis, 2*, 215-220.

Cantrell, R. P., Stenner, A. J., & Katzenmeyer, W. G. (1977). Teacher knowledge, attitudes and classroom correlates of student achievement. *Journal of Educational Psychology, 69*, 192-197.

Cantrell, R. P., Wood, J. L., & Nichols, C. A. (April, 1974). *Teacher knowledge of behavior principles and classroom teaching patterns.* Paper presented at the meeting of the American Educational Research Association, Chicago.

Cook, W. W., Leeds, C. H., & Callis, R. (1951). *The Minnesota Teacher Attitude Inventory.* New York: Psychological Corp.

Durost, W. N., Bixler, H. H., Wrightstone, J. W., Prescott, G. A., & Balow, I. H. (1971). *Metropolitan Achievement Test.* New York: Harcourt Brace Jovanovich.

Flanders, N. A. (1960). *Teacher influence, pupil attitudes, and achievement: Study in interaction analysis.* Minneapolis: University of Minnesota.

Hobbs, N. (1982). *The troubled and troubling child.* San Francisco: Jossey-Bass.

Mitzel, H. E. (1960). Teacher effectiveness. In C. W. Harris (Ed.), *Encyclopedia of educational research.* New York: Macmillan.

Otis, A. S., & Lennon, R. T. (1967). *Otis-Lennon Mental Ability Test.* New York: Harcourt, Brace, & World.

Katzenmeyer, W. G., & Stenner, A. J. (1975). Strategic use of random subsample replication and a coefficient of factor replicability. *Educational and Psychological Measurement, 35*, 19-29.

Ullmann, L. P., & Krasner, L. (1965). *Case studies in behavior modification.* New York: Holt, Rinehart and Winston, Inc.

Robert P. Cantrell, PhD, is Research Consultant for the Positive Education Program in Cleveland, Ohio.
rcantrell8648@sbcglobal.net

24

A Teen Talks: Angie's Story

Angie

Things there were starting to get really tough…. When I went to X High School, things just didn't go right. It was like I was always fighting somebody. Half the time I wouldn't even go to school. Just because I didn't want to be there…. My home life — things were chaotic….

When I started [here at M], I didn't want to be here, I didn't like anybody — to me M was just full of BS. That's how I felt. It's so amazing. I've come too far from where I've started from just to give up now…. I've learned to respect myself and others, and I've also learned that what I did in the community is not accepted — and now I have a better outlook on life. When I was at home [before going to a group home], basically I did what I wanted to do, regardless of who said what and who did what. I just didn't care.

It's like, when I came to M, things just started to change. When I first got here, I was in restraints, I was running away….It's like, I don't know, just the way M is, the way they treat their students is unbelievable…. [T]he staff listens to what I have to say and before a restraint occurs, I'm able to just talk it out instead of being in a restraint. I've just come to realize that through M, I've seen miraculous change in myself — and it's just amazing how the students have changed themselves.

Our school motto from what I've seen is M Magic. When people hear the words M Magic it doesn't have a meaning; it's just two more words. But to me, it's more than just two more words….

I've learned some of life's toughest lessons here at M — and I've learned to win my own acceptance and approval because before I came to M, I didn't feel too good about myself... And to me, what I've learned, through the Re-ED principles that life is to be lived now not in the past, because we can't change the past and not in the future, because the future isn't promised to any of us, and it's like we've got to move forward with ourselves. Even though life is full of ups and downs but it's how we feel, we have to try and overcome our troubles.

At M the Magic is all about respect. The staff listens; it's about choices, it's all about hope. Then it's all about having fun too. For example, when I first came to M even though I didn't respect them, they respected me. That just turned me around, its like wow! These people. No matter how many times I'm disrespectful, they are going to respect me and they are going to help me overcome things and help me learn that respect is a two way street. And it's all about hope because they allow me to know that there's life beyond the rain. I can accomplish anything that I want to accomplish because they encourage me to live up to my fullest potential. They listen to what I have to say, but also I have to listen to what they have to say. We work together as a team so I can accomplish my goals. At the same time we are also having fun. While we're doing this, that, and the other. And they just help me reach my goals while turning it into a game also, but at the same time we're being serious about it because without my diploma, I'm not going anywhere. With my diploma, I'm going places....

I learned to respect myself; I've learned to accept the fact that I don't need to harm myself. Even if I don't stop hurting myself for myself, I need to do it for those who care about me, and that they want me to be stronger than what I was. I've come to accept that I'm worthy, I'm respectable because I'm a young lady and young women should learn to respect themselves. If you respect yourself, then everybody else is going to respect you. The way you feel about yourself, everybody else is going to feel the same about you as you feel about yourself.

To me, any outsider that walks through the doors of M — they will witness and experience the M Magic for themselves.

Part VI

Building and Maintaining Relationships

Building and sustaining constructive human relationships is not easy. Common human emotions interfere – like anger, jealousy, envy, possessiveness. Life gets in the way – repeatedly, with loss, illness, tragedy, threats to financial and emotional survival. And everything gets complicated; above all, our past experiences confuse our attempts to cope. The down sides always loom larger than the ups. We almost seem programmed to see them first and overlook the flip side of the coin. Our own complexity seems to hinder recognition of the basics that essentially make us human.

But how we view an event (or a person) defines it as much as the event (or person) itself. To free ourselves from destructive events or persons, it is necessary to look at them differently and then act differently. Coping is a function of two things: (1) how we see the problem, and (2) the skills we have that provide options for acting on it.

Relationships are essential to being human, to our very survival. Four of the Re-ED principles deal with four aspects inherent in healthy relationships: feelings, trust, group, and community. In helping, relationships between all parties are determiners of success. Forming constructive relationships is critical to every other Re-ED essential — seeing and building on strengths, working with others to reduce ecosystem discord, adding to competence repertoires, valuing the teaching and learning roles, questioning and finding better ways to accomplish goals.

Natural agents in the ecology, such as parents, teachers, and peers, are the major players in our initial learning about relating to others and the development of our ability to create and maintain relationships — one at a time and in groups. What makes for a constructive, long term relationship with another? What makes a group coherent and constructive? All the chapters in Part VI are about positive relationships – creating them, building them, and sustaining them.

Living with Others

Hobbs' own views of human relationships had many thoughtful contributors who influenced Re-ED's conceptualization. He acknowledged indebtedness: *"for the importance of relationship and the significance of time in life to Otto Rank, Jessie Taft, Virginia Robinson, and Carl Rogers; for psychodynamic concepts in general to Sigmund Freud and Anna Freud and their many interpreters; .... for the significance of role and of personal engagement to George Kelly; ... for therapeutic camping and group process to Campbell Loughmiller;...."* (Hobbs, 1982, p.xxvii).

In chapter 25, Thomas Valore describes how groups at high risk for being anti-social become cohesive and constructive in Re-ED. He cites supportive evidence from his own and others' research, and provides guiding principles and practical strategies for working with children and youth in groups. Groups in Re-ED work and play together in an intense mutual experience, and are not to be confused with the transitory groups brought together periodically (hopefully to learn to manage anger, deal with special problems, or progress through a social skills or life skills curriculum).

Chapter 26, which follows, describes the Panthers, a Washington state Re-ED classroom group and staff team who learned how to work and play together. John Perona tells their story from the perspective of a professional who joined the program as the therapeutic approach changed and the students entered. He shares their accomplishments and insights.

In chapter 27, Mary Beth Rauktis, Ana Regina Andrade, and Ann Doucette review the literature on "therapeutic alliance" (TA) of adults in therapeutic roles with children and youth. They describe a series of studies carried out in Pressley Ridge programs, a worthy effort to look at the T-C role through more traditional mental health constructs – the essential similarity between TA and T-Cs' efforts to connect with youth, establish trust, and form a mutual commitment to positive change. They present interesting findings from their research and also pose intriguing questions. Does TA relate to positive student outcomes? What T-C behaviors are associated with both positive TA and positive outcomes?

Finally, chapter 28 provides a striking example of the power of individuals and group relationships to support each other and bring about change, written by Kris Reinbold, Tricia Jump, Mike Oliver, and Lisa Hoyt (all members of the Washington Re-Education Association). They describe how the efforts of a single state staff member and the Re-ED consultant she brought to Washington state from Ohio grew to become a movement with "sticking power." What they shared inspired a few dedicated professionals who sought others and, by systematic design, became a state organization with a self sustaining association that regularly provides training and support for others in roles like their own. Their spirited descriptions give useful detail on the core curriculum and trainer training process that serve as the basis for their trainings, annual conferences, and consultations.

Each of these chapters deals with the differences individuals and groups can make in the relationships and lives of troubled and troubling children and youth. On the following page is a summary of insights on staff supervision provided by Lisa Shepard and Mark Freado.

Supervisors in Mentoring Relationships

Supervisors make the program go. They are the link between what we're supposed to do and what we're actually doing. They ensure that what we do is consistent with Re-ED values.

When Re-ED staff with more than twenty years of experience were asked what was fundamental to their development as helping professionals, nearly all talked about one or more supervisors who helped them through many tough situations they encountered in working with troubled and troubling children and youth with serious needs. They described them as trusted mentors, using these terms:

> *"I never felt stupid for asking a question."*
> *"I felt I could go to him/her about anything; they cared if I got better at my job."*
> *"I understood the rules; even though I felt like I was working without a net, I felt their support."*
> *"It was clear that we were in it together."*

From the supervisees' standpoint, these supervisor/mentors made sure –

We knew the job to be done;

They could teach us the skills necessary to do it;

They were present to observe how we implemented those skills;

They gave timely and clear verbal and written feedback, retraining us as needed;

They created opportunities to enhance and broaden our learning.

Building and maintaining supportive mentoring relationships, with continual reciprocal learning for both parties involved, are critical components in settings helping troubled and troubling children and youth.

— Lisa M. Shepard and Mark D. Freado in Value-Based Supervision, *Reclaiming Children and Youth, 11*:2, summer 2002, pp. 103-105

25

Sharing Adventure, Vicissitudes, and Victories: Creating Cohesive Groups In Re-ED

Thomas G. Valore

Dr. Nicholas Hobbs believed strongly in the power of the group to provide opportunities for troubled and troubling children and youth to relate, connect, and care for one another.

"[T]he sharing of adventure, of vicissitudes, and of victories provides an experience in human relatedness to which most of our students have been alien" (Hobbs, 1982, p. 278).

He was keenly aware of the impact of group forces that promote these experiences. He also lived what he believed. In a biographical study of Hobbs' life, Habel (1998) found the following:

"Hobbs...had a special sensitivity to, and interest in, the plight of the 'outsider.' Mary Thompson Hobbs recounts that her husband made a habit of zeroing in on outsiders at parties–persons who seemed to be unacquainted with other guests–with the intention of integrating them into the group" (p. 217).

Group Work in Re-ED Settings

Group work in Re-ED programs has been a foundation of intervention since 1962 when the first two Re-ED schools, Cumberland House Elementary School and Wright School, opened their doors (Cantrell, Cantrell, Valore, Jones, & Fecser, 1999; Freeman, Henon, Hogan, Kohl, Rousseau, Slagle, & Weinberg, 1971; Hobbs, 1982; Rousseau, 1971). Hobbs believed that group work with troubled and troubling children and youth was so important that he included it as one of the twelve Re-ED principles:

"The group is very important to young people; it can be a major source of instruction in growing up" (1982, p. 22).

Influenced by Campbell Loughmiller's group work with troubled and troubling youth in outdoor settings (Loughmiller, 1965; 1979), Hobbs placed strong emphasis on the power of the group *"in helping each member of the group grow in competence, confidence, self-esteem, and ability to meet the demands of living in home, school, and community"* (1982, p. 332). Given the complexities of the topic, this chapter can only provide a brief overview highlighting some of the salient points of group work in Re-ED, including cohesion building strategies and group meetings.

Three group terms commonly used in Re-ED need defining. The first, *group work*, is working with children in groups to help them improve socially and emotionally; this is the general heading under which all other group related terms fall. For the second term, Re-ED borrows Shaw's (1981) definition of *group*, which states *"a group is defined as two or more persons who are interacting with one another in such a manner that each person influences and is influenced by each other person"* (1981, p. 8). The last term, *group process*, is defined as *"the stages that groups tend to go through, each characterized by certain feelings and behavior"* (Corey & Corey, 2006, p. 148). The American Re-Education Association defines group process in Re-ED settings as the *"deliberate utilization by a team of T-Cs of positive reciprocal influences to help each group member learn behavior management techniques appropriate to responsible living"* (Smith, 1986, p. 22).

Forming Positive, Cohesive Group Cultures

A major goal of Re-ED groups is to form healthy, positive, cohesive cultures that help troubled and troubling children and youth change their behavior and function successfully in their ecology. A significant factor in achieving this goal is *group cohesion*. Group cohesion has at least three different meanings associated with it, including: *"(1) attraction to the group, including resistance to leaving it, (2) morale, or the level of motivation evidenced by group members, and (3) coordination of efforts of group members"* (Shaw, 1981, p. 213). Most sources agree, however, that cohesion refers to the degree of attraction that a group has for its members (Shaw, 1981).

Group cohesion was found to be a significant factor in a variety of contexts including therapeutic groups (Bednar & Lawlis, 1971; Yalom, 1995), task groups (Cartwright, 1968), living units (Moos, 1976, 1979), and classroom settings (Long, Morse, & Newman, 1996; Schmuck & Schmuck, 1983; Vorrath & Brendtro, 1985). Moreover, group cohesion has also been identified as a salient factor in group processes, such as in the achievement of established group goals (Lodahl & Porter, 1961; Rose, 1998), conformity to group norm requirements (Back, 1951; Festinger, Gerard, Hymovitch, Kelley, & Raven, 1952; O'Keefe, Kernaghan, & Rubenstein, 1975), and behavior change (Grotjahn, 1981; Yalom, 1995).

Therapeutic Advantages. Members who participate in highly cohesive groups experience several therapeutic advantages. Studies reveal that highly cohesive groups engage in a greater amount of social interaction (French, 1941; Lott & Lott, 1961), engage in more positive interactions (Schachter, Ellertson, McBride, & Gregory, 1951), exert greater influence over their members (Back, 1951), are more effective in achieving goals (Shaw & Shaw, 1962), and have higher member satisfaction (Gross, 1954).

Schmuck and Schmuck (1983) claim that group cohesiveness among the students is a central feature in developing a positive class-room climate. A cohesive classroom group, according to Schmuck and Schmuck (1983), is *"made up of students who are actively involved with one another, who care about one another, and who help one another"* (p. 153). This type of climate can be powerful in the development of a healthy personality.

Healthy, positive, cohesive cultures are goals not only for class-rooms but also for entire programs that use the Positive Peer Culture (PPC) group methodology. In their specific and comprehensive approach to building positive youth subcultures, Vorrath and Brendtro (1985) also assert the importance of cohesion when working with troubled and troubling youth. They state that *"the greater the cohesiveness, the more impact the group will have on its members"* (p. 114). Staff members using PPC believe that one of the best indicators of a cohesive group is *"that the members gravitate to one another and operate as a unit rather than as individuals"* (p. 116).

Research Findings. Results of a study on group cohesion in Re-ED classrooms (Valore, 1991) corroborate the above findings. The research led to an operational definition of group cohesion and a valid and reliable observation instrument. The study yielded the following results: (a) highly cohesive groups have greater resistance to disruption, (b) highly cohesive groups successfully "graduate" significantly more students to less restrictive settings, and (c) *less cohesive groups have significantly more students who do not make a successful transition into less restrictive settings.*

It is clear that group cohesion is a powerful force wherever youths function in small groups. According to Yalom (1995), group cohesion is "a necessary precondition for other therapeutic factors to function optimally" (p. 49). He further states that "cohesiveness in group therapy is the analogue of relationship in individual therapy" (1995, p. 47). Cohesive groups facilitate therapeutic relationships among the teacher-counselor (T-C), the group members, and the group as a whole. These relationships provide members with a feeling of acceptance that enables them to safely share their feelings and inner thoughts and to help one another. Guiding the development of this necessary component of group process is the T-C.

Importance of the Teacher-Counselor

The most important factor in determining the outcome of group work in Re-ED is the T-C and his or her character, skill, and commitment. In describing the T-C, Hobbs said it best:

"But most of all, a teacher-counselor is a decent adult; educated, well trained; able to give and receive affection, to live relaxed, and to be firm; a person with private resources for the nourishment and refreshment of his own life; not an itinerant worker but a professional through and through; a person with a

sense of the significance of time, of the usefulness of today and the promise of tomorrow; a person of hope, quiet confidence, and joy; one who has committed himself to children and to the proposition that children who are disturbed can be helped by the process of re-education" (1982, p. 82).

These attributes are necessary if the T-C is to guide and influence others, model appropriate and responsible behavior, and deal with problem behavior in an effective and therapeutic manner.

Roles of the T-C. To develop a positive cohesive group, the T-C must remain keenly aware of group processes and cultivate those processes throughout the day. This is where the T-C becomes part scientist, part technician, and part artist. The scientist understands the theory of group work and plans and prepares the day with those concepts in mind – carefully observing and constantly processing what occurs to determine "how things are going." The technician skillfully implements prior plans for developing a positive cohesive unit. The artist creates and capitalizes on spontaneous opportunities to reinforce and exemplify both attitudes and indicators of positive cohesiveness. Within these three roles, the T-C shoulders the enormous task of building a positive group culture with eight to ten different members (a typical size for a Re-ED group), each having different strengths, developmental levels, needs, and disparate cultural beliefs and backgrounds. Once established, this culture becomes an ongoing force that continually helps guide the group. As members, teachers, or situations change, the group modifies somewhat to accommodate the shift. This does not, however, hinder the basic personality or culture of the group. It is this positive and healthy culture and cohesiveness that influences group members to change their behaviors and ecologies.

Leadership of T-Cs. Success by the T-C in developing a highly cohesive group depends not only on the scientist, technician, and artist roles, but also on his or her leadership within those roles. According to Toseland and Rivas (1998), leadership is *"the process of guiding the development of the group and its members"* (p. 91).

On the authoritarian/laissez faire continuum of leadership (Lewin, Lippitt, & White, 1939), the T-C employs a democratic leadership style, viewing leadership as a process for maintaining a delicate and flexible balance between being both a member and a leader while guiding the group toward the goal of shared leadership among all members. For example, in a low cohesive group the T-C may be highly engaged in actively guiding the group (authoritative, but not authoritarian), whereas in a high cohesive group he or she may be intentionally quiet and less active, but never apathetic or uninvolved.

The multiple roles of the T-C in working with troubled and troubling youth in groups cannot be over-emphasized. In addition, the character of the T-C must be beyond reproach, allowing him or her to merit the trust and respect of group members.

Re-ED Cohesion Building Strategies

Developing a group of youths into a cohesive unit not only calls for the specific skills, knowledge, and attributes of the T-C listed above, the task also requires specific cohesion building strategies. Group cohesion building strategies have been, as Rousseau (1971) states, "borrowed, created, structured, and refined" (p. 10), beginning with the earliest pioneers of Re-ED. These strategies can be seen in the early writings of Doncaster (1972), Freeman et al. (1971), "Group Process Manual" (1983), Hobbs (1982), Kaset (n.d.), and West, Albright, Jones, Ransom, and Richman (1980). Over the years the list of strategies has grown and become more formalized, structured, and teachable, resulting in the twelve cohesion building strategies that Re-ED programs commonly use (Valore, 1992). The author has categorized these twelve strategies by function and divided them into the categories of Identity, Infrastructure, Involvement, and Integrity.

Identity

1. Name the group. This first strategy is critical to early guidance of a cohesive and healthy group identity. Because of the importance of the name, groups can take up to a week or more in their decision process. Deciding on a positive and healthy name helps in guiding the group to a positive and healthy group identity, whereas negative names tend to promote a negative and unhealthy group identity.

T-Cs guide the process of naming the group toward the goal of a positive theme (e.g., sports, animals, acronyms, nautical or aviation terms). Positive themes can naturally grow from the name and be used to reinforce the group's identity. With continual attention, these themes become pervasive, infiltrating most systems and activities of the group. Such themes can be used to name positive behavior change systems; for special academic/behavioral awards or recognition; to provide visuals to set up a group behavioral contract; and, for group ceremonies, rituals, and routines.

2. Refer to the group by name. For group members to feel a connection to, or ownership of the name, it has to be used. T-Cs use the group's name throughout the day. Whenever the T-C addresses the group, he or she uses the name, for example, "Okay, the Navigators need to get ready for . . .; T E A M 68 (Together Each Achieves More) will be going to the museum today; Let's see the Mountaineers line up for bathroom break; Looks like it's time for the All Stars group meeting." T-Cs also encourage and reinforce all members' use of the group name.

3. Generate group traditions. As Re-ED groups spend time together, many traditions evolve. These are special group-specific activities, rituals, objects, ceremonies, etc., that lend uniqueness and provide an emotional connection to the group. Traditions help to establish a culture and convey the group's history and legacy by celebrating current and past events. Groups accomplish this by creating and maintaining diaries, photo albums, bulletin boards, and other types of records that describe significant group events. Traditions help to celebrate accomplishments. Secret handshakes, rhythmic and synchronized hand clapping, special cheers, etc., are used to acknowledge academic achievement, behavioral progress, and family and other outside school successes. Traditions can also assist with the transitioning and welcoming of new members to the group. Healthy traditions (e.g., service projects), displayed and described, can create a healthy first impression and reduce a new member's anxiety.

Infrastructure

4. Develop group rules and values. Another way to foster a cohesive group is by developing rules and values. Rules answer the questions "What to do?" and "How to behave?" Rules should be few in number and stated positively, informing the member what to do rather than what not to do.

T-Cs use values to explain "Why?" Values provide the energy and motivation for following specific rules. One without the other loses impact, especially with troubled and troubling youth. Members are more likely to follow specific rules if they are connected to values. For example, one value for the rule *Follow Teacher's Directions* may be that school is a place where people learn. Likewise, the rule *Keep Hands and Feet to Self* would be connected to the value of members' feeling and being safe at all times in school. Additionally, the value behind the rule *Participate with the Group* would be to encourage everyone to be responsible in helping each other. Developing and encouraging values also helps create a culture of caring.

The process of discussing rules and values takes time, but is important for several reasons. In younger groups, it may be the member's introduction to rules, values, and their interrelationships. In older groups, members know the basic rules of a classroom. However, they typically do not understand the connection between rules and values. Developing rules and values articulates each group's code of conduct. Establishing rules also avoids trouble; members can construe an absence or lack of focus on rules as an opportunity to construct their own informal, less desirable, and non-therapeutic ones. Lastly, having members participate in the development of rules reduces their opposition to them.

5. Set group goals. Hobbs stated that *"a group goal was a task that the group as a whole would strive to achieve"* (1982, p. 339). Every member works on group goals every moment of the day. Each group member is responsible for his or her behavior and for the behavior of all other members. The primary group goal of every Re-ED group is to improve the overall functioning of the group, leading to its members' successful transitions from the program. Setting group goals is akin to a mission; the group should strive to articulate their purpose for being a group. The group addresses questions such as "Why are we here?" and "What are we, individually and as a group, trying to accomplish?" There are also less formal goals that the group identifies and explores. T-Cs facilitate discussions around less conventional goals like learning to laugh, play, share, and find joy in each day.

6. Establish group norms. Group norms are expectations for behavior that are different from rules. Rules govern what we should or should not do. Norms, or expectations, are less defined—they govern behavior also, but in a less structured way. They are more like road maps to guide our decisions about how to think and act in accord with our values and beliefs. Norms promote pro-social, responsible, caring behavior, and improved self-esteem. In Re-ED groups, the underlying objective for discussing these expectations is to provide opportunities for altruism and hope. Norms typically discussed and adopted include members' dissatisfaction with their existing behavior and the eagerness to change it by learning new behaviors. Other guiding norms include experimentation with new behaviors, supporting others, and providing helpful and nonjudgmental interpersonal feedback.

Involvement

7. Promote teamwork. T-Cs promote teamwork by recognizing, encouraging, and reinforcing behaviors that cultivate collaboration and cooperation among members. Teamwork is encouraged during academics (e.g., cooperative learning groups), group meetings, outdoor education/recreational therapy, leisure activities, and mealtimes. Each day, T-Cs consider the schedule of tasks to be accomplished and design opportunities for teamwork to occur. As a result, members work together throughout the day to complete academic assignments on time and to improve the group's overall accuracy; increase the group's daily behavior rating average; help each other earn a goal activity, choice time, and field trips; help prepare and serve meals;

and cooperatively accomplish many other tasks that have been created by the T-C.

8. Engage members in various group activities. Although group activities, projects, and camping experiences occur less frequently, they have a powerful effect on increasing the cohesiveness of groups. Group activities mostly occur during structured recreational periods, outdoor education lessons, and camping trips. Group activities such as team building games and initiative tasks are designed to increase the ability of the group to work together cooperatively. Team building games are non-competitive activities ranging from using paper and pencil (e.g., a blank Coat of Arms symbol to be used to describe and share qualities about themselves) to initiating low-risk physical exercises (e.g., engaging in non-competitive volleyball where both sides receive a point for each successful volley across the net).

More intense *initiative tasks* challenge students physically. In these efforts, the T-C produces a problem or obstacle that can only be resolved or conquered successfully by the synergistic engagement of all group members. Re-ED groups use two types of initiatives: natural and organized.

Natural initiatives can happen spontaneously (e.g., the river the group is to cross is running higher than expected) or they can be planned with the creative assistance of the T-C (e.g., challenging the group to scale the large stepped wall of the limestone quarry).

Organized initiatives are tasks developed for the specific purpose of challenging groups. Typically found in Scout camps, these are arranged in a manner similar to an obstacle course, ranging from least to most difficult. Initiative courses are demanding, requiring group members to work as a unit to overcome each obstacle (e.g., helping each member over the imagined "electric fence" until all are on the other side).

Not only do initiatives build cohesiveness, they also allow the T-C to periodically assess the group's level of cohesiveness (the stage at which the group is functioning) and the roles of individual members. During the beginning initiatives, in order to better understand the dynamics of their group (especially less cohesive groups), T-Cs pay particular attention to which members frequently follow an observable, sequenced pattern involving: (a) making an initial haphazard attempt at overcoming the obstacle, (b) exhibiting play behavior and argumentativeness as a result of frustration, (c) seeing the emergence of a leader or leaders, (d) problem-solving and planning by the group, (e) exerting peer pressure to include all members, and finally, (f) performing a cohesive group effort.

Group projects, such as *enterprise units* are employed by the T-C to increase the cohesiveness of the group. One of the most popular Re-ED group projects is the enterprise unit, *"a group activity designed to make learning relevant and meaningful"* (Hobbs, 1982, p. 336). The idea for any enterprise unit initially emerges from the interests of group members. Enterprise units take many forms from a simple small business selling snacks in school, to growing a vegetable garden for the local hunger center, to recording and producing music albums. As the group's idea takes form through Planning meetings (see Re-ED Group Meetings), the T-C begins the process of merging academic content into the project for each member, thereby supporting the academic program. It is the rallying and interdependence of group members working to achieve the goals and objectives of the enterprise unit that increases the cohesiveness of the group.

Value *outdoor experiences.* Based on Campbell Loughmiller's work with troubled and troubling youth in camp settings (1965; 1979) and the Outward Bound Schools in England, therapeutic camping experiences have always been an important element of Re-ED programs. Some Re-ED programs are therapeutic camping programs engaging youth full time in the outdoor camping experience; in most Re-ED programs, camping is part of the therapeutic curriculum. Therapeutic camping accelerates the group process, creating a stronger, more cohesive unit. It does this in the time preceding the trip, during the camping experience, and following the completion of the trip.

In the weeks prior to the camping trip much preparation and planning take place. Skills are learned and practiced, schedules arranged, and menus planned. During this phase there is excitement, anticipation, and mild anxiety that helps members come together and provides motivation to accomplish these preliminary tasks.

During the trip, cohesiveness is intensified because the group is in an environment where everyone depends on each other to make the trip successful. It begins after the unpacking of the gear, when daily living jobs are divided up and assigned to each member. At camp, all group members depend on each other's skills and cooperative behavior to create a living environment that meets basic needs and is comfortable. Cohesiveness is also accelerated because the trip provides time for the group to engage in backpacking, canoeing, High and Low Ropes Courses, and other challenging and cohesion building activities. Furthermore, this extended period also affords the group more time to spend in group meetings discussing goals, solving problems, and assessing all aspects of the trip.

Opportunities for cohesion building do not end when the group breaks camp and the gear is packed and loaded. T-Cs know the trip is not over and that the excitement, energy, and many emotions need to be explored and shared. The debriefing process is a critical component of the camping trip; it helps transfer the cohesion built during the trip into everyday activities of the class. This debriefing process begins informally on the drive home from the trip where members share special moments with each other or with the whole group. T-Cs encourage the talk and prepare them for the upcoming Positives meeting (see Re-ED Group Meetings) by commenting on the conversation "Did you guys hear that statement Joe made? That would be a good one for our Positives meeting later." The Positives meeting is the last activity of the trip. Back at the school after the gear is unpacked, group members gather in a circle to remember and share specific positive highlights of the trip.

On the first morning that classes resume at the center, members also participate in a very important debriefing meeting. The post-camping trip debriefing meeting is customary following every camping trip. During this meeting the group discusses in detail every aspect of the trip, from the planning phase through all activities, both large and small, that occurred on both the trip and the ride home. The debriefing meeting is also the forum for discussing how the trip will be recorded and remembered. Recording and remembering the trip will be achieved in different ways by each group, yet these tasks usually involve writing an account of the trip in the group's diary, posting pictures of special events that took place, and labeling and displaying relics from the trip.

9. Use group contingencies. A group contingency is an understanding or contract among all members in which the consequences for all members of the group depend on the behavior of each individual member. The consequences of group contingencies can be either punishing or reinforcing. Needless to say, Re-ED's focus is the latter. Using reinforcing group contingencies can help turn a negative culture around because it engages the group in pro-social behavior. It can change the thinking of troubled and troubling members from "How can I not get caught doing...(something harmful, offensive, etc.)?" to "How can I get caught doing...(something appropriate, responsible, etc.)?" There are several ways group contingencies are implemented; some examples follow.

T-Cs use group contingencies to improve daily rituals and routines (e.g., "As soon as the Navigators are quiet, we can line up."). Kitchen timers set at random time intervals can be used to "catch the group being good" for general classroom behavior improvement. To support the academic program, group members encourage one another to improve their overall percentage on class assignments. Group contingencies are also used to reduce and extinguish those annoying and disruptive behaviors that surreptitiously occur, such as spitballs and specific disturbing noises. Instead of engaging in the "whodunit" game, T-Cs award points to the group for every X number of minutes that pass without incident. Members are rewarded after accumulating X number of points. Over time, the T-C gradually increases the number of minutes until the behavior has been extinguished.

10. Make group meetings part of the daily schedule. The use of group meetings is probably the most powerful cohesion building technique. Through group meetings the T-C can immerse the members into a feeling of groupness and togetherness. Most group theorists and practitioners concentrate on either the individual or the group as the focus of behavior change. In Re-ED, the basis of group work is ecological, focusing on the individual, the group as a whole, and the home and community that affect each member. There are four basic types of group meetings, the Planning, Positives, Problem-Solving, and Evaluation meetings. A more in-depth look at these four meetings follows this list of cohesion building strategies.

Integrity

11. Model to facilitate cohesive interaction and participation. A solid research base (Bandura, 1971) supports the elements, procedures, and effectiveness of modeling. Its application to forming cohesive groups cannot be overlooked. T-Cs model the group's importance by attending all meetings, showing interest in activities, and exhibiting energy and enthusiasm. T-Cs are very aware that if the adult lacks enthusiasm, so will the members. Some incredibly touching, even "corny," but fun and healthy activities and behaviors have worked wonderfully because of an adult's genuine enthusiasm, participation, and caring.

12. Reinforce cohesive behavior. Cohesive behavior is not typical of group members in programs for troubled and troubling youth. Members who learn new behaviors, or re-learn appropriate and responsible behaviors, require shaping, prompting, and cuing. T-Cs are continually watchful that rules are being followed, norms are taking hold, and traditions are being practiced; they use these moments as opportunities to reinforce members' cohesive group behavior. It is through the T-C's constant attention and reinforcement of cohesive behaviors that group members directly and vicariously learn what desirable group behavior is and then engage in it.

Re-ED Group Meetings

Within Re-ED programs, the use of group meetings is a powerful cohesion building strategy. Through group meetings the T-C can immerse the members in a feeling of belonging and togetherness, creating an environment that helps members gain awareness of their strengths and areas needing change. Group meetings of several types are the most frequently used strategies in Re-ED to harness the power of the group for therapeutic and instructional purposes.

For the past several decades, group work has played an important role in the treatment of emotionally disturbed youth. Through group meetings, therapy has aimed to help children gain awareness of their problems; to express feelings, wishes, and conflicts; and to develop a healthy personality leading to appropriate socialization (Kazdin, 1985). Successful group work is performed in the context of an ongoing therapeutic group milieu (Valore, Cantrell, & Cantrell, 2006) as opposed to the more traditional weekly group therapy or training meetings (anger management or aggression control groups) or informal peer groups (e.g., Boy Scouts, YMCA groups) that Dishion, McCord, and Poulin (1999) found ineffective. The following is an overview of the structure, format, and purpose of the four meetings. It should be noted that the therapeutic power comes from the culture developed through the norms, cohesiveness, and most importantly, the therapeutic alliance between the T-C and group members.

T-Cs incorporate group meetings into their daily schedules to provide opportunities for children to focus on their strengths, develop several skills, and address their irrational thinking or cognitive distortions. Youths practice communication, interpersonal, and intellectual skills that lead to behavior change and emotional growth. Members also learn to identify effective solutions and appropriate behavioral choices through problem solving in group meetings. In groups, members learn to plan and to organize in order to become more productive and to have more manageable and less anxiety producing lives (Hobbs, 1982). Members are able to focus on their positive accomplishments, thereby raising their concepts of themselves and their capabilities (Gallagher, 1979; Hobbs, 1982).

Four Types of Group Meetings

Four types of group meetings have remained central and pivotal throughout Re-ED's history: Planning, Positives, Problem-Solving, and Evaluation. Other topic-specific meetings such as anger control, social skills, character development, etc., can occur or be woven into one of the four meetings, depending on the needs of the group.

Planning Meeting. The Planning meeting prepares and plans for the daily and weekly activities of the group (e.g., scheduling outdoor activities, writing letters, developing a food menu for a camping trip, arranging transportation, buying supplies). In Re-ED residential settings, the Sunday night Planning meeting is reserved for the evening activities of the coming week and is conducted by the night T-C. The day T-C is responsible for the Monday morning Planning meeting during which the group develops plans for the daytime activities of the week. In non-residential settings, the Planning meeting is used to plan for the week's activities as well.

As the least complex and demanding of the four meetings, the Planning meeting serves to enable the novice T-C to increase skills and gain experience in group work. This meeting is also a helpful way to introduce new or low cohesive groups to the group experience, since it is the least emotion-laden of the four meetings. Skilled T-Cs frequently engage new or low cohesive groups in brief Planning meetings prior to most activities, thereby increasing their probability of success in the activity and offering multiple opportunities to practice group skills that will generalize to other meetings.

Positives Meeting. The Positives meeting was originally a major part of the Evaluation meeting held at the end of the day, but because of its importance, it has become a separate meeting. The Positives meeting enhances the self-concept of each member by drawing attention to successes, providing a format and forum for peer reinforcement, and developing communication skills. This meeting typically occurs at the end of each day prior to dismissal to home in community-based settings, or just before bedtime in residential settings or on camping trips. Many possible formats can be used during the Positives meeting. The traditional format begins with one group member stating a specific positive act, deed, or accomplishment about him/herself that occurred that day and one specific "positive" about someone else in the group. After he or she finishes, other members can volunteer a positive statement to him or her. Following the volunteered positives, the member chooses someone else to continue the process. This format continues until every member has participated (including the T-C).

Problem-Solving Meeting. This third meeting teaches group members the processes and techniques for resolving problems and conflicts effectively and peacefully. This type of meeting may be requested when any situation creates a problem for one or more group members, affecting the group. The T-C may call a meeting if he or she determines that a situation calls for a group solution to a group problem (e.g., the increasing classroom disruption during non-academic periods) or that a difficult situation requires a group decision (e.g., how to help the local hunger center during their time of need). Re-ED Problem-Solving meetings are solution-based. When a problem exists between group members or with the behavior of one member that affects the group, solutions leading to responsible, caring behavior are emphasized, rather than solutions based on punishment.

The procedure begins with a request for a Problem-Solving meeting. The group identifies and/or defines the problem and decides whether it requires a group decision. If the problem does require group input, the group assembles. A typical beginning ritual includes a call to order, leader selection, and review of the daily schedule as well as academics and other tasks that need to be completed despite schedule interruption. Following the beginning ritual, there is a statement of the problem from the "complainant" and a defense statement from the "defendant" (if relevant). Next, the group focuses on the solution. The group may also evaluate whether to apply the consequences of breaking existing rules. Lastly, before expectations are set for schedule recovery and the closing ritual, group members vote or reach consensus and commit to the solution. Depending upon the age, stage, cohesiveness of the group, and type of problem, Problem-Solving meetings can be simple "solution-seeking" activities, or highly complex and powerful therapeutic group work. A highly cohesive group of adolescents, for example, may engage in problem-solving discussions around difficult issues in their lives. Such discussions require a safe and trustworthy setting, which the Problem-Solving meeting provides.

Evaluation Meeting. The last type of group meeting, the Evaluation meeting, provides daily feedback to members regarding their overall progress. An individual goal procedure is one central structure for providing feedback. The method is devoted primarily to formulating and/or evaluating a behavior goal and plan for each member. The procedure calls for each member to formulate a short-term goal and to develop a plan that will assist the member in achieving that goal. T-Cs lead members to state their goals positively. Goals are set to accelerate strengths or to build new ones that address needs.

During the meeting, the member states his or her goal and plan, evaluates his or her progress, and receives feedback from other group members, who may be asked to say how they can help the member meet his or her goals. If the member is making progress and the plan is working, the member will continue working on the goal until he or she achieves it (using criteria set by the group). If sufficient progress is not made, then the meeting is used to discuss how to adjust the goal and/or plan. After the member attains the goal, a new goal and plan are developed. A more in-depth look at the individual goal procedure is described in other Re-ED writings on group work (Valore, 1992; Valore, Fecser, Valore, Bockmiller, Siemen, & Warren, 1992; Warren & Maxwell, 1983).

Assessing the Group's Cohesiveness

While engaged in their daily teaching activities, T-Cs are continually observing, listening, and "feeling" for indicators of cohesiveness and non-cohesiveness. Their informal assessment is based on indicators of cohesiveness and non-cohesiveness described by Valore (1991) and on gathering information and asking questions related to the previously described strategies. For example, some questions might include the following. How frequently and how many members use the group name? Are the group's traditions in operation? Are group rules followed and values adopted? Do members refer to the group's purpose or mission? Are group norms embraced so as to see members helping each other with encouragement, hope, and care? Do members eagerly engage in group exercises, often completing tasks with few setbacks or problems? Is the need for using group contingencies decreasing? Are meetings held regularly? Are members punctual and do they exhibit an eagerness to attend?

The cohesiveness of a group can be periodically assessed with objective instrumentation such as the Group Meeting Cohesion Profile (Valore, 1991) and sociometric indices, in particular the L-J Sociometric Test (Long, 1965), or informally on an on-going basis by experienced staff.

Conclusion

In Re-ED, the foundation of group work is ecological, focusing on the individual, the group as a whole, and the outside forces that affect each member. The T-C is continually assessing the group from an ecological perspective. Guiding the group involves knowing each member's individual strengths and needs (academic, social/emotional, behavioral, and cultural) and how those strengths and needs will affect the individual, the group, and the individual's ecosystem.

Group work is complicated and labor intensive. Guiding a group of individuals into a positive, healthy, and cohesive unit takes patience and hard work, but the benefits are tremendous, as one can glean from the following vignette.

An Example of a Classroom Meeting

Following a Problem-Solving meeting in a highly cohesive group of older adolescents, the group was quiet and somber as they returned to their seats. The meeting was called because a music compact disc was missing from a student's desk. There was strong circumstantial evidence that Monica, the new student in the group, had stolen the disc. The group had come together, discussed the problem, and presented the evidence, but Monica denied stealing the disc. The group's discussion centered around the topics of trust, what they valued, and how long and hard they had worked to develop their culture. During the meeting, there was no yelling or screaming, except for Monica's loud cry of denial. The members stated their disappointment that this theft had taken place, that there were no consequences, and that they could do nothing more about the situation since there was no direct proof. They also stated they were saddened that this would set the group back because trust had been broken and they would now have to be watchful of their possessions. The group discussion ended and daily activities resumed.

The next morning, Monica called a Problem-Solving meeting. She began by admitting to the group that she had stolen the disc, by apologizing to the group, and by returning the stolen item. She stated that she disliked stealing, but in her former classroom everyone took what they wanted because that was the way things were. She said that even the teachers in her former classroom told students "better watch your stuff in here." No one seemed to care or to encourage trust.

The group accepted Monica's apology and further discussed the group's history and respected reputation. Near the end of the discussion, one member stated, "When I first came to this classroom from being kicked out of my high school, I was handed trust. I was amazed that I didn't have to earn it. No one ever had given me such a gift before. Today, I think we can give that gift to you."

The meeting ended and students resumed their activities, satisfied this time. Dr. Hobbs would also be satisfied and proud to know of this victory in human relatedness in which the outsider has accepted the invitation to join the group.

References

Back, K. W. (1951). Influence through social communication. *Journal of Abnormal and Social Psychology, 46*, 9-23.

Bandura, A. (1971). *Social learning theory.* New York: General Learning Corporation.

Bednar, R. L., & Lawlis, G. (1971). Empirical research in group psychotherapy. In A. E. Bergin & S. L. Garfield (Eds.), *Handbook of psychotherapy and behavior change* (pp. 812-838). New York: John Wiley.

Cantrell, M. L., Cantrell, R. P., Valore, T. G., Jones, J. M., & Fecser, F. A. (1999). A revisitation of the ecological perspectives on emotional/behavioral disorders. In L. M. Bullock & R. A. Gable (Eds.), *The third mini-library series: What works for children and youth with E/BD: Linking yesterday and today with tomorrow.* Reston, VA: Council for Children with Behavioral Disorders.

Cartwright, D. (1968). The nature of group cohesiveness. In D. Cartwright & A. Zander (Eds.), *Group dynamics research and theory* (3rd ed., pp. 91-109). New York: Harper & Row.

Corey, M. S., & Corey, G. (2006). *Groups: Process and practice* (7th ed.). Monterey, CA: Thomson Brooks/Cole.

Dishion, T. J., McCord, J., & Poulin, F. (1999). When interventions harm. *American Psychologist, 54*(9), 755-764.

Doncaster, J. (1972). *The self government system: The therapeutic use of group process.* Unpublished manuscript. Pittsburgh, PA: Pressley Ridge.

Festinger, L., Gerard, H. B., Hymovitch, B., Kelley, H. H., & Raven, B. (1952). The influence process in the presence of extreme deviates. *Human Relations, 5*(4), 327-346.

Freeman, R., Henon, J., Hogan, E. J., Kohl, J., Rousseau, F., Slagle, R., & Weinberg, S. (1971). *Group process in the Re-Education school.* Unpublished manuscript, A project of: The Information-Dissemination Office, Tennessee Re-Education Program, Tennessee Department of Mental Health.

French, J. R. P. Jr. (1941). The disruption and cohesion of groups. *Journal of Abnormal and Social Psychology, 36*, 361-377.

Gallagher, P. A. (1979). *Teaching students with behavior disorders: Techniques for classroom instruction.* Denver: Love.

Gross, E. (1954). Primary functions of the small group. *American Journal of Sociology, 60*(1), 24-29.

Grotjahn, M. (1981). Group cohesion as a factor in the therapeutic process. In H. Kellerman (Ed.), *Group cohesion* (pp. 247-253). New York: Grune & Stratton.

Group Process Manual. (1983). Unpublished manuscript, Pittsburgh: The Pressley Ridge Schools.

Habel, J. C. (1988). Precipitating himself into just manageable difficulties: An intellectual portrait of Nicholas Hobbs. *Dissertation Abstracts International, 50*(5), 1143A. (UMI No. 8911726)

Hobbs, N. (1982). *The troubled and troubling child: Re-Education in mental health, education and human services programs for children and youth.* San Francisco: Jossey-Bass.

Kaset, L. (n.d.). *Group process, goals, and evaluation rap.* Unpublished manuscript.

Kazdin, A. E. (1985). *Treatment of antisocial behavior in children and adolescents.* Homewood, IL: Dorsey.

Lewin, K., Lippitt, R., & White, R. K. (1939). Patterns of aggressive behavior in experimentally created "social climates." *Journal of Social Psychology, 10,* 271-299.

Lodahl, T. M., & Porter, L. W. (1961). Psychometric score patterns, social characteristics, and productivity of small industrial work groups. *Journal of Applied Psychology, 45*(2), 73-79.

Long, N. J., Morse, W. C., & Newman, R. G. (Eds.). (1996). *Conflict in the classroom: The education of at risk and troubled students* (5th ed.). Austin, TX: PRO-ED.

Long, N. J. (1965). *Direct help to the classroom teacher.* [L-J Sociometric Test, chapter 2]. Washington, D.C.: School Research Project, Washington School of Psychiatry.

Lott, A. J., & Lott, B. E. (1961). Group cohesiveness, communication level, and conformity. *Journal of Abnormal and Social Psychology, 62*(2), 408-412.

Loughmiller, C. (1965). *Wilderness road.* Austin, TX: Hogg Foundation for Mental Health.

Loughmiller, C. (1979). *Kids in trouble: An adventure in education.* Tyler, TX: Wildwood Books.

Moos, R. H. (1976). *The human context: Environmental determinants of behavior.* New York: John Wiley.

Moos, R. H. (1979). *Evaluating educational environments.* San Francisco: Jossey-Bass.

O'Keefe, R. D., Kernaghan, J. A., & Rubenstein, A. H. (1975). Group cohesiveness: A factor in the adoption of innovations among scientific work groups. *Small Group Behavior, 6,* 282-292.

Rose, S. D. (1998). *Group therapy with troubled youth.* Thousand Oaks, CA: Sage.

Rousseau, F. (1971). *Behavioral programming in the Re-ED school.* Unpublished manuscript, Tennessee Department of Mental Health.

Schachter, S., Ellertson, N., McBride, D., & Gregory, D. (1951). An experimental study of cohesiveness and productivity. *Human Relations, 4*(3), 229-238.

Schmuck, R. A., & Schmuck, P. A. (1983). *Group processes in the classroom* (4th ed.). Dubuque, IA: Brown.

Shaw, M. E. (1981). *Group dynamics* (3rd ed.). New York: McGraw-Hill.

Shaw, M. E., & Shaw, L. M. (1962). Some effects of sociometric grouping upon learning in a second grade classroom. *Journal of Social Psychology, 57*, 453-458.

Smith, B. G. (1986) *Ideal Elements of Re-ED*. (1986). Westerville, OH: American Re-EDucation Association.

Toseland, R. W., & Rivas, R. F. (1998). *An introduction to group work practice* (3rd ed.). Boston: Allyn & Bacon.

Valore, T. G. (1991). The group meeting cohesion profile: A reliability and validity study. *Dissertation Abstracts International, 53*(8), 2770A. (UMI No.9238107)

Valore, T. G. (1992). *Group process in Re-ED*. Unpublished manuscript, Cleveland, OH: Positive Education Program.

Valore, T. G., Cantrell, R. P., & Cantrell, M. L. (2006). Competency Building in the Context of Groups. *Reclaiming Children and Youth*, 14(4), 228-235.

Valore, T. G., Fecser, F. A., Valore, C. L., Bockmiller, S., Siemen, K., & Warren, R.S. (1992). *Group Process*. Unpublished manuscript, Cleveland, OH: Positive Education Program.

Vorrath, H. H., & Brendtro, L. K. (1985). *Positive peer culture*. Chicago: Aldine.

Warren, R. S., & Maxwell, M. L. (1983). *Group meetings*. Unpublished manuscript, Cleveland, OH: Positive Education Program.

West, F., Albright, L., Jones, J. M., Ransom, L., & Richman, E. (1980). *Group Process*. Unpublished manuscript, Cleveland, OH: Positive Education Program.

Yalom, I. D. (1995). *The theory and practice of group psychotherapy* (4th ed.). New York: Basic Books.

Thomas Valore, PhD, is Staff Development Director at the Positive Education Program in Cleveland, Ohio. Valore@pepcleve.org

26

Achieving Cohesion: The Panthers Become a Group

John Perona

The Panther story actually begins for me in May 1990, when I began my job as a therapist in a day treatment program in Bremerton, Washington, at Kitsap Mental Health Services. On my first day with my team, I entered a quiet classroom, empty of students. Then, "they" arrived: fourteen adolescents, each with their own sets of problems, attitudes, and emotional needs.

Over the next few months, we team members each played our difficult roles of therapist, special education teacher, and program aide, too often conflicting with what each other was doing. We needed to work more in concert. We were fortunate to get a supervisor, Peggy Thoren, who had a vision for a different kind of team approach. Peggy's first plan of action was to take at least one of us to a Re-ED training session at Evergreen State College. I reluctantly went to the training in the summer of 1991, but I really enjoyed it. I came back more excited than I ever had been following four days of training.

That summer we hired another therapist to replace one who had moved on, and a new program aide. Our team now consisted of five persons. However, instead of a supervisor, two therapists, a special education teacher, and a program aide; we now had five teacher-counselors (just with different training backgrounds).

Over the next few months we adopted the tools Peggy and I were given at the Re-ED training and put them to work in our Madrona Day Treatment Program. Doris Jankowski, the special education teacher, had already attended the training and now she had a team willing to use it. Diane Daniels and Javetta Fleury were new and excited about the tools we shared with them. They did, however, feel that they needed more. In the summer of 1992, we all went to the Re-ED training. From there it became history, the real beginning of the Panthers.

The community meeting took on a whole new meaning, as the students began to help establish an agenda. The students wanted to be more than just the "kids in the Madrona Day Treatment Program." They also wanted to use their skills that were "not traditionally used." This group of young people wanted to have a mascot and be "somebodies." Throughout the weeks to come we would see principles of Re-ED woven into our lives as well as those of the young lives in our classroom. (*"Trust between child and adult is essential....,"* Hobbs, 1982, p. 22.)

These young people dreamed up lots of different mascots and finally agreed not only on the mascot, but its color as well. They chose the panther, but not the mean scary one, instead, one much like the famous Pink Panther. Black, yellow, and green became their colors after much group work to decide how those colors could be used to exemplify "The Madrona Panthers." (*"The group is very important....,"* Hobbs, 1982, p. 22.)

Together this group of youngsters wrote a pledge to become a part of the morning group, a community meeting that gave them a predictable daily ritual and ceremony, beginning the day with a promise to recite, as follows:

"Black is for the darkness, that tries to cloud our day.
Yellow is for the sunshine, that brightens up our way.
Green is for the preservation of the land where we reside.
These are the colors the Panthers hold with pride."
(*"Ceremony and ritual give order, stability, and confidence....,"* Hobbs, 1982, p. 22.)

These young people believed they could make a difference. They decided they would work on goals, not only individually, but also as a group. They devised a level system with ways to display goal achievements and to invite other Panthers to encourage them to reach their goals. (*"The group is very important....,"* Hobbs, 1982, p. 22.)

The Panthers decided that their day should also begin with a commitment to a goal, the sharing of that goal, and the means of attaining it. To make their goals achievable, they wrote long and short-term goals, believing that the short-term goals were stepping-stones to achieving the long-term goals. (*"Life is to be lived now, not in the past....,"* Hobbs, 1982, p. 22.)

As these young people came to feel empowered, they expressed a desire to use their strengths and skills as a group to write a school song. Their joint effort, with the help of one of the teacher-counselors, produced a work of art, sung to a tune they all knew and liked by Boyz II Men. These adolescents, who had been labeled behaviorally and emotionally disabled, would sing this song every day at the end of the Positives Meeting, and again at the end of the day after sharing how they performed their daily goal. (*"Ceremony and ritual give order, stability, and confidence....,"* Hobbs, 1982, p. 22.)

The success rate of these young people increased as they mixed academic enrichment with the positive development of their social skills. Becoming a student in the Madrona Day Treatment Program had a new meaning – it meant becoming a "Panther." A Panther displayed such social skills as working together on projects like "Random Acts of Kindness." The Panthers would clean up city blocks with no need to be recognized or thanked. They had a pancake breakfast to raise money for the victims of the Oakland/San Francisco earthquake and felt great that they could contribute. (*"Feelings should be nurtured....,"* Hobbs, 1982, p. 22.)

Classroom management became a much easier task as those who were fast workers had choices for their extra time. The classroom schedule gave each student a choice to keep him or herself busy instead of bothering classmates. For those students who were struggling or frustrated, the teacher-counselor was near, helping to manage the problem before it became an emotional and/or behavioral explosion. Teacher-counselors roamed the classroom looking for opportunities to help struggling students. Transitions became better than just manageable, and the elements and principles of Re-ED were bearing fruit. These Panthers became a cohesive group, even when inviting new Panthers in and saying good-bye to exiting Panthers.

They decided to have two plays, produce a musical for the Christmas Holidays, and orchestrate four overnight campouts. To understand these plays and the musical production, you must know these young people used their strengths to ensure their plays and music production would become memories embedded in the minds of more than just their peers. The first was *The Christmas Carol*. Bob Cratchet was exchanged for Bobbie Cratchet, and her husband stayed home with Tiny Tim. These young minds were allowed to make changes that met the challenges of today's society. The play was a success. The second play, 'The Haunting of Hathaway House,' was a four-part Sci-Fi comedy. The importance of the teacher-counselors being part of the process became more meaningful to me when these young people convinced me to play Aunt Elizabeth, a matronly aunt. I do not know who got a greater kick out of that, them or me, but it sure emphasized the importance of trust between students and staff. (*"Trust between child and adult is essential....,"* Hobbs, 1982, p. 22.)

The musical production was probably the most memorable, as the fourteen adolescents and five teacher-counselors worked for weeks on it. One boy sang, "Daddy Looked a Lot Like Santa," a girl sang "I Saw Mommy Kissing Santa Claus," and duets with staff and kids pleased the audiences and caused staff hearts to overflow. We performed at two different nursing homes, for parents, for staff, and for the agency. At the end of each performance, we all sang, "Have Yourself a Merry Little Christmas." As we did, we walked out among our audience and shook their hands — all in the room seemed connected. Our students shared later that they felt like they were giving something back to their community, which made them feel like contributors instead of takers. (*"Communities are important....,"* Hobbs, 1982, p. 22.)

This group of adolescents found a way to become a community, accepting new members and creating a ceremony for those who left the community to move on to even more successes. The staff were one, united as "Teacher-Counselors," actively involved in all activities. We found we had a lot to give these young lives, and by allowing them to use their strengths and untapped skills, they helped us discover how much they had to give us.

The five years I spent as a Panther Teacher-Counselor provided me with some of the most successful and precious memories I have. I wanted to tell everyone in the fields of education and/or mental health how wonderfully fulfilling work with emotionally disturbed children and youth can be. Re-ED is so important to me that I became a trainer for Re-ED, an executive board member of WAREA, and a member of AREA. I felt a great desire to write my Panther story for you, hoping you can experience similar joy in your work with troubled and troubling young people.

References

Hobbs, N. (1982). *The troubled and troubling child: Re-Education in mental health, education, and human serices programs for children and youth.* San Francisco: Jossey-Bass, Inc.

John Perona, MSW/LMFT, is a therapist for the children's division of Kitsap Mental Health Services in Bremerton, WA. ajpjp@earthlink.net

27

Therapeutic Alliance and Re-ED: Research on Building Positive Relationships with Youth

Mary E. Rauktis, Ana Regina Andrade, & Ann Doucette

For the past decade, researchers and practitioners have hypothesized that the therapeutic alliance between client and therapist is critical to the therapeutic process. This relationship is defined in terms of a mutual emotional bond between client and therapist, agreement on therapeutic tasks and goals of treatment, and a perceived open, truthful relationship (Doucette & Bickman, 2001).

This chapter discusses how Re-ED and therapeutic alliance (TA) relate, briefly reviews the literature on TA, and describes the TA research performed at Pressley Ridge. It presents findings from this program of research, and discusses implications for Re-ED practice.

Re-ED and Therapeutic Alliance

Although Hobbs never used the term "therapeutic alliance," developing an alliance is consistent with the principles of Re-ED. Re-ED programs believe youth can be "re-educated" to be competent and manage their own behaviors with the help of a professional teacher-counselor. Trust between the youth and the teacher-counselor is *"the foundation on which all other principles rest, the glue that holds teaching and learning together, the beginning point for reeducation"* (Hobbs, 1982, p. 245). For years researchers have not found consistent differences in success between varying approaches to

327

psychotherapy. Wolfe & Goldfried (1988) suggest that alliance may be the "quintessential integrative variable" of therapy.

Hobbs believed that in order *"...to gain the trust of a child, it is necessary to believe that the problem of trust is real and that progress toward* [forming trust] *will mean progress toward the child's learning"* (Hobbs, 1982, p. 250). This is prescient of Shirk and Russell's (1996) observation that relationship and technical processes work in concert, priming increased collaboration with treatment tasks.

Competent teacher-counselors demonstrate *"skillful management of individual children and adolescents, groups, and ecosystems, as facilitators of change"* (Hobbs, 1982, p. 87), using a process of "precision programming." Here teacher-counselors work with children, adolescents, and their ecologies to promote change by (1) a shared process with everyone involved to identify and define problems; (2) enabling agreements on ways to achieve these desired changes; (3) opting for measureable or consensually defined behaviors to detail results; (4) setting target dates for accomplishment of goals; and (5) continually evaluating progress (Hobbs, 1982).

Hobbs also identified the personal characteristics and behaviors of a teacher-counselor that enhance building a relationship. Hobbs described a teacher-counselor as *" ...a decent adult; educated, well-trained; able to give and receive affection, to live relaxed, and to be firm; a person with private resources for the nourishment and refreshment of his own life; not an itinerant worker but a professional through and through..."* (Hobbs, 1982, p. 82).

The process by which a teacher-counselor builds trust is one in which *"She must do what she says she will do....but...her behavior must be sensitively tuned to the uncertainties of a particular child or adolescent....A teacher-counselor must be able to define appropriate limits for a particular student....but again, drawing the limits sensibly and not rigidly.....She will nurture trust...by keeping communication...at an optimum level, being neither aloof nor inquisitive, but clearly concerned"* (Hobbs, 1982, p. 247).

Finally, in Re-ED, the teacher-counselor is the professional responsible for working with children, not someone who does "therapy." All activities, inside the class and out, day and night, should lead to learning and "therapeutic" progress for youths. This approach requires a special kind of person: *"The teacher-counselor is a participant in an emergent situation, not the producer of a designed product. The teacher-counselor must be able to deal freely and confidently with complex transactions among people who are trying to discover satisfactory and satisfying ways to live. A child, his parents, a teacher, and the teacher-counselors themselves are experimenting with the possible in a dynamic system of interpersonal negotiations, some of which succeed and some fail. The balance between success and failure often depends on a teacher-counselor's perceptiveness and ability to act immediately, guided both by an agreed-upon strategy and a private surmise about what should be done"* (Hobbs, 1982, p. 88).

In summary, a Re-ED teacher-counselor is a critical person, a professional who knows the child or adolescent best, and thus can influence, encourage and provide direction for change. Change occurs in the context of a relationship built on trust, with shared understanding of goals and the steps to achieve these goals.

Therapeutic Alliance Literature

Focus on therapeutic alliance and its importance in optimizing treatment outcomes has increased markedly in the past decade (Norcross, 2002; Oetzel & Scherer, 2003). While research continues to focus on adults, youths bring distinct characteristics to intervention settings, differentiating them from traditional populations studied in psychotherapy research (Rubenstein, 1998). Differences between adults and youths can complicate the task of securing sufficient engagement in treatment; child/adolescent developmental stages can add complexity to therapeutic exchanges between a youth and intervening adults. In addition, characteristics of intervening adults (such as the ability to empathize and show genuine interest in the youth without judgment) are considered important to therapeutic relationships with the youth.

Much research with adult populations has investigated clinician and client factors that contribute to enhancing both therapeutic alliance and treatment effectiveness. Therapeutic alliance is thought to develop quickly, typically within the first few meetings. This rapidity makes it even more important to identify characteristics that either enhance alliance or provide barriers to an effective relationship. Strupp (1993) found that clinician judgments and attitudes about clients solidify in the first few sessions of therapy, seldom changing in later sessions. These initial impressions may create a self-fulfilling prophecy (Merton, 1948); clinicians with more favorable attitudes towards clients generally have more positive outcomes with those clients.

Likewise, client attitudes about their clinicians also link to more positive outcomes. Clinicians perceived as caring, empathetic, and genuine are associated with more favorable client outcomes (Garcia & Weisz, 2002). Self-fulfilling prophecies by clinicians potentially influence clinical outcomes for adolescents (Jussim, Eccles, & Madon, 1996), school achievement (Jussim, et al., 1996; Rosenthal & Jacobson, 1968), self esteem (Campbell & Lavallee, 1993), and use of alcohol and drugs (Madon, Guyll, Spoth, Cross, & Hilbert, 2003).

Most recent meta-analyses examining the effectiveness of specific treatment modalities report disappointing results (Ahn & Wampold, 2001, Wampold, 2000, 2001); all treatments appear equally efficacious. Growing evidence indicates that the treatment process, including the nature of the alliance, accounts for any variance in outcomes (Horvath & Symonds, 1991; Martin, Garske, & Davis, 2000; Wampold, 2001). While alliance has been widely studied in adults, child psychotherapy process research has "lagged behind its adult counterpart" (Shirk & Karver, 2003, p. 452; Russell & Shirk, 1998). Children and adolescents bring unique attributes to the therapy process that distinguish them from other therapy populations (Shirk & Saiz, 1992). First, children and adolescents do not voluntarily seek treatment, typically entering treatment because adults recognize the need for intervention. Second, establishing a relationship with an adult helper may be at odds with an adolescent's developmental task of establishing independence from adults (DiGiuseppe, Linscott, & Jilton, 1996; Oetzel & Scherer, 2003). Third, cognitive changes and neurological growth during adolescence may influence impulse control and emotional regulation (Spear, 2000; Walker, 2002).

Yet, creating an alliance is as important for children and adolescents as it is for adults. Among adults, past research has shown that the quality of the relationship relates to premature termination of treatment (Horvath & Symonds, 1991; Martin, Garske, & Davis, 2000). Failure to establish a relationship leading to premature termination, is estimated to range from 40% to 60% for youths (Armbruster & Kazdin 1994). Hawley and Weisz (2003) shed light on this process when they found child caregiver-therapist alliance correlating with both fewer drop outs and more family participation for children being seen in out-patient community mental health centers.

Is TA associated with treatment outcomes for children and youth? In a meta-analysis of 23 studies, Shirk and Karver (2003) found therapeutic relationship modestly associated with treatment outcomes, across both differing treatment types and child development levels. In addition, they found that youth characteristics and methodological factors reduced the association between alliance and outcomes. For example, youth characteristics are not consistent across developmental stages. Cognitive, emotional, physical, and behavioral changes can affect a youth's views of the treatment process and the therapeutic relationship (Kendall, 1984). Developmental stages are also likely to impact the accuracy of self-reflection and reporting. Moreover, many youths with mental health challenges experience cognitive delays that can impede engagement in the therapeutic process (Steinberg & Cauffman, 1996).

Alliance studies use varying data collection strategies, some collecting alliance ratings of the clinician/counselor by only the youth, while others collect dyadic ratings from both youths and clinicians. Few studies collect data at multiple points across the course of treatment. Shirk and Karver (2003) suggest that future TA and outcomes research use longitudinal designs, collecting TA data at multiple points across the treatment. It is equally important to consider characteristics of the therapist in building a sound therapeutic relationship. To establish alliance with youths, adults need to balance appropriate empathy, know when to validate an adolescent's behavior, coordinate candor with a youth's developmental capacities, and understand when and how to confront youths without signaling rejection.

Therapeutic Alliance Research at Pressley Ridge

Pressley Ridge began a collaboration with Vanderbilt University in 1999 to study TA in both Day School and therapeutic wilderness camp settings. Our research examined the processes and outcomes related to building and sustaining therapeutic relationships between teacher-counselors and Pressley Ridge youths.

Methods

Settings and Participants. TA was examined in two settings: a Day School and a therapeutic wilderness camp. The Pressley Ridge Day School provides education and behavioral health treatment to 130 children and youth with DSM-IV diagnoses and functional impairments. It operates on a school-year calendar, and is licensed by the Commonwealth of Pennsylvania to provide both special education and partial hospitalization services. An experiential education component allows teacher-counselors and youths to spend one week at the therapeutic wilderness camp and participate in camping, backpacking and other outdoor activities. The Day School provides intensive, relatively short-term educational and therapeutic services to facilitate successful community adjustment and school reintegration. During the school year of 2000-2001, 68% of these youth lived at home with parents or other relatives, while 32% lived outside their homes for additional services. About 20% of the youth population lived with both natural parents. Most youths met the DSM-IV criteria for behavioral and/or oppositional disorders (75%), while 15% were diagnosed as having attention deficit disorder. More than one-fourth had been adjudicated delinquent.

Forty-five teacher-counselors and liaison teacher-counselors are employed at the Day School. The program consists of 12 self-contained classrooms, each with a capacity for 12-14 youths. Two teacher-counselors (a special educator and a mental health specialist, who may be a special education teacher or professional in another related field) work in each self-contained classroom. Average length of stay for Day School youths is slightly more than two school years, with approximately 50 youths discharged each year.

The therapeutic wilderness camp is located on 1,300 acres of wooded land bordering Ohiopyle State Park in southwestern Pennsylvania. The camp at Ohiopyle is modeled after Campbell Loughmiller's work in Texas (Loughmiller, 1965; 1979). Enrollment capacity is 60 boys, ages 9 to 16 at time of intake. Students are referred by local county agencies including Children, Youth, and Family Services and Juvenile Court. A majority of the youths have been diagnosed with attention deficit and conduct disorder; many have a secondary diagnosis of mood disorder (Maxon, 2003). All have exhibited behaviors so troublesome that a therapeutic placement outside the home is seen as the most appropriate alternative setting. The therapeutic wilderness camping process developed at Ohiopyle temporarily removes youths from their home environments and places them in this new and secure environment. Assignment of a youth to a particular group is based on his age, level of maturity, and physical and emotional characteristics and needs. Youths in each treatment group reside in independent campsites, approximately one-quarter mile apart. Each group designs, builds, maintains, and lives in this semi-permanent campsite, planning and cooking about one-third of its meals. Planning and implementation are important competencies learned as the group deliberates, executes, and evaluates its daily, weekly, and longer range goals. Teacher-counselors and liaisons work non-traditional/flexible hours, enabling them to respond to and meet the daily needs of the youths and families. The teacher-counselors work in teams of three, with each team assigned to a group of 10 youths.

Measures

Therapeutic Alliance Scale (TAS). Doucette and Bickman (2001) developed a multi-respondent, youth-focused Therapeutic Alliance Scale (TAS). The TAS provides three respondent forms (youth, therapist/clinician, and caregiver), and is recommended for use as an assessment of the youth-therapist relationship. The initial scale consisted of 35 items. Subsequent psychometric analyses reduced the final scale to 30 items. The TAS uses a 3-point response scale (disagree, some-

what agree, agree) based on the youth's perspective; the therapist/
clinician and caregiver respondent versions use the same measurement
model. Research done in the Day School and the wilderness camp uses
the dyadic TAS rating between the youth and teacher-counselor.

Initial Rasch analyses, using principal components analysis, revealed two dimensions: (1) items characterizing the therapeutic relationship, and (2) resistance/an unfavorable outlook on therapy in general. The therapeutic relationship dimension measures the mutuality
and empathic qualities of the relationship, as well as the collaborative
working rapport. Examples of the items under each respective dimension are provided below:

1. Therapeutic Alliance
(a) Mutuality/Empathic Qualities: "I like my therapist/counselor."
(b) Collaborative Relationship: "My therapist and I work on my
     problems as a team."
2. Resistance/Unfavorable outlook on therapy:
"My counselor focuses on things that are not important to me."

TA scores combine the mutuality/empathic and collaborative
subscales. Resistance subscale results are reported separately. Reliabilities
(Cronbach's alpha) reported for the TAS subscales (resistance, mutuality, and collaborative relationship) are within acceptable ranges: .83, .86,
and .90 respectively (Bickman, de Andrade, Lambert, Doucette, Sapyta,
Boyd, Rumberger, Moore-Kurnot, McDonough, & Rauktis, 2004).

16 Personality Factor (16 PF). Teacher-counselors' personality
characteristics were measured by the Sixteen Personality Factor Questionnaire (16 PF) (Russell & Karol, 1994), one of the most widely
used normal personality tests (Schuerger, 2000). The 16 PF is a
self-report questionnaire of 187 items categorized into primary and
secondary factors. There are 16 primary factors or dimensions and
4 secondary factors. Primary factors are organized into bipolar scales
(e.g., reserved vs. warmhearted) accounting for where an individual
falls within that dimension. Secondary factors are viewed as broader
influences contributing to the primary factors (e.g., introversion vs.
extraversion). The 16 PF was completed by teacher-counselors at
both the Day School and the therapeutic wilderness camp.

Child and Adolescent Measurement System (CAMS). The CAMS consists of five subscales: acuity, social competence, hopefulness, problems, and victimization. Total scores are created for each problem subscale by averaging all items; total scores for internalizing and externalizing problems are created by averaging internalizing and externalizing items (Doucette and Bickman, 2001). The CAMS was administered to youths in the Day School four times a year; teacher-counselors likewise completed a CAMS for each youth in their classrooms.

Data Collection

TA data were collected in eight Day School classrooms. Once a month, all youths rated the TA for each of the two teacher-counselors in every classroom. All youths in each classroom rated the same teacher-counselor at the same time. To control for time of day, each teacher-counselor was rated at alternating times of day. In turn, both teacher-counselors completed TA ratings once monthly for all youths in their classroom.

At the therapeutic wilderness camp, TA data were collected in each of the six treatment groups over six-week intervals to parallel the staff and youth schedules. All youths rated their TAs for each of the three teacher-counselors once every six weeks by rating one of the teacher-counselors every two weeks. Therapeutic alliance ratings were staggered across three time intervals (early morning, midmorning, and afternoon) to control for time of day. Counselors also performed TA ratings for each youth in the group on the same day as youths completed their ratings for teacher-counselors. A staff person read the questions to the youth at both sites, and the counselor being rated was not present when the questionnaires were completed.

Thus, there were two sources of TA data, Counselor-rated Therapeutic Alliance (CTA) and Youth-rated Therapeutic Alliance (YTA). Both teacher-counselors and youths rated the same concepts for almost all items, as when the teacher-counselor is asked, "I am liked by this youth," while the youth is asked, "I like my counselor."

Qualitative information was obtained regarding perceptions about TA, using focus groups composed of youths from the Day School and the therapeutic wilderness camp, divided into homogeneous groups based on their lengths of stay in the programs. Teacher-counselors participated in a separate series of focus groups, created on the basis of job tenure.

Questions about TA were asked of both groups. For example, one youth question was, "What are the things that a teacher-counselor does that help to build a relationship with you?" A similar question for the teacher-counselor was, "What do you think helps to build a good relationship with a youth?"

To address nested and longitudinal structures of the TA data, we used multilevel models (MLM), also known as hierarchical linear models (HLM) (Bryk & Raudenbush, 1992), random coefficient models (RCM), individual growth models, and mixed models. Because youth and teacher-counselors are nested within classrooms, and classrooms within schools, MLM are the most appropriate models for addressing this hierarchical data structure. MLM are also ideal for examining changes in TA at both the individual level and across groups of individuals simultaneously (Hedeker, Gibbons & Flay, 1994; Littell, Milliken, Stroup, & Wolfinger, 1996; Singer & Willett, 2003). Multilevel model procedures recognize that individuals within one group may be more similar to one another than individuals in another group and therefore explicitly model and account for variability within both individuals and groups. In addition, MLM allows use of all available assessments without omitting cases with missing measurements (Akers, Boyce, Rowley, & Price, 2003).

Qualitative data obtained from the focus groups were tape recorded and transcribed. Transcripts were reviewed by two researchers working independently. They looked for themes across and within groups, then classified the themes into two categories: teacher-counselor behaviors and teacher-counselor personalities.

Findings: What We Learned About TA at Re-ED

What we have learned over the course of this research can be summarized into twelve major points about TA. The reader is referred to the referenced reports or articles in order to learn more about the details of methods and findings.

1. Youths and teacher-counselors have positive relationships.

Both youths and teacher-counselors report positive relationships: their average alliance ratings are higher than 2.0 TA points on a 3-

point scale where 1 indicates poor alliance, 2 is neutral, and 3 is excellent (Figure 1). Alliance ratings vary across classrooms, youths, and teacher-counselors; substantial variation in the ratings across teachers and youths suggests that both teacher-counselors and youths can differentiate how their relationships are doing (Doucette & Andrade, 2003).

Figure 1

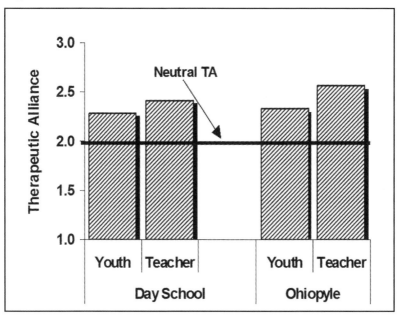

2. Alliance is established early for the youths.

Alliance between the youth and the teacher-counselor is formed early in the relationship (Figure 2). For youths, the relationship stays constant over time (Bickman, de Andrade, Lambert, Doucette, Sapyta,, Boyd, Rumberger, Moore-Kurnot, McDonough, & Rauktis, 2004). If TA forms early and remains relatively constant, teacher-counselors may only have an early "window of opportunity" (Doucette & Andrade, 2003; Doucette, Bickman, & Andrade, 2002).

Figure 2

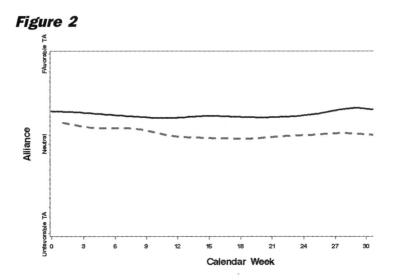

Solid Line= Day School Dashed= Wilderness Camp

3. Youths think differently about TA than do adults.

Teacher-counselors do not accurately perceive how youths view their relationship. On average, teacher-counselor alliance ratings are higher than youth ratings; in other words, teacher-counselors perceive a better relationship than the one described by the youth. Figure 3 shows the discrepancies between TA ratings reported by youths and their corresponding teacher-counselors (Doucette & Andrade, 2003; Doucette, Bickman & Andrade, 2002).

4. Certain 16 PF profiles seem better at fostering TA.

The teacher-counselor personality profile (as measured by the 16 PF) found higher youth reported alliance to be associated with higher levels of: *warmth, flexibility, stability*, and *tranquility*. In addition, *being genuine*, or not focused on "managing appearances," was associated with higher reported youth alliance. This finding was also corroborated by the youths in the focus group interviews (Boyd, Pinkard, Rauktis, & Kurnot, 2003; Doucette & Andrade, 2003).

5. Certain teacher-counselor behaviors foster TA.

If personality is the "trait," then behaviors can be thought of as the "state," more easily influenced than personality. Behaviors associated with higher youth reported alliance include: (a) knowing each youth's

Figure 3

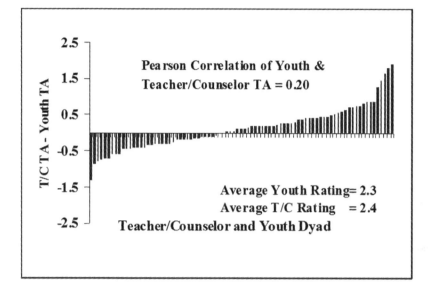

treatment goals and helping the youth to work on those each day, (b) holding youth accountable to program expectations, (c) knowing and implementing treatment program strategies, (d) demonstrating leadership with the youth and the group, (e) keeping events in perspective and modeling this skill, (f) being fair in dealings with youth, (g) demonstrating how to work as part of a "team," and (h) being able to "play" and use humor in an appropriate manner (Boyd, Pinkard, Rauktis, & Kurnot, 2003).

6. Youth symptoms or levels of functioning do not harm TA.

Youths' reported levels of alliance are not affected by their levels of functioning or their internalizing or externalizing symptoms as measured by the CAMS. Youths may be functioning at a low level, or have a high degree of depression or another emotional disorder, and still report that they feel an alliance with a teacher-counselor (Doucette, Andrade, Bickman, Rauktis, Kurnot, & Boley, 2003).

7. Youth age affects TA.

Younger youths report a higher rate of TA improvement than adolescents. To illustrate, if two youths start out reporting low alliance with their teacher-counselor, the younger will show a faster improvement in alliance than the adolescent. Adolescents who initially report lower alliance levels show no improvement or even deterioration over time. This suggests that younger youths believe their relationships with teacher-counselors improve during the school year, whereas adolescents may feel that once their relationship is established, change is more difficult (Doucettte & Andrade, 2003).

8. Teacher-counselors believe in spending time with youth.

Teacher-counselors believe that spending more time with youths will improve their relationships with both adolescents and younger youths, regardless of the youth's response (Doucette & Andrade, 2003).

9. Youths can be resistant and still report high TA.

Although this may appear contradictory, we have found that a youth can report both resistance to, and alliance with, a teacher-counselor. Recall that TA includes liking the teacher-counselor and having a "working" rapport. Being resistant to treatment is measured on a separate subscale. A youth can report both high levels of alliance and high levels of resistance.

Interestingly, while a youth can be both aligned and resistant, teacher-counselors think differently (see Figure 4). With resistant youths, teacher-

Figure 4

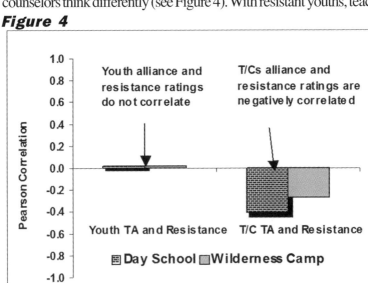

counselors believe it will be more difficult to build alliances (Doucette & Andrade, 2003; Doucette, Bickman & Andrade, 2002). This is an important perceptual difference as well as a critical training and supervision issue. Working with troubled youths can frustrate teacher-counselors. Positive results of their work may not be realized until after the youth leaves, so they may miss the satisfaction of seeing changes in his/her behaviors and then achieving success in school, social, and family life. Thus, it is not surprising that a teacher-counselor may give up, believing that a youth's resistance means, "I am not reaching this kid."

Relationship building with adolescents can be difficult, since adolescence's task is establishing independence. An adolescent's experiences may have led to wariness of adults. Hobbs counsels teacher-counselors *"to accept genuinely the adolescent's need for privacy, autonomy, and idiosyncratic selfhood. Patience, a reserved availability, and a dependable acceptance are part of the adult's needed response pattern"* (Hobbs, 1982, p. 250). Teacher-counselors also need to look to others for support and *"to use private resources for personal understanding and support, especially when the going is tough"* (Hobbs, 1982, pp. 250-251).

10. Experience and education make a difference for TA.

Teacher-counselors with higher levels of education and more years of experience seem to foster better alliance (Doucette & Andrade, 2003; Doucette, Bickman, & Andrade, 2002).

11. Aggression affects TA but this changes over time.

At the first of the Day School year when relationships were new, aggressive youths who underwent restraints report weaker alliances with their counselors, while their teacher-counselors believed relationships with youths were more difficult; youths with aggressive behaviors got less favorable ratings by their counselors than non-aggressive youths. But aggressive youths also believed that their relationships with their teacher-counselors improved over time and alliances got better during the school year. Day School teacher-counselors also believe that relationships improve over time (Doucette & Andrade, 2003).

A different pattern was seen at the therapeutic wilderness camp. As with the Day School, when relationships were new, youths with aggressive behaviors and high numbers of restraints reported weaker alliances with their counselors. However, youths at the therapeutic wilderness camp did not believe that relationships with their corresponding teacher-counselor improved over time. The rate of improvement in alliance was flat for aggressive youths in that setting. While additional analyses need to be performed to determine why TA differs by setting, it may be that the isolation of the camp and its being a residential setting may affect how youths view physical interventions. Youths out in the woods and dependent upon a teacher-counselor may give different meanings to a physical intervention.

12. Restraints affect youth TA.

Using a dynamic method of analysis for looking at restraints and TA over time, we found that youth TA went down temporarily after a restraint, but after a few days returned to the previous level. Thus, youth TA seems to be relatively resilient. Teacher-counselor alliance was unaffected: restraints did not affect teacher-counselor TA (Doucette & Andrade, 2003).

Implications for Re-ED
Practice and Future Research

To anyone who has worked with youths in a Re-ED setting, these findings are probably not surprising. However, while they provide some answers, they also raise additional questions:

1. Do youths with higher levels of TA have better outcomes than youths with lower levels? That is, if a teacher-counselor has a high degree of alliance with a youth, and provides treatment in a Re-ED setting, does this youth function better at home, at school, and in the community?

2. Can we train and supervise teacher-counselors so that they improve their alliances with youths?

3. How do we share results with teacher-counselors and supervisors?

Recruitment, Selection, and Retention

Hobbs believed that *"the teacher-counselor is 'the heart of Re-ED'"* (Hobbs, 1982, p. 92). In the original grant proposal to NIMH, nine personal attributes of teacher-counselors were listed: *"ability to*

*experience, accept and handle feelings with minimum distortion....,
ability to tolerate anxiety without dulling...., ability to exercise
authority.....,ability to refresh..independently of work...., commitment to children...., effective interpersonal relationships with
adults...., skills in general teaching...., skills in special teaching....,
[and] general culture"* (Hobbs, 1982, pp. 97-98). In 1982, Hobbs
added that while he would continue to stress commitment to children,
he would also be disposed to add to the above list the following:
"...[S]ensitive, resolute, creative or *inventive, exuberant* or *zestful* or *quietly purposeful, serious* and *joyous* altogether, *inquisitive, enthusiastic, warm* and *affectionate, stern* even, *professional*
in the demanding sense of that word, *playful* perhaps, *resourceful*
surely, *responsible* and *aware* — aware of themselves, of their world,
of children in all their marvelous simplicity and complexity"* (Hobbs,
1982, pp. 98-99).

Hobbs (1982) believed the best way to select teacher-counselors is to look for evidence of an enduring commitment to children in
the life histories of applicants, look for special interests and skills, and
require a college degree. He advised that self-selection is one of the
most reliable indicators.

Our findings validate that there are personal characteristics correlating with higher alliance with youth. However, much has changed in
our funding and public health systems in the years since Hobbs wrote
The Troubled and Troubling Child. Re-ED is an ecological and competence based approach, while funding is currently based upon a medical model. As early as 1986, the American Re-Education Association identified that inadequate funding limits how a Re-ED program
hires and uses staff (AREA, 1986). Nonetheless, Hobbs may have
been right on target when he advised looking for, recruiting, and selecting teacher-counselors on the basis of certain attributes, in addition to a history of commitment to children. Interviews can be structured to elicit examples of how people respond in certain situations,
and applicants can be asked to write "life histories." Applicants can
do a personality Q-Sort where they sort descriptors (e.g., "organized"; "spontaneous") into piles from "least like" to "most like."

Retaining teacher-counselors who are able to establish alliance is a separate, but important, issue. Personality characteristics of someone who establishes alliance with youth may not be the same as personality characteristics of a good manager. Yet many supervisors and program managers were once teacher-counselors. While some may desire a management position, many seem to transfer since switching to a management position is the best way to increase salary and continue advancing in a career.

Teacher-counselors who want to continue working directly with children and youth need career paths, allowing employees, through education, training, and experience to advance in competence, responsibility, and compensation (Lee, 2003).

Skills Training and Supervision of Staff

While limited research exists on how therapist interventions or behaviors contribute to child or family alliance formation, our research suggests that alliance, particularly for adolescents, is formed early in treatment and may be associated with therapist behaviors. The question then becomes, can a teacher-counselor learn to establish TA?

While studying the effects of structured clinician training on adult client perspectives of alliance, one research group (Hilsenroth, Ackerman, Clemence, Strassle, & Handler, 2002) found that patients rated their TA very positively with graduate clinicians who had received structured clinical training. Specifically, the clinical training focused on training the graduate students to identify patient goals collaboratively and agree on tasks of treatment early in the treatment process. These findings were similar to an earlier study of structured clinical training and alliance (Crits-Christoph, Siqueland, Chittams, Barber, Beck, Frank, Liese, Luborsky, Mark, Mercer, Onken, Najavits, Thase, & Woody, 1998).

How does ongoing supervision impact alliance between a youth and the teacher-counselor? Despite a logical connection between supervisory styles and their impact on training and supervision, most treatment outcome studies have not examined the differential effects of supervisors on patient outcomes (Hilsenroth et al., 2002). The work of Hilsenroth et al. with trainees suggests that supervision which is supportive but also provides structured technical directions, is more effective in promoting alliance. Clearly, examining and training supervisors to provide training that promotes and supports alliance is important future work.

Conclusion

A principle of Re-ED is that the teacher-counselor has the ability to influence, encourage and provide direction for change. Our research has demonstrated that the relationship between youths and teacher-counselors can be observed and measured, and that certain youth and teacher-counselor characteristics affect the relationship. It is as critical now as it was when Project Re-ED was first funded that we identify, train, supervise, and support individuals who work most closely with youths. Fostering a trusting and committed relationship between youths and helping adults is an important part of the Re-ED model and a prerequisite for meaningful change.

References

Ahn, H., & Wampold, B. E. (2001). Where, oh, where are the specific ingredients? A meta-analysis of component studies in counseling and psychotherapy. *Journal of Counseling Psychology, 48*(3) 251-257.

Akers, J., Boyce, G., Rowley, S., & Price, C. (2003, March). *Child and family outcome findings in the Utah Frontiers Project: HLM and triangulation support evidence for positive effects.* Paper presented at The 16th Annual Research Conference: A system of Care for Children's Mental Health: Expanding the Research Base, Tampa, FL.

American Re-EDucation Association. (1986, August). The ideal elements of Re-ED. Westerville, OH: The American Re-Education Association.

Armbruster, P., & Kazdin, A. E. (1994). Attrition in child psychotherapy. *Advances in Clinical Child Psychology, 16,* 81-108.

Bickman, L., de Andrade, A. R., Lambert, E. W., Doucette, A., Sapyta, J., Boyd, A. S., Rumberger, D., Moore-Kurnot, J.

M., McDonough, L., & Rauktis, M. E. (2004). Youth therapeutic alliance in intensive treatment settings. *Journal of Behavioral Health Services and Research.*

Boyd, A. S., Pinkard, T., Rauktis, M., & Kurnot, J. (2003, January). *Establishing favorable relationships between clinicians and youth in therapeutic day school and wilderness camp settings: A qualitative study.* Poster session presented at the Seventh Annual Conference of the Society for Social Work and Research, Washington, DC.

Bryk, A. S., & Raudenbush, S. W. (1992). *Hierarchical linear models: Applications and data analysis methods.* Thousand Oaks, CA: Sage.

Campbell, J. D., & Lavallee, L. (1993). Who am I? The role of self-concept confusion in understanding the behavior of people with low self-esteem. In R. F. Baumeister (Ed.), *Self-esteem: The puzzle of low self-regard* (pp. 3–20). New York: Plenum Press.

Crits-Christoph, P., Siqueland, L., Chittams, J., Barber, J., Beck, A., Frank, A., Liese, B., Luborsky, L., Mark, D., Mercer, D., Onken, L., Najavits, L., Thase, M., & Woody, G. (1998). Training in cognitive and supportive-expressive, and drug counseling therapies for cocaine dependence. *Journal of Consulting and Clinical Psychology, 66,* 484-492.

DiGiuseppe, R., Linscott, J., & Jilton, R. (1996). Developing the therapeutic alliance in child-adolescent psychotherapy. *Applied and Preventive Psychology, 5,* 85-100.

Doucette, A., & Andrade A. R. (2003, October). *Therapeutic Alliance Project: Final Year Report 2002-2003.* The Center for Mental Health Policy, Vanderbilt University.

Doucette, A., Andrade, A., Bickman, L., Rauktis, M., Kurnot, J., & Boley, L. (2003, March). *The Quality of the Therapeutic Relationship and Youth Clinical Characteristics.* Paper presented at The 16th Annual Research Conference: A System of Care for Children's Mental Health: Expanding the Research Base. Tampa, FL.

Doucette, A., & Bickman, L., (2001). *Child Adolescent Measurement System: User Manual.* Unpublished Manuscript. The Center for Mental Health Policy, Vanderbilt University.

Doucette, A., Bickman, L., & Andrade, A. R. (2002, August). *Therapeutic Alliance Project: Final Year Report 2001-2002.* The Center for Mental Health Policy, Vanderbilt University.

Garcia, J. A., & Weisz, J. R. (2002). When youth mental health care stops: Therapeutic relationship problems and other reasons for ending youth outpatient treatment. *Journal of Consulting and Clinical Psychology, 70*(2), 439-443.

Hawley, K. M., & Weisz, J. R. (2003, March). *Engaging Families in Mental Health Services: Focus on the Therapeutic Working Alliance.* Poster session presented at The 16th Annual Research Conference: A System of Care for Children's Mental Health: Expanding the Research Base. Tampa, FL.

Hedeker, D., Gibbons, R. D., & Flay, B. R. (1994). Random-effects regression models for clustered data with an example from smoking prevention research. *Journal of Consulting & Clinical Psychology 62*(4), 757-765.

Hilsenroth, M. J., Ackerman, S. J., Clemence, A. J., Strassle, C. G., & Handler, L. (2002). Effects of structured clinician training on patient and therapist perspectives of alliance early in psychotherapy. *Psychotherapy: Theory, Research, Practice, Training, 39*(4), 309-323.

Hobbs, N. (1982). *The troubled and troubling child: Re-Education in mental health, education and human services programs for children and youth.* San Francisco: Jossey-Bass, Inc.

Horvath, A. O., & Symonds, B. D. (1991). Relation between working alliance and outcome in psychotherapy: A meta-analysis. *Journal of Counseling Psychology, 38*(2), 139-149.

Jussim, L., Eccles, J., & Madon, S. (1996). Social perception, social stereotypes, and teacher expectations: Accuracy and the quest for the powerful self-fulfilling prophecy. In M. P. Zanna (Ed.), *Advances in experimental social psychology* Vol. 28. (pp. 281–388). San Diego, CA: Academic Press.

Kendall, P. C. (1984). Behavioral assessment and methodology. *Annual Review of Behavior Therapy: Theory and Practice, 9*, 39-94.

Lee, N. P. (2003). *The Pressley Ridge Personnel System.* Pittsburgh, PA: Human Resources Department, Pressley Ridge.

Littell, R. C., Milliken, G. A., Stroup, W. W., & Wolfinger, R. D. (1996). *SAS system for mixed models.* Cary, N.C.: SAS Institute.

Loughmiller, C. (1965). *Wilderness road.* Austin, Texas: Hogg Foundation for Mental Health.

Loughmiller, C. (1979). *Kids in trouble: An adventure in education.* Tyler, Texas: Wildwood Book Company.

Madon, S., Guyll, M., Spoth, R., Cross, S., & Hilbert, S. J. (2003). The self-fulfilling influence of mother expectations on children's underage drinking. *Journal of Personality & Social Psychology, 84*(6), 1188-1205.

Martin, D.J., Garske, J. P., & Davis, M. K. (2000). Relation of the therapeutic alliance with outcome and with other variables: A meta-analytic Review. *Journal of Consulting and Clinical Psychology, 68*(3), 438-450.

Maxon, G. (2003). Outcome Report for the Ohiopyle Therapeutic Wilderness Camp, 2002. Pittsburgh, PA: Department of Evaluation & Research, Pressley Ridge.

Merton, R. K. (1948). The self-fulfilling prophecy. *Antioch Review, 8*, 193–210.

Norcross, J. C. (2002). *Psychotherapy relationships that work: Therapists contributions and responsiveness to patients.* New York: Oxford University Press.

Oetzel, K. B., & Scherer, D. G. (2003). Therapeutic alliance with adolescents in psychotherapy. *Psychotherapy: Theory, Research, Practice, Training, 40*(3), 215-225.

Rosenthal, R., & Jacobson, L. (1968). Teacher expectations for the disadvantaged. *Scientific American, 218*, 19–23.

Rubenstein, A. K. (1998). Guidelines for conducting adolescent psychotherapy. In G. P. Koocher, J. C. Norcross, & S. S. Hill (Eds.), *Psychologists' desk reference* (pp. 265-268). New York: Oxford University Press.

Russell, M. T., & Karol, D. L. (1994). *The 16 PF Fifth Edition Administrator's Manual.* Champaign, IL: Institute for Personality and Ability Testing.

Russell, R. L., & Shirk, S. R. (1998). Child psychotherapy process In T. H. Ollendick, & R. J. Prinz, (Eds), *Advances in clinical child psychology.* (pp. 93-124). New York: Plenum Press.

Schuerger, J. M. (2000). The sixteen personality factor questionnaire (16 PF). In C. E. Watkins & V. L. Campbell (Eds.), *Testing and assessment in counseling practice*, 2nd Ed. (pp. 73-110). Mahwah, NJ: Erlbaum.

Shirk, S. R., & Karver, M., (2003). Prediction of treatment outcome from relationship variables in child and adolescent psychotherapy: A meta-analytic review. *Journal of Consulting and Consulting and Clinical Psychology, 71*(3), 452-464.

Shirk, S. R., & Russell, R. L. (1996). *Change processes in child psychotherapy: Revitalizing treatment and research.* New York: Guilford Press.

Shirk, S. R., & Saiz, C. (1992). Clinical, empirical and developmental perspectives on the therapeutic relationship in child psychotherapy: *Development and psychopathology, 4*, 713-728.

Singer, J. D. & Willett, J.B. (2003). *Applied longitudinal data analysis: Modeling change and event occurrence.* New York: Oxford University Press.

Spear, L. P. (2000). Neurobehavioral changes in adolescence. *Current Directions in Psychological Science, 9*(4), 111-114.

Steinberg, L., & Cauffman, E. (1996). Maturity of judgment in adolescence: Psychosocial factors in adolescent decision making. *Law and Human Behavior, 20*(3), 249-272.

Strupp , H. H. (1993). The Vanderbilt psychotherapy studies: Synopsis. *Journal of Consulting and Clinical Psychology, 61*(3), 431-433.

Walker, E. F., (2002). Adolescent neurodevelopment and psychopathology. *Current Directions in Psychological Science, 11*(1), 24-28.

Wolfe, B. E., & Goldfried, M. R., (1988). Research on psychotherapy integration: Recommendations and conclusions from an NIMH workshop. *Journal of Consulting and Clinical Psychology, 56*(3), 448-451.

Wampold, B. E. (2000). Outcomes of individual counseling and psychotherapy: Empirical evidence addressing two fundamental questions. In S. D. Brown & R. W. Lent (Eds.), *Handbook of Counseling Psychology,* 3rd ed, (pp. 711-739). New York: John Wiley.

Wampold, B. E. (2001) *The great psychotherapy debate: Models, methods and findings.* Mahwah, NJ: Erlbaum.

Acknowledgements

Support for this chapter was provided by a grant from The Pressley Ridge Foundation. We are grateful to the youth and teacher-counselors who have supported this research through their participation. Special thanks to the following individuals for their intellectual and practical support and expertise: Scott Finnell, PhD, Len Bickman, PhD, Richard Reed, Clark Luster, Lynne Boley, Mary Lynn Pleczkowski, Luke McDonough, David Rumberger, A. Suzanne Boyd, PhD, and Joyce Kurnot-Moore. Finally, special thanks to Jim Doncaster and Jim Akers, PhD for their careful reading and editing of this chapter.

Mary E. Rauktis, PhD, LSW, is former Director of Evaluation and Research Department at Pressley Ridge in Pittsburgh, PA, and currently Assistant Professor at the University of Pittsburgh School of Social Work, Child Welfare Research and Training Program in Pittsburgh, PA.
    mar104@pitt.edu

Ana Regina Vides de Andrade, PhD, is a Research Associate at the Center for Evaluation and Program Improvement and a Senior Lecturer in Economics, Department of Economics at Vanderbilt University in Nashville, TN.
    ana.andrade@vanderbilt.edu

Ann Doucette, PhD, is a Research Professor at The George Washington University Medical Center in Washington, DC.
    doucette@gwu.edu

28

Starting a Grassroots Movement: Washington Re-EDucation Association (WAREA)

Kris Reinbold, Tricia Jump,
Mike Oliver, & Lisa Hoyt

Washington Re-EDucation Association (WAREA) is a multidisciplinary group of individuals, brought together because of a common need -- to help youth with emotional, behavioral disabilities (E/BD) and the staff who work with them. Much like a Re-ED classroom, we have gone through the forming, storming, norming, and performing stages (Stanford, 1977), and we keep working to learn from each stage and continue to cycle through them as we grow. The following is a brief account of our development to date. We have come a long way, but know where we want to go and look forward to what is ahead.

Planting the Seed

Our story starts with one person who found a magic seed. She brought it home to plant in the fertile soil of Washington State and now is able to clearly see the fruits of her labor through growth in many different fields of care for "our children and youth." We give Mary Sarno, an administrator from the Washington Department of Social and Health Services (DSHS) full credit for connecting with Re-EDucation and making it her mission to bring it to the children and staff of Washington State. She was first introduced to Re-EDucation at an American Re-EDucation Association (AREA) conference at

UCLA in the summer of 1986 when she met Rico Pallotta, then the Executive Director of the Positive Education Program (PEP) of Cleveland, Ohio and Mary Lynn Cantrell, an early Project Re-ED teacher-counselor and PEP's Director of Training at the time. Mary Sarno was amazed by PEP's "no eject, no reject" policy and the principles of Re-ED.

Charged with energy and determination, Mary started to plant the seed of Re-ED in Washington. Her vision was to create a continuum of services with a Re-ED focus, ranging from public schools to 24-hour residential care for troubled and troubling youth. With support from the network of Re-EDers she met at the conference, she began by bringing consultants in and sending groups of people from Washington to visit PEP in Cleveland for their summer training. Dr. Frank Fecser was the key person from PEP to provide trainings and consultation in Washington, helping programs that worked with Children with E/BD to maximize their efforts to serve these youth. From 1987 to 1995, he consulted with over 500 education and mental health staff in 20 different school districts and mental health agencies throughout the state of Washington. During these consultations and some additional training provided by Frank and PEP staff, the founding members of WAREA were introduced to the ideals and principles of Re-EDucation.

From 1987 to 1990, Mary Sarno was able to send Washington State staff from diverse programs to PEP in Cleveland to experience Re-ED first hand. Kris Reinbold of the Shoreline School District and Melody Harless of Mental Health North, working in a collaborative Day Treatment Program in Shoreline, were two of the lucky few to attend PEP's 1990 summer training. Kris recollects, "At the end of our first year of working together, we went to PEP's Summer Institute in Cleveland. When we walked into the Eastwood K-12 Day Treatment Center, we were simply amazed how the whole school was connected and staff worked together as teacher-counselors. Things ran like clockwork. It felt so familiar, like going home to a place you've known forever. It was very reinforcing to see what we were trying to do with our own program — put into words, systems, and principles. We learned so many things and were inspired to go home and implement new strategies — and to increase our expectations of both our students and staff. It was like a big 'Ah Ha!'"

In 1991, Mary and Frank decided to bring PEP's summer training to Washington to expose more educators and clinicians to the Re-ED model. Topics included in these trainings were behavior management, communication and conflict management, group process, working with the child's ecology, and an overview of the Re-ED philosophy. After a few trainings, Frank had some local practitioners help present with his PEP staff. These first few "Re-EDers" had many discussions about how these summer institutes in Washington could have a more "homespun" feel to them, with even more local people taking charge of them. The soil was prepared and fertilized for more planting.

After three summers of trainings, Frank had developed a group of practitioners in Washington State who had the Re-ED momentum going, and were interested in collaborating to help spread the word and the strength of Re-ED's structures and principles. With his encouragement, this group of 19 people consulted with a lawyer, an accountant, and a financial institution about starting a small non-profit organization called Washington Re-EDucation Association (WAREA).

The original Steering Committee consisted of staff from Shoreline School District, Mental Health North, Edmonds School District, Seattle Children's Home, Child Treatment and Study Program, Kitsap Mental Health, Issaquah School District, the Department of Social and Health Services (DSHS), and the Puget Sound Educational School District. Our first executive board members were: Mary Sarno, *Past-President*, Bridget Walker, *President*, Lou Ann Hepp, *President-Elect*, Melody Harless, *Treasurer*, and Joyce Houser, *Secretary*. Bridget Walker recalls, "The biggest challenge was just finding the time to pull people together."

An Organization of Individuals

We were, and still are, a group formed of individuals, "working in the field." This early group of practitioners represented a full continuum of service opportunities for the troubled and troubling youth in the Seattle area, from public schools to residential care. There are many individuals within our organization worth noting and praising for their efforts and commitment to Re-ED and WAREA. We are all individuals who want to see change in our state so that troubled and troubling children are guided in a predictable, positive, and caring way that facilitates changes in their lives. Each of us believes that Re-ED is the vehicle to drive that change. We each have witnessed transformations in our personal and professional environments.

Collective Action

Several key factors helped our organization move forward after a lot of coaxing and encouragement from "Father Frank." The first factor was a commitment from our school districts' and mental health agencies' administrators to provide both resources and time to get together as a group to brainstorm ideas. We had monthly board meetings and were able to focus as a committee on group process, business procedures, goals for the future, and what to do first!

In 1995, our first undertaking as an organization was to host a 2-day summer training session focusing on the principles, structures, and best practices of Re-ED, following the format and information provided at the PEP summer institute. We worked to make this information our own, and developed a core curriculum as the basis for our future trainings. During the initial development phase, it was important for us to define our mission statement:

"We are a group of educators, clinicians, and administrators whose concern is the welfare of troubled and troubling children and youth in the state of Washington. Our purpose is to promote, encourage, and support the use of Re-EDucation principles and practice in a variety of settings and modalities."

The by-laws and articles of incorporation for a non-profit organization that we wrote had to clearly define what our business would involve. There were no large agencies practicing Re-EDucation in Washington State. WAREA made it possible for individual practitioners to represent their school districts or mental health agencies in ways that would give strength and diversity to Re-ED in Washington. Through WAREA, we wanted to: (1) create "Master Trainers" to present the Re-ED ideas to a wide variety of people in many different settings; (2)

provide a forum to share ideas, concerns, and support to help us deal with the day-to-day issues of working with troubled and troubling youth; and (3) help change things on a broader policy/ bureaucratic level to make life better for "our kids,"their families, and those who work with them.

In addition to the invaluable work of Frank Fecser and Mary Sarno, WAREA received generous grants from the Washington State Department of Social and Health Services (DSHS), and more recently from the Washington State Office of Superintendent of Public Instruction (OSPI), allowing us to provide trainings at greatly reduced costs. The result has been that our trainings have been offered to well over 4,000 people as of this writing. As we continue our work, we are fortunate to have several local school districts include WAREA trainings and consultations in their budgets.

Planting More Crops

Training Others

Washington Re-EDucation Association's original focus was training local practitioners in the Re-EDucation philosophy. As practitioners and members of WAREA, we had adopted a philosophy about how to approach our work with troubled and troubling children. Our jobs were dispersed around the state within different programs, school districts and mental health organizations. As we began to create a core-training curriculum, one of our first tasks was to determine operationally how our programs supported kids and how this information could be presented in a sequential training. We decided that some of the key elements necessary to create successful Re-EDucation Programs were: Re-EDucation's Historical Background, The Nine Psycho-Educational Stages of Re-EDucation (Long, 1986), The Conflict Cycle (Long, Wood, & Fecser, 2001), Structure and Predictability within the Classroom, Group Development, Effective Instructional Techniques, Behavior Management, Experiential Education, Social Skills, and Team-building for Professionals (which we added a few years later). Components of the curriculum are summarized following.

Re-EDucation's Historical Background. Re-Ed's philosophy and strategies have been refined through study and time, and they are the foundation of all the other components included in our training. Hobbs' 12 guiding principles reflect what is important in the lives of children. In teaching the origins of Re-ED, we emphasize four key components: Joy, Teacher-Counselors, Just Manageable Difficulty, and Ecology.

Hobbs (1982) knew how important being positive and experiencing *joy* were to troubling kids and the adults helping them. He referred to staff as *Teacher-Counselors*, because he knew that professionals working with children and youth with E/BD had a dual role. Hobbs pointed out that crises did not necessarily wait for the 50-minute therapy hour, and that educating and being therapeutic with the child were each adult's responsibility. The concept of "*Just Manageable Difficulty*" tells us the importance of challenge and competence in each of our lives. When a child has made significant gains in behavior and performance, we encourage him/her to go slightly further, instead of backing off. When a child or adult is operating at the level of "just manageable difficulty," they eventually learn to encourage themselves to move forward, to make the gains necessary to become a productive member of society. Hobbs also encouraged professionals to look not just at the child, but also at the *ecology* each one defines. A child's behaviors do not happen in a vacuum, and all the adults surrounding and supporting the child need to be included in programming and planning. His goal was to create a support network for that child in his/her own community that would be there long after they left the Re-EDucation programs.

Kris Reinbold remembers, "I think one of the greatest aspects of our program was the collaboration between teachers and counselors, and the sense of community that developed both with the staff and the students. When substitute teachers would come into our classroom, the greatest compliment was that they could not tell which one of us was the teacher. Being the youngest in the group, I was their last choice. When the time called for it, which it often did, the therapist would take over the reading group and the teacher would finish up the social skills lesson. It was just a free give-and-take, not an awkward struggle to try not to step on each other's professional toes. This meshing of roles helped to create an amazing sense of community." [Re-ED Principle: *"Communities are important for children and youth, but the uses and benefits of community must be experienced to be learned"* (Hobbs, 1982, p. 23).]

Communities are important for adults as well, allowing us to support and learn from one another. "Getting together" is important. Community building takes time, a great deal of effort, and presents many challenges, but once found, it makes everything else seem to work more smoothly. It is this sense of community and collaboration that has brought WAREA together and keeps it working toward a future together. A participant from one of our trainings said, "It continues to amaze me how you can tie it all back to the 12 Principles, etc. It is all so valuable."

Nine Psycho-Educational Stages of Re-EDucation. Dr. Nicholas Long published the results of a four year study conducted at the Rose School in Washington D.C. (Long, 1986). He was looking to see if any pattern existed in healing for the E/BD child, and if so, what a teacher-counselor could do along the way to support the child's growth and progress. Four major findings within the study were: (a) behavioral and academic changes are not linear, rather they ebb and flow; (b) learning evolves around significant interpersonal relation-ships; (c) the quality of the teacher-student relationship is critical to the process of pupil change; and (d) the success of the program is also dependent on the stability of the child's home and community life. Long also describes how a child might act at each of nine psycho-educational stages, as they make progress toward return to a main-stream setting. WAREA has found that the knowledge and understanding of these stages has given us tools to help children make significant gains. We teach and model the appropriate teacher-counselor strategies for each stage as part of our training.

The ninth stage is known as Attachment and Sadness, when students are so proud of their accomplishments, but worried about leaving a place where they have found so much success. Kris Reinbold recalls, "When I think of the program's greatest successes, I flash back to pictures of our students on 'Graduation Day.' One of the tasks we gave our graduating students was for them to think back about what they were like when they first came to our program, or before they came. Then they had to compare it to what they were like now and tell us what they were choosing to do differently, and what they hoped to continue doing. This was a very powerful moment for those students and for everyone else in the room sharing this ceremony with them. Their faces were filled with such pride and joy that it just filled the room. I know, that no matter where they are today, they will always look back to their time with us and remember at least one happy time in their life." [Re-ED Principle: *"Ceremony and ritual give order, stability and confidence to troubled children and adolescents whose lives are often in considerable disarray"* (Hobbs, 1982, p. 23).]

The Conflict Cycle. When working to help E/BD youth, inevitably there will be conflict. Members of WAREA knew that without specific training for dealing with conflict, professionals would be ill prepared to work with this special population. Furthermore, without this knowledge, they could inadvertently escalate a small situation into a larger one. Nicholas Long explained this unintentional escalation phenomenon as the Conflict Cycle Paradigm (Long, 1996). Understanding this paradigm is critical in a Re-ED classroom. The Conflict Cycle begins with a stressful incident, which in turn drives a student's thoughts, typically based on irrational thought patterns or core belief systems; these irrational beliefs in turn drive feelings and thoughts that may soon result in observable behavior. When the behavior materializes, this is the point when the teacher-counselor's response is crucial. An adult's reaction to the child's behavior can either create a second stressful incident or diffuse the incident. The usual reaction of most adults in that situation typically escalates conflict; de-escalation requires a different mindset. Understanding the teacher-counselor's role in conflict is critical to successful programming. A participant in our training commented, "This training has totally changed my perception on how I can better help my students. Thank you so much for providing me the skills to become a better advocate for my kids."

Structure and Predictability within the Classroom. When developing the training curriculum, members of WAREA felt that helping practitioners create a structured, predictable classroom was critical for success. We also felt strongly that there wasn't one "correct" way to have a classroom set up. There are elements that make programs successful, but the teacher-counselor and the group of children within the program determine how they are implemented.

One of the key elements in this area of training is the organization of the environment. There should be no surprises in an E/BD program. These kids already have too many surprises within their lives. When unexpected things happen, inappropriate behaviors increase. By creating predictable environments, we are able to support the child's education and healing. Key components for the environment include schedules, rules, routines, and rituals.

Group Development. When WAREA began speaking to colleagues within our field, there was an overall tendency to avoid group work with students. Professionals reported that attempts they made to develop group projects usually ended with big behavior challenges. Teachers and counselors believed they were better able to manage E/BD kids if the instruction and social skills training were individualized. Although this approach usually made life easier for the adults, the kids had fewer opportunities to socialize and try out new skills.

WAREA members felt strongly that group work be included as part of our core training, as it was in the PEP summer trainings. We introduced participants to the four stages of group development: forming, storming, norming, and performing (Stanford, 1977), which illuminates the idea that sometimes group problem situations get worse before they get better. Knowing there are such steps in group development can encourage practitioners to persevere when group work is becoming difficult.

We provided participants with information about the key elements for effective classroom meetings and how to facilitate a variety of other meetings: check-in meetings, problem-solving meetings, positives meetings, planning meetings, goal setting and goal evaluation meetings. One participant said, "I love it when you relate things back to our own group process."

Effective Instruction Techniques. Successful E/BD classroom programs are a marriage of two key elements: effective behavior management techniques and high quality academic instruction. If either one is missing, the classroom tends to have difficulty. Some training programs for professionals working with the E/BD population only include behavior management. We felt that we also needed to include training on effective instructional techniques to make our training complete. We borrowed from Madeline Hunter's (Hunter, 1991) model describing the elements of a lesson, then addressed appropriate ways to modify and adapt curricula for different learners, including a strong focus on assessment for both academic and behavioral concerns. Information from assessment results support teacher-counselor decision-making about how to help students become more proficient — academically, behaviorally, and socially.

We also address the fact that troubled and troubling behaviors tend to escalate when a student experiences continued academic failure. Many mental health professionals are not required to take classes on best practices in instructing clients on social skills or learning new behavior skills. Kris Reinbold remembers one of her student's reaction when the Re-ED principles of joy and competence combined to make a difference, "A 4th grader with mild developmental delays, working on a challenging math task, exclaimed with such glee, 'Wow! I am so smart! I didn't use the number line! I didn't use my fingers! And I didn't even use my head to figure out that problem!' For that one moment his world was a wonderful, happy place." [Re-ED Principle: *"Competence makes a difference; children and adolescents should be helped to be good at something, and especially at schoolwork"* (Hobbs, 1982, p. 23).]

Behavior Management. Training can provide practitioners with some basic tools to create a successful environment for children and youth with E/BD. Consistent implementation of just a few of the core components of the training, changing classroom structure and staff responses, can alleviate some behavior problems.

We also teach some basic behavior management techniques, with ideas for their implementation. We know that if you want to change a negative behavior, you must teach and encourage the child to use a replacement behavior that fulfills the same need the negative behavior was seeking to fill. Sometimes a stable and structured environment is not enough for the child to make the significant changes that are necessary for him/her to be successful in school, work, or home. When a child experiences recurring problems, something more individualized and intensive may be needed. Thus, we have participants practice designing individualized contracts to facilitate behavior changes for children.

We offer advanced trainings that include Life Space Crisis Intervention (Long, Wood, & Fecser, 2001) and Functional Behavioral Assessment and Positive Behavioral Support (Sugai & Lewis, 1999) classes. Life Space Crisis Intervention (LSCI) is a structured way that adults can talk with a child after a crisis to illuminate problems in a child's thinking and patterns of self-defeating behavior. Through several interviews the adult can help the child recognize and change these patterns of behavior. WAREA Board member and trainer, Tricia Jump remembers one of her students who learned so much with the help of LSCI, behavior supports, and the Re-ED principles.

"When I first came into contact with this fifth grader and his family, all avenues had been exhausted. He was failing, prone to violent outbursts, disrespectful, vulgar, and often unaccounted for during the school day. At home he was a handful as well. His mom told me she would leave the house just to get away from him. When he arrived in my class he was like a feral animal. He would spit threats like a tiny wild cat when pushed to complete assignments or play games at recess with the rest of the class. Physically he was only the size of a third grader. He had had six operations to repair and improve his hearing. He was diagnosed with bi-polar disorder and attention deficit hyperactivity disorder for which he is medicated both in and out of school. Academically, he was two grade levels behind. Did his illness and behavior cause his academic deficit? Or did the academic deficits cause his behaviors? At this point, it no longer mattered. I found, despite the pending lawsuit his family had against his home school, his mom was extremely supportive; she learned to trust us. He would have a blowout and go home with a poor daily score. The account of the incident we gave was the same as his. This was new for them. No matter what his problems, or the problems he caused, his mom still protected and defended him against those who attacked. I didn't attack. I reported — communicated. He did the same. He soon found that feelings were supported and nurtured. Events were transitory. He could move on with his day, recover, and it wasn't being held over his head. He was allowed his mistakes and not judged for them. As he graduated from the program on a sunny Thursday afternoon, his regular education teacher, the principal, the health clerk, the music teacher, and numerous other adults throughout the building attended the ceremony to wish him well and congratulate him on his accomplishments. He is well liked, accepted, productive — and sorely missed."

Experiential Education. The Pacific Northwest is a wonderful place for outdoor activities. We have a plethora of trails and mountains practically at our back door. Many of us found ourselves taking kids out of the classroom to experience success in other ways such as a ropes course, building boats, painting garbage cans in our neighborhoods, or adopting a wolf or a whale. Our experience has shown that briefly removing children who are continually failing from the academic or residential environment that may represent failure to them, and giving them opportunities to experience success, can serve to facilitate the generalization of those successes back into the original, previously negative, environment. We incorporate this concept into the WAREA curriculum. We teach educators and clinicians to add games and problem solving to the social skills lessons. We present the Full Value Contract (Rohnke, 1984) to participants, a model that keeps each person safe, supports the notion of "challenge by choice" (in which a participant can opt out of an uncomfortable situation while still being a member of the group), and supports positive interactions of each child with both the adults and their peer group. Experiential education is fun for kids, fun to teach, and fun to learn.

Social Skills. There are times when a child chooses not to do the right thing; then there are times when a child does not know the right thing to do. When children have emotional and behavioral disabilities, the adults who come in contact with them often assume that they know how to behave, but are just choosing not to do it. If the same scenario took place with the learning disabled child who is not able to multiply, teachers would not say that he really knows how to do it but is choosing not to show those skills. They would continue to teach different strategies to support that child until s/he learned the skill of multiplication. We keep trying to find new ways of helping our students learn and choose new behaviors and social skills.

We found that many classrooms in our area did not have comprehensive social skills programs. We knew from experience that children we were working with needed to learn social skills specifically and intentionally. Within our trainings we describe strategies for teaching new skills, role playing, giving feedback, generalizing the new skill across environments, and debriefing a learned skill. We make suggestions for published curricula and explore ways to incorporate social skills instruction into the classroom schedule.

Team Building for Professionals. We do not work alone, nor could we survive this job without the support and encouragement of a team of people. Programs supporting children and youth with E/BD are usually composed of many professionals, each with their own ideas, strategies, and philosophies. When those ideas oppose one another, programs can become dysfunctional, making changes for children difficult. Learning to communicate as professionals is imperative to the success of our students. We have created a curriculum to assist professionals in developing an understanding of others' perspectives and to communicate with one another.

The basis for this curriculum draws heavily from the book, *Dealing with People You Can't Stand* (Brinkman & Kirschner, 1994). Tricia Jump recalled her journey to build a team with her elementary school building staff: "I would say our greatest accomplishments follow our greatest challenges. Just manageable difficulty, conflict to coping, and teachable moments abound in the face of adversity. Learning and living with the twelve principles, I had to teach not only my students but also my colleagues their meaning and value. The Re-ED Principle, *"Life is to be lived now, not in the past..."* (Hobbs, 1982, p. 23) was a hard one that we achieved together.

"The year before I arrived, a petition was drafted and signed by the entire general education staff of the building demanding the removal of the E/BD program from 'their' school. They were tired of putting up with 'those kids,' and let the administration and teacher's union know about it. I worked diligently at first just to have staff acknowledge my presence (they would walk by and not even glance my way); later they warmed up to me and my students as real people.

"I started a group compliment chart. Each time another person outside of our class gave us a compliment we recorded it. We needed to be good at something. They soon started to add up and we became the specialists' favorite class!

"The Re-ED principle of trust comes to mind, in that trust is indeed essential not only between child and adult but also between colleagues as well. We built the trust up over the two years I was there, and when it was time to move into the new building, they hated to see us go."

Trainer Development

When we first began, Frank Fecser from PEP in Cleveland would come to Seattle and work with WAREA to develop both our curriculum and our trainers. Frank would ask each trainer to present their materials to him and the other trainers. After each presentation, the group would give feedback to the trainer on content, presentation style, materials, and also help develop more activities to highlight the concepts. WAREA would also videotape the presentations so that the presenter could take the tape to review and then use to make necessary changes. This process would occur in the form of one or two day retreats. Through this intensive process, the original core members became master trainers.

WAREA knew it was important that we develop a system to support our trainers and cultivate new trainers. Once we had a core curriculum, WAREA was ready to bring in new trainers. But the system that developed the original core group was neither time nor cost effective. WAREA believes that it is important to have trainers who are front line professionals who are already experienced in assisting children with E/BD. However, some of these professionals might have little or no experience in training adults, and we needed consistent training content.

Through trial and error, WAREA developed a system that both supports and encourages new trainers while protecting the integrity of our materials and organization. During our training conferences we began giving new recruits opportunities by pairing them with an experienced trainer. To prepare the trainer-in-training, the master trainer would help develop materials, presentation technique, and timing through a few individual meetings. During the final meeting time the trainer-in-training would present this small concept to the larger group of experienced trainers as if at a conference. If ready, the trainer-in-training would then present this small concept to an audience at a conference.

Through coaching, direct observation, and evaluation, WAREA gives the new trainer critical feedback in order to ensure he/she is ready to continue taking on more material. By pairing them with master trainers we allow them the opportunity to practice in small steps, and place them in the ranks when they are both confident and competent. Fifteen trainers in our state have become master trainers, and we are actively working to increase these numbers.

Consultation

Consultation has always been part of WAREA's services. While working with individual practitioners and small staff teams during trainings, WAREA also worked with organizations and school districts. Many times participants left trainings feeling excited about changes they were going to incorporate within their programs, only to be discouraged by a larger systems issue that hindered the transformation they had envisioned. They often asked for additional help.

From the outset, WAREA has been working in close contact with school districts, mental health agencies, day treatment facilities, residential treatment centers, and parent groups. The need within these organizations is growing exponentially as schools and agencies struggle with diminishing resources and a growing population of troubled youth. They needed assistance. Dr. Frank Fecser helped us develop the consultation part of our organization, helping us structure our consultation model and develop it as part of our organizational business. For two days we trained in the skills necessary for consulting and how to promote this through WAREA. We began slowly because we did not want to advertise a service that we were not yet equipped to handle.

If a district/agency wants training around a topic that is within our core curriculum, we charge a training rate. If that same organization wants specific materials developed around their needs and/or wants us to make specific observations and suggestions, we charge a consultation rate. We also negotiate specific services through our Service Coordinator.

Conferences

Conducting conferences is WAREA's bread and butter. Providing these venues for practitioners allows us to share the Re-ED philosophy on a greater scale in the state of Washington. Currently, WAREA's five-day conference curriculum provides participants with practical and usable information to help them get their school-based programs up and running. The format for the conference allows 35 - 40 participants opportunities to see how the information can be used in their own settings. Typically, much of the content has real-use application within their settings. A week of training involves both didactic information and opportunities to practice the skills presented. In small groups, participants make decisions about the effectiveness and relevancy of their daily routines in their own settings, through the use of experiential education principles and techniques, sometimes using the Full Value Contract (Grimm, 1993) as a way to establish group norms. We keep to this limited participant number because it allows us to meet their needs while connecting with them personally and professionally.

Branching Out

In addition to the annual conferences, WAREA trainers also present through a variety of other venues, such as both the Washington State and the National Council for Exceptional Children (CEC) conferences. We send presenters to both the Bi-Annual AREA and Off-Year AREA conferences, and hosted the Off-Year AREA conferences ourselves in 1997 and 2003. Our members have also presented at Council for Children with Behavior Disorders (CCBD) conferences, both here in Washington and nationally. Our trainings at these conferences are always well attended, needing extra handouts and extra chairs. We continue to receive extremely positive feedback from evaluations of our presentations.

Even before WAREA became an official organization, founding WAREA member Bridget Walker started attending the AREA meetings. She has now served as national AREA's President-Elect, President, and Past-President. Our connection to other AREA programs that are on the cutting edge of new ideas, who have been using Re-EDucation for decades, and who give us something to strive for, has been essential to WAREA's development and our plans for the future. AREA and its constituents have supported WAREA on many different levels. We would not be where we are today without their guidance.

Planning for More Plantings

Organizational Structure of WAREA

We see our organization developing in accord with the foundations discussed elsewhere in this book in Drs. Bridget Walker and Frank Fecser's chapter entitled, "Elements of An Effective Re-EDucation Program for the 21st Century."

First, we worked very hard on our *philosophy and systems* approach. Our mission statement and our core values drive the decisions of our group. We have developed and continue to refine our guidelines, policies, roles, responsibilities, and procedures.

Next, we focused on *structures*, both fiscal and programmatic. We developed a budget, based on expenditures over the last five years. We are trying to gather more funding through grants from a variety of different organizations. Marketing ideas have included producing a brochure, creating a website, attending and presenting at conferences, and connecting with individuals at school districts and mental health agencies. Currently, our most effective advertisement is via word of mouth; "once they've seen us, they tell their friends."

Other structures include policies on anti-discrimination, anti-harassment, and trainer's ethics agreements. We also have developed application procedures for joining the WAREA Board and for becoming a WAREA trainer, as well as a sequenced curriculum of procedures for trainers-in-training.

Climate and group process is the next tier in the foundations that Frank and Bridget describe. This area is one of the most important and most challenging for WAREA, calling for a delicate balancing of friendship and business. When people of similar values, beliefs, and commitments towards a cause come together, there can be magic. WAREA has become a family. All of us cherish this aspect of our organization. With so many decisions to make as a group, however, it's not possible to please everybody all of the time. Things can be taken more personally than intended and feelings hurt. We have had five retreats, both on our own and facilitated by others, to work through a number of group development needs: establishing norms, seeing others' perspectives, developing operating principles. WAREA is diligently trying to work through tough issues with grace and determination, recognizing it is a long, hard, and cyclical process.

Individualization, the inner box of Walker and Fecser's essentials for the Re-ED foundation, points up the critical focus on the individual. WAREA is solely made up of individuals, as opposed to representatives of the large or small, new or long-standing organizations who are part of AREA. This frequently adds an extra dimension to our needed activities. Our individuals have their own jobs and lives that take priority over the business of WAREA, and so they should in life's big picture.

All of us have changed jobs since we first joined WAREA. Several have gone on to get more formal education, some have moved from the mental health field to education, one has gone from an instructional assistant position to that of administrator, but each of us takes Re-ED with us wherever we go. As life happens to each of us, the level of time and energy we are able to devote to WAREA fluctuates greatly. We are always working on ways to make it easier to attend board meetings, trying to attract new Board members and trainers, and are ever mindful of trying to make sure our trainings and consultations remain top notch. We know that the numbers of children and youth with E/BD will not be decreasing any time soon in Washington. And we know that more and more of these kids are being served in settings with fewer and fewer resources. WAREA is committed to supporting the programs and staff that work with these children to the best of our abilities; it gets more challenging each year.

Technology

Our organization has been working diligently to consolidate and solidify WAREA training materials and copyright those materials for the training and consultation services we offer. Lisa Hoyt and Pat Connolly have taken on the challenge of bringing us into the 21st Century. They have created professional Power Point presentations for each of our training areas, preparing CDs of those presentations that are easily transferred and utilized by any trainer within our organization. Tricia Jump has created a website, http://www.warea.org, to display our mission statement, affiliations, pertinent links, and information on upcoming trainings. The website has been helpful in connecting others to our organization through its content, e-mail, and 24/7 availability.

Handling Growth

We learned that the demand for our services far outweighed what any of us could do on a voluntary basis. In the fall of 2002 we began contracting with one of our members, Mary Ann Lyons, as WAREA's Service Coordinator. She has been invaluable for our growth and the fine-tuning of our business. Having a specified contact person, both for districts/agencies requesting services and for participants searching for information on our organization, has been invaluable. She is the glue that holds our enterprise together: managing phone contacts, mail, e-mail requests, contracts with outside organizations, insurance, conference registration and coordination, and a million other things that we don't know about, but appreciate being accomplished so we don't have to worry.

Visions for Future Harvests

WAREA has always discussed the idea of opening our own day treatment facility, from the ground up, incorporating the Re-ED principles and philosophy within the program. We understand this is a daunting task. There are giant hurdles to overcome, such as funding, insurance, and site availability. Our vision for our day treatment facility is that it could be a training site for new teachers, counselors, and visiting professionals, part of a larger teacher-counselor training program at higher institutions of learning, while operating at the cutting edge of research and development. Already, we have substantial connections with the University of Washington. Several board members have completed their masters degrees or are working on their doctoral programs in E/BD. Others are teaching there, incorporating Re-ED curriculum into the training of new special education teachers. Some of our members are hosting interns from universities to help with new teacher training. As the Project Re-ED Panel of Visitors noted, it is important for Re-ED programs to build and maintain ties with institutions of higher learning (Hobbs, 1982). Such ties are investments into children's futures for both entities, service programs and universities.

Fields of Dreams

You have just read the story of a magic seed and how it has proliferated over nearly two decades, still this is just the beginning for Re-ED in Washington. WAREA is documented proof that one person with one idea can make a world of difference for thousands of others. We are forever indebted to Mary Sarno, "Mother Mary," and Dr. Frank Fecser, "Father Frank," for their never faltering ideas, encouragements, and visions for us and for the children and youth with emotional and behavioral disabilities whom we serve. Our wish for you is that you take this small seed of an idea and make it grow wherever you are.

References

Brinkman, R., & Kirschner, R. (1994). *Dealing with people you can't stand: How to bring out the best in people at their worst.* New York: McGraw-Hill, Inc.

Grimm, D. (1993). Resources: *A guide to challenge kit construction, use, sequencing, and full value.* Unpublished master's thesis, Evergreen State University, Olympia, WA.

Hobbs, N. (1994). *The troubled and troubling child.* Cleveland, OH: American Re-EDucation Association.

Hunter, M. C. (1991). Generic Lesson Design: The Case For. *Science Teacher, 58*(7), 26-28.

Long, N. J. (1986). The nine psychoeducational stages of helping emotionally disturbed students through the Re-EDucation process. *The Pointer, 30*(3), 5-20.

Long, N. J. (1996). The conflict cycle paradigm: How troubled students get teachers out of control. In N. J. Long & W. C. Morse (Eds.), *Conflict in the classroom* (5th ed., pp. 526-532). Austin, TX: Pro-Ed.

Long, N. J., Wood, M., & Fecser, F. A. (2001). *Life space crisis intervention: Talking with students in conflict.* Austin, TX: Pro-Ed.

Rohnke, K. (1984). *Silver bullets: A guide to initiative problems, adventure games, and trust activities.* Dubuque, IA: Kendal/Hunt Publishing.

Stanford, G. (1977). *Developing effective classroom groups: A practical guide for teachers.* New York: Hart Publishing.

Sugai, G., & Lewis, T. J. (1999). What works for children and youth with E/BD: Linking yesterday to tomorrow. In L. M. Bullock & R. A. Gable (Eds.), *The third mini-library series: What works for children and youth with E/BD: Linking yesterday and today with tomorrow.* Reston, VA: The Council for Children with Behavior Disorders.

Kris Reinbold, MEd, is a special education teacher in Seattle, WA, for BRITE (Behavior Re-EDucation in a Therapeutic Environment), the Shoreline School District's day treatment program.
krisreinbold@msn.com

Tricia Jump, MEd, is an E/BD teacher in the Bethel School District's self contained intermediate elementary PATHS program, located in Graham, WA.
ljump@bethelsd.org

Mike Oliver,MEd, is the Program Facilitator at Renton Academy, a therapeutic public school program for students K-12 who exhibit social, emotional, and behavioral challenges, located in the Renton School District just outside Seattle, WA.
Mike.oliver25@renton.wednet.edu

Lisa Hoyt, MEd, is the Director of Renton Academy, a therapeutic school for students with Emotional and Behavioral Disabilities that uses Re-Education as their philosophical framework located in the Renton School District in Washington State.
Lisa.hoyt@renton.wednet.edu

Part VII

Questioning and Growing

Data-Based Decision Making

Rapid learning requires that we build upon the ideas and work of others, recognizing and valuing what others have discovered before us. Our human tendencies to value only what we have sought and found by ourselves prove counterproductive. We seem best served by continually searching and incorporating new learning, avoiding "having all the answers" since no one ever does. Nicholas Hobbs showed us how by asking hard questions, by working to find answers in research and in the wisdom of others, and by growing as we ask even more. We seek information to use at all levels - child, group, program, system.

Hobbs credited many thinkers for historical and scholarly contributions to Re-ED's development. Among them, he recognized indebtedness *"for specific techniques of working with disturbed children to Carl Fenichel, William Glasser, Norris Haring, Frank Hewitt, Nicholas Long, William Morse, and Fritz Redl...."* (Hobbs, 1982, p. xxvii). The search continues.

Re-ED is an open paradigm with a pragmatic bent. It started as a philosophy which became an approach, made operational by stated principles and tested strategies. Elements of other approaches with demonstrated efficacy were incorporated where they were consistent with Re-ED basics. Hobbs said frequently, "Re-ED re-invents itself daily," implying a dynamism that responds adaptively to individual needs of children and families — and to changes in the child and family serving fields (Hobbs, 1982, pp. 30-31).

On the page following this introduction, Claudia Lann Valore reflects on the necessity for programs to sustain their commitment for responsiveness to change. Her experiences, ranging from teacher-counselor to program administrator, provide a broad perspective on Re-ED's questioning culture.

Reports on Research To Date

Re-ED started with a commitment to research their first program efforts rigorously. Chapter 29 begins Part VII by summarizing the initial research Laura Weinstein conducted on the original Re-ED venture in two short term residential "schools." Her 312 page report described this extensive program of data collection and analysis, following the children across entry, discharge, and follow-up. Chapter 30 presents the second rigorous research on the Re-ED approach, this time applying the principles and practices in public schools from five school districts spread across Tennessee. The research design provided results of interventions on students' behavior and achievement, on teachers' knowledge, attitudes, and classroom behaviors, and on special services required for students in experimental schools compared to control schools. Other findings explored how training by Re-ED support staff working with classroom teachers produced gains in both teachers' knowledge and problem solving processes.

Chapter 31 presents the empirical efforts of Pam Meadowcroft and her colleagues to define Re-ED and determine if the thinking of Re-ED staff differs from staff in more traditional mental health programs. The differences found may help establish a method for measuring treatment fidelity with Re-ED principles and practices which can be used in more current effectiveness studies – across the range of Re-ED adaptations.

In chapter 32, Robert Cantrell summarizes follow-up studies from the early Re-ED programs over the years since the original research. Whitaker School was established in 1981 as a result of the Willie M. case in North Carolina which mandated mental health services for dually diagnosed, adjudicated youth. Ray Newnam, Joseph Murphy, Asenath Devaney, and Stephen Hooper close Part VII by describing Whitaker School's two follow-up studies and their results in chapter 33.

A Questioning Culture

Re-ED's practices largely developed by searching for what works when facing a present challenge – whether posed by a child or a system of care in need of help. Re-ED began as a response to a nationwide absence of care for troubled and troubling kids of crisis proportions. It continues to seek answers for today's children and families in need. Newer practices were developed, adopted, or adapted over the years as they emerged from various disciplines (psychology, education, social work, medicine, etc.) where they were already evidence supported or promising responses to current needs.

Re-ED is not dogmatic; there is no formula or set of steps. It is a pragmatic, principles-driven philosophy of learning, teaching, treatment, and care for children and youth that provides a solid, enduring, values-based foundation to ground an agency, school, or program. It is (somewhat uniquely) able to accommodate the vast and often constricting range of state or local contextual variables -- funding, compliance, service delivery options, client or student base, and community needs, to name a few. It can work in schools, in community-based mental health agencies, in residential settings, and in other networks of care (governmental or private) for children and families.

Like the amazing brain, Re-ED possesses plasticity. It constantly reinvents itself through its flexible, malleable, and responsive nature. This is its strength, and most likely accounts for its durability and sustainability in the face of the constantly changing world of service providers in all our social systems. Paradoxically, this very strength is also its Achilles Heel – hard to describe succinctly, and impossible to reduce to a formulaic treatment model for easy replication or research. Nevertheless, Re-ED can be described and validated with evidence from the field. As adaptable as it is, there are "non-negotiables"-- characteristics and practices of Re-ED programs that clearly set them apart from other treatment and education programs and providers.

Despite the technology and information now available, helping professions and systems of care are struggling in the face of rules, regulations, compliance requirements, and mandates -- often unfunded. A values-based approach that can, with dogged determination, be implemented within the very real context of system realities and constraints across time and place is needed more than ever. Re-ED has this history. We are determined to continue to create its future by continuing to reinvent it every day and to document evidence that it works.

--- Claudia Lann Valore

29

The Original Re-ED Venture into Ecological Change: Laura Weinstein's Research on Project Re-ED

Robert P. Cantrell & Mary L. Cantrell

[Editors' note: The following chapter is our attempt to paraphrase and condense the 312 pages of Dr. Weinstein's final Re-ED report into a document that captures the original efforts and their results, while providing Re-EDers a sense of continuity with those who first blazed this trail. For omissions and lapses of important points we apologize. The original author of this study did a careful and thorough job. We think she "got it right."]

Dr. Laura Weinstein began her final report on the evaluation of the original Re-ED project with a succinct, first page footnote: "*...the emphasis in the Re-ED orientation on disturbance within a social system rather than within an individual child makes the use of any label which describes the child as if he were an isolated entity inconsistent with the basic philosophy*" (Weinstein, 1974, p. 1). More than 30 years later these words still remind us of what Re-ED's continuing, quintessential approach to those children most professionals persist in labeling as "emotionally disturbed" should be.

Congruent with the above declaration, the 1974 report documented rigorous research designed to: (a) evaluate the effects of the Re-ED approach, and (b) examine the outcomes of changes made in the eco-systems within which Re-ED students functioned. This repeated testings evaluation design documented how students' behavioral, academic, and family discordances were eased by Wright School (Durham, North Carolina) and Cumberland House (Nashville, Tennessee) Re-ED staffers. Their partnered interventions led to functional, sustainable patterns so that Re-ED children could return to their families and home schools in a timely fashion. The average length of stay was 8.1 months (SD = 2.8 months). For practical purposes, especially proximity to the research staff, the research reported emphasized Cumberland House students, their families, home schools, and referring agencies.

Re-ED residential schools operated groups populated by eight students, two teacher-counselors, a liaison teacher-counselor for communications with others in the child's social system, and a night aide to watch over the students during their sleep. An arts and crafts instructor helped fill out the curriculum. One of the teacher-counselors taught the students during the day; the other teacher-counselor spent less structured time outside the classroom with students in varied activities. Students went home on week-ends and holidays to involve home social systems throughout the Re-ED experience. An active camping program expanded students' physical competencies and provided added opportunities for group process interventions.

The Re-ED Intervention Process

Hobbs and colleagues lent their best thinking to the Re-ED intervention process. Re-ED's infancy began with a commitment to recruiting *"decent adults"* who were *"natural child workers"* (Hobbs, 1982, pp. 82 and 96) to work with, and within, each child's ecology. This was a far more radical, non-medical model approach to dealing with troubled children and their daily surroundings than was customary at the time. In attempting to capture effects of this ecological enterprise without mandating an evaluation structure that would eventually shape therapeutic interventions, Weinstein chose to use measures that would document the results of ecological interventions that proved successful.

Hobbs articulated 12 principles and some associated strategies which arose inductively over time as Re-ED staffers gained experience. Students also benefited from their teacher-counselors' exposures to some of the best thinkers of the time. Both students and their families learned additional cognitive and emotional competencies by coping with "just manageable difficulties" (Hobbs, 1971). Many of these new coping challenges were deliberately structured and encouraged by thoughtful teacher-counselors to initiate growth which leads to the personal enhancements of accomplishment, effectance, and independence. Whether it was learning how to rappel down a cliff face, use mathematics to divide a pizza equitably, or resolve disputes within a group, skills were acquired in context with others.

The Research Schema

Out of this fruitful mix developed an ethos committed to cautious openness to new ideas, to newly minted research results, and most importantly, to testing all new procedures against tried-and-true principles of healthy human interactions. Dr. Weinstein wisely avoided trying to measure such a young, ephemeral, rapidly evolving treatment process too narrowly. Instead, she cast her evaluation net widely to track the results of such efforts. Weinstein's (1974) evaluation of the original Re-ED schools and their effects on students was comprehensive. She gathered data on most of the variables that have since become commonplace to work in the field. She sought to document Re-ED effects using a broad range of benchmarks to legitimize this broad, unconventional approach for the larger mental health community. It is an upstream effort that continues to this day.

Re-ED Students

Students originally admitted to Re-ED residential "schools" (N = 122) were white males between six and twelve years of age. When Cumberland House opened in 1962, public schools were racially segregated and remained so until close to 1970. The Cumberland House student population was broadened in its racial and gender composition about 1965. Males were initially chosen since most children in treatment centers for emotionally disturbed children have historically (about 80%) been males. Later, the age limits and racial/

ethnic identifications were extended, and some females were admitted. The children came from across Tennessee or North Carolina; they were typically referred by an agency or professional person (usually a mental health center or child psychiatrist in private practice).

These enrolled children were too disturbed to be treated as out-patients. Usually their problems were sufficiently severe that the child was about to be removed from school and/or separated from his parents, but his needs were not so severe as to require hospitalization or constant surveillance. Primary behavioral difficulties were not to have originated from brain damage, mental retardation, or autism. Both extremes of the socioeconomic continuum were represented by these target children. Many had experienced instability and trauma in the past. Almost all of the target children had posed significant behavior problems in school; most had severe academic problems as well.

Comparison Groups

Limited project resources restricted the use of a completely randomized design for placing disturbed children into comparison groups. Instead, students for an "untreated disturbed" (UD) comparison group were nominated by principals from the Nashville-Davidson County schools system. The second comparison group was formed of "normal" (N) children age-matched from the same classroom as a boy selected to be part of the "UD" group. Project research staff searched the school's records to find a child in each UD child's same classroom whose characteristics (i.e., age, intelligence, socioeconomic status as measured by education / occupation of parents) were not significantly different from a nominated UD child. They were hoping to pair a classmate who was roughly similar (except for the absence of special problems) to each UD child. Paired lists were then discussed with the school's principal; if the principal agreed on the similarity, the N child was accepted as a member of that UD-N pair.

Characteristics of Groups and Difference Codes

Data on many entering variables were collected to find differences or similarities in the three student comparison groups (R, UD, N). In lieu of the large table detailing numeric means, standard deviations, percentages of comparisons or exact significances between the

Re-ED, UD, and N groups provided in her final report's Table 1 (Weinstein, 1974, pp. 16-35), our Tables 1 and 2 (at the end of the chapter) will detail variables and briefly describe their relationships. All entries use the referencing codes provided in Table 1. Abbreviations of the variables indicate the direction and presence of significant comparison results (minimum alpha required for all significant results: $p < .05$). Table 2 provides details on results of the analyses comparing 70 measurements on characteristics of Re-ED, UD, and N children. The code sequences use UPPER case (i.e., R, UD, or N) to indicate that Re-ED, UD, or N was the larger result in the statistically significant comparison. Lower case (i.e., r, ud, or n) indicates the smaller result in the comparison. Use of all lower case superscripts (i.e., rud, udn, etc.) indicates non-significant differences between those designated groups. For example, Table 2 reports for analysis (1) that there was no significant difference between the three groups for age in months at enrollment.

Comparison Group Similarities and Differences

Home interviews, Symptom Checklists, Social Maturity Scales, and Semantic Differential measures were completed by the mother(s) of boys in the Re-ED and both control groups. Project staff members conducting the interviews were unaware as to which control group children were assigned. There were no significant differences among the Re-ED disturbed, the UD, and the N group boys at enrollment on (a) age, (b) I.Q., (c) education and occupation of the father, (d) education of the mothers, (e) number of siblings, (f) mean grade in school for boys in regular classes, or (g) mean grade when the boy stopped normal progress in school.

Other, significant differences were obtained between the Re-ED and UD boys when compared with the N group: (a) significantly fewer N boys had mothers who worked outside the home (including working full time) than the other two groups, (b) significantly fewer N boys were from an orphanage or adopted, and (c) significantly more N boys had lived with biological parents throughout their lives. Ninety-one per cent of the N children lived with both biological parents, as opposed to 49% of the Re-ED and 61% of the UD children. More Re-ED and UD children were either adopted, lived with a parent and step-parent, one parent, or neither parent than was true for the N group.

Significantly fewer N boys' families had sought behavioral-emotional help for their boys from any source. Significantly fewer N boys had received medications for behavior problems, or had been enrolled in a special class, or had failed one or more grades, or had not made usual school progress. N students had significantly more positive sociometric nominations by peers and significantly fewer negative nominations from peers in classroom sociometrics.

Testing Intervals and Schedules

The basic evaluation strategy of the Re-ED research was the collection of baseline data prior to students' enrollment at Re-ED, then collection of data on the same measures at discharge and again at approximately six and eighteen months following discharge. Data for Re-ED children were later compared with data collected on the same measures at comparable time intervals for the comparison groups (UD and N children). To conserve limited resources, comparison group data collection was started only after preliminary results on the initial cadre of Re-ED children had shown that the program was being effective and measures were sensitive to change. Comparison and R group data were all collected from others in the children's ecologies (family members, school personnel, school records, classmates) and from the children themselves (in one-on-one testing sessions).

Time frame lags similar to those used for R children were used for comparison groups (i.e., initial, six, and eighteen months). Although similar, these measures were not on the exact same schedule or at the same times as they were for Re-ED students. Re-ED children's testings were tied to their referral and entry sequence. Comparison children's testings occurred in annual Rounds, with time lags between their three testings which were close to those of Re-ED students at entry, follow-up 1 and follow-up 2. R children had an additional set of tests at their time of discharge.

Re-ED Pre- and Post-Treatment Test Results: Measures and Findings

To maximize clarity in the service of brevity, only results that were significant will be presented, omitting most statistical details. This rule of thumb on reporting only significant results will be violated only where the finding of *no significant differences* among all three groups (R, UD, N) supports the efficacy of the Re-ED program. An example would be where R versus N results were significantly different on a measure at pre-test but not significant at the discharge post-test, indicating the Re-ED children became more like the "normal" students during their Re-ED experience (Weinstein, 1974, p. 61).

Child Measures

The measures described in the paragraphs below were chosen in an attempt to capture Re-ED's effectiveness with variables often implicated in a child's being perceived as "emotionally disturbed." They have the added advantage of being *"potential indicators of how Re-ED works"* (p. 61). Of course, the *"ultimate criterion of Re-ED's effectiveness...is the increased acceptability of the child's behavior, in his normal environment, to his family, school, peers, and community"* (p. 61).

Self-Concept Scale

This measure was adapted from work by Rogers (1931) and Bower (1960). The child was asked to respond to 12 items in which an imaginary child is described under various conditions. The child is asked to compare himself to the imaginary child as the R child himself *is at present* (Self as is) and as he might *wish to be* (Ideal Self). Then he is asked for repeated comparisons of how much his mother might wish him to be, and how much his father might wish him to be like the child described. Choices range from 3 (very much) to 0 (not at all). The *Self vs. Ideal Self* discrepancies, and differences in perceived *expectations by Mother and Father* compared to his own "Self as is" perception, provide measures of the child's perceived discrepancies from standards set by himself and his parent(s) for his behavior.

The Re-ED students' testings prior to entry and the UD children's initial tests did not differ significantly on the self-ideal discrepancy measured by the Self Concept Scale. On these pre-tests, the self-ideal discrepancies for each of the two disturbed groups were greater than the self-ideal discrepancies of the N children.

In analyses of pre- to post-test changes, the Re-ED group showed a greater, and significant, decrease in their discrepancy scores between pre-test and post-test relative to the changes pre- to post-test for the UD students ($\underline{t} = 1.90, p <0.05$) or when compared with the N ($t = 3.13, p <0.001$) children. The UD and the N groups did not differ in amount of change between initial and post-tests ($t = 1.12$).

Only the Re-ED group changed significantly from pre-test to post-test ($t = 3.44, p <0.001$) on the Self-Concept (i.e., self-ideal discrepancy) measure. The UD group did not change in self-ideal discrepancy scores from pre-test to post-test ($t = 0.97$), nor did the N children ($t = 0.59$). At post-test, the self-ideal discrepancy remained higher for the UD than for the N children. At post-test the Re-ED and N children did not differ significantly. The post-test comparison between the UD and Re-ED children did not reach significance.

Need for Approval

Epstein (1964) developed this social desirability measure; it was added to the battery to serve two purposes: (a) as a covariate for the self-reported Self-Concept measures when children described themselves in a suspiciously positive manner, and (b) as a check for intervention-produced changes in Self-Concept for children scoring high initially on Need for Approval, compared with those who did not score high on Need for Approval initially.

No independent results are reported on this measure. Although need for approval showed an r = -.48 with self-ideal discrepancy scores (but not with any other self report measures), using Need for Approval as a covariate when analyzing Mother-Father discrepancies or Locus of Control did not affect the results for those measures.

Locus of Control

This measure was adapted from Rue Cromwell's (1963) work on attribution patterns which individuals use to explain events that occur in their lives. Two belief patterns predominate: (a) an *internal locus of control*, meaning that the individual tends to assume that events that impact him (or reactions to him by others) are due to his own behaviors, and (b) an *external locus of control*, in which the individual tends to believe that he has no control over events and that they are due to forces external to his actions (such as luck, chance, or others). Results for this measure and for the next two measures are reported following descriptions of the next two measures.

Matching Familiar Figures Test (MFFT)

This test of cognitive behavioral impulsiveness (Kagan, Rosman, Day, Albert, & Phillips, 1964) measured where the child was functioning with respect to *cognitive reflection before acting* vs. *acting before reflecting*. The child was timed in choosing a perfect match to a line drawing sample from six alternative drawings. A lower time score implied impulsiveness.

The Spiral Test

Ritter and Colvin (1959) developed this measure of motor impulsiveness. The task required the child to trace between the lines of a spiral from beginning to end without lifting the pencil, cutting across lines, retracing, or stopping. The child is then asked to repeat the task, but this time by going as slowly as he could. The score was the timed difference between the two trials, with the inability to go slower under instructions implying greater motoric impulsiveness.

Results for Self-Concept, Locus of Control, and Two Impulsiveness Measures

R versus N comparisons at pre-test were unfavorable to R students, but not at post-test for Self-Concept Scale discrepancies (Self-Ideal discrepancies, Mother-Father discrepancies) and Locus of Control (external/internal).

R versus UD comparisons at pre-test were not different on the Self-Concept Scale (Self-Ideal discrepancies), but were favorable to R at post-test on the Self-Concept Scale (Mother-Father discrepancies), Locus of Control, and measures of impulsiveness (Matching Familiar Figures Test and Spiral). These results supported the Re-ED effectiveness hypothesis without confirming a competing hypothesis that changes could have occurred through maturation with the passage of time (UD condition).

UD versus N comparisons were all favorable to N students on both pre-tests and post-tests for the Self Concept Scale (Self-Ideal discrepancies and Mother-Father discrepancies) and Locus of Control.

Social Schemata

Kuethe and associates (Kuethe, 1962; 1964; Kuethe & Weingartner, 1964) posed this task as a way of tapping into individuals' learned beliefs about social relations. The child is asked to place figures on an open surface in any manner they choose. Adults, when given this task, tend to place child figures nearer adult female figures than they do with adult male figures.

Weinstein (1965) found characteristic differences in placement preferences between Re-ED and UD vs. N children on this task, when compared with a control task of placing a pair of rectangles on the same surface. Weinstein (1968) found that when a child placed the father-child figures closer together than they placed the mother-child figures, this pattern was associated with indices of anxiety and school underachievement. Also, Weinstein (1967) found that children who placed the rectangles closer together than they did the human adult-child figures were more likely to feel greater differences between their behaviors and the parental standards being held for them.

Academics

School Records: Metropolitan Achievement Tests

Academic accomplishments have been a major part of the Re-ED stratagem for ecological change from Re-ED's beginning. Next to family processes, school provides children a major tool for measuring themselves against the expectations of adults and other children. Not all children entered Re-ED with academic problems, but those with academic problems were helped to achieve significantly more than UD children who had also been nominated for the project. This was especially true for reading. Comparable evidence was not found for Re-ED treatment's differential effects on arithmetic achievement between the two groups. No data were reported on teaching processes (including academic curricula within the Re-ED programs) that might have differed from those used within regular classes attended by UD controls.

[Editors' note: *Arithmetic results may reflect a curricular confusion in schools at the time, the era that introduced elementary grades to "The New Math," which was comparatively more theoretical and abstract. Districts and classrooms varied in their use of "traditional arithmetic" or "new math" textbooks; many children lacked smooth transition from one to the other curriculum.*]

Continued Academic Progress

Both Re-ED and UD control students were behind grade norms prior to the beginning of the Re-ED project; overall, neither group "caught up" to grade level expectations by the project's end. They both continued to lag behind expectations, but at significantly different rates of academic retardation. Significantly more of the Re-ED children were functioning at the month for month rate of academic accomplishment after Re-ED than the UD group. The Re-ED group, who prior to entering Re-ED had started from further behind than UD students, slowed their rate of falling behind academically across testings.

The UD children, however, continued their statistically significant slide towards ever greater academic retardation relative to their peers. Overall, the Re-ED group surpassed the UD group by the first follow-up and continued to surpass them by the second follow-up (significantly across testing periods for all comparisons except arithmetic). These results confirm the repeated finding in the literature that untreated disturbed children continue to fall behind academically without special intervention.

When the analyses turned to rates of learning, significantly more Re-ED children were achieving at the month for month reading and arithmetic rates than were the untreated group. After Re-ED clients returned to their home schools, they continued to make academic progress, but not sufficiently to overcome the lags they had previously experienced. It appeared to Weinstein (1976/1969) that *"...learning at the normal, expected rate after Re-ED is sufficient only if the children have completely closed the gap between themselves and their peers during Re-ED -- if on leaving Re-ED they are performing at grade level. This did not occur; after Re-ED the children were about as academically retarded compared to their classmates as they had been at enrollment. The Re-ED program had succeeded in affecting the children's motivation for learning and ability to learn; it had not been able to make up for their initial retardation"* (p. 427).

However, some students' monthly rates of learning had progressed to the point where they were learning as rapidly as would be expected of N children.

[Editors' note: This finding produced the attempt to put Re-ED principles into a preventive effort, ultimately becoming the Prevention-Intervention Project (PIP), detailed in a separate chapter of this book. PIP's emphasis was on trusting the judgment of classroom teachers to refer children for help who were demonstrating early signs of behavioral and academic distress, and thus prevent their falling further behind academically.]

Parent Measures

The Symptom Checklist

Parents rated the frequency with which problem behaviors commonly used to describe disturbed children had occurred for their child over the preceding two weeks. The overall score was calculated using the total number of symptoms observed multiplied by the number of times the parents had observed each problem occurring. Round 1 ratings on this measure were performed after the children had been nominated for the study (or R children were referred). Round 2 ratings were gathered one year later (at follow-up 1 for the R group). Round 3 ratings were gathered two years after initial nominations had occurred (follow-up 2 for the R students).

Symptom differences comparing parents' ratings of Re-ED students with those by parents of UD and N children were largest at the Round 1 testing. Re-ED children had significantly more symptoms than UD or N children. By the Round 3 symptom ratings, parents' ratings of their Re-ED children had dropped by more than a third, a far greater decrease than for the UD or N groups. Nevertheless, the Re-ED symptom ratings remained significantly higher than the parents' ratings of the other two groups across Rounds 1 through 3.

Social Maturity

Thirty-four items of this measure were adapted from the Vineland, incorporating many of its variations as developed by Cain, Levine, Tallman, Elzey, and Kase (1958), Doll (1947), and Farber (1959). It was scored by counting the number of "usual" behaviors the child displays as reported by the child's mother and father. Results showed that all three groups improved across Rounds 1 through 3. The differences between the Re-ED and UD groups (significant in Round 1) were no longer significant in Rounds 2 and 3, although both the Re-ED and the UD groups continued to lag behind the N group in social maturity increases from Rounds 1 through 3.

Semantic Differential

This measure was selected as one means of measuring *"disturbance within a social system rather than within an individual child"* (Weinstein, 1974, p. 1). This Semantic Differential measure was based, in part, upon the polar adjectives (e.g., fast-slow) developed by Becker (1960) from his factor analyses of ratings about children by parents and teachers, to which Weinstein added an "activity" dimension. Each parent's view of their child's characteristics on this Semantic Differential measure was obtained separately at three points in time: (1) when the child entered the Re-ED program (or became a member of a comparison group), (2) at the six month follow-up (Round 2 for comparison students), and (3) at the eighteen month follow-up (Round 3 for comparison children).

Each time the Semantic Differential measure was administered, the parent (or other ecological agent) was first asked to answer all items for how the child's personal traits/emotions were viewed at present. This was followed by a second questioning for all items, asking how the parent (or other) would prefer the child to be. Differences per item between the two administrations (squared to eliminate negative numbers) could be interpreted as discrepancies between parents' current perceptions and their idealized expectations across five areas concerning their child: (a) affect, (b) emotional lability, (c) emotional control issues, (d) self-assertiveness, and (e) general activity level.

Items were compared for parental perceptions of changes toward congruence (i.e., differences between "as is" and "ideal" becoming smaller) across the time between initial and later testings. Between Rounds 1 and 2 the Re-ED group's parents reported a 40% drop in differences between "as is" and "ideal" for their children. Neither of the other two groups demonstrated even half that amount of improvement. Even so, it was only after Round 1 that the Re-ED group was no longer significantly different from the UD group. The N group continued to be more "normal" than either the Re-ED or the UD groups across all three testing rounds.

As Weinstein (1976/1969) states, changes could have occurred *"... in any one of three different ways: the child's behavior could have 'improved' (i.e., become more like his parents' expectations) while his parents' expectations remained unchanged; the parents' expectations could have become 'more realistic' (i.e., more like the child's behavior) while the child's behavior remained unchanged; or both the child's behavior and his parents' expectations could have changed in ways which made them more congruent"* (p. 421).

One could argue that if both parents began viewing their child as: (a) showing significantly fewer inappropriate behaviors, (b) becoming significantly more socially competent, or (c) significantly less discrepant from parental expectations and standards across time, any of those changes are fruitful examples of the Re-ED ecological approach that aims toward reducing discordances within the child's ecology.

Teacher and Referring Agent Change Ratings

Across similar time frames, referring agencies rated both Wright School (73%) and Cumberland House (89%) graduates as being either moderately or greatly improved. Likewise, teachers gave Re-ED graduates from both schools significantly higher improvement ratings on "role behavior," "disruptiveness," "feelings of personal distress," "work habits," and "relationships with other children" than had their teachers at the time of Re-ED enrollment (Weinstein, 1976/1969).

Conclusions

The goal of this study was to evaluate how effective a Re-ED short-term residential school would be in improving disturbed children's behavioral and academic adjustments. The data clearly indicate that the Re-ED residential intervention led to positive changes in attitude, behavior, and learning by children with "severe emotional disturbance." Initial testings of all three groups confirmed the R children to be clearly far more troubled and/or troubling than either the UD or N students. *[Editors' note: Not all of the reported analyses are described in detail in this chapter. These conclusions are drawn from Dr. Weinstein's own Conclusions section, each of which are supported by detailed findings in the 1974 report.]*

Self Concept

Re-ED students at discharge, when compared with a comparable set of UD students, *possessed more positive self-concepts and stronger beliefs that their behaviors could affect their situations.* Re-ED students at discharge also viewed their parents as being in greater agreement about standards and expectations for their children.

Impulsivity

Students initially categorized by Re-ED staff as acting out or impulsive *learned control over their motor behaviors,* as measured by changes in: (a) the pre-post latency of response on the Matching Familiar Figures Test (which implies the presence or absence of time taken to evaluate or cognitively reflect on choices before acting), and (b) pre-post time-to-completion changes on the Spiral Test (which implies ability to deliberately and slowly control motoric actions as directed).

Behavior Ratings

Following the Re-ED experience, Re-ED students were *viewed by their regular school teachers as better adjusted behaviorally* when compared with reports by teachers of UD children. This comparison difference held for Re-ED students whether they had less severe or more severe behavior problems when they had entered Re-ED.

Academics

Re-ED students needing academic remediation before their Re-ED experience *performed closer to grade norms after Re-ED than did students in the UD group* on standardized achievement tests. *More Re-ED students learned at the usual, expected, month-for-month rates after Re-ED than untreated controls.* This was particularly important since students with emotional disturbance typically fall further behind academically over time (as this study's UD children demonstrated).

Global Improvement Ratings by Staff

Ninety-four per cent of the Re-ED students were judged as moderately or greatly improved by Re-ED staff at discharge; 88 per cent of the Re-ED students were rated as moderately or greatly improved by involved referring agency staff.

Parental Ratings of Improvement

Eighteen months after discharge from Re-ED, *mothers reported "a good deal of improvement or great improvement"* (Weinstein, 1974, p. 205) when compared with pre-Re-ED levels for 73 per cent of the Re-ED students. *Fathers reported comparable levels of improvement for 81 per cent* of the students.

Although Re-ED students improved more than UD controls on their respective mothers' rating scales, this improvement was not large enough to surpass initial differences between Re-ED and UD control mothers' ratings of their children. Before Re-ED, mothers of Re-ED students rated them significantly more negatively than mothers of UD controls rated their children. Total rated improvement denoted by Re-ED mothers was not sufficient for Re-ED students to achieve significantly more positive ratings than were received by the UD children after Re-ED. It is unclear whether rating differences between the two sets of mothers reflected student differences, mother perception differences, or differences in conditions under which ratings occurred.

Sociometric Ratings

Although the adults' ratings indicated that Re-ED helped students more closely meet adults' expectations, *sociometric data from classmates showed no discernible improvement attributable to Re-ED in Re-ED students' relationships with regular school peers on return to home schools.* Peers represent unforeseen future ecological demands; program effectiveness within Re-ED for changing students' behaviors did not generalize automatically to improved social relations in the public school environment. Additional future effort and experiment in this arena should be worthy endeavors. One suggestion is that Re-ED programs consider providing children with additional experiences in guided interaction with N children before discharge.

Overall Results

Overall, the data suggest *important improvements in Re-ED children's basic attitudes, school behaviors, and learnings.* Not all children improved, however, or became free of problems. After the Re-ED experience, the *children, though they did better than the UD group, continued to differ on most measures from the N group* (children designated by their schools as being free of behavior problems).

These differences between Re-ED graduates and other groups were not surprising. The Re-ED program does not attempt to both remediate and then complete a disturbed child's re-education. By making the program more economically feasible while also reducing the time the child is separated from his everyday social world, *Re-ED's goal is less intrusive and perhaps more realistic: sufficient improvement so that the child can continue to develop appropriately* at his home, his school, and his community. Over time, the re-education process started at Re-ED is expected to continue – a journey far more enduring than the course of this study.

Follow-up Results

Follow-up data on R students following their discharges were collected at two points, since determining whether improvements would continue was important. *Improvements were generally sustained at six and 18 months post discharge.* However, *children with academic skills so far below grade expectations that they had problems coping with schoolwork experienced deteriorations in their behaviors.*

"Spontaneous Improvement?"

"Spontaneous improvement" apologists (e.g., Levitt, 1957) suggest that most disturbed children get better without special intercession. The *UD students in this study did not confirm this hypothesis*, with the only exception being mothers' ratings on the Symptom Checklist and the Semantic Differential in the last two testing rounds. However, as Weinstein points out, during this time period the "untreated" disturbed children were not devoid of interventions by parents, the private treatment sector, and the schools. Even so, two-thirds of the UD group were originally rated by their teachers as having behavioral difficulties extending from fairly severe to very severe. After two years their behaviors were once more judged by their teachers to be fairly severe or very severe. Furthermore, at the two year follow-up period the percent of UD students judged as having very severe problems had not decreased.

Only those UD children who had no academic difficulties connected with their behavior problems were likely to improve behaviorally over time. The majority (59%) of the UD children *without* initial academic deficits shifted from being behaviorally rated as fairly severe or very severe to being rated as mildly problematic or not problematic over a two year span.

By contrast, only 21 per cent of the UD students with initial academic difficulties shifted from a behavioral rating of fairly severe or very severe to being rated as mildly problematic or not problematic over a two year span. *"Indeed, in contrast to children with initial academic difficulties, UD children without initial academic problems were doing as well on the behavior ratings after two years as comparable children who spent time in a Re-ED school"* (Weinstein, 1974, p. 207). Based upon these findings, it would appear that Re-ED-oriented programs engaged in preventive work within public school settings should focus heavily upon ensuring that behaviorally problematic children achieve academic competence quickly, while aiding with behavioral interventions.

These studies confirmed the value of Re-ED's ecological approach (which includes families and emphasizes skill building) in changing the trajectories of children who were moving toward ever more serious problems. These changes apparently led in directions more in accord with the enhanced functioning hoped for by both the children and the families themselves.

References

Becker, W. C. (1960). The relationship of factors in parental ratings of self and each other to the behavior of kindergarten children as rated by mothers, fathers, and teachers. *Journal of Consulting Psychology, 24,* 507-527.

Bower, E. M. (1960). *Early identification of emotionally handicapped children in school.* Springfield, IL: Charles C. Thomas.

Cain, L. E., Levine, S., Tallman, I., Elzey, F., & Kase, D. (1958). *Study of the effect of special day training classes for the severely mentally retarded.* Report the Commissioner of Education, United States Department of Health, Education and Welfare.

Cromwell, R. L. 1963). A social learning approach to mental retardation. In N. R. Ellis (Ed.), *Handbook of mental deficiency: Psychological theory and research.* New York: McGraw-Hill.

Doll, E. A. (1947). *Vineland social maturity scale manual of directions.* Minneapolis: Educational Test Bureau.

Epstein, R. (1964). Need for approval and the conditioning of verbal hostility in asthmatic children. *Journal of Abnormal and Social Psychology, 69,* 105-109.

Farber, B. (1959) Effects of a severely mentally retarded child on family integration. *Monographs of the Society for Research in Child Development, 24*(2, Serial No. 71).

Hobbs, N. (1971, May). *The art of getting into trouble.* Commencement address to the graduating class of Peabody Demonstration School. Reprinted in Hobbs, N. (1974). A natural history of an idea: Project Re-ED. In J. M. Kaufman, & C. D. Lewis (Eds.), *Teaching children with behavior disorders* (pp. 164-165). Columbus, OH: Charles E. Merrill.

Kagan, J., Rosman, B. L., Day, D., Albert, J., & Phillips, W. (1964). Information processing in the child: Significance of analytic and reflective attitudes. *Psychological Monographs, 78*(1, Whole No. 578).

Kuethe, J. L. (1962). Social schemas. *Journal of Abnormal & Social Psychology, 64*(1), 31-38.

Kuethe, J. L. (1964). Social schemas and the reconstruction of social object displays from memory. *Journal of Abnormal & Social Psychology, 65*(1), 71-74.

Kuethe, J. L. & Weingartner, H. (1964). Male-female schemata of homosexual and non-homosexual penitentiary inmates. *Journal of Personality, 32*, 23-31.

Levitt, E. E. (1957). The results of psychotherapy with children: An evaluation. *Journal of Consulting Psychology, 23*, 189-196.

Ritter, A. M., & Colvin, R. W. (1959). *Impulse control as related to intellectual and social functioning of retarded children.*Paper presented at the meeting of the American Psychological Association, Cincinnati, September.

Rogers, C. R. (1931). *Measuring personality adjustment in children nine to thirteen years of age.* New York: A. M. S. Press.

Weinstein, L. (1965). Social schemata of emotionally disturbed boys. *Journal of Abnormal Psychology, 70,* 457-461.

Weinstein, L. (1967). Social experience and social schemata. *Journal of Personality and Social Psychology, 6,* 429-434.

Weinstein, L. (1968). The mother-child schema, anxiety, and academic achievement in elementary school boys. *Child Development, 39,* 257-264.

Weinstein, L. (1969). Project Re-ED schools for emotionally disturbed children: Effectiveness as viewed by referring agencies, parents, and teachers. *Exceptional Children, 35*(9), 703-711.

Weinstein, L. (1974). *Evaluation of a Program for Re-Educating Disturbed Children: A Follow-Up Comparison with Untreated Children.* Washington, D. C.: Department of Health, Education and Welfare. (Available through ERIC Documentation Reproduction Service, ED-141-966.)

Weinstein, L. (1976). Project Re-ED schools for emotionally disturbed children: Effectiveness as viewed by referring agencies, parents, and teachers. In N. J. Long, W. C. Morse, & R. G. Newman (Eds.). (1976). *Conflict in the classroom: The education of emotionally disturbed children* . (3rd ed.) (pp.420-428). Belmont, CA: Wadsworth. (From *Exceptional Children,* vol. 35, no. 9, May 1969, pp. 703-711. Reprinted by permission of The Council for Exceptional Children and the author).

Laura Weinstein, PhD, designed, carried out, analyzed, and reported the extensive research done on Project Re-ED. She later worked on the staff of the National Institute of Mental Health.

Robert P. Cantrell, PhD, is a research consultant for the Positive Education Program in Cleveland, OH
   rcantrell8648@sbcglobal.net

Mary L. Cantrell, PhD, is a research consultant for the Positive Education Program in Cleveland, OH.
   mlc8648@sbcglobal.net

TABLE 1. Comparison Results Referencing Codes

Abbreviations	Abbreviation Definitions
na	not asked for or not applicable
n s	none of the Re-ED, UD, or N groups differed significantly from one another
rud	Re-ED vs. UD do not differ significantly from one another
rn	Re-ED vs. N do not differ significantly from one another
Rna	Re-ED comparisons not applicable with UD or N groups
udn	UD vs. N do not differ significantly from one another
Rudn	Re-ED was significantly higher on this variable than either of the UD or N groups
Rud	Re-ED significantly higher than UD group
Rn	Re-ED significantly higher than N group
UDrn	UD was significantly higher on this variable than either Re-ED or N groups
UDr	UD significantly higher than Re-ED group
UDn	UD significantly higher than N group
Nrud	N was significantly higher on this variable than either Re-ED or UD groups
Nr	N significantly higher than Re-ED group
Nud	N significantly higher than UD group

TABLE 2. Statistical Results Across Comparison Groups

Result Abbreviations	Statistical Comparisons Across Re-ED, Untreated Controls, & Normals
(1) ns	Age (in months) at enrollment
(2) ns	Mean intelligence test score
(3) ns	Mean rank of Father's education
(4) ns	Mean rank of Father's occupation
(5) ns	Mean rank of Mother's education
(6) rud Rn UDn	Mean % Mother Works Outside Home
(7) ns	Mean rank of Mother's Occupation if Employed
(8) rud Rn UDn	Mean % Mother Works Full Time
(9a) rud Rn UDn	Percent Parents in Household: Child from Orphanage or Home for Dependent Children
(9b) rud Rn UDn	Percent Parents in Household: Child Adopted (vs. all others)
(9c) rud Rn UDn	Percent Parent plus stepparent, or single parent, or neither parent (vs. all others).
(10) rud Nr Nud	Percent Child lived with bio parents continuously total life
(11) Rud Rn UDn	Mean N of Differing Parental Situations Child Has Experienced (1 - 4+)
(12) ns	Mean N of Siblings
(13) ns	Percent Sibling Status (i.e., only, eldest, middle, youngest)
(14) rna UDn	Percent Parents Get Along (poorly/very poorly)
(15) rna Nud	Percent Parents Agree on Child Management Methods
(16) rna UDn	Percent Child Gets Along with Siblings (poorly/ very poorly)
(17) rna udn	Percent For child's sake Mother Would Like to Change
(18) rna UDn	Percent For Child's Sake Mother Would Like Father/Father Figure to Change
(19) rud Rn UDn	Percent Families Having Sought Help for Child's Emotional/Behavioral Problems from Physicians
(20) Rud Rn UDn	Percent Families Having Sought Help for Child's Emotional/Behavioral Problems from Psychological/Psychiatric/Social Workers/ Social Agencies
(21) Rud Rn UDn	Percent Families Having Sought Help for Child's Emotional/Behavioral Problems from

TABLE 2. (continued)

	any sources listed in (19) or (20)
(22)maUDn	Percent Families Having Sought Help for Child's Emotional/Behavioral Problems from School Personnel (i.e., teachers, principals, school psychologists, school social workers)
(23) Rud Rn UDn	Percent Families Having Sought Help for Child's Emotional/Behavioral Problems from any sources listed in (19) through (22)
(24) ns	Mean Age of Child (in years) when Mother First Realized Child Needed Special Help
(25) Rud Rn udn	Age of Child When First Seen by Helping Agency
(26)	Mean Age (in years) When He Entered Re-ED (10.2 years, s.d. = 1.2)
(27)	Percent Agencies Referring Child to Re-ED (75% Mental Health or Child Study Center, 25% all others)
(28) Rud Rn UDn	Percent Children Given Medications for Behavior Problems (prior to Re-ED)
(29) rud rn UDn	Percent Children in Trouble with Law Enforcement
(30) Rud Rn udn	Percent Mothers Having Received Professional Psychological Help for Problems Not Related to Child
(31) rud Rn udn	Percent Fathers Having Received Professional Psychological Help for Problems Not Related to Child
(32) UDr Nr udn	Percent Enrolled in Regular Class in School
(33) Rud Rn UDn	Percent Children Having Spent Time in a Special Class
(34) ns	Mean Grade in School for Children in Regular Class
(35) rud Rn udn	Mean Expected Grade Placement for All Project Children
(36) Rud Rn UDn	Mean Number of Times Child Failed a Grade
(36a) Rud Rn UDn	Mean Percent Children Having Failed One or More Grades
(37) rud Rn UDn	Mean Number of Grades Retarded for Children in Regular Classes (R = -0.6 UD = -0.4 N = -0.2)

TABLE 2. (continued)

(38) Rud Rn UDn	Percent Children Having Not Made Normal Progress in School
(39) ns	Mean Grade Where Child Stopped Normal School Progress (R = 1.8,UD = 1.7, N = 1.4)
(40) rna UDn	Percent Children Having Been Seen by School Psychologist
(41) rna UDn	Percent Children Having Been Seen by School Social Worker
(42) rna UDn	Percent Children Having Been Seen by School Psychologist and/or School Social Worker
(43)	Percents for **UD only:** (a) 10% placed in smaller classes (b) 24% placed with more appropriate teacher (c) 1% placed in a more appropriate school (d) 50% adjusted curriculum within regular class (e) 27% separated from classmates sometime each day (f) 23% relaxed discipline/usual requirements for behavior in school
(44) rna UDn	School Requested Parents Obtain Outside Help for Child
(45a) rna UDn	School Requested Outside Help for Child's Behavior
(45b) rna UDn	School Requested Outside Help for Child's Academics
(46) rud Nr Nud	Child Is No More Troublesome in Class than Most Children
(47) rud Rn UDn	Percent for neither praise nor criticism appear to affect behaviors/attitudes
(48) rud Rn UDn	Percent children in Danger of Suspension, Expulsion, or Exclusion
(49a) rna UDn	Mean Self-Control Ratings (below average) Given by Teacher at End of School Year
(49b) rna UDn	Mean Dependability Ratings (below average) Given by Teacher at End of School Year
(49c) rna UDn	Mean Cooperation Ratings (below average) Given by Teacher at End of School Year
(50) rud Rn UDn	Percent Child's Being Rejected by Other Children in Class
(51) Rud Rn UDn	Percent Personal Distress Felt by Child
(52) rud Nr Nud	Mean Child's Ability Ratings Compared with

TABLE 2. (continued)

	Others His Age (1 = Far Above Average to 5= Far Below Average; R = 3.1, UD = 3.3, N =2.8)
(53) rud Nr Nud	Mean Child's Achievement Level Compared with Other Children in Class (1 = Far Above Average to 5 = Far Below Others in Class; R = 3.9, UD = 3.9, N = 2.7)
(54) rna Nud-only	Mean Percent Achievement Ratings (5 point scale from "complete misfit" to "above average," excluding Re-ED children from ratings as "not applicable"— Ratings favor N children)
(55) rna UDn-only	Percent Ratings of Child Being Retained or Socially Promoted (excluding Re-ED children from ratings; ratings favor N children)
(56) rud Nr Nud	Mean Percent Use of Potential (1 = Full Capacity Work to 3 = Seldom Uses Abilities Fully; R = 2.6, UD = 2.6, N = 1.3, N children's low ratings more favorable)
(57) Rud Nr Nud	Mean Percent Receptiveness by Parents to Suggestions from School (Parents of N Children most receptive, Re-ED next most receptive, UD least receptive)
(58) rna UDn	Percent Current/Earlier Teachers Have Reported Behavior Problems in School (Re-ED pupils were not applicable for this question, for UD Children 93% of teachers had reported problems vs. 35% for N students)
(59) rna UDn	Percent Teachers' Reports about Current School Behavior (miscellaneous listing of concerns, all significantly more frequent with UD students, R not applicable)
(60a) rna udn	Mean Earliest grade for Teacher-Reported Behavior Problems in School (UD mean = 2.1, N mean = 2.5, ns; Re-ED children not applicable)
(60b) rna udn	Percent times First Grade Teacher Reported Behavior Problem to Mother (UD = 55%, N = 40%, ns; Re-ED children not applicable)
(60c) rna UDn	Percent of all children in the respective groups that First Grade Teachers Reported Behavior Problems to Mother (R = na, UD=51%, N=14%)

TABLE 2. (continued)

(61) rna UDn — Percent Teachers Reported Behavior Problems in Every Grade (wave 2 mothers only as respondents; UD = 53%, N = 3%, R = na)

(62) rud Rn UDn — Percent Mothers Saying Teachers Reported Problems with Child's Schoolwork this Year (R = 63%, UD = 49%, N = 12%)

(63) Rud Rn UDn — Percent School Requested that Mother Obtain Outside Help for Child (R = 84%, UD = 24%, N = 2%)

(64a) Rud Rn UDn — Percent School Requested Outside Help for Behavior (R = 83%, UD = 19%, N = 0%)

(64b) rud Rn UDn — Percent School Requested Outside Help for Academics (R = 10%, UD = 9%, N = 2%)

(65a) Rud Rn UDn — Mother-Mentioned Problem: School Behavior/ Attitudes

(65b) rud Rn UDn — Mother-Mentioned Problem: Getting child to study, do homework, show interest in school

(65c) Rud Rn UDn — Mother-Mentioned Problem: "Problems getting along with others" (p. 33)

(65d) Rud Rn UDn — Mother-Mentioned Problem: "Acting-out, aggressive, belligerent, headstrong, temper, no self-control" (p. 33)

(65e) Rud Rn UDn — Mother-Mentioned Problem: "Important rule or law-breaking behavior" (p. 33)

(65f) rud Rn UDn — Mother-Mentioned Problem: "Doesn't apply himself, short attention span, restless, impatient, demanding, careless, daydreams" (p. 33)

(65g) Rud Rn udn — Mother-Mentioned Problem: "Worried, anxious, withdrawn, no self-confidence, unhappy, nervous, fearful" (p. 33)

(66) rna Nud — "Does Mother Feel Child Has ... Fewer Problems than Other Boys His Age" (p. 33)

(67) rud Rn UDn — Mother's Rating of: "Child is not working up to ability" (p. 34)

(68) rna Nud — "Does Mother Feel Child Needs Special Help for His Problems" (answer: No) (p. 34)

(69) rud Nr Nud — "Number of Positive [Sociometric] Nominations by Classmates" (p. 34)

(70) rud Rn UDn — "Number of Negative [Sociometric] Nominations by Classmates" (p. 35)

30

The Prevention Intervention Project: Validating Re-ED as a Model for Mental Health in Public Schools

Robert P. Cantrell & Mary L. Cantrell

As the Project Re-ED short term residential programs completed their eight year grant and shifted to state funding, the Prevention Intervention Project (PIP) began using Re-ED principles and practices to prevent students' behavioral and/or academic problems from escalating to more severe levels. This was accomplished by teaching public school teachers to use the Re-ED model to conceptually unravel, then initiate remedies within, children's problematic ecologies. PIP's task involved training public school support teachers quickly in the Re-ED approach, providing intensive follow-up to these support teachers as they learned to help classroom teachers with troubled pupils, and evaluating the impact of these efforts on support teachers, classroom teachers, and pupils. This chapter presents the goals, operations, and results of another Re-ED application, this time in public schools.

Implementing Re-ED in Public Schools

Problem and Setting

The troubled and troubling children served and taught in Re-ED's short term residential schools of the 1960s demonstrated positive changes in their homes and home schools after their sojourn in the care of talented and creative teacher-counselors (Weinstein, 1974). These children had been identified earlier by their parents and teachers as

403

posing or experiencing serious problems. Admittedly, thousands more across the nation were at risk of developing similar problems. These students could, at some point, need specialized services, separating them from their peers and sometimes from their families. Could this Re-ED approach that had worked with seriously troubled children within a residential setting be used to *avoid* residential or special class placement? What if trained educators used the Re-ED approach earlier with troubled students within a regular school setting?

Proposed Solution: The Prevention Intervention Project

Teacher-counselors (T-Cs) trained within Project Re-ED (in conjunction with Peabody College, the Tennessee Department of Mental Health, and the North Carolina Department of Mental Health; Hobbs, 1982) were highly successful in changing the behaviors of troubled children inside a short term, 5 day residential setting (Weinstein, 1974). The residential structure of Re-ED, however, limited the numbers of youngsters who could be served. Residential treatment was, and remains, costly. PIP's primary purpose was to determine whether similarly trained T-Cs could be successful within a public school setting, providing a cost-effective prevention alternative.

Aside from parents, teachers are the most plentiful resource per child for behavior change. They are nearly continuous presences in the lives of children, yet good instruction within school walls seldom meets all areas of each child's needs. Occasional parent-teacher conferences cannot substitute for a daily working relationship between schools and homes for those children who need this collaboration most and early. Problematic behaviors brought to school or developed there during the first days and weeks can quickly chip away at an otherwise optimal social-emotional-educational mix. Soon a first grader eager to go to school can morph into a storm warning with a "reputation" as he enters second grade.

The project focus during the first four years of PIP operation was to provide Re-ED trained support staff (i.e., "support teachers" or STs) to assist regular classroom teachers in analyzing problems and planning interventions, enabling pupils to function effectively within the mainstream of education. By so doing, classroom teachers should acquire problem solving skills applicable for use with all children, resulting in a lower referral rate from regular education to special education and extra-school services.

Intervention. PIP aimed toward both preventive work with children who appeared to be on the road to more serious difficulties, and children already in difficulty within their classrooms. Classroom teachers were the primary referral source. No diagnostic tests were administered to screen for acceptance into the program; a teacher needed only to approach a support teacher with a concern about a child for him or her to be considered. Each teacher in the experimental schools was informed that this request for consideration was not a "hand - off" process to STs who would then assume responsibility for the child; rather, all children referred to PIP would receive teamwork effort. The STs, the referring classroom teacher, and the principal were part of the problem analysis and intervention teamwork for problems that were best handled at school. Parents were added to the team when interventions outside of school were needed.

The team approach grew from the behavioral, ecology-based belief that child problems arise within the complex interactions a child experiences every day with peers, family members, neighborhood situations, and teachers – all with sets of expectations. As these external issues develop, they can be exacerbated by the internal complexities of emotions, skill-demand discrepancies, and skewed (or realistic) interpretations of events. Unique issues often arise as these complexities are played out each day. Because of their seemingly ever-changing nature, sometimes these troubling interactions seem to have no easy solutions – they require a team approach.

We needed interventions tailored to each child's unique strengths and difficulties, not a standardized, one-size-fits-all intervention to which all referred children would be exposed. Those types of grouped interventions may be easily tested for efficacy statistically, but we would have learned little about why they worked or failed with individual children. Nor were standardized interventions ecologically defensible;

too many children had too many different combinations of external and internal complexities.

However, project planning required a concise explanation of our goals and objectives for officials in the Tennessee Departments of Mental Health and Education. Initially, these officials were thinking along the lines of a mental health curriculum that could be shoe-horned into a public school setting. We were thinking more along the lines of what was later articulated so well by Nicholas Hobbs:

> *"One of the important early ideas in project Re-ED was that there should be no orthodoxy, no fixed explanations, no set ways of doing things, no dogma.... There are... certain pervasive concepts that form Re-ED programs.... [that] are not so much fixed principles as they are working hypotheses about how to help disturbed children and their families.... The concepts have never existed as restraints on discovery, on invention.... [but rather depend upon] the people who have committed themselves to it, their rational and intuitive grasp of a loosely defined set of principles, and their ingenuity in inventing each day what the Re-ED program should become"* (Hobbs, 1978, p. 65).

Therein lay the challenge: to intercept and re-direct the problem trajectories of children before the public education system ejected them from normalizing pathways within regular school into "special" programs. Ultimately, we wanted to keep as many students out of Re-ED residential programs as possible. The proposed program had to (a) remain sufficiently generic to be applicable for a wide range of complex problems, and (b) produce results that would be empirically justifiable.

General Goals. The Prevention Intervention Project (PIP) tested whether the principles, ecological change concepts, and strategies defining teacher-counselor roles as developed within Project Re-ED could be successfully transplanted into five selected public school districts and generate positive changes with troubled children.

Project staff assisted district contact persons in selecting teachers from their systems who would become "Support Teachers" (or STs) within the two experimental schools in each district. Two STs were assigned to each district, working together with both target schools.

Training for the STs was provided by a group of program consultants selected from the Tennessee Department of Mental Health's Re-ED residential programs. These Program Consultants (PCs) planned training and supported the STs in their work with children, teachers, and families. The PCs were, in fact, the transmitters of the Re-ED culture and problem solving tools to STs operating in these new roles.

PIP Project Structure and Function

Dr. Charles MacDonald initiated an early attempt to transfer the Re-ED approach from its residential beginnings to a public school setting when he was Director of the Children's Division for the Tennessee Department of Mental Health. In the early 1970's, children's mental health in Tennessee had embraced the Re-ED model. The state mental health leadership had accepted it as the preferred approach for dealing with disturbed children and youth. Residential Re-ED programs were attached to mental hospitals across Tennessee and were largely granted freedom from the structural and procedural strictures of the medical model.

PIP was also a response to a search the Nixon administration had initiated for a project that could demonstrate cooperative funding and shared administrative control across differing state and federal programs. Dr. MacDonald approached the governor of Tennessee with the idea that Re-ED in the schools might be such a venue. The governor broached the idea with his federal contacts and PIP became a possibility, assuming it could meet the stringent grant application guidelines posed by the various federal funding agencies that would be involved.

Funding

PIP was funded cooperatively by: (1) the Elementary and Secondary Education Act (ESEA), Title III (Section 306), U.S. Office of Education; (2) the Education Professions Development Act, U.S. Office of Education; (3) the Bureau of Education for the Handicapped (BEH, now OSED), U.S. Office of Education; (4) Tennessee ESEA III; (5) BEH through the Tennessee Department of Education; (6) the Tennessee Department of Mental Health; (7) the Tennessee

Department of Education; and (8) five Tennessee school systems: Metropolitan Nashville-Davidson County, Memphis City, Kingsport City, Robertson County, and Hamilton County.

The proposal's funding began July 1, 1971. Metropolitan Nashville-Davidson County Public Schools was the recipient agency with the Tennessee Department of Mental Health, Division of Children and Youth, as the contract agency for training, consultation, and evaluation.

Participating School Districts

PIP was implemented in five Tennessee school systems seen as representative of school system types across the nation. The Memphis city school system typified the large urban school district. The Hamilton County School System was a suburban school district surrounding Chattanooga, Tennessee. The Kingsport City Schools served a smaller city. The Robertson County schools were in a low density rural area around Springfield, Tennessee. The Nashville - Davidson County schools were situated within a large metropolitan form of city - county government.

These school systems were chosen to represent the widest possible range of Tennessee's socioeconomic levels, cultural and ethnic groups, and community organizations. PIP's administrative arrangements with each of the five school systems differed dramatically, offering project staff contacts with project schools across systems by way of differing administrative pathways (special education, curriculum and instruction, program and staff development, or pupil personnel services). In addition, active involvement with the Tennessee State Departments of Education and Mental Health, as well as with the Citizens Advisory Committee selected from separate geographic regions of the five completely independent school systems, helped prevent dominance over project activities by any one location.

Delineating Interventions

In essence, the Re-ED approach practices ecological enhancement and problem solving within the framework of a strong philosophical basis which: (a) builds on current strengths, (b) develops competencies through positive experiences, and (c) demonstrates deep respect for children and families. Before the project could be funded we needed to explain what this approach entailed, how we proposed to intercept and re-direct the problem trajectories of troubled and troubling children in public schools, and how we planned to do this in a manner sufficiently generic as to be applicable for a wide range of complex problems.

Looking for logjams. One helpful concept Re-ED uses (informally attributed to the University of Oregon's Gerald Patterson) refers to a logging practice in the northwest U.S. of floating cut timber downriver to a sawmill. Floating logs, attempting to pass obstacles or negotiate a bend in the river, clump together around the first log to stop at the obstacle. Loggers learned that a stick of dynamite strategically placed near a key log can free the whole clump to continue downstream.

"Logjam" became a useful metaphor for children's problem complexes and the "key operants" that tend to build that complexity. Families (and classrooms) often get "stuck" using repetitive, non-productive ways of interacting. Conflicts tend to increase the emotional charge attached to everything associated with the logjam, including steps leading up to it, players in the interchanges, and the consequences (most often punishments in some form for one or more players). If a more successful method for dealing with a key log can be introduced, often other seemingly unrelated conflicts associated with emotional residue from the logjam also disappear.

Modeling Problem Solving. The funders' requests for detail led to intensive reflection on how to articulate and systematize the Re-ED processes used while intervening successfully with troubling children in public schools (Cantrell, 1969; Cantrell, Cantrell, Huddleston, & Wooldridge, 1969). Could the problem solving strategies used with parents and teachers be captured to form a flow chart of Socratic-like questions (Cantrell & Cantrell, 1980), serving as templates to reveal core patterns within complex problems? Such a guide would approximate Simon and Newell's (1965) conceptualizations of how humans solve problems, so we labeled the resulting set of flowcharts a "heuristic," the word used by Newell and Simon (1972) in their work. This "heuristic" described the process PIP would follow with schools for "ecological diagnosis and intervention," and representatives of the mental health and education state departments deemed it a viable explanation for submission in the proposal for PIP's federal funding.

Working through Natural Agents. In previous work with families concerned about a child's behavioral difficulties (Cantrell, et al., 1969), the problem solvers typically never knew what the children looked like, nor were their problems observed directly. Instead, we relied upon the natural agents' observations, re-framed through careful questioning into a functional analysis of cues, behaviors, and attendant consequences within each child's ecology. This questioning approach conveyed several subtle messages. First, it became clear to all parties involved in the meeting who the most knowledgeable persons were about the child's behaviors — the parents and/or teachers. As visitors and potential helpers, professionals could ask for forgiveness of our ignorance, with repeated statements like, "Let me be sure I understand what you're saying," or "What exactly does s/he do when s/he's 'Xing'" (using their term, not our translation).

Careful amalgamation and analysis of respondents' answers to these questions led to determination of what seemed to be key areas within each child's social ecology that were amenable to needed change. Only after identifying key logs and resources did we tentatively propose something couched in speculation, such as, "What do you think would happen if you were to do Y, when s/he did X?" If we had done our part well, the parent and/or teacher would often agree to a tryout. If the situation was still filled with anger, it sometimes was necessary to back-track and try a different approach.

The most successful interventions seemed to hinge around "gently" teaching natural agents how to cope successfully, without any hierarchy of "expertise," or taking responsibility away from natural agents. Success in helping them solve their own problems would "teach them how to fish," instead of providing them with a fish for that day, cooked the way we liked it. The strategy for the heuristic was to attempt to capture the problem solving tactics in a form that could be transmitted to others in hopes they could resolve problems more quickly, benefiting from others' experiences, both successes and failures.

Analyzing Discord. The flow chart consisted of: (a) questions that STs would pose to teachers, parents, principals, the children themselves, and others who might have observed the behavior(s) *in situ* and (b) subsequent questions for consolidating the obtained information into objectives and intervention activities. Thus the heuristic worked like a template to guide STs through functional behavioral analyses in each of the major ecological domains of most children and youth: social behaviors, academics or other skills, home problems, neighborhood issues, and/or community based conflicts. Each analysis section used descriptions reported by parents or teachers of potential/present strengths and difficulties to feed into a planning section. Questions posed were designed to help STs develop a thorough understanding of the situational logjam *before* jumping into intervention. Interventions thrown at situations quickly without thorough analysis were more likely to fail. And, more importantly, each adult failure would likely teach the child lessons best not learned, especially since the child was likely to learn powerful and destructive control - counter control measures during these failed adult attempts.

STs learned to listen carefully after asking this first question: "How can we be of help?" By attending to first concerns, several overt and covert messages appeared to be given: (a) we're listening; (b) we're taking your concerns at face value; and (c) when it's your turn to listen, we hope you'll listen, too. But tackling the biggest logjams head-on as the ST's first intervention was often not the best choice, at least not until STs had developed a grapevine-fed reputation for competence. If anything went awry, the intervention itself could easily be blamed and participants might abandon the effort before it had a chance to work. For this reason, STs were often advised to begin with a less ambitious intervention. This gave everyone an opportunity to fine-tune their own part in the intervention, often uncovering missing information that was not mentioned or remembered during the initial interviews. Successes strengthened trust and encouraged perseverance towards overcoming other more difficult obstacles.

The prime example of this strategy was the way we introduced the STs to their schools' staffs. After the usual introductory in-services to introduce PIP, we waited until a less timorous teacher referred the first child from her classroom for ST help. Out of the usual litany of concerns voiced by a teacher we advised the STs to choose a highly visible, yet more rapidly modifiable behavior with first graders, such as out-of-seat behaviors. By combining data gathering observations with in-class prompting of the teacher to differentially attend more to the child when s/he was seated than when wandering (assuming, of course, that teacher attention was the operating reinforcer), the STs could demonstrate their ability to be of help to the teacher. Afterward, the staff grapevine usually helped move matters along.

The Support Teacher Role

PIP intervention teams were comprised of STs, classroom teachers, parents, principals, neighbors, and/or community resources who met consensually as needed. The STs were the coordinating hub of each team, as well as the diplomatic glue that held each team together by maintaining focus on the child's needs and on each member's interests. The charge for that role was not easily carried out. It was clear from PIP's earliest negotiations with the involved school systems that the Re-ED concept of working with the child's total ecology would not be easily spliced into the educational belief structures of most teachers. This seemed even more true of 1970's era principals; many had difficulty accepting an outreach mind-set for working with parents, much less with other non-school individuals who might be primary influences in the lives of these children. This struggle and confusion seemed to grow largely out of premises that adults often hold about children. One set of premises arises from educators' beliefs (often negative) about the worlds from which troubled children arise. The second set seems affected by the educators' own personal and scholastic histories, most having been successful students who grew up wanting to be educators. Beliefs about how children should perform as students, paired with lowered expectations from their beliefs about the homes of "problem kids," often led to a tendency to give up on problem students prematurely.

Principals expressed concerns about the family/community liaison functions of the new support teacher role. How could principals account for where STs were during the day if they didn't clock into the school building in the morning and clock out when they left after the last bell? Negotiating compromises with these and other usual school practices was time consuming, but critical. We finally agreed that STs would be allowed to spend up to 50% of their work time outside the school walls. This loosened the public school structure sufficiently to enable selected staff to work with parents and other community agents outside the school walls and school time strictures. But clearly, STs would need to be visibly successful — quickly.

Preparation and Startup Activities

Support Teacher Selection

Project planners envisioned a variation of the teacher-counselor role already functioning within the residential Re-ED programs. To staff PIP, we wanted to find teachers indigenous to each of the five school systems and provide them with additional training, followed by continuous consultation and feedback as they worked with regular school teachers.

PIP district contact persons assigned by each project school system were already highly placed within their administrative hierarchies. They issued invitations to classroom teachers who were interested in exploring other role opportunities within their school system. We met with groups of these interested teachers and promised them that in this new role they would work harder than they had ever worked before, but they would have support from Re-ED teachers who had "been there and done that." They would get feedback about the impact their efforts had on children, and they would never view troublesome pupils the same way again. This first group meeting separated the curious from those undeterred by challenge.

Next, we held individual interviews with prospective STs. We were looking for individuals with energy, a sense of humor, and a broad set of life experiences relative to their ages. We sought persons who had been employed in non-education jobs at some time prior to teaching, particularly jobs that had socialized them to life experiences of others in the broader society outside schools, enabling them to relate to significant others within children's ecologies. If conversant with at least some of the day-to-day concerns of these significant others, STs could more easily broach school issues.

Our expectation was that many parents who would become key members of the intervention team for helping their child continued to harbor mixed feelings about the way school had affected their own lives. Now, perhaps, school would be intruding once more through the lives of their children, sometimes evoking painful memories. We could not expect them to lay aside their own past pain merely because we had promised to help their child. Thus, it was important to impress upon STs that they were expected to work as part of a team effort that would include the child's parent, teacher, and any "significant other" persons who would need to work congruently with the team to produce changes.

These early interviews with candidate groups ultimately helped us persuade the classroom teachers that STs would not serve as quasi-supervisors. We wanted to use the school grapevine to good advantage. As STs started with classroom teachers who were trying to cope with "troublesome" children and were willing to try out any source of help, we were able to help produce changes that made teachers' jobs easier and more successful. Word eventually spread, and STs were gradually welcomed into more and more classrooms.

At times teachers wanted to use STs as tutors for children in need of additional help. The STs responded by starting programs where they showed older children who volunteered as tutors how to work effectively with those less skilled, making themselves even more widely effective in classroom teachers' eyes.

Support Teacher Training and Ongoing Support

In seeking solutions to problem behavior situations, experienced Re-EDers tend to think of "core patterns" as habits of interacting that members of the child's social ecology have fallen into, perhaps inadvertently, but from which they cannot distance themselves in order to problem-solve dispassionately. Case studies from the literature or from our own experience helped provide possible solutions, but repertoire transfer of possible solutions (the benefits of Re-ED experience) to new PIP STs was challenging. PIP used Re-ED "Program Consultants" (or PCs) to train and support the project's STs as in-school mental health/educational change agents. The PCs were experienced practitioners whose skills and beliefs had been formed by working successfully with troubled children using the tools honed within the residential Re-ED model.

Viewing Discord. PCs tended to conceptualize troubled and troubling children as being active participants in sometimes stable, sometimes unpredictable, sometimes turbulent ecologies. These trainers viewed ecologies experiencing unmanageable discord as constantly shifting systems of behavioral, educational, social, familial, communal, biological, neurological, and even economic elements. In short, anything and everything that did (or might) affect the child was a legitimate area for appreciation, understanding, or concern, if not intervention. Viewed this way, the child did not "own" more than his/her fair share of the problems of concern, nor did others. Both the child and the others participated in the discord, and all had strengths to use in contributing to discord resolution. The target child became the focal point for accomplishing these altered patterns of interaction.

Training the STs. During the planning grant period, program consultant (PC) staff developed six training program modules (i.e., ecological planning, program relevant evaluation, academic programming, behavioral principles and contingency management, evaluation techniques, and group processes). The PCs served as initial trainers and later as ongoing consultants to the STs in the new roles they held in their home school districts. All ten STs were brought to the central Re-ED unit in Nashville and trained intensively for 240 hours spread across six weeks during the summer of 1971.

Guiding and Reporting Analyses. Near the end of this initial training, STs were given the heuristic to use as a case-reporting instrument. This guide helped STs untangle complex situations into sets of key issues to be resolved. They started by identifying the major players (e.g., parents, teachers, the child, or others in the child's ecosystem) who would be asked for interviews. Space was provided on the heuristic forms to record information following interviews, including places to code each informant's role in the child's ecology. Overlapping reports from independent observers provided an informal measure of concurrent validity for information about shared concerns.

STs separately interviewed principal players about an important, clearly remembered problem episode. The episode would be taken apart step-by-step, using a behavioral timeline of who did what, where, when, and what happened afterward. This reporting of major episodes at the interview's beginning accomplished several immediate, important goals: (1) being asked to report on these concerns in detail validated for STs that the parent(s) or teacher(s) were major sources of helpful information leading to potential solutions, (2) parents' and teachers' concerns were tacitly acknowledged as important rather than trivial by "experts;" (3) the sequence of concerns expressed gave the STs some insight into the parents' and teachers' perceived hierarchy of behaviors that would, or would not, be tolerated in their settings; (4) the descriptions of concerns and their accompanying contingencies gave STs information needed to pick ecological logjams for timely, hopefully rapid, intervention successes.

Providing Structures for Mentoring. The PCs were more than trainers. Once the initial support teacher training phase was completed, follow-up structures enabled PCs to serve as mentors to STs. Four mechanisms helped this process: (a) periodic long distance phone consultations about target children, (b) the heuristic case record procedures (described below), (c) periodic site visits by PCs to support teachers' schools, and (d) periodic refresher workshops complete with the popular "Yay-Boo" sessions, when each team told of a particularly successful intervention (Yay) and then presented the details of a child's problems (Boo) for which they were soliciting suggestions from the other teams.

These mechanisms provided formats for intensive feedback, consultative backup, and tracking interventions geared to resolving each child's problem(s). The core of the tracking system was the heuristic case record. The STs mailed photocopies of their heuristics (one for each child on their caseload) at periodic intervals to the program consultant assigned to their team for that period (as PCs rotated across teams monthly). New information on each heuristic was always dated as it became known and recorded. PC staff called the STs on a regular basis to discuss each case, as well as make periodic on-site visits to school sites across Tennessee. In this fashion we kept an intensive training program active long after the initial six weeks training period had passed, and more importantly, assured treatment fidelity of the Re-ED process. After about two years of this process, most STs had cognitively incorporated the problem-solving structures embedded in the heuristic into their own professional problem-solving templates.

Tracking Interventions. Heuristic forms also provided basic data for program evaluation and research. Through these completed records, we could track *when* each bit of information was obtained, and when each objective was met, reviewed, or dropped. We could also compare patterns of interventions and their ultimate differential effectiveness. Days lapsed between treatment milestones provided interval level data for statistical analyses.

Introducing PIP to Schools

Many activities were designed to introduce and initiate PIP staff and functions each project year. Meetings with district level administrators had been ongoing before and during the first project year. Principals' meetings were introduced soon afterward, and then meetings involving other staff whom STs were to approach (i.e., school psychologists, counselors, etc.). The project evaluator, sometimes accompanied by the school district administrator assigned to the project, met frequently with principals individually to introduce the concept of the project and to answer questions and concerns directly.

The two weeks prior to schools' opening were busy ones for PCs and STs. The PCs rotated through each experimental school, providing in-service training to local classroom teachers in each of their own specialty areas. At this time PCs introduced the local STs who would be available to help teachers with children causing concerns in classrooms. Because this teacher training schedule was well received, it was maintained throughout the project's four years.

Operation and Expansion

Experimental and Control Schools

Each of the 5 cooperating school systems designated 2 experimental schools and 2 control schools: one active control and one hold-out control. Active control schools provided classroom observations plus teacher and pupil testings on the same schedule as experimental schools. Observed students in the active control schools were nominated by teachers on the basis of their being "behaviorally active." No other requirements for students observed in the active control schools were specified. Hold-out control schools had no classroom observations but did provide teacher and pupil testings. These control school arrangements provided comparative data for project evaluation. Only in the experimental schools did STs help formulate intervention strategies to deal with academic, behavioral, and/or other ecological difficulties presented by each (target) child referred.

Actively teaching an ecological approach to problem-solving, along with intensive follow-up from experienced Re-ED PCs, enabled us to reinforce the original training and track the treatment process. We could then link the changes the treatment process produced between pre-testing and post-testing for STs, classroom teachers, and the children in their schools.

Support Teacher Assignments and Targets

Starting with grade one in year 1, PIP added a grade each succeeding year, while continuing to help teachers and target children with whom STs had worked previously. This basic method of operation was repeated each year.

Year 1. The first year of operation focused on grade one teachers and pupils. That year PIP STs worked in the experimental schools with 37 teachers and 183 target children (out of 723 total first graders). In the active control schools 18 teachers and 36 nominated children (out of 710 total first graders) were observed. No attempts were made to match "target" children in the experimental schools and "nominated" children in the active control schools, since target children moved in and out of that designation as interventions began and ended.

Year 2. Project year 2 focused on second grade as the target grade, while continuing first grade services. During this second year of project activities, the Tennessee Legislature passed a law mandating "education for handicapped children in public schools" (Tennessee Code Annotated Section P.L. 839). The new law entirely changed service delivery under the Tennessee Department of Special Education, suggesting a mainstreaming and non-labeling approach which closely resembled the PIP objectives. These new priorities led to wider use of project staff, including consultations on the development of new programs for students with "handicapping conditions" throughout the state.

Year 3. Year 3 focused on grade three plus an expansion to target grade seven in junior high schools. Ten additional support team teachers were trained to staff the junior high component. An experimental junior high school and a control junior high school were selected in each school system. The 20 support teams worked with 1,485 pupils during Year 3 for an average of 74 pupils per support teacher, a rough ratio of STs to pupils served.

Year 4. Year 4 expanded the target grades to K-4 at the elementary level and 7-9 at the junior high level. Also, during the fourth year of operation a special grant from the State Department of Education required PIP to train up to 100 teachers in five centers throughout the state, using a refinement of the training modules used with the STs previously. The six-week summer training used the previously trained support team teachers, with consultation from PCs.

Maintaining Treatment Fidelity

The growing pressures for evidence-based treatment practices have received much attention in recent years and have been credited with influencing psychotherapy practices and training programs (Miller & Binder, 2002). In the attempt to address these concerns about treatment fidelity, many training programs developed treatment manuals to be used as a common framework for training. These manuals hopefully defined the ongoing task of verifying implementation of prescribed treatments and monitoring their effects on therapeutic outcomes.

The rationale for the origin of the heuristic had similar routes, but was designed to extend beyond the stage of manual-based training received during the initial six weeks. Intensive, training-based follow-up was provided STs as they began working with children and with members of each child's ecosystem. The treatment goal was minimal intrusion for maximal effect, relying upon ecological re-direction and the belief that *"Time is an ally"* (Hobbs, 1982, p. 22) for developmental forces to build momentum in proactive ways, once positive interventions began.

The heuristic worked as an organizing template for both the STs and their continuing instructors, the PCs. It provided a common format for reporting behavioral objectives that STs had formulated in consultation with the target child's regular classroom teacher and/ or parents. Sometimes heuristics were written for a target group where the same problems and interventions were appropriate for more than one student.

The PC staff tracked changes through the eyes of STs who reported information with associated dates on the heuristic. With this version of manual-based training, PCs were able to help STs see how the dynamics for a specific target child related to what had been taught in the training sessions. The transition from didactic instruction to daily practice was therefore continuous and virtually seamless. This treatment consultation and tracking process standardized the transmittal of Re-ED treatment procedures to support team teachers in training and hindered the treatment "drift" plaguing so many past attempts to replicate successful intervention treatments.

Parenthetically, some later data analyses appeared to tell us that this heuristic process required about two years' active usage before cognitive templates for successful ecological problem-solving were well established in the problem-solving repertoires of STs. At this point STs streamlined their heuristic reporting and began completing only key items of the short form version of the heuristic.

PIP Research and Evaluation

Design

Medley and Mitzel (1959) had long before suggested parameters for the three most important criteria in investigating teacher effectiveness. They prescribed inclusion of: (a) presage variables (e.g., measurement of teacher personality, knowledge, and other characteristics), (b) process variables (e.g., teacher behaviors, student behaviors, and teacher-pupil interactions), and (c) product variables (measures of student change, e.g., achievement). All three were included in PIP's project objectives, data collections, and analyses. Evaluation activities included on-site classroom observations, supervised testing of teachers and students, and monitoring of individual casework data as developed by STs in their respective work sites.

Presage. Demographic, professional experience, and university preparation information were recorded for teachers. Teacher pre-tests described their entering behavioral knowledge and attitudes towards students and teaching.

Process. Guiding all project processes and procedures were the 12 Re-ED principles and other concepts critical to the Re-ED philosophy. These statements of belief about the components of successful living provided no technical guides. The heuristic operated within the Re-ED philosophy to help STs clarify problematic situations and design individualized ecological interventions, focusing the core tools from behavioral science and learning theory on achieving successful results. The heuristic also provided the prime case datasets for program evaluation research activities (Cantrell & Cantrell, 1977).

Product. Pre/post-year testings measured pupils' IQs and academic achievement, as well as teachers' behavioral knowledge and attitudes towards teaching. The inclusion of year-long classroom observations rounded out the presage, process, and product research paradigm, much as incorporated by Cantrell (1969) in a prior school system research program.

All pupils were evaluated on the Metropolitan Achievement Test (Durost, Bixler, Wrightstone, Prescott, & Balow,1971) and the Otis-Lennon IQ test (Otis & Lennon, 1967). Teacher testing employed the Minnesota Teacher Attitude Inventory (Cook, Leeds, & Callis, 1951) and the Alternative Classroom Strategies Inventory or ACSI (Cantrell & Cantrell, 1969).

PIP's Classroom Observation Schedule was designed as a modified form of the Flanders Scale of Classroom Interaction (Flanders, 1960). Independent data collectors assigned to each school system were trained to an inter-rater reliability criterion of 80%. Over 3,000 hours of classroom observations were performed, many with accompanying videotaped verification for reliability checks. These were recorded, entered, and analyzed in the evaluation process. Testing results and observations were compared in a research design based on a pre vs. post and an experimental vs. control basis to determine statistical and educational significance of the project activities.

Project Objectives and Evidence of Effectiveness

PIP underwent the extensive ESEA Title III validation process in 1975 and was approved for national dissemination as an exemplary program with highest ratings in all categories from the validation team. Summaries of validation studies follow, including (1) ST training gains, (2) classroom teachers' learning and student maintenance in regular schools, (3) ST problem solving, (4) pupil classroom behavior, and (5) pupil academic performance.

Objective 1. STs Gain in Behavioral Knowledge and Training Content: *Re-ED-trained STs will demonstrate gains in (a) behavioral knowledge applied to classroom problem situations, and*

(b) knowledge of a broad range of options for academic, behavioral, and other ecological interventions.

Procedures. The Tennessee Department of Mental Health would train "support" teacher personnel in Re-ED's ecological analysis and intervention techniques for work with classroom teachers, students, parents, and community agencies. This objective was to be considered met successfully if STs made statistically significant gains on the ACSI and on a series of multiple choice items pertaining to the training module content between the initiation of training and the end of training. (Information on ACSI reliability and evidence of construct validity, content validity, and predictive validity is available from the authors.)

Results. At the point of the ESEA Title III validation study, two groups of STs had been trained and were working in the project: (a) an elementary group ($N = 10$) who were in their fourth project year, and (b) a junior high group ($N = 10$) who were finishing their second project year of activity. Both groups had made statistically significant pre- to post-training on (a) the ACSI, a measure of knowledge of behavioral principles, and (b) multiple choice items concerned with major concepts from each of the training program modules (ecological planning, program relevant evaluation, evaluation techniques, group processes, behavior management, and academic programming).

The STs showed mean growth on the behavioral knowledge and training module probe measures; their scores also became significantly more homogeneous pre- to post-training. On the measure of teacher attitudes (MTAI), STs in both groups also became significantly more homogeneous pre- to post-training in their attitudes about children and teaching. This increased homogeneity indicated that, for all these measures, trainees scoring in the lowest ranges at entry raised their scores, as did the others, but did so at an even higher degree of improvement.

Objective 2. Classroom Teachers Maintain Students in Regular Classrooms: Experimental classroom teachers working with Re-ED-trained STs will learn to be more successful in main-

taining troubled and troubling students within regular education services in public schools than will teachers in control schools without Re-ED support.

Procedures. Support team teachers would help classroom teachers learn to maintain behaviorally and academically troubled students within the regular classroom. The accomplishment of this objective was to be evaluated by: (1) Classroom teachers making statistically significant behavioral knowledge gains on the ACSI as a function of their consultative contacts with STs for solving children's problems (see Studies 1 and 2 below), and (2) Maintenance of behaviorally and academically discordant students in the regular classroom as measured by significantly fewer ($p < .05$) students being referred for psychological or special education services by teachers in experimental schools than by teachers in control schools (Study 3 below).

Results. Since classroom teacher involvement in the experimental schools was voluntary so far as teacher referrals of students were concerned, this first knowledge gain variable was measured on two levels using the ACSI. Test results were analyzed: (a) for scores from repeated testings of all experimental teachers, relative to control school teachers in Years 1 and 2, and (b) as a function of the amount of contact time experimental school teachers had with STs in the resolution of children's problems. This hypothesis was supported by the results of both analyses.

Study 1: Comparison of experimental school and control school teachers' scores. In the first study, a significant interaction ($F = 3.67$, df = 2, 124, p < .05) was obtained between experimental and control teachers across pre-year 1, post-year 1, and post-year 2 behavioral knowledge results. The control school and experimental school teachers scored at approximately the same level in knowledge during the initial testings. Experimental school teachers, after a full year's work with STs in resolving pupils' problems, achieved a statistically significant increase in knowledge, while control teachers' behavioral knowledge remained roughly unchanged.

Study 2: Classroom teacher gains when working with STs. This study added the results for grade two experimental teachers at the end of project year 2. Here it was possible to look at the ACSI results for experimental teachers based upon which year(s) they had worked with STs on behalf of referred target children.

These four teacher groups were significantly different in ACSI knowledge overall ($F = 3.69$, $df = 3, 55$, $p < .05$):

(1) The greatest growth in behavioral knowledge occurred with those teachers who had worked with STs in both years 1 and 2.

(2) Next in knowledge growth were the teachers who had worked with STs in year 1 only.

(3) The third group, those second grade teachers who had not worked with STs year 1, but then referred children and worked with STs in the team efforts during year 2 made a large spurt in behavioral knowledge by the end of that year, although they had scored the lowest of the four groups on ACSI pre-testing.

(4) Teachers who had not worked with STs in either year 1 or year 2 stayed relatively the same, but overall were the lowest performing ACSI knowledge teachers of the four experimental school teacher groupings by the end of year 2.

Interestingly, STs' own knowledge gains on the ACSI measure across testing points showed the most knowledge growth of all those tested. Each year's results showed significant growth, probably as a function of the continued consultative support from PIP PCs, added knowledge from feedback about their interventions with classroom teachers and pupils, and, of course, repeated testings on the same knowledge measure.

Study 3: Student referrals to district special services. One independent measure of the effectiveness of ST-classroom teacher teamwork in maintaining behaviorally, academically, and other-ecologically troubled students within regular classrooms was the differential numbers of students referred to psychological services units by experimental and control school teachers. These data were gathered from psychological service units' referral records from the respective experimental and control schools within each of the school systems.

Across the five school systems, 85 students were referred for presumed intellectual handicaps, underachievement, and/or emotional handicaps. More than four times as many first graders ($N = 34$ control vs. $N = 8$ experimental) and two times as many second graders ($N = 29$ control vs. $N = 14$ experimental) were referred by control school than by experimental school teachers (chi-square = 19.78, $p < .001$).

Objective 3. Support Teachers' Systematic Problem Solving Improves Outcomes: When STs adhere to the Re-ED-based ecological analysis and intervention procedures they were trained to use in their public school work with troubled children, they will produce significantly better pupil outcomes in less time than when they are not systematic.

Procedures. We tested the efficacy of structured problem solving through the date-sequenced use of heuristic case records. An ecological case record for each target child (or group) was created by transforming the problem-solving heuristic flow charts into a series of questions with room for dated answers. In this manner, we could track how well STs understood and implemented the techniques they had been taught. We could also track the dated sequences STs used in their interventions. If, for example, they initiated an intervention before they had uncovered a clear pattern of how the problem situation habitually occurred and was consequated, it seemed likely they would eventually have to "backtrack" when their intervention was not working successfully. On the other hand, if they obtained a clear picture, with similar patterns of information from both parents and teachers, they could probably be more confident that interventions would produce generalized changes across domains.

Results. STs were significantly more successful with problematic ecologies when they followed the heuristic's sequentially prescribed areas for gathering information about the dynamic interactions of the situation before generating possible interventions. Days lapsed to objectives met was the criterion measure. Each new bit of information was dated on the heuristic when it was obtained or implemented. It was a relatively simple task to divide each support teacher's cases into sequential versus non-sequential blocks for statistical analysis by checking that dates on the analysis sections were earlier than dates on the intervention sections and vice-versa.

The research used heuristic records STs completed during their first year of work in either junior high or elementary schools. Resulting outcomes for students (N = 183) were affected by sequential vs. non-sequential work patterns (Cantrell and Cantrell, 1977). When heuristic case analysis and planning information were completed in the appropriate sequence (i.e., when all involved participants were interviewed before interventions were initiated), behavioral objectives for children with learning problems were met in significantly less time ($F = 5.74$, $df = 1, 101$, $p < .025$) than for students where information and/or planning was incomplete or out of sequence.

Objective 4. Pupils Improve in Classroom Behavior: *Observed classroom behaviors of students in PIP experimental classes will demonstrate more productive and less disruptive or non-attentive behavior than pupils in control school classes.*

Procedures. STs would work with students, and where needed, their families, in the alleviation of behavioral problems which were either currently or potentially a hindrance for the pupils' optimal school performance. This goal would be met if target children referred to STs for behavioral intervention over the academic year's span exhibited a statistically significant decrease in observed disruptive and non-attentive classroom behaviors compared with controls.

Results. Data collectors performed independent classroom observations of teacher-pupil interactions in both experimental and control school classrooms. A data collector-criterion rater coefficient of ratings agreement (inter-rater reliability) was maintained at the 80+% level. Classroom observations took place, on average, twice per month, each for an observation period spanning 30 minutes. During project year 2 experimental school students referred to STs because of behavior problems became significantly less disruptive and non-attentive, while control school students increased in disruptive and non-attentive behavior across the school year to a final level higher than the experimental school students (interaction $F = 3.95$, $df = 2, 58$, $p < .05$).

During project year 3 similar significant results were found when junior high experimental and control schools and their STs were added to PIP. A significant experimental versus control groups by repeated observations interaction was obtained ($F = 5.11, df = 1, 77, p < .05$). Both elementary and junior high experimental school disruptive students showed a significant drop in disruptive and non-attentive behaviors. While control school students demonstrated an increase in these behaviors between the first half of the year and the second half of the year's observations, their final disruptive and non-attentive levels did not exceed those of the experimental school students. This is likely associated with control group students' having been nominated for observation by control school teachers solely on the basis of their being "behaviorally active." Control group students were not matched with experimental school behavior problem students on any other dimension.

Control school students increased in disruptive and non-attentive behaviors across both project years 2 and 3, while experimental school target students' rates of these behaviors consistently dropped. These changes may well be related to observed differences in experimental teacher behaviors. Additional teacher-pupil interaction research (Cantrell, Wood, & Nichols, 1974) reported significant differences between high and low behavioral knowledge teachers in the relative proportions of praise to criticism they used in class. High behavioral knowledge teachers used more praise than criticism while conducting their classes; low behavioral knowledge teachers used more criticism than praise.

Objective 5. Pupils Gain in Academic Performance: *Standardized tests of academic achievement will show differentially improved scores by students in experimental classrooms where STs worked with experimental classroom teachers and others on the students' behalf, compared to control school students functioning at similar I.Q. levels.*

Procedures. One major project objective was to determine if experimental school first-graders would achieve higher academically by the end of the school year than first graders in control schools whose teachers did not receive the Re-ED-based support. Further details are in Cantrell and Cantrell (1976) and the ESEA Title III Validation Report (1975).

Results. Multiple regression procedures used beginning of the year IQ scores (Otis-Lennon) and academic achievement scores (Metropolitan Achievement Test, or MAT, primer level) to predict end of year achievement scores for each student in both experimental and control schools. Residual achievement gain scores (defined as differences between predicted academic scores and achievements actually obtained) served as the dependent variable for this analysis. Students were grouped on the basis of two variables: (1) their beginning Otis-Lennon IQ scores (low IQ range: 50-90, mid IQ range: 91-104, and high IQ range: 105-135), and (2) whether they attended experimental schools or control schools. Residual achievement scores were used as the dependent variable in a 3 by 2 ANOVA. A significant experimental vs. control result was obtained ($F = 11.78$, $df = 1, 1072$, $p < .001$), as well as a significant IQ levels result ($F = 18.83$, $df = 2$, 1072, $p < .001$).

Each IQ level of experimental (E) school students achieved higher residual means than did their control (C) school counterparts (E low = -3.39 vs. C low = -8.06; E mid = 6.93 vs. C mid = 0.92; E high = -.51 vs. C high = -3.12). Interestingly, the variability of scores at each level of the E IQ groups was also lower than for the C IQ groups, indicating more homogeneous achievement within experimental school first grade classes; even students scoring lower at entry made relatively rapid gains.

Follow-up of these year 1 first grade teachers showed similar effects in year 2 with their next year's students. Teachers requested we drop IQ testing for these young students, so percentile scores were used rather than residual scores. Again in year 2, first grade students in experimental schools entered second grade with significantly higher MAT mean percentile scores on Word Knowledge ($F = 3.41$, $p < .10$) and Numbers ($F = 36.56$, $p < .001$) after their year with experimental teachers, even though they had entered first grade with readiness percentile scores that were lower than those of control school students.

Summary and Conclusions

The funds provided PIP from federal and state sources enabled Re-ED principles and practices to be subjected to rigorous experimental test within public school settings. School systems involved ranged from large city systems to rural, and covered all regions and demographics present in the state: east (Kingsport City, small city), west (Memphis, urban), north (Robertson County, rural), south (Hamilton County, suburban Chattanooga), and central (Nashville, city-county government). *The positive results obtained across all five districts support the replicability of the Re-ED ecological approach as used within PIP in regular public school settings.*

Objectives Achieved

All project objectives were achieved at levels of statistical significance:

Objective 1. Support Teachers continued to make significant gains in behavioral knowledge throughout all their years working in PIP, using skills they had learned through training and consultation.

Objective 2. Classroom Teachers made significant gains in behavioral knowledge as they worked with STs on behalf of target children. They also maintained their students in their regular classes, evidenced by significantly fewer referrals to psychological or special education services than were made by control school teachers.

Objective 3. In those cases where STs adhered to the Re-ED based ecological analysis and intervention procedures they were trained to use in their public school work, they achieved significantly more pupil objectives in less time.

Objective 4. Observations of target students in experimental schools demonstrated significantly more productive and less disruptive or non-attentive classroom behavior across time than did observations of pupils in control school classes. This is likely related to the higher proportions of praise to criticism found in the behavior of high knowledge teachers.

Objective 5. Students in first grade experimental classrooms achieved significantly higher residual academic gains on a standardized achievement test across all three IQ score ranges, than did control school students functioning at similar intellectual levels. Similar results were obtained for experimental school first graders during the subsequent project year.

In sum, Re-ED trained STs helped teachers provide ecologically relevant interventions, enabling target students to avoid falling into deleterious patterns of behavior and academic distress. There was no need for classroom teachers to go through a complicated referral process to certify a student's needs, or wait for students to worsen before specialized help was made available. Team interventions planned and carried out with the investment of parents, teachers, principals, and STs were sufficient for these children to escape more restrictive alternatives. Our access to multiple data sources enabled us to investigate the effects of PIP's training paradigm. The results of our analyses were consistently positive and highly encouraging, suggesting that broadly applicable, Re-ED based training can be specified and its effects verified.

References

Binder, J. L. (1993). Observations on the training of therapists in time-limited dynamic psychotherapy. *Psychotherapy, 30,* 592-598.

Brunswik, E. (1947). *Systematic and representative design of psychological experiments; with results in physical and social perception.* Oxford, England: U of California Press.

Brunswik, E. (1955). Representative design and probabilistic theory in a functional psychology. *Psychological Review, 62,* 193-217.

Cantrell, M. L. (1974). Maladaptive behavior as a function of skill/demand discrepancies: An empirical investigation of the competence model. (Doctoral dissertation, George Peabody College for Teachers, 1974). *Dissertation Abstracts International, 35,* 7718-7719

Cantrell, R. P. (1969). Efficacy of In-Service Training of Teachers in Operant Techniques. (Doctoral dissertation, George Peabody College for Teachers, 1969). *Dissertation Abstracts International, 30*(10-A), 1970, 4301.

Cantrell, R. P., & Cantrell, M. L. (1969). *Alternative Classroom Strategies Inventory.* Unpublished test.

Cantrell, R. P., & Cantrell, M. L. (1975). Heuristic case study. In W. C. Rhodes (Ed.), *A study of child variance: Exercise book.* Ann Arbor, Michigan: University of Michigan.

Cantrell, R. P., & Cantrell, M. L. (1976). Preventive mainstreaming: Impact of a supportive services program on low and middle I.Q. pupils in public school first grades. *Exceptional Children, 42,* 381-386.

Cantrell, R. P., & Cantrell, M. L. (1977). Evaluation of a heuristic approach to solving children's problems. *Peabody Journal of Education, 54*(3), 168-173.

Cantrell, R. P. & Cantrell, M. L. (1980). Ecological problem solving: A decision making heuristic for prevention - intervention education strategies. In J. Hogg & P. Mittler (Eds.), *Advances in mental handicap research.* Vol. 1. Chicester, England & New York: John Wiley.

Cantrell, R. P., Cantrell, M. L., Huddleston, C. M., & Wooldridge, R.L. (1969). Contingency contracting with school problems. *Journal of Applied Behavior Analysis, 2,* 215-220.

Cantrell, R. P., Wood, J. L., & Nichols, C. A. (April, 1974). *Teacher knowledge of behavior principles and classroom teaching patterns.* Paper presented at the meeting of the American Educational Research Association, Chicago.

Cook, W. W., Leeds, C. H., & Callis, R. (1951). *The Minnesota Teacher Attitude Inventory.* New York: Psychological Corp.

Durost, W. N., Bixler, H. H., Wrightstone, J. W., Prescott, G. A., & Balow, I. H. (1971). *Metropolitan Achievement Test.* New York: Harcourt Brace Jovanovich.

Flanders, N. A. (1960). *Teacher influence, pupil attitudes, and achievement: Study in interaction analysis.* Minneapolis: University of Minnesota.

Hobbs, N. (1978). Perspectives on Re-Education. *Behavioral Disorders*, 3(2), 65-66.

Hobbs, N. (1982). *The troubled and troubling child.* San Francisco: Jossey-Bass.

Medley, D. M., & Mitzel, H. E. (1959). Some behavioral correlates of teacher effectiveness. *Journal of Educational Psychology, 50*, 239-246.

Miller, S. J., & Binder, J. L. (2002). The effects of manual-based training on treatment fidelity and outcome: A review of the literature on adult individual psychotherapy. *Psychotherapy: Theory, Research, Practice, Training. 39*(2), 184-198.

Munger, R. L. (1991). *Child mental health practice from the ecological perspective.* Appendix 6. New York: University Press of America.

Newell, A., & Simon, H. A. (1972). *Human problem solving.* Englewood Cliffs, NJ: Prentice-Hall.

Otis, A. S., & Lennon, R. T. (1967). *Otis-Lennon Mental Ability Test.* New York: Harcourt, Brace, & World.

Rhodes, W. C. (1975). Exercise 10. *A study of child variance: Exercise book.* Institute for the study of mental retardation and related disabilities. Ann Arbor, MI: The University of Michigan.

Simon, H. A., & Newell, A. (1965). Heuristic problem solving by computer. In M. A. Sass & W. D. Wilkinson, (Eds.), *Computer augmentation of human reasoning.* Washington, D. C.: Spartan.

Weinstein, L. (1974). *Evaluation of a Program for Re-Educating Disturbed Children: A Follow-Up Comparison with Untreated Children.* Washington, D. C.: Department of Health, Education and Welfare. (Available through ERIC Documentation Reproduction Service, ED-141-966.)

Acknowledgements:

Special recognition is given to Dr. Charles Watts who negotiated agreements from multiple funding agents for a single set of reporting requirements in the project's early days. Dr. Richard Gardner was the first project director; he was followed by Wayne Pyle in that role. Robert Cantrell was PIP's Director of Research and Evaluation.

The PIP Program Consultants were:

Bev Lee Lewis, Frank Rousseau, Melanie Hampton,
Mary Lynn Cantrell, Emma Jean Hogan , Linda Odum,
Louise MacKay, Mary Bell

The PIP Support Teachers were:

Chattanooga:	Estelle Cunningham, Myra Longley Burgess, Carolyn Chandler, Wallace Tallent
Memphis:	Jean Bynum, Mary Bell, Agnes McIntyre, Sue Isom, John White
Springfield:	Ruth Cage, Dick Pelley, JoAnn Webster, Myrtle Mills, Catherine Holman
Nashville:	Louise MacKay, Nancy Steranka, Bettye Otey, Marian George Susan Bertram, Richard Randolph
Kingsport:	Irene Hageman-Cook & Lawrence Cook

Explanation of the problem-solving heuristic is available as flow-charts in Hogg and Mittler (1980), as a case example in Rhodes (1975), and in adapted case format as Appendix 6 of Munger (1991). More information can be obtained from the authors. Feel free to use or adapt the heuristic to your needs; we request you credit the authors, to avoid our cncountering copyright problems in subsequent uses we may make of the heuristic.

Robert P. Cantrell is Research Consultant for the Positive Education Program in Cleveland, Ohio. rcantrell8648@sbcglobal.net

Mary Lynn Cantrell is Research Consultant for the Positive Education Program in Cleveland, Ohio. mlc8648@sbcglobal.net

31

Defining a Re-ED Model: Fidelity Measurement for Principles Based Services

Pamela Meadowcroft, Mary Lynn Cantrell, & Robert Cantrell

Over 40 years ago, Nicholas Hobbs developed Project Re-ED as a way of showing how an ecological approach to serving children and youth with serious emotional problems could work more effectively for less cost than more traditional mental health treatment strategies. Intervention's task in Re-ED was *"helping the significant members of the ecosystem, including the child or adolescent, take the steps necessary to enable the system to work reasonably well - that is, within tolerable levels of discord"* (Hobbs, 1982, p. 183). The ecological approach considers individuals to be *"...nested within a complex network of interconnected systems that encompass individual, family, and extra familial (peer, school, neighborhood) factors with interventions necessary in any one or combination of these systems"* (http://www.mstservices.com/text/treatment.html, p. 1). Hobbs further recommended choosing *"the model provided by education with its emphasis on health rather than on illness, on teaching rather than on treatment, on learning rather than on fundamental personality reorganization, on the present and the future rather than on the past, on the operation of the total social system of which the child is a part rather than on intrapsychic processes exclusively"* (Hobbs, 1982, p. 16).

Re-ED Services

The original Project Re-ED occurred within a short term residential group setting. Over the following decades Re-ED has been adapted to a wide variety of service settings for a broader range of youths than was originally imagined. Most Re-ED programs are now community based, occurring in children and youths' own homes, schools, and therapeutic foster homes rather than residential group settings. The children served are not only youngsters with mental health issues as in the original project, but also younger children, older youths, teen mothers, sibling groups, and whole families. All are likely dealing with combinations of serious and persistent mental health issues, cognitive deficits, histories of adjudication, or other basic needs.

Characteristics of a Re-ED approach to working with children and their families (Cantrell, Cantrell, Valore, Jones, and Fecser, 1999) include: (a) values based decision making, employing guiding principles defined by Hobbs in his early work; (b) emphasis on pragmatic interventions rather than one theory of psychological functioning (Re-ED programs view their work as always evolving, rather than a fixed model); (c) focus on skill building or developing competence in all those involved, rather than on child and family pathologies; (d) careful choices of language in talking and thinking about programs and interventions for children and families, using the most affirming, least damaging, health oriented language possible; (e) use of well planned activities so that children's and their families' days are full and purposeful; (f) recognition that some of the most important therapeutic agents for a child and family are already in their lives; (g) awareness of the need for systematic data in ecological intervention and program planning; and (h) building interventions based on the child and family's strengths, using positive goals and strategies.

Recommended Dissemination

Given Re-ED's distinguishing characteristics, it is one of the earliest strengths based approaches to children's mental health, a move away from deficit models, now the mantra of many children's and family's service systems. Early on, Re-ED was recognized as an approach to the treatment of children with serious emotional disturbance worthy of emulation when the Joint Commission on Mental Health of Children (1970) strongly endorsed it. The two initial field tests were each subjected to rigorous research and demonstrated high levels of effectiveness, relative to control groups. The first program of research occurred in the two original five day residential school sites in Tennessee and North Carolina, and the second in the five school districts spread across Tennessee, urban to rural, that participated in the adaptation of Re-ED to public schools. Yet despite its early history and demonstrated promising approach to serving children and their families effectively, Re-ED remained and remains remarkably unknown.

Re-ED's not being widely adopted can be partly attributed to professionals' thinking of Re-ED as short term residential care for emotionally troubled young children (based on the initial demonstration projects' two residential settings). These assumptions of Re-ED as a group approach to intervention in residential settings probably slowed its broad application. This was a time of active movement toward community based services. Funding resources necessarily flowed to the development of "Systems of Care" and implementation of Public Law 94-142 (later IDEA). Hobbs' pioneering advocacy for keeping troubled and troubling youngsters as close to home as possible and working in partnership with families was largely unrecognized in its relationship to achieving these two important national goals.

Despite the development of the American Re-ED Association (AREA) in 1981, widespread dissemination of Re-ED as an attractive approach to working with a broad range of children's and families' needs still did not occur. AREA programs and Re-ED trained professionals actively created a wide range of adaptations of the original programs to public school needs, in-home services, treatment foster care, and other varied populations of children with seriously troubled behavior. As these adaptations expanded, and some other existing programs sought to adopt and apply Re-ED's approach, a question arose with increasing frequency: "What exactly defines a Re-ED program?"

Expert Re-ED practitioners emphasized that Re-ED was a set of values and principles without a firm set of highly specified practices or program structures that could easily define a model. Many felt that because Re-ED is "always becoming," establishing a measure for Re-ED fidelity would be counter to one of its key values. There was reluctance to define a "model" in measurable ways, with some thinking that such specification could hamper creative programmatic adaptations. Concern regarding the ideological drift and practice variations of Re-ED programs mounted, however, when some isolated programs began labeling their approach as consistent with Re-ED while engaging in practices that directly contradicted the Re-ED beliefs. Concern for Re-ED fidelity came to be coupled with Re-ED practitioners' awareness of increasing pressure to demonstrate the effectiveness of the approach in its new applications. The time had come to define and measure the effectiveness of a Re-ED "model," not a simple task for a values and principles driven approach.

Defining a Service Model

By "model" of service we mean a *"theory of action explicating the mechanisms through which the program will achieve its desired outcomes"* (Mowbray, Holter, Teague, & Bybee, 2003, p. 315). Models of children's services characteristically show an integrated set of principles, practices, and procedures that can be transported (via training and practice manuals or processes) to new staff and new settings. It is the ability both to replicate the set of practices and principles and to measure the occurrence of these that defines a "model."

A model, once described sufficiently for replication, can then be tested to see if it produces positive outcomes for those served. If such testing shows its effectiveness, the model is then based on evidence and could come to be considered *evidence based*. Few models of human services have reached "evidence based" stature. The level of empirical rigor involved requires multiple replications which consistently demonstrate statistically significant improvement of clients receiving highly specified treatment, as compared to control client groups who receive a different treatment or none (with raters blind to group membership). Results are then assumed applicable only to clients essentially the same in all major aspects as those participating in the studies. Unfortunately, such research is expensive and funding is extremely limited. In addition, service providers, striving to meet the community's service needs, find it difficult to meet both restraints on subject selection and controls required by rigorous research designs. Therefore, most models are developed as a set of *best practice* standards which may or may not be based on empirical evidence acquired from rigorously controlled research.

"Best practices" can be defined as guidelines or practices driven more by clinical wisdom, experts' opinions, or other consensus approaches that may not include systematic use of available research evidence. Best practices provide program implementers with a description of program structures, activities, or replicable features that, if followed, meet a standard of quality defined by a set of experts. Nearly all nationally accrediting groups create their best practice standards based on an expert consensus approach, although there is growing interest in validating standards with existing research evidence. Best practices, until they are tested and demonstrate that they actually produce improved client outcomes, may or may not produce more effective programs. They nonetheless narrow the range of acceptable practice to that which a group of seasoned experts have deemed useful and effective from their own experiences.

Thus, in defining and empirically validating a Re-ED model, both evidence and best practice are relevant; two phases of development are needed. The first phase would define a measurable set of best practice standards deemed characteristic and essential for true Re-ED practice. The second phase would empirically test these essential features to determine if programmatic adherence produces positive outcomes for the children and families served. A third phase could then rigorously test the effectiveness of validated Re-ED programs as compared to other models or no treatment controls.

The Re-ED Essentials Project

The American Re-ED Association, with support from the Pressley Ridge Foundation and the Positive Education Program, asked the authors to develop a reliable method for measuring fidelity to a Re-ED model and, then, to test the model's effectiveness. We described the task as two research targets: Phase I Developing a set of Re-ED best practices and a method for measuring adherence, and Phase II Demonstrating evidence for the Re-ED model by determining if degree of Re-EDness proves to be associated with positive outcomes; both are needed in preparation for the more rigorous research studies required to establish Re-ED as an Evidence Based Practice in Phase III. AREA's Board recognized that Re-ED values and principles are manifested in the actions and cognitive views of people in Re-ED programs; in this way Re-ED can be measured and operationally defined. Furthermore, ingredients for specifying a Re-ED model exist: (a) a long history of practice, (b) dozens of expert practitioners, (c) a well defined literature describing the model's values and beliefs, (d) training materials that describe applications of these beliefs, and (e) indications that key essentials of Re-ED frequently lead to positive outcomes for even the most complex children and family needs.

Project Purpose

The Essentials Project focuses on developing easy to use measurement tools that will: (a) provide definitional clarity on current Re-ED programs by identifying essential elements, (b) facilitate communication about what Re-ED is today, and what it is not, (c) allow for a diagnostic tool that programs can use in self study and quality assurance, (d) assist in strengthening existing programs and in replication efforts, (e) verify programs included in major AREA publications as Re-ED consistent, and (f) serve to quantify the work of Re-ED sites in research studies' validating the effectiveness of the model. Eventually, the tools used to measure a program's level of "Re-EDness" objectively will provide AREA with a guide for certifying Re-ED programs, should the need arise.

First, defining the Re-ED model of today (i.e., its "best practices" or Re-ED standards) requires identifying its essential ingredients, components, or prescribed elements. Essential elements can be beliefs, values, practices, program structures, and/or the program standards believed to be characteristic of Re-ED (and especially important for positively impacting children and families served). The second step establishes indicators of these essentials (i.e., measures of treatment or model "fidelity"). With such measures, the degree to which programs adhere to essential ingredients of a defined model can be determined.

Seeking a Means for Validation

Once a program's level of Re-ED fidelity is measurable, it is then possible to link it with service outcomes. Mowbray et al. (2003) found Chen's (1990) observations on this evaluation issue useful: *"Without documentation and/or measurement of a programs adherence to an intended model, there is no way to determine whether unsuccessful outcomes reflect a failure of the model or a failure to implement the model as intended"* (p. 317). Establishing criteria by which a program shows adherence to the Re-ED model will enable the Re-ED approach to be more consistently replicated and researched.

But establishing a set of Re-ED essentials requires that they contain broadly applicable elements. Since Re-ED is not a singular set of practices occurring in similar settings with similar populations, we cannot use many of the customary approaches for measuring treatment fidelity to a specified model. Fidelity criteria are often composed of easy to measure structural components of a model. Mowbray et al. list staffing levels and characteristics, case load size, frequency and intensity of contacts, budget, procedure codes, and such items as components of structure (Orwin, 2000), adding that these *"require less subjective judgment and can often be obtained through existing documentation.... [In contrast,] process criteria include program style, staff client interactions, client client interactions, individualization of treatment, or emotional climate"* (Mowbray et al., 2003, p. 329).

Since Re-ED programs today have few common structural components, yet share a common philosophy and orientation to treatment, it follows that Re-ED fidelity criteria are likely to be comprised of process measures, such as organizational climate, staff, and adult-child interactions. These process measures require more subjective judgments, based more on observations, interviews, and/ or surveys, and less on existing written documentation. *"Process criteria may be more difficult to measure reliably, but more significant in terms of program effects"* (Mowbray et al., 2003, p. 330). Models with a lengthy research history conclude that drift occurs less on the easy to measure structural components (such as caseload size or hours of service) and more on process components, such as treatment characteristics (Teague, Bond, & Drake, 1998; Henggeler, Roland, Schoenwald, & Hoagwood, 1998). The move toward model definition in terms of proven principles (process measures) could maximize model adaptability, yet maintain the prescriptive rigor necessary for ongoing model development and effectiveness research.

Thus, Re-ED programs need a tool that ascertains whether a particular service or program's operations are consistent with the best current view of the principles or essentials in Re-ED beliefs and practices. This Re-ED tool must be useful regardless of location, population, or type of service provided (e.g., group residential, foster care, community support, special education). The tool should be able to identify adherence to Re-ED principles and practices, even in service programs whose staff have no prior knowledge of Re-ED.

The tool must be quantifiable. Its usefulness is greatly enhanced if it produces "scores" of some kind which can be used for validating the tool during its development, in programmatic self study and development planning, and later in research demonstrating the effectiveness of Re-ED approaches and services. Numerical ratings in each domain enable the ultimate development of profiles, and later a "short form" of the tool which contains the minimal number of items needed to discriminate.

Research Questions

The Re-ED Essentials Project began with the following set of research questions: (a) What is Re-ED? (b) Is a Re-ED approach different from current standard approaches to treatment for children?

(c) What are Re-ED Best Practices? (d) Can program fidelity with Re-ED Best Practices be objectively measured? (e) Are there program and population variations that cannot produce fidelity with Re-ED Best Practices, and if so, why? (f) Does Re-ED make any difference in the lives of kids and families? (g) Can Re-ED become identified as an evidence based set of practices?

Phase I: Defining and Measuring the Re-ED Model of Today

Step One: Identification of the Re-ED Essentials

Board members from AREA suggested 27 *Re-ED Experts* to begin identifying and validating key ingredients of today's Re-ED programs. An "expert" was defined as an individual recognized as demonstrating Re-ED values and leadership in an agency that the board considered was providing Re-ED services. Often these Re-ED agencies had leaders trained by Hobbs and colleagues in the early programs. Typically the Re-ED experts were in agency leadership or supervisory positions, having had many years experience within a Re-ED program. Interviewers of this group of experts asked the following questions, "What would you see in a Re-ED program that you wouldn't see in a non-Re-ED program relative to the following program domains: (a) program / service values, (b) leadership, (c) staff selection / training / roles, (d) role of non-staff adults, (e) assessment, and (f) interventions / treatment."

Based on the transcriptions of the interviewees' responses, common themes emerged. A set of 100 brief statements of Re-ED essentials was created from three sources: (a) these interviews, (b) the Re-ED principles listed in Hobbs defining book, *The Troubled and Troubling Child* (1982), and (c) themes from the more recent description of Re-ED in a Council for Children with Behavioral Disorders monograph (Cantrell, Cantrell, Valore, Jones, & Fecser, 1999). Examples of some of the statements are: "Organizational hierarchy lacks rigidity; staff relationships are informal and collegial;" and "Efforts are made to minimize the number of uninvested adults engaged with the child."

To create an initial *Re-ED Essentials Survey*, each of the 100 items was categorized under one of the following eight program domains: (a) Common principles, (b) Service delivery structure: Staffing principles, (c) Service delivery structure: Supervision principles, (d) Service delivery structure: Principles of training and selection of staff, (e) Service delivery structure: The role of non-staff adults, (f) Therapeutic components: Orientation to assessment, (g) Therapeutic components: Intervention principles, and (h) Commitment to program improvement.

Step Two: Refining the Essentials List

We then sent the Re-ED Essentials Survey to 27 *Re-ED Experts* and 14 additional *Re-ED Practitioners*, with instructions to rate each item on a three point scale, as "essential, desirable, or nonessential" for a Re-ED program. Practitioners with substantial experience with various types of Re-ED programs, locations, and populations were selected. Their responses would add to the face validity of the initial Re-ED Essentials Survey. We hoped their responses would help us eliminate less essential items. To further this elimination process, we also selected five experts in mental health services who were not familiar with Re-ED (*Non-Re-ED Experts*), anticipating that their responses, when compared with those of the Re-ED Practitioners, could tell us which items were typically seen as essential in Re-ED's view of good service.

We also encouraged all who completed the surveys to provide comments for improving, eliminating, or adding items. Finally, we followed up the completion of these surveys with in-depth interviews of one Re-ED Practitioner and one Non-Re-ED Expert to understand better why they responded to each item the way they did. Analysis of responses from the Re-ED Experts, Re-ED Practitioners, and the five Non-Re-ED Experts led us to three major conclusions described below.

1. Non-Re-ED experts and Re-ED staff did rate items differently. Priority items for the Re-ED Practitioners that provided these ratings differed from those of the Non-Re-ED Experts. For example, none of the items related to assessment and evaluation were in the Re-ED

Practitioners' top rankings, whereas these items were consistently ranked higher by the Non-Re-ED Experts. This lack of emphasis on evaluation among Re-ED Practitioners seemed surprising until we reviewed the evaluation history of Re-ED programs. Other chapters in this book describe Laura Weinstein's (1974) comprehensive evaluation and follow up research studies on Project Re-ED and Robert Cantrell's (1976) evaluation and research on the Re-ED public school adaptation; both were extensive and yielded positive results. Early Re-ED program staff, however, set ecological goals with parents and performed "program relevant assessments" for children and families; they did not use the results of traditional diagnostic assessments. They were influenced by the appearance of "behavior modification" in the mid-1960's, and adopted an expectation for collection and use of individual child and goal attainment data. Subsequent Re-ED programs were established to provide badly needed services, but almost invariably no funds for research or evaluation were provided in funding streams. As a result, the early descriptions of Project Re-ED and subsequent literature on the model do not emphasize program-wide evaluations or any focus on aggregated outcomes of services. Nor do they use mental health disagnostic categories as major determinants in program relevant assessment. Hence, lower ratings on these items might have been anticipated. Nonetheless, in an era newly emphasizing evidence based services, we did expect greater inclusion of items related to program effectiveness.

2. Some Re-ED hallmarks are no longer consistently interpreted by Re-ED staff. Re-ED programs and those who have been instrumental in teaching Re-ED principles and practices need to address increasing misinterpretations of some original Re-ED hallmarks even among seasoned Re-ED personnel. Some Re-ED experts commented on these items, saying that the item may have been significant forty years ago, but with managed care or with advances in research, the principles are now questionable. The two most frequently mentioned are discussed below.

"Intelligence can be taught." One Re-ED responder stated a belief also held by others, saying, "If intelligence can be taught means that we can raise a kid's IQ, then I don't agree with this at all." Apparently, these more recently trained mental health workers were not exposed to exciting research unfolding between the 1930s and the 1970s, and confirmed by later studies to date. During the mid 1930s and 1940s, researchers at the Iowa Child Welfare Station (H. M. Skeels, Marie Skodak, and H. B. Dye) placed 13 seven to 30 month old children, then considered unsuited for adoption because of intellectual disability, on a ward with developmentally delayed women. Twelve similarly aged children who scored somewhat higher on the measure of intelligence used were left in the orphanage.

The women and attendants on the ward played and talked with the placed children. The children remaining in the orphanage were cared for by ward workers, without exposure to the stimulation of additional human interaction provided to those on the ward. This research was reported in the literature, culminating in a long term followup study (Skodak & Skeels,1949; Skeels, 1966). At the 1968 convention of the American Association on Mental Deficiency, Harold Skeels and Marie Skodak were presented the prestigious Joseph P. Kennedy Award by a member of the original experimental group, all of whom had made sufficient intelligence gains while on the ward to warrant foster home placement. The presenter was then in his sophomore year in college. None of his counterparts in the control group of infants remaining in the orphanage ever left the institution; all continued to function in the developmentally delayed range of intelligence. This finding led to their subsequent research providing long term followups on adopted children formerly at risk of intellectual delays.

Skeels, and Dye (1939), Wellman, Skeels, and Skodak (1940), and others who contributed to these research efforts were attacked for their findings, largely because their research was not in line with statistical views or interpretations of how such early stimulation studies should be designed and analyzed. McNemar (1940), a leading statistician in those years, criticized the Iowa studies and *"...concluded that the case for the effect of changes in environment on the IQ has been 'demolished'"* (p. 63). The picture of a college sophomore presenting the Kennedy Award to these researchers, however, does much to diminish the statistical "demolishment" of this meaningful series of outcome studies.

Increases in IQ scores as a function of early stimulation and training, found by Susan Gray (Gray & Klaus, 1970; Gray & Ruttle, 1980), formed the basis for Head Start programs around the country. Gray provided a highly enriched preschool experience for children from inner city poverty areas, and gave toys to their mothers with ideas on how to play with them at home. The children showed remarkable gains in measurable IQs, as well as improved school performance on entering public school.

Later, Reuven Feuerstein demonstrated that stimulus deprived Jewish orphans from war ravaged European countries could be taught to use explicit cognitive structures in problem solving. This groundbreaking work was then confirmed, using the same techniques with Israeli soldiers (Feuerstein, 1979; 1980).

Hobbs' faith in the power of teaching and learning was based on the most recent research results of the period, a wide collection of intelligence stimulation research studies reported near the time of Re-ED's beginnings by J. McVickers Hunt (1961) and others.

"Re-ED programs are based on the postulate that intelligence can be taught, that children and adolescents can be helped to increase their capacity for problem solving and for making good choices in the living of their lives. We regard as myth the idea, now firmly rooted in American thought, that intelligence is immutable. We assume, instead, intelligence is a dynamic evolving and malleable capacity for making good choices in living" (Hobbs, 1982, p. 265).

Hobbs, and other special education and mental health practitioners from within the broader psychoeducational approach, have a substantial research base showing that seriously troubled and stimulation deprived children can experience intellectual growth, given appropriate guidance and stimulation. The astounding rate of brain growth during the first three years of life has become a commonly accepted basis for infant stimulation and child care activities (Nash,

1997). Magnetic resonance imaging studies have found continuing structural changes in the brain through age 15 (Thompson, Giedd, & Woods, 2000), with other studies confirming functional brain changes to age 25 and beyond (Sowell, Thompson, & Holmes, 1999; NIH publication No. 01-4929, 2001). Indeed, there currently is information that intellectual stimulation is vital to postponing the onset of dementia (Shiel & Schoenfield, 2004; Verghese, Lipton, Katz, Hall, Derby, Kuslansky, Ambrose, Sliwinski, & Buschke, 2003).

Intelligence is thus not a fixed entity; old, quasi-folklore beliefs about fixed intelligence must give way to newer, empirically verified ways of producing change for children and adolescents.

"Time is an ally." This traditional Re-ED hallmark also inspired a number of comments from survey responders: "[This principle is] increasingly threatened and may need to be redefined in this new managed care context." "What success is achievable in a much shorter time, given that our services are becoming more and more time limited?" "What are the implications for follow through and creating less dependency on staff relationships and more emphasis on community building?"

Hobbs' *Time is an ally* addresses the benefits of allowing normal developmental processes time to evolve in a positive and growth supportive setting:

"From childhood through adolescence, the individual grows steadily in stature, in intellectual capacity, in physical skill, in knowledge, in sensitivity. These years may prove to be optimum for providing corrective experiences for children who have been given a poor psychological start in life, ... young people are still open to to experience and change, and...they have surplus energy to support the operation....In Re-ED we try at least to avoid getting in the way of the normal restorative processes of life" (Hobbs, 1982, p. 258).

Some incorrectly assume this principle states or implies that merely the passage of time spent in treatment is helpful, even though children and youth do not simply grow out of serious problems, and seldom are well served away from home and community. A better statement of the principle might be: *Time is an ally when used to make positive changes in the life of a child.*

Forty years ago, long before our current managed care revolution, Hobbs crafted this principle to underscore the value of intervening early and keeping treatment interventions short by maximizing how staff used time when working with troubled kids. Wright School, the only remaining Project Re-ED short term residential treatment center, maintains to this day a four to six month length of stay with positive followup outcomes (Fields, Farmer, Apperson, Mustillo, & Simmers, 2006).

Some current day Re-ED programs have evolved into longer term treatment programs which are increasingly threatened by managed care time constraints. This trend is likely a natural product of underfunded community based alternatives who can only accept children and youth deemed most in need. Although these Re-ED programs are largely not residential, this is an evolution that Re-ED experts should carefully consider. Hobbs said clearly that long term treatment and removal from one's family and community could in fact be damaging to a troubled child's recovery or adjustment:

"What to make of time may well be the most important practical and theoretical decision confronting a staff responsible for designing a program to help disturbed children and adolescents....A long stay in a treatment center may actually slow down the process of learning to be oneself, to be effective, to be mature....In planning Re-ED, we resolved to do everything possible to cut down the length of stay, to separate children from their families and schools...only as long as we are clearly helping, and only up to the point where the system can operate in a reasonably satisfactory manner without our assistance" (Hobbs, 1982, pp. 257-259).

Longer treatment time is not necessarily an ally. Unfortunately, adequate funding streams for liaison roles to facilitate family, school, and community services during treatment, transition, and followup was, and remains, a continuing problem for Re-ED programs of all kinds.

Similar uncharacteristic responses to other Re-ED historic hallmarks led us to conclude we need training methods for Re-ED practitioners to assure that these principles are understood and implemented in terms of today's environment and knowledge. Items where interpretations vary widely or are commonly misinterpreted should be investigated and then either dropped as no longer essential, or more likely (as in the above examples) explained and practiced more accurately.

3. Most Re-ED responders viewed most items as essential.
We could not eliminate any of the 100 items based on results from the Re-ED practitioners and experts; their responses showed highly consistent agreement that most of the 100 items were essential or at least desirable. Even though we had responses from five Non-Re-ED Experts, they were too few to provide us with any statistical comparison power. Thus, differences between their responses and the Re-ED Experts, while qualitatively valuable, did not help us determine a reduced set of key Re-ED essentials. In retrospect, had we used a five or seven point scale instead of a three point scale, the survey might have produced greater spread among the Re-ED responders' ratings of the essential elements. We may have found some items to be less essential and, therefore, dropped them. However, even with a larger scale, we may not have had any item elimination because others (e.g., Holter, Mowbray, Bellamy, MacFarland, & Dukarski, 2004) working to develop criteria for model fidelity, report that experts rate most of the elements of their models as critical or essential. In addition, though expert consensus is often used to develop fidelity criteria for a model, their criteria may pose some problems.

"In the absence of established empirical findings, opinions of experts may change significantly (sometimes appropriately) over time, and the predictive utility of expert opinion may [therefore] be quite low….Still, where a proven model is not available and the research base is limited, expert opinion may be the only, if provisional, alternative" (Mowbray, et al., 2003, p. 326).

Despite Re-ED's early efficacy research, the lack of a research base for the key ingredients of a Re-ED model forces us to rely on experts' opinions as a starting point. We did take an additional step to validate the essentials as unique to Re-ED programs by increasing the number of Non-Re-ED mental health practitioners asked to rate the items so that statistical comparisons between Re-ED practitioners / experts and Non-Re-ED responders could be conducted.

Step Three: Re-ED vs Non-Re-ED Practitioners' Ratings

The most valuable set of Re-ED essentials would empirically differentiate Re-ED from Non-Re-ED beliefs and practices. Such a determination requires comparing Re-ED Experts' and Practitioners' opinions about what is essential with ratings by children's service experts who know nothing about Re-ED. Doing this, we had to be prepared to drop historic hallmarks from a Re-ED essentials list if those principles were rated equally important by Re-ED and Non-Re-ED professionals. If Re-ED principles had generally been embraced by children's services over the past several decades, then we would not be able to differentiate Re-ED programs from non-Re-ED programs. And if we couldn't differentiate between Re-ED programs and other approaches to children's services, then we might not find that Re-ED produces better results than other approaches. Thus, developing a set of discriminating Re-ED essentials became, well, essential.

Twenty-four experienced professionals working in a traditional mental health facility that served children responded to the same Re-ED Essentials Survey as their Re-ED practitioner counterparts. They were asked to indicate if an item was essential or desirable to their own clinical orientation or practice (thus, not rating items relative to their being essential ingredients of a Re-ED approach).

Analyses comparing this group of 24 more traditional *Non-Re-ED Practitioners* with the Re-ED survey responses revealed marked, significant differences. Results showed that Re-ED practitioners hold different opinions about what is important for effective mental health intervention. The first statistical analysis showed that of the 100 items on the Re-ED Essentials Survey, 39 items significantly differentiated Re-ED practitioners from Non-Re-ED practitioners. Content analysis and grouping of these items separating Re-ED thinkers from Non-Re-ED thinkers showed that all 39 concepts could be logically grouped under one of six categories. Because the validation work on the 39 essential items continues, we provide below only a brief description of each of the six Re-ED dimensions.

1. Wellness, Strength, and Joy. Emphasizing pathology can reinforce belief in the pathology's permanence and strengthen its destructive components. On the contrary, replacing a pathology or compliance view with a focus on current positive elements of daily experience can help the child grow, experiencing strength and building wellness.

2. Working within Children's Ecologies. Children's strengths and problems exist in context. They result from complex interactions in which every member of the child's world both teaches and learns from each other. Anyone seeking to help the child must also seek an alliance with those within the child's ecological unit. All critical eco-system members can be gradually involved in addressing problems constructively, working for positive change and employing strengths as intervention resources.

3. Competence: Teaching & Learning. Experiential learning contributes to both the origins of serious emotional disturbance and to its amelioration. The more we know about how teaching occurs, the more we are able to help troubled and troubling children learn and change. We all learn through the groups we are socialized within and in the context of communities. Natural agents acting as children's teachers exist in each child's life. These agents can themselves learn how to become more positive contributors. Other needed "teachers" can be found or recruited to work within children's worlds; helping children build competencies is a critical function of Re-EDucation.

4. Frontline Workers as Primary Agents of Change. Change occurs through one on one interactions carried out by natural agents of those interactions in the child's world. Teacher-counselors and others providing direct services to the child are carefully selected for their commitment to positive change. To enhance these growth oriented interactions, these agents require ongoing support, training, and supervision. Ideally, supervisors have accumulated positive experience in direct service which helps them in two critical ways: (1) they know how to assist front line staff to develop decision making skills, and (2) they value direct service workers and recognize their role's difficulty.

5. Creating and Enhancing Relationships. Troubled kids often have problems forming and maintaining relationships with others. This is one of the most critical skills adults need for social functioning. When trust in caretakers or peers has never been established or has been broken, learning or re-learning to let others become important in one's life is difficult, but critical. Sincere, caring, and informed strategies help trustworthy adults impart this complex skill set.

6. Questioning as a Culture to Assure Innovation. Life itself is dynamic, with change a constant - especially in today's world. To persevere in refining our helping skills, we must be open to new information. We must be willing to question our own effectiveness, assumptions, and operations; even if it marks us as "irreverent revolutionaries." Building and maintaining a questioning culture becomes a primary and continuing goal, while we simultaneously create and operate stable, but vital, service structures and operations. The beauty of uncertainty lies in its possibilities.

Step Four: Using Re-ED Essentials to Measure Treatment Fidelity

A preliminary tool for measuring fidelity to the above Re-ED essentials is now complete. The *Framework for Assessing an Agency's Level of Re-EDness* contains a section of essentials for each of the six dimensions. Each essential provides indicators along a four point scaled continuum from meeting the essential to not meeting it at all.

Overall, the Re-EDness framework has multiple indicators, each with a four point rating scale for Re-ED adherence. These can be used for program self assessment. Scrambled items, each with randomly ordered indicators, make up the self assessment (titled, *Staff Assessment of Your Program's Key Features*). Scores from staffs' choices of indicators most like their program can be averaged and profiled for each of the six key Re-ED dimensions. A single score for each of the six Re-ED dimensions gives program managers and staff a way to prioritize areas for program improvement, if they choose to strengthen their adherence to the Re-ED model.

Determining an evidence base for Re-ED requires independent measurement of each program's fidelity to those essential elements which are not available from the program's self assessment. As we continue to develop measurement protocols and test this tool in program sites, the measurement process will be progressively improved.

Program sites will include some that are thought to adhere closely to a Re-ED model and others that are thought to do so less closely. Measuring degrees of fidelity to these essentials will require ways for eliciting staff and child interactions so that independent evaluators can observe the degree to which each essential is being met.

All sites that participated in round one of the measurement development provided a standard set of baseline information being used in content analysis, protocol development, and reliability studies. Baseline data and data sources were collected before sites completed self assessments. Transcribed case presentations, vignettes presented to staff for their responses, reviews of child records, and interviews with staff, children, and families are all current components of Re-ED fidelity measurement being tested. Reliable and valid measures of model fidelity are critical for Phase II of the project. Here program outcomes will determine if degree of Re-ED fidelity is related to positive outcomes, thus empirically validating the Re-ED Essentials. Phase II once again poses the risky, big question: Do Re-ED philosophy and practice make a difference for kids and families?

Conclusion

Our initial work on developing a valid tool for measuring a programs "Re-EDness" is promising. With additional data, we believe that the Re-ED Essentials Survey will not only improve the quality of Re-ED program development, but will also enable us to differentiate Re-ED programs from more traditional mental health programs, whether or not a program overtly espouses Re-ED. But even if these promising prospects are realized, the Re-ED Essentials Survey and Framework for Agency Assessment are not the reason we undertook this assignment. They are merely a means to an end. Assessed compliance to any list of standards for best practices based on expert opinion does not mean that compliant programs with high fidelity to Re-ED are automatically effective, although research studies detailed in this section and the preceding section of this book support the efficacy of various combinations of the Re-ED approach. Adherence to the Re-ED essentials will simply mean that a program uses these practices in providing its services. Model fidelity criteria become powerful prescriptions only when proven relevant to positive outcomes for students and families served. When research demonstrates that high levels of Re-ED model fidelity are necessary for producing good outcomes for students, then adherence to each of the Re-ED essentials is likely to translate into improved effectiveness of a program.

All six essential aspects may be more effective than any one or few by themselves, a case where the whole is greater than the sum of its parts. Nevertheless, a final step, determining which Re-ED essentials contribute most to good outcomes is critical. One item, *"Trust between child and adult is essential,"* was investigated in collaborative research studies between Pressley Ridge and Vanderbilt University. By developing ways to measure "trust between child and adult" this measure may be used to determine if trust actually relates to positive outcomes for kids (see chapter 27). A similar research agenda for each of the final, short set of Re-ED essentials, may not only improve the development of all Re-ED programs, but also contribute to improving all children's services. We can imagine a set of program principles necessary for positive outcomes for troubled and troubling children that may have started as hallmarks of Re-ED programs, but eventually become proven hallmarks for a wide variety of effective services.

References

Cantrell, M. L., Cantrell, R. P., Valore, T. G., Jones, J. M., Fecser, F. A. (1999). A revisitation of the ecological perspectives on emotional/behavioral disorders. In L. M. Bullock & R. A. Gable (Eds.). The third mini-library series: *What works for children and youth with E/BD: Linking yesterday and today with tomorrow*. Reston, VA: The Council for Children with Behavior Disorders.

Cantrell, R. P. & Cantrell, M. L. (1976). Preventive mainstreaming: Impact of a supportive services program on pupils. *Exceptional Children (April)*. 381-386.

Chen, H. (1990). *Theory-driven evaluations*. Thousand Oaks, CA: Sage.

Feuerstein, R. (1979). *The dynamic assessment of retarded performers*. Baltimore: University Park Press.

Feuerstein, R. (1980). Instrumental enrichment: An intervention program for cognitive modifiability. Baltimore: University Park Press.

Fields, E., Farmer, E. M. Z., Apperson, J., Mustillo, S., & Simmers, D. (2006). Treatment and posttreatment effects of residential treatment using a Re-Education model. *Behavioral Disorders, 31*(3), 312-322.

Gray, S. W. & Klaus, R. A. (1970). The early training project: A seventh-year report. *Child Development, 41*(4), 909-924.

Gray, S. W. & Ruttle, K. (1980). The family-oriented home visiting program: A longitudinal study. *Genetic Psychology Monographs, 102*(2), 299-316.

Henggeler, S. W., Roland, M. D., Schoenwald, S. K., & Hoagwood, K. (March, 1998). *Getting outcomes with MST: Implications for treatment and transportability and dissemination*. Paper presented at the Children's Mental Health Research Conference, Tampa FL.

Hobbs, N. (1982, 1994). *The troubled and troubling child: Re-EDucation in mental health, education and human services programs*. First Edition, San Francisco: Jossey Bass.

Second Edition, Cleveland, OH: American Re-EDucation Association.

Holter, M. C., Mowbray, C. T., Bellamy, C., MacFarland, P., & Dukarski, J. (2004). "Critical Ingredients" of consumer run services: Results of a national survey. *Community Mental Health Journal, 40 (1)*, 47-63.

Hunt, J. McV. (1961). *Intelligence and experience.* New York: Ronald Press.

Joint Commission on Mental Health of Children. (1970). *Crisis in child mental health: Challenge for the 1970s.* New York: Harper & Row.

McNemar, Q. (1940). A critical examination of the University of Iowa studies of environmental influences upon the IQ. *Psychological Bulletin, 37,* 63-92.

Multi-systemic Therapy Treatment Model. Retrieved May 12, 2000 from http://www.mstservices.com/text/treatment.html .

Mowbray, C. T., Holter, M. C., Teague, G. B., & Bybee, D. (2003). Fidelity criteria: Development, measurement, and validation. *American Journal of Evaluation, 24*(3), 315-340.

Nash, J. M. (1997). Special Report: Fertile Minds. *Time, 149*(5). National Institutes of Mental Health. (2001). *Teenage brain: A work in progress* (NIH Publication No. 01- 4929, http://www.nimh.nih.gov/publicat/teenbrain.cfm).

Orwin, R. G. (2000). Assessing program fidelity in substance abuse health services research. *Addiction, 95*(Suppl. 3), S309-S327.

Shiel, W. C. & Schoenfield, L. J. (2004). Dementia prevention: Brain exercise. Retrieved January 21, 2006 from http://www.medicinenet.com.

Skeels, H. M. (1966). Adult status of children with contrasting early life experience. *Monographs of the Society for Research in Child Development, 31*(3), 1-65.

Skeels, H. M., & Dye, H. B. (1939). A study of the effects of differential stimulation on mentally retarded children. *Procedures of the American Association on Mental Deficiency, 44,* 114-136.

Skodak, M., & Skeels, H. M. (1949). A final follow-up study of one hundred adopted children. *Journal of Genetic Psychology, 75,* 85-125.

Sowell, E. R., Thompson, P. M., & Holmes, C. J. (1999). In vivo evidence for post-adolescent brain maturation in frontal and striatal regions. *Nature Neuroscience, 2*(10): 859-861.

Teague, G. B., Bond, G. R., & Drake, R. E. (1998). Program fidelity and Assertive Community Treatment: Development and use of a measure. *American Journal of Orthopsychiatry, 68,* 216-232.

Thompson, P. M., Giedd, J. N., & Woods, R. P. (2000). Growth patterns in the developing brain detected by using continuum mechanical tensor maps. *Nature, 404* (6774): 190-193.

Verghese, J., Lipton, R. B., Katz, M. J., Hall, C. B., Derby, C. A., Kuslansky, G., Ambrose, A. F., Sliwinski, M., & Buschke, H. (2003). Leisure activities and the risk of dementia in the elderly. *New England Journal of Medicine, 348,* 2508-2516.

Weinstein, L. (1974). *Evaluation of Program for Re-EDucating Disturbed Children: A Follow up Comparison with Untreated Children.* Washington, D.C.: Department of Health, Education and Welfare. (Available through ERIC Document Reproduction Service, ED 141 966.)

Wellman, B. L. Skeels, H. M., & Skodak, M. (1940). Review of McNemar's critical examination of Iowa studies. *Psychological Bulletin, 37,* 93-111.

Pamela Meadowcroft, PhD, of Meadowcroft Associates, Inc., is affiliated with the Graduate School of Public and International Affairs, University of Pittsburgh in Pittsburgh, PA. PMeadowcroft@aol.com

Mary Lynn Cantrell, PhD, is a Research Consultant for the Positive Education Program in Cleveland, Ohio. mlc8648@sbcglobal.net

Robert P. Cantrell, PhD, is a Research Consultant for the Positive Education Program in Cleveland, Ohio. rcantrell8648@sbcglobal.net

32

Follow-up Studies from the Project Re-ED Sites

Robert P. Cantrell

Weinstein (1974) reported positive results from Re-ED's first follow-up investigations in her original project evaluation (see chapter 29). Of the two original schools, Cumberland House in Nashville, Tennessee, and Wright School in Durham, North Carolina, only Wright School remains active and thriving. This remaining Project Re-ED school recently completed an effectiveness study which is reviewed below. Two of the other three follow-up studies in this chapter (Lewis, 1982, 1988) were conducted for the Nashville Project Re-ED site, Cumberland House. The third (Lewis, 1984) studied adolescent students from an outgrowth program on the Cumberland House grounds, Crockett Academy. By 2004, both Nashville sites were closed and students were transferred into programs within Tennessee's regional mental health systems.

Wright School Follow-up Study

The effectiveness and follow-up study of the Wright School program (Fields, Farmer, Apperson, Mustillo, and Simmers, 2006) used the Externalizing Subscale of Achenbach's (1991) Child Behavior Checklist (CBCL) and Epstein and Sharma's (1998) Behavioral and Emotional Rating Scale (BERS) to evaluate progress of 98 students. They compared data on these measures initially collected at admission with students' progress at discharge, then at three months and six months post-discharge.

Significant student improvements were found on both the CBCL and the BERS between admission and discharge. Furthermore, these improvements were sustained six months out from discharge,when compared to scores at admission. Younger students changed more than older students. Students experiencing longer treatment durations (> 198 days) achieved significantly higher rates of normal BERS scores.

Results were further scrutinized using three main interpretations of "improvement:" (a) total score changes tested against the probabilities that they had occurred by chance, yielding the above results; (b) a more stringent interpretation of "significant" change (at least one standard deviation above or below admission levels); and (c) change that put students into the "normal" range, as defined by the norms of the measures used.

Using the stringent definition of improvement (b) above, more than 50% of the children discharged improved significantly on both the CBCL and the BERS during treatment. Slightly fewer than half (43% CBCL, 40% BERS) changed less than one standard deviation during their treatment period.

Both the CBCL and BERS indicated marked improvements using (c), the absolute rather than relative criterion, i.e., percentages of discharged students functioning at the "normal" range on the measures when discharged. Only 9.6% of the students fell within the normal range at admission on the CBCL; at discharge, 55.6% achieved "normal" status. For the BERS, 21% scored at the normal level at admission, progressing to 73% normal at discharge. For those entering the program at the "low/abnormal" level on the BERS, 63.9% scored in the normal range at discharge, with over 58% remaining in the normal category at both three and six months post-discharge.

Multiple regression procedures were used to determine whether demographic variables contributed to a child's progress to the "normal" level by discharge. Demographics did not appear to be associated with improvement on the CBCL Externalizing scale by discharge. However, this was not the case for the BERS. Students who were male, younger, and from higher SES families were significantly more likely to progress to the "normal" level by discharge.

The median length of stay for all students discharged in this study was 192 days. The authors pursued answers for why more (70%)

long-term students (> 192 days before discharge) remained in the "normal" range at the six months follow-up period than did short-term students (45%). Although long-term students received more follow-up services during the three months following discharge than short-term students (< 192 days before discharge), these additional services during the three month follow-up period did not explain the sustained improvements noted. The two groups did not receive significantly different total numbers of services recommended or received by the six months follow-up period. Ascher, Farmer, Burns, and Angold's (1996) Child and Adolescent Services Assessment (CASA) was used to identify services received or recommended.

This was a needed and informative Re-ED efficacy study. Weinstein (1974) recommended that Re-ED workers concentrate on disturbances within a social system, including within-child changes. It is likely that Wright School liaison workers helped produce needed changes within families for their long-term students, thus explaining the ultimate stabilization and maintenance of "normalcy" in these social systems during the six months follow-up period. Lewis (1982, 1984) found something similar to this hypothesis with his early follow-up studies: both family and other agency supports increased over time for successfully discharged students.

Lewis (1982) Follow-up Study

W. W. Lewis conducted a follow-up study of two groups of children in treatment at Cumberland House. Both groups had been monitored for actively ongoing ecological variables while the children were in treatment. Although both groups made good progress during treatment, one did well during follow-up, while the other did not. Lewis attempted to tease out which ecological variables contributed to the divergence of ecological functioning between the two groups.

Blind ratings of case records emphasized rating each individual who had some role in each child's life (e.g., family members, friends, school workers, agency representatives, etc.), highlighting each person's ongoing support or stress in the child's life at the child's admission and again at discharge from treatment.

Differential weights were assigned to five categories of support or stress provided by participants in the child's ecology: (a) Major support (+2), (b) Minor support (+1), (c) Neutral (zero weight), (d) Minor stress (-1), and (e) Major stress (-2). Reliability checks on the ratings using independent raters were within acceptable ranges (i.e., 78% for exact rating for the same category and 92% for adjacent categories). Support and stress ratings for key actors in each child's ecology were put into two support/stress ratios, one for admission information and one for discharge information.

Three ecological areas discriminated significantly (Wilcoxon rank sum test) between successful (S) and unsuccessful (U) groups: (a) support/stress ratios at discharge (S > U), (b) family contacts per month (S > U), and (c) percent positive family contacts (S > U).

Lewis reanalyzed the discharge support/stress scores to see if differences between the S and U groups could be due to differential changes in support from family versus community agencies. Results showed that *both* family support and agency support had increased more for the S group during enrollment than for the U group.

Lewis concluded that positive changes in child support by both family and community agencies as treatment progressed was the determining factor in differentiating the successful group from the unsuccessful group. He could not pinpoint why some children's ecosystems were resistant to change while others were permeable to change.

Lewis (1984) Follow-up Study

In this follow-up study, two adolescent groups (composed from 89 consecutive admissions to Crockett Academy) were compared for indicators of their continued progress six weeks after discharge using the 20% most improved contrasted with the 20% least improved (N = 18 per group). Each had been rated by professional staff members on severity of their symptoms in (a) school academics, (b) school behaviors, (c) home and family life, and (d) community life.

Like the Lewis (1982) results, the most improved group had received significantly more support from their receiving ecology than the group making the least improvement. Both groups had been similar on admission, with no differences at admission on involvement with juvenile court, number transferred from Corrections, number of prior hospitalizations, prior months in group homes or institutions, or age at admission. There were also no differences in months since help had first been sought for problematic behaviors nor differences in treatment durations.

Further, the successful group had received more ecological support while they were in treatment (i.e., more parent contacts with staff or with the adolescent while the adolescent was in treatment). This apparent pattern of continuously developing synergistic support from within each adolescent's enveloping ecology seemed once again to be a deciding factor for successful outcomes.

Lewis (1988) Follow-up Study

The third follow-up study in this series investigated the effects of ecological supports being present for a child returning from residential treatment at Cumberland House. Liaison teacher-counselor (LTC) ratings of students' characteristics and ecological status at admission were used to predict LTC ratings on these same variables at follow-up 6 months after discharge. Ratings covered key elements of each child's ecology thought to be contributing to success or failure in post-treatment adjustment. These included:

(a) "Family Problem Index" consisting of present/absent judgments for each of six potential family problems: *"...abandonment or divorce by a parent, physical or sexual abuse, family member in corrections, physical illness of a parent that interfered with functioning, family member diagnosed mentally ill or mentally retarded, and family dependent on public housing"* (Lewis, 1988, p. 103);

(b) "School Climate Rating" using a 5 point scale assessing how easily staff could be approached, staff morale, how forthcoming staff were with information about the student being assessed, how amenable staff members were to requests for adapted schedules and other plans geared to the needs of the child, how well staff followed through on agreed-upon plans, and a global judgment about the care taken to maintain the appearance of the school;

(c) "Community Resources Ratings" using a 5 point scale to rate how the family used community services, educational resources, and *"church, health and dental health, mental health, juvenile court, organized recreation and informal recreation resources"* (Lewis, 1988, p. 103);

(d) "Mother Behavior ratings and Father Behavior ratings" using a 5 point scale for assessing each parent's limit-setting skills, appropriateness of each parent's use of praise and punishment, whether (and how) parents set expectations for the child's behaviors, whether they demonstrated respect for opinions expressed by the child, how helpful each parent was in solving their child's personal difficulties, and whether each explained to the child their reasons for decisions and delivered consequences;

(e) Discharge Adjustment Ratings using a 5 point scale to document liaison teacher-counselors' predictions of how well each student would adjust to home situations upon his/her return, predictions on how well each student would adjust to school situations upon her/his return, judgments about how much improvement the student had undergone, and how much interactions at home had improved;

(f) Follow-up Ratings using a 5 point scale for judgments about how well the student was actually adjusting to home and school six months post discharge, plus how much improvement was noted in the student and in the home setting following treatment.

Reliability checks on the ratings procedures were accomplished by re-rating the ecological domains above by the same liaison teacher-counselor for 30 discharged students, two weeks after each of the original ratings had been performed. Reliability results ranged from 75% to 93% agreement with a median rating of 82%.

Chi-squares compared LTCs' ratings at entry and follow-up for 82 students. Results showed that families where fathers were rated higher on behavior management skills at admission were demonstrating better *home adjustment* ratings at follow-up. By contrast, children of mothers who received higher ratings on behavior management skills at admission demonstrated higher ratings on *school adjustment* at follow-up.

There was no non-treatment control group who underwent the same ratings on the same variables at admission and at six month follow-up. Without a control group, interpretations of the relationships between ratings at admission and ratings at the six months follow-up period cannot infer definitively that community conditions at admission alone could have produced the same ecologically positive results noted in this study. Community treatment effects were confounded with residential treatment effects. This calls into question the interpretation made in the following statement by the 1999 Surgeon General's Report on Children's Mental Health about the Lewis (1988) study: *"This suggested that interventions in the child's community might be as effective as placement in the treatment setting"* (Department of Health and Human Services, 1999, p. 171). The analyses in the Lewis study were based solely on a treatment group that had experienced treatment within the residential program *plus* treatment within the community/ecological settings. The Re-ED approach commits to working with each child's ecology, as well as with the child while he/she is enrolled in the Re-ED residential schools.

Lewis (1988) used ratings at discharge compared with ratings at six months follow-up by liaison teacher-counselors. His interpretation of these findings was, *"this study and the earlier pilot studies [1982, 1984] suggest that ecological change can occur as a part of the treatment process, and is an important factor in later adjustment"* (p. 105). Here again, it is difficult to estimate the size of the ecological change that accompanied Re-ED residential treatment without similar measures on a comparable control group across similar follow-up time periods.

However, Lewis's hypothesized effect of ecological change as part of the Re-ED-based treatment process has empirical support in the experimental vs. control school studies of the Prevention-Intervention Project (see chapter 30). These results support the *"...interventions in the child's community"* statement made above in the 1999 Surgeon General's Report, since PIP's ecological interventions were conducted solely within the child's community. Although the PIP children's problems were generally not as severe as those of the children in the Re-ED residential programs, the purpose of PIP was a combination of prevention and intervention to preclude more restrictive treatment placements for troubled children. Ecological changes included significantly increased classroom teachers' behavioral knowledge as their contacts with PIP Support Teachers increased. These knowledge gains were in turn linked to significant improvements in both target children's behaviors and target children's academic achievement gains for both elementary and junior high school students (tables 5, 6, and 8 in PIP's ESEA Title III Validation Report, 1975).

Discussion

The studies reviewed showed that the engagement of the child's ecology is a key element in treatment, as opposed to the older, more traditional comparisons of residential schools versus community-based interventions. Some studies reviewed showed correlated changes within the child's ecology as treatment progresses; others showed similar results from an experimental vs. control group research standpoint. This continuing theme showing the worth of ecological engagement repeats itself across more than 40 years of mental health interventions within troubled ecologies.

All four studies, the Wright School study (Fields, et al., 2006), Lewis (1988), and the Lewis (1982, 1984) studies of how support/stress ratios work with families and agencies, support Weinstein's (1974) contention that social systems should be addressed for a complete treatment picture, rather than exclusively within-child issues.

The results reported within this book are compelling: the Re-ED approach works, especially as implemented by well-trained, decent adults working cooperatively with indigenous adults who are important to each target child's world. Providing Re-ED students with continuing parental and local encouragement is essential across each phase of treatment and in melding them back into their home ecologies. Follow-up contacts and assistance can help maintain long term gains. These research results provide hope for solving a heretofore discouraging aspect of mental health involvement for troubled and troubling children and adolescents — maintaining progress long after treatment has ended. Re-ED staff members might consider referring to these research results as a way of encouraging broad and continuing support from members of the child's ecology. Such supports can produce both early and lasting impacts on children's mental health progress.

References

Achenbach, T. M. (1991). Manual for the child behavior checklist/4-18 and 1991 profile. Burlington: University of Vermont, Department of Psychiatry.

Ascher, B. H., Farmer, E. M. Z., Burns, B. J., & Angold, A. (1996). The Child and Adolescent Services Assessment (CASA): Description and psychometrics. Journal of Emotional and Behavioral Disorders, 4, 12-20.

Department of Health and Human Services (1999). *Mental health: A report of the Surgeon General.* Washington, D.C.: Author.

Epstein, M. H., & Sharma, J. (1998). Behavioral and emotional rating scale: A strength-based approach to assessment. Austin, TX: Pro-ED.

Fields, E., Farmer, E. M. Z., Apperson, J., Mustillo, S., & Simmers, D. (2006). Treatment and posttreatment effects of residential treatment using a Re-Education model. *Behavioral Disorders, 31*(3), 312-322.

Lewis, W. W. (1982). Ecological factors in successful residential treatment. *Behavioral Disorders, 7*(3), 149-156.

Lewis, W. W. (1984). Ecological change: A necessary condition for residential treatment. *Child and Youth Care Forum, 13*(1), 21-29.

Lewis, W. W. (1988). The role of ecological variables in residential treatment. *Behavioral Disorders, 13*(2), 98-107.

Weinstein, L. (1974). *Evaluation of a Program for Re-Educating Disturbed Children: A Follow-Up Comparison with Untreated Children.* Washington, D. C.: Department of Health, Education and Welfare. (Available through ERIC Documentation Reproduction Service, ED-141-966.)

Robert P. Cantrell, PhD, is a Research Consultant with the Positive Education Program in Cleveland, OH rcantrell8648@sbcglobal.net

33

Follow-Up Outcomes for The Whitaker School: Re-Education for Youth from Multiple Service Systems

Ray Newnam, Joseph G. Murphy, Asenath Devaney, & Stephen R. Hooper

The North Carolina Adolescent Re-Education program began operation in October of 1980 as a part of the settlement agreement between the parties in a lawsuit entitled, Hunt vs. Willie M. et al. The plaintiff's complaint in the suit was that children and youth with serious emotional disorders were not receiving appropriate mental health treatment in the state's juvenile corrections system. This Re-Education Program was primarily developed to provide long-term residential treatment for the Willie M. population who were deemed too aggressive to be served in the community. In 1981 the North Carolina Re-Education program was renamed The Whitaker School, a name more sensitive to the needs of students and families.

This chapter presents characteristics of the Whitaker program and outcomes from Whitaker's follow-up studies of its discharged youths. Results are compared with outcome studies from other residential programs.

This chapter was supported by the North Carolina Division of Mental Health, Developmental Disabilities, and Substance Abuse Services, and by grants awarded to The Clinical Center for the Study of Development and Learning from the Administration on Developmental Disabilities (#90DD043003) and the Maternal Child Health Bureau (#MCJ379154A).

Requests for reprints should be directed to Dr. Stephen R. Hooper, The Clinical Center for the Study of Development and Learning, CB# 7255, University of North Carolina School of Medicine, Chapel Hill, NC 27599-7255; e-mail address Stephen.hooper@cdl.unc.edu

The Whitaker School

The Whitaker School is a state funded residential treatment program that reflects the principles of the Re-Education model (Hobbs, 1982). Systems theory is a cornerstone of this model, with the treatment components based on a definition of emotional conflict as arising from ecological discord and reflecting both interpersonal difficulties and system level deficiencies. The Whitaker School program maintains a daily census of 36 students (20 males and 16 females), ranging in age from 13 through 17. Available slots are filled on a first-come-first-served basis, with enrollment decisions made by Whitaker's director and/or the Director of the North Carolina Division of Mental Health, Developmental Disabilities, and Substance Abuse Services. Severity of disturbance is generally the major consideration for placements of students. Clients typically have exhausted available community services. Students experiencing severe medical difficulties or acute psychosis are excluded from admission until their medical needs are met. Students entering Whitaker receive medications and ongoing pharmacological monitoring as needed from a consulting psychiatrist.

The Whitaker School operates as a non-medical alternative treatment program to serve those adolescents needing mental health services who have not been served successfully in more traditional existing community-based programs, public or private.

The 335 students served in Whitaker from August 1992 to February 2005 were between 12 and 17 years old; each entered the program with an extensive history of serious difficulties. Half had experienced documented abuse, and about three-quarters had attempted suicide. On average, they had 3.6 prior hospitalizations (with as many as 20) and 3.83 out of home placements (with as many as 25). The mean number of psychiatric diagnoses received per child was 2.79, with as many as 6 given to an individual child. Virtually all were multi-system involved and came with Individual Educational Plans for special education services. Almost half were in the custody of the Department of Social Services. They remained in Whitaker for an average of 289.57 days, ranging from 33 to 766 days. Over 70% of students were admitted directly from another state psychiatric or juvenile facility. An additional 20% were referred by their communities following discharge from another state facility (Hooper, Murphy, Devaney, & Hultman, 2000).

While many treatment components are similar to other residential treatment programs, the Re-ED emphasis on community involvement prior to, during, and after treatment makes this program unique within the wide array of available residential treatment models. Whitaker offers community and family oriented services that begin while the student is still in residence, facilitating discharge planning and community involvement. The Liaison Teacher-Counselors (LTCs) at Whitaker School coordinate services with the Local Management Entities (formerly known as the area mental health centers) and the families/ primary guardians.

Individual intervention plans are implemented within a structured therapeutic environment using a peer group process model. This provides: (a) a clear feedback system for adolescents to facilitate effective communication and conflict resolution, (b) several psychoeducational groups, (c) an eight-hour per weekday educational component with individual education plans, (d) individualized behavior management programs, (e) community-based individual and family therapies, (f) recreation and leisure skills training, (g) prevocational development, and (h) ongoing community consultation and support via the LTCs. Additional diagnostic evaluations (e.g., speech-language, audiological, neuropsychological assessment services) can be conducted via consultants as needed. The program's pre-vocational training program works to re-integrate students into their home communities.

Residential Treatment Outcome Studies

Discussions of "outcome" from any treatment experience tend to create vigorous debate regarding definitions, collection of specific outcome data, and ultimately, interpretation of these data (Forness & Hoagwood, 1993; Green & Newman, 1996). Despite the many point-counterpoints offered, descriptive outcome data are critical to understanding program impacts on those served. Tracking individual outcomes after discharge from residential treatment is difficult, but critical to understanding treatment program effects on individuals as they re-integrate into the community. Examination of outcomes can impact how programs are administered - affecting specific treatments, management of resources, fiscal health, and even the program's ongoing existence. Pfeiffer and Shott (1996) stated that outcome data offer some accountability for a program's efforts and its cost effectiveness. Some leaders demand such evidence (Goocher, 1997).

Various residential treatment program models exist; reviews are available for many (Curry, 1991; Lyman & Campbell, 1996; and Zimmerman, 1990). Some provide outcome data (e.g., Basta & Davidson, 1988; Bruns, Burchard, Froelich, Yoe, & Tighe, 1998; Chamberlain & Reid, 1998; de Leon, Wexler, & Jainchill, 1982; Friman, Clark, Soper, & Sinclair, 1996; Gilliland-Mallo & Judd, 1986; Greenbaum, Dedrick, Friedman, Kutash, Brown, Lardieri, & Pugh, 1996). Holden, Friedman, and Santiago (2001) pushed for greater availability and range of community-based treatments. Several studies document positive benefits persisting from one to five years post-discharge (Blackman, Eustace, & Chowdhury, 1991).

Joshi and Rosenberg (1997) stated that children showing oppositional, defiant, or conduct-disorder seemed to make the least progress in residential treatment, suggesting that current residential centers may be unable to cope with acting-out behaviors. This observation failed to address variability issues across residential treatment settings and the differing interventions they use. *Residential treatment, as a term, only states the continuity of time youths spend in the setting.* Residential programs vary widely, as do their lengths of stay and their patterns of success or failure.

Studies with Positive Outcomes

Thompson, Smith, Osgood, Dowd, Friman, and Daly (1996) provided follow-up data on 503 children treated in the Father Flanagan's Boys Home four years earlier. Interviews with these students revealed better school performance and a more positive attitude toward school than those of a comparison group not placed in the program. The authors suggested that for long term, positive impact, troubled children and adolescents may need a treatment environment with consistent home and school contingencies over an extended period of time. More recently, Larzelere, Dinges, Schmidt, Spellman, Criste, and Connell (2001) examined the effectiveness of mental health treatment at the Girls and Boys Town residential treatment center. Their 43 clients showed objective gains on the Child Behavior Checklist (CBCL) (Achenbach, 1991), a teacher behavior rating scale, and the Children's Global Assessment Scale (DSM-IV-TR, 2000); the youths maintained their gains 10 months post-discharge. Similarly, Landsman, Miriam, Groza, Tyler, and Malone (2001) compared two residential treatment models. They described a family-centered residential treatment model that showed more success in achieving permanency outcomes 6 to 12 months post discharge to reunification and adoption placements than those in the regular residential treatment program.

Leichtman, Leichtman, Barber, and Neese (2001) discussed follow-up data at 3 and 12 months post discharge for 23 adolescents with severe behavioral disturbance in an intensive short-term residential treatment program. The program, offering pharmacological, psychological, group, and family therapies, demonstrated significantly increased rates of success between admission and discharge which were maintained through the year after discharge. The program's key factors in success were their work with families who made commitments to their adolescents, to community involvement, and particularly to discharge planning.

Negative Outcomes in Residential Treatment Studies

Despite these relatively positive findings, challenges to residential treatment by home/community-based treatment initiatives continue to mount (e.g., Holden, Friedman, & Santiago, 2001; Mattejat, Hirt, Wilken, Schmidt, & Remschmidt, 2001). To illustrate, Hoagwood and Cunningham (1992) found that 63% of children and adolescents who had been served in a residential treatment facility had made little or no progress at discharge; conversely, more positive outcomes were associated with shorter lengths of stay and the availability of community-based services for the student and family. Similarly, Asarnow, Aoki, and Elson (1996) found that residential treatment was associated with repeated placements in similar settings and increased dependency on state agencies. These authors noted that the rate of re-placement in similar settings was 32% one-year post discharge, 53% two-years post discharge, and 59% by the third year post discharge. Conduct problems (e.g., assaultive behaviors, truancy, property destruction, drug use) and school failure were the primary reasons for returning to a residential setting. Further, when residential treatment programs were subdivided into custodial and/or punitive models, wherein individuals "do time for their crime," extremely high rates of recidivism have been reported. For example, the California Youth Authority reported an 84% re-arrest rate within three years of discharge from a custodial residential treatment facility, with about 40% of adult prisoners being graduates from secured detention facilities (Smith & Associates, 1997).

Re-Education and Student Outcomes at Program Completion

Several studies conducted over the years addressed the effectiveness of the Re-Education residential treatment model (Hobbs, 1982; Lewis, 1982, 1988; Lochman, Bennett, & Simmers, 1988; Weinstein, 1974; Wilson & Lyman, 1983). Both Weinstein (1974) and Lewis (1988) report follow-up data with positive results for Re-ED "graduates." Lochman et al. (1988) used staff ratings of behavior problems, a self-esteem tool, and academic achievement testing. They found lessened hostility and anger in the students as defined by staff ratings, increases in reading and math skills, and improved student feelings of control over the environment at program completion.

The authors also noted that students with affective difficulties were those associated most directly with a decrease in behavioral difficulties at program discharge.

Post Program Outcomes at The Whitaker School

North Carolina's Re-Education Program at The Whitaker School has undertaken a major effort to evaluate the success or failure of students after program completion. We tracked a number of our students post program completion, some cross-sectionally and some longitudinally, to determine what happens to them once they leave our program.

Hooper, Murphy, Devaney, and Hultman (2000) provided initial evidence about how these adolescents fare post discharge. In this study, outcome data were collected on 111 students, ages 13 through 16, at approximately 6, 12, 18, or 24 months post-discharge in a cross-sectional fashion (i.e., one follow-up point per student). These students comprised 74% of all admissions over a five year time period.

The average length of stay for these students was approximately 9 to 10 months. Given the complexities of defining outcome, a simple, but multidimensional definition of outcome was employed. Ratings by community professionals documented each adolescent's status in three major ecological domains: School, Legal, and Level of Care. Students were rated by their community case managers (employed in community agencies) as functioning either satisfactorily or unsatisfactorily from the time of discharge in each of the domains (i.e., School = in school/graduated or not; Legal = new legal trouble or not; Level of Care = residing in a higher level of care, such as a juvenile detention center, or not). A rating of satisfactory did not necessarily imply that the adolescent was doing well in a respective domain, but that they were still functioning in an at least modestly adaptive manner.

The sample was 67% male and 60% Caucasian adolescents. The average educational status of the mothers/primary caregivers averaged at about the 11th grade level. The adolescents had received, on average, three psychiatric diagnoses on admission. These diagnoses covered most of the major psychiatric categories. The most frequent primary psychiatric diagnoses in this sample included: Conduct Disorder, Attention Deficit/Hyperactivity Disorder, Major Depression, and Post-Traumatic Stress Disorder.

About 85% of the sample were receiving some type of pharmacological management upon admission to the Whitaker program. All students entering the program received a variety of special education services. Over 80% of the sample had experienced some type of documented abuse, and about 85% had been living in an out-of-home placement prior to enrollment in Whitaker's Re-Education Program.

Cross-Sectional Study: Overall Outcomes

The criterion for success post discharge was defined as satisfactory performance in all three domains (School, Legal, and Level of Care). Nearly 58% of the students were rated as performing satisfactorily in all three domains across all reporting periods sampled (6, 12, 18, or 24 months). Rates varied from 69.2% of students who were rated at 6 months post discharge to 29.4% of those rated at 24 months post discharge. Only two students (1.8%) received unsatisfactory ratings in all three domains for their single rating episode, and only 8 students (7.2%) received unsatisfactory ratings in two domains. Nearly all students (98.2%) received satisfactory ratings in at least one domain following discharge for their one reporting period.

When the criterion for overall outcome status was changed to include cross-sectionally sampled students who received *satisfactory ratings on any two of three domains*, the overall rates of success on follow-up increased to 90.1%, and ranged from 97.4% at 6 months post discharge to 70.6% at 24 months. The Legal Domain probably represents the area of most concern to the general public. When the criterion was again modified to include a satisfactory rating in the Legal Domain plus at least one other domain, the overall success rate between 6 and 24 months post discharge was 77.5%. These cross-sectionally sampled ratings, grouped by months since discharge, demonstrated consistent rating decreases across 6 months to 24 months post discharge.

Success in Specific Domains. When the number of domains rated as satisfactory per child is disregarded, a majority of the students received satisfactory ratings in each of the School, Legal, and Level of Care domains. Overall, 79.3% of the students received satisfactory ratings in the School Domain across all time periods, with rates ranging from 94.9% at 6 months (the highest) to 47.1% at 24 months (the lowest). A "satisfactory" rating in this domain indicated that the student graduated, received a GED, or was attending school on a relatively regular basis. In the Legal Domain ratings, 80.2% of students were "satisfactory," with rates ranging from 85.7% at 12 months (highest) to 64.7% at 24 months (lowest). Satisfactory ratings in this domain indicated the student did not engage and/or get caught engaging in illegal activity. In the Level of Care domain, 86.5% were rated as "satisfactory," with success rates ranging from 88.6% at 12 months (highest) to 82.4% at 24 months (lowest). These percentages reflect that the student did/did not require a more restrictive level of care post discharge.

Successful versus Unsuccessful Students. Using the most stringent definition of success, students were grouped into those who were successful (satisfactory in all 3 domains; $N = 64$) versus those who were not ($N = 47$). Using months lapsed since discharge as a follow-up covariate, the groups were compared across key demographic, ecological, and psychoeducational variables to determine their differences. Table 1 shows that the two groups differed significantly on Verbal IQ, Full Scale IQ, reading, writing, and number of diagnoses at admission. In addition, chronological age and CBCL Internalized Score approached significance. These findings suggest that successful students manifested the following: higher intelligence, particularly verbal abilities; higher reading and writing skills; more Axis I psychiatric diagnoses upon admission into the program; and possibly more internalizing symptoms. In addition, the most successful students were more likely to be younger and female when compared to the less successful students.

Longitudinal Follow-Up Data

Following the above study, we continued to track many of these individuals ($N = 82$) post program in order to learn more about what happens to students discharged from The Whitaker School. All students had follow-up data for the 6 and 12 month time points; 73.2% had follow-up data for the first three time points; 46.2% had data for all four time points. Preliminary analyses of these data suggested that success rates remained relatively constant across time points and domains when compared with cross-sectional findings. When success in all three domains was required for designation as "successful," nearly 59% of the observations were rated as satisfactory across all follow-up time points. The largest group of successful ratings was the 64% rated as satisfactory in all 3 domains at the 6-month time point; the smallest group was the 42% successful at the 24-month time point post discharge.

When the criterion for overall outcome status was modified to include students receiving satisfactory ratings on any two of three domains, the overall success rates increased, as expected, to about 89%. When the criterion was changed to include a satisfactory rating in the Legal Domain plus at least one other domain with a satisfactory rating, the overall success rate was about 74%.

We collapsed ratings across all time periods and examined each domain separately. A majority of the students received satisfactory ratings in each of the three domains. Within the School Domain, about 85% of the students received satisfactory ratings over the various time points. Within the Legal Domain, about 74% of the students received a satisfactory rating across the various time points. The rate of students not requiring increased Level of Care post-discharge was approximately 83% across all time points. Taken together, these preliminary rates compared favorably to those obtained from our cross-sectional study.

Support for CASSP Values

The cross-sectional and longitudinal findings by Hooper and colleagues present some of the first descriptive post-discharge outcome data for adolescent students receiving residential treatment services in a publicly funded state facility operating under the guiding principles of the Re-Education model. Using a dichotomous rating (i.e., satisfactory versus unsatisfactory), approximately 58% of the students received satisfactory ratings by their community case managers in all three domains across all four follow-up points sampled. This percentage increased to about 78% when the definition was modified to include satisfactory ratings in the Legal Domain plus one other domain, and to nearly 90% when any two out of three domains were rated as satisfactory. While the overall success rates tended to decrease over time the longer an individual has been discharged, it is less likely that the program will continue to impact

Table 1.
Differences between Successful and Unsuccessful Students Across Selected Demographic, Psychoeducational, and Social-Behavioral Variables Controlling for Follow-up Time Point.

Variable	Successful (n = 64)		Others (n = 47)		F-Value
	Mean	SD	Mean	SD	
Demographics					
Chronological Age (yrs.)	14.92	1.01	15.31	1.29	2.07+
Number of Diagnoses	2.59	1.08	2.83	1.32	3.39*
Number of Placements	4.03	1.64	4.40	2.51	1.60
Maternal Education (yrs.)	10.67	1.94	10.96	1.14	0.97
Psychoeducational					
Verbal IQ	85.34	11.93	79.06	11.59	5.03**
Performance IQ	85.97	13.19	84.87	15.28	1.86
Full Scale IQ	84.64	12.78	81.51	13.18	3.00*
Reading	82.69	13.41	77.96	13.84	3.08*
Mathematics	77.28	11.27	75.09	11.06	2.04
Writing	81.30	15.00	80.17	11.69	3.59*
Social-Behavioral					
CBCL Internalized	74.05	5.89	68.58	6.62	2.21+
CBCL Externalized	75.30	4.85	73.89	6.11	1.34
CBCL Total	77.05	6.25	75.19	6.97	1.74

Note. The specific follow-up time point was used as the covariate in the MANCOVA, with all data being collected at the time of admission into the program. Scores for the psychoeducational variables have a mean = 100, SD = 15, with higher scores reflecting a more intact performance; scores for the social-behavioral variables have a mean = 50, SD = 10, with lower scores reflecting a more intact functioning; $*p < .05$; $**p < .01$; $+p < .10$.

the individual's life *without active follow-up support programs funded in home communities.*

These findings are encouraging and far more positive when compared with outcome data from the California Youth Authority and other "boot camp" types of treatment (Peters, Thomas, & Zamberlan, 1998). Results also provide support for the Child and Adolescent Service System Program (CASSP) values which target student/family orientation, community-based collaboration, continuum of care, and alternative placements for youth experiencing serious emotional and behavioral disturbance (Duchnowski, Johnson, Hall, Kutash, & Friedman, 1993). More specifically, the various nuances of the Re-Education model are consistent with the key components advocated by the Center for Effective Collaboration and Practice (1998) for successful treatment outcomes (i.e., community-based planning, transition services, interagency collaboration).

Differences between students deemed successful at the specified follow-up points versus those deemed unsuccessful were interesting, particularly as these differences suggest what intrinsic and/or extrinsic factors might be affecting outcomes for adolescents in their typical ecological settings. Indeed, the Report from the Surgeon General (Department of Health and Human Services, 1999) noted that this type of information should provide ongoing guidance for determining which characteristics will influence outcomes following participation in a residential treatment program. In addition, the cross-sectional findings by Hooper et al. (2000) are consistent with those of Curry (1991) and others (e.g., Lochman et al., 1988). Namely, key characteristics of successfully treated individuals at Whitaker included being female and younger, having higher IQ and literacy skills, having fewer psychiatric diagnoses, and manifesting more internalizing behaviors.

Surprisingly, no differences were found on other key ecological variables, such as history of abuse and living with biological parents (Hooper et al., 2000), particularly given earlier follow-up findings from Project Re-ED schools (Lewis, 1988). Perhaps these variables represent less modifiable aspects of an adolescent's life,

multiple-system adolescents, who frequently "fall between the cracks" and then later pose significant problems for the community. Available literature does suggest that communities adhering to system of care principles provide improved and better connected services (Hernandez, Gomez, Lipien, Greenbaum, Armstrong, & Gonzales, 2001).

Evaluation Strategies (on a shoestring budget!)

It is imperative that all programs provide concrete evidence of their effectiveness. The two studies above furnish emergent evidence of the success of Whitaker students once they leave our program and return to their respective communities. These studies have provided support for continuation of the program over the past several years, and they clearly have reinforced programmatic offerings within The Whitaker School (e.g., pre-vocational offerings). Data collected for program evaluation also assist with program modifications that contribute to improved performance. While many program evaluations are conducted as an after-thought, or on a "shoestring budget," these data are critical to determining programmatic changes and/or even program continuation. In this regard, it would be important for policy makers to mandate and fund evaluation initiatives for all state-funded programs. Findings from such endeavors could result in more evidence supported program offerings within a system of care.

Legislative Support

Similarly, it is important to get program evaluation findings into the hands of legislators—especially those inclined to support such concerns and issues. For example, funding is a key challenge facing programs such as The Whitaker School, especially use of Medicaid dollars to support treatment efforts. While Medicaid dollars can be employed for residential treatment programs using a decidedly medical model, these public monies currently cannot be used to support programs with an ecological or skill building focus. For programs such as The Whitaker School, where some degree of success has been demonstrated, it would seem critical that use of Medicaid and related funds be re-examined for cost effectiveness. Modifications of regulations may be necessary for evidence backed practices to receive public funds, securing efficient mental health services for some of our neediest future citizens.

Summary and Conclusions

This chapter provides an overview of the development and ongoing operation of the North Carolina Re-Education Program for adolescents, a residential treatment program called The Whitaker School. Two post program outcome studies were presented for adolescents who were Whitaker residents. Each was served in this secure, state operated treatment program. It is neither a juvenile correction, nor a medical/state hospital facility. Initial findings suggested a relatively higher rate of successful re-entry of students back into their communities post discharge compared with other types of residential treatment programs reported in the literature. Data from this chapter suggest that programs employing a noncustodial approach with an ecological and psychoeducational focus, not only provide security for society in the short run, but can offer potential longer term benefits for both youths and society at large.

The community-based orientation of this Re-Education program facilitated community re-entry for adolescents. Re-entry is a key issue of advocates for cost effective and evidence based mental health policy, addressing specific concerns raised by the Surgeon General (Department of Health and Human Services, 1999) about the difficulties inherent in community re-entry. These data suggest that a community-based orientation increases the chances that a student will: (a) function in a more adaptive fashion once he/she leaves the treatment environment, (b) integrate some of the benefits derived from residential treatment into their adaptive functioning, and (c) later require less intense mental health services. For students with severe and persistent mental health problems and high needs for both intensive support and multisystem involvement, the presence of a program such as Whitaker's with its community involvement can deflect the trajectory of these severe problems from more intensive and/or restrictive types of intervention (Hooper et al., 2000).

Unfortunately, programs for child and adolescent mental health treatment are frequently competing for funding with other service entities. For example, in the state of North Carolina the entire Juvenile Crime Code has been rewritten to focus on stiffening punishment and penalty options, without regard to the presence or absence of demonstrated effectiveness in changing youth behavior or increasing security for citizens. Services dealing with juvenile crime have only recently begun to add mental health components to their programs. Increased funding for such programs, and for community-based mental health services in general, will be critical for serving children and adolescents with severe mental health needs. All components will be more functional when they are embedded within a comprehensive system of care.

Tracking student progress during treatment and through post-discharge is critical to supporting these efforts. The Re-Education model appears to hold good potential for positive outcomes. The Whitaker School will continue to work with communities to facilitate positive community adjustment for its adolescent constituents.

References

Achenbach, T. M. (1991). *Manual for the Child Behavior Checklist/ 4-18 and 1991 profile*. Burlington, VT: University of Vermont, Department of Psychiatry.

Asarnow, J. R., Aoki, W., & Elson, S. (1996). Children in residential treatment: A follow-up study. *Journal of Clinical Child Psychology, 25*, 209-214.

Basta, J. M., & Davidson, W. S. (1988). Treatment of juvenile offenders: Study outcomes since 1980. *Behavior, Science, and Law, 6*, 355-384.

Blackman, M., Eustace, J., & Chowdhury, T. (1991). Adolescent residential treatment: A one to three year follow-up. *Canadian Journal of Psychiatry, 36*, 472-479.

Bruns, J., Burchard, J. D., Froelich, P., Yoe, J. T., & Tighe, T. (1998). Tracking behavioral progress within a children's mental health system: The Vermont Community Adjustment Tracking System. *Journal of Emotional and Behavior Disorders, 6*, 19-32.

Center for Effective Collaboration and Practice (1998). Delinquency: Effective programs from across the nation. *Reclaiming Children and Youth, 7*, 125-126.

Chamberlain, P., & Reid, J. B. (1998). Comparison of two community alternatives to incarceration for chronic juvenile offenders. *Journal of Consulting and Clinical Psychology, 66,* 624-633.

Curry, J. (1991). Outcome research on residential treatment: Implications and suggested directions. *American Journal of Orthopsychiatry, 61,* 348-357.

de Leon, G., Wexler, H. K., & Jainchill, N. (1982). The therapeutic community: Success and improvement rates 5 years after treatment. *International Journal of the Addict, 17,* 703-747.

Department of Health and Human Services (1999). *Mental health: A report of the Surgeon General.* Washington, D.C.: Author.

Duchnowski, A. J., Johnson, M. K., Hall, K. S., Kutash, K., & Friedman, R. M. (1993). The alternatives to residential treatment study: Initial findings. *Journal of Emotional and Behavior Disorders, 1,* 17-26.

Forness, S. R., & Hoagwood, K. (1993). Where angels fear to tread: Issues in sampling, design, and implementation of school-based mental health services research. *School Psychology Quarterly, 8,* 291-300.

Friman, P. C., Clark, T., Soper, S., Sinclair, J. (1996). Maintaining placement for troubled and disruptive adolescents in voluntary residential care: The role of reduced youth-to-staff ratio. *Journal of Child and Family Studies, 5,* 337-347.

Gilliland-Mallo, D., & Judd, P. (1986). The effectiveness of residential care facilities for adolescent boys. *Adolescence, 21,* 311-321.

Goocher, B. E. (1997). A comment on "Residential treatment and its alternative:" A call to action. *Child and Youth Care Forum, 26,* 53-55.

Green, R. S., & Newman, F. L. (1996). Criteria for selecting instruments to assess treatment outcomes. *Residential Treatment for Children and Youth, 13,* 29-48.

Greenbaum, P. E., Dedrick, R. F., Friedman, R. M., Kutash, K., Brown, E.C., Lardieri, S.P., & Pugh, A.M. (1996). National adolescent and child treatment study (NACTS): Outcomes for children with serious emotional and behavioral disturbance. *Journal of Emotional and Behavior Disorders, 4,* 130-146.

Hernandez, M., Gomez, A., Lipien, L., Greenbaum, P. E., Armstrong, K. H., & Gonzales, P. (2001). Use of the system-of-care practice review in the national evaluation: Evaluating the fidelity of practice to system-of-care principles. *Journal of Emotional and Behavioral Disorders, 9,* 43-52.

Holden, E. W., Friedman, R. M., & Santiago, R. L. (2001). Overview of the national evaluation of the comprehensive community mental health services for children and their families program. *Journal of Emotional and Behavioral Disorders, 9,* 4-12.

Hoagwood, K., & Cunningham, M. (1992). Outcomes of children with emotional disturbance in residential treatment for educational purposes. *Journal of Child and Family Studies, 1,* 129-140.

Hobbs, N. (1982). *The troubled and troubling child.* San Francisco: Jossey-Bass.

Hooper, S. R., Murphy, J., Devaney, A., & Hultman, T. (2000). Ecological outcomes of adolescents in a psychoeducational residential treatment facility. *American Journal of Orthopsychiatry, 70,* 491-500.

Joshi, P. K., & Rosenberg, L. A. (1997). Children's behavioral response to residential treatment. *Journal of Clinical Psychology, 53,* 567-573.

Landsman, M. J., Miriam, J., Groza, V., Tyler, M. & Malone, K. (2001). Outcomes of family-centered residential treatment. *Child Welfare, 80,* 351-379.

Larzelere, R. E., Dinges, K., Schmidt, M. D., Spellman, D. F., Criste, T. R., Connell, P. (2001). Outcomes of residential treatment: A study of the adolescent clients of Girls and Boys Town. *Child & Youth Care Forum, 30,* 175-185.

Lee, R. E. (1996). FIRO-B scores and success in a positive peer-culture residential treatment program. *Psychological Reports, 78,* 215-220.

Leichtman, M., Leichtman, M. L., Barber, C. C., & Neese, D. T. (2001). Effectiveness of intensive short-term residential treatment with severely disturbed adolescents. *American Journal of Orthopsychiatry, 71,* 227-235.

Lewis, W. W. (1982). Ecological factors in successful residential treatment. *Behavior Disorders, 7*, 149-156.

Lewis, W. W. (1988). The role of ecological variables in residential treatment. *Behavior Disorders, 13*, 98-107.

Lochman, J. E., Bennett, C. L., & Simmers, D. A. (1988). Residential Re-Ed treatment of highly aggressive youth: Preliminary indications of effectiveness and the precursors of improvement. *Educational Treatment of the Child, 11*, 52-62.

Lyman, R. D., & Campbell, N. R. (1996). *Treating children and adolescents in residential and inpatient settings.* Thousand Oaks, CA: Sage Publications.

Mattejat, F., Hirt, B.R., Wilken, J., Schmidt, M.H., & Remschmidt, H. (2001). Efficacy of inpatient and home treatment in psychiatrically disturbed children and adolescents. Follow-up assessment of the results of a controlled treatment study. *European Child and Adolescent Psychiatry, 10* (Supplement 1), 171-179.

Peters, M., Thomas, D., & Zamberlan, C. (1998). *Boot camps for juvenile offenders: Program summary.* Washington, DC: OJJDP.

Pfeiffer, S. I., & Shott, S. (1996). Implementing an outcome assessment project: Logistical, practical, and ethical considerations. *Residential Treatment of Children and Youth, 13*, 71-81.

Smith, D. C. and Associates, Kaplan McLaughlin Diaz, Kitchell CEM (1997). *Arizona Juvenile Detention Master Plan Supplement.* Tucson: Arizona Supreme Court Administrative Office of the Courts Juvenile Justice Services Division.

Termini, A. M. (1991). Ecologically based interventions in residential and school facilities: theory or practice? *Adolescence, 26*, 387-398.

Thompson, R. W., Smith, G. L., Osgood, D. W., Dowd, P. T., Friman, P. C. & Daly, D. L. (1996). Residential care: A study of short and long-term educational effects. *Child Youth Services Review, 18*, 221-242.

Weinstein, L. (1974). *Evaluation of a program for re-educating disturbed children: A follow-up comparison with untreated children.* Washington, D.C.: Department of Health, Education, and Welfare, Bureau for the Education of the Handicapped.

Wilson, D. R., & Lyman, R. D. (1983). Residential treatment of
    emotionally disturbed children. In C. E. Walker, & M. C.
    Roberts (Eds.), *Handbook of clinical child psychology* (pp.
    1069-1088). New York: John Wiley and Sons.
Zimmerman, D. P. (1990). Notes on the history of adolescent inpatient
    and residential treatment. *Adolescence, 25*, 9-38.

*Ray Newnam, PhD, is Senior Psychologist of The Whitaker School in Butner,
North Carolina.*
    ray.newnam@ncmail.net

*Joseph G. Murphy, PhD, is the Director of Residential Programs and Related
Schools in the Sheppard Pratt Health Systems, Jefferson Schools in Jefferson,
MO.*
    jmurphy@thejeffersonschool.org

*Asenath Devaney, EdS, is the Clinical Director at The Whitaker School in
Butner, North Carolina.*
    asenath.devaney@ncmail.net

*Stephen R. Hooper, PhD, is a Professor in the Department of Psychiatry, and
the Associate Director of The Clinical Center for The Study of Development
and Learning at the University of North Carolina School of Medicine in
Chapel Hill, North Carolina.*
    Stephen.hooper@cdl.unc.edu.

Part VIII

Looking at Re-ED Past, Present, Future

Past: Choosing to Think and Act Differently

This section concludes with Frank Fecser's description of Re-ED as he has experienced it for over thirty years. The emotion attached is not atypical of practitioners of this approach. They see the fruits of their labors on a daily basis, taking joy in the successes and feeling pain when interventions miss the mark. Their emotional investment tends to be reinforced. The authors try to avoid overstating the case, but hope readers understand their enthusiasm for what they believe makes real differences in lives.

It is impossible to describe Re-ED without hearing from children and families--or without talking about Nicholas Hobbs. This difficulty exists, even though, as he said, "Re-ED was constructed by many people and is still in the process of being invented by others... The vital essence of Re-ED is that it is a self renewing institution, always in the process of becoming. Thus, no one can rightly claim to be its founder" (Hobbs, 1974, pp. 145-146). But Re-ED began with him.

Chapter 34 provides a tribute to Hobbs which summarizes his professional contributions. In chapter 35 following, Clark Luster provides a historical overview of Re-ED as it began with the thoughts of Hobbs and his colleagues in the 1950's, established the initial programs in the 1960's, expanded and added community based adaptations through the 1970's, and collaborated as a national organization in the 1980's. Ever since, adapted Re-ED services have continued and expanded across the nation.

In "Growing Up Re-ED" (chapter 36) Connie Mills summarizes the reflections of Youth Villages' administrators describing how they encountered Re-ED ideas, accessed the assistance available in other Re-ED programs, and became a multi-state program which essentially provides a continuum of care for the children and youth they serve.

Present: Helping Programs and Schools Help Students

Today's Re-ED programs reflect the approach's most salient contributions to helping troubled and troubling students. These include: (1) the ecological systems approach to viewing a child's world and the efforts needed to maximize strength and minimize discord, (2) emphasis on competence which places importance on enhancing the skills of ecosystem members, and (3) focus on natural expectations and expeditious interventions in natural settings (or as close to them as possible). This latter view was new in the late 1950s but no doubt was shared by others. By the mid 1960's and early 1970's it was beginning to change the human service field — with court cases, public policy, and budget decisions giving evidence of that change.

Hobbs was particularly concerned with the isolating effects of the field's categorical systems. He pointed out the extraordinary consequences of definitions and the labels we use. *"Once a verbal commitment has been made in describing a child, there follows inexorably a chain of actions that may be less related to the primary data of behavior than to social arrangements made to care for generic types of children"* (Hobbs, 1974, pp. 165-166). Being called "sick" makes illness the child's lot and compliance with treatment the key to "cure," yet it is vastly different if the child sees medications as causing his improvements rather than helping his *efforts* to improve. Being called "bad" or "delinquent" leads to correction or punishment, yet paying for your misdeeds is different from changing your interpretations of events and learning new behaviors. *"What a child is labeled often seems fortuitous, yet the consequences of the naming are of great moment in determining what then happens to him"* (Hobbs, 1974, p. 166). Re-ED programs often serve children and youth with multiple and serious labels, but they see them as children rather than labels, each with strengths, needs, and characteristics, like other children. Staff walk a difficult tightrope — knowing what the labels mean professionally and using them in recording and reporting as required, but making sure they avoid thinking or speaking of the children as if they were the same as their labels. One of the important functions of the national organization is to serve as a forum where service providers can remind each other why they seek to operationalize their philosophy, rather than be shaped toward a different philosophy by the regulations of a funding source.

In chapter 37, Mark Freado introduces the American Re-Education Association and its fourteen current sponsoring programs. A description of each of these members follows, with information about their locales, missions, staff, children, youth, and families served. Services they provide are outlined, and a brief history of the agency is provided.

"Beyond Our Borders," chapter 38 by Scott Finnell and his colleagues, describes a forward thinking effort started at Pressley Ridge some years ago when visitors from Europe requested training at Pressley's U.S. sites. Later they jointly sponsored extension sites and training /consultation services overseas. These efforts are expanding to new horizons today, operating service programs with indigenous staff and providing evaluation services.

When asked in 1974 to evaluate Project Re-ED's accomplishments, Hobbs described what he saw as contributing to Weinstein's positive results. He followed the description by saying, "We have hard data to substantiate these claims. Indeed, these are the most substantial data known to us that validate the effectiveness of a treatment program for children…. From one perspective, Project Re-ED could be declared a success. Yet it is just as readily manifest that Re-ED [as short term residential treatment] does not offer a solution of what to do about the disturbed child" (Hobbs, 1974, pp. 155, 161). He saw promise in adaptations, continually informed by new research, to all kinds of services meeting community needs — particularly in the public schools.

"We start with the assumption that each day is of great importance to young people; when an hour is neglected, allowed to pass without reason and intent, teaching and learning go on nevertheless, and the child or adolescent may be the loser. In Re-ED, no one waits for a special therapeutic hour. We try, as best we can, to make all hours special. We strive for immediate and sustained involvement in purposeful and consequential living."

(Hobbs, 1982, pp. 242-243)

"The continuing vitality of the Re-ED program springs, in part at least, from an understanding that every person involved in the program is responsible for inventing what Re-ED should become. The challenge is intellectually and personally demanding…."

(Hobbs, 1982, pp. 30-31)

34

Nicholas Hobbs

1915-1983

To the many Re-EDers who knew him, Nicholas Hobbs was the Nick who wanted to hear how "the kids" and "the families" were doing; who loved camping himself and wanted to know about the latest group's foray into the wilds; who enjoyed a party even if he was one of the earliest to leave; who taught us by example to focus on positive solutions, to avoid dwelling on the negative aspects of any problem. To those less fortunate than to know him, Hobbs was the consummate writer whose words seemed to express their own feelings and beliefs better than they could have - an inspiration who cared about our students even before we were there to care for them ourselves, someone who seemed to see the future we live in now, though a potentially better one than we know at this point. He taught us that many people have gifts to help us with the troubled and troubling kids we worry about and work for - professionals with wisdom, information, and strategies to offer; community and neighborhood folks who, more often than not, would join in efforts to help someone if we asked; family members and students, each of whom could teach us as we learned together.

Directly or indirectly, Nick was friend, model, teacher to all of us. Many of us were largely unaware of his work outside Re-ED, summarized in the following citations for two awards given him by the American Psychological Association (APA) in 1980:

1980 APA Citation of Nicholas Hobbs for Distinguished Professional Contributions to Public Service:

"Few can match Nicholas Hobbs' record of utilizing psychological knowledge in the public interest and social policy. Among his outstanding contributions are the now famous Project Re-ED, an educational approach to the residential treatment of emotionally disturbed children, his service as the first director of selection for the Peace Corps, his leadership in studying the classification of children, his creation of the Center for the Study of Families and Children at Vanderbilt University, and his service to the government in many capacities. As chair of the Committee on Ethical Standards and as president of APA he has rendered distinguished service."

1980 APA Citation of Nicholas Hobbs for Distinguished Contributions to Psychology in the Public Interest:

"Early in his career, Nicholas Hobbs made a strong commitment to bettering the lives of children as the most productive application of psychology in the public interest. This commitment continues today in his effort to formulate public policy and legislation through projects he directs at the Vanderbilt Center for the Study of Families and Children. He has pioneered in assembling academicians and practitioners of all disciplines to study public policies affecting children. Always intrigued by novel ideas, he has over the years departed from many traditional concepts. He has been an innovator in the treatment of emotionally disturbed children, applying psychological principles to their reeducation in home-like residential centers. He has expanded the concepts of this program to all children with special needs. He directed the Project on the Classification of Exceptional Children, the foundation of the Education for All Handicapped Children Act, and has developed new approaches to assessment and classification.

In positions of leadership throughout his career, he has served children, his profession, and the public at large through continuous executive and advisory roles in professional associations, national commissions, councils, foundations, and UNESCO. He took the lead in the empirical development of APA's first code of ethics. A lucid writer, accomplished scholar, master teacher, dedicated nurturer of young professionals, creative problem solver, and skilled administrator, Nicholas Hobbs possesses the remarkable combination of abilities needed to transform good ideas into actual programs for children. He is an inspiration to all who ascribe to his dedication of The Futures of Children:
To the children of our nation
Whose hope lies in our caring
And whose futures are our trust."

References

Hobbs, N. (1982). *The troubled and troubling child.* San Francisco, CA: Jossey-Bass.
Hobbs, N. (1975). *The futures of children: Categories, labels, and their consequences.* San Francisco, CA: Jossey-Bass.

35

The History of Re-ED

William Clark Luster

Today, Re-ED is a values and principles based approach to helping troubled and troubling children and youth, and their families, through diverse service arrangements. The national organization which serves as its virtual meeting place represents work in 19 states, the District of Columbia, and 3 European nations -- daily serving more than 40,000 children and their families.

The history of the Re-Education movement is the story of the people and the ideas that affected the lives of many thousands over the last four and a half decades. A large number were touched directly by Re-ED ideas and practices -- as a child, a family member, or a practitioner within a Re-ED program. Others, some of whom may be unfamiliar with the term "Re-ED," have come to embrace what is essentially Re-ED thinking as best practice in working with troubled and troubling children and their families. What began as a ray of hope in the hearts of Re-ED explorers in the mid-1950s became a foundation for today's ideal system of care for children and families across our nation and beyond. Wellness based, family involved, competence focused, skill building, short termed, community connected, individually and ecologically oriented -- each is becoming a hallmark concept of today's accepted best practice in child and family service. Over time the field is coming to share Re-ED's strong sense of the potential and importance of ecosystem members and direct care providers (like teacher-counselors) as therapeutic agents. These concepts were galvanized by those early explorers into the Re-ED approach - beginning its first services in 1962 with the university based *Project for the Re-Education of Emotionally Disturbed Children.*

In many ways Re-ED explorers were revolutionaries. Dr. Nicholas Hobbs and others (William C. Rhodes, Wilbert W. Lewis, and Lloyd Dunn) were external to the then traditional service system for children. They were academics and researchers, no longer providing direct service, with radical ideas about "parents as partners" and "community connectedness." They rejected concepts of cure in favor of "skill enhancement" and "successful living" - new ideas in children's mental health. They began to discuss the potential of a treatment "school" for children with severe behavioral and emotional difficulties, one where specially selected and trained teachers were both teachers and counselors for small groups of children. They proposed that students go home on weekends, that staff "liaisons" work with the families and home schools to help visits home be productive and to prepare for the child's successful return as soon as possible.

Early in Re-ED, the view of families' roles held by staff was significantly different from the usual view of the day. As the years passed, family members' roles expanded to include new program functions as well. The development of that role is detailed in *Part III: Strengthening Families and Ecologies.* An overview and historical timeline for those changes is provided in the Introduction to Part III, rather than in this chapter. Families are critical for children, and Re-ED works to support or supplement their critical functions, as described in chapters 8-12.

In retrospect, early Re-ED leaders clearly made efforts to reform the children's mental health system. Given the 1950s' lack of system capacity, the absence of mandate and adequate public policy, sparse human resources for training, research, or clinical service, and the extreme scarcity of program offerings for children and families in need, almost any serious attempt at resource enhancement could successfully impact the status quo -- and Re-ED did.

Nicholas Hobbs and Other Early Explorers

No discussion of Re-ED history or tradition can begin without considering the role that Nick Hobbs played in Re-ED's first 30 years. There may ultimately have been a Re-ED without Hobbs, but were it not for his national stature, his prescient vision and clarity, his rational and pragmatic ideas, his openness to change and input from others, and his confidence that appropriately selected and well trained young adults (teacher-counselors) would make a difference in the lives of children and families, Re-ED would look significantly different today. Or it might not exist at all.

Born in 1915, young Nicholas was reared in a socially concerned Southern family which lost its financial resources in the Depression. Aspiring to be a teacher, he won a competitive scholarship to The Citadel where he earned a B.A. in English. After two years as a high school teacher in his home state of South Carolina, Hobbs began graduate work at Ohio State University where he worked with Sidney Pressey, originator of the first teaching machine, and with Carl Rogers, one of the most innovative therapists of the day.

During World War II, he interrupted his doctoral studies to join the U.S. Army Air Force, where he rose to the rank of colonel. He served in the Army Air Force Psychological Research Program where he helped develop tools for selecting the most appropriate enlistees for Army aircraft roles, matching recruit skills and aptitudes with wartime needs. Person-task matching became a strong, lifelong professional interest and skill area for Hobbs. His predilection for selection was again tapped in the late 1960s with his appointment as the first Director of Selection and Research for the Peace Corps. Later in Re-ED, this interest led to his notion that certain people may well have a propensity to do the work of Re-ED. He believed that there were natural teacher-counselors, trained by life and open to learning.

After the war, Hobbs finished his doctorate, and in 1946 was appointed as director of the Clinical Psychology Training Program on the faculty of Columbia University. While there, he met and married psychologist Mary Thompson Hobbs. Dr. Mary Hobbs was a valued intellectual partner throughout Nick's career.

The Hobbs moved to Baton Rouge in 1950 where Nick taught at Louisiana State University before going to Nashville where he became chair of the Department of Psychology at George Peabody College for Teachers (now part of Vanderbilt University). It was at Peabody that Hobbs led other "explorers" through the 1950s and 1960s to create what would become Re-ED. He was also to become the founding director of the John F. Kennedy Center for Research on Education and Human Development established there.

In 1954, Hobbs directed a survey of children's mental health resources for the Southern Regional Education Board. The study confirmed the national dearth of resources available to address children's mental health needs. Many who were troubled and troubling spent years of their young lives in large custodial institutions. The study group's concluding report queried the effectiveness of the traditional psychotherapeutic model and pointed out that high cost, uncertain outcomes, and scarcity of qualified manpower required other solutions. The study called for new cost-effective models, whereby existing pools of professionals might be trained to serve troubled youngsters in a variety of settings, including the public schools.

Besides site visits to some deplorable psychiatric hospital programs (euphemistically named children's mental health programs), Hobbs learned about, or visited, state-of-the-art programs run by skilled innovators: Fritz Redl's early Pioneer House in Detroit, William C. Morse's Fresh Air Camp in Michigan, Campbell Loughmiller's camp for boys in Texas, and later, Nicholas Long's Hillcrest Children's Center and Rose School in Washington, D.C. These bright spots for children made meaningful contributions to the development of Re-ED.

In 1956, Hobbs, as part of a federal Joint Commission on Mental Illness and Health, studied promising programs in Western Europe. He was particularly taken by ideas related to the "educateur" role (Hobbs, 1982, pp. 84-86). The educateur was a professionally trained child-serving generalist whose list of competencies would include many skills found in social work, education, psychology, psychiatry, and counseling curricula.

In collaboration with psychologists William C. Rhodes and W. W. Lewis, Hobbs developed one of Re-ED's enduring hallmarks -- an ecological approach to understanding human behavior, thinking, and emotions. This approach views the child as part of an interlocking system of people and settings where lack of fit causes discordance. "Lack of fit" can be defined as a mismatch between the needs of anyone or any component in that system and the availability of resources for meeting those needs. Solutions often involve identifying an ecological inadequacy or member skill deficits, and creatively using available strengths or resources to increase "fit." This ecological approach demanded that the system be addressed, rather than solely addressing the child's symptoms. Within Re-ED, the ecological bias fostered the liaison staff function (the liaison teacher counselor) to help families, home schools, and communities minimize discord. Later, inside and outside Re-ED, similar new program job functions appeared: "case manager," skill or job coach, family care coordinator, court or school liaison.

By the early 1960s, Hobbs began to articulate a children's mental health program model that encompassed:

The teacher-counselor role as a primary change agent in the life of the child, supported by more specifically trained specialists in mental health, education, health, or other fields;

A skills and strengths focus within each child's unique ecological system, with a treatment planning approach to address enhanced skill acquisition as a vehicle for change;

Partnership with parents and other natural support systems to allow the child to be served in as normal a setting as possible, or for as short a time as possible where home removal proves necessary;

Expectation that the service model will grow and change, as knowledge expands, stimulated by research, wisdom, and energy -- with appreciation for the life expanding functions of joy.

Hobbs and colleagues asked the National Institute for Mental Health to fund a new kind of therapeutic school -- where the language of health is consciously employed and "teacher-counselors" create lively experiences for coaxing kids into health; where "students" stay as short a time as necessary, and go home on weekends with their home goals to help everyone prepare for the ultimate return; where "liaison teacher-counselors" work in partnership with families and community agents to achieve mutual goals for the child to soon return home successfully. No longer were parents to be viewed as "sources of contagion," but as responsible collaborators in making the system work.

Project Re-ED: The 1960's

In 1961, the National Institute for Mental Health funded Project Re-ED to create and evaluate two such "schools." At the first Re-ED staff Gatlinburg conference, Hobbs reported that the eight year support for Project Re-ED was the largest grant ever given to fund a demonstration project within NIMH. Over the next several years, faculty at Peabody were recruited, graduate students were selected, and two facilities opened: Cumberland House Elementary School in fall 1962 (Nashville, Tennessee) and Wright School in spring 1963 (Durham, North Carolina). They were created as research centers, staff training sites, and child and family treatment centers — treatment in the Re-ED sense. Faculty (Wilbert W. Lewis and others) were selected to provide Re-ED trainees with needed skills. Laura Weinstein joined this faculty to seize the research opportunities provided by the project for important new information.

The Peabody faculty was joined in 1965 by William and Diane Bricker, coming from the University of Oregon where they worked with Gerald Patterson applying social learning theory and behavior change techniques to help children with significant behavior problems and their families. They invited Re-ED staff and graduate students to work with them, employing these strategies with especially difficult problems of Cumberland House students (Bricker, 1967). The Brickers' efforts to extend these behavior change skills reflected a particularly Re-ED compatible view of behaviorism -- emphasizing skill based interventions directed at accelerating positive behaviors rather than decelerating problematic behaviors. Like Hobbs, they valued individual choices and skill building over punitive compliance training. Nashville Re-EDers soon shared their behavioral orientation with other Re-ED staff across Tennessee and elsewhere.

In the late 1960s Re-ED began to expand beyond the historical scope of a university based demonstration project funded primarily by the NIMH grant. The project's success and momentum created demand that the model be replicated in additional settings and with different populations. Re-ED could no longer be two small programs, serving 32 youngsters in Tennessee and 24 in North Carolina. After eight highly successful years of research and demonstration, in 1970 the project received an unqualified endorsement from the Joint Commission on Mental Health of Children, saying: *Because of its proven effectiveness, in terms of both cost per child and success in restoring the child to home, school, and community, the commission recommends that the Re-ED model be adopted and extended as one of the many needed kinds of services for emotionally disturbed children."* Re-ED was poised for growth.

Growth in Tennessee: 1965 to 1975

Between the late 1960s and the mid 1970s, the thrust to expand the Re-ED programs picked up speed. Tennessee's Department of Mental Health embarked upon the expansion of Re-ED model programs throughout the state. In addition to Cumberland House in Nashville, Re-ED Centers were established in Memphis (Sequoyah Center), Chattanooga (Moccasin Bend), and Knoxville (Riverbend School). These new programs expanded the model by serving the older adolescent population and more children with multiple and the most severely challenging problems. By the 1970s, all Tennessee's Re-ED programs were subsumed into the state psychiatric hospitals as their children's units.

In 1969, Tennessee also saw the beginning of a Re-ED compatible program when the Regional Intervention Program (RIP) opened at Peabody College, teaching mothers to help their own preschoolers learn new behaviors. Later, the mothers helped other mothers learn the same skills, requiring fewer professional staff than in traditional programs. RIP began to receive state funding, and moved into Nashville facilities. Long term followup of these children showed their significant gains maintained over years (Strain & Timm, 2001).

RIP's parent implemented programs operate throughout Tennessee today and in some agencies elsewhere.

Over the 10 year period from 1965 to 1975, Re-ED residential programs in Tennessee expanded service capability from 32 children in Nashville to hundreds statewide in the four major geographic areas of the state. Federal funding for a Re-ED Institute to promote dissemination and explore community-based adaptations provided a six year base for sharing information and hosting visitors interested in viewing Re-ED programs. One of the outgrowths of the Institute was the empirically examined and validated field test of Re-ED principles, practices, and roles in public schools (described in chapter 30). From 1970 to 1975, the Prevention Intervention Project successfully adapted Re-ED's approach to involving families and home schools as ecological change agents across Tennessee in 5 school systems. As the grant neared its end, the national validation team studying the project and its data recommended national dissemination and replication. The limited funds available, however, were of necessity directed elsewhere, helping localities meet the broad and underfunded new mandates for free public education and community-based mental health services for all children.

During this period of growth, however, several factors threatened the spread of Re-ED practices.

Unforeseen Barriers

Unexpected factors and events appeared which posed real barriers to the expansion of the Re-ED model. The first factor was the changing economic and political climate in the United States. The beginning of the 1960s heralded hope for the elimination of poverty, mental illness, and disease. By the end of that decade, the country was torn by the death of a beloved President and other leaders, along with an unpopular war in Southeast Asia. Fiscal resources and manpower which could have addressed social concerns were redirected to military priorities.

Secondly, in 1967 Dr. Hobbs left Peabody College and Re-ED, moving literally "across the street" to become Provost of Vanderbilt

University. He remained in that position until 1975 and at Vanderbilt until 1982, always a Re-ED friend and mentor but removed from the forefront of Re-ED's next generation of programs. He returned attention to Re-ED in time to complete *The Troubled and Troubling Child,* his Re-ED book published in 1982, the year before his death from cancer.

But the third, and possibly the most damaging factor to establishing Re-ED as a national model, was the move of Re-ED Centers into and under control of the Department of Mental Health in both Tennessee and North Carolina with new funding structures. The funding shift from the NIMH demonstration grant to state mental health dollars and federal Medicaid funds was a significant change -- likely both blessing and curse. The blessing of state supported program expansion allowed increasingly diverse populations of children and their families (both in terms of needs and geographic locations) to be served. But the shift of funding to federal Medicaid required extensive "medical model" reporting requirements and restricted programming capabilities. Re-ED program efficiency suffered, and creative interventions Re-ED staff had formerly used to benefit children and families were sorely curtailed by funding regulations. For example, time spent serving families was often no longer fundable for programs serving children. Now, four and a half decades later, only the original Wright School in North Carolina maintains its base of state support. Cumberland House closed, as did the original, prolific state model programs funded by mental health in Tennessee. The requirements of mental health Medicaid funding proved to be antithetical to Re-ED practices -- greatly increasing costs by substituting or adding staff with other credentials and emphasizing expensive medical model reporting.

Additional funds were not available. States were preoccupied with funding new federal mandates for both free appropriate public education for all and community based programs to serve individuals leaving state psychiatric hospitals. Nevertheless, the Re-ED concept continued to develop, serving exceptional youngsters of all ages in a variety of settings from public schools to residential treatment facilities.

Expansion to New Arenas and New Areas

Simultaneously the ideas of Re-ED grew beyond the boundaries of North Carolina and Tennessee, where later pioneers spread Re-ED's influence to other children's services.

Pennsylvania, 1967. At Pressley Ridge, people connections pre-dated the actual development of Re-ED. Nick Hobbs and Dr. John Gorsuch (Pressley Ridge Board member employed at U.S. Steel) served together in the Army during World War II. Their ongoing relationship brought Re-ED to Pressley Ridge in 1967 when staff trained at Peabody College and Project Re-ED (Bill Willis, Carol Tomlinson, and others) launched the Re-ED model in Pressley's Day School for troubled kids. In 1975, Tennessee Re-ED's Riverbend School Director, Clark Luster, became Executive Director of Pressley Ridge where he remained for the next 27 years, before retiring to consult with new Re-ED programs elsewhere. During that time, Pressley Ridge developed a number of innovative services, including PRYDE (Pressley Ridge Youth Development Extension), an early therapeutic foster care program that rapidly became a national model. They also established Wraparound services to meet the needs of many children and families in the seven states they serve.

Pressley Ridge was home to a series of other Re-ED pioneers. Deborah Simmers (now director of Wright School in Durham, N.C.), Mark Freado (Executive Director of the American Re-Education Association), Dr. Andy Reitz (Child Welfare League), and Dr. Pamela Meadowcroft (Meadowcroft & Associates, Inc.) all have long standing connections to Re-ED. Each has helped shape Re-ED's diverse modern day adaptations, having started or established their earlier professional careers at Pressley Ridge.

Ohio, 1971. In 1970, Rico Pallotta and Lee Maxwell of Cleveland, Ohio heard Charlie McDonald (Director of Tennessee Re-Education Programs) and Robert Slagle (Director of Project Re-ED Dissemination) share Re-ED ideas at a two day conference in Cleveland. After each visited Tennessee Re-ED programs, Pallotta asked Maxwell to join him in adapting the Re-ED philosophy in Ohio, forming the Positive Education Program (PEP).

Today PEP is an award winning agency in the greater Cleveland area, serving over 3,000 youngsters aged birth to 22 years and their families each year in more than fifteen service programs (providing day treatment, early childhood intervention, and community support services).

PEP's development illustrates the expanding role of families in Re-ED services, beginning by partnering with parents through liaisons and parent support/training groups. They soon moved on to create a parent support role at their central office (first, a parent education coordinator and later family services specialists). They brought the first of several parents with a child in the program onto the PEP Board of Trustees where they have been represented since. About 1987 PEP started a central office Parent Advisory Council; later, Parent Advisory Boards were formed in each center. Also in 1987, a parent was hired as the first day treatment center Family Services Aide; by 1990, parents of PEP students were Family Service Aides in each of the Day Treatment Centers. Parent satisfaction surveys became part of PEP's annual evaluation process about 1982. Every year since, well over 90% of responding parents express satisfaction with the services their children and family receive. PEP parents collect the surveys and also contact other parents for the one year follow-up studies.

Early on at PEP, Re-ED's experience was tapped by recruiting Fred West from Tennessee's Riverbend School to come to Cleveland in 1975. After five years at PEP, Fred West became the first Re-ED Director of the Centennial School at Lehigh University in Bethlehem, Pennsylvania.

Virginia, 1978. Virginia school officials from 8 school districts in the Norfolk area established the Southeastern Cooperative Educational Program (SECEP) under the direction of Robert Lawrence. Hearing of Project Re-ED, Lawrence visited Tennessee Re-ED residential programs and met early Re-ED pioneer, Bob Slagle, who sent him to see PEP's day treatment centers in Cleveland. After the PEP visit, Lee Maxwell (PEP associate director) consulted in Virginia with the SECEP day treatment schools over a period of years. In 1981 SECEP added an innovative autism program serving youngsters in public schools near their homes. After directing the autism program for a year, Judith Green became SECEP's Executive Director in 1985. The agency joined AREA as a sponsoring agency member in 1983. Since then, it has added services at the schools' requests until today SECEP is a Re-ED agency operating five programs that serve more than fifteen hundred children and youth each day.

North Carolina, 1980. North Carolina's Department of Mental Health established Whitaker School in 1980 as a sister school just 15 miles from Wright School. Their creation was in response to the Willy M. federal class action suit on behalf of older students in juvenile justice facilities who needed mental health services. Whitaker remains, like Wright School, a totally state funded, non-Medicaid reimbursable, Re-ED program.

A National Organization: AREA, 1981. With the spread of Re-ED programs and professionals, the need for a joint forum of support and communication led to a group proposing the creation of the American Re-Education Association. The final section of this chapter describes AREA's creation and development in more detail.

Tennessee, 1986. Another significant Re-ED program grew in many ways from the seeds of Tennessee Re-ED, again with Bob Slagle's consultation. In 1986 Youth Villages was formed by the merger of two small residential treatment facilities. Today, still headquartered in Memphis, the agency serves more than 11,000 children and youth each year in service programs in nine states and the District of Columbia. Youth Villages, under the longtime leadership of Patrick Lawler, has become much of what Nick Hobbs and the other Re-ED explorers envisioned 50 years ago – defining their services in terms of the needed continuum of care, and fostering kids' and families' continuing success past their enrollment in a Youth Villages service site. Youth Villages became a major provider of MST services (Multisystemic Therapy, Henggeler, 1993) to families inside and outside Tennessee. In 1996 Youth Villages made an agency wide commitment to support or find permanent families for every child and youth they serve. They consistently strive to meet that goal, and celebrate each child when the goal is attained. They describe their Re-ED journey in chapter 36.

Washington, 1992. After attending the 1986 AREA conference at UCLA, Washington state mental health staffer Mary Sarno sent area professionals to PEP's summer training in Ohio, later arranging with Frank Fecser to bring Re-ED summer training west. A core group formed there incorporated as the Washington Re-Education Association, set up their own statewide training program, and joined AREA as a sponsoring member in 1992. In chapter 28, they tell how they started a grassroots network for professionals serving troubled students in schools and agencies statewide.

Pennsylvania, 1992. When Whale's Tale executive Chris Smith recognized clear conjunctions with Re-ED's philosophy and AREA's mission, the Pittsburg program joined AREA as a sponsoring agency. After their 2000 merger with the Parent and Child Guidance Center, the new organization became FamilyLinks and maintained its affiliation, with John Amato serving on the AREA Board.

West Virginia, 1996. Stepping Stones was founded in 1975 to provide a group home for boys with special needs and has expanded services since to meet many needs for WV's troubled and troubling children. After discovering Re-ED in the early 1980's and recognizing its kindred philosophy, director Susan Fry later received an AREA mailout for the 1996 conference. Staff attended, and the program soon joined the organization as an AREA sponsoring agency.

Tennessee, 1997. Centerstone's director for children's services, (John Page, a former staff member at Crockett Academy, the adolescent program on Project Re-ED's Cumberland House grounds) and others were instrumental in seeking AREA agency membership for Centerstone when it was formed in 1997. Their actions as liaisons secured the Re-ED time capsule for AREA's protection when Cumberland House closed in 2003, and the grounds were sold.

Oregon, 2002. ChristieCare, in existence since 1859, began dramatic changes in the 1990's to serve Oregon children most in need. They consolidated residential services and placed them in the community. They worked with the many community-based services needed by the young people they served, and created other services not available in the communities. During this time, consultations from

W. C. Luster led them to the organization and AREA conferences. They joined as a sponsoring agency member in 2002, and Kit Kryger of ChristieCare is AREA's current president.

California, 2002. Charis Youth Center originated in Carol Fuller Powell's 1978 creation of a private school to adequately serve boys with special needs in the San Francisco Bay area. The U of Kansas' Achievement Place and Peabody's Project Re-ED served as models for the program. After conference attendance and AREA consultations, Charis became an AREA agency member in 2002.

West Virginia, 2004. The Youth Academy began serving troubled children in 2002. The Re-ED experienced staff who began the program under Steven Fairley's direction, maintained both their commitment to the principles and practices and contacts with Re-ED agencies. In 2004 they became a sponsoring agency member of AREA.

Texas, 2005. Cal Farley's met Re-ED through colleagues trained as Life Space Crisis Intervention trainers and through an old friend and former employee who became Pressley Ridge's chief executive. After visiting Re-ED facilities and extensive contacts, they joined AREA as an agency member in 2005. Mark Strother serves as their Board member.

The American Re-Education Association (AREA)

By the early 1980s, with the diminished leadership role of the Tennessee Department of Mental Health and Peabody College, Nick Hobbs' poor health, and the potential growth of and need for Re-ED programs, a vehicle for support of Re-ED programs became necessary. In April of 1981 a group of Re-ED pioneers attending the Council for Exceptional Children's national convention in New York City met to discuss the future of Re-ED. Rico Pallotta, Mary Lynn and Bob Cantrell of PEP in Cleveland, OH; Clark Luster of Pressley Ridge School in Pittsburgh, PA; Fred West of Centennial School in Bethlehem, PA; Debbie Simmers who was starting the Whitaker School in North Carolina; Dick Yell of Wright School; Bill Lewis and Beverly Lee Lewis from TNMH; and others were present. The group agreed to launch the American Re-Education Association (AREA).

The purpose of AREA was to: (1) serve as a source of information and communication for current and developing Re-ED programs; (2) preserve the history of Re-ED; (3) provide training and research related to Re-ED; (4) celebrate the success of Re-ED programs; and (5) recognize important achievements relevant to Re-ED, none more important than the daily work of Re-ED teacher-counselors with troubled children and families. As a result of AREA's efforts, programs and schools from the east to the west coasts are implementing the Re-ED philosophy and practices.

AREA does its work through part-time staff and a Board of Directors. Mark Freado, Executive Director, has served AREA staff since 1996. The organization's activities include technical assistance and training, a periodic newsletter, grants to teacher-counselors for special projects, and support of research and dissemination. One special effort was initiated by a Nashville group of early Re-ED affiliated professionals, forming to celebrate Re-ED's thirtieth year of operation and calling themselves The Nicholas Group. They approached AREA to serve as the organizational vehicle for submitting a proposal to produce media about the Re-ED approach. With the direction, commitment, and skilled efforts of their member Dee Newman, a Robert Wood Johnson Foundation grant was secured to produce a PBS special titled *Crisis of Care*. This video product highlighted Re-ED program services which exemplify needed components in a comprehensive system of care for children and families with mental health needs. Another special project was the 1994 reprinting of Hobbs' 1982 book, *The Troubled and Troubling Child*, when it was no longer in print after several re-printings by Jossey Bass.

Early on, Re-ED conferences became an effective and popular means of support and dissemination. Since 1982, in even numbered years there is a large national Biennial Conference attended by professionals interested in Re-ED. The First AREA Conference was held at Cumberland House in Nashville in August 1982. Larry Thompson, Director, and other Cumberland House staff hosted the conference. Clark Luster of Pressley Ridge Schools was the founding first president of AREA. Nicholas Hobbs and Campbell Loughmiller received the first and second Lifetime Achievement Awards. Other conferences which followed are summarized in Table 1.

Often in odd numbered years, smaller topical conferences are offered by an agency or group largely for their own staff, but invite other AREA members as well. For example, WAREA started their statewide summer training conferences in 1995; twice they expanded the conference and offered off year conferences in Washington state. Wright School, Stepping Stones, and others have sponsored topical conferences. This year, ChristieCare is holding an off year conference in Portland focus on *Frontiers of Healing*.

Table 1

AREA Conference Year & Site (Host Program)	AREA Presidents	Lifetime Awards
1982 Nashville, TN (Cumberland House)	Wm. Clark Luster (Pressley Ridge)	Nick Hobbs Campbell Loughmiller
1984 Bethlehem, PA (Centennial School)	Lee Maxwell (Positive Education Program)	Charles MacDonald Frank Hewett
1986 Los Angeles, CA (UCLA)	Betsy Burke (California DMH)	Mary Hobbs W. W. Lewis
1988 Cleveland, OH (PEP)	Fred West (Lehigh University)	Nelle Wheeler Nat Winston
1990 Norfolk, VA (SECEP)	Mary Lynn Cantrell (PEP)	Nick Long Laura Weinstein
1992 Pittsburgh, PA (Pressley Ridge)	Pat Lawler (Youth Villages)	Betsy Burke William (Bill) Morse
1994 Nashville, TN (Youth Villages)	Rico Pallotta (PEP)	Jeanie Williams Robert F. Cole
1996 Cleveland, OH (PEP)	Judith Green (SECEP)	Bob Slagle Rico Pallotta
1998 Norfolk, VA (SECEP)	Chris Smith (Family Links)	Mary Lynn Cantrell
2000 Seven Springs, PA (Family Links)	Frank Fecser (PEP)	Ira Lourie Robert Cantrell
2002 Nashville, TN (Centerstone)	Bridget Walker (WAREA)	Wm. Clark Luster Larry Brendtro
2004 Baltimore, PA (Pressley Ridge)	John Page (Centerstone)	Beverly Lee Lewis Matt Timm
2006 Memphis, TN (Youth Villages)	Kit Kryger (ChristieCare)	Frank Wood

A Collaborative Bent

Re-ED programs function with an interconnectedness of spirit and people, bound together by the values that define Re-ED practice. If one were to trace the creation and growth of the more than 25 member agencies of the American Re-Education Association (working in 19 states, the District of Columbia, and 3 other countries) serving approximately 30,000 children and families each day, the trail would lead to Nicholas Hobbs and the early Re-ED explorers at Peabody College, Wright School, and Cumberland House. Each of AREA's Sponsoring Programs is described in some detail in chapter 37.

A substantial group of Re-ED explorers and pioneers have devoted their careers and much of their lives to the work of Re-ED. Seldom, if ever, has a successful Re-ED program been the result of an agency's search for the Re-ED model or reading written material. Instead, the expansion and success of Re-ED programs has evolved from person-to-person learning and the Re-ED principles. Over the years Re-ED programs expanded into new geographic and program areas through this network of relationships. Many of these programs succeeded – and helped the troubled and troubling children and youth they served to succeed as well. We hope to continue this helping network for each other and for other interested programs and individuals, expanding our ability to help through more written and visual media which increase our accessibility. If you have any inclination to do so, please consider joining us.

References

Bricker, D. D. (Ed.) (1967). *Cumberland House Studies in Behavior Modification*. Nashville, TN: Department of Mental Health, State of Tennessee.

Hobbs, N. (1982). *The troubled and troubling child*. San Francisco, CA: Jossey-Bass.

Hobbs, N., Dokecki, P., Hoover-Dempsey, K., Moroney, R., Shayne, M., & Weeks, K. (1984). *Strengthening families*. San Francisco, CA: Jossey-Bass.

Henggeler, S. W. (1993). Multisystemic treatment of serious juvenile offenders: Implications for the treatment of substance abusing youths. In L. S. Onken, J. D. Blaine, & J. J. Boren (Eds.), *Behavioral treatments for drug abuse and dependence: National Institute on Drug Abuse Research Monograph 137*. Rockville, MD: NIH Publication No. 93-3684.

Strain, P. S., & Timm, M. A. (2001). Remediation and prevention of aggression: An evaluation of the Regional Intervention Program over a quarter century. *Behavioral Disorders, 26*(4), 297-313.

Wm. Clark Luster, MEd, is currently retired and consulting part-time with children's programs.
cluster148@aol.com

36

Growing Up Re-ED

Prepared by Connie Mills

When Patrick Lawler first heard about Re-ED, he was the administrator of a small residential treatment campus that employed a handful of people and annually helped 40 children. More than 20 years later, Youth Villages has grown to touch the lives of more than 11,000 children and families each year through the work of more than 1,400 employees in 45 locations in 33 cities across nine states and the District of Columbia. From one program in 1986, Youth Villages now operates a nine-program continuum of services – all built on a Re-ED foundation.

"Re-ED is the philosophical base for everything we do at Youth Villages," Lawler says. "In a way, it's like our religion, the mindset that we use to view the children who come to us and what is possible for them – despite their challenges. Re-ED is what gives kids hope and what allows our counselors and staff to truly believe that success is achievable for every child and family who come to us."

Recently, Lawler sat down with many of the officers and directors who played a part in the history of Youth Villages to remember the ways the Re-ED philosophy influenced the growth and development of the organization.

Introduction to Re-ED

Patrick Lawler, *chief executive officer*: "I read a great quote recently: 'I'm not young enough to know everything.' When I came to Youth Villages in 1980, I was young enough to think that I knew it all. I thought I had a vast amount of knowledge about kids – not about running a company, a nonprofit – but about dealing with troubled kids. I talked to many directors of local programs to get advice about running an organization, but not so much about taking care of kids – because I thought I knew how to do that already.

"I had worked at Tall Trees (a youth development center) during college before joining the Memphis and Shelby County Juvenile Court as a probation counselor. In our first few years, we basically did the kind of things that they did at Tall Trees. We had two group counseling sessions each week, individual counseling once a week and tried to get the kids to bed every night, have time to read a book, have three meals a day and get them to school."

A chance meeting with Bob Slagle, one of Nicholas Hobbs' original teacher-counselors, changed his way of thinking. Slagle told Lawler about Re-ED and invited him to the second conference of the American Re-Education Association in 1984 at Lehigh University in Pennsylvania. The meeting opened Lawler's eyes to new possibilities in helping children.

Lawler: "I realized that I really didn't know very much about the most effective ways to help emotionally troubled children. I fell in love with the whole idea of Re-ED. It was the first time I had really thought about developing a system or a model to use in treatment.

"I also had the opportunity to see and meet young counselors and teachers who were working in a wide variety of programs: residential, group homes, wilderness programs, foster care, day treatment programs and schools. I was just amazed. I came home to Memphis and began using Re-ED."

Learning More

Over the years, Re-ED conferences and the help of Re-ED members and sustaining organizations played an important role in how Youth Villages worked with the children in its care.

Bob Slagle was Youth Villages' first training consultant. He eventually came to the Memphis campuses once each month, helping develop the Youth Villages Re-ED programs by working with teacher-counselors and leadership. Ralph McDaniels, an early Re-EDer, also helped with training at Youth Villages and specifically assisted when the organization expanded for the first time, taking over a Middle Tennessee residential program.

Lawler: "We learned more about Re-ED by attending conferences. At a conference at Pressley Ridge's Wilderness School in 1987, we spent three days in the wilderness camp. It was the first time I had really spent time in a Re-ED program, and I saw that Youth Villages really wasn't doing Re-ED properly. I thought that the only way to move forward was to get the top members of our team out to a Re-ED program so that they could see for themselves."

Tim Goldsmith, *chief clinical officer***:** "We actually went out and visited other Re-ED programs and spent days there learning. We would observe and actually sit in during the whole group process and watch 'pow wow.' We stayed in the camps, slept in the tents, really got involved. When we came back, we got it. We understood what Re-ED was really all about. At that point, we reworked everything."

Lawler: "We have revised and improved our programs many times through the years. We re-evaluate, choose to do things differently, find a more effective, better way."

In the late 1980s, leadership at Youth Villages began noticing a change in the severity of problems children faced who were referred to the organization for help. Youth Villages had to change to help these children with more severe emotional disturbances.

Lawler: "We had been helping mainly 'street kids,' children with neglect or delinquency issues, children from the inner city. We began to see children who had serious emotional and behavioral problems. We wanted to find ways to help those children. Early on as an organization, Youth Villages survived because we were willing to take the kids no one else wanted – the children with the most serious challenging behaviors. We've continued to do that, and one of the primary reasons that we've been successful with these changing populations is our commitment to Re-ED – our belief that every child can be helped.

"In the 1980s, we were seeing kids with sexual behavior problems, and we went to the state and said that we wanted to begin a program to help those children. At that time, the state was sending most of those kids to correctional facilities. But state leaders knew that the children didn't need to be there, that they caused problems in that setting and were being taken advantage of by older youth."

Facing Long Waiting Lists

Lawler: "Our only continuing complaint from our major customer, the state of Tennessee, was that we couldn't take more children. We had long, long waiting lists. Openings were infrequent because it was rare for children to go home from our programs."

Following Pressley Ridge's lead, Youth Villages began tracking children who had been discharged from the program to see how they fared after going home. Although the research was not scientific, it was still disturbing. Counselors who called the families at about a year post-discharge found that many children who had completed the residential program successfully at Youth Villages were not able to maintain success in their own homes. Instead, many came back to Youth Villages, ended up in other out-of-home treatment programs, or worse, in the juvenile corrections system.

Lawler: "Our kids just were not doing very well when they went home to their families. Our success rates were somewhere around 55 to 60 percent – which is about the rates that residential-only programs still record now."

Youth Villages counselors at this time did not have many opportunities to work with families. Unlike the Project Re-ED five-day programs, where children went home to their families every weekend, children receiving treatment at Youth Villages only went home on infrequent passes. Treatment was almost completely child-focused.

While there were problems for kids who went home to their families after treatment at Youth Villages, other children never got the chance to go home – or to grow up in a home-like setting – at all.

Goldsmith: "[These other children] had no biological family, and, at that time, there was no foster care in Tennessee for our children – for kids with emotional and behavioral problems. When the state put out a request for proposals for treatment foster care, we decided to start a program of our own."

Once again, Youth Villages reached out to other Re-ED organizations for help in developing the new program.

Goldsmith: "We went first to the Re-ED group and began

looking at foster care programs run by Re-ED organizations. Pressley Ridge and its director, Clark Luster, were influential in Youth Villages' [foster care] program development."

Lawler: "We had the opportunity to start up large – to help 120 children immediately in the new program. Most everyone agreed that it was better to start smaller and build up to help more children. Clark was very supportive. I remember him saying that, sometimes, non-profit organizations move too slowly: 'Maybe, we should be more aggressive when the need exists,' he said. He made us feel like we could do it. Clark helped us lay out an initial plan for the new program and gave us manuals for their foster care program, PRYDE – Pressley Ridge Youth Development Extension."

Goldsmith: "To me, this was the beginning of the Youth Villages sense of urgency when it comes to helping more children, to starting needed programs. The idea that if we're going to do something, we're going to do it quickly and in a large way."

Lawler: "But we never started a program 'big' intentionally. When we have done that, it's because that's the way the opportunity was presented."

Goldsmith: "Yes, but we choose to take the initiative. Many times, we were the only organization that saw an opportunity and expressed interest."

Cliff Reyle, *chief officer for human resources, information technology and communications*: "It's that 'can-do' spirit that Youth Villages has. When I tell our story to business people, they assume that we planned our growth. In recent years, we've helped 20 percent more children every year, but there has never really been a plan. The secret of our growth has been simple. We respond to op-portunities, and we focus on growth in areas where children's needs aren't being met. The organization made a strategic decision to provide the help to children that others couldn't or weren't providing. That's one of the key points about Youth Villages: we help children and families that other organizations don't want to deal with or don't know how to help."

The foster care program was Youth Villages' first step away from its core residential programs. The next step, also in 1993, began when Lee Rone, who had just completed his MBA from Vanderbilt University, conducted a survey of child welfare professionals in the rural West Tennessee counties adjacent to Youth Villages' residential campuses in Memphis. The survey determined that the greatest regional need was for intensive home-based help for the families of troubled children. There was no program of that type in Tennessee, so Youth Villages decided to develop one. In a strategic search for a program model, Youth Villages discovered Multisystemic Therapy (MST). Youth Villages was the first agency to use the therapy on a large scale outside of clinical trials. Today, the Youth Villages Intensive In-Home Services Program reaches a broader population than standard MST, including children in the juvenile justice, child welfare, and mental health populations.

Putting the Focus on Families

Lawler: "Our adoption of MST represented a complete change in our thinking about the best way to help troubled children. For many years, the prevailing wisdom in child welfare was that child-focused therapy and out-of-home placements were the best approaches. MST offered us scientific evidence that intensive, family-based therapy can be a major part of the solution for many seriously troubled teens and their families. Before, most children's mental health providers saw the family as the 'problem.' We now know that the family is the solution.

"If you read Re-ED, if you read Nick's book, he talks about the family systems, but all of the early Re-ED programs were residential-based or school-based, and there wasn't an emphasis on keeping children at home, providing treatment in the home."

[Editors' note: Unusual for the day, however, all the early Re-ED programs provided liaison roles whose specific function was to work with families; the goal of the 5 day residential programs was to work toward the child's return home within 4 to 6 months. Hobbs saw parents as true experts on their children, rather than as sources of contagion. Other Re-ED programs developed in the 1970s specifically served parents and used

parents to train and support other parents. Some of these family-focused programs are described in Part III. From a Re-ED perspective, MST is highly valued and has never known how "Re-ED" it is.]

Goldsmith: "Our programs weren't even like most Re-ED residential programs. Those projects [the Project Re-ED centers] were in essence [operating like] boarding schools; children lived on campus and went to school during the week and then went home on weekends where they could practice what they had learned [and where family members were practicing what they had learned as well]. We knew that we had to do much more with the families than just send the kids home. The families of our children need much more intensive work."

Lawler: "It was important to us that MST was consistent with Re-ED. We found out that Dr. Scott Henggler, who developed MST, had studied Nicholas Hobbs' work and knew the background of Re-ED. He was familiar with many of the people who had worked on Re-ED [ideas] in the early days in Europe [when Hobbs made international visits]."

Goldsmith: "We saw immediately that MST was a good complement to Re-ED. MST was more research-based, had the clinical, scientific studies to back it up and had a lot more structure than Re-ED did. But the Re-ED philosophy was completely compatible with the MST treatment model."

Lawler: "Hobbs said: 'In Re-ED, we work not with individual children but with ecosystems, of which a particular child is the defining member. However, standardized procedure for classification of ecosystems is not yet available.'

"With MST, we now had at our disposal the standard, the structure that Hobbs sought for working with children and families. MST fills in the blanks in Re-ED." *[Editors: MST has indeed filled in some important blanks, but sadly, a service-based system for classifying ecosystems is still lacking.]*

Hughes Johnson, *director of performance improvement*: "Both MST and Re-ED emphasize the importance of positive and caring relationships, structure, learning – in school, through activities, and in daily life through positive peer relationships, individual problem solving, and communication skills. In a residential setting, the teacher-counselor is the primary agent for change. In our intensive in-home program, it is the parents and family members.

"In our training for employees, we identified five points where Re-ED and MST intersect: 1. Successful living is healing; 2. Ecological paradigm; 3. Positive attitudes and adventures; 4. Metaphorical imperative; 5. Creativity.

"Nick Hobbs emphasized the importance of ecology and that therapy be focused on the interactions between children and other significant people in their lives. He understood that children's behaviors make sense in the context of their life situations: what MST calls finding the 'fit.' The MST model provides concrete ways to assess and intervene in each 'system' surrounding the child. That's what Hobbs would call the ecosystem.

"Hobbs realized that institutions tend to create the very problems they are supposed to alleviate. This is the paradox of the cure causing the illness. In today's world we know that removing a child from his home and placing him in a facility with other kids can institutionalize the child and motivate antisocial behavior. Focusing on the principles of Re-ED helps organizations steer away from practices that cause that sort of unintentional negative consequences. Finally, Hobbs believed in creativity: in searching for individual interventions for each child. The teacher-counselor must create and innovate to bring Re-ED to life. In MST, the family counselor is charged with doing whatever it takes to help a child and family find success."

Lawler: "Re-ED's principles and the central ideas of MST became the framework for Youth Villages in many ways."

Youth Villages began developing its MST-derived intensive in-home program in 1993, starting the program before any children had been referred to the program.

Lee Rone, *chief operating officer*: "Referral sources would say, 'That sounds interesting,' but not refer a child to us. Finally, a few referral sources gave us a shot, and we got started. But the program struggled.

"A grant from the Plough Foundation, a Memphis philanthropy, provided start-up funding for the new program, particularly important because we hired counselors before we had cases. We peaked at about 50 cases in the summer of 1995 and then dropped down to about 15, and we still had a complete staff to pay. Then, the state declared a financial crisis, and a new governor came in."

Lawler: "That was the turning point."

Crisis Forces Change

Lawler: "In the summer of 1995, we got word from the state of Tennessee that they were going to cut our funding – and funding for all the children's mental health programs in the state – by 10 to 15 percent. At the same time, they were interviewing managed care companies, and we knew that if they hired a managed care company, there would probably be another 15 percent cut to pay for their fees.

"We started a critical discussion with state leaders. We showed them the outcome data that we had accumulated in the first few years of the in-home program, and they liked what they saw. In the course of about 90 days, a handful of our directors sat at a table and built the Youth Villages Continuum of Care, a system designed to provide the most effective care to each child in the least restrictive setting. We integrated all of our programs. Instead of operating separately, each program – residential, foster care, home-based – would work together to help the child and family.

"The continuum approach allowed us to help more children for the state of Tennessee at a lower cost to them. We had been paid about $185 per day for residential treatment; we agreed to a set fee of $120 a day for children in our continuum. The new continuum would allow Youth Villages to place a child in residential treatment, treatment foster care, a group home, or in our in-home program. We were given the freedom to move children through our continuum and to work with families after they returned home. We had to move kids to a less restrictive, less expensive treatment setting within our continuum – or we would have gone broke. We had convinced the state that they shouldn't be buying beds; they should buy outcomes, successful outcomes. We envisioned a continuous treatment approach that ended with the child living successfully in his own home or an adoptive home.

"As part of the continuum, we agreed to take all the children the state referred – not just the easy cases. We also guaranteed them 80 percent success rates at one-year post-discharge. We knew that we could do that based on the data that we had generated during the first 18 months of operating the in-home program.

"In short, we told the state we would take the hardest kids, treat them for less money and guarantee that they would be successful."

Lawler: "Although it sounded great, in about six or seven weeks, we had a disaster on our hands. Our staff were fighting one another – even in court! There were actual cases of Youth Villages staff coming before a Juvenile Court Judge and arguing against one another as to whether a child should go home: foster care vs. in-home. The foster care staff would argue that the kids should stay in foster care; the family counselors would argue that the child should go home. It was chaos. Both of those programs were fighting the residential staff who didn't think kids were ready to leave the campuses at all.

"Finally, in December of that year, I ended the war. We started over. We rewrote every job description. We changed people's jobs, reallocating staff from residential and foster care to the in-home program. We reduced staff in residential. We trained every employee in MST. We even added a value to our Mission and Values: 'Children are raised best by families.' Before, we believed that we were in the business of raising other people's children. It was a big move – the big change – that made Youth Villages what it is today."

Goldsmith: "We had to let some people go. There were foster care counselors who just didn't believe that kids should go home to their parents. They believed that the children were better off in foster care. The same thing was true for residential. We had staff there who philosophically believed that they were in the business of raising those poor children and keeping them safe from their horrible families.

"You could see that attitude in the initial assessments of the children in residential treatment. The residential staff evaluated the kids and concluded that about 25 per cent could go home. The family counselors came in and assessed the same children and said that 75 per cent could go home. It was a totally different way of looking at children – and their parents. In the end, we got about 65 percent of those kids home."

Johnson: "That was a time of real cleansing. People who didn't believe in the new approach had to leave. And everyone who was hired new bought into the changed Youth Villages philosophy."

Goldsmith: "We had an all-staff meeting and had them break into small groups and talk about how they could work together to get kids home. After that, we began to move forward. We believe that children should be with their families. It's our number one value. We staked the financial viability of the organization on it.

"We went to every office and did presentations to the staff to let them know why we wanted to do things differently. Sonja Schoenwald from MST Services went with us and answered all the hard questions people had."

Rone: "Sonja was very direct, very blunt, about what works and what doesn't. She'd talk to an audience of residential treatment and foster care staff and say: 'Where's the data that shows that what you are doing works? There's no data.' That was part of our attempt to acculturate. We did the MST supervision model for everyone, for foster care, residential. We changed our entire consultation process."

[Editors: This is an excellent illustration of how poorly Re-ED professionals have disseminated the controlled research findings from its early days and how few resources have been found or committed to research in Re-ED services ever since. AREA is striving to remedy both of those omissions, as some of the chapters in this book describe, largely in Part VII.]

Goldsmith: "We changed the whole treatment approach – the way we do treatment plans. It was an organizational change; it was consistent with Re-ED but a much more structured approach to treatment" *[compared to what had been ongoing in this program].*

Lawler: "We set up the continuum as a three-year pilot project. About six months into it, the state adopted our approach and told all the other providers in the state that they had to be continuum providers or take another cut in fees. Most of the large providers followed our lead within a few months."

It was apparent almost immediately that the foster care program as constituted had to change in order to function as part of the continuum. Under the new approach, foster parents would have to be able to help children who were "stepping down" from residential care and had significant mental health issues and problem behaviors. Youth Villages changed to a more structured treatment foster care program that put more emphasis on providing support to foster parents and helping children improve their behavior.

Goldsmith: "Before we changed the program in 1996, the average age of the child in foster care was 11; we had very few teenagers and very few children who were stepping down from a more restrictive setting. Our foster parents then were really just babysitters. To make foster care a viable part of a continuum built on the concept of 'step downs,' our foster parents had to do more. We needed to create a program that was child and family focused and provided more training and support for foster parents.

"In building the new program, we used every principle of Re-ED. In traditional Re-ED *[the short-term, 5-day residential treatment centers]*, the teacher-counselor is the major catalyst for change in the life of a troubled child; in our foster care program the foster parents fill that role, but work as part of a team of professionals focused on helping a child overcome functional deficits.

"Included in the team are the child, foster parents, birth parents, a child counselor, behavior specialist and clinical supervisor. Our program also adapted a family-systems approach. In helping the child, counselors work in every system around a child – the school, peer group, neighborhood and community — analyzing how each component affects the child's behavior and planning interventions that change what Nick Hobbs might view as the child's 'ecology.' Counselors use the principles of Social Learning Theory and Cognitive Behavior Therapy in helping the child learn to identify the drivers for behavior and make changes.

"The use of the Re-ED philosophy and our own model, developed based on best practices, has allowed Youth Villages to help children stepping down from our residential campuses move toward success. We have been able to find and train parents who can help these children. In 2000, we began an adoption program at Youth Villages. We have found that the highest percentage of adoptive parents for our children have come from our own foster care program."

Although Re-ED was most influential in the development of Youth Villages' new programs, it also was an underlying influence on the organization's development in other key areas.

Re-ED's Impact on Employees

Lawler: "Before 1986, 1987, we hired house parents to work with the children in residential treatment; most of them were in their 50s and 60s. We had a couple of counselors who were younger, but they were even older than the typical counselor at Youth Villages now.

"When I visited Re-ED organizations, I saw many young people – just out of college – working with the troubled children. We began moving that way. We found that the young teacher-counselors needed more guidance because of immaturity, but they did have energy, enthusiasm and a willingness to learn.

"Re-ED also influenced my early management practices. In the early 1980s, all we talked about was Re-ED. We read the books; we studied; we practiced; we hired consultants; we talked about how things worked. I began implementing the Re-ED philosophy in management. I thought if the whole concept of structure, education and democracy is working with kids, why don't we utilize some of the same concepts in management!

"We started having structured activities and offering more for staff. I began to get the staff more involved in making more decisions, instead of making all the key decisions myself. If we had an employee who needed to improve, we phrased it in positive terms. Youth Villages became a very positive, affirming place to work, and we continued that over time.

"One of the most important parts of our employee relations was developing a mission and values that we all could use for guidance in our everyday decisions, and in setting the strategic course of the organization. If you think back on our history, choosing the Re-ED treatment philosophy was our first step in becoming a better organization."

Re-ED's Influence on Technology

Lawler: "In 1989, I was invited to an AREA board meeting in the Tampa area. Tampa Bay Academy offered free accommodations, so I stayed there. I walked around and talked to the kids and the staff. Everyone there had computers on their desks, and an electronic information system. All the children's records were there. So, when Tim started talking about moving to an electronic system, I had already seen how one functioned in a Re-ED organization."

Reyle: "At that time, we recognized that if we were going to do any kind of meaningful research, we had to move away from the paper format. Tim had a vision for that. When I joined [Youth Villages], he was already looking for ways to get those records in electronic form. With data in an electronic form, we'd be able to do research, to analyze outcome results on different programs. Because we made the right moves early, we've had things in place as we've grown."

Goldsmith: "Our technology system has allowed Youth Villages to develop a strong research department. In the last nine or 10 years, we've invested an enormous amount in research and the outcome evaluation process. And we don't do outcome evaluation just to say that we do it. The data we develop is actively used to improve our programs and services."

Re-ED and a Culture of Learning

Lawler: "Around 1985, 1986, we were at a Re-ED meeting, and Mary Lynn Cantrell was sitting next to me at dinner. She asked, 'What have you been reading lately?' No one had ever asked me that question before, and I said, 'Well, I think I read an article in *Sports Illustrated* on the way up here on the airplane.' All of the

Re-ED people were so smart, so committed to learning as much as possible about how to best run their organizations, how to best help children. I became committed to continual learning, too.

"Over the years, I've read many books that have changed Youth Villages. One of the most important was '*Demystifying Baldridge.*' Two of the four people who wrote the book live in Memphis. So, we ended up hiring them to consult and work with us. Our customer service focus dates from this time."

Reyle: "Customer service and the training is woven into the Youth Villages culture. I think it's unique that we deal with these things broadly across the entire organization. It's not easy because our counselors and staff have multiple customers on many different levels. But it has had a lasting impact on the organization for people to think of their work in total-quality-customer-service terms."

Goldsmith: "We pursued a United Way Award for Total Quality Management, which we later received. We spent a lot of time on these issues, and it did drive us to begin the whole measurement piece. It was the genesis of the type of performance measurement that we do now – which is a hallmark of Youth Villages."

Johnson: "And the fit for me is that most of the things we now measure relate to customer satisfaction issues. We measure many performance issues and meet every month to go over our numbers. We watch our numbers because we know they affect the way our customers feel and think about us, and what they require of us."

Goldsmith: "There is actually a customer service value in our Mission and Values statement. That's unique for a nonprofit. People often value treating their patients well, but they don't really think of them as customers. Customer service drives much of what we do. Our staff still go out and do customer service, and we still call it customer-service calls, not 'talking to the people who fund us.'"

Johnson: "We keep a scorecard that shows how we're doing in many different areas, and it's reviewed each month. We constantly raise the bar. We have Core Indicators and an annual planning process. We're always striving to do our jobs better, with an eye toward improving the outcomes for the children and families we help."

Lawler: "The drive toward measuring our performance and constantly improving systems has allowed us to have good systems in place that we have used to begin new programs and to replicate our programs in other locations. It doesn't mean that we learn something important at every monthly review of our Scorecards, but we know where our problems are and have good systems that allow us to improve our processes and prevent some problems from ever occurring. That's critical when you're dealing with the safety and treatment of children."

[Editors' note: Because of their leadership, this staff has been able to use corporate terminology without losing their focus on children and families. They reap the benefits of useful corporate strategies while maintaining a view that places people first, well above the bottom line - a critical and admirable characteristic in a non-profit 'company.' Few manage that feat so well.]

Re-ED in a Growing Organization

Lawler: "Adopting the Re-ED philosophy was the first step Youth Villages took toward becoming a better organization, to becoming the organization it is today. People think of us as always being entrepreneurial, growth-oriented, but that really isn't true. Our growth has always been very Re-ED — focused on helping meet the needs of children who are not receiving the help they need to live successfully."

Every Youth Villages expansion has been in direct response to the needs of children; often it is spurred by the desperate needs of one child. A boy named Brian led the organization to develop intensive residential treatment; Nate, abandoned by his mother and suffering from Down syndrome, was the impetus for the Youth Villages family-based program for children with developmental disabilities. Youth Villages' drive to help more children each year goes back to a teenager named Phillip.

Lawler: "Phillip touched Youth Villages at about the time that I was first learning about Re-ED. A board member called and said: 'I have a friend whose son is having problems, will you talk to her?' The mother brought her son to see me, and he was in trouble and needed help. He was depressed, using drugs. He needed a residential placement, but we were full. I encouraged the mother to call community health centers, even gave her the right telephone numbers. A few weeks later, I called to see how things were going, and the boy seemed better.

"A month went by. Then at 7:30 one morning that board member walked into my office. He sat down and looked at me, and I could tell he wasn't happy. Then he asked me if I remembered Phillip. Of course I did.

"He killed himself last night," the man said.

"I felt really horrible about it. Later, I started thinking that we had to expand the program and try to help more children. We were able to help only 40 children at that time. Only 40. When Youth Villages was formed in the merger, we could help 80. But there were still so many children on the waiting list. Every time I saw that list, I thought about Phillip.

"That's the one thing that we as Re-ED organizations need to remember. There are so many children who have serious emotional and behavioral problems who aren't being helped by philosophically sound programs — or they are receiving no help at all.

"We feel driven to help more children each year. It's not a business decision; it's a moral imperative."

Connie White Mills, BA, is Public Relations Manager at Youth Villages in Memphis, Tennessee
connie.mills@youthvillages.org

37

Re-ED Programs and the American Re-EDucation Association

Mark D. Freado

From its idealistic beginnings in two residential programs in Tennessee and North Carolina in 1962, Re-ED has endured, evolved, and expanded. Since 1982 the American Re-EDucation Association (AREA) has been the formal body through which Re-ED continues to grow and thrive. The headquarters of the national association is located in Westerville, OH.

The programs described on the following pages are the sponsoring members of our association; they operate services in 17 states, the District of Columbia, and three foreign countries. Sponsoring members of AREA actively support the association; their executives comprise the board of directors. Staff members from sponsoring agencies actively contribute to the growth and development of Re-ED by participating on AREA committees for training, research, and communication.

Re-ED programs touch the lives of tens of thousands of children, youths, and families each year through a wide array of services. Some member agencies continue to operate residential programs with on-site educational components; others also work in public school settings, or as independent day treatment programs. Still others run therapeutic/ treatment foster care, intensive in-home, or family preservation programs, and many offer case management services. The principles and practices that form the core of the "Re-ED Approach" have proven to be responsive to an increasingly diverse range of needs.

Re-ED agencies sometimes operate services developed elsewhere which are consistent with its core beliefs and practices. Identity issues are minimal since Re-ED was never a set of manualized procedures describing a tight service structure. Re-ED is more a set of essential beliefs with related practices around which any number of service structures could be organized.

Member agencies have histories ranging from nearly two centuries old to as recent as this decade. Several charter member agencies have Re-ED histories pre-dating the inception of the American Re-EDucation Association. Other organizations have become sponsoring members much more recently. AREA agencies may be large, multi-state, and international. They may be single programs working in urban or rural settings; or they may be grassroots organizations made up of like-minded professionals from throughout a community or region. In the spirit of re-inventing Re-ED every day, these organizations adapt their services to meet the changing needs and challenges of the children, youth, families, and communities they serve.

Sponsoring Member Agencies include:

Cal Farley's, Amarillo, TX
Centerstone, Nashville, TN
Charis Youth Center, Grass Valley, CA
ChristieCare, Marylhurst, OR
FamilyLinks, Pittsburgh, PA
Positive Education Program, Cleveland, OH
Pressley Ridge, Pittsburgh, PA
Southeastern Cooperative Educational Programs, Norfolk, VA
Stepping Stones, Lavalette, WV
Washington Re-EDucation Association, Lynnwood, WA
Whitaker School, Butner, NC
Wright School, Durham, NC
Youth Academy, Fairmont, WV
Youth Villages, Memphis, TN

Other organizations join AREA as associate members. These members include those with extended commitments to Re-ED who benefit from our communications, training events, and conferences. They may also include organizations that have recently decided that Re-ED provides the philosophical foundation that will help them develop their services more effectively. These agencies work in some of the same and an additional two states.

Associate Agency Members include:

Beacon School, Greenville, TN
Children's Home of Wheeling, Wheeling, WV
Elwyn, Elwyn, PA
Grandfather Academy, Banner Elk, NC
Helen Ross McNabb Center, Knoxville, TN
Kitsap Mental Health, Bremerton, WA
Northwest Children's Home, Lewiston, ID
Rutherford County Schools / Special Education, Lavergne, TN
Sipe's Orchard Home, Conover, NC
Woodhouse Academy, Milford, CT
Youth Enhancement Partnership, Olympia, WA

Individual memberships in AREA are available for professionals who may not be affiliated with an AREA member agency or who may work independently but value being affilitated with an organization that operates from a strength-based perspective for clients. AREA's membership roles include individual members who have been part of our association since its inception, or those who were former employees of AREA member agencies who want to remain connected to the organization.

We welcome anyone who is a Re-EDer, even if the term is new to them. If you are one of us, you will recognize yourself in what we believe and what we do. Join us.

For information about membership in AREA please contact:
Mark Freado, MA, Executive Director
American Re-EDucation Association
259 N. State Street, Suite 200
Westerville, OH 43086-1331
Phone: 614-783-6314
Fax: 775-261-5462
Email: mdfreado@re-ed.org
Or visit us on the World Wide Web at: www.re-ed.org

Cal Farley's

Dan Adams, LMSW
President & CEO

Cal Farley's, 806-372-2341
1-800-687-3722 • Fax: 806-372-6638
600 W. 11th, Amarillo, TX 79101
www.calfarley.org

Locations: Cal Farley's helps at-risk boys and girls realize their full potential through programs, services, and activities provided at no charge to parents and without fees from government agencies. Sites are located at multiple locations across Texas. Families residing in the United States are eligible for services.

Mission: The Cal Farley organization provides professional programs and services, in a Christ-centered atmosphere, to strengthen families and support the overall development of children.

Provenance: Cal Farley's is a non-profit organization. All programs and services are provided at no cost to children and families. This has been made possible through generous donations from individuals, corporations, and foundations across the country.

Staff and Services: In 1939, our founder, Cal Farley, began working to provide services to children and families. His mission of giving a child a "shirttail to hang onto" is the historic foundation of ongoing program and service development. Today our staff team provides residential services to more than 300 young people in two programs: Cal Farley's Boys Ranch and Cal Farley's Girlstown, U.S.A. Many more families and children are served annually through after-care and community-based services.

Cal Farley's is a non-profit organization dedicated to helping children become well-balanced, responsible, and productive. All of our programs and services have been made possible through generous donations from individuals, corporations and foundations across the country.

Residential Programs

Our modern residential campuses are located in the Texas Panhandle region. Boys and girls reside in nurturing, structured group home environments. They are engaged in a variety of academic, vocational, spiritual, and adventure programs designed to help them become responsible and resilient individuals. The Boys Ranch campus provides services to boys and girls from pre-school through high-school. Girlstown, U.S.A. cares for girls ranging in age from 10 to 18. All residents receive medical, optical, dental, and emergency services as needed. Capacity at the Boys Ranch campus is 275 children in residence. The average length of stay for residents who graduate from the Boys Ranch High School is four years. For the 56 girls residing at Girlstown, the average length of stay is four years for those girls graduating from high school while in residence. For those who return home prior to graduation, the average length of stay is 1.5 years. Our campuses provide a variety of services for families with children in residence. Families benefit tremendously from parenting workshops, guidance pertaining to goal attainment, and in-home services. Casework staff provide an initial point of contact for youngsters when they first come to Boys Ranch or Girlstown, often resulting in a lasting and trusting relationship.

Model of Leadership & Service

The Cal Farley Model of Leadership and Service outlines six critical areas of need for all children and youth in care: *safety, belonging, achievement, power, purpose,* and *adventure.* A young person whose needs are consistently met over time is more likely to adopt the spiritual and moral values that imbue the Cal Farley's environment. These values are the bedrock of lifelong resiliency.

Educational Services

The campus of the Boys Ranch Independent School District (BRISD), which is fully accredited by the Texas Education Agency, is contiguous to and integrated with the Boys Ranch campus. BRISD provides a full K-12 academic and vocational curriculum. Students have the opportunity to develop healthy attitudes toward education and are encouraged to achieve their full potential. Programs are provided for students having difficulties in regular classrooms.

Similarly, the Academic Center at Girlstown provides a motivating environment for girls who require a self-paced program, especially those who require assistance in being reintegrated into mainstream classrooms. The mainstream classroom environment, located at local public school campuses, enables students to enjoy the normative opportunities for academic and social development.

Cal Farley's joined the American Re-Education Association in 2005.

Centerstone

David C. Guth, Jr.
Chief Executive Officer
Robert Vero,
President and Chief Operating Officer
John Page,
Vice President for Child, Adolescent and Family Services

Centerstone, 615-463-6627
Fax: 615-463-6603
PO Box 40406, Nashville, TN 37204-0406
www.centerstone.org

Locations: Centerstone provides behavioral healthcare in 67 facilities throughout the Middle Tennessee region.

Mission: Centerstone's mission is to create and sustain the highest quality behavioral health services for championing individuals, families, and communities.

Staff and Services: Centerstone, a non-profit organization, helps children, adolescents, adults, and seniors who suffer from a myriad of behavioral health challenges, along with their families. We are Tennessee's largest, and the nation's ninth largest, behavioral healthcare organization providing a full range of mental health services, substance abuse treatment, and related educational services for people throughout the Middle Tennessee region. Centerstone's Child and Family Services serve approximately 8500 children and families each year through the work of our 298 staff.

Mental Health Counseling Services (Outpatient) - All ages

Professional staff provide counseling/therapy services for individuals, families, couples, and groups needing help with depression, stress, anxiety, divorce, anger management, grief, and/or other concerns. Overall services include therapy, case management and medication management for clients in the Middle Tennessee region.

Family Centered Services - Ages 11-18

Adolescents in state custody for out of home treatment of severe behavioral problems reside in group homes or foster homes which serve as both temporary placements and primary treatment program sites. The overall goal of treatment is to return the adolescent to their home and community as soon as possible. The principles of Re-Ed and the Circle of Courage guide all aspects of these services to youth and family. Assessments, treatment planning, counseling, medications (as needed according to medical evaluations), and case management services assist in reunifying the adolescent with family members. If reunification is not possible, then program staff assist with adoption services or transition to independent living.

Preferred Options – ages 18 and under

Preferred Options is an "intensive family preservation service" for children and adolescents diagnosed with a serious emotional illness who have not benefited from treatment in a less intensive service setting, such as outpatient therapy. Services are provided in the home and community with the goal of 1) improving interpersonal and family functioning, and 2) reducing likelihood of inpatient psychiatric hospitalization or entry to state custody. Preferred Options works to increase a family's ability to solve their own problems and advocate for themselves.

Project BASIC
(Better Attitude and Skills in Children) - Ages 5-8

This school-based program serves elementary school children (grades K-3). It is designed to enhance the students' interpersonal skills, as well as helping to identify possible SED children.

Project STAR
(Standing Tall And Resilient) - Ages 10-16

Project STAR is a school-based prevention program that serves middle and high school aged youth. The program, funded by the Tennessee Department of Health and the Metro Nashville Health Department, focuses on helping students and their families prevent the development of problem behaviors, such as substance use, violence, and premature sexual activity. Project STAR has three components: facilitating social learning of small groups using curricular training, service learning through community-helping activities, and parent involvement.

Regional Intervention Program
(RIP) - Ages 6 and younger

This nationally recognized, parent-implemented program helps parents learn and work directly with their own children where there are concerns regarding a preschool child's behavior or development. Experienced parents who have completed RIP, along with professional staff, successfully provide training and support to newly enrolled families.

Responsible Parenting Project
Females, ages 12-18

The program provides education and support to teenage parents of children, age birth to four years. The 8-week course provides a supportive environment, with classes during school hours, in-home visits, and a 24-hour "Warmline."

School-Based Mental Health Counseling Services
Ages 18 and under

On-site counselors help students cope with their emotional or behavioral problems. The program combines individual and group counseling with parent and teacher consultations. Priority is given to students in special education classes and severe or moderate behavioral intervention classes, or those at risk of entering those classes.

A Brief History of Centerstone

For over 50 years, Centerstone has provided professional behavioral health services and advanced programs to people who suffer with mental illness and emotional problems. Centerstone consists of 67 facilities in 22 Middle Tennessee counties and is the largest behavioral healthcare organization in the state. We were formed in 1997 through an affiliation, later followed by a merger in June 2000, of five prominent community mental health centers: Dede Wallace Center and Luton Mental Health Services (each based in Nashville), Harriet Cohn Center (based in Clarksville), Columbia Area Mental Health Center (based in Columbia), and Highland Rim Mental Health Center (based in Tullahoma). Once the merger was complete in July 2000, we began a transition period to allow our clients, employees, and communities to adapt to our new, unified operation and identity. During this period, individual centers operated jointly but under their own names as affiliates of Centerstone. At this time, all of our facilities officially adopted the name Centerstone. Some of our locations still retain a reference to their original names at their site, in honor of the individuals after whom they were named. These facilities include the Dede Wallace Campus, Ella Hayes Center, Frank Luton Center, and Harriett Cohn Center.

Centerstone has been a sponsoring organization member of AREA since 1997.

Charis Youth Center

Carol Fuller Powell, EdD
Executive Director

Charis Youth Center, 530-477-9800
Fax: 530-477-9803
714 W. Main Street, Grass Valley, CA 95945
www.charisyouthcenter.org

Locations: Troubled and troubling adolescents, and their families, are served in the Sierra Nevada Foothills.

Mission: Charis Youth Center provides therapeutic, residential, educational, and vocational services to students with learning disabilities and emotional challenges from age 13 to 22 years. This special needs population includes adolescents and their families; adolescents in transition to lesser restrictive environments through the Transitional Housing Program; young adults in independent living, 18-22 years of age, with case managers; and young adults in re-entry, preparing and linking to community support agencies for their transition into society as productive and contributing citizens.

Charis is committed to partnership with families and their community as a valuable colleague and resource. Charis works to expand services to meet the growing and changing needs of youth and their families. Charis seeks to hire, train, and develop the most talented and competent people available.

Staff and Services: Each year Charis' more than 50 staff serve an average of over 40 youth. Services include:

Residential Treatment Services

The Residential Treatment Programs (California's Rate Classification Levels 12 and 14) provide 12 to 18 month care and treatment to youth with emotional challenges. Youth referred to the program generally have histories of multiple placement failure. Referrals come from Departments of Mental Health, Probation, Social Services, and Education throughout California. Youth placed in the program receive individualized treatment consisting of a structured behavioral plan implemented by residential counselors and mental health workers at a staff-to-youth ratio of no more than 1 to 2 in the RCL 14 program and 1 to 3 in the RCL 12. The residential program is goal driven and outcome based for maximizing skills and progress. In addition, mental health services are provided through individual, group, and family therapy by licensed/registered mental health professionals and mental health staff. Ongoing medical, dental, hearing, and eye treatment, as well as periodic psychiatric and psychological evaluations, are available for each youth. The objective of the program is to prepare the youth to return to either a less restrictive environment, their family's home, or independent living.

Educational Services

Charis Youth Center's Non-Public Special Education School provides a 12-month/235-day school year program. All teachers hold a Specialist Credential and have had experience working with the emotionally challenged population. The student to staff ratio is 2 to 1, which allows for intensive individualized and small group instruction. This ratio helps staff remediate the difference between a student's current functioning level and their potential performance level. The educational psychologist and special education teachers use standardized tests and direct assessment to determine the present functional level for developing an Individual Educational Program (IEP), curriculum placement, progress and performance monitoring, and instructional planning. Curriculum is geared to each student, using a multi-modality and level approach with supportive materials to help achieve success. The State Frameworks and Standards are used in developing approved curriculum for High School Graduation Credits. Charis works with the local school districts to administer all performance tests including the High School Exit Exam/Project. In addition, there is an Individualized Transitional Plan (ITP) for each student. All students work with the treatment team and faculty to develop their Positive Behavioral Plan (PBP) using the Functional Analyses and Day Treatment Program data.

Mental Health Services

Charis Youth Center provides comprehensive specialty mental health services that include Day Treatment Intensive, Day Rehabilitation, Medication Support, and Mental Health Services. Charis' Mental Health Services provide a thorough assessment of each youth's mental health status, the development of a comprehensive treatment plan and interventions, and an integrated approach to alleviating symptoms related to the youth's identified DSM IV diagnosis. Adolescents placed in Charis' program have typically experienced numerous placement failures in less restrictive environments. For many of these youth, the mental health interventions they receive through Day Treatment and Day Rehabilitation Programs, Medication Support Services, and Mental Health Services are critical to their success in a community-based program, and aid in avoiding placement in a more restrictive setting, such as a Community Treatment Facility or acute hospital. Charis' Mental Health Services are designed to provide interventions which reduce the symptoms of the youth's mental disability and improve or maintain his/her functioning consistent with the goals of learning, development, independent living, and enhanced self-sufficiency.

A Brief History of Charis Youth Center

In 1972 a young mother and regular education teacher of home economics was confronted with a personal and professional dilemma. Carol Fuller Powell, founder and Executive Director of Charis Youth Center, realized that the educational system was unable or unwilling to provide adequate services to her son with special needs. By 1978 her frustration turned to passion and a determination to do something about it. She began to provide school services for boys in a room donated by a church in Hayward, CA.

In 1984 Charis was incorporated, changed from a private school to a licensed non-public school, and began to expand into residential services by opening the first group home. Charis Youth Center treatment programs were developed to serve youth and families challenged by emotional, economic, and systemic problems that could not be effectively served in other settings.

In the San Francisco Bay Area, the agency grew to a staff of more than 110, with 5 residential sites, a large Non-public School, a Day Treatment Program, and a high school based mental health program. In 1997 the organization relocated to its present location in the Sierra Foothills serving adolescents from various California counties, including Placer County, Nevada County, Sacramento County, Yuba/ Sutter County, and neighboring communities. Two empirically based programs were used to develop the Charis Youth Center operations. One program was Achievement Place (1972) developed at the University of Kansas. The other program carefully studied and used to develop Charis Youth Center was Project Re-ED (researched by Weinstein, and reported in 1974).

Charis Youth Center became a sponsoring organization member of the American Re-EDucation Association in 2002.

ChristieCare

Lynne Hume Saxton
Executive Director

ChristieCare, 503-635-3416
Fax: 503-697-6932
P.O. Box 368, Marylhurst, OR 97036-0368
www.christiecare.org

Locations: ChristieCare is based in Marylhurst, Oregon, with satellite locations in Portland, Oregon City, and Lincoln City. Children and families across Oregon also receive services in their respective home communities.

Mission: ChristieCare creates and delivers mental health solutions that promote enriched, full lives for children and families.

Staff and Services: ChristieCare offers an array of treatment programs for children and families experiencing mental health challenges. A dedicated staff of over 200 specialists (including teacher counselors, therapists, psychiatrists, registered nurses, and special education teachers) provide care to approximately 1,000 children each year.

Intensive In-Home Support and Stabilization

This program supports children and families living throughout Oregon by creating environments in which families and their natural supports identify their needs. Professionals and families work together to meet these needs so that the family can thrive with only the natural support of family and friends. ChristieCare partners with Options Counseling Services of Oregon, Inc. to deliver this program.

Treatment Foster Care

Children placed out-of-home receive treatment foster care from highly trained foster parents, backed by daily clinical support from ChristieCare and 24-hour access to professionals and other resources. These professionals team with the child's family and community to deliver care, helping children transition to less restrictive settings.

Therapeutic Day School

In partnership with the Clackamas Education Service District, ChristieCare operates a therapeutic school for children who require a behavioral treatment component to their education. This program, which emphasizes family participation, focuses on developing academic and emotional skills for transition to less restrictive educational settings.

Children's Receiving Center

The center offers short-term 24-hour emergency shelter care for children removed from homes suspected of abuse, neglect, or criminal activity. By intervening to prevent unnecessary placements, this center provides case managers crucial time to plan and locate the best placement for a child or sibling group; it keeps sibling groups intact, provides immediate health assessments for each child, maintains school attendance and regular activities as much as possible, and involves family and community in treatment and placement decisions.

Assessment and Evaluation Services

This program focuses on each child's strengths and needs by medical, educational, psychosocial, recreational, and psychiatric assessments. Families and caregivers are part of all assessments and treatments. We provide intensive care coordination for safe and effective transition of children back to their home communities.

Crisis and Planned Respite

This effective alternative to out-of-home placement is offered to families when a child's behavior/other stress factors produce a crisis or a crisis threat in the home. Designed for a length of stay less than 72 hours, this program enables a child and family to disengage from stressful interactions by providing a safe, supervised place for the child until the home stabilizes. This service is available 24/7.

Psychiatric Residential Treatment Services (PRTS)

Residential Treatment

This program provides a full range of intensive therapeutic services including individual, group, and family therapy; skills training; special education; medical services; and therapeutic recreation. Each child's treatment plan focuses on building self-esteem, trust, and positive behavioral patterns. Children are reintegrated into communities through volunteer service and/or vocational and work experiences.

Secure Residential Treatment

This program provides a secure, therapeutic setting for children whose suicide ideation, self-harm behaviors, or other factors threaten their safety. Children and families receive intensive psychiatric and therapeutic services matched to their needs. A strength-based individualized plan builds skills and provides children with opportunities for successful, community based experiences.

Stabilization and Transition Services

This secure setting provides services for children whose more acute safety needs may require one-on-one staffing, additional medical support, or other individualized support.

Subacute Care

This short-term, intensive treatment program provides crisis stabilization and psychiatric assessment to children requiring more intense containment and care than psychiatric residential treatment. Its objective is to prevent psychiatric hospitalization, rapidly resolve crisis situations, and transition children to a lower level of care.

Alaska Native & Native American Services

In partnership with tribal agencies and guided by their representative advisory council, this program provides culturally responsive psychiatric residential treatment for Alaska Native and Native American youth and families on a wooded 42-acre site along the Clackamas River. Treatment focuses on emotional, spiritual, cultural, educational, and physical needs in collaboration with children, families and communities.

A Brief History of ChristieCare

In 1859 the Sisters of the Holy Names of Jesus and Mary founded ChristieCare to provide long-term care and education for children who had lost their parents or whose families were otherwise in crisis. In the 1960s, ChristieCare became a secular, independent agency as its mission shifted to serving children with mental health challenges. Operations passed to a professional staff governed by a Board of Directors. Two residential cottages were built, and an intensive care unit opened in 1979 to meet the needs of Oregon's most troubled children.

Innovations in the 1990s marked dramatic changes at ChristieCare. After earning accreditation by the Joint Commission on Accreditation of Healthcare Organizations in 1991, the agency continued to expand services by opening a secure unit and a group home. Since 2003 ChristieCare has opened a short-term emergency shelter facility, a therapeutic day school, a sub-acute program, and several community based services across Oregon. The agency continues to collaborate and partner with others to serve children as they move from one level of care to another, ultimately helping them succeed in their homes, schools, and communities.

ChristieCare has been a Sponsoring Agency of AREA since 2002.

FamilyLinks

Fred Massey
Chief Executive Officer

Family Links, (412) 661-1800
Fax: (412) 661-6525
250 Shady Avenue, Pittsburgh, PA 15206
www.familylinks.org

Locations: FamilyLinks serves children, families, and individuals throughout southwestern Pennsylvania.

Mission: FamilyLinks is a caring link joining resources of families and communities to build hope, health, and strength. Its vision is that communities will care, families will succeed, and individuals will reach their full potential with FamilyLinks as a primary partner and catalyst for change.

Staff and Services: FamilyLinks is a non-profit social service agency. It provides a broad array of human services for children, families, and individuals. These include mental health; alcohol and other substance abuse treatment; developmental disability services;

crisis intervention; emergency shelter; residential treatment; independent living, housing assistance and community support services; youth and family development programs; adult community services; and school-based prevention services. The 475 FamilyLinks staff serve 10,000 children, families, and individuals throughout southwestern Pennsylvania each year.

Mental Health Services

Wraparound Program.

Mental health services are coordinated for children with severe emotional disabilities to assist in supporting the child so that s/he can succeed in daily living at home, at school, and in the community.

Family Based Mental Health Program

Interventions, support services, and therapy in the home, school, and community are provided for consumers/families experiencing significant emotional/behavioral disturbances.

Mobile Crisis Intervention Services

Through emergency face-to-face triage, Mobile Crisis Workers intervene and stabilize intense and sometimes unimaginable crises, with scheduled follow-up visits to ensure stability and linkages with necessary supports.

Alcohol and Other Drug Treatment Services

Outpatient Treatment Services

Specific counseling and interventions are geared to the needs of the individual and the family as they enter treatment and move through recovery.

Day Treatment Services

Intensive outpatient and day treatment are provided for chemically dependent women, particularly mothers, pregnant women, and their families.

Family Treatment Center

This residential treatment program for substance dependent mothers and pregnant women, ages 18 and older, and their children, operates within an intensive therapeutic environment.

Youth and Family Development Services

Adolescent Semi-Independent Living Program

This service provides supervised independent apartment living for youths, ages 15-18, together with meals, counseling, education, and life skills training.

Children's Treatment Center

This residential treatment facility for young males, ages 11-15, focuses on reunification with the family while insuring client safety, educational achievement, and mental health family support.

Youth Emergency Shelter Services

This program provides short-term shelter, assessment, treatment planning, and a comprehensive school program for neglected and abused youth, in conjunction with the child welfare system.

McKeesport Teen Parent Treatment and Shelter Program

This bridge housing program for teen mothers and pregnant teens, ages 15-18, helps teen parents achieve competencies in basic parenting and life skills.

RESPOND

This residential treatment program provides services for youth who are dually diagnosed with mental health and developmental disability needs.

Mental Retardation Services

Independent Support Coordination

This service coordinates support for persons with mental retardation, including their families in the assessment, planning, referral, and advocacy processes.

In-Home Support Services

Coordination of Home and Community Based services allows individuals with developmental disabilities to live in the least restrictive environment possible.

A Brief History of FamilyLinks

FamilyLinks was established in 2000 as a result of the merger between The Whale's Tale and Parent & Child Guidance Center. Both the Parent & Child Guidance Center and The Whale's Tale were originally (PCGC in 1956; TWT in 1970) configured with similar family-based visions of providing a comprehensive and long-term approach to serving troubled children, adults, and families. From a client perspective, a merger of the two agencies resulted in the most comprehensive collection of prevention, intervention, and rehabilitation services for Western Pennsylvania's residents. From an agency perspective, a merger meant that the two agencies were able to build capacity, eliminate duplicative services, and consolidate two administrations into one.

The Whale's Tale had been a Sponsoring Organization of AREA since 1992, and FamilyLinks maintained that association after the merger.

Positive Education Program

Frank A. Fecser, PhD
Chief Executive Officer

PEP Central Office, 216-361-4400
Fax: 216-361-8600
3100 Euclid Avenue, Cleveland, OH 44115
www.pepcleve.org

Locations: PEP provides services throughout Northeast Ohio.

Mission: Positive Education Program helps troubled and troubling children and youth learn and grow successfully through the Re-ED approach, blending quality education and mental health services in participation with families, schools, and communities.

Staff and Services: PEP's more than 600 staff members impact the lives of 3,000 children and their families each year. Services provided include:

Day Treatment

The Re-ED philosophy provides the framework that creates a therapeutic environment where there are expectancies for normal, healthy behavior, where competence is stressed, and where energy is focused on finding and building strengths that promote positive growth. Individual and group meetings, lessons, and activities are used to teach new ways of perceiving, thinking, feeling, and behaving. Individualized programming builds functional skills and academic competence that promote cognitive and social-emotional growth and development.

Positive Education Program's *Day Treatment Centers (DTCs)* serve school-age children diagnosed with serious emotional disturbance in an integrated educational and mental health environment. PEP's ten centers – *Eastwood, Greenview, Harbor, Hopewell, Midtown, Phoenix Place, Phoenix Point, West Bridge, West Shore, Willow Creek* - are located across Northeast Ohio and are able to serve children with multiple disabilities. These centers annually help over 700 students from more than 50 school districts.

While all ten centers specialize in working with children and youth with serious emotional, social, and behavioral challenges, four have additional specialties:

Phoenix Place and *Phoenix Point* specialize in serving children and youth with significant cognitive delays.

Harbor serves children and youth experiencing significant developmental disabilities and a considerable impairment in communication; the majority have diagnoses within the autism spectrum.

Midtown Center for Youth in Transition is designed to meet the specific needs of troubled teens transitioning to adulthood.

Community Support

Connections provides case consultation, care management, and community support services to children and youth who have been diagnosed with a serious emotional disturbance, are multi-system involved, and either removed or at imminent risk of removal from their families and communities. The overwhelming majority of Connections' 300 clients each year are involved with the Department of Children and Family Services and/or the Juvenile Court.

Tapestry, a community-wide initiative currently funded by a large federal grant, is designed to bring more support to more families, thus reducing their reliance on the County's public systems. Among Tapestry's primary goals are increased voice and choice from parents and other caregivers who support these children, with an emphasis on services provided by local neighborhood-based organizations and the more traditional service providers. PEP is the first mental health agency to pilot Tapestry.

Early Childhood Services

PEP operates two *Early Childhood Centers (ECCs)*, one on Cleveland's east side and one on the west. Centers serve families with young children from birth to kindergarten age with serious behavioral difficulties, by providing short term educational and therapeutic services to the child and the family. Professional staff serve as teachers and consultants to families, believing that support for the adults in a child's environment will positively influence the child's ongoing development. Trained parents teach newly enrolled parents the skills that enable them to help both themselves and their children.

PEP is a Cuyahoga County provider of *Help Me Grow On-going Home Visiting* which provides support and services to promote the well being of children birth to three who are at risk for developmental delay, abuse, or neglect.

Day Care Plus provides consultation services and technical assistance to child care providers and support for families with children experiencing difficulties in the child care setting. Working with staff, parents, and all agencies involved, Day Care Plus Consultants develop a seamless and effective program for children experiencing social, emotional, and behavioral difficulties.

Consultation and Training for Schools and Programs

PEP Assist is a consulting and training service provided to schools and programs, designed to teach best practices for working with at-risk children. Serving more than 40 schools each year, PEP staff develop innovative programs and staff development opportunities so that children with severe and challenging behaviors may be served successfully in their school of residence. Since 1981 PEP has operated a *Summer Institute*, providing summarized information on the Re-ED philosophy and practices employed in PEP services.

A Brief History of PEP

In April of 1970, Rico Pallotta and Lee Maxwell separately attended a conference in Cleveland; later they discovered both were impressed by the message of two early Re-EDers on how to reach troubled children. Dr. Pallotta secured funds to take several multidisciplinary groups of Cleveland professionals to Tennessee to visit the Re-ED programs, hoping to bring Re-ED ideas to Cleveland.

In 1971, PEP was created at the request of area school districts to provide consultation and training to help them with their most challenging students. It quickly became apparent that districts needed specialized centers dedicated to meeting the educational needs of their most troubled and troubling students. In 1975, PEP opened its first Day Treatment Center, providing a blended educational and mental health program. In 1976, PEP opened its first Early Childhood Center. Other services followed, as the community requested assistance.

PEP has grown in size and reputation. Locally and nationally, PEP has been recognized for its excellent programming. In 1996, the U.S. Department of Education identified PEP's Day Treatment Centers as one of six model special education programs in the country. In 2000, the U.S. Departments of Education and Justice recognized PEP as a model program providing intensive interventions to troubled students. In 2003, Positive Education Program won the Woodruff Prize, a local honor bestowed upon an agency demonstrating excellence in mental health care.

Positive Education Program was one of the founding organization members of the American Re-EDucation Association in 1981.

Pressley Ridge

B. Scott Finnell, PhD, LCSW
President and Chief Executive Officer

Pressley Ridge, 412-872-9400
Fax: 412-872-9478
5500 Corporate Drive, Suite 400, Pittsburgh, PA 15237
www.pressleyridge.org

Locations: Headquartered in Pittsburgh, Pennsylvania, Pressley Ridge's therapeutic programs and services are offered in Pennsylvania, West Virginia, Maryland, Ohio, Virginia, Delaware, Kentucky, Texas, the District of Columbia, and internationally in Portugal and Hungary.

Mission: To improve the adjustment and achievement of children and youth with troubling behaviors through effective programs that focus on all aspects of their lives; to lead in the development of innovative programming through evaluation, research, and outcome measurement; to champion initiatives to improve the system of care for children, youth, and their families

Staff and Services: Pressley Ridge's 1,000+ employees serve 4,000 children and families annually.

Residential Treatment Services

Pressley Ridge's Pennsylvania, West Virginia, and Ohio facilities are the primary locations for the residential treatment services. These programs serve children and youth who require out-of-home care and treatment. Residential sites vary from single homes to campus and wilderness-based programs. By developing strong, therapeutic relationships and nurturing children's feelings, we ensure that children and their families have the skills and supports necessary for successful living. These include the development of problem solving and communication skills. Family involvement, including liaison services, regular family conferences, and supported home visits, are heavily emphasized. Individualized and peer group support activities are also encouraged.

Treatment Foster Care

Pressley Ridge Treatment Foster Care concentrates on creating a sense of permanency while developing individualized treatments within professionally trained foster parents' homes. The intensity of services is adjusted to children's needs, allowing them to remain in the same family setting as their situation improves. Treatment foster care is an alternative to intensive residential treatment. In addition, treatment foster care provides a continuum of care services including: emergency shelter short-term care and longer-term placement, respite services, step-down, and adoption services. Treatment foster care is provided in each state served by Pressley Ridge.

Educational Services

The children and youth referred to Pressley Ridge have serious emotional disturbances and diagnosable mental illnesses. Students are required to attend classes regularly, which also serves to provide more consistent exposure to treatment. Providing integrated educational and mental health services in this manner, helps students meet their goals of less troubling behavior, more effective social functioning, and improved academic performance. In addition, Pressley Ridge provides specialized educational services for emotionally disturbed deaf children and for children with autism. Pressley Ridge operates the DaySchool, three other free-standing educational sites, and provides education as part of the residential programs.

Community-based Services

Pressley Ridge community-based services are designed to keep seriously troubled children at home, in their schools, and with their families. Many interventions are available to help families learn to maintain their integrity and manage everyday problems. Community-based services focus on strengthening, preserving, and maintaining the family unit. Pressley Ridge provides short-term and intensive services with a goal of decreasing the needed level of support provided to the child and family, as the scope and purpose of the services provided vary. These services utilize a values based, ecological approach to treating youth within the context of family and community life inclusion.

The Pressley Ridge Institute

The Institute provides training, consulting, and applied research to teach professionals how to provide effective treatment for children who have mental, behavioral, or developmental disabilities. The Institute's clinical training programs, centering on Life Space Crisis Intervention (LSCI) and Response Ability Pathways (RAP), teach staff members how to provide effective, values based treatment to troubled children. Leadership training, using the Situational Leadership II model, is available for managers. Specialized consulting services can assist with clinical program planning, leadership issues, and meeting accreditation standards.

Pressley Ridge International (PRI)

Pressley Ridge International has flourished as a training program to connect professionals who work with troubled children around the world. More than 100 treatment specialists from 23 countries, including South Africa, Botswana, Argentina, El Salvador, Brazil,

Cambodia, Malaysia, Portugal, Belgium, Greece, Czech Republic, Hungary, Ukraine, Bulgaria, and Russia have been part of this training program thus far. Pressley Ridge also has experienced multi-year success with the Pressley Ridge Portugal Training Center. As a result of those efforts, PRI established a training hub in Hungary called the Central and Eastern Europe Training Center and Demonstration Site.

A Brief History of Pressley Ridge

Pressley Ridge is a 175-year-old nonprofit children and family services organization offering services to troubled and troubling children. Created from a merger of two prominent Pittsburgh orphanages, Pressley Ridge traces its roots back to 1832. Those orphanages, the Protestant Home for Children and the Pittsburgh and Allegheny Home for the Friendless, merged in 1969. At the time of the merger, a study was carried out under the direction of Nicholas Hobbs, PhD, then Provost of Vanderbilt University. The results of the study led the newly blended Board of Directors to adopt the Re-EDucation philosophy as the model for the therapeutic services provided for troubled children.

Pressley Ridge is fully accredited by the Council on Accreditation (COA), a national body that verifies that the organization's services meet the highest standards of care for children and families.

In 1981, Pressley Ridge was one of the founding organization members of the American Re-EDucation Association and continues in this leadership role today.

Southeastern Cooperative Educational Programs (SECEP)

Judith N. Green, PhD
Executive Director

SECEP, 757-892-6100
Fax: 757-892-6111
6160 Kempsville Circle, Suite 300B, Norfolk, VA 23502
www.secep.net

Locations: SECEP serves children in Virginia's Hampton Roads Cities: Chesapeake, Franklin, Isle of Wight, Norfolk, Portsmouth, Southhampton, Suffolk, and Virginia Beach.

Mission: SECEP functions as a regional public school serving school districts in Virginia's Hampton Roads Cities by providing programs for the children with special needs. Guided by a solid commitment to the growth of children, comprehensive educational programming is provided for a diverse population of students with challenging needs through high quality instruction within a safe and nurturing environment.

Staff and Services: SECEP employs over 700 professional and classified employees to serve more than 1500 special education and alternative education students. SECEP manages eight centers for the Re-ED/Alt-ED programs, and operates over 100 ACP/EBICS classrooms located in public school buildings throughout the eight Hampton Roads cities. The REACH program operates in two sites with 12 classrooms.

The Re-ED Program

SECEP's Re-ED Program is a day school for students identified with serious emotional disturbance. The program follows the principles of Re-ED developed at Peabody College. It emphasizes the development of each child's social and academic competencies through a structured school program designed to enable students to be successful. Career and Technical Education Services in horticulture and culinary arts are available to selected students. Re-ED staff consider it crucial to work with the family, the neighborhood, community service agencies, and the school to which the child will return. SECEP's six Re-ED Schools are located in Chesapeake, Norfolk, Portsmouth, Suffolk, and Virginia Beach. Each site serves both children and adolescents.

Educational & Behavioral Interventions for Challenging Students Program (EBICS)

The EBICS Program serves students who exhibit aggressive and/ or severe disruptive behavior and are diagnosed with mental retardation. The program utilizes a functional, structured, skill-oriented curriculum. The major program goal is to prepare students to function as independently as possible in the most complex and least restrictive community, domestic, vocational, and recreational environments. Each classroom, with four to six students, is staffed with a certified special education teacher and a school/community trainer or a teaching assistant. A principal and support staff provide supervision, direct support, and overall program development to each of these classrooms operating in local school buildings spread across the eight Hampton Road cities.

Tidewater Regional Alternative Education Program (TRAEP)

The Tidewater Regional Alternative Education Program (TRAEP) provides academic instruction to at-risk children who have been expelled from school, who have had multiple, long-term suspensions, or who are in need of a transitional placement when returning from a state learning center. Special education services are provided by certified special education teachers to students who need both alternative education and special education. These students receive educational services at four alternative school locations: Norfolk, Portsmouth, Virginia Beach, and Suffolk.

Instruction is adjusted to the individual learning needs of the students and focuses on a core curriculum of Social Studies, English, Math, and Science, adhering to the Standards of Learning (SOL) established by the Virginia Department of Education. Students in grades 6-12 receive academic services, with credit track classes available for grades 9-12. Students also receive daily pro-social skills training. In their group settings, students model, role play, and practice a wide range of pro-social skills necessary for re-integration into their home-school setting.

Autistic Children's Program

The Autistic Children's Program provides services for children and youth who have autism, autism spectrum disorder, or a disability that is related to autism (preschool to age 22). Established in 1981, the program uses structured, skill-oriented training tailored to the student's strengths and weaknesses. The Autistic Children's Program currently operates classrooms in seven cities. Each class of six to seven students is staffed with a certified teacher and teacher assistants. An individualized educational program (IEP) is developed for each student. The principal, support staff, and teachers implement the IEP as a team.

Raising Expectations and Abilities for Children with Complex Health Needs (REACH)

Established in 2004, the REACH Program provides high quality instruction with integrated assistive technology, speech therapy, and occupational and physical therapies. The goal of the program is to maximize the potential of students with complex medical needs who live in residential settings. Currently, the program operates in a hospital and a home for disabled children. The program strives for close integration between the child's home, school, and residential facility in meeting goals identified in each child's individualized educational program (IEP). Emphasis is on building meaningful relationships and active learning, with qualified team members fostering an environment that provides safety, security, dignity, and respect for the students.

A Brief History of SECEP

In 1978, the school systems of Chesapeake, Franklin, Isle of Wight, Norfolk, Portsmouth, Southampton, Suffolk, and Virginia Beach established the Southeastern Cooperative Educational Programs (SECEP), with financial assistance from the Virginia Department of Education.

The organization provides a formal structure through which the participating school systems can plan and operate programs for children with special needs. SECEP is a public body established in accordance with the Code of Virginia which provides for the establishment and operation of jointly owned schools.

SECEP has been an organizational member of the American Re-EDucation Association since 1983.

Stepping Stones

Susan Fry
Executive Director

Stepping Stones, (304) 429-2297
Fax: (304) 429-8365
P.O. Box 539, Lavalette, WV 25535
www.steppingstonesinc.org

Locations: Stepping Stones is located in Wayne County, 20 minutes from Huntington, WV, and serves children from a variety of West Virginia regions.

Mission: Stepping Stones helps kids realize their potential:

We believe in the resiliency of kids. We want our kids to develop an "I can" attitude. Building on their strength; we challenge each child to reach for their potential physically, emotionally and spiritually. Our message is Simple...Kids Can.

We go the extra step. Our kids come first...no exceptions. We do not give up on kids. We stick. At Stepping Stones we fight for our kids, no matter what.

566

We believe in family and community. We believe that the family role is an integral part of the child's treatment. It is simply not good enough that a child does well while he is with us; the true measure of success is gleaned when he returns to his home and community successfully.

Kids need a safe, stable, and structured environment. A safe home and nurturing adults are critical to a child's well-being. Regular meals, a time to play, a time to study, knowing that there is someone who cares enough to say "no" and mean it... rituals are both comforting and necessary in a child's development.

We appreciate the joy in every day. A sunset, a joke, a shared meal. We believe it is healthy to identify the positives in every day; to laugh at ourselves and to have fun together. We believe that every good day is a stepping stone to the morrow.

Education is a must. We support the child and his opportunity to be successful in the public school setting both academically and socially. Education is the first step; everything else will then fall into place.

WV kids and families deserve our best. We believe that challenge can be motivating for our kids, staff, and Program. We look at challenge as an opportunity for growth. We are responsible for adhering to the highest standards in child care; everyday, in every policy; during every phone call....

Staff and Services: Stepping Stones generally employs twenty staff who provide services to about sixty children and their families each year.

Residential Services

Stepping Stones is a Level One/Level Two Therapeutic Residential Program. Services are geared toward male youths, ages 11-17 years, who may have experienced a multiplicity of behavioral and/or emotional traumas. Youths must be able to function within a highly interactive Group Process environment. The Home first prioritizes care for youths from Wayne, Cabell, Lincoln, and Mingo counties and then youths from West Virginia's Region II.

Transitional Living Program

Stepping Stones provides Transitional Living Services for six youths (male or female) in scattered site apartments. Eligible youths must meet the criteria set forth under the WV Transitional Living Program. Each youth must be referred from Region II. Stepping Stones works with each youth to locate community living settings that are accessible to educational and vocational opportunities.

Parent-Education Program

This grant-funded service targets at-risk families in Wayne County. Stepping Stones works closely with Wayne County Department of Health and Human Resources and holds weekly group sessions throughout Wayne County.

The Next Step Program

The Next Step is a family-centered, community focused program designed to minimize out-of-home care placements. The Next Step is a "residential without walls" program implemented via evening and weekend programming. The Next Step is an alternative to out-of-home care, enabling youths to remain/return to their home settings with a safety-net of professional/parent partnership and support. The Next Step is comprised of three distinct levels of programming. The youth is placed in one of the three following Programs based upon his/her identified treatment needs. Service intensity reflects the youth's individualized needs:

The Intensive Community Prevention Program (ICP)

Supportive Community Reintegration (SCR)

Supportive Community Aftercare (SCA)

Family Partnership

The Next Step targets families for intervention according to their individual strengths, resources, and circumstances. This strength-based approach is critical in promoting the maintenance of the natural family; the family will be included in every step of the treatment intervention during programming. Emphasis is focused on family reintegration,

with all efforts made to support the natural family in their community environment. A cohesive community system will allow the youth and family to enhance coping skills and have opportunities to "practice" these skills in a supportive environment.

A Brief History of Stepping Stones

Founded in 1975, Stepping Stones was born in an era of immense social welfare growth in West Virginia. From a small seven bed group home that provided very basic residential care to its now highly intensive, nationally accredited therapeutic treatment approach for youth and families, Stepping Stones has continued to be a resilient program dedicated to best practice.

Overarching all Stepping Stones programs is the ecological focus of the Re-Ed model. A chance attendance at a conference about Re-ED in Gatlinburg, TN in the early 1980's introduced the philosophy to Stepping Stones. That experience provided a basis for our foundation. Even though *The Troubled and Troubling Child* influenced every nuance of Stepping Stones' programming, it was not until 1996 that the American Re-Education Association found Stepping Stones through a conference mailing, and consequently, that Stepping Stones found a home.

Re-ED fit. The agency understood that you do not *make* a Re-ED Program; you find Re-ED or Re-ED finds you. Stepping Stones absorbed Re-ED's strengths-based approach and fashioned programs that were engaging, relevant, and focused on resiliency. Using Hobbs' descriptions as a guideline, Re-ED shaped our service delivery, unified the kids, families and staff, and promoted the identification of individual and program outcomes.

Washington Re-EDucation Association (WAREA)

Mary Ann Lyons
Services Coordinator

WAREA Coordinator, (206) 230-5292
Fax: (425) 482-2392
PO Box 37 , Lynnwood, WA 98046-0037
www.warea.org

Locations: WAREA is a state-wide association that serves professionals who work with troubled and troubling children and youth across the state of Washington.

Mission: Our concern is for the welfare of troubled and troubling children and youth in the state of Washington. Our purpose is to promote, encourage, and support the use of Re-EDucation principles and practices in a variety of settings and modalities.

Staff and Services: WAREA is a grassroots organization composed of teachers, mental health professionals, researchers, and administrators throughout Washington state who are committed to integrating Re-ED principles and practices in their work helping both troubled and troubling children and youth, and the professionals who serve them. We represent both education and mental health services, as well as teacher education programs. WAREA members serve students, families, and professionals in 15 agencies, school districts, and institutions of higher learning throughout the Puget Sound Area. Since 1992 we have provided training, consultation, and technical assistance to over 2000 "teacher-counselors."

The North Star Elementary PATHS (Parents and Teachers Helping Students) Program

This special education program for children with emotional or behavioral disabilities is located in a general education elementary school and has a strong focus on experiential education.

Coweeman Middle School

Re-EDucation is integrated into all aspects of the special education program at this rural middle school through the supports provided by its special education resource teacher.

Madrona Day Treatment Program at Kitsap Mental Health

This elementary and secondary day treatment program is located on the campus of a residential hospital for children and youth with the most significant behavior and mental health needs. It serves students from the residential program as well as those referred by surrounding school districts.

Behavior Facilitation and Support Specialist

The District Behavior Facilitator provides consultation and training to staff in all the elementary programs for students experiencing Emotional and Behavioral Disability throughout a large suburban school district.

Cedar Valley Community School

For the Cedar Valley Dean of Students, Re-ED principles and practices provide the foundation of her interactions with students and staff in this diverse K-8 school.

University of Washington, Graduate Program in Emotional and Behavioral Disability

As the Practicum Supervisor for graduate students seeking special education certification, this WAREA member introduces the principles and practices of Re-EDucation to both cooperating teachers and graduate students, as well as within graduate courses offered by the program.

Salmon Bay Middle School

Re-EDucation is the foundation for the services and supports provided to staff and students in this urban middle school by the special education resource teacher.

Children's Crisis Services Team at Kitsap Mental Health

As Supervisor of the Children's Crisis Team in this regional mental health center, this WAREA member infuses Re-ED into both the role of supervisor and when working directly with children and youth in crisis situations.

The BRITE (Behavior Re-EDucation in a Therapeutic Environment) Program at Syre Elementary School

This special education day treatment program for children experiencing emotional or behavioral disabilities is located in a general education elementary school and is built on the Re-ED philosophy.

Child and Family Counseling, private practice

This mental health professional integrates the philosophy of Re-ED into her work with adults and children in the Puget Sound region.

The BEACONS Project at the University of Washington

The Project Coordinator links Re-ED to school-wide positive behavior supports as a part of a federal and state funded training project for schools and districts throughout Washington State.

Sumner Junior High Program for Students with EBD

This special education program is located on the campus of a general education junior high and has a strong parent involvement focus.

A Brief History of WAREA

Incorporated as a nonprofit organization in 1994, WAREA provides conferences, training, consultation, and technical support to school districts, mental health agencies, or other programs interested in improving their services for students with, or at-risk of developing, emotional or behavioral concerns. WAREA integrates Re-ED into every service or training we provide. To date WAREA has trained thousands of teachers, counselors, paraprofessionals, treatment staff, and administrators. Topics of our trainings include: Life Space Crisis Intervention (LSCI), Group Process and Development, Effective Instruction, The 9 Stages of Re-EDucation, Classroom and Program Management, Effective Supports for Students with Emotional and Behavioral Disabilities, Positive Behavior Supports, Functional Behavior Assessment, the Conflict Cycle, Experiential Education, and other related concepts. Additionally, WAREA has provided consultation to numerous programs throughout the state.

WAREA joined the American Re-Education Association in 1992.

Whitaker School

Jeff Lenker, MSA, MED
Director

Whitaker School, (919) 575-7927
Fax: (919) 575-7895
L Street, Butner, NC 27509

Locations: Whitaker School serves North Carolina youths referred because they need a secure setting due to their severe behavioral and emotional disabilities.

Mission: The Mission of Whitaker School is to provide the best possible Re-EDucation services to those behaviorally and emotionally disturbed youths of North Carolina needing secure residential care. Whitaker School provides excellence in diagnosis, treatment, and education. Its personnel facilitate the development of strong, effective, community-based resources through an ecologically based approach so that youths may return to maintain successful, productive lives in their home communities.

Staff and Services: Whitaker School has about 65 staff who serve 18 students, ages 13 to 17, in a secure and intensive residential treatment setting. Whitaker School uses the Re-ED philosophy to create a safe and therapeutic environment in which deeply troubled children can experience success and develop the skills necessary to return to normal, functional lives in their home communities. Whitaker School's programming is both strength-based and incentive-based. Individualized programs are developed to meet students' emotional, psychological, and educational needs. Residential programming is designed to promote a "positive peer culture" in which students are responsible to each other for the success of the group as a whole. Individual and group therapies help students resolve specific areas of concern. From the time of admission, linkages are established with community-based visitation resources so that students can consolidate their gains in a normalized environment.

Residential Treatment

Whitaker School's Residential Treatment component is composed of two units. Each unit has nine students, five males and four females. Since Whitaker is a secure, residential facility, our units are open seven days a week, 365 days a year. Whitaker has a staff to child ratio of one-to-three during the day and one-to four overnight. Whitaker serves children of average intelligence who have severe emotional and behavioral disturbances. Many of the children have severe learning disabilities and language disorders as well. Whitaker's programming is designed to facilitate the development of students' skills to enable them to return to public schools and function in a home environment.

Educational Services

Whitaker School's nine teachers provide educational services for the students. All teachers are certified. Students receive credit for all coursework accomplished during their stay at Whitaker School, which offers a Standard Curriculum, an Occupational Course of Study for eligible students, and a GED Prep program. Whitaker students' academic functioning ranges from elementary grades to high school. All students receive individualized instruction based upon their academic abilities. Residential and educational staff work together to ensure a seamless treatment milieu. Residential personnel work closely with educational staff to help students achieve individual educational objectives.

Diagnostics

Whitaker School employs two clinical psychologists, one school psychologist, a licensed professional counselor who specializes in risk assessment and treatment with sex offenders, a social worker who specializes in the assessment and treatment of substance abuse, a neuropsychological consultant, and a speech and language specialist. Interdisciplinary treatment teams allow Whitaker School to develop and implement highly specific treatment plans for maximizing the student's successes in school, with peers, in the community, and within the family.

Therapy

Each student has an individual therapist with whom they meet twice a week. Therapists are trained in a wide range of individual specialty areas across therapists, allowing Whitaker School to address the needs of each student, including therapy groups for students with specific problems such as anger, grief, and sexual aggression. Whitaker School also provides art therapy for all students.

Vocational Training

Whitaker School has a well developed vocational program offering a variety of different experiences for students who can benefit from work training. This vocational programming provides occupational assessments and appropriate work experiences for students for whom work is an appropriate modality for their development.

A Brief History of Whitaker School

The North Carolina Adolescent Re-EDucation program began operations in October of 1980. Over almost three decades Whitaker has evolved to adapt to the changing landscape of mental health services in North Carolina. Whitaker was originally established in response to a class action lawsuit filed against the state of North Carolina. This lawsuit was brought to address the needs of severely emotionally and behaviorally disturbed children who were repeatedly sent to training schools rather than receiving appropriate treatment. Whitaker School provided an effective, strength-based approach to treating these children who had, heretofore, been considered untreatable by the psychiatric community. In the ensuing years, Whitaker had as many as four units, including an MRMI Unit and an Independent Living Unit. In 2005, the State of North Carolina moved 18 of Whitaker's beds to a facility for the developmentally disabled to establish a larger MRMI Program. Whitaker School now has 18 beds and continues in its original mission. Whitaker's current population is somewhat more psychiatrically disturbed and neuro-cognitively impaired than the original population. Whitaker School is now in its 26th year of providing quality services to the children of North Carolina. Despite plans for closure, upsizing, downsizing and changes in administration, Whitaker continues to be a vital component in the array of children's services in North Carolina.

Whitaker School joined the American Re-Education Association in 1981.

Wright School

Deborah A. Simmers, MEd
Director

Wright School, 919-560-5790
Fax: 919-560-5795
3132 North Roxboro Road, Durham, NC 27704
www.wrightschool.org

Location: Wright School accepts children and youth referred from across the state of North Carolina.

Mission: Wright School provides best practice, cost-effective residential mental health treatment to North Carolina's children and youth, ages six to twelve, with serious emotional and behavioral disorders, and supports each child's family and community in building the capacity to meet children's special needs in their home school and community.

Staff and Services: Continuing to use the original Project Re-ED model, Wright School's 43 staff provide 5-day residential mental health treatment and special education services. Students are referred through local public mental health management entities across the state of North Carolina, using a bed allocation system based on population.

Residential Services

The program maintains an enrollment of 24 children and youth. Students admitted usually have severe behavior problems both at home and at school. All interventions are designed to maximize each child's capacity to be successful not only in the treatment milieu, but in the home, school, and community. Liaison teacher-counselors teach families and their formal and informal support systems to better understand, become more skillful, and build capacity to meet the special needs of their children in the life domains of home, school, and community. Therefore, children spend five days at Wright School in a rigorous treatment milieu and two days at home practicing, with their caretakers, new skills and strategies to manage symptoms and stressors.

Academics and School

Because Wright School is a residential program, it is staffed by teacher-counselors who work with children throughout the day, evening, and overnight. Though activities vary throughout the course of the day, treatment goals are consistent and teacher-counselors target educational and cognitive behavioral intervention strategies to meet each child's individual needs in a seamless manner across day and evening programs.

Consultants

Consultants in a variety of fields (for example, psychiatry, psychology, and occupational therapy) are available and used when needed. They provide assessment and consultation to teacher-counselors more often than they provide direct service.

Evaluation Findings

In a series of yearly caretaker and family satisfaction surveys carried out by North Carolina's Division of Mental Health, 98% of Wright School families gave the highest ratings possible to statements indicating that they liked the services they received from Wright School, would continue to choose Wright School for services, and would recommend the treatment program to others.

In 2004 Wright School completed a four-year treatment outcomes evaluation. Parent reports indicated significant reductions in children's severity of externalizing symptoms and significant increases in their interpersonal strengths. Almost 60% of children moved into the normal range from the clinical range on standardized measures of behavior (CBCL) and of child strengths (BERS). Although there was some deterioration of gains over time, these significant improvements in children's strengths and behavioral symptoms were sustained for at least six months after leaving Wright School's treatment program.

A Brief History of Wright School

Wright School is one of the two original Project Re-ED programs and is the oldest continuously operating Re-ED program. Since 1963, Wright School has provided strength based, child and family centered mental health residential treatment, originally under a National Institute of Mental Health (NIMH) grant awarded to Nicholas Hobbs and Peabody College for Teachers (now part of Vanderbilt University). Since 1968, Wright School has continued as a state operated program under the statutory authority of the North Carolina Secretary of Health and Human Services through the Division of Mental Health, Developmental Disabilities, and Substance Abuse Services.

Wright School and other Re-ED programs purposefully use the language and interventions of wellness and education, and include families as full partners and participants in the treatment process. We work to develop strong community ties before, during, and after a child is admitted. Many Re-ED tenets, though "revolutionary" in the early 1960s, are now defined in the best practice literature and have gone on to inform the federal CASSP initiatives and System of Care (SOC) methodologies.

In 1981 Wright School was one of the founding organization members of the American Re-Education Association.

Youth Academy

Steven W. Fairley, MSW
Executive Director

Youth Academy, Phone: (304) 363-3341
Fax: 304-363-3342
#3 Crosswind Drive, Fairmont, WV 26554
www.youthacademywv.com

Locations: Youth Academy in Fairmont, West Virginia, serves children and families throughout the state of West Virginia for the residential program and in West Virginia's Regions I and III for in-home services.

Mission: Youth Academy is a community-based organization dedicated to serving children and their families. It is the philosophy of Youth Academy that children are best served when their families are included in the therapeutic process. We believe in:

Commitment to Service...by acknowledging that the easy way is not always the best way, and challenging ourselves to find positive solutions.

Education …as the cornerstone to constructive change.

Outcomes…that are evidence-based.

The Individual…Every child matters!

Community…by developing a sense of belonging which values the client as a member of the community and each community member as an investor in the mission of the Youth Academy.

Respect…that is earned by staff and fostered in clients.

Communication…as essential in delivering efficient and effective services.

Re-Education…as the foundation on which programming is delivered.

Family…as being a vital and inherent component of a child's success.

Safety and Well-Being…as the first component to treatment.

Trust…as sacred and essential.

Innovation…in programming to create a challenging environment that guides a child and family to reach their potential.

Staff and Services: Youth Academy operates a 22-bed (level II) residential treatment facility for children ages 12-17. The services provided through Youth Academy's program are performed by 34 trained staff. Master's degreed personnel provide clinical services and coordinate bachelor level and paraprofessional level staff, as well as providing and coordinating clinical services.

Community Family Intensive Treatment (CFIT)

Community Family Intensive Treatment (CFIT) is designed to provide an array of services to assist struggling families. This model is a combination of Social Necessity and Medical Necessity services (as designated by those West Virginia funding streams). The combination of these services allows the child and/or family to receive specific attention to their needs, rather than a predetermined course of treatment. A comprehensive assessment allows services to be individualized to provide the most appropriate service and/or treatment. Youth Academy's comprehensive approach includes behavioral health services (provided through the WV Clinic, Rehabilitation, and Targeted Case Management model), as well as Social Necessity services when assessments have deemed them necessary.

CFIT provides a wide array of services, ranging from preventive in-home and intensive out-patient (IOP) to reunification services for those times when a family is regrouping after an episode of out-of-home care. Additionally, while participating in the pilot phase of West Virginia's Comprehensive Assessment Planning Service (CAPS), Youth Academy experienced both the need for, and benefit of, CAPS to its clients. Youth Academy provides CAPS services as well by combining them with Medical and Social Necessity services.

Caseloads are maintained at the lowest level to ensure the staff attention necessary to reach the highest level of success. The staff work closely with the West Virginia Department of Health and Human Resources and other community stakeholders to provide services previously identified as needed to resolve issues facing the community.

A Brief History of Youth Academy

Youth Academy began operation in 2002. Though a relatively new organization, Youth Academy's commitment to the principles of Re-Education is obvious. Executive Director Steve Fairley cut his teeth in the child care industry by working for an organization steeped in the philosophies and practices of Re-Ed. The Youth Academy Management Team has more than 45 years combined experience working in Re-Ed organizations. Whether treating children in the 22-bed facility in Marion County, West Virginia or delivering in-home services to children and families, Youth Academy practices and preaches learning as the cornerstone to change.

Steve has committed Youth Academy to being a leader in the area of outcomes in West Virginia. His presentations to various groups and committees in West Virginia have demonstrated Youth Academy's devotion to showing outcomes while remaining dedicated to Re-Ed philosophy and practices which value data-based decision making.

Youth Academy's approach to treating children and families is based in the time tested principles of Re-Ed with a respect for evolution to meet their changing needs.

Youth Academy has been a Sponsoring Organization member of AREA since 2004.

Youth Villages

Patrick W. Lawler
Chief Executive Officer

Youth Villages, (901) 251-5000
Fax: (901) 251-5001
3320 Brother Bvld., Memphis, TN 38133
www.youthvillages.org

Locations: Headquartered in Memphis, Tennessee, Youth Villages is a private nonprofit organization that provides services throughout Tennessee as well as in Alabama, Arkansas, Mississippi, Texas, North Carolina, Massachusetts, Virginia, Florida and Washington D.C.

Mission: Youth Villages helps children and families live successfully.

Staff and services: Youth Villages employs more than 1,300 staff who work in 45 locations in 33 cities and help more than 11,000 emotionally troubled children and their families each year. The organization offers a continuum of programs and services–all consistent with the Re-ED philosophy–helping children with emotional and behavioral problems and their families find long-lasting success. The latest information about the organization is available at www.youthvillages.org.

Intensive In-Home Services

Youth Villages' acclaimed intensive in-home services program provides intensive treatment for troubled children and families in their own homes. The program model is derived from *Multisystemic Therapy (MST)*, one of the nation's premier evidence-based treatment models. The MST model complements the Re-ED philosophy and in effect adds structure to Nicholas Hobbs' work in the area of "liaison" counselors and his emphasis on the role of parents and work in a child's natural ecology. In 1994, Youth Villages was the first organization to replicate MST on a large scale outside of clinical trials, and Youth Villages quickly became the world's largest provider of MST. Youth Villages has always provided intensive in-home treatment to a broad population of youth and families from across the child welfare, mental health, and juvenile justice systems and has maintained consistently high success rates across populations and locations. Currently in East Tennessee, North Carolina, and Washington, D.C., Youth Villages has intensive in-home services teams which are specifically licensed to provide MST, thus serving a population involving primarily juvenile justice oriented problems. Youth Villages provides intensive in-home services in Tennessee, Florida, Virginia, Mississippi, Alabama, and North Carolina, as well as in Dallas, Washington, D.C., and the Boston, Massachusetts, area. Altogether Youth Villages' intensive in-home services program serves more than 2,500 children and families per year.

Treatment Foster Care

The Youth Villages Treatment Foster Care Program allows children with emotional and behavioral problems to receive help from specially trained treatment parents in stable homes. Youth Villages recruits parents and gives them extensive initial and continuing training. Our counselors and behavior specialists provide 24-hour-a-day support.

Adoption

Begun in 1999, the Youth Villages Adoption Program works with the Tennessee Department of Children's Services to find permanent homes for Youth Villages children who have adoption as a goal. Our counselors in other states support the adoption process in their own communities as a way for children to find permanency when ties with their biological parents have been severed.

Residential Treatment

Counselors on three open residential campuses use the Re-ED treatment approach to help troubled children learn successful behavior patterns. This enables children and their families to identify, understand, and cope with their individual challenges, as well as develop skills for success in less restrictive settings. When children complete their residential treatment, they return home with support from the Intensive In-Home Services program or "step down" to less restrictive environments (such as foster care or a group home).

Intensive Residential Treatment

In 2003, the Youth Villages Center for Intensive Residential Treatment began providing help to children and youth who suffer from the most serious emotional and behavioral problems, such as suicidal or self-harming conditions, psychotic symptoms, sexual behavior problems, and behavioral issues complicated by chronic medical problems. The open, light-filled center features four courtyards, allowing the facility to help a wide range of children with a variety of problems and needs. The center includes school rooms and safe outdoor play areas. A shortage of intensive treatment alternatives for girls led Youth Villages to develop plans for a Girls Intensive Residential Treatment Center. The center will open in 2009.

CHOICES

The CHOICES program supports children with developmental disabilities, allowing them to grow up in families, not institutions. Children live with their own families or in homes with resource parents specially trained by our counselors. The program measures its success by increased quality of life for both children and their families.

Group Homes

The Youth Villages Group Homes, located in West and Middle Tennessee, include Project Safe Place, the Mid-South's only runaway and homeless shelter for teens. Group homes allow young people to receive mental health support while they learn to live successfully in the community. Older teens learn independent living and life skills, including how to budget, prepare meals, shop for groceries, use the public transportation system, and find and keep a job.

Transitional Living

The Transitional Living program provides help to young people who are aging out of foster care or state custody and lack a viable support network. Transitional Living specialists help young people find housing, health services, and employment, and learn to meet their basic living needs. The program has operated since 1999 through an initial grant and continuing support from the Day Foundation and other private donations, including payroll donations by Youth Villages employees. In 2007, the State of Tennessee matched a challenge grant from the Day Foundation, offering the first sustained state funding for young people in the program.

Specialized Crisis Services

Begun in June 2003, the Youth Villages Specialized Crisis Services provides assessment and evaluation of children and youth who are experiencing psychiatric emergencies. The counselors refer children and youth who are experiencing psychiatric emergencies to the most appropriate, least restrictive treatment option with an emphasis on intensive home and community-based help. In its first year, the program diverted nearly 75 percent of the children evaluated from psychiatric hospitalization to more appropriate and effective community care; the average daily census in Tennessee's acute treatment facilities for children declined by 36 percent.

A Brief History of Youth Villages

Youth Villages was founded in Memphis, Tennessee in 1986 with the merger of two small residential treatment facilities that together helped 80 children a year. Although its roots are in residential treatment, Youth Villages became a pioneer in the use of evidence-based, in-home treatment services to allow children to receive help in the least restrictive, most effective environment possible--preferably their own homes.

Youth Villages has been a sponsoring member of the American Re-EDucation Association since 1986.

38

Beyond our Borders: Pressley Ridge brings Re-ED back to Europe

B. Scott Finnell, Scott W. Erickson,
Mary Beth Rauktis, Andrea Gruber,
& Kátia Almeida

Pressley Ridge is the first Re-ED organization to offer services and supports in Europe. In doing so, the organization looked to the legacy of Nick Hobbs for the vision and within Pressley Ridge for the talent and determination to make the vision a reality. Re-ED has deep roots within Western European models for treating children with emotional disturbances. In putting together the basic tenets of Re-ED, Hobbs was stimulated in part by the 1956 study of the Joint Commission on Mental Illness and Health (JCMIH) examining children's mental health programs in Western Europe. From this report, Hobbs said, "came a suggestion of a possible new approach to the problem" (Hobbs, 1982, p. 15).

European Contributions to Re-ED

After World War II, France needed to care for thousands of orphaned, homeless, handicapped, and emotionally disturbed children. There were few professionals to care for such large numbers. Those concerned invented new ways to respond to these children's needs. One important development produced a new profession called the *educateur*. Similarly, Scotland placed children who were too disturbed to adapt to new homes after being evacuated from London during the bombing into a residential treatment center near Glasgow. Educational psychologists whose training compared to the French educateurs staffed the program. This professional role had no counterpart in the United States. The JCMIH respected these European models and recommended to Congress that, *"Pilot studies should be undertaken in the development of centers for the reeducation of emotionally disturbed children, using different types of personnel than are customary....The schools would be operated by carefully selected teachers working with consultants from the mental health disciplines"* (Joint Commission on Mental Illness and Health, 1961, p. 259, cited by Hobbs, 1982, p. 15).

This recommendation from the JCMIH to Congress had Hobbs' imprint, as Vice-Chair of the Joint Commission's Board of Trustees. In 1956 Hobbs studied mental health programs for children in Italy, France, England, Scotland, Belgium, and Holland. Hobbs' observations greatly expanded his sense of possible alternatives to the current hospital model for treating disturbed children in the United States (Habel, 1988).

Since there was no parallel professional role to the educateur in the United States, Hobbs designed the teacher-counselor based on this new role, but with an important difference. The French educateur is a skilled childcare worker, but not a classroom teacher (that role is left to the professeur). Teacher-counselors would facilitate learning for children, despite their emotional disturbances (Hobbs, 1982).

European Needs and Pressley's Response

Current European Needs

There are a number of reasons that children's services based on Re-ED are now emerging in Europe. While programs to help troubled and troubling children in Western Europe are numerous and effective, this is not true for Southern and Eastern Europe. In those regions, there are significant problems subsequent to the demise of dictatorial regimes, the formations of new nations, ethnic conflicts, and issues related to the immigration and social exclusion of populations such as immigrated African-Europeans and the traditionally nomadic Roma. Since existing social structures in some of these countries are limited, needs are great, opening many chances to provide new services to disturbed children and their families.

Portugal is one of the poorest countries in the European Union. It is just now emerging from the effects of Salazar's long dictatorship, during which social services received little attention. Portugal is now part of the European Union, increasing opportunities for economic aid to develop services for children with emotional disturbances and their families. For many years Portugal has placed children into institutional care, where treatment and professional training of childcare workers were based on approaches other than the European educateur. Portuguese government agencies and professionals became interested in the teacher-counselor approach, especially for working with the large Portuguese-African immigrant population.

Social services for children and families are somewhat similar in Central and Eastern Europe, where many new democracies emerged after the collapse of the Soviet Union. Democratic institutions in many countries are stressed by limited economic opportunity and by the large number of young people who have little to do other than school. Social service networks for children and families in countries like Ukraine (where less than half the population even support the idea of democracy) and Hungary (just entering the European Union) have not matured enough to replace activities once organized by the Young Pioneers under the Communist regimes. Central Europe faces serious challenges as the formerly nomadic Roma population integrates into schools and society as a whole. The Roma group is perceived to be outside the mainstream of national cultures and Roma children are often identified as troubled and troubling in the school systems.

In the early 1990s, Pressley Ridge introduced Re-ED to several countries in Europe. Since then, hundreds of professional and governmental decision makers have learned about Re-ED principles and their implementations. In recent years, Pressley Ridge has started programs in Portugal and Hungary, providing training, consulting, evaluation, and direct services to troubled children and their families. The remainder of this chapter describes Pressley Ridge's international efforts and details two of its programs in Portugal and Hungary.

Pressley Ridge's Early International Efforts

Pressley Ridge was founded in Pittsburgh, Pennsylvania in 1832 in response to a cholera epidemic. Early services focused on orphanage care, but over the past half century, Pressley Ridge has evolved into an organization that serves over 4,000 children annually in seven states and the District of Columbia.

Pressley Ridge was one of the first organizations outside Project Re-ED's two pilot programs to adopt Nicholas Hobbs' new treatment philosophy. In the early 1960s, a Pressley Ridge board member who knew Nicholas Hobbs from their WW II work together suggested they investigate this new approach. This resulted in a new Day School for troubling children, opening in 1967. Since then, every program developed by Pressley Ridge has used Re-ED as its foundation.

Pressley Ridge's international services began in 1983 with a chance encounter between one of its teacher-counselors and an adult student from the Portuguese juvenile justice ministry who was in a training program at the University of West Virginia. The Pressley Ridge staff member told this person about the exciting program where he worked and the difference it made in children's lives. Over the next ten years, informal exchanges between Portuguese child care professionals and Pressley Ridge laid the foundation for the formal introduction of Pressley Ridge and Re-ED into Europe.

By 1996, Pressley Ridge was convinced that Re-ED principles were applicable to children around the world. This led to Pressley Ridge's second phase of international activity known as the Pittsburgh International Children and Families Institute, or PICFI. This program model operated in two segments similar to a university year, fall and spring. The fall segment's activities brought political leaders and decision makers from different countries to Pittsburgh to be oriented to Re-ED principles, to learn about Pressley Ridge's services, and to see Re-ED being implemented in its different programs. Participants learned how non-profits function in the United States. The fall session lasted about two weeks with Pressley Ridge often partnering with the University of Pittsburgh to teach non-clinical aspects of the training. Afterwards, participants returned to their countries and sent practitioners to Pressley Ridge in the spring where they spent two weeks to two months intensively training in program specific methods.

The PICFI program operated from 1996 to 2003 when Pressley Ridge evaluated the program's impact. During this seven-year period, more than 100 professionals from 23 countries had come to Pittsburgh and attended training sessions. These professionals had then created 33 "Pressley Ridge-like" programs in 13 countries. The PICFI alumni estimated that about 4,000 children received Re-ED-like services in their countries based on the program models they had learned at Pressley Ridge. The review revealed that the training made a profound difference in the individual practitioners' lives. However, sustainability of programs in their native countries was less than ideal, probably due to insufficient infrastructure and to the limited time that individuals were able to spend learning at Pressley Ridge. Leaving their families and jobs for an extended period of time was problematic; also, it was very difficult for these individuals to initiate and sustain change in their institutional cultures without continuing support. Thus, while the Pressley Ridge leadership believed that the international program had great value, it needed a different strategic focus.

Pressley Ridge International Today

Following the PICFI evaluation, Pressley Ridge's senior leadership visited Hungary, Macedonia, and the Ukraine. If Pressley Ridge's international work was to achieve maximum impact, it had to be anchored in countries able to sustain and support efforts. The strategy was to first build on established relationships and then develop relationships with countries with adequate infrastructure.

Creating a non-governmental organization, or NGO, in Portugal allowed Pressley Ridge to actually provide services in that country. The NGO, similar to a 501(c)(3) in the United States, offered two benefits: it would demonstrate the effectiveness of Pressley Ridge programs and more professionals could be trained without their having to leave home. The NGO in Portugal was created in 2004 and is directed by a Portuguese national who worked extensively at Pressley Ridge prior to her employment. This model, allowing the hiring of local "experts" committed to Pressley Ridge values, provides for a better understanding of how Re-ED and Pressley Ridge programs can work within the Portuguese culture.

After a group of Hungarian nationals strongly urged Pressley Ridge to continue working with them, Pressley Ridge also established an NGO in Hungary and hired a director for Central and Eastern Europe. Hungary's acceptance into the European Union and its development of infrastructure for social systems enabled them to provide for services to a large number of troubled children.

Pressley Ridge reached an agreement with the Ukranian city of Donesk to train their social workers. In 2004, Pressley Ridge sent senior staff to train the Ukranian professionals in community-based models of care and experiential methods. A Special American Business Internship Training (SABIT) grant also enabled a social worker from the Ukraine to spend six months at Pressley Ridge.

Pressley Ridge Portugal

Before the NGO, Pressley Ridge had staff in Portugal and trained hundreds of Portuguese professionals and direct care workers in Re-ED principles and Pressley Ridge program models. Since 2001, Pressley Ridge has trained and supervised the clinical teams of Santa Casa Da Misericordia De Lisboa, a government child welfare organization with residential homes, foster care programs, adoption and community-based services. Pressley Ridge Portugal has also trained public school and support staff in several cities, as well as residential child care staff of Crescerser, another NGO. Finally, Pressley Ridge teaches four graduate courses at the University of Minho, Institute of Child and Family Studies, where graduate students are introduced to the work of Nicholas Hobbs, his Re-ED principles and their application to families with children and troubled adolescents.

While training and education continue to be a major focus of Pressley Ridge's efforts in Portugal, in 2004 it began an after-school program for African-Portuguese urban youths from low-income families. Called Trilhos Alternativos, the program is based in a "loja social" (social house) in Lisbon's African-Portuguese neighborhood, Estrada Militar do Alto Damaia. At the loja social, adults learn to read and write Portuguese and participate in family activities while youths can attend after-school programs and participate in social groups. The loja provides a safe place for families to be together and offers services and resources to help them to function more successfully in the Portuguese culture. The African-Portuguese have second-class status, occupying the least desirable neighborhoods, working for minimal wages, and surviving on a day-to-day basis. Many feel they have fewer rights than "white" Portuguese, and that values of the Portuguese culture compete with African values (Sarmento, Almeida, Rauktis, & Bernardo, 2006).

The idea for the Trilhos Alternativos ("alternative paths" or AP) began when loja staff identified some youths whose poor social skills, truancy, and oppositional behaviors put them at risk of being excluded from the loja. When loja staff asked Pressley Ridge Portugal to provide additional services to these youth, Trilhos Alternativos was born.

AP seeks to re-integrate youth socially into their community through experiential learning of social and emotional skills, using motivation systems, and teaching pro-social skills through modeling and coaching. The program works from several Re-ED values, including treating youths in environments as similar to their own as possible and that trust is essential.

Also, AP believes that teacher-counselors can promote change as role models for youth who will learn better through opportunities for personal growth. A clinical psychologist serves as the AP supervisor/coordinator. Two teacher-counselors also have psychology backgrounds. A ratio of two adults to eight children with a third adult added during outdoor activities is maintained. AP sessions last ninety minutes twice a week; an outdoor activity occurs one weekend a month.

AP Program Components

The AP program has four key components: (1) a motivation system, (2) working with families, (3) group activities, and (4) experiential activities. These were enacted for all groups at loja social.

The Motivation System. This system encouraged youth to participate in activities, to follow rules, and to learn and practice new personal and social skills. Points are awarded only for positive behaviors which are then exchanged for colored beads, each representing a different number of points and type of skill. The beads are strung and hung on the wall for display and can be used to purchase soccer balls, tennis shoes, and other highly valued goods.

Working with Families. This includes meeting with family members individually as well as informal family gatherings organized around a craft activity, allowing families to share a fun activity and provide support for one another. When youth miss AP meetings, teacher-counselors try to re-engage youth and families in the AP activities.

Group Activities. Group activities reflect the Re-ED principle that the group is important to adolescents. All AP activities occur in a group. Every session begins with a planning meeting, followed by an activity. A sample AP activity was creating games for the loja social's "Tournament." The group had to brainstorm, select games, and then create the games they would play. The exercise required working cooperatively, communicating and taking turns, attending to the task at hand, etc. Other group activities include organized games, debates, and role playing.

Outdoor Experiential Activities. These expose youth to situations they would not normally encounter, such as archeology and rock climbing. Since these activities occur in new environments, they challenge youth to use their developing skills.

Cultural Variables. While the AP program is based on what we know to be effective for Pressley programs in the U.S., cultural differences must be taken into account. U.S. programs use a more visual approach, often posting reinforcing statements on the walls. In the Portuguese culture such input is typically shared face-to-face. How reinforcement is used and how problem solving is taught also differ. Students and teachers are not used to applause or overt positive feedback. They may not be well received, so reinforcement and praise must be delivered in a less obvious way. Finally, Portuguese professionals tend to be more "problem focused" than their American counterparts. It is not possible to go directly to training unless time has been spent discussing challenges. As a result, extra training time must allow for discussion of problems, active listening, and modeling alternative approaches to problems.

AP Evaluation

Because the Alternative Path program is still evolving, the evaluation focused on three key questions: Were youth participating or dropping out of AP? Was the motivation system effective? Were social skills improving? Data collection began prior to the beginning of AP (September 2004) and continued until the end of the 62 sessions (July 2005), a 10-month period. Initially, AP included 10 youths but two left early, institutionalized by a prior court decision. The remainder maintained until the sessions ended. Since this is a voluntary program, and youth can choose to attend, absence of drop-outs was a positive outcome. The group's mean for sessions attended was 42 of the 62 possible sessions (SD=12.68). As for the program's motivation system, participants could win a maximum of 220 good-behavior points if they won five points in all 62 sessions. The average number of total points awarded was 145.75 (SD = 55.20).

Social skills changed while youth were in the AP program. Teacher-counselors conjointly completed an observational checklist of students' social skills at three time points: before the program started (Time One), in March 2005 (Time Two), and at the last session (Time Three). Group means increased for all six social skills from evaluation Time One to Time Two, and from evaluation Time Two to Time Three. There was a statistically significant difference for all six social skills; the group showed significantly better social skills by the end of the program than in the beginning. While this was true for all appraised social skills, the greatest improvements were seen in behavioral alternatives to aggression ($p < .005$) and dealing with stress ($p < .005$).

A critical question concerned the effectiveness of the motivation system. Creating and maintaining these systems requires a great deal of time and attention. Did the motivation system have any impact? Not surprisingly, a significant, positive correlation occurred between the number of sessions attended and the number of motivation points earned ($r = .91, p = .01$). However, the relationship between motivation points earned and social skills development was non-significant.

Nevertheless, there was a strong positive correlation, given the small sample size, between the number of sessions attended and advanced social skills at the end of the program. This was true for both the average number of sessions attended ($r = .79$, $p = .02$) and the sum of sessions attended ($r = .83$, $p = .01$). The data trends suggest that the motivational system may play an indirect rather than direct role in the development of social skills. Attending a series of sessions to earn points until they have enough points to purchase something increases the youth's exposure to social skills. It is not the points that associate with better skills; rather, it is cumulative time in the social skills intervention.

These interpretations should be accepted with caution since correlations are inherently non-causal; this research design does not allow for causal conclusions. It could be that more socially skilled youth are more likely to attend group, rather than students getting more skilled socially because they attend group, although increases across time by all group members provides some argument for the intervention. Additional research needs to be conducted to understand how motivation systems work with Portuguese students. However, the AP staff is encouraged by the evaluation results and has used them, as well as their observations and feedback from the participants and families, to continue to improve the program.

Pressley Ridge Hungary

Pressley Ridge launched its operations in Hungary by signing a letter of cooperation with the mayor of Ferencvaros in the Ninth District of Budapest. The agreement allowed Pressley Ridge to support the District's efforts to transform the traditional elementary Lenhossek School (grades 1 to 8) into one modeled on the Pressley Ridge Day School and based upon Re-ED principles. The school resides in the heart of Ferencvaros and serves a significant Roma population.

The Roma are an ethnic group found in most European countries; the total population is estimated at 7 million to 9 million persons, with 80% of Roma living in Central, Eastern, and Southeastern Europe (Liddle, 2006). Traditionally nomadic, their lifestyle was irrevocably altered as modernizing European nation states forced many Roma to settle permanently in urban areas. Eliminating their traditional life patterns has contributed to social problems. High rates of crime and substance abuse are prevalent, and in many countries, Roma are ten times more likely to live below the poverty line than non-Roma (Liddle, 2006).

In Hungary, Roma youths comprise about 15% of the total primary school population. Stigmatization and misdiagnosis often work to channel them into "special schools" designed for the mentally and physically handicapped. Accordingly, gaps in educational achievement are stark; 70-80 percent of Roma have less than a primary education (Liddle, 2006). Traditional educational approaches have not changed the educational outcomes for Roma youths. The district's leadership believed that Re-ED approaches could help the school to positively impact the lives of Roma youths and their families.

Traditional Education in Hungary

Historically, Hungary's school system follows the Prussian educational model: very knowledge-focused and requiring students to passively absorb teacher presented information. Hungary's teacher training system is similarly rigid. Graduating teachers have thorough knowledge of their subjects, but are not equipped to handle difficult classroom situations when they do not have all their students' undivided attention. This rigidity was further strengthened by Hungary's socialist regime, which also had a knowledge-focused and strict approach to education. As a result, a teacher's goal for teaching seems distilled to one mandate: "I must deliver subject material given for an academic period to students. If it is completed, then I did my job and it does not concern me whether actual learning takes place or not."

Hungarian students face a similar inflexibility in their learning. They must master a vast amount of information across their 18 years of compulsory education. They are then tested for their ability to remember and apply that information. Those able to understand and process the information progress through the system with success, but for those students with limited capabilities for whatever reason, learning is difficult and frustrating. The education system does not provide alternate strategies and coping skills for their success in daily life. Of course, there are exceptions to the rule, with some creative and affectionate educators trying innovative programming within their educational system. Also, educational reform is being discussed at the governmental level. But the current system generally forces both teachers and learners into situations where they are almost doomed to failure - especially for students with undeveloped skills and capabilities. Therefore, when Re-ED is mentioned or Pressley Ridge's approach is introduced, one question is always asked, "When can we start?"

Re-ED in a Hungarian School

The educational model is being phased into Lenhossek School. The first year focused on the 5th grade class. Each year the incoming 5th grade class will be added to the program until by 2008, grades 5 through 8 will be transformed. Interestingly, the intrinsic appeal of the Re-ED model has begun affecting other grade levels. Sixth grade teachers are partially applying the model by changing teaching approaches, and many lower grade classrooms are now using some elements.

The "Pressley Program" supervisor studied in the Pressley Ridge Day School in Pittsburgh for 10 months. She supervises and trains teachers and liaisons in the Re-ED principles and oversees the program's implementation. The District committed almost 100,000 U.S. dollars to hire supervisors and liaison personnel to work with students and their families. Pressley Ridge, along with providing the model and initial training, provides weekly consultations through its Director of Central and Eastern European Operations. Pressley's professional staff also provide training regularly, both in Pittsburgh and in Hungary; they also help evaluate the program's effectiveness.

Evaluation of the Pressley Program in Hungary

While the program is just finishing its first year, initial results and teacher satisfaction have been impressive. Early data clearly show that as students gain more control over their behaviors, their attendance and performance improve. Teachers also report that youth in the program have fewer behavioral issues and an improved focus on academics.

As educators in Hungary learn about Re-ED and the Pressley Day School program, they instantly realize what a powerful tool it is. For those who are naturally talented educators, Re-ED provides validation for their work and beliefs. For those for whom teaching appears to be more of an effort, Re-ED prescribes simple, manageable steps, and a usable framework. Many teachers in Lenhossek School who previously struggled now report small but noticeable improvement in students' behaviors. This, in turn, increases these teachers' motivation to work with these troubled youths.

Continuing and Future Challenges

The continuing challenge is how to implement the Pressley education model. Simply taking a Pressley Ridge program and replicating it in Hungary does not work. We took the Pressley Ridge Day School model and tried to fit it with the administrative and cultural framework of the Hungarian education system. Time was spent adapting the model for the Lenhossek School, training the teachers, and introducing the methods into the classroom. However, it did not seem to "click into place" easily. Fortunately, Re-ED has another value that aids its implementation in other cultures: it calls for each program that wants to operate according to Re-ED principles to be constructed anew, with flexibility to re-invent itself if needed. Pressley and Lenhossek educators are finding answers they need by reviewing each Re-ED principle and measuring what is done at the school against Re-ED's principles.

New initiatives are also underway. The school at Bona Kovacs Karoly in Northern Hungary plans to introduce the Pressley Ridge educational model, based on Re-ED principles, in their incoming 5th grade class. The Kornis Klara Children's Home and Vocational School in Budapest is planning to start a preparatory class in the fall of 2006 for youths who need to be better prepared for vocational study. The program for this class will also be built on the Pressley Ridge education model.

Finally, Pressley Ridge is committed to work with Hungary to find ways to reduce the Roma's social exclusion. The Pressley Ridge Hungary program works closely with the Ferencvaros District Council on rehabilitating a slum area, where Pressley will train the mentors working with families in the area. In conjunction with The Open Society Institute's Roma Cultural Participation Project, the Pressley program is training Roma mentors to work with Roma youth. It is also developing a Roma Youth Leadership Program to use experiential activities to develop the leadership skills of Roma youth.

Conclusion

Pressley Ridge's work in Europe began with a chance encounter and developed by carefully building relationships over a twenty-year period. When an evaluation found that sustainability was problematic, Pressley Ridge re-focused and became more strategic in providing training, support, and consultation. Pressley Ridge made a long-term commitment in Europe by creating NGO's and implementing effective programs in the African-Portuguese and Roma communities.

A common question asked is, "Why work in Europe when there are so many children, youth, and families that need help here in the United States?" This is a legitimate question that highlights how, in the world's wealthiest and most powerful nation, there are many children who have unmet needs for care, nurturance, health, and happiness—the basic tenets on which our democracy is built. It also identifies the tension between reaching out and reaching in: How do we meet the needs of children in the United States as well as those of others in the world?

Our response is that we are increasingly becoming a connected world. One can trace the roots of terrorism and violence that the world is experiencing to poverty, to intolerance, and to need; these are the conditions that support extremism. As 9/11 and the bombings in London and Madrid made clear, our world is connected, and a bomb detonated in one country affects people all over the planet. Helping European professionals who are committed to children to provide education, safe homes, and communities not only touches and improves children's lives; it may also make the world a safer and more humane place.

It is a testament to the power of Re-ED values that so many European professionals, when they learn of Re-ED and Pressley programs, ask "When can we begin?" A strengths-based approach that focuses on solutions, the power of relationships, and the importance of community is one that is fundamentally sound and universally understood. The values of Re-ED also aid in its transfer to other cultures because, at its heart, it is a philosophical approach that looks at what is working and what can be adapted rather than what is wrong and should be fixed. It is also an approach that promotes mutual learning. In our twenty years working in Europe, we have learned far more than we ever taught. In conclusion, "going beyond our borders" and bringing Re-ED back to Europe has affirmed the power of Re-ED to transform lives and systems.

References

Habel, J. C. (1988). Precipitating himself into just manageable difficulties: An intellectual portrait of Nicholas Hobbs. *Dissertation Abstracts International, 50*(5-A), 1143.

Hobbs, N. (1982). *The troubled and troubling child.* San Francisco: Jossey-Bass. (reprinted in 1994 by AREA).

Liddle, M. (2006). *The Roma leadership project* (unpublished paper). Pittsburgh, PA: Pressley Ridge Institute.

Sarmento, P., Almeida, K., Rauktis, M. E., & Bernardo, S. (2006). *Promoting social competence and inclusion for at-risk African-Portuguese youth: Taking alternative paths.* Manuscript submitted for publication.

Acknowledgements

This work was supported in part by The Pressley Ridge Foundation. We acknowledge the excellent work of Patricia Sarmento in Portugal and of Nicoletta Kovacs in Hungary, and thank Jane-Ellen Robinet for her editing assistance.

B. Scott Finnell, PhD, LCSW, is President-CEO of Pressley Ridge.

Scott W. Erickson, PhD, is Executive Vice President and Chief Financial Officer of Pressley Ridge, Pittsburgh, PA.

Mary Beth Rauktis, PhD, LSW, is former Director of Research and Evaluation at Pressley Ridge in Pittsburgh, PA, and currently Assistant Professor, University of Pittsburgh School of Social Work, Child Welfare Research and Training Program, Pittsburgh, PA.

Andrea Gruber, MPIA, is Director of Central and Eastern European Operations, Pressley Ridge.

Kátia Almeida, MBA, is Director of Pressley Ridge Portugal.

Requests for information should be directed to: the Research and Evaluation Department of Pressley Ridge, 530 Marshall Ave., Pittsburgh PA 15214, 412-321-6995

The Future:

Helping More Children and Families
– and Doing It Better

Re-ED's contributions since 1962 to the fields serving troubled and troubling children and youth, and their families, have been notable, but of course they are by no means exclusive. Re-ED professionals continually find others whose work expands their own views and who think much as they do. Occasionally, these others later point up the utility of Re-ED's ecological competence approach as an integrated view, a values-based set of principles and practices with the adaptability for application to the wide variety of children and families we serve. Their recognition of the need for such a comprehensive approach encourages us to place these principles and practices in the literature, more accessible to others.

An Integrated Comprehensive Approach

An approach may be emerging from the collective intelligence in our field, an integrated approach where the whole exceeds the sum of its parts. Its template would incorporate the basic factors that typically contribute to building strengths as well as identifying those that create major discord in a child's ecosystem. Being child, family, and system oriented, it should be comprehensive and sufficiently flexible for intervention planning across the span of child and family needs. If bolstered by data, such an approach could provide aggregated information for informed policy decisions and serve as a planning base to meet the needs of identified populations. Given future instrumentation and statistical models which allow more functional analysis of complex ecological variables, these data could inform our helping repertoires as well.

Re-ED may offer the foundation for one such approach.

Evidence Based Services

Recently, AREA's Board committed themselves to present evidence existing for the Re-ED approach, established early and continued only in smaller efforts since. Positive outcomes evaluation has become insufficient in today's search for Evidence Based Programs. Yet it is unlikely that a collection of EBPs provides a comprehensive solution for troubled children, either. Funding of EBP model replications offers the high likelihood of yet another incomplete system of care with splintered programs, where children and families who do not meet the strict criteria used in researched demonstration programs again fall between the cracks. Given the certainty of limited funds, we need cost effective, evidence based approaches adaptable across the full breadth of needs, with funding and regulations that sponsor less disciplinary exclusivity and more integrated programming.

The distinguished professionals who served as the 1980 Panel of Visitors assessing Re-ED's first twenty years made an astute recommendation regarding program funding. *"The panel has grave concerns about programs where sources of funding, usually through third-party payment arrangements, have been allowed to distort the fundamental philosophy of reeducation, to impose on programs alien expectations as well as superfluous personnel, and to run up costs unconscionably. Where such situations exist, they should be rectified as rapidly as possible, and the mistake should not be repeated in the establishment of new programs around the country"* (Hobbs, 1982, p. 367). Their concerns were prophetic of the struggle most service programs experience to stay cost effective, viable, and need responsive, given the complexities and restrictions of today's funding structures. The added layers of cost required both for compliance on the part of programs and for oversight on the part of system components significantly decreases the funds available for badly needed services, already underfunded. Since these programs meet basic needs in their communities, this is a detrimental condition for our nation which requires rapid and serious attention.

University / Practitioner Affiliations

One future development in Re-ED could accelerate the national achievement of a cost effective child helping system. Strengthening and re-establishing multiple and meaningful university / Re-ED service affiliations was recommended by the Panel of Visitors in both 1969 and 1980 (Hobbs, 1982). At present, the Peabody connections no longer exist. Although some limited collaborative activities occur elsewhere, the closest link with an institution of higher education is WAREA's relationship with the special education training program at the University of Washington where Re-ED content is part of the curriculum. There is a variety of training available from AREA programs themselves, but requests asking which universities offer Re-ED training programs can no longer be answered readily. Ideally, there would be an infusion of Re-ED training content on ecological competence for the many disciplines that serve troubled children and families, as well as re-education training programs embedded within special education and psychology as there were at Peabody in the early years. The crossover learning of such affiliations promises important mutual benefits to service providers and to university trainers, as well as to those receiving the training.

Teacher trainers in our field have long been concerned about the relatively small proportion of their graduates who stay in the classroom. Re-ED tends to support longevity in the job, unlike the high staff turnover typical in many schools and programs serving troubled and troubling students. On tough days, staff invariably ask, "Why am I doing this?" At such a time, it is easy to choose escape and seek greener pastures elsewhere. Many Re-ED staff know why they stay. At first it is the collegiality that makes the difference, teammates who provide support and alternatives for rough situations. Over time, these growing successes build lifelong commitments, along with an increasing focus on the rewarding elements of the work — "making a difference."

Advancing the State of the Art – and the Science

"[T]oday, although progress has been made throughout the country, the problem of what to do to help emotionally disturbed children remains a major challenge to the nation" (Hobbs, 1974, p. 161). The statement remains true in the 21st century. Although more skills and more workers are available, the nation's resources are invested elsewhere. Yet, helping only makes sense – for the children and for us all. Troubled students themselves wish to become productive, contributing, tax paying citizens in their communities. And society wants to be protected from the acts of desperate and deeply troubled individuals. Helping helps everyone, as a cost effective investment in the future.

Despite our profound respect for the enlightening potential of quantified information, Albert Einstein's oft-quoted statement about data is notable: "Not everything that can be counted is important, and not everything that is important can be counted." The continuing evidence for the broad based, comprehensive approach Re-ED offers to help troubled and troubling children and youth, and their families, comes from a variety of sources:

Two rigorous empirical investigations (residential and public school),
Recent follow-up studies in separate sites,
Practitioner views, with enthusiasm for the work and its outcomes,
Parent reports of support from their own participation,
And stories from troubled youth who want to tell others.

After more than four and a half decades of helping, Re-ED is represented by a lively national organization of large and small service providers, located from the nation's east to west coasts, whose members want to add to this evidence base — as we continue to meet the needs of children and families in our communities and beyond.

--- the Editors

What is Re-ED?

"It is said that Re-ED is hard to describe. That is true. Re-ED is a state of heart as much as a state of mind – as much spiritual as it is intellectual. It begins with an attitude of unconditional caring – not just for troubled and troubling children, but for all people.

"It incorporates a sense of limitless hope sprinkled with naiveté and energized by boundless enthusiasm. When it comes to children, Re-ED is blind in one eye and has stars in the other. Re-ED never says never. Re-ED is not good at finding the disease or sickness or weakness in people. Re-ED targets personal strengths and builds on them. Re-ED sizes up what's working, what's resilient, and then nurtures that part so that it takes up more and more space in a child's life.

"Re-ED doesn't blame kids for their problems; it recognizes that the problems kids cause are not the causes of their problems; that kids can never feel completely whole if they are not gaining knowledge and skill academically, because, as Hobbs noted, that is the business of children.

"Re-ED understands that in the life of a child, it is temporary; that the group, the community, the family, the ecology are all important. Re-ED does not stop at the four walls of the classroom; and when at its best, Re-ED is infinite, carrying its influence far into the child's future. Re-ED is a talisman crafted carefully by the loving, patient hands of teacher-counselors and gifted to the spirit of the child.

"It is unforgettable, irreversible and enduring. It is the backbone of our past, it nourishes our daily work, and it guides our future."

— Frank A. Fecser

Frank Fecser, PhD, is Chief Executive Officer of the Positive Education Program in Cleveland, OH.   Fecser@pepcleve.org.
Reprinted with permission from *Reclaiming Children and Youth*, vol. 11, Number 2, Summer 2002, p. 124.

Names Index

610

616

About and By Nicholas Hobbs
Hobbs, N. / Nicholas / Nick

Content Index

Quantum physics, 176
Questioning, 2, 4, 11, 44, 199, 296, 373-375, 388, 410, 453

R

Re-ED: adaptations, 3, 374; agencies, 377, 443, 509, 532; classroom(s), 139, 141, 142, 159, 165, 172, 179, 296, 302, 351, 358, 563, 605; compatible view of behaviorism, 501; concept, 113, 390, 409, 412, 504; conferences, 510, 515; essentials, 4, 26, 439-444, 450-455; fidelity, 374, 435, 438, 441, 443, 454, 455; group meetings, 309, 310, 312; groups, 296, 299, 300, 305, 307, 308, 397; history, 3, 313, 445, 496, 498, 510; ideas, 354, 490, 496, 505, 520, 557; intervention, 25, 377, 390; organization(s), 2, 255, 256, 258, 517, 521, 526, 527, 530, 583, 588; philosophy, 2, 3, 108, 112, 129, 131, 137, 220, 227, 252, 281, 353, 356, 366, 421, 454, 505, 508, 510, 514, 520, 526, 527, 529, 554, 557, 572, 575, 583, 585; practice(s), 42, 182, 327, 342, 354, 375, 408, 439, 440, 442, 443, 503, 504, 512, 583; practitioners, 66, 437, 438, 444, 445, 450-452; principle, 33, 34, 48, 111, 223, 345, 357, 358, 360, 364, 525, 595, 600; programs, 1-3, 25, 27, 41-43, 45, 49, 52, 53, 56, 65, 66, 74, 125, 139, 141, 159, 160, 172-174, 187, 201, 204, 217, 220, 221, 227, 246, 248, 251, 255, 257, 258, 260, 280, 299, 304, 309, 312, 327, 370, 374, 375, 386, 392, 406, 407, 413, 436-445, 447, 449, 451, 454, 455, 465, 470, 490, 491, 502, 503, 505-507, 509, 510, 512, 515-517, 519, 520, 531, 557, 563, 580, 605; residential, 187, 222, 313, 377, 378, 390, 406, 407, 413, 415, 465, 487, 503, 506, 520; school(s), 36, 44, 64, 65, 183, 201, 299, 320, 377, 378, 393, 395, 396, 401, 403, 424, 445, 459, 465, 479, 563, 600; services, 7, 222, 257, 436, 443, 490, 506, 510, 524, 527; settings, 52, 139, 222, 299, 300, 465; sites, 1, 217, 440, 459; staff, 1, 2,

27, 45, 73, 134, 138, 201, 218, 227, 252, 266, 298, 374, 390, 391, 444, 445, 466, 501, 504, 509, 563, 605; teacher-counselor, 252, 328, 329, 352; training, 182, 322, 323, 374, 431, 508, 605; values, 252, 298, 440, 443, 594, 601
Re-EDers, 41, 52, 175, 206, 352, 353, 376, 414, 493, 501, 557
Reading, 49, 85, 150, 173, 174, 176, 184, 188-190, 193, 199, 275, 286, 350, 356, 385, 386, 473, 476, 512, 527
Regional Intervention Program (RIP), 64, 65, 67-68, 99, 124-127, 502-503, 513, 540
Re-inventing Re-ED, 373, 489, 406, 492
Relationship: building, 47, 254, 259, 328, 341; development, 259
Research: base, 312, 345-347, 447, 450, 451; based principles of learning, 177; evidence, 172, 439; findings, 302, 524; group, 318, 344, 379, 466; literature, 80, 184, 283; questions, 442; results, 65, 302, 378, 447, 466; studies, 26, 440, 445, 447, 455
Research and Training Center, 100, 145
Research-based, 177, 279, 520
Response Ability Pathways, 255, 263, 560
Results, 26, 37, 101, 105, 110, 113, 116, 167, 182, 193, 209, 210, 217, 220, 222, 225, 270, 282, 288-290, 302, 328, 330, 334, 342, 357, 360, 374, 376, 378, 380-384, 386, 388, 392, 395, 397, 398, 403, 406, 422-429, 431, 438, 445, 450, 451, 457, 460, 462, 464-466, 468, 479, 481,487, 527, 561, 597, 599
Role models, 134, 253, 259, 594
Role of a teacher-counselor, 53
Rose School, 357, 499
Rule, 91, 133, 149, 268, 269, 271, 272, 274, 275, 277, 278, 306, 382, 402, 599
Rules, 147, 154, 176, 182, 197, 254, 269, 270, 276-279, 298, 306, 307, 312, 315, 316, 359, 375, 594

S

School: achievement, 280, 330; behavior(s), 168, 185, 392, 400-402, 428, 462, 571; day, 2, 115, 160, 270,